The Writer's Choices
with Handbook

The Writer's Choices
with Handbook

Second Edition

Leonora Woodman
Purdue University

Thomas P. Adler
Purdue University

Handbook by
Mary Berthold
University of Wisconsin—Madison

Scott, Foresman and Company
Glenview, Illinois   London   Boston

An Instructor's Manual is available. It may be obtained through a local Scott, Foresman representative or by writing to English Editor, College Division, Scott, Foresman and Company, 1900 East Lake Avenue, Glenview, Illinois 60025.

Cover illustration: Fran Lee

Literary acknowledgments begin on page 575.

Library of Congress Cataloging-in-Publication Data

Woodman, Leonora.
    The writer's choices.

    Includes index.
    1. English language—Rhetoric.   2. English language
—Grammar—1950–   I. Adler, Thomas P.   II. Title.
PE1408.W66   1988b   808′.042   87–23485
ISBN 0–673–18840–X

123456-RRC-929190898887

Preface

*T*he second edition of *The Writer's Choices* continues to rely heavily on student work as the source for models, from sentences through paragraphs to complete essays. Some of the paragraphs and essays appear in two drafts because we also believe that principles of editing are often best learned during the process of revising. For this reason, we give revising special emphasis in *The Writer's Choices,* primarily by asking students to edit the work of other students. In our own teaching, we have found that the relationship between peer editing and self-editing is reciprocal: students who learn to edit well learn to write and revise well. Peer editing also has a psychological advantage in that it builds students' confidence by giving them an instructional role and helping them see how other students are managing the composing process.

Our title points to another basic emphasis. Throughout this text, we encourage students to see that *choice* is fundamental to the composing process. We begin by providing an overview of what choice in writing entails, and then suggest techniques for making choices during the exploratory stage. Moving on to drafting and editing, we show that choice involves judgment; it implies that in the writer's view, one alternative is better or more effective than another. The abundant editing activities that invite students to compare drafts of the same essay stress this point. So, too, do the "Exploring Choices" sections following each essay. Our experience suggests that when students examine choice in a rhetorical setting, they are better able to grasp the idea that to be effective choice must be guided by the writer's purpose, occasion, and audience.

In part, *The Writer's Choices* was written by students. However inexperienced student writers may be, they have in abundance wit, honesty, and, above all, imagination. We think that our student writers will recognize and respond to these resources as their own.

NEW TO THIS EDITION

In preparing the second edition of *The Writer's Choices*, we have tried to incorporate the revisions most often suggested by the teachers and students who successfully used the first edition in the classroom. These revisions include:

- substantially reshaping Chapter 2 by discussing two additional prewriting techniques;

- incorporating a new section on illustration as a pattern of development;

- expanding the material on descriptive and critical abstracts;

- providing over a dozen additional professional essays for analysis;

- presenting a case study to demonstrate for students the various stages of prewriting, drafting, and revising an essay;

- and adding a chapter on writing the book review.

SPECIAL FEATURES

Student Examples

Fifty complete student essays—some in two drafts—and many more student sentences and paragraphs enrich the text. Sections called "Exploring Choices" following each student essay stress the writer's rhetorical and stylistic choices and ask students to consider other choices the writer might have made. "A Style Aside" following selected paragraphs similarly stresses language alternatives.

Professional Essays

To the generous sprinkling of professional models contained in the first edition are added well over a dozen new professional essays for analysis—making the second edition of *The Writer's Choices* a complete rhetoric *and* reader.

Peer Editing

Systematic attention is given to building editing skills—from editing paragraphs, sentences, and words to the whole essay. Sections called "Tips for Self-Editing" summarize the skills taught in each chapter and remind students how to apply editorial techniques consistently throughout their own work. Part 3, "A Peer Editor Workshop," considers the editor's tone and phrasing in the context of edited student essays, shows how writers revised on the basis of the editor's comments, and provides essays in first draft for students to edit.

Invention Strategies

The text explores a variety of invention techniques—freewriting, on-the-spot observing, journal-keeping, brainstorming, clustering, the pentad, and the topics—all illustrated by student work. New to this edition is a case study that describes the various stages of the composing process from prewriting through drafting to revising.

Activities

The text's abundant, engaging, and practical activities encourage active student involvement. Besides the constant attention to drafts and editing, there are many small-group, in-class activities: a holistic scoring exercise based on four student essays; a thesis-building activity based on examples of southwestern humor; a word choice activity based on personal ads.

Writing Assignments

Writing assignments for paragraphs and essays appear in every chapter, often illustrated by student models.

Scope

Special chapters focus on persuasion, the essay exam, the book review, the controlled research paper, and the library research paper. The chapters on research explain both the MLA and APA documentation methods and demonstrate each in the work of three student writers.

Handbook

The longer hardcover edition includes a comprehensive and innovative handbook dealing with problems student writers often encounter. It also considers language effectiveness—the choices writers have within accepted conventions. Again, student work illustrates these choices. Each section of the Handbook also contains an editing acitvity.

The Teacher's Choices: An Instructor's Manual

An extensive resource text for teachers accompanies *The Writer's Choices*. In addition to providing guidance for using the text, *The Teacher's Choices* presents alternative syllabi, supplementary activities, additional examples of both student and professional writing, and an annotated bibliography based on the focus of each chapter. All the material designed for students has been classroom tested.

ACKNOWLEDGMENTS

The initial evolution and current revision of *The Writer's Choices* have amply confirmed two of its key principles: that writing is always a matter of rewriting, and that a good reader is the writer's best resource. It is with pleasure that we acknowledge our debt to the many reviewers whose incisive comments guided the development of our book over the years. We are grateful to these instructors and their student writers not only for their advice but also for confirming our long-held belief that student writing is a powerful instructional tool that helps make students more alert and attentive and confident of their own writing powers. We would especially like to thank Donna Kaye and the two reviewers, Elizabeth Steinberger of Metropolitan State College and John Collins of Glassboro State College, whose extended commentaries guided our thinking in the initial stages of preparing this second edition. To Constance Rajala and Anne Smith, we extend our thanks for their continued interest and support. We owe a special debt to our editor, Lydia Webster, for her discerning eye and her discriminating judgment.

We also thank Harold Woodman and Winifred Adler, our partners in all that we do, for their patience and understanding during every stage of this project.

Perhaps our greatest debt is to our student authors. Whether signed or unsigned, their work provides the foundation of this book. We thank them for having taught us that however arduous the teaching of writing may be, its rewards are beyond measure.

Leonora Woodman
Thomas P. Adler

Overview

Contents

Part 2   MAKING CHOICES
The Shape of Expression

4   CHOOSING PARAGRAPHS   151

WHAT IS A PARAGRAPH?   *152*

SENTENCES THAT MARK NEW PARAGRAPHS   *153*

PARAGRAPH UNITY AND THE TOPIC SENTENCE   *154*

Composing Effective Topic Sentences   155

Part 3   *MAKING CHOICES*   281
A Peer Editor Workshop

9   WRITING THE BOOK REVIEW   375

THE ELEMENTS OF A REVIEW   376

SAMPLE REVIEWS (FICTION)   377

REVIEWING NONFICTION   380

SAMPLE REVIEWS (NONFICTION)   381

ORGANIZING A REVIEW   386

Bibliographic Headnote   *386*
Lead Paragraph   *386*
Body of the Review   *388*
Conclusion   *388*

A SAMPLE REVIEW   388

10   WRITING THE CONTROLLED RESEARCH PAPER   391

THE NATURE OF CONTROLLED RESEARCH   392

A CASEBOOK: PRIMARY SOURCES   393

" 'Out, Out—' "   *394*
"Auto Wreck"   *395*

A CASEBOOK: SECONDARY MATERIAL   396

Descriptive and Critical Abstracts   *397*

REFERENCES WITHIN THE CONTROLLED RESEARCH PAPER   403

A SAMPLE CONTROLLED RESEARCH PAPER   404

A Casebook: The NCAA Statement of Academic Requirements   *408*

11 WRITING THE LIBRARY RESEARCH PAPER   413

The Writer's Choices
with Handbook

But writing itself is one of the great, free human activities. There is scope for individuality, and elation, and discovery, in writing. For the person who follows with trust and forgiveness what occurs to him, the world remains always ready and deep, an inexhaustible environment, with the combined vividness of an actuality and flexibility of a dream. Working back and forth between experience and thought, writers have more than space and time can offer. They have the whole unexplored realm of human vision.

—*William Stafford*, **Writing the Australian Crawl**

1

MAKING CHOICES

Some Fundamental Considerations

WRITING AND EDITING: ELEMENTS OF CHOICE

WRITING AND THINKING

BECOMING A WRITER-EDITOR

RECOGNIZING GOOD WRITING

ELEMENTS OF CHOICE

Choosing a Purpose

Choosing a Structure

Choosing a Voice

Knowing Your Reader

Writers describe the process of composing in different ways. Some compose entirely in their heads, feeling no need to go through several drafts before approving what they have written. The celebrated philosopher Bertrand Russell stated that after thinking intensely for an entire year about a series of lectures he had agreed to give, he called in a secretary and proceeded "to dictate the whole book without a moment's hesitation." Similarly, the American poet Wallace Stevens composed many of his finest poems during his daily walk to his office, revising only for punctuation and spelling after he had dictated them to his secretary. William Faulkner confessed that he put off writing as long as he could (owing to laziness, he admitted), but once he began, he found it fun, writing "so fast that somebody said my handwriting looks like a caterpillar that crawled through an inkwell and out on to a piece of paper."

More often, however, writers struggle to get their ideas down on paper. Impatient with the notion that writing is spontaneous joy, Wolcott Gibbs once observed that the only man he "ever knew who claimed that composition caused him no pain was a very bad writer, and he is now employed in a filling station." S. J. Perelman confessed at the end of his career that unlike technicians "who are supposed to become more proficient with practice," he found "the effort of writing . . . more arduous all the time." And the desire to escape from the labor of writing prompted the British novelist Anthony Trollope to advise all writers to attach a piece of cobbler's wax to the seat of their chairs to keep themselves securely fastened. The excuses many writers will invent to keep from filling the blank page are aptly described by John Steinbeck:

> Doc brought a package of yellow pads and two dozen pencils. He laid them out on his desk, the pencils sharpened to needle points and lined up like yellow soldiers. At the top of the page he printed: OBSERVATIONS AND SPECULATIONS. His pencil broke. He took up another and drew lace around the O and the B, made a block letter of the S and put fish hooks on each end. His ankle itched. He rolled down his sock and scratched, and that made his ear itch. "Someone's talking about me," he said and looked at the yellow pad. He wondered whether he had fed the cotton rats. It is easy to forget when you're thinking.
>
> Watching the rats scrabble for the food he gave them, Doc remembered that he had not eaten. When he finished a page or two he would fry some eggs. But wouldn't it be better to eat first so that his flow of thought would not be interrupted later? For some days he had looked forward to this time of peace, of unbroken thought. These were the answer to his restlessness: peace and the life of the mind. It would be better to eat first. He fried two eggs and ate them, staring at the yellow pad under the hanging light. The light was too bright. It reflected painfully on the paper. Doc finished his eggs, got out a sheet of tracing paper, and taped it to the bottom of the shade below the globe. It took time to make it

neat. He sat in front of the yellow pad again and drew lace around all the letters of the title, tore off the page, and threw it away. Five pencil points were broken now. He sharpened them and lined them up with their brothers.

—"The Creative Cross," *Sweet Thursday*

DISCUSSION QUESTIONS

1. Is Doc's writing experience similar to or different from your own? Recall the last time you wrote something and describe the way you worked.

2. Have you ever found that you worked more easily on one piece of writing than on another? Compare your working habits and explain why one piece was easier to complete.

WRITING AND THINKING

Obviously, it is impossible to generalize about the psychology of writing from the accounts of professional writers. Some work rapidly; some struggle for every word. Most student writers are likely to find more in common with the gropers and the grumblers. This is not cause for despair: if you found Doc's writing habits similar to your own, you can feel assured that you are much like many writers, even those whose pen is their livelihood. In fact, the difference between you and professional writers is one of degree and not of kind. Though writers who have worked long and hard at their craft have a degree of polish which you, a less experienced writer, may not yet command, they, like you, go through stages of thought that are the same for everyone who puts pen to paper. One of these stages is simply getting started—finding something to write about. Even then—even after the idea seems to have been discovered—the very act of putting thoughts into written words often stimulates other and perhaps different ideas, which in turn suggest new beginnings. In some mysterious way, the process of making thought visible in words enables you to understand what you really think—even to discover ideas you did not know you had. As William Stafford once said, "A writer is not so much someone who has something to say as he is someone who has found a process that will bring about new things he would not have thought of if he had not started to say them."

Writing is a dynamic process that weaves back and forth between thought and words. For convenience this process is divided into the stages of *prewriting* (the discovery of ideas), *writing* (the recording of ideas), and *revising* (the refining of ideas). In practice, though, such divisions are often blurred because discovery is a continuous process that occurs at every stage. Often, the very act of writing prods writers to discard, modify, or expand the ideas with which they began. And because thought and expression are so closely related, changes in one often require changes in the other. As a result, revising goes hand in hand with discovery. Though you may think of revising as the last stage in the writing process, good writers will also revise during the actual composing process, as well as after they have completed their first draft. Often they will write three or more drafts before they are satisfied. For them, no word or idea is final until it has been thoroughly reviewed, rethought, and rewritten.

Because revision is fundamental to good writing, we give it special emphasis in this text. We do this by asking you to become a writer-editor. The assumption is that the better a writer you become, the better an editor you will be, and vice versa. Becoming a writer-editor will help you become a perceptive critic not only of others' writing but of your own writing as well.

BECOMING A WRITER-EDITOR

All of us enjoy having our writing read. If we are genuinely involved in what we write, we want to communicate our thoughts and feelings to others. We are eager to have readers share our ideas, and we feel extremely gratified when they do. Sometimes, however, our readers' responses tells us that we have not succeeded, or that we have succeeded only partially. The meaning of passages that seemed clear to us may be questioned. Some of our words may be judged inappropriate; perhaps we've included too much detail or too little; perhaps we haven't provided a clear idea of what our essay is about. Whatever the problem, the message from our readers is clear: we need to revise.

At first such negative responses may make us feel discouraged or even angry. This is understandable, for writing is an expression of the deepest self; when it is questioned, we may feel threatened. Mature writers, however, are able to accept and even welcome criticism. They have learned that not only do serious writers seldom succeed with their first try but that a good reader, one who reads with care and offers specific suggestions for change, is invaluable. This is the role of the editor, a critic-friend.

Editors are very important to writers. A good editor can help writers arrange their ideas for maximum effect, eliminate material that does not contribute to their ideas, clarify their thought, and choose better words and phrases. They can also identify specific strengths, indicating, perhaps, that certain features of style create a desired effect or illuminate a central idea.

Many professional writers seek and follow editorial advice, often from other writers. T. S. Eliot, an Anglo-American poet and critic, was so grateful for the editorial assistance of Ezra Pound, a fellow poet, that he dedicated his poem *The Waste Land* to his editor-friend. Similarly, Ernest Hemingway revised the opening chapter of his novel *The Sun Also Rises* following the editorial advice of F. Scott Fitzgerald, another distinguished American writer. The novel established Hemingway as a writer of the first rank.

Student writers also benefit from the editorial advice of informed readers. In this text you will find many student essays. If you enjoy these essays, keep in mind that most were rewritten many times after a reader had commented on each draft. The final versions represent the end of a revising process that benefited at each stage from the guidance of a skilled editor.

In the following chapters, you will find many activities designed to improve your editing skills. Before you begin, however, it is important to understand what an editor does. Many people think that an editor is a proofreader who eliminates errors in spelling, punctuation, and sentence structure. Editors do this, of course, but it is not their major task. Their main task is to see if writers have achieved their purposes. Does the writer have a good idea that is clearly stated, adequately supported, logically developed, effectively described and explained? Do the language and arrangement meet the needs of intended readers? In the editorial activities that appear in many of the chapters, you will learn what editors look for. These activities will help you become a skilled reader of other students' writing. In the process you will also become a better reader and editor of your own work. The sections called "Tips for Self-Editing" will help you see the connection between editing the work of others and editing your own writing.

RECOGNIZING GOOD WRITING

Robert M. Pirsig, author of *Zen and the Art of Motorcycle Maintenance,* tells how a composition instructor helped his students understand that they had an intuitive sense of what good writing was—that, in fact, they could identify quality in writing as well as he could. To illustrate this, the instructor read from two student papers, one a superb piece, the other a poor one. He then asked students to determine which essay was better, and, of course, students overwhelmingly chose the finer piece. To reinforce the students' confidence that they were indeed good judges of writing, he then devised the following exercise:

> He read four student papers in class and had everyone rank them in estimated order of Quality on a slip of paper. He did the same himself. He collected the slips, tallied them on the blackboard and averaged the rankings for an overall class opinion. Then he would reveal his own rankings, and this would almost always be close to, if not identical with the class average. Where there were differences it was usually because two papers were close in quality.

Pirsig's assumption that you can identify excellence in writing even before you have completed a course in composition is appealing and valid. Test it by ranking the following essays. Unlike Pirsig's model, these essays are all on the same topic. The students who wrote them responded to the following assignment: *Write a letter to Mr. X, a Chinese student who will soon come to the United States to study. Although Mr. X knows English well, he is unfamiliar with American culture. Before he arrives, he would like to know something about American currency. In your letter to him, explain the value of the American penny.*

After you have read the letters, rank them according to their relative excellence (give a 1 to the best essay, a 4 to the least effective essay). Then compare your ranking to that of the other students in the class. You'll probably agree about which one is best.

Letter A

Dear Mr. X,

Before you come to America, I would like to inform you about a little piece of my country's heritage. A very little piece. In our currency there is a coin called the penny.

Easily distinguished because of its copper-red color, the penny has been around for ages. The penny is indirectly related to the accumulation of years of its existence. As the number of years escalates, the value of the penny diminishes.

The uses of the penny are very restricted. Pennies have no monetary use unless, like used stamps, they have been collected over a very long period of time. If a penny is very old, it may be worth a considerable amount of money. If you are fortunate enough to find a penny minted from the 1850s to 1909, you will have an object valued at nearly five dollars. This is an increase of 500 percent. Again, like stamps, old pennies in good shape can reap rich rewards if you find the right buyer.

The penny by itself is worthless. It now takes at least two pennies to buy one piece of gum. The penny is worth only one hundredth of a dollar and we all know how little the American dollar is worth today.

In closing, I would like to say that if you happen to find a penny, check the date. If it is not extremely old, find the nearest wishing well and pitch it in. It will do as much good in there as in your pocket. Even more, perhaps, because you never know. You might get your wish.

Best wishes,

Mary Losey

Letter B

Dear Mr. X,

I understand you'll soon be coming to the United States to study. Let me welcome you. Let me, too, tell you something about the American penny, which you'll find in abundance once you get to our shores.

When the penny is new, it is the most colorful piece of United States currency. It is copper and very shiny, but if you happen to get an older minted penny, it will be brown and the luster will be dull. The penny is the only American coin that has this color. All other coins are silver and are easily distinguishable from the penny.

Years ago the penny had many practical uses. It was used to buy simple things such as thread, bobby pins, buttons, and even fruit. Because of inflation, though, we can no longer use the penny to buy these useful objects.

Today we cannot buy many things with a penny. It is used mostly to make change. Change is the amount given back to people after they pay excess for something. Other uses today for the penny are for candy machines and gum.

Even though the penny is one hundredth of one dollar, you can see from its uses today that the penny isn't worth a "plugged nickel."

Sincerely,

Roger Luesch

Letter C

Dear Mr. X,

I'm pleased to have this opportunity to give you some information about the American penny. I'll start off with the way it looks. Circular in shape, the penny has a diameter of approximately one centimeter, and it is just a bit under two millimeters thick. Its copper composition may have turned from its original shiny orange to a dull brown-orange, depending upon its date of mint. The staunch profile of Abe Lincoln (America's sixteenth president who was responsible for ending slavery), with the motto "In God We Trust" above his head, graces one side of the coin, while the Lincoln Memorial is displayed on the other.

Turning now to the value of the American penny, let me say right away that its value is next to nil because it is one hundredth of the American one dollar bill. You can afford a stick of chewing gum if you own it, but little else. In fact, some Americans believe the penny is a foe because its monetary value is so low. They get little for it and would rather do without it than have it fall inside a purse or fall out of a pocket in church. Others, though, see through its insignificant value and consider it a friend. It satisfies a child's desire to carry cash. It satisfies many superstitious citizens who believe that a discovered penny means a lucky day. It serves as that coveted piece in a checker game when all the other checker pieces have been lost. It is a handy tool in instances when the screwdriver has not been returned to the junk drawer.

So the value of the American penny depends more on personal estimates than on the value assigned it in the American currency table. After all, America prizes individualism; just as individuals quarrel about almost everything, so, too, do they disagree about the value of the penny.

Sincerely,

Sheila Hanley

Letter D

Dear Mr. X,

   To tell you about the American penny, I'll start off with a popular adage: "Find a penny, pick it up, and all the day you'll have good luck." Good luck is almost all a single penny can provide the American consumer today. Though it continues to remain in our system as a basic coin, the penny really pleases only the small child at the gum ball machine!

   This piece of currency is the only piece in our monetary system that is not silver in color. If you come across a new penny, it will be a bright and shiny copper color. But because the penny has been with our country for many years, we often come upon older pieces that have become dull and almost brown from age.

   The penny feels very light in your hand. And when you rub its front surface, the top half of our former president, Abraham Lincoln, gives it a smooth though bumpy texture. The profile of this long-nosed, bearded man sits beneath the words, "In God We Trust."

   If you still aren't sure you can identify this coin, watch closely to see which piece is left behind by the customer in a grocery store. That's the penny.

Good luck,

Kim Cassady

WRITING SUGGESTIONS

Try a ranking session using papers from your class. Choose a topic and write for about fifteen or twenty minutes. When you have finished, join four or five other students and read the papers of each member of the small group. Select the paper you think most effective and give it to your instructor. Your instructor will number the papers and read them aloud. You will then rank them, giving a 1 to the best essay, a 2 to the second-best essay, and so on.

Here are some topics you might want to consider. Remember that ranking works best when the class writes on a common topic.

1. Pick a popular restaurant and try to convey its unique atmosphere and flavor.
2. Write a letter of support for one of your teachers who is a candidate for "The Best Teacher Award."
3. Explain to your classmates the advantages (or disadvantages) of working part- or full-time while attending college.
4. Write a parody of a job rejection letter. The following amusing example may give you some ideas.

> Thank you for your interest in our opening.
>
> However, the Selection Committee announces that the position has been awarded to an Apple II computer. This computer has been serving as Information Organizer at this college for the past two years.
>
> Please do not interpret this decision as a reflection on your qualifications. In fact, the entire committee was most impressed with you. Your style of dress for your interview was appropriate, your posture good, and your manners quite cordial. You remembered everybody's name and possessed an unbelievable amount of knowledge about our university.
>
> But let's be realistic. An Apple II computer doesn't haggle over salary, request additional vacation dates, or groan at the thought of serving on All-Campus Committees. I wish you success in your continued job search.
>
> —*Chronicle of Higher Education*

ELEMENTS OF CHOICE

In ranking the letters addressed to Mr. X, you may have put yourself in his shoes, trying to decide which letter would have been most likely to give you the fullest and clearest guide to the American penny. If so, you were already assuming the editor's role: you saw the letters as written to fulfill a specific purpose—explaining the value of the American penny to a foreign student who was unfamiliar with American currency—and by matching the purpose to the content and style of the various letters, you were able to evaluate their relative effectiveness. You compared what the writers said and how they said it to their overall reason for writing. In effect, you were considering the *process* of composing as well as the *product* composed.

To use your editorial skills effectively, and to make informed decisions in your writing, you will need to understand the elements of this writing process. Writing consists of interrelated elements that reflect the writer's choice of aim, structure, tone, voice, and audience. How well a paper succeeds often depends on how well these choices blend to produce a sense of unity and wholeness. Examining each component more closely will help explain how they interact.

Choosing a Purpose

Purpose in writing refers to the writer's major *aim* (or goal). A keen sense of purpose helps writers determine what to say as well as how to say it.

You probably know from your own writing experience that the writer's major *aim* can vary. Perhaps you've recently written to the editor of the campus newspaper complaining about the parking regulations on campus; in that case your primary purpose would have been to *persuade* your readers that something needed to be changed. Or, in framing an essay response to an American history exam, you may have sought to *explain* and *evaluate* the development of American labor laws. If you've recently written a set of instructions designed to help your readers do something, your aim would have been to *instruct*. Or perhaps in writing an autobiographical essay for your classmates you wished to *express* a facet of your own experience.

These purposes may, of course, overlap. In complaining about parking regulations, you might have had to explain how these regulations had changed. Or you might have used a personal anecdote to illustrate how you missed an exam because you couldn't get into a parking lot. Still, your major purpose—to persuade your readers that parking regulations needed to be changed—would have shaped the overall design of your letter.

You'll see the varied aims of writing in the following introductory paragraphs written by students. For each, try to determine the writer's purpose and speculate on how the rest of the essay would likely be developed.

Paragraph A

Sunday morning again. I roll over and glance at the illuminated dial of my alarm clock on the desk. Seven twenty-three. The party-wearied half of my consciousness begs for more sleep, only to be overruled by a sudden sweep of pure insanity. From somewhere deep inside of me comes the command, "Go run." As if powered by some alien force, I rise automatically, putting on my gym shorts, a worn turtleneck and a battered pair of Adidas. I steal into the dark dormitory hallway, leaving my soundly sleeping roommate undisturbed.

Paragraph B

Etched in American political philosophy and expressed in the United States Constitution is the right of the American people to be free of the intrusive acts of government. Nevertheless, no people in the world are scrutinized, measured, counted, and interrogated by as many poll-takers, social-science researchers, and government officials as are Americans. As information-recording systems have become cheaper and more efficient, the government's appetite for data has led to the development of complex, computerized data systems which are fast becoming a threat to personal privacy.

Paragraph C

Two hundred years after it was first brought to the New World, the tomato stands as one of America's favorite vegetables. No home garden seems complete without a row of these lush, vigorous plants spilling out from the garden plot onto the lawn or towering above the garden from their wooden stake tower. Though it is susceptible to frost damage, the tomato is a relatively easy plant to grow. Any home gardener can successfully raise tomatoes if he remembers to follow certain procedures during the tomato-growing season.

Paragraph D

Trypanosomiasis, better known as sleeping sickness, is a painful and many times fatal disease that infects a wide area across Central Africa. Carried by the tsetse fly, the disease at one time was known only in a few isolated areas. But as felled tropical forests gave way to moisture-laden savanna woodlands—excellent breeding grounds for the moisture-hungry tsetse—the disease gradually spread. Above all, the advent of colonialism in the nineteenth century spurred its growth; for the colonialist built modern transportation systems that helped introduce trypanosomiasis to many previously uninfected regions. Today, the disease attacks more than ten thousand people each year, seven thousand of whom die from its ravages. As a result, many of the nations affected have embarked on elaborate programs of control, diagnosis, and treatment.

EXPLORING PURPOSE

1. Point out the sentences in paragraphs B, C, and D that summarize the writer's major purpose.
2. How does paragraph A differ from the other three? What is its implicit purpose?
3. Consider whether this hypothetical conclusion to paragraph D would change the writer's purpose: "Unfortunately, many of the rulers of these countries have not addressed this problem; they are more interested in private gain than in public service."

Choosing a Structure

Your choice of purpose will also influence the structure or overall organization of your essay. You are familiar with the structure of a building, of a dam, of an automobile—of countless manufactured objects and mechanisms. Structure is the key element in various types of organizations created to reflect religious, political, educational, or economic life. You expect to find structure in the supermarket, in games and sports, in books and films. It is difficult to imagine life without structure.

Structures are divisible into parts, all of them linked to one another to form a harmonious unity based on the purpose for which they were designed. Each part of an automobile engine contributes to the functional requirements of a moving vehicle—the purpose for which each was made and assembled. No part is extraneous; none has been randomly selected. So, too, a composition is composed of interrelated sentences and paragraphs, all chosen to reflect the writer's overall purpose.

Structure is a broad word that refers to the arrangement of sentences and paragraphs within the essay; the arrangement of the components will be examined in greater detail later on. As introduction, examine two student paragraphs to see how the writer's purpose shapes the way each paragraph is organized.

Paragraph A

    As I trudged through the doors of St. Marie Hospital on a
    bleak November morning, I signed wearily. "This is insane," I
    mumbled. I could not for the life of me figure out why I came
    back day after day. I continually subjected myself to a
    physically and emotionally exhausting job that was full of
    disappointment. After all, being a nurse's aide wasn't a very
    glamorous line of work. My main responsibility was to keep
    the patients happy and clean. That meant that I spent eight
    hours a day bathing and cleaning up patients, emptying
    bedpans, making beds, and running menial errands for patients
    as well as nurses. My tasks were everything that a nurse and
    janitor would not do. I found myself at the bottom of the
    pecking order. I received complaints from the doctors, the
    nurses, and the patients. A lot of my work went unnoticed,
    and my efforts went unappreciated. I realized that I had not
    decided to become a nurse's aide for the sake of receiving
    gratitude. However, a little thanks now and then would have
    done wonders for my self-esteem. Now, as I walked down the
    empty hall, all I could hear were the steady hum of the
    overhead fluorescent lights and the quiet breathing of the
    sleeping patients. Once again, I mumbled, "What am I doing
    here? I should be home asleep, enveloped by the warmth and
    security of my comforter."

Paragraph B

    At the turn of the century, Williamsport, Indiana was a
    bustling town, vibrant and alive on the banks of the Wabash
    River. But in the last three decades, Williamsport has
    gradually died. Today, three blocks of storefront buildings
    line its main street, their two- and three-story facades only
    remnants of a once-bold, ornate Victorian architecture.
    Helplessly victimized by time, the unloved and abandoned

buildings crumble and lean. The once–proud opera house, dated
1894, sags miserably; once a center of entertainment and
culture, it now accommodates a dingy laundromat in its main-
floor lobby. Today Williamsport is a mere shell of the
community where farmers used to converge to trade, bank, shop,
and spend their leisure time. Eyeing these once–majestic
buildings, a visitor might wonder what has caused their
plight. Why has this town been neglected and rejected by local
residents?

EXPLORING CHOICES

1. How would you characterize the purpose of each paragraph? Explain the writer's intention.
2. Explain the subject of each paragraph. Determine if the sentences of each paragraph contribute to the subject the writer has chosen.
3. In part, paragraph B is organized around contrast. How does this organization serve the writer's purpose?
4. What signals tell you that paragraph A is organized chronologically? How does this organizational pattern serve the writer's purpose?

A STYLE ASIDE

1. Explain why the writer uses direct dialogue with similar content at the beginning and end of paragraph A. Try eliminating this dialogue. What difference in effect do you find?

2. In paragraph A you'll find a sentence with a series of participles ("bathing," "cleaning," "emptying," "making," "running"). Try dividing this sentence into two sentences. What difference in effect do you find?

3. In the first sentence of paragraph B, the writer has put the adjectives "vibrant" and "alive" after the noun they modify. Why do you think this was done? What would be the difference if the adjectives had been placed before the noun where we usually expect to find them?

4. In paragraph B the writer writes that the buildings are "helplessly victimized by time." They are described as "once-bold" and "once-proud." Can buildings literally be victims or bold or proud? What type of language is the writer using here?

Choosing a Voice

Your writing purpose will also entail choosing a *voice,* the "self" you wish the audience to perceive. Its close companion is *tone,* your attitude toward your subject and audience. You can see both at work in your everyday behavior. Consider the many voices you adopt each day in response to different people and situations. You will use one voice with an intimate friend, another with a prospective employer, yet another with a professor. In each case, your attitude toward your audience will determine the relative formality of the words you chose, the pitch, stress, and intonation of your voice, even your gestures and facial expressions. You might also choose to color your message, adjusting your tone from caustic to solemn to argumentative, for example. In making these choices, you would probably also choose (consciously or unconsciously) an image of yourself you wanted to project. To an intimate friend, you might want to appear worldly and sophisticated; to a prospective employer, self-assured and responsible; to a professor, thoughtful and hardworking. You would find, in short, that your voice, tone, and projected self-image interacted dynamically to fit your purpose.

This same interaction is usually the case in good writing; we say *usually* because voice is a point on a continuum ranging from personal to impersonal. Some writing purposes require a degree of detachment in which the writer disappears into the subject. The paragraph on trypanosomiasis (p. 13), for example, is relatively impersonal because the writer aims to explain the "control, diagnosis, and treatment" of the disease rather than to express a personal attitude toward it. In later chapters you'll see that some writing purposes encourage the expression of a personal voice while others encourage anonymity.

To see how voice, tone, and self-image may interact, look at a letter addressed to the editor of a local newspaper. Its aim is to persuade readers to follow a course of action. As you read, notice that the author's tone is satirical and ironic: the writer actually means the opposite of what is said. To emphasize the irony, the author adopts a cool and impersonal voice, projecting the image of someone who wants to solve a serious problem. In fact, this assumed voice allows the author to discredit the ideas which seem to be advocated.

Dear Editor,

   The growing number of muggings in the United States, a figure that has more than doubled in the past fifteen years, prompts me to write this letter to clear up some of the misconceptions concerning this problem. I feel that the so-called "victims" of these crimes are themselves primarily responsible. Saying "I was mugged" is just an excuse people invent to cover up their own irresponsibility. Going about after dark, chatting among themselves or staring dreamily into a soft night's breezes, acting as if the streets and parks belonged to the citizenry, they deliberately court danger. Moreover, people will do this even when they have been warned not to. They always claim a good excuse—"I had to go to the community board meeting" or "It was just such a beautiful evening" or "But I don't get off work until after dark"—but these excuses just hide the real reason. Actually, these people are just irresponsible, covering up for their lapses in judgment.

Furthermore, no one recognizes the beneficial effects of mugging. What system to redistribute the wealth of this country could be more simple? The involuntary emptying of pockets by members of society temporarily deprived of funds saves them the time and overall nuisance involved with seeking some other sort of employment. As well, these effective "get rich quick" schemes keep potential muggers well-financed and therefore off public welfare roles. Finally, the chance that you might be mugged presents a great deterrent to those citizens who fancy that they have the right to come and go when and how they choose. Without the threat of getting mugged, our parks and streets might be clogged with people at all hours—people talking, laughing, and socializing with each other; this would create terrible interference with important public services, such as collection of litter and street cleaning.

If unrestrained muggings could carry so much potential benefit, why not decriminalize this particular offense? The money saved by not having to incarcerate and retrain convicted muggers could go to buying every citizen a heavy-duty lock, so that we can all continue to hide out in our own homes.

While this proposal is still in the planning stages, I think it will win widespread support because intelligent people will quickly grasp the logic of my position. It could certainly go a long way in solving the so-called crime dilemma.

Please sign this letter

"Concerned"

A STYLE ASIDE

1. Note the use of the dash in the first paragraph. What purpose does the dash serve?

2. In the first draft of this essay the writer used the following introductory sentence: "With the growing number of alleged muggings in the United States, a figure which has more than doubled in the past fifteen years, I feel compelled to write this letter focusing on some of its inequitable misconceptions and offering a solution to the growing problem of muggings." Point out the changes the writer made in the revision. Which version do you prefer? Why?

Write a paragraph or two in which you propose something likely to be considered outrageous (for example, eliminating traffic lights or reinstituting child labor). In doing so, project an image of yourself as a reasonable and judicious critic.

Knowing Your Reader

You have seen that purpose influences the writer's choice of structure, and of voice and tone. Another important element that influences choice is the reader or audience.

Having a keen sense of audience can help assure the clarity of what you are saying, the meaning you want to convey. This is especially important because, unlike speaking, writing is a private activity: writers have no audience that they can actually see while they are composing their messages. Consider the difference this makes. In ordinary conversation, the lift of an eyebrow, the gesture or grimace, the stress, pitch, and intonation of the voice, the pause in which silence is itself expressive—all help to convey meaning. Try transcribing a taped conversation, and you will find much of it puzzling because the speakers probably relied in part on nonverbal strategies to communicate their ideas. Moreover, in conversation, you get an immediate response that tells you whether or not your audience has understood what you are saying. If you think they haven't, you can repeat your message, perhaps by rephrasing what you have already said or by beginning again with a different set of verbal and nonverbal strategies. You can do this many times until you are confident that your audience has grasped your meaning.

These advantages of speaking are not available when you write. In writing, every shade of meaning must be expressed in words, with the aid of punctuation. Moreover, you can change ideas and words while you are revising, but once you have submitted the final copy, you can no longer alter what you have said.

Lacking a tangible audience to respond to your ideas puts special demands on you as a writer. You need to create an audience in your head so that, in effect, you become two voices, one recording and one listening. Between the two voices there is a continual dialogue on many levels. One that is fundamental, especially to beginning writers, is the question of how well an intended meaning has been communicated. A writer who is sensitive to the hypothetical reader will ask such questions as: Does this word really express my meaning? Do I need to add further detail to explain my meaning? Should I rearrange my sentences or paragraphs to clarify my meaning? Does my punctuation capture the tone that is basic to the meaning I intend? This kind of dialogue can help save you from the surprise you may feel when a meaning you thought was self-evident is questioned by a reader.

In addition to helping you clarify your meaning, your hypothetical reader can also help you shape and clarify your purpose. Of course, the way you perceive this reader may change, depending on your writing aim. The easiest way to see this is to imagine the same reader for several different kinds of messages. Say, for example, that you decide to write a letter to your good friend Carl to tell him about some of your recent activities. With this purpose in mind, you would probably adjust your voice and tone to fit your specific audience. You would also select the kind of material that would be likely to interest him. Knowing that Carl was an avid jogger, you might include an account of a recent race in which you had participated. Or, if you and he shared an interest in motorcycles, you might tell him about the new bike you had recently purchased. In either case, the interests of your reader would influence the content of your letter even though your focus would be on your personal experiences.

Now, change your purpose: you are writing the letter to Carl to persuade him to pay back money he has borrowed. You want to influence him to do something, to listen to your appeal and to act on it. With this purpose in mind, you might not be as interested in examining the experiences you and he share (though they may certainly be a part of your message) as you would be in analyzing his personality: is he easily angered, excessively proud, sympathetic to the needs of others, or somewhat selfish? How might he react to your request? Would he honor it or meet it with hostility? What about the state of his finances? Can he spare the money, or is he short of cash? Being sensitive to the quirks of Carl's temperament and his values and financial situation would be crucial in helping you frame a suitable appeal.

Now change your purpose once again. You are an amateur photographer with considerable skill and experience in taking and developing pictures. Knowing this, your friend Carl, who is interested in taking up the developing end of the hobby, has written to you asking you how to begin. While framing your letter to him, you find that you are continually asking yourself if he will understand your instructions. This time you are not so much concerned about Carl's interests or temperament as you are about his level of knowledge. Compared to Carl, you are an expert with special skills accumulated over a period of time. He, in contrast, is a novice. And so you find yourself asking, Do I need to explain this word? Will this allusion be clear? Do I need to add further details about this stage of the process? At all times you perceive your reader from the point of view of the specialist who is advising a relative nonspecialist on the procedures he must follow.

You can see from the preceding examples that depending on your writing aim, you will, at different times, want to consider:

The reader's knowledge. How familiar is my reader with the material I am presenting? What common knowledge can I take for granted? What must I explain or define?

The reader's interest. How much reader interest in my subject can I assume? How much must I cultivate?

The reader's attitude.   Is my reader receptive to the material I am presenting? Is my reader hostile? Or is my reader simply neutral?

The reader's expectations.   Is my proposed essay governed by certain conventions that a knowledgeable reader would expect to find? Do I need to arrange my material in a certain way because essays of the type I am writing are generally arranged in this way?

EXPLORING CHOICES

Audience

1. The writers of advertisements are especially adept at devising appeals directed toward a specific audience. Examine the ad for the Audi on the following page. The questions that follow will help you determine the audience for which the ad was written.

   a. Why do you think the ad emphasizes where the car was made? How is this information meant to influence a prospective buyer? What kind of prospective buyer would want to know this?

   b. Why does the subtitle invoke the concepts of "modern" and "ancient"? How are these contrasting terms reaffirmed in the ad itself? How do they capture the values of the audience for this ad?

   c. Why do you think the writer uses the phrase "feverishly concocted" in the first sentence instead of a phrase like "quickly made"? Why is the notion of instability emphasized immediately? To what is it contrasted in the rest of the ad? What does this contrast tell you about the audience?

   d. In the second sentence, the writer uses the phrase "hyperbole aside." What does this phrase mean? What kind of an audience would be likely to understand the phrase?

   e. The writer calls the Audi "an aerodynamic tour de force." Who would be likely to buy something called a "tour de force"?

   f. Characterize the amount and quality of technical information in the ad. Who might want and understand this information?

   g. The writer calls the Audi "an ethical GT machine." Can a machine be ethical? What does this phrase tell you about the values of the audience?

   h. The writer concludes by calling the Audi the "Coupe du jour." Why do you think he borrows this French phrase? Why not a phrase taken from German or Spanish? How does the phrase help characterize the audience for the ad?

2. The power of the word to influence the public prompted the Ford Motor Company to consult Marianne Moore, a distinguished American poet, for assistance in devising a name for a new series of cars it sought to market in the mid-fifties. This exercise contains some of the correspondence between Ford and Miss Moore. Note in the first letter

"The Coupe."

A masterpiece of modern design from an ancient Bavarian town.

To a world weary of redesigned and restyled automobiles feverishly concocted for these unsettling times, the new Audi Coupe is refreshment itself.

It is, hyperbole aside, a genuine masterpiece in advanced automobile design. Ahead of conventional grand touring cars.

The Coupe is a beneficiary of the innovative engineering that went into the Audi 5000 and 4000 series automobiles. All of its systems and components have been carefully thought out and developed.

This high performance GT machine offers an invigorating ride, with outstanding quickness and tracking.

The Audi Coupe classic low-front, high-back wedge shape is an aerodynamic tour de force.

Standing still the Coupe looks fast. It is as fast as it looks. 0 to 50 in just 7.4 seconds.

Heart of this performance is the CIS fuel-injected, 5-cylinder engine invented by Audi; this efficient engine has been further refined to give the Coupe exceptional compressive power. No less sophisticated is the 5-speed transmission and the front-wheel drive, which in all candor is without peer. Audi pioneered front-wheel drive half a century ago, long before it became fashionable.

Yet all of this exhilarating performance is accomplished without sacrificing economy. The Coupe is an ethical GT machine, truly responsive to the energy dilemma: EPA estimated [21] mpg. 36 mpg estimated highway. Its cruising range also is impressive: [331] estimated miles per tankful. Highway range, 568 estimated miles. From its 15.8-gallon tank.

Inside the new Coupe the biomechanical engineering by Audi's scientists is immediately evident.

The ambience of the interior with its excellent ergonomics and thoughtful instrumentation gives the driver a comforting sense of command.

The Coupe is another reminder that when innovative automotive ideas are required by the times, Audi engineers are already one step ahead.

In every way, the Coupe is pure fun. Pure Audi. A masterpiece of relevant, state of the art engineering and all from the century-old village of Ingolstadt, Germany. It is, indeed, the Coupe du jour.

For your nearest Porsche Audi dealer, please telephone toll-free (800) 447-4700. In Illinois, (800) 322-4400.

*Use "estimated mpg" for comparison. Mileage and range vary with speed, trip length, weather. Actual highway mpg and highway range will probably be less.

PORSCHE+AUDI
NOTHING EVEN COMES CLOSE

how the head of Ford's Marketing Research Department describes the connotative associations he wishes the prospective name to have.

October 19, 1955

Dear Miss Moore:

This is a morning we find ourselves with a problem which, strangely enough, is more in the field of words and the fragile meaning of words than in car-making. And we just wonder whether you might be intrigued with it sufficiently to lend us a hand.

Our dilemma is a name for a rather important new series of cars.

We should like this name to be more than a label. Specifically, we should like it to have a compelling quality in itself and by itself. To convey, through association or other conjuration, some visceral feeling of elegance, fleetness, and advanced features and design. A name, in short, that flashes a dramatically desirable picture in people's minds.

Over the past few weeks this office has confected a list of three hundred-odd candidates which, it pains me to relate, are characterized by an embarrassing pedestrianism. We are miles short of our ambition. And so we are seeking the help of one who knows more about this sort of magic than we.

As to how we might go about this matter, I have no idea. One possibility is that you might care to visit with us and muse with the new Wonder which now is in clay in our Advance Styling Studios. But, in any event, all would depend on whether you find this overture of some challenge and interest.

Should we be so fortunate as to have piqued your fancy, we will be pleased to write more fully. In summary, all we want is a colossal name (another "Thunderbird" would be fine). And, of course, it is expected that our relations will be on a fee basis of an impeccably dignified kind.

Respectfully,

Robert B. Young
Marketing Research Department

a. Though Mr. Young does not identify the particular consumer for whom the new series of cars is intended, he does specify the qualities he wishes the name of the car to embody. Are these qualities universally desirable, or appealing to a particular type of buyer?

b. Mr. Young's letter is intended as a request: he is attempting to persuade a distinguished poet who does not ordinarily write advertising copy to use her talent in an unorthodox way. To do so, he adopts a particular mode of appeal. What is it? How would the mode of appeal differ if he had begun his letter in the following fashion: "We are writing to request your assistance in developing a name for a new series of cars we are planning to market"?

c. Note that Mr. Young three times uses the verb *might: might care to; might be intrigued with; how we might go about this matter*. What effect on his intended reader is this verb of possibility intended to have? Is it in keeping with Mr. Young's description of his letter as an *overture*?

d. In paragraph 3 Mr. Young uses two sentence fragments. What are they? Assuming they are deliberately chosen, what is their effect? Do you think Mr. Young was wise to violate standard grammar, given the reader he was addressing?

e. In the final paragraph, Mr. Young uses the phrase *piqued your fancy*. Can you think of an alternative phrase which would mean the same thing but would have a different effect?

3. If you thought Mr. Young's letter was likely to achieve its intended purpose, you were right. Here is Miss Moore's response:

October 21, 1955

Let me take it under advisement, Mr. Young. I am complimented to be recruited in this high matter.

I have seen and admired "Thunderbird" as a Ford designation. It would be hard to match; but let me, the coming week, talk with my brother who would bring ardor and imagination to bear on the quest.

Sincerely yours,
and your wife's,

Marianne Moore

A week later, Miss Moore submitted her first list.

October 27, 1955

Dear Mr. Young:

My brother thought most of the names I had considered suggesting to you for your new series, too learned or too labored, but thinks I might ask if any of the following approximate the requirements.

THE FORD SILVER SWORD

This plant, of which the flower is a silver sword, I believe grows only in Tibet, and on the Hawaiian Island, Maui on Mount Háleákalá (House of the Sun); found at an altitude of from 9,500 to 10,000 feet. (The leaves—silver-white—surrounding the individual blossoms have a pebbled texture that feels like Italian-twist back-stitch all-over embroidery.)

My first thought was of a bird series—the swallow species—Hirundo or phonetically, Aërundo. Malvina Hoffman is designing a device for the radiator of a made-to-order Cadillac, and said in her opinion the only term surpassing Thunder-bird would be hurricane; and I then thought Hurrican Hirundo might be the first of a series such as Hurricane aquila (eagle), Hurricane accipiter (hawk), and so on. . . .

If these suggestions are not in character with the car, perhaps you could give me a sketch of its general appearance, or hint as to some of its exciting possibilities—though my brother reminds me that such information is highly confidential.

Sincerely yours,

Marianne Moore

a. Note that Miss Moore seems not to be concerned with the prospective buyer in her search for a name. What seems to be her main concern?

b. Would you agree that the names Miss Moore submitted are "learned" and "labored" as her brother suggests was true of the names she did not submit?

c. Miss Moore draws her examples from nature. Do you think they are as successful as other names of cars that are also drawn from the physical world?

4. A year after the correspondence started, Miss Moore received the following letter informing her of the name that had been chosen. Note how the writer develops suspense before he divulges the name. Why do you think he does so? Is the effect intended to be ironic?

November 8, 1956

Dear Miss Moore:

Because you were so kind to us in our early and hopeful days of looking for a suitable name, I feel a deep obligation to report on events that have ensued.

And I feel I must do so before the public announcement of same come Monday, November 19.

We have chosen a name out of the more than six-thousand-odd candidates that we gathered. It has a certain ring to it. An air of gaiety and zest. At least, that's what we keep saying. Our name, dear Miss Moore, is—Edsel.

I know you will share your sympathies with us.

Cordially,

David Wallace, Manager
Marketing Research

WRITING SUGGESTIONS

1. Write a letter to a respected member of your community asking this person to contribute a substantial amount of time or money to a worthy project you are supporting. Then write a letter making the same request to a friend your own age. What difference do you find in the mode of appeal and style between the two letters?

2. Invent a product (practical or otherwise) for which you see some need and give it a name. Consider the likely buyers and write an ad designed to make your product attractive to them. Exchange your ad with your fellow students and have them determine what type of buyers you had in mind.

THE WRITING PROCESS

*T*he many choices writers must make in the course of developing an essay do not arise at the same time. Choosing a purpose, for example, usually precedes the process of composing a rough draft. And purpose, in turn, depends on first choosing a subject and exploring the various ideas it suggests. In this chapter you will find techniques that will help you make these preliminary choices. You'll also see how these early choices are linked to drafting—the tentative shaping of your material—and to revising, the review and possible reformulation of your initial draft.

CHOOSING A SUBJECT

The essayist Stephen Leacock once asked himself how writers found their ideas. Do ideas, he wondered, arise from inspiration—"effortless and inevitable"—or must they be courted with "a great deal of deliberate effort"? Citing his own experience, Leacock concluded that ideas come from a combination of both inspiration and effort, but probably there's no ideal combination that applies in all cases. Just as writers differ in how they compose, so, too, do they differ in how they get their ideas.

In some cases, of course, writers don't need to do much searching for an idea or subject. Journalists, for example, regularly respond to specific assignments that define their subject and even their purpose. Writers for specialized magazines or journals write on subjects already defined by the special interest of their periodical and the expectations of their readers. Usually, they think less about finding a subject than about developing a subject already proposed.

Your own writing experiences will probably fit both patterns. At times in your college career you will be expected to write on an assigned subject: you may be asked to respond to an essay question, to write a lab report, to do an analysis of a literary work, to compose a detailed term paper. You may even be instructed to arrange your material in a particular fashion: to compare and contrast two figures, events, or theories; to marshal evidence in support of one thesis as opposed to another; or to trace the causes of an event or pattern of behavior. However structured these assignments may be, though, you will still need to show that you know what you're talking about. You'll want to demonstrate from the fullness of your response that you've thought about the subject seriously and that you've gathered a rich array of ideas and information about it.

If you are given an open assignment that asks you to select your subject and to develop it in any way you choose, you will need to do additional planning. For beginning writers, Leacock's deliberate effort is more fruitful than waiting passively for the inspired thought. Before you begin to write, you can use a variety of strategies that will help you think of a subject attractive enough to whet your interest and prod your imagination. Other strategies described in the following pages will show you how to examine your subject closely so that you can determine what you want to say and how you want to say it. Whether your assignment is restricted or free, using these exploratory strategies will help you make wise and informed choices when you begin composing.

Exploring Memories

When asked where he got his ideas for his novels and short stories, William Faulkner replied that "the writer collects his material all his life from everything he reads, from everything he listens to, everything he sees," and he stores it away in a kind of "filing cabinet" for future use. Though Faulkner's filing cabinet was probably more generously crammed than most, his view that all writers possess a storehouse of accumulated experience from which to dig out an appropriate subject can help you explore the possibilities of your own past.

If you think of your filing cabinet as a kind of memory box, you will have grasped one means of finding a subject to write about. Jerome Bruner, the distinguished psychologist, says that the mind is able to store a huge quantity of information; the principal problem of human memory is not storage but retrieval. Some memories fade quickly, some remain vivid for years. This is true not only of people we have known or of events we have lived through but of books we have read, ideas we have thought about, and subjects we have studied.

Why the mind retains some memories and not others is imperfectly understood. Some evidence suggests that we remember particular experiences because they are tinged with feeling. Think of moments in your life that have remained vivid even though they may have occurred when you were a child. Ask yourself why you remember these moments. Is it because, in each case, your emotions were stirred? This connection between emotion and memory can be of great use to you. Not only can it suggest a subject to write about but it can help you generate the rich detail that will recreate the experience for your reader.

Exploring Interests

Professional and personal interests can also be a rich source of material for writing. For example, you are attending college to train in a particular field. Though many factors may have influenced your choice, one, certainly, is that you find the field attractive—it already holds some interest for you even though you are just beginning your training. Perhaps this interest was stimulated by your reading, perhaps by courses you took in high school, perhaps by the recommendation of a trusted friend, relative, or teacher.

Whatever the source, you've accumulated some knowledge that can be tapped. Your interest in becoming a nurse, engineer, computer specialist, or teacher suggests that you already have some familiarity with a profession that you can explore in your writing.

Personal interests can be equally useful in your writing. Perhaps you enjoy sailing or spelunking or chess. Perhaps you are a collector of stamps, porcelain figurines, or old LP records. You may enjoy making model airplanes or developing your own photos or weaving rugs. Or you may be an avid fan of a particular sport or celebrity. Each of these is a potential subject for writing.

Following is a list of subjects our students have recently chosen to write about. Does the subject give you some hint of the student's professional or personal interests? Which (if any) subject interests you? Why? Explain elements of your own background that account for your interest.

Resurfacing Bridge Decks	Wildlife Protection
Downhill Skiing	The Electric Car
UFOs	Cheese-making Technology
WWI Aircraft	Nursing Specialties
Teaching Gifted Children	Marriage Customs of the Navaho
The Circus Aerialist	Indians
Breeding Thoroughbred Horses	

A tip for exploring: Freewriting.   To tap your personal resources, try some *freewriting*. As the name implies, freewriting means putting thoughts on paper without worrying about spelling, punctuation, sentence structure, or the logical connection of ideas. When you freewrite you simply write nonstop for about ten minutes, putting down nonsense or "can't think" or anything—just so you keep pen to paper. When you've finished, you can reread what you've written to see if there's the kernel of an idea you can use.

Freewriting can focus on a subject you've already selected, or it can help you discover a subject. Jon's freewriting illustrates how it can be used to generate an idea.

> Hot. Hot. Too hot to write. But I have to write. Have to. Have to. What to write? Hot. Too hot for spring. Air conditioning not on. Everything runs by the calendar around here. Wish the pool was open. Good day for swimming— swimming in the quarry. We'd swing from the

> rope tied to a branch of the oak tree and land
> smack in the middle. Thrilling to hit the water.
> We'd pretend we were pelicans looking for dinner.
> Or paratroopers sailing to a landing. Steve was
> always the last. Had to get up courage. Wonder
> what happened to him? Moved out west after
> his junior year. He changed after that Amish
> baby got killed. So did I. Guilt maybe. Maybe
> growing up. Can't believe we did those rotten
> things. Maybe it's time to stop. Don't like to
> think about that Amish kid.

Looking over his freewriting, Jon saw that he had hit on several possibilities. The idea of the quarry was attractive. He could write about the imaginary world he and his friends had loved to create. The other possibility was the thought of the Amish baby, a memory he almost wanted to suppress. Though he had hit a raw nerve, he decided to write about that experience because, unlike the first, it had made a deep impression on him, powerfully shaping his attitude toward people different from himself. He wrote the following paragraph:

JUST A SIMPLE WAY OF LIFE

Ever since I can remember, the Amish have been the butt of jokes. On more than a few occasions, my friends and I got our jollies on a boring night at the expense of these gentle people. We would take an air-pressure fire extinguisher and put it in the back seat of one of our cars. The driver of the car would spot the blinking hazard lights of a buggy in the distance and alert the man on the extinguisher. We would then slowly approach our prey until we were right beside it. Whoosh—Ca! went the fire extinguisher. "Dumpkopf!" went the thoroughly soaked buggy driver (we always got a kick out of being cursed in low German). These hilarious pranks got wilder and wilder until one night a few of the local boys discovered some broken clay tiles in the back of their pick-up truck and thought that nothing would be more fun than throwing tiles at Amish buggies. These boys wound up killing

three-month-old Eliza Schwartz that night. That changed my
attitude completely. Before, I'd always thought of the Amish
as almost things--almost inhuman. When the baby died, I found
myself thinking that maybe her parents hurt like regular
people.

Examining People, Events, and Objects

A keen interest in the world about you can also yield subjects for writing.
Examine the people you know or those you've read about in books, magazines, and the newspaper. What makes them tick; what are their motives,
their lifestyles, their influence on other people or events? Or consider an
event that concerns you, whether close to home—a university decision to
increase the student activity fee—or relatively remote—a State Department
decision to restrict overseas travel to a particular country. Observe the
landscape or a man-made object, concentrating on shapes, sounds, and textures. Developing this habit of close observation can help you see that all
experience, no matter how trivial, is grist for the writer's imagination.

A tip for exploring: On-the-spot observing.   A good way to train your
powers of observation is to do some *on-the-spot observing*. You'll need a
notebook in which you can jot down your immediate impressions. As with
freewriting, you won't need to worry about writing in sentences. Simply put
down your perceptions in whatever order they occur and however abbrevi-
ated they may be. Right now you are just making an inventory; later, you can
go back and arrange your impressions to get the effect you want.

You can do your on-the-spot observing anywhere—in a supermarket, a
classroom, a bus station, places where people are likely to congregate—or
in a lonely country spot. You can choose to observe people, objects or the
landscape. It's not *what* you observe that counts most but the quality of
your impressions. When you're observing purposefully, you'll want to
record shapes, sounds, smells, and textures—the sensory details that will
help you compose a vivid and persuasive account of what you've observed.
Even more, though, you'll want to interpret your subject in order to capture
the feeling or mood it evokes. Your goal will be to describe your response
to what you are observing, not merely to record appearances.

Sometimes, interpretation and recording will occur simultaneously.
You'll know right away how you feel about the subject you're observing. At
other times, however, you won't be able to decide how you really feel until
you review your notes and think about what they mean.

Jim's on-the-spot observing illustrates the postponed response. He decided to observe his study, a place he had worked in for three years but had
never really examined closely. With notebook in hand, he made an inventory of its features, but it was not until he reread his notes that he decided
how he felt about the familiar setting.

Here are Jim's notes and the paragraph based on them. As you read his
paragraph, note especially how his interpretation of random impressions

gives them meaning and coherence. Note, too, how every detail he chooses to include contributes to his interpretation.

My Study

A three- by four-yard utility room

A cylindrical water softener in one corner—
    two torpedo-shaped steel containers
    hooked to it

water softener is wheezing and sputtering—
    going through its cycles

lit by a two-hundred-watt bulb without a
    shade

light is in the ceiling—turned on by pulling
    a long, white shoelace

one wall concrete block, other walls a dull
    tan wallboard

concrete block covered with light brown stains—
    reminds me of blood

ten pipes cover the upper half of the concrete
    wall

pipes are tarnished copper and steel, water
    dripping from them

floor is concrete, gray, cold

salt crystals litter floor—dropped on way to
    water softener

odor damp and moldy

My study at home is a loathsome place aptly nicknamed the
"hole." A three- by four-yard utility room, it is lit by a
two-hundred-watt bulb without a shade to combat its glare.
The wall opposite the entrance is a concrete block from the
floor to halfway up. Originally painted white, it is now
splotched with light brown stains that crisscross its many
cracks, like blood that has trickled down from above, dried
and faded with time. The upper half of the wall is hidden by
ten pipes, ranging from two to five inches in diameter. Like
cobras under the spell of a snake charmer, they stretch their
clammy necks upward and then crisscross the wood-plank ceiling
in a network of tarnished copper and steel. The other walls
are just dull tan wallboard coarsely locked together with
rusty nails and rough wooden beams. The gray floor is hard,
cold, and gritty with salt crystals dropped when salt has been
hauled to the water softener inside the room.

Using the Library

You might think of the library as a place to go when you've already chosen
your subject. If you've been assigned a library paper that involves research,
you may first select a subject and then use library resources to gather
relevant material. Using the library in this way is, of course, productive, but
if you think of the library as a place that can *introduce* you to ideas and subjects, you will see that it has broader uses. Think of the library as a place to
leaf through all kinds of printed materials. Go to the periodical room and
leisurely examine current magazines and journals, preferably those you've
never seen before. Skim the editorial and opinion columns of recent newspapers. Stop at the new book shelf and review recent publications. If your
library has open stacks, take a walk through them, stopping occasionally to
look through bound periodicals and books. At first, this random sampling
may seem purposeless and desultory, but in time you'll find yourself recalling ideas you've unconsciously stored. These ideas may be the beginning
of an effective essay.

Keeping a Journal

Try recording your thoughts daily in a journal. Your journal can be a kind
of cedar chest in which you preserve and store everything you've thought
and read, everything you've seen or heard. Your entries should be free and
wide-ranging: record an amusing jingle you heard on a television commercial, a pungent phrase or passage you've heard or read, a response to a
movie you've seen. Examine and evaluate the people you've met, the places

you've been, the food you've eaten, the arguments you've had. Above all, speak in your own voice. Don't let your journal become a laundry list of events ("Got up at seven, had toast and coffee for breakfast, caught the bus . . .") that could happen to anyone. Concern with the *what* of experience encourages the passive eye of the reporter who deliberately remains anonymous. You can avoid this facelessness by cultivating the active and critical eye. Consider the *how* and the *why* of your experiences; examine their significance for you. Think of your journal as a place where you can grouch or laugh or simply muse. The subject of your journal is you, and your voice is different from any other.

Writing daily in your journal will sharpen your writing skills. Even if you write rapidly without attention to form and style, simply putting your thoughts down on paper will increase your control of language. Moreover, your journal can be a rich source of ideas for writing. Professional writers often testify that many of the ideas they use in their work first appeared as journal entries. They enter their ideas and impressions quickly, sometimes without reflection and usually without thought of creating a polished piece of writing. Commenting on her journal, Virginia Woolf notes, "If I stopped and thought, it would never be written at all; and the advantage of the method is that it sweeps up accidentally several stray matters which I should exclude if I hesitated, but which are the diamonds of the dustheap."

A tip for exploring: Exploring impressions. You too may find diamonds in the dustheap if you think of your journal as a treasure house of potential subjects for writing. Foraging in your journal may uncover an idea, image, or experience that you can work into an effective essay. One way to develop the material you've recorded is to explore your impressions before you begin to write by asking yourself questions that will help you recall shapes, sounds, movements, colors, and textures. The example that follows shows how one student used these questions to sharpen her impression of a person, but, actually, they can be applied to objects as well.

To see how Meg explored her impressions in order to transform a journal entry into a polished piece of writing, let's examine her journal entry first:

> Friday. Waited impatiently in line today to mail Aunt Martha the robe she'd forgotten to pack. Had to get to class. What's holding up the line? Well, I saw the hitch when I peered around the people in front of me. In front of the counter stood

a tiny, elderly woman in a black cloak and a gray hood. Her thin shoulders were slightly hunched. She could barely hear the clerk when he asked for eighty-two cents. She pulled out her red purse (of all things) and fumbled around for a bill. When the clerk handed her the change, she asked for it in stamps. By this time, the clerk was impatient. "Window six," he advised her gruffly. When the woman groped her way toward the stamp counter, I saw something remarkable. This aged lady was wearing bright cherry-red stockings.

Though the entry is not especially effective, it has the core of a good idea. Reflecting on what she had written, Meg saw that she had been especially surprised by the cherry-red stockings—suggesting health and vigor—worn by a frail figure who could barely hear or move. She decided that this tension between what she had expected and what she had actually seen would be the focus of her paper.

To reconstruct the episode with the emphasis she wanted, she began to explore her subject, using the following questions as her guide:

What did X wear? What was the color, shape, and texture of her clothing?

Black cloak and gray hood. Cloak seemed several sizes too large. Covered with lint. Hood came to a peak, like the hood of a sweatshirt. Carried a red leather purse with a gold clasp. And those cherry-red

> stockings. Seemed to be made of cotton.
> Bunched around the ankles. Probably held
> up by elastic that had come loose.

How did X look? What was the shape of her body, the shape and color of her eyes, her hands and legs? What was the texture and color of her skin, her hair?

> Hands gnarled, blue-veined, shiny-knuckled.
> Tiny — stood eye level with the window.
> Skin shriveled like onion-skin paper.
> Transparent, waxy. Shoulders thin
> and hunched. Wore glasses with thick
> lenses. Magnified her eyes.

How did X move?

> Fumbled with her purse. Hands moved slowly.
> Seemed to have a tic — kept nodding.
> Could barely walk — tottered is the word.

How did X speak?

> Voice quivered and quaked. Couldn't hear well.
> Clerk had to repeat instructions. She was
> like his echo. Repeated his words.

With her notes before her, Meg began to write her essay, keeping her focus in mind. As you read the essay, consider her choice of details. Why do you think she kept some and discarded others? How does the effect she wished to achieve account for her choice?

```
              CHERRY-RED STOCKINGS

    I glanced up at the clock.  It was 9:15. Lord, I would be
late for class if I didn't get to the parcel post window
quickly.  I peered around the people in front of me to see
what was holding up the line.  There, at eye level with the
window, stood a tiny figure in a black coat and gray hood.
The thin shoulders were hunched slightly forward, the hood
inclined at an angle toward the clerk inside the parcel post
window.  "How much?  How much did you say?"  quavered a voice
from inside the hood.
    "Eighty-two cents."  This came clearly enunciated, each
syllable with a slightly higher pitch and stress.  The
quavering voice carefully pronounced, "Eighty-two cents."
Then, after repeating it two or three times as though trying
to remember what it signified, the hood began to nod.  The
nodding stopped.  There was a flutter of movement within the
cloak and a red purse emerged, clutched in one shiny-knuckled
old hand.  Then the other hand pushed clear of the cloak's
folds and ten slow-moving fingers went to work on the gold
clasp.  After a moment, the red purse came open and the hands
pulled out a crumpled bill.  The clerk promptly pushed
eighteen cents across the counter.
    "Next!"  the clerk commanded.  The hood didn't budge.
    "Give it to me in stamps."
    "You get stamps at window six," said the clerk.  The hood
inclined toward the clerk.
    "What's that?"  quavered the voice within the hood.
    "Window six.  Stamps."  The clerk was shouting now.
    Again the hood nodded several times, and then the tiny
figure turned away from the window toward the back of the post
office.  I turned to watch her totter toward window six.  She
wore glasses that made her eyes swim huge behind the lenses
as though they were astonished at everything on the other
side of the glass.  And below the gray hood, below the black
cloak, there were two thin legs--in bright cherry-red
stockings.

                                        --Meg Newcomer
```

EXPLORING A SUBJECT

Meg's essay illustrates how exploring a subject before composing can transform a fragmentary journal entry into an effective piece of writing. In this case, Meg explored her sensory impressions, but exploration can also focus on ideas and concepts and can help you assemble rich and varied material about your subject. Even if you feel you know your subject intimately, you may fail to tap all its possibilities until you've thought about it in a systematic way. A period of exploration can be valuable, too, because it can help you refine your purpose. Obviously, subjects can be treated in different ways. Any of the subjects listed on p. 28, for example, can be examined from a variety of perspectives. The student who wrote about UFOs decided to argue that UFOs were the products of disordered imaginations, but he could have taken a different tack, perhaps explaining the nature of UFOs or classifying the types of UFOs supposedly sighted. Once you select your subject, you can make a more intelligent choice of purpose if you take the time to gather as much material as you can about your subject. Here is one method you can use to do this.

Brainstorming

Most of us think of a brainstorm as an idea that arises out of the blue. It might be ordinary or it might be sublime, an inspired thought on what to name your cat, or—of weightier consequence—Archimedes' sudden discovery that the volume of an object could be measured by its displacement of water. At first glance, the brainstorm appears disembodied and unattached, a flash of thought strangely alien to the way the mind ordinarily works. If, however, you thought about it, you would realize that thinking depends on multiple links that we often make unconsciously. What seems to be a moment of insight—a sudden idea, isolated and spontaneous—is, in fact, connected to other ideas stored in the mind.

For writers, the moment of insight is useful; indeed, a fortunate few recognize their purpose instinctively and begin writing without thinking too much more about it. For most writers, however, the moment of insight comes only after they have systematically retrieved what they know about their subject and discovered links and relationships among their ideas. Unwilling to leave the brainstorm to chance, they cultivate it deliberately.

In bare outline, brainstorming is associational thinking that encourages a random listing of every bit of information that comes to mind about a subject. The completed list is a kind of inventory or data bank from which writers abstract a purpose and a central idea, selecting only those points that are relevant to their aim and theme and discarding the rest.

Here is how one student used brainstorming to gather material for a paper about industrial robots:

called "workers of the future"

good workers — don't require coffee breaks
or pay raises

will work anywhere, anytime

good for factory assembly work — packaging,
sorting, inspecting, testing

auto industry uses them most now

expensive — I think prices range from
$25,000 to $90,000 (have to look this up)

costs about $5.00 an hour to operate a
single robot

break down easily — technicians have to
be trained to run and repair them

not yet widely used, but some experts
say they'll be in every factory in the
country by 1990

most robots now are blind, but researchers are developing vision systems (computer-
linked cameras)

future robots will be "intelligent" — will
interact with their environment

robots are now building other robots

will take away jobs — people need to be
retrained to handle them or to do other
kinds of work

Clustering

Clustering is a way to discover ideas and to show how they are related. It can be used independently, or it can follow brainstorming. Used in conjunction with brainstorming, it can help you organize the material you've already generated.

Clustering helps you see how ideas may be grouped based on something they share. It also helps you see what further work you need to do to expand what you already have. The method is graphic. Begin by placing a circled topic in the middle of a blank page. Then divide your topic into related subtopics. Circle these and connect them to the main topic. Next, expand each subtopic with additional related material. Circle these as well and connect them to the subtopic.

Following is an example of how one student used clustering to plan an essay about the role of biomechanics in athletic performance:

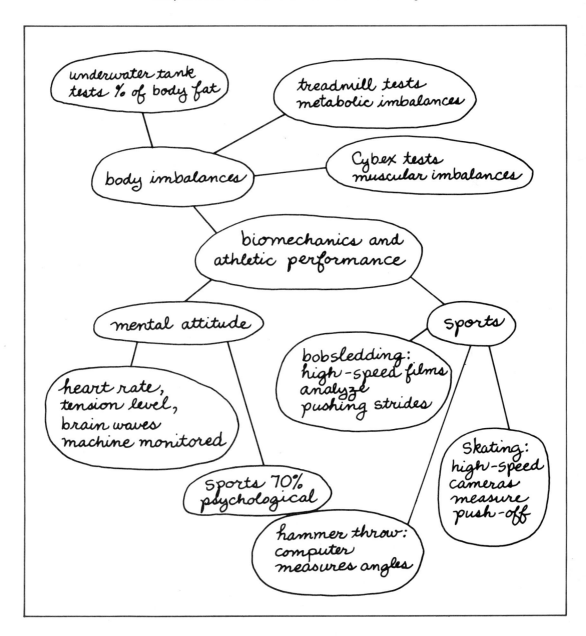

Using the Topics

Another way to tap the possibilities of a subject is to use the topics of invention. The *topics*—the word is a loose translation of the Greek *topoi*—are a figurative map of mental processes. We use them every day when we do such things as compare, contrast, classify, define, and illustrate. If, for example, you debated the advantages and disadvantages of a variety of cars before you made your final choice, you were using one of the topics: comparison and contrast. Or if you pegged an acquaintance as a party-goer, you were using another topic: classification. These and the other topics described in the following pages are not only common ways of thinking which we use almost instinctively, but are also useful strategies for generating ideas. The topics are a means of self-teaching, of using your own powers to examine and explore the accumulated resources stored in your mind.

Following are the notes of one student who used the topics to generate ideas for a paper on epilepsy. Nancy chose the subject because a member of her family had the disease. The notes respond to the commonly asked questions used in the topics of invention. Note that the questions are grouped under six headings: definition, comparison and contrast, classification, illustration, cause and effect, and process.

Definition

1. How does the dictionary define X?
2. What is the etymology of X? When was X first used?
3. What is the general meaning of X? Can its meaning be divided into specific characteristics or attributes?
4. Has the meaning of X changed over time? Will recording this change help clarify X?
5. What are some synonyms for X? Are these synonyms exact, or approximate?

Response

    Dictionary defines epilepsy as a "chronic disease of the nervous system, characterized by convulsions and, often, unconsciousness." Word comes from the Greek epi, meaning "upon," and lambanein, meaning "to seize." Its ancient name was "sacred disease." Also called "the falling sickness." Some people call it a "fit" or "seizure," but I don't think that's accurate. From what I've read, these words describe what the observer sees, not the actual disorder itself. A.M.A. describes it as "a massive build-up of electrical impulses in the brain."

Comparison and Contrast

1. Has X changed over time? If so, what was it like in its earlier form?
2. Has X remained the same over time? If so, what features have remained constant?

3. Is X viewed or practiced differently in different cultures? If so, how?
4. What is X most like? What is it least like?

Response

> Disease hasn't changed, though people's attitudes toward it
> have. In classical times, epileptics were thought to be in
> direct communication with God during a seizure. Idea of
> supernatural powers continued into the Middle Ages. Also
> thought to be contagious. Later, epileptic was thought to be
> possessed by the devil. Sometimes put in institutions for the
> insane. Today, we no longer hold these views. Many people
> are still afraid of the epileptic, though, because they don't
> know much about the disease. I guess the disease can be
> compared to a fuse box when the circuits are overloaded.

Classification

1. Does X consist of distinctively different parts?
2. To what class does X belong? How can this class be labeled or categorized?
3. Does X resemble other things? What is the basis of their shared characteristics?

Response

> Epilepsy is a disease of the central nervous system. Other
> neurological disorders are Parkinson's disease, cerebral
> palsy, and chorea. Three kinds of epileptic seizures. Most
> serious is the "grand mal." Victim suffers convulsions and
> loss of consciousness. Less serious is the psychomotor fit.
> Patient not unconscious but in a kind of dream. Behaves like
> an automaton. Also the "daydreaming seizure." Common in young
> children. Suffer a blackout for five to twenty seconds.

Illustration

1. What are some representative instances of X?
2. What is the supporting evidence for X?

Response

> A lot of famous people had epilepsy: St. Paul, Alexander the
> Great, William the Conqueror, Julius Caesar, Napoleon,
> Dostoevsky. Dostoevsky describes his own affliction through
> the character of Prince Myshkin in The Idiot. Some people
> interpret St. Paul's blackout on his trip to Damascus as an
> instance of epilepsy. Eight hundred thousand people in the
> United States suffer from epilepsy.

Cause and Effect

1. Can X be explained by its effects?
2. Can X be explained by its causes?

3. Has X changed? What has caused the change?
4. What are the consequences of X?

    No organic cause for epilepsy known. Can be brought on by
measles, mumps, and chicken pox. Also alcoholism, severe
injuries to the head, lead poisoning, and birth defects. Not
contagious. Seems to run in families. Does not affect
intelligence, though some people think it does. Once thought
to be caused by an evil spirit. Symptoms of epilepsy haven't
changed, but methods of treatment have. Invention of
electroencephalograph taught us a great deal about the
disease. At one time, disease was treated by applying a hot
iron to the head or by making a small opening in the skull.
Today, the disease is treated with drugs known as
anticonvulsants. The disease is sometimes devastating.
Victim feels like an outcast.

Process

1. Can X be divided into stages?
2. Can X be made? What sequence of steps must be taken in its production?
3. Can X be done? What steps must be followed to do it?

    "Grand mal" attack can be divided into three parts. First
victim feels a tingling in the hands or smells something
strange. This is the warning part. Next comes the fit.
Muscles of the chest and of the rest of the body contract,
victim screams, and face becomes blue-gray. When convulsions
start, the arms, legs, and trunk muscles jerk and the tongue
is sometimes bitten. When the fit is over, the victim falls
into a deep sleep. He won't remember his fit when he awakens.

The Pentad

The *pentad,* often called the dramatistic method, suggests that the interactions of real people resemble the interactions of characters in a play. According to the philosopher Kenneth Burke, who developed the technique, we can examine human behavior from five vantage points:

Act—What exactly was done?
Agent(s)—Who did it?
Agency—By what means?
Scene—Where (in time and place)?
Purpose—Why?

As an inquiry technique, the pentad can be a useful way to gather ideas about a subject. Here is how a student used it to generate material for a paper on training thoroughbred horses.

What exactly was done?

Racehorses were trained. That means conditioning--a schedule of walking, galloping, working, a certain diet, being at the track or kept up in the barn, having legs wrapped, attended to.

Who did it?

The responsible person is the trainer. He or she is licensed by the racing organization, but in reality training involves more than just the trainer, no matter how talented that person is. Training involves the teamwork of grooms, horse walkers, exercise or gallop boys (whatever their sex, they're called boys), owners, veterinarians, sometimes the jockey.

By what means?

A lot of money and a lot of work on the part of all the people listed above working from 5 A.M. to 10 or 11 P.M. How much money? A cheap cheap horse costs $1500 (can sometimes be bought ''on the cuff,'' to be paid for out of its winning purses) and maintaining a horse at the track costs a minimum of $15-20 a day. An average priced horse is $15-20 thousand. There's also a variety of paraphernalia that goes along with training--including everything from an eight-horse van to a tack box filled with a variety of bridles, bits, reins, saddles, medicines, salves, bandages to such things as buckets, rubber mats, ropes, and so on.

Where (in time and place)?

The racing season usually extends from March to November, but there are few tracks with seasons of more than ninety days, so racetrack people have to move around a lot. Where are the best places for racing? That depends of course on how good your horses are, but generally the East Coast and West Coast have most of the country's best racetracks, although there are several in the Great Lakes states--Ohio, Michigan. There's even a nice track in Omaha, Nebraska--Aksarben (read it backward). Specifically, most training occurs at a racetrack daily during the racing season. It's exciting to watch--there are the muted colors of the horses, the tack, the people in their old work clothes, the soft brown of the freshly plowed

track, the clean whites of the distance poles, the brighter
colors of the grandstand. It's cool, usually, because it's
early. It's quiet except for the thudding of hooves and the
splattering of dirt clods raised by the horses, the breathing
(sometimes labored) of the horses, the creaking of saddles,
the slapping of leather, the riders yelling to their horses--
coaxing, scolding. This is a highly romantic memory, of
course, that also reminds me of another whole side of the
racetrack, one not so glamorous.

Why?

Good question. The lure of big money fast is always there,
but so few people around the racetrack have a truly and
consistently middle-class income that I think the real reason
is something else. A love of the horses, maybe, or the lure
of adventure. The life of a Gypsy. Maybe they have no
training for anything else.

LIMITING A SUBJECT

After you've used a method of exploration to gather material about your
subject, you may find your harvest puzzling. The assortment of ideas and information may, in fact, strike you as haphazard and diffuse, hardly conducive to an organized piece of writing. If, however, you remember that you
need to be selective in determining which items to use and which to discard, you will have begun the task of *design*.

Purpose and Thesis

To sift through your material intelligently, you first need to determine your
major purpose. Let's say that you've explored the subject of athletic scholarships and you've assembled a respectable collection of material. You are
now in a position to choose a purpose, but note some of the options you
have. If you argue that athletic scholarships encourage academic fraud, your
purpose will differ considerably from explaining how athletic scholarships
evolved. And both, in turn, will differ from a paper instructing the reader
on how to get an athletic scholarship. Though there might be some overlap,
each purpose requires a different decision about the content to include.

A second principle of design, and one closely related to purpose, is the
thesis of an essay, a key idea that expresses your attitude or point of view.
Keep in mind, though, that purpose determines whether or not a thesis is
necessary. A straightforward list of how to get an athletic scholarship (or
bake a cake or drive a car) or a description of how a cathode ray tube (or
zoom lens or typewriter) works usually will not need a thesis. If, however,

you want to express a point of view or to uphold the validity of an opinion, you will need to formulate a thesis that summarizes the idea you are presenting.

The thesis is not only the best guide to the selection of material, but it can also assure the orderly development of the essay. To exploit its many rhetorical uses, try in the planning stage to formulate a single sentence that tersely captures the idea you intend to develop. Such a thesis statement may or may not appear in your actual essay, but if you devise it before you begin to write, it will help you define what you want to say.

A thesis is an interpretation.   The most important feature of a thesis statement is that it reflects your interpretation of a subject; it does not merely state your subject but affirms your attitude toward it. Unlike a statement of fact, which is self-evident and easily verifiable, a thesis statement expresses a point of view or opinion and is hence problematic or debatable. "American football is played on a field 360 yards long and 160 feet wide" is an expression of fact. It may appear in a paper about football, but it cannot be the unifying element of an essay; it states an element of the game that can be measured and therefore requires no defense. In contrast, a sentence such as "Football players must be cunning as well as agile" contains the kernel of an arguable proposition; it announces that the writer has judged the subject and is prepared to defend a point of view.

A thesis is a conclusion.   The thesis statement also expresses a conclusion. If affirms that the writer has examined the particulars of a subject and has arrived at a generalization summarizing their significance. Making generalizations is, of course, something you do every day. Think of how you sum up your assessment of someone or something by generalizing your impressions. Perhaps you recently left a college classroom, relieved that the hour had finally ended. If you muttered "What a bore" as you headed for the door, you would have captured the quality of a thesis statement. The particulars that led to your judgment might have been that the instructor spoke in a monotonous voice, or read from lecture notes without once inviting discussion, or rambled and was unprepared. Whatever the reasons, you recognized a pattern among these things. You then concluded on the basis of your experience that the word *bore* best reflected the total quality of your instructor's individual acts. You observed your instructor, discerned a common element in your instructor's behavior, and then generalized your experience. In other words, you formulated a thesis.

Developing an Effective Thesis

A thesis is restricted and precise.   Understanding the general features of a thesis statement can help you shape and develop your material if you keep in mind that to be effective, a thesis must be restricted and precise. If you compose a thesis that requires a far more elaborate discussion than you have space for, you need to narrow it, perhaps selecting one of its components to discuss, perhaps discarding it altogether. A good rule of thumb for developing a restricted thesis is to move down the ladder of generality. You may, for example, want to write about foreign imports because you feel strongly that they pose a threat to the American economy. But if you phrased your objections in a sentence such as "Foreign imports threaten the jobs of many Americans," you would soon discover that the notion of foreign imports includes so many products from so many countries that you would be unable to consider the subject in depth in a relatively brief essay. A better way to phrase your objections would therefore be to specify the foreign imports you want to consider, as, for example, "Japanese automobile imports have severely affected the U.S. auto industry" or "The Korean and Taiwanese textiles now flooding the American market have depressed the American textile industry."

In addition to being sufficiently restricted, an effective thesis is also precise. A rule of thumb in this case is that a thesis should be specific enough to guide the development of the essay. Look at some that are too general because they rely primarily on a summarizing adjective: "My grandmother is a remarkable person"; "My neighborhood is depressing." Though statements such as these express an interpretation of a subject, they are too vague to be of much use unless they are immediately followed by a subthesis that specifies their meaning. For example: "The most remarkable woman I have ever known is my grandmother Rosina. After my grandfather died, Rosina suddenly shed her submissive image and became an independent woman." Or "My neighborhood is depressing. The sterile atmosphere caused by too much uniformity, excessive cleanliness, and constant self-awareness is chilling."

In each example, the second sentence reduces the generality of the opening statement and gives the writer a firmer grasp of how to develop the essay. For the first writer, the idea of independence will control the selection of material. Similarly, the writer of the second example now has a three-part subthesis that not only guides the choice of content but suggests its arrangement as well.

FOLLOW-UP ACTIVITY

You have seen that a thesis statement reflects the writer's conclusion that certain events or experiences or ideas share a common pattern. Apply this thinking process to the following tales, anecdotes, and jokes drawn from American frontier humor of the mid-nineteenth century. Try grouping these selections according to a common idea one may share with another and then decide what each group suggests about the values and character of the American backwoods people. Phrase your conclusion as a thesis statement inclusive enough to cover all the qualities you've discerned. For example, your statement might begin: "Samples of frontier humor suggest that the American backwoodsman of the mid-nineteenth century. . . ."

Selection A

I'm that same David Crockett, fresh from the backwoods, half-horse, half-alligator, a little touched with the snapping-turtle; can wade the Mississippi, leap the Ohio, ride upon a streak of lightning, and slip without a scratch down a honey locust; can whip my weight in wild cats,—and if any gentleman pleases, for a ten dollar bill, he may throw in a panther,—hug a bear too close for comfort, and eat any man opposed to Jackson.

Selection B

A traveler stopped at a cabin where a woman and her daughter, both barefooted, were boiling hominy in an iron pot over an open fire in the yard.
The mother shouted, "Look out there, Sal! You're standing on a coal of fire."
Sal looked up and without moving asked, "Which foot, Ma?"

Selection C

A son was born to a frontier couple. The parents wished to find out what his future was to be. They placed before him a bottle, a Bible, and a silver dollar. If he grasped the bottle first, they would know he was going to be a drunkard; if he took the Bible, he would be a preacher, or at least a deacon; if he reached for the coin, he would be a successful businessman, in all probability a banker.
When the objects were laid out in reach of the infant, he grabbed all three simultaneously, from which fact the father inferred that his son would be a politician.

Selection D

I come from high up on the Guadalupe;
The higher up you go the wilder they get;
I come from the head of the creek.
Born on the Guadalupe,
Raised on a prickly pear,
Quarreled with an alligator
And fought with a grizzly bear

I'm wild and woolly and full of fleas;
I've never been curried below the knees.
I'm a wolf with a barb-wire tail;
I'm a wolf and it's my night to howl.

Selection E

A man was struggling to get through an especially muddy stretch of country road when he saw a hat lying on the ground. It looked like a pretty good hat and he dismounted to pick it up. Leaning out cautiously over the mudhole, he seized it by the crown and a voice from beneath called out, "Hey, what are you doing there?" The hat was on a man's head.
"Do you need any help?" the wearer was asked.
"No, thank you," he replied. "I'm riding a mighty good horse and I guess I'll make it through."

Selection F

A farmer in the Camp Springs community in Scurry County has raised a stalk of corn so high he was unable to count the number of ears on it. His eldest son was sent up the stalk to ascertain the amount of corn. The stalk grew so fast that the corn, boy and all, disappeared heavenward, the last report being that the boy had already thrown down three bushels of cobs and shucks.

Selection G

A lawyer, wishing to show his interest in a laborer, asked how he was getting along.

"Oh, I reckon I ain't got nothin' to complain about," said the laborer. "Last week I planted corn for old man Johnson and he paid me forty cents a day and grub. Monday I split rails for Pete Henderson and made fifty cents. And yesterday I mended Widder Jones's roof and she paid me two bits."

"How long did it take you to mend the roof?"

"I worked all day."

"You didn't do so well to work all day for twenty-five cents."

"I got all the money she had. A lawyer couldn't have done no better."

Selection H

"Who killed Abel?" asked a circuit rider of a small boy by way of testing his knowledge of the Bible.

"I don't know nothing about it," replied the boy. "My folks has jest moved here last week."

"Better watch him, Parson," observed an old-timer. "I ain't accusing him, but he sounds mighty suspicious to me."

Selection I

A man hired a lawyer to represent him in a damage suit. After months of litigation, he secured judgment for $2,000. The lawyer handed him a silver dollar.

"What is this for?" asked the client.

"That is the balance coming to you after deducting court costs and attorney's fees."

"What's the matter with this dollar? Is it counterfeit?"

Selection J

A Presbyterian home missionary came to a cabin and engaged a woman in conversation.

"Are there any Presbyterians in this country?" he asked.

"Naw, I jest couldn't say about that," replied the woman. "These woods is full of all kinds of varmints, but I ain't paid much attention to 'em. My husband, he's out with the dogs now. If he was here, he'd know. He keeps his hides on the south wall of the cabin. You might go around there and see if he's got any Presbyterian hides nailed up. I know he's got foxes and bars and painters, and I know if there's any Presbyterians in the country, he's caught some of 'em before now."

"My good woman, you seem to be in the dark."

"Yes, I been after my old man for months to saw me out a winder, but he won't do it."

"You don't understand. Have you ever had any religious convictions?"

"Naw, nor my ole man neither. He was tried once for hog-stealing but he warn't convicted."

—From Mody C. Boatright, *Folk Laughter on the American Frontier*

EXPLORING AND INTERPRETING: A CASE STUDY

If you keep in mind that a thesis is an interpretation of a subject, you'll see that its formulation can grow out of the exploration process. In fact, exploration is more than the collection of material; in its broadest sense it implies a way of thinking that begins with the gathering of data and ends with a creative interpretation that finds a pattern in the seemingly random. Indeed, Jacob Bronowski, the mathematician and writer, shows that these stages of thought occur whenever the human mind begins to synthesize and interpret experience. Following is his version of how this type of thinking accounted for the theoretical formulations of Johannes Kepler and Sir Isaac Newton, two thinkers who laid the foundations of modern astronomy:

> Recall the example of the work of Kepler and of Newton: the steps are there to be re-traced. *The first step is the collection of data:* here, astronomical observations. Next comes the creative step which Kepler took, *which finds an order in the data by exploring likenesses.* Here the order, the unity, is the three laws by which Kepler described the orbit, not of this planet or of that, but simply of a planet.
>
> Kepler's laws, however, put forward no central concept; and the *third step is to create this concept.* Newton took this step when, at the center of astronomy, he put a single activity of the universe: the concept of gravitation.
>
> —*Science and Human Values* (emphasis added)

Note that Bronowski discerns three stages of thought: (1) collecting data; (2) exploring likenesses; and (3) creating a concept. We have rephrased these stages to make them (1) *collecting and recording;* (2) *grouping and classifying;* and (3) *interpreting.* In the discussion that follows, you will see how one student interested in developing an essay about farming used brainstorming to collect and record her ideas, and clustering to group and classify them. These intial steps completed, she considered various ways to interpret her material. The interpretation she chose helped her formulate her purpose and thesis.

Collecting and Recording: Brainstorming

When she began, Lisa was sure that the subject interested her—she had been raised on a farm and knew the farming way of life intimately—but she was uncertain of how she wanted to treat her subject. She therefore began randomly, jotting down whatever ideas came to mind.

Decline in farming population: less than
    four percent today compared to ninety
    percent 100 years ago.
Farmers like being close to nature.
Farmers borrow heavily; always in debt.
Farming expensive: huge investments in
    machinery, fertilizer, seed, etc.
Farm children leaving the farm, pursuing
    other careers.
Sense of community among farming
    families—always willing to help one
    another.
Farm prices unstable—makes farming risky.
Farm bankruptcies have risen twenty
    percent this year.
Advances in farming technology.
Advances in weed-and-insect control
    chemicals; in fertilizers, hybrids, etc.
Today one farmer can feed 68 people in
    contrast to the 15 he fed in 1950.
Farmer important—key to human survival.
Average farm size larger today than 50 years ago.
Fewer farms today than 50 years ago.
Fewer competitive pressures in farming.

Grouping and Classifying: Clustering

When Lisa had completed her list, she went on to the second stage, grouping and classifying. In this stage, she used clustering to organize her material, grouping items according to an element or idea they shared. In the center of a blank page, she placed her topic, farming, and circled it. She then examined her data to see if she could find subtopics that would help her group her material. Some items, she saw, were related to farm income and farm expenditure—what farmers had to spend to run their business and, conversely, what they could expect to receive in return for their product. This suggested that one subtopic could be economics. Accordingly, she placed it (circled) in her cluster picture, showing its connection to her main topic.

Another group seemed to have in common the element of change: farming was different now from what it had been in the past. She saw, though, that these changes were not alike: some pertained to land, technology, and productivity, while others pertained to people. She decided, therefore, to consider change under three subtopics: changes in the size and number of farms; changes in farm methods and productivity; and changes in farm population. She therefore inserted these (circled) in her cluster picture and linked them to her main topic. Finally, she saw that a number of items pertained to the positive aspects of farm life. Identifying these as advantages, she added the heading to her cluster page.

Once Lisa had her subtopics, she then inserted the items on her brainstorming list, connecting each to a relevant subtopic. Pictured on the following page is how her cluster picture looked when she had completed the stage of grouping and classifying.

Interpreting: Developing a Thesis

In the final stage—interpreting—Lisa studied her cluster picture to determine her purpose and thesis. Clearly, she had a variety of options. The notion of change suggested that she could adopt a comparative approach to explain how current farming practices were different from those of the past. Or she could focus on the advantages of farming life, perhaps using anecdotes drawn from personal experience to support her point of view. Or she could write on farm management, explaining the economic hazards farmers face in trying to make farming profitable. At first, she toyed with the last option, since many of her items suggested that farming had become an increasingly risky business. But then she saw that many of her subtopics were causally related; she noted, for example, that the growth of farm technology had changed farming from a labor-intensive to a capital-intensive operation, accounting in part for the decline in the farming population and for the growth of larger farms. Once she recognized this, she saw that what she really wanted to do was to generalize her own experience. She was, in

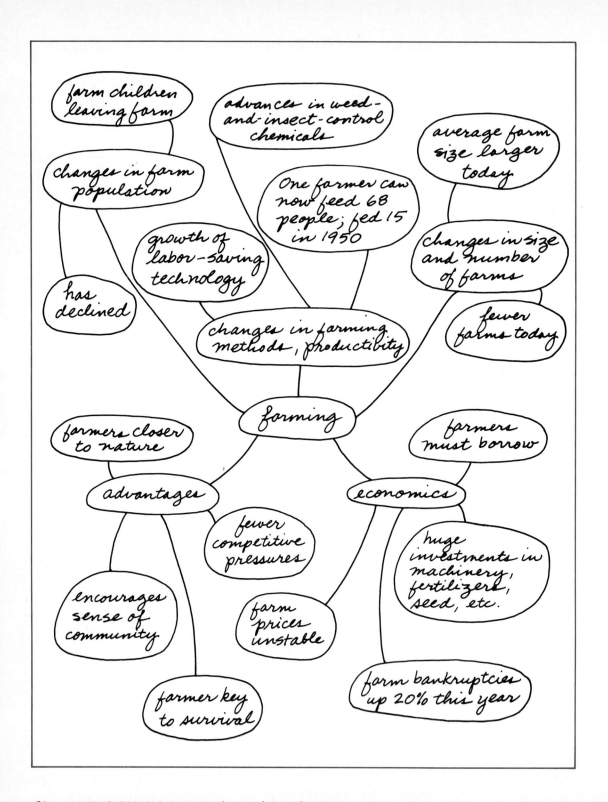

fact, one of the statistics she had cited, a farm child who was attending a university to train as an engineer. She had no intention of returning to the farm. The question she then posed was: Why? Why had she and many other farm children like her elected not to pursue farming as a career? Responding to her question, she developed the following tentative thesis: "Farm children are leaving the farm to pursue other careers because farming has become too chancy a way to make a living."

Choosing an Audience

Once Lisa had her tentative thesis, she then considered her possible audience. She could, of course, write for farm children like herself, but then she would be examining a problem that was already familiar to most of them. As a result, what she had to say might not be of much interest. A better alternative, she thought, would be to direct her essay to those who were unfamiliar with what farming entailed and who, as a result, might have misconceptions about the relative prosperity of farmers. So she determined to write for the nonfarming audience. Choosing such readers, she thought, would allow her to use her special knowledge to build a persuasive case for the riskiness of farming.

DRAFTING AND REVISING: A CASE STUDY

Having chosen her purpose, thesis, and audience, Lisa was ready to write her first draft. Like most writers, she knew that she would probably rewrite her draft many times over before she felt confident that she had written an effective essay. But now she needed to get her ideas down on paper. To help her see how she could arrange her material, she drew up the following informal outline:

```
Farm population down--young people don't take up farming

Farm children going to college--learn about opportunities for
other careers

Really want to go into farming, but farming is risky

Farmers go into debt--have to borrow large sums of money

Farmers often can't pay back debt--income doesn't match
expenses

Farmers don't have fringe benefits

Farmers work long hours

Fewer farmers needed because of technological advances
```

Using her outline as a guide, Lisa wrote her first draft. When she had finished, she read it carefully and then reread it, this time revising as she went along, either by noting what she needed to change or by making the actual changes. Here is how her first draft looked when she had marked the elements she wanted to revise.

ugh! *The Disappearing Farmer*
~~THE DECLINE OF FARMING~~

1   A century ago, farmers constituted
approximately ninety percent of the total labor   *dull intro!*
force in America. Today, less than four percent
of the people employed are farmers. Even in the
last thirty years the farming population has
decreased more than any other sector of the labor
force. Strong influences of the society and
economy are discouraging young men and women from
entering the farming field.

2   With increasing opportunities for young adults
to continue their education beyond high school,
many farmers' children are pursuing careers
unrelated to the farm. Once they reach college,
sons encounter a ~~vast~~ variety of subjects to
study. Encouraged to expand their interests,
they grow apart from the farm. Unlike *the farm children of* fifty
years ago, they are no longer expected to follow
father's footsteps. Likewise, daughters no
longer remain at home to cook and clean. As a
result of women's liberation movements, more of
them are
~~the female population is~~ attending college,
learning to become
~~pursuing careers of~~ lawyers, doctors, engineers,
and mechanics.

3   Many young people would take up farming if they

could. They know ~~that~~ there are rewards to *some of these ideas could go in my conclusion*

farming. If you ask them, most will say ~~that~~

there's a personal satisfaction in being

independent, or they'll tell you that they like

the lack of competition, or they'll talk about

their love of nature and the thrill of working

outdoors. They leave not because they want to

but because they have to. The bottom line is

money. They're afraid they won't be able to earn

their living by farming.

There's plenty of evidence for their fears.

4   ∧A farmer's livelihood depends on investment.

probably not obvious to my reader

The <u>obvious machinery</u> must be replaced frequently

to produce high quality crops. In addition, the

farmer also needs to buy tools and materials to

repair his buildings and grounds. Therefore, a

farmer must constantly borrow money, but often he

finds that he cannot pay back his debt because he

can't earn enough money from the sale of his

crops. Even if a father can help his son start

farming by lending machinery, very few fathers

can afford to give land to their sons any longer,*;*

they need every acre themselves.

5   A farmer's fuel bill alone is enough to disuade *s* *put in ¶ above — same ideas*

anyone from farming. Also, fertilizer costs are

outrageous. But these ~~prices~~ *costs* must be ~~paid~~ *borne* to

continue planting corn and soybeans. On the

other hand, a farmer depends on high prices ∧to *for his products*

earn money, but in today's economy, farm incomes
for a good many farmers do not match farm costs.
When even the most financially stable farmers are
beginning to worry, it is easy to see why many
young men and women are choosing other careers.

6   Another reason many young adults decide not to
farm is that ~~there are~~ *farmers have* no unions to ~~demand a~~ *protect them.*
~~raise in the market price of corn and beans for~~
~~the farmer.~~ No benefits such as free insurance,
free dental care, or free doctor services are
available. The farmer works seven days a week,
twelve hours a day, putting in a work week longer
than the work week of any unionized worker. As a
result, young adults ask themselves why do ~~we~~ *they would*
want to spend ~~our~~ *their* lives in a profession that
involves grueling work and is at the mercy of
Mother Nature when ~~we~~ *they* can make more money *and work fewer hours* in a
profession outside the farm. The answer is
obvious.

7   ~~Along with high prices,~~ Technological advances   *probably have to tell my reader more about this*
have been the main reason for the decline of
farmers in the United States. Fewer farmers are
required to produce the same amount of
agricultural products. Today, one farm worker
can support sixty-two people as opposed to the
fifteen he supported in 1950. Breakthroughs in
plant and soil research are leading to big

business farms, wiping out the small farmer. *There is simply no demand for farmers.*

8   In this [fast-paced, profit-minded society,

farmers are at a disadvantage. They simply can't

compete.] As a result, the farmers of the

nineteenth century have become the doctors,

pilots, and factory workers of the twentieth

century.

not sure I've discussed this

Revising Patterns

If we examine Lisa's revisions carefully, we can see that they can be grouped according to some element they share. One group shows the connection between content and concern for audience. Phrases like "obvious machinery" (paragraph 4) and "technological advances" (paragraph 7) bothered Lisa because she had not sufficiently illustrated them for her intended readers—the nonfarming audience that probably knew little or nothing about farming life. Another group concerns organization: Lisa questions whether the placement of paragraph 3 is effective; whether paragraph 5 should be incorporated in paragraph 4 since both have the same main idea.

Still another group addresses clarity and logic. "Learning to become" replaces "pursuing careers" in paragraph 2 because Lisa sees that college students do not yet pursue careers. The substitution of "costs" for "prices" (paragraph 5) makes the substituted word consistent with what has been discussed earlier. Inserting "and work fewer hours" (paragraph 6) provides parallelism between the first and last part of the paragraph. The transition inserted in paragraph 4 clarifies its relationship to paragraph 3.

Revising for effectiveness is still another group. Lisa changes her title to "The Disappearing Farmer," thereby highlighting the human element in her discussion. She questions her introduction and conclusion, finding the first dull, the other misleading. She adds a final sentence to paragraph 7 that tersely sums up the idea she is discussing. Grammar and mechanics, finally, constitute another group: Lisa is careful to correct problems with punctuation, spelling, and usage throughout.

The Final Draft

Lisa wrote two more drafts before she was satisfied with her work. Here is her final draft. As you read it, consider what further changes she made.

WHERE ARE THE FARMERS?

1   A century ago, farmers constituted approximately ninety percent of the labor force in America. Then, the son of a farmer was expected to follow in his father's footsteps. More than likely, he would complete his education (usually no more than elementary school) and then turn immediately to earning his livelihood on the farm. Today, in contrast, those farm sons are attending college, training for careers unrelated to the farm. Likewise, farm daughters no longer remain at home; more and more of these young women are training to become lawyers, doctors, engineers--even mechanics. Today, less than four percent of the people employed are farmers. Even in the last thirty years, the farming population has decreased more than any other sector of the labor force.

2   The reasons for this decline of interest in farming are many, but one, certainly, is the advance in farm technology. Four-wheel-drive tractors have replaced horses. Eight-bottom-blade plows have replaced single, horse-drawn hoes. Electronically controlled harvesters--fast and efficient--have replaced hand-held scythes. As a result, it is now possible for one farm worker to support sixty-two people in contrast to the fifteen he supported in 1950. There is simply a declining need for farmers.

3   Another reason why farming has become less attractive to the young is its cost. A farmer's livelihood depends on investment. The obvious machinery--combines costing over thirty thousand dollars, tractors topping twenty thousand dollars, pickup trucks priced at ten thousand dollars, plows, planters, rotary hoes--must be replaced frequently to produce high-quality crops. Moreover, the farmer must also buy lumber to repair buildings, grease to oil machinery, wrenches to tighten bolts, hammers to pound nails, and nails to build fences. To do all this, he must constantly borrow money, but often he finds that he cannot make ends meet. To pay his bills, he depends on high prices for his products, but in today's economy, farm incomes for a good many farmers do not match farm costs. When even the most financially stable farmers are beginning to worry, it is easy to see why many young men and women are choosing other careers.

4   Another reason many young adults decide not to farm is that farmers have no unions to protect them. Nor do they enjoy fringe benefits such as free insurance, free dental care, or free medical services. The farmer works seven days a week, twelve hours a day, in one work week putting in more hours than a unionized worker puts in in two. As a result, young

adults ask themselves why they would want to spend their lives
in a profession that involves grueling work and is at the
mercy of market fluctuations when they could enjoy greater
security with less labor in a profession outside the farm.
The answer is obvious.

5   Granted, there are many rewards to farming: the personal
satisfaction of being independent, the lack of competitive
pressure, the thrill of working outdoors. However, these
advantages are overshadowed by the anxiety many farmers feel
about a farm economy that is unstable and often depressed. As
a result, the young are lured to less insecure professions.
However nostalgic they may be about the farming way of life,
they know that the compensations of farming lag far behind its
risks. No wonder, then, that the farmers of the nineteenth
century are changing increasingly into the blue- and white-
collar workers of the twentieth century.

—Lisa Eller

EXPLORING CHOICES

1. Examine Lisa's revised title. Is it more effective than her second choice of title? Explain.
2. Examine the introduction. How does it differ from the introduction of the first draft? Which is more effective? Why?
3. Paragraph 7 of the first draft appears as paragraph 2 of the final draft. Evaluate the effectiveness of this change.
4. What details has Lisa added to paragraphs 2 and 3? Why do you think she added them?
5. Examine the conclusion. Where had Lisa included this information in her earlier draft? Evaluate the change.

A REVISING CHECKLIST

The checklist on the following page provides a guide to revising. It will be useful to you when you begin your own revising. Subsequent chapters in this text will give you added practice and will help you become an acute reader of your own work.

CONTENT AND AUDIENCE

Have I fulfilled my purpose? Do I have a main point that is clearly and precisely stated?

Have I developed my ideas fully? Are they sufficiently supported by specific examples, details, and information?

Have I considered my readers' knowledge of my subject? Have I given them enough information? Too much information?

ORGANIZATION

Have I arranged my material in the best possible order?

Is each paragraph related to the main idea?

Have I used strong transitions to connect my paragraphs?

CLARITY AND LOGIC

Is my word choice clear and accurate?

Are my sentences connected? Have I used a variety of coherence devices?

Does each sentence follow logically from the preceding sentence?

Does each paragraph have a clear focus?

Are the ideas in each paragraph related to each other?

Does each paragraph follow logically from the preceding paragraph?

EFFECTIVENESS

Is my title effective? Will it capture the reader's attention? Does it reflect the theme of my essay?

Is my introduction effective? Does it forecast what my essay will be about?

Does my conclusion effectively restate my case? Does it interpret what I've already said in a fresh way?

Are my sentences varied? Have I alternated sentence openers? Have I varied sentence length?

Is my word choice effective as well as accurate?

GRAMMAR AND MECHANICS

Are my sentences complete? Are they punctuated accurately?

FOLLOW-UP ACTIVITY

Examine the following versions of a student essay. Point out how the thesis of the revision differs from that of the first draft. Determine which is better and explain why by discussing the content and development of each version.

First Draft

THE UNDERWATER WORLD

1   Exploring the depths of the ocean is an adventure that should be missed by no one. From the standpoint of the average person, the ocean is nothing more than a bunch of water. When this mass of water (which accounts for three-fourths of the earth's surface) is closely examined, it is found to contain some of the most vivid colors your mind could ever imagine. Not only the tropical sea life and the coral reefs but also the water itself make up this beautiful underwater world.

2   The surface of the water is crystal blue with rolling swells. As you descend through the water, you will encounter a feeling of total freedom, one that can be compared to nothing on land. It is this feeling, along with the unmistakable smell of the fresh ocean water air, that makes it the inviting environment it is.

3   The creatures that inhabit this huge body of water are themselves equally as fascinating. From the brilliantly colored queen angel fish to the fluorescent green moray eels, there is a feeling of lively awareness. The barracudas with their pointed noses and needle-like teeth move slowly in large schools, casually observing the surroundings. The normally broiled red lobster sits flamboyantly colored in front of the opening in the coral reef. The animals of the underwater world come in many different shapes, sizes, and colors, which enhance this already illustrious world.

4   The ocean floor also adds to this tropical fantasy land. The bottom is covered with beige crystal sand. The sand forms a huge design that flows with the current. The coral reefs

are colorful rock-like configurations. They have roughly
textured surfaces with razor-sharp barnacle growths on them.
The barnacle formations give the reef color and definition.
The reef itself serves as a home for many of the sea
creatures, particularly lobsters and eels. It is a form of
protection in which they can recede into the cavities and
crevices when confronted with danger. There are also various
types of plants and shells which give added character to this
dynamic underwater world.

5   It is extremely difficult to describe something as awesome
as the ocean in words. It is one of those things that must be
personally witnessed to capture its true beauty, but I am sure
many people will never understand this feeling.

Revision

A WORLD OF THE UNEXPECTED

1   I've been scuba diving for almost two years now, and every
dive has been an adventure. From Sweetwater Lake in Brown
County, Indiana, to Franz Park in New Paris, Ohio, to the
Atlantic Ocean off Key Largo and West Palm Beach, I've always
been amazed by the variety and brilliance of undersea life.
It's in diving in the ocean, however, that I have been most
surprised by what I've seen. Somehow, animals look different
in the water than they do when they're out of their natural
environment.

2   Undersea, the starfish, for example, is not the stiff,
fragile, lifeless animal sold in a souvenir shop but a mobile
and flexible sea creature. Last Christmas when I was scuba
diving off Key Largo, I saw a starfish in its natural
environment. Much to my surprise, this five-armed underwater
animal was able to move about, although very slowly. It is
propelled by suction cups that line the bottom of each arm.
These suction cups act as feet and move simultaneously, giving
the starfish its mobility. In its natural state, the starfish
has a smooth, rubbery, flesh-like surface much different from
the rough, hard-textured surface of its lifeless state. Its
color, too, is different: underwater, the starfish is a
brilliant golden brown rather than the bleached color of the
one we have at home. Having seen a starfish in its natural
environment, I now know that the one preserved is only a pale
copy.

3   Another underwater animal that surprised me was the lobster.
We associate lobster with the flamboyant red delicacy that is
served at our favorite restaurant. Sitting on your plate, it
looks fierce and mean, with its bugged eyes and deadly
scissors-like pinchers. This being my perception, I hardly

recognized the first lobster I saw off the coast of West Palm
Beach. Its basic body shape was the same; however, it lacked
its flamboyant red color and its deadly pinchers. Instead, it
was a vivid purple and had two tentacles approximately six
inches long in place of the pinchers. Lobsters use these
tentacles to keep unwanted objects at a safe distance. I was
also surprised by the way the lobster moved. I always thought
it got around by walking. Was I ever surprised the first time
I tried to catch one; it dashed from me in a brief second.
Lobsters, I learned, propel themselves by quickly curling
their tails for thrust.

4   Seeing these underwater animals in their natural environment
upset all my old ideas. For the first time, I saw that live
creatures were far more beautiful than their dead imitations.
Now that I've had a taste of the real thing I won't settle
for less. Museums and souvenir shops may satisfy some, but
for me diving into the depths of the ocean is the only way to
know what marine life is really like.

—Tom Spivey

YOU ARE THE EDITOR

The writer of the following essay decided that his purpose would be to explain to the general reader the significance a particular place had for him.
He chose to write about his neighborhood, but note that he neglects to
develop a thesis that would connect the details he provides. As a result, the
essay rambles from one thought to another. As editor, your task is to help
the writer improve his work. The Editorial Guide that prefaces the essay
will point out the matters you need to look at closely.

EDITORIAL GUIDE

1. Does the essay have a clear thesis? If not, can you suggest one in sentence form and advise the writer where it should be placed?
2. Is the thesis adequately supported? If not, can you suggest additional
supporting details and advise the writer where to place them?
3. Are all the details relevant to the writer's thesis? If not, can you advise
the writer what should be eliminated?
4. Are the details in the right order? If not, can you suggest the order in
which they might be arranged?
5. Does the title reflect the thesis of the essay? If not, can you suggest an
alternative?

DRUMMOND STREET

Drummond Street, a friendly residential area, provides me with memories of the past. I spent my childhood days there and learned to appreciate the simple things it stood for.

Drummond Street is in the central part of town. I remember arguing with my friends that it is in the north end of town, but they said the south. So we compromised and said the middle of town.

It is a small street made up of only two blocks. At the end of the street is an Army Reserve Office. The neighborhood would get together there to play football, only to be run off the grounds by the janitor.

The residents of the block were either very old or very young. As kids, we looked up to the old folks, especially to Pop McDowell and his swinging chair. Pop would always welcome kids to come and talk to him, either about their problems or his. Sitting in his chair made us feel like we were on top of the world because Pop was the toast of the neighborhood.

Drummond Street has a beauty that you cannot appreciate unless you lived there. Rows of maple and oak trees extend for the two blocks, acting as a shelter against attack. When bats would come out at night, we would find the nearest tree and hide underneath its broad limbs for safety.

Watching a day go by on Drummond Street may not seem to be exciting, but for me it was. Getting up early in the morning meant chirping birds. The smell of bacon and eggs on the griddle, with Mom cooking her heart out, was a sign of a good day, a day to be outdoors.

As the day progressed, we would play our mischievous games, ranging from sneaking into old lady O'Brien's vegetable garden to harassing the bumblebees in Brown's garage. It was fun being together with friends. But the summertime was the only time to be together every day. When school was in session, there was a change of scene as well as season. Drummond Street was no longer busy with little kids playing.

Drummond Street has many good memories as well as bad. It gave me friends as well as enemies. Most of all, it let me grow up in better conditions than many and to see life from the good side. Although I lived there for only fifteen years, I will carry the spirit of Drummond Street with me forever.

WRITING SUGGESTIONS

1. Many companies publish in-house newsletters for their employees. Imagine that you are working for such a company and write an article for the newsletter outlining the working conditions that promote

employee satisfaction and productivity. Support your thesis with details drawn from direct observation, the comments of other employees, and reading.

2. Think of one or more regulations in the federal income tax law that you consider inequitable (your thesis) and write a letter to a member of Congress outlining the reasons for your objections (the support for your thesis).

3. Describe a place you've visited that surprised you because you expected one thing and found another.

4. Describe a person you know well by singling out one feature of his or her personality. Support your thesis with the details that helped you formulate your conclusion.

2
MAKING CHOICES
The Shape of Expression

CHOOSING A PATTERN OF DEVELOPMENT

*I*n Chapter 2, you saw how students used different strategies of invention to select and explore a subject. You also saw that these preliminary explorations helped them determine what they wanted to say and how best to arrange their material. For example, the student who decided to explain why fewer farm children were choosing farming as a career discovered that she was tracing the causes of an event, and so she used a *cause-and-effect* pattern to develop her essay. Another, who wanted to explain epilepsy, found that the topics helped her to *define* and *classify* epileptic seizures as well as to *compare and contrast* public attitudes toward the epileptic. In each case, the writers found that exploring their subject provided them with certain patterns that could help them develop their material.

Depending on your purpose, you may need to combine several developmental patterns in a single essay—as Robert Brustein effortlessly does in "Reflections on Horror Movies" below. Brustein's *overall purpose* is to convince his readers that many classic horror movies not only entertain but also speak to the popular imagination by expressing an ambivalent attitude toward science and scientists. To accomplish this, he employs classification as his *major* developmental *pattern,* yet he also uses several other patterns along the way. As you read the essay, you will notice, in fact, that each paragraph has its own purpose and its own pattern (or patterns).

REFLECTIONS ON HORROR MOVIES

1   Horror movies, perennial supporting features among Grade B and C fare, have recently been enjoying a vogue, a fact in which I shamelessly rejoice. I have been hopelessly addicted to them since the age of eight when my mother, with great anxiety lest I be traumatized for life, accompanied me to see Frederic March in *Dr. Jekyll and Mr. Hyde.* Since then, I guess I have seen about two hundred horror films but, although my mother had a couple of bad nights, I have always remained impervious to the inviting promise of their advertising ("Will Give You Nightmares FOREVER"). My satisfactions are more simple. Horror films give me pleasure by their very faults: the woodenness of the acting, the inevitability of the plot, the obstinate refusal to make any but the most basic demand on my mind. I can suggest nothing more remedial after a night of agony at the theatre than a late horror show at a 42nd Street flea pit.

Purpose: to introduce subject and its appeal and suggest thesis in broad terms.
Patterns: narration of autobiographical anecdote; effect (pleasure) from certain causes.

2   It may seem a little graceless of me, in view of the enjoyment I have derived from these films, to analyze their "cultural significance" and run the risk of stifling any pleasure you (or I) might seek from them in future. But it has occurred to me over the years that, aside from modest shock motives, horror films always try to involve us in certain underground assumptions. They have been serving up a mess of cultural pottage whose seasoning gives science (and sometimes even all knowledge) a bad taste. Since I attended these films with childlike innocence, I consider these added motives an impudence, and I retaliate by pointing out to you what the hidden images are.

Purpose: to indicate arrangement of evidence.
Pattern: classification (three categories).

Purpose: to explain chief characteristics of first category.
Patterns: illustration; narration of figure's genesis in myth; process by which devil became scientist.

Purpose: to explain central figure of Mad Doctor.
Patterns: comparison/contrast (Faustus and Frankenstein); description of monster.

3   The horror movies I am mainly concerned with I have divided into three major categories: Mad Doctor, Atomic Beast, and Interplanetary Monster. They do not exhaust all the types but they each contain two essential characters, the Scientist and the Monster, toward whom the attitudes of the movies are in a revealing state of change.

4   The Mad Doctor series is by far the most long lived of the three. It suffered a temporary decline in the forties when Frankenstein, Dracula, and the Wolf Man (along with their countless offspring) were first loaned out as straight men to Abbott and Costello and then set out to graze in the parched pastures of the cheap all-night movie houses, but it has recently demonstrated its durability in a group of English remakes and a Teenage Monster craze. These films find their roots in certain European folk myths. Dracula was inspired by an ancient Balkan superstition about vampires, the werewolf is a Middle European folk myth recorded, among other places, in the Breton *lais* of Marie de France, and even Frankenstein, though out of Mary Shelley by the Gothic tradition, has a medieval prototype in the Golem, a monster the Jews fashioned from clay and earth to free them from oppression. The spirit of these films is still medieval, combining a vulgar religiosity with folk superstitions. Superstition now, however, has been crudely transferred from magic and alchemy to creative science, itself a form of magic to the untutored mind. The devil of the vampire and werewolf myths, who turned human beings into baser animals, today has become a scientist, and the metamorphosis is given a technical name—it is a "regression" into an earlier state of evolution. The alchemist and devil-conjuring scholar Dr. Faustus gives way to Dr. Frankenstein the research physician, while the magic circle, the tetragrammaton, and the full moon are replaced by test tubes, complicated electrical apparati, and bunsen burners.

5   Frankenstein, like Faustus, defies God by exploring areas where humans are not meant to trespass. In Mary Shelley's book (it is subtitled "A Modern Prometheus"), Frankenstein is a latter-day Faustus, a superhuman creature whose aspiration embodies the expansiveness of his age. In the movies, however, Frankenstein loses his heroic quality and becomes a lunatic monomaniac, so obsessed with the value of his work that he no longer cares whether his discovery proves a boon or a curse to mankind. When the mad doctor, his eyes wild and inflamed, bends over his intricate equipment, pouring in a little of this and a little of that, the spectator is confronted with an immoral being whose mental superiority is only a measure of his madness. Like the popular image of the theoretical scientist engaged in basic research ("Basic research," says Charles Wilson, "is science's attempt to prove that grass is green"), he succeeds only in creating something badly which nature has already made well. The Frankenstein monster is a parody of man. Ghastly in appearance, clumsy in movement, criminal in behavior, imbecilic of mind, it is superior only in physical strength and resistance to destruction. The scientist has fashioned it in the face of divine disapproval (the heavens disgorge at its birth)—not to mention the disapproval of friends and frightened townspeople—and it can lead only to trouble.

6   For Dr. Frankenstein, however, the monster symbolizes the triumph of his intellect over the blind morality of his enemies and it confirms him in the ulti-

Purpose: to show that
relationship between
scientist and monster
implies criticism of
experiential
knowledge that
would make man a
usurper of the divine;
to restate thesis.
Patterns: narration of
monster's actions;
illustration.

mate soundness of his thought ("They thought I was mad, but this proves I am the superior being"). When it becomes clear that his countrymen are unimpressed by his achievement and regard him as a menace to society, the monster becomes the agent of his revenge. As it ravages the countryside and terrorizes the inhabitants, it embodies and expresses the scientist's own lust and violence. It is an extension of his own mad soul, come to life not in a weak and ineffectual body but in a body of formidable physical power. (In a movie like *Dr. Jekyll and Mr. Hyde,* the identity of monster and doctor is even clearer; Mr. Hyde, the monster, is the aggressive and libidinous element in the benevolent Dr. Jekyll's personality.) The rampage of the monster is the rampage of mad, unrestrained science which inevitably turns on the scientist, destroying him too. As the lava bubbles over the sinking head of the monster, the crude moral of the film frees itself from the horror and is asserted. Experimental science (and by extension knowledge itself) is superfluous, dangerous, and unlawful, for, in exploring the unknown, it leads man to usurp God's creative power. Each of these films is a victory for obscurantism, flattering the spectator into believing that his intellectual inferiority is a sign that he is loved by God.

Purpose: to define
central figures of
subcategory.
Patterns: description;
illustration; contrast
of scientist and
monster with types in
earlier movies.

7   The Teenage Monster films, a very recent phenomenon, amend the assumptions of these horror movies in a startling manner. Their titles—*I Was a Teenage Werewolf, I Was a Teenage Frankenstein, Blood of Dracula,* and *Teenage Monster*—(some wit awaits one called *I Had a Teenage Monkey on My Back*)—suggest a Hollywood prank but they are deadly serious, mixing the conventions of early horror movies with the ingredients of adolescent culture. The doctor, significantly enough, is no longer a fringe character whose madness can be inferred from the rings around his eyes and his wild hair, but a respected member of society, a high school chemistry teacher *(Blood of Dracula)* or a psychoanalyst *(Teenage Werewolf)* or a visiting lecturer from Britain *(Teenage Frankenstein).* Although he gives the appearance of benevolence—he pretends to help teenagers with their problems—behind this façade he hides evil experimental designs. The monster, on the other hand, takes on a more fully developed personality. He is a victim who begins inauspiciously as an average, though emotionally troubled, adolescent and ends, through the influence of the doctor, as a voracious animal. The monster as teenager becomes the central character in the film and the teenage audience is expected to identify and sympathize with him.

Purpose: to provide
evidence for
preceding.
Pattern: narration of
specific plot.

8   In *I Was a Teenage Werewolf,* the hero is characterized as brilliant but erratic in his studies and something of a delinquent. At the suggestion of his principal, he agrees to accept therapy from an analyst helping maladjusted students. The analyst gets the boy under his control and, after injecting him with a secret drug, turns him into a werewolf. Against his will he murders a number of his contemporaries. When the doctor refuses to free him from his curse, he kills him and is himself killed by the police. In death, his features relax into the harmless countenance of an adolescent.

Purpose: to analyze
meaning of this type
of horror film, in
which distrust of
science is seen in

9   The crimes of the adolescent are invariably committed against other youths (the doctor has it in for teenagers) and are always connected with those staples of juvenile culture, sex and violence. The advertising displays show the male monsters, dressed in leather jackets and blue jeans, bending ambiguously over the diaphanously draped body of a luscious young girl, while the female

antiauthoritarian impulse— particularizes thesis. Patterns: description; illustration; effect on adolescent spectators.

teenage vampire of *Blood of Dracula,* her nails long and her fangs dripping, is herself half dressed and lying on top of a struggling male (whether to rape or murder him it is not clear). The identification of sex and violence is further underlined by the promotion blurbs: "In her eyes DESIRE! In her veins—the blood of a MONSTER!" *(Blood of Dracula);* "A Teenage Titan on a Lustful Binge That Paralyzed a Town with Fear" *(Teenage Monster).* It is probable that these crimes are performed less reluctantly than is suggested and that the adolescent spectator is more thrilled than appalled by this "lustful binge" which captures the attention of the adult community. The acquisition of power and prestige through delinquent sexual and aggressive activity is a familiar juvenile fantasy (the same distributors exploit it more openly in films like *Reform School Girl* and *Drag-Strip Girl*), one which we can see frequently acted out by delinquents in our city schools. In the Teenage Monster films, however, the hero is absolved of his aggressive and libidinous impulses. Although he both feels and acts on them, he can attribute the responsibility to the mad scientist who controls his behavior. What these films seem to be saying, in their underground manner, is that behind the harmless face of the high school chemistry teacher and the intellectual countenance of the psychoanalyst lies the warped authority responsible for teenage violence. The adolescent feels victimized by society— turned into a monster by society—and if he behaves in a delinquent manner, society and not he is to blame. Thus, we can see one direction in which the hostility for experimental research, explicit in the Mad Doctor films, can go—it can be transmuted into hatred of adult authority itself.

Purpose: to explain characteristics of second category. Patterns: contrast (Atomic Beast with Mad Doctor); illustration.

10   Or it can go underground, as in the Atomic Beast movies. The Mad Doctor movies, in exploiting the supernatural, usually locate their action in Europe (often a remote Bavarian village), where wild fens, spectral castles, and ominous graveyards provide the proper eerie background. The Atomic Beast movies depend for their effect on the contemporary and familiar and there is a corresponding change in locale. The monster (or *thing,* as it is more often called) appears now in a busy American city—usually Los Angeles to save the producer money—where average men walk about in business suits. The thing terrorizes not only the hero, the heroine, and a few anonymous (and expendable) characters in Tyrolean costumes, but the entire world. Furthermore, it has lost all resemblance to anything human. It appears as a giant ant *(Them!),* a prehistoric animal *(Beast from Twenty Thousand Fathoms),* an outsized grasshopper *(Beginning of the End),* or a monstrous spider *(Tarantula).* Although these films, in their deference to science fiction, seem to smile more benignly on scientific endeavor, they are unconsciously closer to the antitheoretical biases of the Mad Doctor series than would first appear.

Purpose: to furnish detailed example of category. Pattern: narration of plot.

11   All these films are similarly plotted, so the plot of *Beginning of the End* will serve as an example of the whole genre. The scene opens on a pair of adolescents necking in their car off a desert road. Their attention is caught by a weird clicking sound, the boy looks up in horror, the girl screams, the music stings, and the scene fades. In the next scene, we learn that the car has been completely demolished and its occupants have disappeared. The police, totally baffled, are conducting fruitless investigations when word comes that a small town nearby has been destroyed in the same mysterious way. Enter the young scientist-hero. Examining the wreckage of the town, he discovers a strange fluid

which when analyzed proves to have been manufactured by a giant grasshopper. The police ridicule his conclusions and are instantly attacked by a fleet of these grasshoppers, each fifteen feet high, which wipe out the entire local force and a few state troopers. Interrupting a perfunctory romance with the heroine, the scientist flies to Washington to alert the nation. He describes the potential danger to a group of bored politicians and yawning big brass but they remain skeptical until word comes that the things have reached Chicago and are crushing buildings and eating the occupants. The scientist is then put in charge of the army and air force. Although the military men want to evacuate the city and drop an atom bomb on it, the scientist devises a safer method of destroying the creatures and proceeds to do so through exemplary physical courage and superior knowledge of their behavior. The movie ends on a note of foreboding: Have the things been completely exterminated?

Purpose: to determine whether scientist has changed.
Patterns: description; contrast; illustration.

12   Externally, there seem to be very significant changes indeed, especially in the character of the scientist. No longer fang toothed, long haired, and subject to delirious ravings (Bela Lugosi, John Carradine, Basil Rathbone), the doctor is now a highly admired member of society, muscular, handsome, and heroic (John Agar). He is invariably wiser, more reasonable, and more humane than the boneheaded bureaucrats and trigger-happy brass who compose the members of his "team," and he even has sexual appeal, a quality which Hollywood's eggheads have never enjoyed before. The scientist-hero, however, is not a very convincing intellectual. Although he may use technical, polysyllabic language when discussing his findings, he always yields gracefully to the admonition to "tell us in our own words, Doc" and proves that he can speak as simply as you or I; in the crisis, in fact, he is almost monosyllabic. When the chips are down, he loses his glasses (a symbol of his intellectualism) and begins to look like everyone else. The hero's intellect is part of his costume and makeup, easily shed when heroic action is demanded. That he is always called upon not only to outwit the thing but to wrestle with it as well (in order to save the heroine) indicates that he is in constant danger of tripping over the thin boundary between specialist and average Joe.

Purpose: to emphasize change.
Pattern: definition of "new" monster.

13   The fact remains that there is a new separation between the scientist and the monster. Rather than being an extension of the doctor's evil will, the monster functions completely on its own, creating havoc through its predatory nature. We learn through charts, biological films, and the scientist's patient explanations that ants and grasshoppers are not the harmless little beasties they appear but actually voracious insects who need only the excuse of size to prey upon humanity. The doctor, rather than allying himself with the monster in its rampage against our cities, is in strong opposition to it, and reverses the pattern of the Mad Doctor films by destroying it.

Purpose: to show continuity in attitude towards science.
Patterns: process of how monsters came to be; illustration.

14   And yet, if the individual scientist is absolved of all responsibilty for the thing, science somehow is not. These films suggest an uneasiness about science which, though subtle and unpremeditated, reflects unconscious American attitudes. These attitudes are sharpened when we examine the genesis of the thing, for, though it seems to rise out of nowhere, it is invariably caused by a scientific blunder. The giant ants of *Them!,* for example, result from a nuclear explosion which caused a mutation in the species; another fission test has awakened, in *Beast from Twenty Thousand Fathoms,* a dinosaur encrusted in polar icecaps;

the spider of *Tarantula* grows in size after having been injected with radioactive isotopes, and escapes during a fight in the lab between two scientists; the grasshoppers of *Beginning of the End* enlarge after crawling into some radioactive dust carelessly left about by a researcher. We are left with a puzzling substatement: science destroys the thing, but scientific experimentation has created it.

Purpose: to analyze "thing" as symbol for bomb. Patterns: contrast; definition (of scientist vs. theoretician).

15   I think we can explain this equivocal attitude when we acknowledge that the thing "which is too horrible to name," which owes its birth to an atomic or nuclear explosion, which begins in a desert or frozen waste and moves from there to cities, and which promises ultimately to destroy the world, is probably a crude symbol for the bomb itself. The scientists we see represented in these films are unlike the Mad Doctors in another, more fundamental respect: they are never engaged in basic research. The scientist uses his knowledge in a purely defensive manner, like a specialist working on rocket interception or a physician trying to cure a disease. The isolated theoretician who tinkers curiously in his lab (and who invented the atom bomb) is never shown, only the practical working scientist who strives to undo the harm. The thing's destructive rampage against cities, like the rampage of the Frankenstein monster, is the result of too much cleverness, and the consequences for all the world are only too apparent.

Purpose: to support preceding symbolic reading. Pattern: narration of two detailed examples.

16   These consequences are driven home more powerfully in movies like *The Incredible Shrinking Man* and *The Amazing Colossal Man,* where the audience gets the opportunity to identify closely with the victims of science's reckless experimentation. The hero of the first movie is an average man who, through contact with fallout while on his honeymoon, begins to shrink away to nothing. As he proceeds to grow smaller, he finds himself in much the same dilemma as the other heroes of the Atomic Beast series—he must do battle with (now) gigantic insects in order to survive. Scientists can do nothing to save him—after a while they can't even find him—so as he dwindles into an atomic particle he finally turns to God, for whom "there is no zero." The inevitable sequel, *The Amazing Colossal Man,* reverses the dilemma. The hero grows to enormous size through the premature explosion of a plutonium bomb. Size carries with it the luxury of power but the hero cannot enjoy his new stature. He feels like a freak and his body is proceeding to outgrow his brain and heart. Although the scientists labor to help him and even succeed in reducing an elephant to the size of a cat, it is too late; the hero has gone mad, demolished Las Vegas, and fallen over Boulder Dam. The victimization of man by theoretical science has become, in these two movies, less of a suggestion and more of a fact.

Purpose: to distinguish third category from other two. Pattern: narration about two movie scientists.

17   In the Interplanetary Monster movies, Hollywood handles the public's ambivalence toward science in a more obvious way, by splitting the scientist in two. Most of these movies feature both a practical scientist who wishes to destroy the invader and a theoretical scientist who wants to communicate with it. In *The Thing,* for example, we find billeted among a group of more altruistic average-Joe colleagues with crew cuts an academic long-haired scientist of the Dr. Frankenstein type. When the evil thing (a highly evolved vegetable which, by multiplying itself, threatens to take over the world) descends in a flying saucer, this scientist tries to perpetuate its life in order "to find out what it knows." He is violently opposed in this by the others, who take the occasion to tell him that

such amoral investigation produced the atom bomb. But he cannot be reasoned with and almost wrecks the entire party. After both he and the thing are destroyed, the others congratulate themselves on remaining safe, though in the dark. In *Forbidden Planet* (a sophisticated thriller inspired in part by Shakespeare's *Tempest*), the good and evil elements in science are represented, as in *Dr. Jekyll and Mr. Hyde,* by the split personality of the scientist. He is urbane and benevolent (Walter Pidgeon plays the role) and is trying to realize an ideal community on the far-off planet he has discovered. Although he has invented a robot (Ariel) who cheerfully performs man's baser tasks, we learn that he is also responsible, though unwittingly, for a terrible invisible force (Caliban) overwhelming in its destructiveness. While he sleeps, the aggressive forces in his libido activate a dynamo he has been tinkering with which gives enormous power to kill those the doctor unconsciously resents. Thus, Freudian psychology is evoked to endow the scientist with guilt. At the end, he accepts his guilt and sacrifices his life in order to combat the being he has created.

Purpose: to analyze 18
role of the "monster."
Patterns: narration of
three plots;
comparison.

The Interplanetary Monster series sometimes reverses the central situation of most horror films. We often find the monster controlling the scientist and forcing him to do its evil will. In *It Conquered the World* (the first film to capitalize on Sputnik and Explorer), the projection of a space satellite proves to be a mistake, for it results in the invasion of America by a monster from Venus. It takes control of the scientist who, embittered by the indifference of the masses toward his ideas, mistakenly thinks the monster will free men from stupidity. This muddled egghead finally discovers the true intentions of the monster and destroys it, dying himself in the process. In *The Brain from Planet Arous,* a hideous brain inhabits the mind of a nuclear physicist with the intention of controlling the universe. As the physical incarnation of the monster, the scientist is at the mercy of its will until he can free himself of its influence. The monster's intellect, like the intellect of the Mad Doctor, is invariably superior, signified by its large head and small body (in the last film named it is nothing but brain). Like the Mad Doctor, its superior intelligence is always accompanied by moral depravity and an unconscionable lust for power. If the monster is to be destroyed at all, it will not be done by matching wits with it but by finding some chink in its armor. This chink quite often is a physical imperfection: in *War of the Worlds,* the invading Martians are stopped, at the height of their victory, by their vulnerability to the disease germs of earth. Before this Achilles heel is discovered, however, the scientist is controlled to do evil, and with the monster and the doctor in collaboration again, even in this qualified sense, the wheel has come full circle.

Purpose: to 19
recapitulate and
expand on thesis that
a suspicion of
scientific research
underlies horror
films.

The terror of most of these films, then, stems from the matching of knowledge with power, always a source of fear for Americans—when Nietzsche's Superman enters comic-book culture he loses his intellectual and spiritual qualities and becomes a muscleman. The muscleman, even with X-ray vision, poses no threat to the will, but muscle in collaboration with mind is generally thought to have a profound effect on individual destinies. The tendency to attribute everything that happens in the heavens, from flying saucers to Florida's cold wave, to science and the bomb ("Why don't they stop," said an old lady on the bus behind me the other day, "they don't know what they're doing") accounts for the extreme ways in which the scientist is regarded in our culture: either as a protective savior or as a destructive blunderer. It is little wonder that America exalts the physician (and the football player) and ignores the physicist. These issues, the issues of the great debate over scientific education and basic research, assert themselves crudely through the unwieldy monster and the Mad Doctor. The films suggest that the academic scientist, in exploring new areas, has laid the human race open to devastation by either human or interplanetary enemies—the doctor's madness, then, is merely a suitable way of expressing a conviction that the scientist's idle curiosity has shaken itself loose from prudency or principle. There is obviously a sensitive moral problem involved here, one which needs more articulate treatment than the covert and superstitious way it is handled in horror movies. That the problem is touched there at all is evidence of how profoundly it has stirred the American psyche.

—Robert Brustein

In the following pages, you will see how other writers—both professional and student—have used the various patterns to develop effective essays. For convenience, each pattern is presented separately, though in practice patterns are often intertwined, as an analysis of the Brustein essay has shown. Examining the patterns separately will, however, help you gain control of their basic structure so that when you have occasion to use them in your writing, you will be able to manage them skillfully, suiting pattern to purpose, either to develop paragraphs or to shape the whole essay.

NARRATION

The story is possibly our earliest encounter with shaped expression. Even before we can read, we are enchanted by fairy tales, fables, or myths that tell of wondrous places and people. Later, our tastes may change: for some, detective fiction is eternally fascinating; for others, science fiction is the favorite type of story; for still others, historical novels or romances are required reading. Even in nonprint media, the story has special prominence: think of television, with its soap operas, police tales, and situation comedies—all of which rely on fictional events arranged in narrative form.

The Structure of Narration

Narration follows a time sequence; it moves from one event to another in an order resembling the rhythms of everyday life. We arrange our lives according to time; we sleep and awaken at certain hours, take our meals according to the clock, make and keep appointments scheduled by time. For these reasons, chronological order is usually a comfortable pattern, easily mastered by most beginning writers.

Mastering a pattern, however, is not always enough. After all, simply listing events in the order in which they happened may lead to writing which describes life without interpreting it. Most of us would find this boring. We expect to find meaning in what we read, as well as in what we do or live through. We want, in short, to analyze experience, to understand why something happened or what effect it produced. For this reason, a narrative does not simply list events but conveys their significance, either explicitly or implicitly. Usually, this significance becomes apparent when some conflict—either internal or external—is worked through and resolved. The conflict and its resolution lead to an insight that helps us understand ourselves and others.

The structure of a narrative generally has three parts: the *exposition* announces place, time, actors, and theme; the *complication* describes the conflict and its corresponding events; and the *resolution* ends the conflict and sums up its meaning, either directly or indirectly.

Essays for Analysis

Essay A

The following essay, written by Ernest Davis, a college freshman, describes a contest that marked an important moment in his life. As you read the essay, consider how the event changed the author's conception of himself.

THE PENALTIES OF PRIDE

1   Racing in the streets is illegal, and the punishment, if caught doing so, is usually suspension of one's license for at least one year. Quite a detriment, yet sometimes an adolescent's pride is more powerful than any written law imaginable.

2   It was spring about a year ago, but it seems like just yesterday that the black Kawasaki appeared in my high school's parking lot. I had been expecting him. I didn't know who he was exactly, but the word on the street was that he was some wealthy punk from our rival school. It didn't really matter; boy and bike melted into one being, and he was the black Kaw.

3   I had heard from friends that he had just bought a brand-new 44 ILD Kaw, a bike on the cutting edge of technology, and at the time one of the fastest midsized bikes on the market. My bike, in contrast, was a decade-old stormer from another time and another school of thought. It was as heavy as new bikes twice its size, although when new it had been a technical wonder with twin cams and 9 1/2-to-1 pistons. The 450 cc Honda had since fallen into my hands and had been reworked. It now boasted a Jardine header, K.C. alloy sprocket, King and Queen seats, sissy bar, and drawn-back handlebars lowered in the rear and extended in the front. A chopper.

4   With all my modifications, I had gained considerable speed,
and with this an unofficial title as the fastest midsized bike
in the area. That was why the black Kaw was looking for me.

5   It was lunch time at school, and we were outside relishing
the spring's new-found warmth when the black Kaw came
screaming across the tarmac of the parking lot. He came to
rest at the corner of the area reserved for motorcycle parking
and flipped up his black face mask to expose an extremely
young-looking face, blond hair streaming down to his
shoulders, and intense, almost icy-blue eyes. He didn't look
old enough even to have his license. He gave his gurgling
ride a blip of gas and pulled across the lot. A challenge had
been made on my home ground. My friends, excited by the
possibility of a good race, forgot their lunches and
girlfriends; they followed in tight formation behind me.

6   The black Kaw stopped in front of us and a quick exchange of
bike identities was made. Still no names. The race site
chosen was U.S. 205, an all but deserted stretch of straight,
smooth highway on the outskirts of town. The event picked up
an almost carnival atmosphere as word spread. People started
to pile into anything that moved and was going to U.S. 205.

7   It was warm out, but I wore my letter jacket for the
protection the leather sleeves offered. Throwing on my
helmet, I gave my bike a quick check and then kicked it to
life. It spit flames rearward as it backfired, but then
caught hold solidly and roared in protest. We left en masse
to the site of final truth. The race had become more than a
personal confrontation; it had become a school vs. school
event in which we both represented our individual schools.
There was no backing out now even if I had wanted to.

8   Arriving at U.S. 205, the spectators went to the accepted
finish line one-half mile down the road. My best friend
stopped his bike along the road with us to serve as the
starter. The black Kaw looked atune, and I nodded as we both
nervously revved our engines. I had raced on this strip at
least fifty times, yet I still swam in the warm waters of my
own sweat, and my stomach knotted unbearably.

9   He was in the left lane, I in the right, as my friend came
between us and raised his arms. Everything is automatic now.
My tach needle sweeps towards its 9500 rpm red line as my
friend yells "Three!" over the deafening roar and lowers his
arm. We hurl down the lane like rockets with near neck-
breaking acceleration. He jumps to an immediate lead because
of his bike's lightness, but I rapidly gain ground. I start
to pass the black Kaw by. He glances over, but I can't see
his face for the mask. I don't need to see it. I know what
it would show—frustration and anger.

10   I'm at 122 mph with the finish line dead ahead when I hear a loud "plafumf." My skin instantly crawls as I frantically search my gauges for the cause. Looking back, I see black smoke belching from the black Kaw. His inexperienced urgency on the throttle had blown his head gasket. I give him my condolences, and he limps home on his wounded steed. I've won, I'm the hero of the day.

11   I remain undefeated, but for how long? How long before I blow a gasket, a rod, or worse, a tire or chain? An accident that would send me down onto the abrasive surface of some deserted two-lane. It was after this, my last race, that I decided to leave the title I had fought so many times to retain to those who were foolish and reckless enough to let their pride and machines rule their destinies.

—Ernest Davis

EXPLORING CHOICES

Content and Organization

1. Note that the first paragraph announces the theme of the narrative. How is the theme reaffirmed in the resolution?
2. Explain the function of paragraphs 3 and 4. How are they different from paragraphs 2 and 5?
3. Point out the structure of the essay. Which paragraphs carry the exposition, the complication, and the resolution?
4. Note the title of the essay. How does it reaffirm the essay's theme? Do you find its alliteration effective?

Style

1. Point out the sentence fragments in paragraphs 3, 6, and 11. Do you find them effective? What justification would you offer for their use?
2. Note that the writer switches to the present tense in paragraph 9. Why do you think he did so? Do you find this shift acceptable? Why or why not?
3. In paragraph 7 the writer says his bike "spit flames." Can a bike literally "spit"? What language device is the writer using? Point to a sentence in paragraph 10 that illustrates the same device.
4. Note the description of the writer's bike in paragraph 3. Do the details persuade you that the writer is knowledgeable about motorcycles?
5. Point out the verbs you think especially effective. Give reasons for your choices.

The next essay comes from *The Big Sea,* an autobiographical work by the distinguished American poet Langston Hughes. In this selection, Hughes describes a "conversion" experience that inspired a sense of remorse.

SALVATION

1   I was saved from sin when I was going on thirteen. But not really saved. It happened like this. There was a big revival at my Auntie Reed's church. Every night for weeks there had been much preaching, singing, praying, and shouting, and some very hardened sinners had been brought to Christ, and the membership of the church had grown by leaps and bounds. Then just before the revival ended, they held a special meeting for children, "to bring the young lambs to the fold." My aunt spoke of it for days ahead. That night I was escorted to the front row and placed on the mourners' bench with all the other young sinners, who had not yet been brought to Jesus.

2   My aunt told me that when you were saved you saw a light, and something happened to you inside! And Jesus came into your life! And God was with you from then on! She said you could see and hear and feel Jesus in your soul. I believed her. I had heard a great many old people say the same thing and it seemed to me they ought to know. So I sat there calmly in the hot, crowded church, waiting for Jesus to come to me.

3   The preacher preached a wonderful rhythmical sermon, all moans and shouts and lonely cries and dire pictures of hell, and then he sang a song about the ninety and nine safe in the fold, but one little lamb was left out in the cold. Then he said: "Won't you come? Won't you come to Jesus? Young lambs, won't you come?" And he held out his arms to all us young sinners there on the mourners' bench. And the little girls cried. And some of them jumped up and went to Jesus right away. But most of us just sat there.

4   A great many old people came and knelt around us and prayed, old women with jet-black faces and braided hair, old men with work-gnarled hands. And the church sang a song about the lower lights are burning, some poor sinners to be saved. And the whole building rocked with prayer and song.

5   Still I kept waiting to *see* Jesus.

6   Finally all the young people had gone to the altar and were saved, but one boy and me. He was a rounder's son named Westley. Westley and I were surrounded by sisters and deacons praying. It was very hot in the church, and getting late now. Finally Westley said to me in a whisper: "God damn! I'm tired o' sitting here. Let's get up and be saved." So he got up and was saved.

7   Then I was left all alone on the mourners' bench. My aunt came and knelt at my knees and cried, while prayers and songs swirled all around me in the little church. The whole congregation prayed for me alone, in a mighty wail of moans and voices. And I kept waiting serenely for Jesus, waiting, waiting—but he didn't come. I wanted to see him, but nothing happened to me. Nothing! I wanted something to happen to me, but nothing happened.

8   I heard the songs and the minister saying: "Why don't you come? My dear child, why don't you come to Jesus? Jesus is waiting for you. He wants you. Why don't you come? Sister Reed, what is this child's name?"

9   "Langston," my aunt sobbed.

10   "Langston, why don't you come? Why don't you come and be saved? Oh, Lamb of God! Why don't you come?"

11   Now it was really getting late. I began to be ashamed of myself, holding everything up so long. I began to wonder what God thought about Westley, who certainly hadn't seen Jesus either, but who was now sitting proudly on the platform, swinging his knickerbockered legs and grinning down at me, surrounded by deacons and old women on their knees praying. God had not struck Westley dead for taking his name in vain or for lying in the temple. So I decided that maybe to save further trouble, I'd better lie, too, and say that Jesus had come, and get up and be saved.

12   So I got up.

13   Suddenly the whole room broke into a sea of shouting, as they saw me rise. Waves of rejoicing swept the place. Women leaped in the air. My aunt threw her arms around me. The minister took me by the hand and led me to the platform.

14   When things quieted down, in a hushed silence, punctuated by a few ecstatic "Amens," all the new young lambs were blessed in the name of God. Then joyous singing filled the room.

15   That night, for the last time in my life but one—for I was a big boy twelve years old—I cried. I cried, in bed alone, and couldn't stop. I buried my head under the quilts, but my aunt heard me. She woke up and told my uncle I was crying because the Holy Ghost had come into my life, and because I had seen Jesus. But I was really crying because I couldn't bear to tell her that I had lied, that I had deceived everybody in the church, that I hadn't seen Jesus, and that now I didn't believe there was a Jesus any more, since he didn't come to help me.

—Langston Hughes

EXPLORING CHOICES

Content and Organization

1. How does Hughes create and sustain tension in this selection?
2. What does this essay reveal about the differences between the adult's perspective and that of the children?
3. What are the differences between Westley's conversion and the author's?
4. Where does Hughes come closest to explicitly stating his thesis?
5. Does the conclusion strike you as the insight of a twelve- year-old, or of an adult looking back? Explain.

Style

1. What would be the difference in effect if this were narrated in the third rather than in the first person?
2. Notice Hughes' use of short sentences, especially in paragraph 13, and of one-sentence paragraphs (5 and 12). What is the purpose of these? What is the importance of the brief second sentence for the selection as a whole?

3. Point out Hughes' transitional devices and his use of repetition. What do these contribute to the essay?

Essay C

The prominent American theater director Alan Schneider recounts, in this passage from his autobiography *Entrances,* being uprooted from the rural area where both his parents were doctors in a tuberculosis sanatorium. After arriving in Baltimore, he undergoes a religious ritual that was drained of all significance for him.

From ENTRANCES

1   My parents always told me that they left the sanatorium so that I wouldn't have to go to the second-rate high school in Thurmont. I'd had a look behind its peeling yellowed walls and watched some nervously bored students cut up a frog in a dingy underground dungeon of a biology lab, deciding immediately that I would hate everything about the place. My loving mother sympathized and began a subtle but persistent campaign to persuade my father to move to more civilized climes. . . .

2   When the Playground Athletic League in Baltimore announced that it was looking for a physician couple to examine Maryland high-school students for TB and other diseases, Dad immediately expressed interest. The pay was more than both my parents made at the sanatorium, and somebody said that if we located in a sprawling suburb called Forest Park, I could attend a good high school.

3   We moved to Baltimore in the late summer of 1930. The Depression was on, and Dad had lost three hundred dollars in Cities Service gold bonds, but no sad thoughts remained. After Sabillasville Elementary, Forest Park High School was huge (2400 students), overpowering, and incomprehensible. I was lost, unsure, and alone, and afraid to share my concerns with my parents, who had abandoned their rich and fruitful lives for my sake. Reeling from the double task of adjusting not only to a large city but to a big-city school that taught Latin, literature, and something called "civics," I was also approaching my thirteenth birthday, with just enough time for a crash course in the ritual of a Bar Mitzvah. My family was not religious in any way; we were Jewish because other people felt we were. I do not recall a single occasion in Russia or Sabillasville where we even spoke of going to synagogue. Nevertheless, the fact of my Bar Mitzvah was neither discussed nor questioned. No one, certainly, ever knew how terrified I was of botching the whole ceremony. Having to memorize what seemed like half the Torah in a language that was utterly incomprehensible, I regretted more than once forsaking Thurmont's frogs.

4   On the day of my Bar Mitzvah, I awoke earlier than usual to find, most disappointingly, a fountain pen beside my bed rather than the usual birthday toy or book. A chemistry set eventually materialized, however, threatening my prompt departure for the synagogue. My reading of the Torah didn't shock anyone but myself. I was appalled at having to move the hand-pointer vaguely on cue from line to line, intoning words of whose meaning I had no idea, and realizing that I was in no way serving my religion or my country or my inner self, but only

acting out an agreed-upon pretense. The rabbi—a staunch liberal, an orator of eminence, and a leader of the Baltimore Reformed Judaism community—shook my hand warmly and took off on a rousing sermon, of which I recall not one word.

5   What bothered me most, however, was the party afterward. Our middle-floor apartment was far from large, and my bedroom was minimal—a cot-sized bed, a small desk, some books, and a sort of stamp collection. Over the bed there was a small framed magazine print of a teenager reading in bed, the glow from his bedside lamp lighting up the kind of youthful idealized Norman Rockwell countenance I always yearned to possess. I kept that print for years until the plays of Thornton Wilder took its place in my heart.

6   The party was held in the living and dining rooms and attended by all my parents' friends. I spent the whole afternoon in my bedroom, among coats thrown over my bed, the door closed, playing quietly with my chemistry set and talking with the one friend my father had allowed me to invite. Through the wall, I heard the laughter and revelry of all those so-called adults celebrating *my* coming of age.

7   My mother did bring us some tea and extra-large portions of cake, but that did not dispel the dreariness of the occasion. She was radiantly happy and looked especially youthful and beautiful in a long white evening dress she had bought for the occasion. I could not bring myself to tell her how empty I felt. I have never, except on rare occasions, set foot in a synagogue again, although the day my son should have been Bar Mitzvahed—and wasn't—was hard to take. Away from him, in California somewhere, I watched the film *Sunday, Bloody Sunday,* with its moving Bar Mitzvah scene, and wept without stop.

—Alan Schneider

EXPLORING CHOICES

Content and Organization

1. Schneider tells you that his family was in no way religious, and yet they subject him to being Bar Mitzvahed. Why?
2. What does the ceremony mean to the boy? Why is it traumatic for him?
3. How does the boy's attitude differ from that of the parents? When the boy himself becomes a parent, has his attitude changed?
4. What is Schneider's thesis? What, if anything, prepares you for the last sentence?

Style

1. Schneider's writing seems distanced, objective, and unemotional throughout. Why is this appropriate? Would it have been more forceful if it had been less so? Explain.
2. Contrast Hughes' and Schneider's style and tone, and their impact upon you as reader.

Think of a moment in your life that you associate with tension or lack of harmony. The moment may have been potentially catastrophic, such as a near-drowning or a serious automobile accident; or it may have been a relatively routine event that would have gone unnoted had it not been linked in your mind to something you had learned or understood for the first time. Before writing, use the strategies of invention outlined in Chapter 2 to help you recall the details of the moment. When you begin writing, keep in mind the three-part structure of narrative. You may, of course, modify this structure to suit your purpose, but remember that the reader must be able to follow the sequence of events easily.

DESCRIPTION

Imagine that a police officer is asking you to describe a robbery you have just witnessed. He asks you dozens of questions about the thief's height, weight, coloring, hairstyle and length, facial expressions, type and condition of clothing, and so on. To answer, you exercise visual recall, relating what you saw. But if, to take another imaginary situation, you are a camper in a national forest and you alert forest rangers to a fire that is about to break out, it's likely that your warning might be triggered more by your senses of smell and hearing than by your sense of sight. In both cases, though, you would use your senses to describe people, objects, and events.

The use of our senses in everyday life parallels the use of our senses in writing. Depending on purpose, you can use your senses either to give detailed information about something without letting your personal feelings intrude, or you can allow them imaginative play, attempting in your description of a scene or thing to create an atmosphere or feeling. The first kind of description is called *scientific* or *technical:* its focus is on the object itself and the writer's voice is seldom or never heard. The second is called *impressionistic,* implying that the writer's personal response to the object being described is uppermost. The first seeks to explain to or inform the reader about the essential features of the object while the second, though it still seeks to describe the object, nevertheless involves a personal point of view.

Consider, for example, the difference in descriptive purpose in the following two passages:

Description A

    Clam is an animal whose soft body is covered with a protective shell. Clams live on the bottom of oceans, lakes, and streams in many parts of the world. They feed on tiny water plants and animals called *plankton.* Clams have a large organ called a *foot,* which they use to burrow in mud or sand. Their shell is two parts that are called *valves.* A *ligament* fastens the valves together. The growth lines on the valves show how the shell has enlarged from time to time. The *mantle,* a fleshy part of the body just inside the shell, secretes the shell material. The space between the main body of the clam and the mantle is called the *mantle cavity.* The clam has gills that hang into the mantle cavity. . . .

Clams are valuable as food. The Indian name *quahog* is sometimes given to the hard-shell clam. This clam was used as *wampum* (money) by the Indians. It is a salt-water clam and is found in mud and sand from Canada to Florida.

—World Book Encyclopedia

Description B

```
    More difficult to find were the quahogs and not until we
were older did my father teach us, one by one, how to find
them.  Adults considered them more of a delicacy than the
other clams and either ate the meat raw or ground it for
chowder.  Hard-shelled clams, quahogs have no necks and keep
their mantles inside their tightly closed shells.  They, too,
burrow in the mud, but only under several inches of water, for
they keep a ridge of shell above the surface of the mud.  In
order to find quahogs, my father, in goggles and bathing suit,
floated face down along the shoreline where the water was a
foot deep.  The water being too murky to see through, he
pulled himself along, feeling the mud with his hands for the
telltale ridge.  When he found one, he loosened the
surrounding mud with his fingers and pulled the quahog out of
its hiding place.  This was a slow, arduous process, demanding
too much patience for most of us children. But my father was
motivated by his love for the results of his labors,
especially enjoying the sweet flavor of the small quahogs'
meat, called cherrystones, as he swallowed them raw.
                                            --Student paragraph
```

Examining both passages, you can see that the focus of the first is entirely on the object; the reader knows nothing of the writer's relation to, or experience with, the thing being described. The emphasis is on what a clam *is* rather than on what impression it makes. In contrast, the second subordinates the object to the writer; though the quahog is described, it is described only as the writer encountered it as an event in her own life. The first passage tells us a great deal about the object by isolating it and treating it as a thing of nature; the second tells us how the object is perceived and assimilated in human experience.

When your aim is to express your personal response to the world, you will often use description to set forth its textures, colors, sounds, and scenes, creating for the reader images that capture the qualities observed.

Description of this sort requires that you look closely and write precisely if you wish the reader to share your perceptions. The need for detail in descriptive writing is especially important for beginning writers, because the temptation is to tell how something affects you or to summarize its features in bare outline rather than to show how it actually looks, feels, or sounds. Consider, for example, the difference between the following two paragraphs, both of which record the same scene:

Paragraph A

```
    At one end of the lake is a hill.  At the other end, the
lake runs out over a small waterfall.  A wooden plank bridge
crosses the lake's outlet.  The remains of three stone L-
shaped supports indicate that a park bench used to overlook
the falls.
```

Paragraph B

```
    At one end of the lake is a hill, its sides worn down by the
sled runners of the neighborhood kids.  At the other end, the
lake runs out over a small waterfall.  In spring, when the
water is high, the lake surges over the rocks in a smooth,
glassy sheet, but now the water foams through the rocks
beneath a fender of ice.  The splintery rails of the wooden
plank bridge that crosses the lake's outlet below the falls
are tattooed with first names, pairs of initials, and dates.
Three stone L-shaped supports, sandpaper-rough to the touch,
are all that is left of the park bench that used to overlook
the falls.
```

In both paragraphs, the student writer attempts to describe specific features of the scene rather than just say that it was awe-inspiring, uplifting, or magnificent—adjectives that substitute the writer's response for the thing perceived. The second paragraph, however, is much fuller and richer. Note, for example, how the "hill" of the first sentence is specified by a detail describing its contours. The inserted third sentence picks up the perception of the waterfall and expands it, describing its changes in spring and winter and capturing a sense of motion in the verbs *surges* and *foams*. In the fourth sentence, the adjective *splintery* appeals to the sense of touch, as does the phrase "sandpaper-rough to the touch" of the final sentence. Finally, the bridge rails appeal vividly to our visual sense because the writer includes the image of graffiti.

The Structure of Description

Although description will often be an important part of your writing, it will become the major strategy when you are concerned with expressing your personal impressions of the world. Descriptive essays based on personal response, like the narrative essays examined earlier, suggest the significance of what is being described. The author of "Barbie Doll" (p. 162), for example, arranges her description of a person around a dominant impression that expresses an interpretation of the subject. As a result, the essay begins with a thesis (the dominant impression) and develops by exploring various aspects of the thesis.

Essays for Analysis

Essay A

Philip D. Miller, a student writer, lived in the Philippines for a year when his father served in the U.S. Army Air Force. In his essay, he re-creates the sense of imprisonment he felt during that year. Consider, as you read, how each detail he selects contributes to his feeling of isolation.

THE FORT

1   The high crime rate in the Philippines can make life a nightmare of restrictive rules. When I lived there for some two years with my family, we stayed in a village of about two hundred houses completely surrounded by a chain—link fence topped with barbed wire and constantly patrolled by guards dressed in blue uniforms and carrying shotguns. To leave or enter this "fort," you had to present a special card and pass at the solitary main gate where you were checked for stolen items and made to prove your eligibility for being there. Even after you left the gate and started walking towards your house, you took the chance of being stopped by guards who again checked your credentials. If for some reason your pass was not in order, as once happened to me, you were taken to the guardhouse. Since I was an American and young, I was able to talk my way out of trouble, but many others were not so lucky.

2   At home, the environment and atmosphere were just as threatening as the village itself. My house, for example, was encircled by a wall made of concrete with sets of white iron bars bolted into the cement. The only way a person could enter the yard was through a high metal gate that could be opened only from the inside. A small silver intercom speaker was implanted in the wall, and only after someone from inside the house was assured that it was your voice on the speaker were you allowed to enter the yard. Our yard was about twenty square feet and was covered with roses, petunias, and daisies, all of which were surrounded by vines covering every available space left over by the plants. It all looked as though flowered wallpaper had been glued to the ground, rather than like a garden all crammed together. The house itself looked

every bit as forbidding as the house wall, in that the windows were covered with bars, the doors all had two shiny locks, and four white pillars stood dull-looking, seemingly more appropriate as fort ramparts than as supports for a house. At night security lights shone from behind bushes and around corners, making one question if they were there to keep people out or to imprison them within.

3   The whiteness of everything gave the feeling that the house was as impersonal and sterile as an old fort that had been newly whitewashed. The bars were a constant reminder that it was just as hard to leave the house as it was to enter. One time, my friend's father caught a robber in his bedroom and had only to lock the door and call the police, even though the windows were wide open. The bars made escape impossible. The vines in the front yard seemed as though they waited, hoping that someone or something would slip off the walk so that they could quickly snatch just one more victim.

4   Eventually, I came to overlook all these fences and barriers, though I always felt their underlying presence, as when I would be lying in bed and the security lights would cast shadows against the wall as they shone through the barred windows. I often wondered who was really protected from whom. Was it they from us, or were we being caged in a fort only to await their inevitable entry into our protected surroundings?

—Philip D. Miller

EXPLORING CHOICES

Content and Organization

1. Point out the thesis in the first paragraph. How does this thesis control the development of the essay? What principle of order (spatial, temporal, etc.) is the writer using?
2. Note the transitional sentence that opens paragraph 2. How does this sentence point to what has been said earlier as well as introduce a new idea?
3. Point to the transitional sentence *within* paragraph 2. How does this sentence help the writer move from one perception to another?
4. Note the title and point out its appearance within the essay. Does the title capture the essay's thesis? Explain.
5. Point out the writer's use of example and detail to support his thesis. Does he use enough to persuade you that he is knowledgeable about his subject?
6. Note the spatial order of paragraph 2. How would you characterize it? You may want to examine the patterns of spatial order on p. 164.

Style

1. Point out the writer's use of personification in paragraph 3. How does the image contribute to the writer's thesis?
2. Point out the comparison the writer uses in paragraph 2. Does the comparison contribute to the writer's thesis?
3. Point out the verbs and nouns the writer uses throughout his essay to reaffirm his thesis.
4. Note that the writer concludes the essay with a question. Do you find this conclusion effective?

Essay B

The following essay by Carl T. Rowan, a distinguished statesman and journalist, describes a teacher who influenced him deeply. As you read it, note especially how Rowan uses abundant detail to develop Miss Bessie's character.

UNFORGETTABLE MISS BESSIE

1   She was only about five feet tall and probably never weighed more than 110 pounds, but Miss Bessie was a towering presence in the classroom. She was the only woman tough enough to make me read *Beowulf* and think for a few foolish days that I liked it. From 1938 to 1942, when I attended Bernard High School in McMinnville, Tenn., she taught me English, history, civics—and a lot more than I realized.

2   I shall never forget the day she scolded me into reading *Beowulf.*

3   "But Miss Bessie," I complained, "I ain't much interested in it."

4   Her large brown eyes became daggerish slits. "Boy," she said, "how dare you say 'ain't' to me! I've taught you better than that."

5   "Miss Bessie," I pleaded, "I'm trying to make first-string end on the football team, and if I go around saying 'it isn't' and 'they aren't,' the guys are gonna laugh me off the squad."

6   "Boy," she responded, "you'll play football because you have guts. But do you know what *really* takes guts? Refusing to lower your standards to those of the crowd. It takes guts to say you've got to live and be somebody fifty years after all the football games are over."

7   I started saying "it isn't" and "they aren't," and I still made first-string end—and class valedictorian—without losing my buddies' respect.

8   During her remarkable 44-year career, Mrs. Bessie Taylor Gwynn taught hundreds of economically deprived black youngsters—including my mother, my brother, my sisters and me. I remember her now with gratitude and affection—especially in this era when Americans are so wrought-up about a "rising tide of mediocrity" in public education and the problems of finding competent, caring teachers. Miss Bessie was an example of an informed, dedicated teacher, a blessing to children and an asset to the nation.

9   Born in 1895, in poverty, she grew up in Athens, Ala., where there was no public school for blacks. She attended Trinity School, a private institution for blacks run by the American Missionary Association, and in 1911 graduated from

the Normal School (a "super" high school) at Fisk University in Nashville. Mrs. Gwynn, the essence of pride and privacy, never talked about her years in Athens; only in the months before her death did she reveal that she had never attended Fisk University itself because she could not afford the four-year course.

10   At Normal School she learned a lot about Shakespeare, but most of all about the profound importance of education—especially, for a people trying to move up from slavery. "What you put in your head, boy," she once said, "can never be pulled out by the Ku Klux Klan, the Congress or anybody."

11   Miss Bessie's bearing of dignity told anyone who met her that she was "educated" in the best sense of the word. There was never a discipline problem in her classes. We didn't dare mess with a woman who knew about the Battle of Hastings, the Magna Charta and the Bill of Rights—and who could also play the piano.

12   This frail-looking woman could make sense of Shakespeare, Milton, Voltaire, and bring to life Booker T. Washington and W. E. B. DuBois. Believing that it was important to know who the officials were that spent taxpayers' money and made public policy, she made us memorize the names of everyone on the Supreme Court and in the President's Cabinet. It could be embarrassing to be unprepared when Miss Bessie said, "Get up and tell the class who Frances Perkins is and what you think about her."

13   Miss Bessie knew that my family, like so many others during the Depression, couldn't afford to subscribe to a newspaper. She knew we didn't even own a radio. Still, she prodded me to "look out for your future and find some way to keep up with what's going on in the world." So I became a delivery boy for the Chattanooga *Times*. I rarely made a dollar a week, but I got to read a newspaper every day.

14   Miss Bessie noticed things that had nothing to do with schoolwork, but were vital to a youngster's development. Once a few classmates made fun of my frayed, hand-me-down overcoat, calling me "Strings." As I was leaving school, Miss Bessie patted me on the back of that old overcoat and said, "Carl, never fret about what you *don't* have. Just make the most of what you *do* have—a brain."

15   Among the things that I did not have was electricity in the little frame house that my father had built for $400 with his World War I bonus. But because of her inspiration, I spent many hours squinting beside a kerosene lamp reading Shakespeare and Thoreau, Samuel Pepys and William Cullen Bryant.

16   No one in my family had ever graduated from high school, so there was no tradition of commitment to learning for me to lean on. Like millions of youngsters in today's ghettos and barrios, I needed the push and stimulation of a teacher who truly cared. Miss Bessie gave plenty of both, as she immersed me in a wonderful world of similes, metaphors and even onomatopoeia. She led me to believe that I could write sonnets as well as Shakespeare, or iambic-pentameter verse to put Alexander Pope to shame.

17   In those days the McMinnville school system was rigidly "Jim Crow," and poor black children had to struggle to put anything in their heads. Our high school was only slightly larger than the once-typical little red schoolhouse, and its library was outrageously inadequate—so small, I like to say, that if two

students were in it and one wanted to turn a page, the other one had to step outside.

18   Negroes, as we were called then, were not allowed in the town library, except to mop floors or dust tables. But through one of those secret Old South arrangements between whites of conscience and blacks of stature, Miss Bessie kept getting books smuggled out of the white library. That is how she introduced me to the Brontës, Byron, Coleridge, Keats and Tennyson. "If you don't read, you can't write, and if you can't write, you might as well stop dreaming," Miss Bessie once told me.

19   So I read whatever Miss Bessie told me to, and tried to remember the things she insisted that I store away. Forty-five years later, I can still recite her "truths to live by," such as Henry Wadsworth Longfellow's lines from "The Ladder of St. Augustine":

> The heights by great men reached and kept
> Were not attained by sudden flight.
> But they, while their companions slept,
> Were toiling upward in the night.

20   Years later, her inspiration, prodding, anger, cajoling and almost osmotic infusion of learning finally led to that lovely day when Miss Bessie dropped me a note saying, "I'm so proud to read your column in the Nashville *Tennessean*."

21   Miss Bessie was a spry 80 when I went back to McMinnville and visited her in a senior citizens' apartment building. Pointing out proudly that her building was racially integrated, she reached for two glasses and a pint of bourbon. I was momentarily shocked, because it would have been scandalous in the 1930s and '40s for word to get out that a teacher drank, and nobody had ever raised a rumor that Miss Bessie did.

22   I felt a new sense of equality as she lifted her glass to mine. Then she revealed a softness and compassion that I had never known as a student.

23   "I've never forgotten that examination day," she said, "when Buster Martin held up seven fingers, obviously asking you for help with question number seven, 'Name a common carrier.' I can still picture you looking at your exam paper and humming a few bars of 'Chattanooga Choo Choo.' I was so tickled, I couldn't punish either of you."

24   Miss Bessie was telling me, with bourbon-laced grace, that I never fooled her for a moment.

25   When Miss Bessie died in 1980, at age 85, hundreds of her former students mourned. They knew the measure of a great teacher: love and motivation. Her wisdom and influence had rippled out across generations.

26   Some of her students who might normally have been doomed to poverty went on to become doctors, dentists and college professors. Many, guided by Miss Bessie's example, became public-school teachers.

27   "The memory of Miss Bessie and how she conducted her classroom did more for me than anything I learned in college," recalls Gladys Wood of Knoxville, Tenn., a highly respected English teacher who spent 43 years in the state's school system. "So many times, when I faced a difficult classroom problem, I asked myself, *How would Miss Bessie deal with this?* And I'd remember that she would handle it with laughter and love."

28   No child can get all the necessary support at home, and millions of poor children get *no* support at all. This is what makes a wise, educated, warm-hearted
teacher like Miss Bessie so vital to the minds, hearts and souls of this country's
children.
                                                                    —Carl T. Rowan

EXPLORING CHOICES

Content and Organization

1. What overall impression does Rowan create of Miss Bessie through the
   specific physical details he provides? How do her actions either bear
   out or contradict this impression?
2. How do Miss Bessie's actions support the more abstract descriptive
   phrases such as "towering presence," "informed, dedicated teacher,"
   and "essence of pride and privacy"?
3. What is the main point of the essay? To what extent is it a description of
   something larger and more universal than one teacher?
4. There are two time frames in the essay; what are they? What purpose is
   served by concluding with the recent past? How would the total effect
   have differed if Rowan had ended his remembrance with paragraph 19?
5. Explain the connection between reading, writing, and dreaming. How
   does what Rowan reveals about himself clarify this connection.?

Style

1. How dependent is Rowan upon adjectives? Categorize them as either
   concrete or abstract.
2. Rowan uses the dash frequently. Evaluate the reason for and effectiveness of this in specific instances.
3. What stylistic purpose is served by quoting Miss Bessie's own words?

WRITING SUGGESTION

Using the strategies of invention described in Chapter 2, gather as many details and examples as you can of a place or person you know well. From
these, single out a quality that you feel best expresses the atmosphere or
character of the place or person. Before you begin to write, decide what
method of organization would best suit your purpose. In developing your
impression, try to use sensory details to make your description vivid and
exact.

ILLUSTRATION

Illustration is a useful way to give writing substance and texture. To illustrate a point is to use examples that help make the point concrete and specific. Most of us do this frequently. Suppose you're telling a friend about a movie that impressed you deeply. You might begin by sketching its outlines, but then, to back up your response, you would probably search for details to illustrate each feature you thought especially fine.

In writing, examples are especially important: they help to clarify and support a concept, and they often make the concept memorable. How many examples you will need to use often depends on context. At times, a single example will serve your purpose. At other times, you may need to use multiple examples. The following paragraph, taken from an essay that argues against indiscriminate whale hunting, presents a single example to support the author's point that products made from whale oil can be made from an alternative source:

> Actually, some of these products can be supplied in other ways. Take, for example, sperm oil, which comes from the head of the sperm whale. The oil is used to oil everything from automatic transmissions to machine tools, and it performs superbly because it forms a bond when it is applied to metals. Now, however, a promising substitute has appeared in jojoba oil, which comes from a bean that grows wild in arid regions of California, Arizona, and New Mexico. In fact, jojoba oil is superior to sperm oil in some cases. Sperm oil is used as an antifoam in the manufacturing of antibiotics and penicillin. When jojoba oil is substituted, it not only works spectacularly, but it increases the production of these drugs by ten to twenty percent. —Student paragraph

In the following paragraph, the writer uses multiple examples to illustrate how each member of her family is a pack rat—the main point of the passage:

> We are all of us incurable pack rats. Mom has some little treasure from every memorable day in her life—a candle from each birthday, at least three baby teeth, the movie ticket stub from her first date, and the first love letter Dad ever wrote her. My own collecting habits center on every pet I've ever owned. I have my first dog's collar and tags, hair from my guinea pig, a chip from the shell of my box turtle, hair from my horse's tail, and two teeth from my first cat. Even Susie, my eight-year-old sister, has the hoarding instinct:

she saves money. Her idea of an afternoon's entertainment is
rolling coins into paper money holders Mom obtains from the
bank. And then there's Dad, with two suitcases full of old
comic books and World War II paraphernalia.

—Student paragraph

The Structure of Illustration

Some of your essays will, more obviously and emphatically than others, employ a pattern of assertion plus illustration to back up that assertion. This
organizational pattern usually includes a statement of your thesis in the introduction, followed by three or four paragraphs with the topic sentence in
each of them supported by two or three or four examples. It is one of the
easiest to master, and is therefore probably one of the first that you learned
to use. When you do employ it, you will want to make certain that you provide a sufficient number of relevant examples to illustrate your points, and
that you arrange those examples—both within individual paragraphs and
within the paper as a whole—for maximum effect, which means most likely
in an ascending order of importance.

Essays for Analysis

Essay A

In the following selection, E. B. White, who was one of America's best
loved essayists and stylists, considers people's reticence to commit themselves openly, both in writing and in life, by using the pronoun "I."

A STUDY OF THE CLINICAL "WE"

1   A recent article on grammar, which I read in a magazine, has led me to the
preparation of a paper on the clinical "we." The clinical "we" is a bedside form
in use among practical nurses, who find, in the sound of the plural, a little of
the faded romance that still attaches to life. It is also used universally by baby
nurses, who think of themselves in groups of four.

2   Unlike the editorial "we," which is a literary device used to protect writers
from the fumes of their own work, the clinical "we" is simply a spoken form,
and is rarely written. A baby nurse employs the "we" in the belief that no single
person could have as much special knowledge as she has, and that therefore
when she speaks it must be three other people too. Thus, when I once asked a
baby nurse if she wouldn't please put a hat on my son before she took him out
in a sandstorm that happened to be raging at the moment, her reply was: "We
never put hats on him after June first." "You and who else don't?" I remember
answering. It was my first clash with the clinical "we."

3   Since then I have studied it, not only in baby nurses but in dentists' assistants,
ward witches, and the developers of X-ray plates. It is common to all of them,

but hospital nurses use it to denote the patient, not the nurse. I know of one hospital case in which the sudden use of the clinical "we," in the presence of an elderly gentleman convalescing from an operation, threw him into a paroxysm that proved a serious setback to his recovery. It was early in the morning, and a pretty little Southern nurse, coming into his room, sang out: "We didn't change our pajamas this morning, did we?"

4   "No, let's do it right now!" replied the aged patient somewhat bitterly. The wry joke so excited him that he had to be given a sedative, and later a talking to.

5   It is probably apparent from the above examples that the clinical "we" can seldom be taken lying down, but almost always provokes a rejoinder. In hospitals the "we" is merely an unattractive figure of speech in a world of strange and unattractive details, but in the home it is intolerable. To live under the same roof with a user of the "we" is a fairly good test of a man's character. During the winter of 1931 I employed twenty-two baby nurses, one after another, before I found one who could make a sentence beginning with the word "I." I used to call them "we- uns." Every morning I would go upstairs to the nursery. "Morning, Nurse," I would say, "how you feeling?"

6   "We are just fine, sir," would be the courteous but silly reply.

7   "Canst make a sentence beginning with the word 'I'?" I would ask.

8   "We never make sentences that-a-way, sir," she would say. So I would fire her and get another. Finally a little Irish girl named McGheogheoghan (pronounced McVeigh) came along, and one morning I went up and asked how she was feeling.

9   "I feel terrible," she answered.

10   That nurse is still with us, and grows, I am happy to say, more singular every day.

—E. B. White

EXPLORING CHOICES

Content and Organization

1. White employs a number of examples to illustrate his point. Can you see any reason(s) for the order in which he presents them?

2. Does the fact that White limits himself to discussing practical nurses and baby nurses restrict the application of his diagnosis? Why or why not?

3. What, if anything, justifies White's attributing so much import to seemingly so unimportant a problem?

4. What does White seem to be implying about the relationship between the language people use and the social situation in which they find themselves?

5. This essay first appeared over a half-century ago. In your experience, what groups of people today are still prone to falling into "the clinical 'we' "?

Style

1. How would you describe White's tone in this essay? Point out particular words and phrases that helped lead to your conclusion.
2. White peppers his essay with reconstructed conversations. What would have been the difference in effect if he had used only narration without adding dialogue?
3. Comment on the appropriateness of the pun in White's concluding sentence.

Essay B

In the following selection, Lewis Thomas, a medical doctor and essayist, uses many examples to support the point that in nature, as well as in human life, death is a hidden phenomenon.

DEATH IN THE OPEN

1   Most of the dead animals you see on highways near the cities are dogs, a few cats. Out in the countryside, the forms and coloring of the dead are strange; these are the wild creatures. Seen from a car window they appear as fragments, evoking memories of woodchucks, badgers, skunks, voles, snakes, sometimes the mysterious wreckage of a deer.

2   It is always a queer shock, part a sudden upwelling of grief, part unaccountable amazement. It is simply astounding to see an animal dead on a highway. The outrage is more than just the location; it is the impropriety of such visible death, anywhere. You do not expect to see dead animals in the open. It is the nature of animals to die alone, off somewhere, hidden. It is wrong to see them lying out on the highway; it is wrong to see them anywhere.

3   Everything in the world dies, but we only know about it as a kind of abstraction. If you stand in a meadow, at the edge of a hillside, and look around carefully, almost everything you can catch sight of is in the process of dying, and most things will be dead long before you are. If it were not for the constant renewal and replacement going on before your eyes, the whole place would turn to stone and sand under your feet.

4   There are some creatures that do not seem to die at all; they simply vanish totally into their own progeny. Single cells do this. The cell becomes two, then four, and so on, and after a while the last trace is gone. It cannot be seen as death; barring mutation, the descendants are simply the first cell, living all over again. The cycles of the slime mold have episodes that seem as conclusive as death, but the withered slug, with its stalk and fruiting body, is plainly the transient tissue of a developing animal; the free-swimming amebocytes use this organ collectively in order to produce more of themselves.

5   There are said to be a billion billion insects on the earth at any moment, most of them with very short life expectancies by our standards. Someone has estimated that there are 25 million assorted insects hanging in the air over every temperate square mile, in a column extending upward for thousands of feet, drifting through the layers of the atmosphere like plankton. They are dying steadily, some by being eaten, some just dropping in their tracks, tons of them around the earth, disintegrating as they die, invisibly.

6   Who ever sees dead birds, in anything like the huge numbers stipulated by the certainty of the death of all birds? A dead bird is an incongruity, more startling than an unexpected live bird, sure evidence to the human mind that something has gone wrong. Birds do their dying off somewhere, behind things, under things, never on the wing.

7   Animals seem to have an instinct for performing death alone, hidden. Even the largest, most conspicuous ones find ways to conceal themselves in time. If an elephant missteps and dies in an open place, the herd will not leave him there; the others will pick him up and carry the body from place to place, finally putting it down in some inexplicably suitable location. When elephants encounter the skeleton of an elephant out in the open, they methodically take up each of the bones and distribute them, in a ponderous ceremony, over neighboring acres.

8   It is a natural marvel. All of the life of the earth dies, all of the time, in the same volume as the new life that dazzles us each morning, each spring. All we see of this is the odd stump, the fly struggling on the porch floor of the summer house in October, the fragment on the highway. I have lived all my life with an embarrassment of squirrels in my backyard, they are all over the place, all year long, and I have never seen, anywhere, a dead squirrel.

9   I suppose it is just as well. If the earth were otherwise, and all the dying were done in the open, with the dead there to be looked at, we would never have it out of our minds. We can forget about it much of the time, or think of it as an accident to be avoided, somehow. But it does make the process of dying seem more exceptional than it really is, and harder to engage in at the times when we must ourselves engage.

10   In our way, we conform as best we can to the rest of nature. The obituary pages tell us of the news that we are dying away, while the birth announcements in finer print, off at the side of the page, inform us of our replacements, but we get no grasp from this of the enormity of scale. There are 3 billion of us on the earth, and all 3 billion must be dead, on a schedule, within this lifetime. The vast mortality, involving something over 50 million of us each year, takes place in relative secrecy. We can only really know of the deaths in our households, or among our friends. These, detached in our minds from all the rest, we take to be unnatural events, anomalies, outrages. We speak of our own dead in low voices; struck down, we say, as though visible death can only occur for cause, by disease or violence, avoidably. We send off for flowers, grieve, make ceremonies, scatter bones, unaware of the rest of the 3 billion on the same schedule. All of that immense mass of flesh and bone and consciousness will disappear by absorption into the earth, without recognition by the transient survivors.

11   Less than a half century from now, our replacements will have more than doubled the numbers. It is hard to see how we can continue to keep the secret, with such multitudes doing the dying. We will have to give up the notion that death is catastrophe, or detestable, or avoidable, or even strange. We will need to learn more about the cycling of life in the rest of the system, and about our connection to the process. Everything that comes alive seems to be in trade for something that dies, cell for cell. There might be some comfort in the recognition of synchrony, in the information that we all go down together, in the best of company.

—Lewis Thomas

Content and Organization

1. What is the author's thesis, and where does he state it?
2. Where in his essay does Thomas begin to illustrate the point that death in animate nature is ordinarily "hidden"?
3. Why does he present his examples in the order that he does?
4. How do human beings, in their treatment of the fact of death, seem to imitate other animals?
5. What, according to Thomas, is the effect of death's being "hidden" rather than "out in the open"?
6. How well does the author succeed in making you see and know death as something concrete? Point to specific details in the essay that help make an ordinarily taboo subject seem less extraordinary, even natural.

Style

1. How does Thomas make his scientific data understandable to the lay reader? Do you need to know the precise definitions of all his terms, such as "amebocytes" and "synchrony," to understand the meaning? Explain.
2. Some paragraphs, specifically 2, 3, 9, and 11, are more general than others. What is the purpose of these paragraphs? Describe their tone, and then suggest why it is appropriate.
3. Comment on your reaction to the word choice of the concluding phrase: "the best of company."

WRITING SUGGESTION

Demonstrate the existence of some correctable social problem or ill—it might be lack of attention to the needs of the handicapped or the elderly, senseless humiliation of the poor, lack of adequate public services, censorship of books or videos, etc.—on your campus or in your community by presenting evidence in the form of illustrative examples.

PROCESS

Sometimes your purpose may be to explain the stages or phases of a process. Such a purpose may take the form of giving directions (how to do it), or of giving information (how it is done). In the first case, the aim is to instruct the reader in how to make or do something: how to make a pot roast, how to develop film in a home darkroom, how to organize and start a restaurant, how to perfect the breaststroke. In the second case, the purpose is to explain how something is done or how something happened, without expecting the reader to undertake the process described. Explanations of how a bill becomes a law, or of how meat is processed for consumption, or of how utopian communities in the United States developed do not aim to give directions but seek rather to broaden readers' understanding.

A process paper requires close attention to the expectations, interests, and degree of knowledge of the audience. If you are writing a direction-giving paper, it is likely that you will be addressing readers who are relatively naive about your subject and who therefore expect you to give them precise instructions. Directions that do not provide an exact sequence of steps or do not describe each step clearly are likely to confuse and frustrate the reader. Moreover, you will also have to define special terms that may be unfamiliar. It is also useful to tell your readers why they need to perform a certain step or what hazards they may encounter if they don't perform the step as you have outlined it. Such consideration will not only establish your expertise and credibility, but will contribute as well to your readers' understanding; instead of merely obeying instructions, they will be encouraged to reflect on them.

The Structure of Process

If your purpose is to explain a process or to instruct your reader, you will find a chronological pattern the most appropriate, since it reflects the order in which the steps occur. Your chief transitional signals in an essay of this sort are likely to be the ordinal numbers—*first, second, third*—or adverbs of time such as *before, after, meanwhile, during, next.* If your emphasis is on the thing being done rather than on the person doing it, you will find the passive voice useful (such as, "the first step is taken"). If, however, you choose to instruct your reader, you will be likely to use the active voice (such as, "you take the first step") because your emphasis will be on having someone do something.

Essays for Analysis

Essay A

The following editorial appeared in the *Los Angeles Times.* As you read it, consider how the writer's instructions on converting temperatures are designed for readers of a daily newspaper.

FIGURING IT OUT BY DEGREES

1   Most of the rest of the world reckons temperature on the Celsius or centigrade scale, and Celsius is even seen occasionally in this country on electric time-and-temperature signs outside banks.

2   But the usual method for converting from Fahrenheit to Celsius is cumbersome, difficult to remember and hard to do in your head. In degree of difficulty among algorithms, it is second only to extracting a square root with pencil and paper.

3   It turns out that there is a better, easier way to do it that is rarely taught, though it should be.

4   The almanac gives the standard method. "To convert Fahrenheit to Celsius," it says, "subtract 32 and multiply by 5/9. To convert Celsius to Fahrenheit, multiply by 9/5 and add 32."

5   The first problem with this method for converting temperature scales is that it is really two methods, and some people (us included) can never remember which is which. To go from Fahrenheit to Celsius, you subtract first and then multiply. To go from Celsius to Fahrenheit, you multiply first and then add. What's more, in one case you have to subtract, and in the other case you have to add.

6   If you do the steps in the wrong order, or if you add when you're supposed to subtract, or the other way around, you get the wrong answer.

7   Here's the better way to do it.

8   Regardless of whether you're going from Fahrenheit to Celsius or Celsius to Fahrenheit, add 40 to the temperature.

9   If you're going from Fahrenheit to Celsius, multiply by 5/9. (That's easy to remember because the Celsius numbers are smaller. The boiling point of water is 212 degrees Fahrenheit but only 100 degrees Celsius.)

10   If you're going from Celsius to Fahrenheit, multiply by 9/5. (That's also easy to remember for the same reason. Fahrenheit numbers are larger.)

11   Then subtract 40.

12   The number that's left is the answer. And that's all there is to it. This method works in either direction for any number.

13   For example: To convert 212 degrees Fahrenheit to Celsius, add 40, giving 252. Multiply by 5/9, giving 140. Subtract 40, leaving 100. So 212 degrees Fahrenheit is 100 degrees Celsius, which is correct.

14   If you want to convert 0 degrees Celsius to Fahrenheit, add 40, giving 40. Multiply by 9/5, giving 72. Subtract 40, leaving 32. So 0 degrees Celsius, the freezing point of water, is 32 degrees Fahreneheit, which is also correct.

15   Why does this method work? The Fahrenheit and Celsius scales cross at −40 degrees. That is, both scales are the same at −40. By adding 40 to start, this point of equality is shifted to 0. Then the multiplication can be carried out directly, without having to add or subtract anything before or after. Finally, subtracting 40 shifts the two scales back to their correct positions.

16   The real question is, why is this method a secret? It's much superior to the standard method, which nonetheless continues to be the standard method. Nor is the regular method conceptually easier than the add-40-subtract-40 method of doing it. Adding or subtracting 32 isn't any more enlightening to students about what is going on than adding and subtracting 40.

17   Textbook publishers and teachers should switch. If there's a better way to do something, why not do it?

Content and Organization

1. Do you find any steps in the process as the writer explains it in paragraphs 8 through 11 confusing? If so, what words could you add to make the process clearer?

2. The primary purpose of this editorial is to instruct the reader in how to do something. Yet it uses process analysis as a component of a larger aim. What is this aim, and where does the writer first state it? Where is the argument repeated, and is the repetition effective?

3. What does the introductory paragraph, taken by itself, lead you to believe the editorial's argument will be? Since this is not, finally, the author's thesis, is the introduction inappropriate? Why or why not?

4. Are you convinced that the proposed process is indeed easier than the one it is intended to replace? Why or why not?

Style

1. Why does the author choose to write in the second person ("you")? Would some other person have been equally as effective?

2. The editorial writer often employs colloquial phrasing, such as "it turns out," "what's more," "here's the better way," etc. Why is this tone adopted here?

3. Is there any reason for the succession of relatively short—even one-sentence—paragraphs, other than that this essay was originally written to appear in a newspaper?

Essay B

The student author of the following selection uses knowledge he gained while holding a summer job in a Hollywood studio to describe how animated cartoons are made.

NOT KID'S PLAY

1   It's Saturday morning. You awake, flip on the television set, and flop onto the sofa to watch a cartoon. You may chuckle, smile, or just stare stonily at the flashes of color and motion before you. Probably, you'll never think to ask how an animated cartoon is made, what materials are used in its production, or what types of people are involved in the process of giving life to drawings. Like most people, you may even believe that the cartoon is merely a simple form of entertainment, suitable for children and therefore unworthy of serious consideration. If, however, you're somewhat more curious, you may learn that making animated cartoons is a highly sophisticated process, no less organized and specialized than the assembly of an automobile.

2   As in any intricate process, the making of a cartoon begins with careful, detailed planning. First, the story to be depicted is written down, its ideas and reasons explicitly stated. In other words, an "animation script" is made. Directly after, with this script as a guide, the "storyboard," consisting of the drawing and dialogue of each scene, is tacked up to a wall. In reality, the storyboard is just an enlarged and elaborate comic strip. In feature films such as Disney's Snow White and the Seven Dwarfs, several hundreds of these sketches are used to clarify the entire plot. After this storyboard is scrutinized and pondered, every movement of every character in every situation is entered into the "workbook," along with dialogue and sounds, and the number of film frames necessary to produce the desired result is tabulated. The purpose of the workbook is to facilitate the synchronization of picture with sound which occurs later on. The voluminous collection of data suggests that not even the most punctual train engineers calculate their arrivals and departures as thoroughly as the animators calculate each movement of their characters.

3   The sound-track charts and "dope sheets," which connect the frame actions to the bars of the music and order of photography respectively, are also produced at this time. Meanwhile, the animation director is constructing the "model sheets." These are drawings used as standards depicting the appearances of the characters in various bends, twists, and turns, their relation in size and shape to one another, and their colors. Now, after the intricate planning with script, storyboard, workbook, sound-track charts, dope sheets, and model sheets, the actual "life giving" begins.

4   In general, the animation of a lifeless drawing is achieved by copying one drawing several times over, yet minutely varying each in some respect. During a quick flashing of these drawings in succession, the eye, bewildered by the quick movement, views the small variations as a smooth, continuous motion. However, one second of film-time requires 24 of these minutely varied drawings for smooth motion. This number quickly multiplies to 14,400 in just ten minutes! A mind-boggling 477,000 drawings were photographed to produce Disney's Snow White.

5   When the second step of the process—the execution of the cartoon—is undertaken, the workers complete their task in an assembly-line fashion, specializing themselves in a way that would please even Henry Ford. First the "key animator" swings

into action. He is the one who draws the "key" or important drawings (perhaps five out of the twenty-four needed per second). Following close after are the assistant animators or "in-betweeners" who, as masters of forgery, copy the key sketches while incorporating the minute variations essential for the motion. After the flood of drawings sweeps past the in-betweeners, they are snatched up by the "inkers" who, being careful not to smudge (they wear white gloves), trace the drawing onto clear plastic celluloid sheets ("cels") with black ink. Upon drying, the cels travel to the painters who dab opaque colors onto their backs as the model sheets instruct. The reason for painting on the backs is that when the cels are turned right side up again, the paint appears to lie within the ink lines. These steps, however, increase the chance that the cels have gotten out of sequence; thus, it is up to the "checker" to make sure the cels are in order and to ready them for photographing. The cameramen, their rostrum cameras capable of photographing one frame at a time, now film each separate cel pegged down onto a pre-painted background. As the strips of film come straggling in, the editor slices out mistakes and eventually splices together the entire film.

6   These films are now ready to be pumped into your home. If you find them silly or foolish or predictable, you are probably right: great themes are not often treated in an animated cartoon. If, however, you take a moment to recall the painstaking process needed to produce them, you may find something to applaud. Animated cartoons require much skill and talent--perhaps more than the medium warrants.

--James A. Burrell

EXPLORING CHOICES

Content and Organization

1. If the writer's aim had been to teach his readers how to make an animated cartoon, what changes would he have made in the essay?
2. To whom is this essay addressed: to the specialist or to the intelligent layperson? Give reasons for your answer.
3. For the most part, this essay is organized chronologically, that is, it describes events in the order of their occurrence. Why is this organization appropriate to the writer's purpose?
4. Apart from the introduction and conclusion, the essay divides into two major sections. What are they? How do the writer's subject and purpose account for this division? How does the last sentence of paragraph 3 connect the two sections?

Style

1. Note that the first and final paragraphs use the second person *(you)*. Compare them to the following introduction which does not use the second person. Which do you consider more effective? Why?

   ```
   Though it is fair to say that the entire adult population of
   the United States has at one time or another watched an
   animated cartoon, it is equally likely that most people are
   unaware of how an animated cartoon is made, what materials are
   used in its production, or what types of people are involved
   in giving life to drawings.  They may even think that making a
   cartoon is a simple matter when, in fact, it is a highly
   sophisticated process, no less organized and specialized than
   the assembly of an automobile.
   ```

2. Note the frequent use of the passive voice: "An animation script is made"; "The storyboard is tacked up." Try changing each instance of the passive voice to the active voice. What difference in emphasis do you find? Why do you think the writer prefers to use the passive voice?
3. What methods are used to achieve coherence? Mark each paragraph in detail to illustrate the use of transitional devices. What type of transitional word or phrase appears most often? Why?
4. Find the words enclosed in quotation marks. Why are they so marked?
5. The writer uses a comparison in paragraph 1. What is it? Do you find it repeated elsewhere?
6. A number of words and phrases are immediately followed by phrases such as *the reason for, the purpose of.* What function do these phrases serve?
7. Note the title. Does it accurately reflect the writer's theme and purpose?

WRITING SUGGESTION

Each of us is a specialist, if you consider a specialist someone who has particular knowledge about a subject, the kind usually not shared by the general population. Being a specialist need not mean having an academic degree testifying to your expertise. What it does mean is that you have studied something so closely or done something so frequently that you have perfected understandings and skills beyond those that most people have. Perhaps you are a motorcycle buff familiar with a range of models and able to customize your own bike. Or you may be a dedicated spelunker who has not only explored many caves but has taught others to perfect their spelunking skills. Or you may be a specialist in weaving who has designed handcrafts that decorate your home—even, perhaps, the local art museum. Whatever the hobby or special interest, your familiarity with it testifies to your special knowledge.

Using the rich background you have in your special field, write a process essay that will introduce the general reader to your specialty. If your interest involves doing something, you may want to consider a direction-giving essay. If, on the other hand, you want to show how something is done, you will want to consider an information-giving essay. In either case, keep your audience in mind: explain terms that you think may be unfamiliar, and give as many reasons as you can for the steps you are describing.

CAUSE AND EFFECT

A writing purpose that questions an object or event, perhaps in an attempt to pinpoint its origin, entails causal reasoning. We seek causal explanations when we diagnose a problem or probe human motives: Why did I not get elected president of the Swim Club? Why won't my car start? Why has my closest friend suddenly turned cool? We also seek to determine effects: What is the effect of smoking, of going on crash diets, of excessive drinking? Attempts to answer these questions can often involve a complicated chain of reasoning. For example, the student who sought to find out why farmers were a vanishing breed in the essay "Where Are the Farmers?" (Chapter 2) reasoned that the decline in the farm population (an effect) could be attributed in part to advances in technology (a cause) which in turn increased the cost of farming (an effect). She found, however, that the increased cost of farming—the effect of technological change—was also a cause, since it had the effect of pricing the least wealthy farmers out of the market.

Causal relationships are not always easy to establish. The most common hazard is oversimplification, the belief that one cause is sufficient to explain a particular effect, or vice versa. If, for example, you've been consistently late for your Saturday job, you may plead a faulty alarm clock as an excuse (the proximate or direct cause), only to realize that the real reason for your tardiness is that you've become bored (the remote or indirect cause). To take a less personal example, it is possible to argue a causal relationship between television violence and real-life violence—as many have done—only if one concedes that there are many other features of contemporary American life that also encourage violence.

Because causal reasoning is so often used to interpret and explain experience, cause and effect is commonly found in all types of writing. At times, it will constitute the writer's major purpose, at other times it will be used in conjunction with a purpose that is not primarily concerned with causal explanations. Consider, for example, the following three student paragraphs, the first taken from a narrative based on personal experience, the second from a paper seeking to explain the role of the militia in colonial America, the third from an essay opposing the breakup of big oil companies.

Paragraph A
Effect
Cause 1

Cause 2

Cause 3

Gradually, the thrill of driving and caring for my car began to wane. Insurance payments seemed to grow with each billing, even though I had never had an accident. A few expensive speeding tickets, as well as the embarrassment of having my name appear in the paper in the "traffic court" news, also helped wean me from my adolescent passion. And then there was that spring evening when I found myself surrounded by a bunch of smartalecks heckling me while I tried to fix my rear wheel that had come off in the midst of traffic. Feeling vulnerable and alone, I vowed then and there that the flashy pleasures of car-owning were not for me.

Paragraph B
Mistaken cause

Writer's view of the true causes

According to British accounts of the time, General Braddock's stunning defeat in the 1755 campaign against the French posts of Fort Duquesne and Crown Point was caused by panic among the colonial American soldiers who served with him. The claim appears to be false. Braddock advanced too quickly, he advanced without adequate intelligence, he ordered his troops in the march in a long, thin line (flanks were left unguarded, a mistake in the wilderness), and, worst of all, he failed to secure high ground before entering into battle. It was a recipe for disaster.

Paragraph C
Cause

Effect 1

Effect 2

Effect 3

Those who advocate the breakup of the big oil companies are unaware of or unconcerned about the serious consequences of such a move. In the first place, it would take years to implement. During that time, there would be absolutely no capital formation. Affected companies would be unable to engage in oil exploration or to increase their production, with serious consequences for the motorist, the homeowner, the economy, and for the companies themselves. Research on alternative sources of energy would be discouraged. Foreign dependence would be insured. No one would gain except, perhaps, those who like to see the big brought small.

Examining these paragraphs, you can see that the focus of each is different. In the first, the self is at the center of the stage: the writer uses causal analysis to examine a personal experience. In the second, the writer disappears into the subject; it is still interpreted, to be sure, implying an intelligence at work, but the writer's aim is not to explore a personal event but to explain the subject. In the third, the focus is on the audience because the writer wishes to persuade readers to adopt a course of action, in this case, to pressure Congress to vote against impending legislation ordering the breakup of big oil companies. You can see, then, that cause and effect, like many of the other patterns, can serve a variety of purposes.

The Structure of Cause and Effect

There are two major patterns in cause-and-effect essays. Each is illustrated in miniature in two of the preceding paragraphs. Paragraph A begins with an effect (the writer's waning interest in his car) and then lists three causes that contributed to the effect. In paragraph C the pattern is reversed. The writer begins with a cause (the possible breakup of big oil companies) and then suggests three effects that the cause would have. In an extended causal analysis essay, these patterns are supplemented by an introduction that states the thesis of the analysis and a conclusion that reaffirms the thesis and interprets the assembled evidence.

Essays for Analysis

Essay A

In the following essay, the student writer attempts to trace the causes of a personal dilemma, using the effect-to-cause pattern. Note that to trace the origin and development of this dilemma, she arranges her causes chronologically.

HE, SHE, HIM, HER . . . WHO?

1   I've always admired teachers, parents, salesmen, businessmen, TV personalities, and even peers with a command of the English language. I do not have such good fortune. I have to think, stumbling in the midst of a thought to keep my pronouns straight. He's, she's, him's, and her's don't come out easily in my sentences; I have to contemplate, analyze the relationships, and make sure my pronouns are correct before I proceed with my sentence, and even then I sometimes get lost. There are reasons for this problem of careful pronoun choice. I have been conditioned to be cautious.

2   At one time I had no problems. Like everyone else, I used pronouns automatically, matching gender to referent with ease. But one spring I began to have trouble choosing him or her in a sentence. It all began with those scraggly cats.

3   At the time of my impending impairment, we lived next door to a big, old, unkempt-looking house. Inside lived an old

woman and fifty pet Pomeranians and toy poodles, or so rumor
had it. To keep rats and mice away from the house she had a
few cats out back who grew in number each spring. When their
number increased to a point where many could not find enough
food, some would stray over the fence from the tangled briars
to our neatly mowed lawn and huddle close to our patio window.
The eyes of many were red and puffy with mucous—like fluid
clogging the corners shut. Their ribs showed as they walked.
How could we fail to feel compassion for these pathetic
creatures? Though wild, the hungry cats and kittens allowed
us to come close to them and touch them. One kitten in
particular was afraid to take food but appeared to need it
more than any, so we made a special effort to nurse it.
Maybe, too, the kitten's appearance is what attracted us to
it. It was a version of Charlie Chaplin with a black slit
centered across its nose, its face a pale white. Even its
shy, lonely movements reminded us of Charlie Chaplin. Thus,
we immediately began to call the kitten Charlie.

4   Charlie grew friendlier and more and more amusing as he
played games with us. We liked him——until he began to swell
at the abdomen the following spring. Yes, as it turned out,
we had never checked the back end of that cat to determine its
sex. He was just Charlie, because he looked like a Charlie
and that had to be his name. That mistake was not so hard to
live with until we found we had made another mistake. It
became apparent that Charlie's mate was an ugly grey and white
patched cat that had sore eyes and a very sickly—looking pink
nose. This pathetic thing we called Bernice out of fun
because it looked like all those women we had heard called
Bernice. But as feminine as Bernice looked, she wasn't a
female. She was a he. And Charlie was a she. From our
discovery, however, came no changes in names. Charlie
continued to nurse her kittens and Bernice continued to search
for food for them.

5   It is easy to see that reassociating a male name with the
female gender and a female name with the male gender could
make anyone's mind go TILT. As I told someone about Charlie
or Bernice, I had to utter my sentence carefully to make sure
my pronoun references were correct. I was learning to be
cautious.

6   The study of a foreign language did not alleviate my
problem. In Spanish, all nouns are either feminine or
masculine and are therefore preceded by the article la or el
respectively. La nouns have an a at the end of the word,
which made the concept of a noun such as window——la ventana——

being feminine, a bit easier to handle. El nouns have an o at the end as in the word for summer--el verano. Remembering which inanimate objects were masculine and which were feminine put a heavy tax on my thinking. Later I found that I could not even trust the rule that words ending in a were feminine and those ending in o were masculine. The word for day--día--they told me, was masculine, thus requiring the antecedent el. El día. That just wasn't right. The only way I could be correct with my pronoun assignment now would be to consider my sentences carefully and to speak slowly.

7   Dare I even mention that I also took Latin? The horror of that experience was remembering case endings. Sometimes a plural masculine word could refer to both males and females. My confusion with Latin endings was not mine alone, though. We've all been told that alumni are a group of female alumnae and male alumni. A male graduate is an alumnus and a female graduate, an alumna. The tedious deciphering of endings again was wear and tear on my circuits.

8   The final blow came when I was a junior in high school and the town I lived in became involved in a bitter dispute over the granting of tenure to an elementary school music teacher. The news reports seemed to avoid confusion, but whenever I tried to explain the case I became hopelessly entangled. The problem this time? A sex change operation. This music teacher was a man, but now he, Paul, was a she, Paula, and she had his voice and strikingly resembled him, but she wanted to be considered as a separate person from him and she wanted to have his tenure. His wife, now her wife, was very supportive of his decision to become a she and together they tried to live with their children. He, the music teacher, now a she, had to earn money somehow in the meantime and in order to do this, she sang in nightclubs, singing in that same masculine voice I had heard when I was a student of his.

9   Considering the language problem this sex change created for me, one can easily see why this person was not granted a position in the same school system. The students would be confused because they had known this person as a man before. How could the eleven- and twelve-year-old students accommodate such a change?

10   I still find it very difficult to talk about my former music teacher. My friends avoided this problem by jokingly referring to the person as shim, because the efforts to make ourselves understood by using proper references to he or she were too burdensome. That experience, along with my training in the Spanish and Latin languages and my nursing of the

kittens, has confused me to the point where I can't make
logical distinctions. My proper sense of gender has been
destroyed. Listening to someone explain his family relations
strains me, and I want to do without figuring it out.

11   The scars I still carry with me. I'm just wondering how
anyone else has managed to escape such problems. Perhaps
school teachers, parents, salesmen, businessmen, TV
personalities, and my peers were the smarter ones. They
checked the sex of the stray cat before adopting it and naming
it, avoided the study of foreign languages (particularly
Spanish and Latin), and had music teachers who were satisfied
with their lives in their naturally assigned gender.

—Brenda Brumley

EXPLORING CHOICES

Content and Organization

1. The writer seeks to understand the causes of a personal problem. What is the problem? How many causes does she cite?
2. What principle of order is the writer using in citing the causes?
3. Note the title. Does it alert the reader to the problem treated in the essay?
4. Explain the transitional devices the writer uses in the opening sentence of each paragraph.
5. Examine the opening and concluding paragraphs. What major idea do they share? How does the concluding paragraph summarize the content of the essay? Where else does such a summary appear? Can you justify the repeated summary?
6. Evaluate the evidence the writer summons to explain her problem. Is it persuasive? Is it subject to external verification?
7. What idea is repeated in the final sentence of paragraphs 1, 5, 6, and 7. How does this repetition help to unify the essay?
8. How is paragraph 2 related to paragraphs 1 and 3? What function does it serve?
9. In paragraph 3, the writer calls the cats "pathetic creatures." What evidence does she provide in support of her estimate?

Style

1. This paper was written in several drafts. In the final draft, the student revised the word order of a number of sentences. Following are several examples of original and revised sentences. Which do you consider more effective? Before deciding, examine the context of each sentence and consider such matters as tone, emphasis and coherence.

Paragraph 3

> Original: An old woman lived inside with fifty pet Pomeranians and toy poodles . . . .
>
> Revised: Inside lived an old woman with fifty pet Pomeranians and toy poodles . . . .
>
> Original: Maybe, too, we were attracted to the kitten by its appearance.
>
> Revised: Maybe, too, the kitten's appearance is what attracted us to it.

Paragraph 4

> Original: She was a he and Charlie was a she.
>
> Revised: She was a he. And Charlie was a she.

Paragraph 7

> Original: Studying Latin also compounded my difficulty.
>
> Revised: Dare I even mention that I also took Latin?

Paragraph 8

> Original: The problem this time was a sex change operation.
>
> Revised: The problem this time? A sex change operation.

Paragraph 11

> Original   I still carry the scars with me.
>
> Revised: The scars I still carry with me.

2. Substitution can often help determine the relative effectiveness of a writer's choices. Following are several phrases the writer used. Try to think of alternatives for them and then evaluate the writer's choice in light of your substitutions.

Paragraph 3   impending impairment
unkempt-looking house

Paragraph 4   until he began to swell at the abdomen

Paragraph 6   put a heavy tax on my thinking

Paragraph 7   tedious deciphering

Paragraph 8   bitter dispute

Paragraph 8   whenever I tried to explain the case I became hopelessly entangled

Essay B

In the following essay, a free-lance writer examines his past, trying to understand and assess the reasons for a course of action.

WHY DID I EVER PLAY FOOTBALL?

1   Coach kept running the halfback sweep through the projector, clicking the stop, rewind and forward buttons as he dwelled on each "individual break-down" by our defense. Princeton had gained 20 yards on the play and our individual mistakes added up to a "total Yale breakdown." Gallagher and I sat with the other sophomores, savoring the embarrassment of the first-stringers.

2   The last individual to break down on the play was the defensive safety who started ahead of me. Yale's sports publicity department was touting him as a "pro prospect," but during the 11th screening of his mistake, he protested that he was not sure how to defense a sweep. After three years on the varsity, our NFL-bound star didn't know how to play your everyday end run.

3   "The first rule," Gallagher said as loudly as he could, "is don't get hurt." Suppressed laughter spread through the room. Everyone knew "the films don't lie" and that "newspaper clippings don't make tackles"; that "you have to want it," even in the Ivy League.

4   I'm not entirely sure why I played football; it might have been because of those great clichés. I certainly didn't enjoy hitting people the way Gallagher did. He liked to bury his helmet into a quarterback's ribs and drive him into the turf. As he returned to the huddle, there would be a strange expression on his face, somewhere between a grimace and a smile. After a game he would be sore, bruised and bloodied, like the other linemen and linebackers, while I would feel about the same as I did after an uneventful mixer at Vassar.

5   Defensive safeties are not supposed to make a lot of tackles, especially when the people up front are good, which ours were, and that was just fine with me. Still, some of my most vivid memories are of moments of intense pain. Once in junior year I found myself in a dreaded position: one-on-one with a fullback charging as swiftly as his bulky legs would carry him. He was 10 yards away and closing fast. He was also growling. "His S.A.T. scores must be beauts," flashed through my mind and the urge to flee became acute. Thousands of eyes were watching—including Coach's camera. If I blew it I would have to see the replay at least a dozen times.

6   Suddenly I was moving sideways through the air, pain jolting my body, the fullback forgotten. I hit the ground writhing, clutching my side and pulling my knees up to my chest. There was no air in my lungs. For a moment the world stopped at my skin. I wanted to stay crumpled up on the ground, but one of our linemen pulled me to my feet with one hand and half-carried me to the huddle. It must have been their end who hit me. I had seen him split out wide, then I forgot about him. He weighed over 200 pounds; I went about 160. What was I thinking of, playing football? I didn't hear our captain call the defensive signals, but fear slowly returned as the pain subsided. If that quarterback were smart he would try a pass in my zone. The pass never came. Thank God we were playing Harvard.

7   Continuing to play football was not a particularly rational thing for me to do. In sixth grade I was as big and strong and fast as anyone our six-man team faced. And jocks were popular then. By college virtually everyone I played against was bigger and stronger, and the consensus on campus in the late 1960s was that we were a bunch of neofascists, at best. So much for "Boola, Boola."

And when it wasn't a physically grinding ordeal, practice, too, could be as boring as Archeology 101.

8   Saturday's approach would turn my insides to mush, but the day I dreaded most was Sunday, film day. "Now I want everyone to watch the tackling technique on this play," Coach would say. "Holahan, I hope you squeeze your dates harder than this." Gallagher laughed the loudest.

9   Oh, I had my moments, usually when the people up front either played badly or were overmatched. Then I got a workout and there was no place to hide. Against Dartmouth, senior year, I turned positively vicious after watching their halfback gloat over one of our players lying injured on the field. I started burying my helmet into people even if they didn't have the ball. Once I made that halfback groan in pain. I also said some ugly things about his mother. I intercepted two passes. And the next day brought sweet soreness; so that's how Gallagher felt after every game.

10   There were other players who must have had a tougher time figuring out why they were playing football; high-school hotshots who couldn't crack the second string, but who hung on. Some who didn't play in games, never expected to, maybe never even wanted to, for blocking and tackling are clearly unpleasant experiences. A few were not in the least bit athletic. Who knows, they may have been doing it for their résumés, but I suppose they had their moments too, when things would happen that could never take place in Archeology 101. For me, Coach's films had something to do with why I continued to play.

11   Sunday afternoon was both a social and a moral occasion—funny, embarrassing, depressing or happy, depending on how the team had done and how each player had performed. Every fall Sabbath was a new Judgment Day. What was shown on the screen was often harsh, but always just. I could fool professors and pass courses without working very hard, but no one could slip anything past that camera. If I played well Saturday, I knew it; still, the camera confirmed it. There was no place to hide in that room, no big linemen up front to take the heat. Film immortalized shirking efforts.

12   I have often thought of driving 40 minutes to New Haven and digging up that old Dartmouth game, going back 14 years to see a younger, stronger, less cautious me. The temptation seems to grow each year, but I will never do it. It would be cheating the camera to look only at that one film.

—David Holahan

EXPLORING CHOICES

Content and Organization

1. What are some reasons that probably did *not* govern Holahan's decision to play football? Where in the essay are these mentioned?
2. What seems to have been the primary reason why he did play, and in what ways did playing affect him?
3. How does Holahan appear to feel about the truth that his "most vivid memories" of the game center on the "moments of intense pain"?
4. Explain what Holahan means when he says that the filmed replay of a game became "both a social and a moral occasion."

5. Why does the writer feel "it would be cheating" if he went back and looked at only one game film?

6. Explain whether or not Holahan's subject matter limits his likely audience in any way. What can the essay still say to someone who has never participated in competitive sports?

Style

1. The first person *I* occurs frequently in this memoir; what techniques does Holahan use to maintain variety and to keep the repetition from becoming boring?

2. Holahan's narrative moves so easily between the present and the past that he does not need to use many transitional words. Explain how he effects his transitions.

3. What does the inclusion of the word "Ever" add to Holahan's title? Would the title lose anything if that word were omitted?

Essay

In the following selection, the student author seeks to persuade the reader to adopt a particular course of action. To show how the course he is advocating would lead to desirable consequences, he uses a cause-to-effect pattern.

BANISHING THE TRAFFIC JAM

1   The traffic jam is one of the more depressing features of modern urban life. On any business day, autos, trucks, cabs and buses fill the city streets to capacity and beyond, making already difficult living and working conditions even more unpleasant. No one can deny that the perpetual crush of heavy traffic is injurious to health, to emotional well-being, and to aesthetic sensibilities. Even hardheaded practical considerations--the efficient transport of people and products--demand some sort of viable alternative.

2   Serious problems call for radical solutions: in this case, the daytime banning of vehicular traffic from major business districts. Strenuous objections are bound to be made--many of them perfectly legitimate--but it seems to me they are far outweighed by the benefits that would accrue to the vast majority of city dwellers.

3   First of all, the vehicular traffic ban would provide an immediate boost to our currently floundering, unprofitable system of mass transit. Increased ridership would help provide the incentive and the capital for broadening and improving subway and bus service--the gradual decay of which is largely responsible for the glut of traffic in the first place. One could also anticipate increased federal aid for

mass transit, since decreased auto use coincides with national priorities of fuel conservation and environmental protection.

4   Another advantage, then, is the decline in consumption of gas and other petroleum products. The amount of fuel required to move several tons of metal per drive is clearly wasteful; such gross inefficiency would be largely eliminated by greater utilization of mass transit. Iron, rubber, and other precious raw materials would also be more economically employed.

5   Whatever the practical advantages, the most important benefit of banning vehicular traffic from major business districts would be realized in what has come to be known as the "quality of life." Foremost among these is reduction of automotive exhausts, the single greatest cause of air pollution. One can look forward to an enormous improvement in air quality with the banning of downtown auto use—— particularly since slow-moving, traffic-snarled vehicles emit the largest quantity of noxious gases and solid waste matter. Not only would downtown districts become more habitable, but, with the concomitant decline in pollution-related illnesses, we could anticipate shrinking hospital rolls, improved overall health, and increased average life span.

6   When similar proposals have been submitted in the past, both private and public interests have voiced strong opposition. Merchants fear that business would suffer should customers be denied access by car to goods and services, while drivers are reluctant to give up the convenience and comfort of their own autos for the claustrophobic confines of bus and subway. I can only respond that the thriving commerce of such European capitals as Copenhagen and Amsterdam, where cars are banned from certain districts, suggests that economic consequences can be minimized; and an upgrading of public transportation should make private auto use less attractive by comparison. If we follow these already existing models, there is a good chance that living in the city would become not only tolerable, but desirable.   ——Jonathan Breslaw

EXPLORING CHOICES

Content and Organization

1. Point to the writer's thesis. In what paragraph does it appear? Why did the writer not include it in his introductory paragraph? Consider the function of the first paragraph in formulating your answer.
2. How many advantages to his proposal does the writer cite? Are they sufficient to persuade you of his argument? Can you think of other advantages he might have cited in support of his point of view?

3. Chart the cause-and-effect pattern in paragraph 3, paying particular attention to the way in which causes become effects and vice versa.
4. Point out the climactic order the writer uses. Do you find this order effective? Explain.
5. Who would be the likely audience for this essay? The city council of a large metropolitan area? City dwellers in general? A personal friend? Merchants in a downtown metropolitan area? Explain your choice.
6. Where does the writer address opposing arguments? Do you find his response to these arguments convincing? Explain.

Style

1. Note the writer's use of the dash in paragraphs 2 and 3. Could the writer have substituted a comma for the dash in each case? Explain.
2. The two clauses of sentence 2 in paragraph 4 are joined by a semicolon. Why do you think the writer uses this punctuation mark? Could he just as well have separated these clauses with a period? Explain.
3. Try substituting "smothering quarters" for "claustrophobic confines" in the second sentence of the final paragraph. Which do you prefer? Why?
4. Note the writer's use of the first person in paragraphs 2 and 6. Try rephrasing these sentences to eliminate the first person. Do you find a difference in effect? Explain.

WRITING SUGGESTIONS

1. Consider a sport or hobby you're interested in and try to analyze how you developed your interest.
2. Examine a community problem (housing, public transportation, parking, and so on) and suggest a solution. Determine the effects that would follow from your solution.
3. Trace the development of public interest in foreign cars or imported wines.
4. Consider the effects of the computer on education, business, or farm management.

COMPARISON AND CONTRAST

You will often find occasion to organize and develop an essay by comparison and contrast. In a class you may be asked to compare the molecular structure of two compounds; or to contrast the architectural styles of two buildings; or to compare and contrast the tragic heroes in Shakespeare's

King Lear and Arthur Miller's *Death of a Salesman.* Your employer or supervisor might want a comparative analysis of the advantages and disadvantages of two approaches to advertising a product; or a comparison and contrast of the coverage and cost-effectiveness of different dental insurance plans for employees. At times, you may wish to use the pattern to explain a subject to your readers or to express a facet of your own experience; at other times, you may use it to make a judgment about the items being compared. In each instance, you would use the comparison-and-contrast pattern to express, explain, or argue a central point, not merely to list similarities and differences.

The Structure of Comparison and Contrast

You can choose one of two organizational plans when you develop an essay by comparison and contrast: the *block pattern* (the comparison of wholes) or the *alternating pattern* (the comparison of parts). The block pattern requires that you take one of the two items being compared and contrasted and examine it in full, turning next to a full examination of the second item. Organizing a paper in this way can benefit the reader if the items being compared and contrasted are complex, or if the reader is unfamiliar with the items being examined.

The alternating pattern requires that you move between the two items, discussing them point by point. Though this structure is somewhat more difficult to organize because it requires more transitional signals, it is easier for readers to follow since they need not refer to what has been said earlier, often the case when the block pattern is used. Whichever pattern you use, you need to be equitable to both sides. If you mention a certain detail in your discussion of one item, you must mention it in your discussion of the other.

The following is how the two organizational plans would look in outline form if you chose to compare and contrast the news coverage of two newspapers.

Block Plan
Introduction (including thesis)
A. *The Chicago Tribune*
    1. Foreign news
    2. Financial news
    3. Sports news
    4. Local news
    5. Entertainment news
B. *USA Today*
    1. Foreign news
    2. Financial news
    3. Sports news

4. Local news
5. Entertainment news
Conclusion

Alternating Plan

Introduction (including thesis)
1. Foreign news
   A. *The Chicago Tribune*
   B. *USA Today*
2. Financial news
   A. *The Chicago Tribune*
   B. *USA Today*
3. Sports news
   A. *The Chicago Tribune*
   B. *USA Today*
4. Local news
   A. *The Chicago Tribune*
   B. *USA Today*
5. Entertainment news
   A. *The Chicago Tribune*
   B. *USA Today*
Conclusion

Essays for Analysis

Essay A

Just as a cause-and-effect pattern can serve different purposes, so, too, can a comparison-and-contrast pattern. Note how Denise Gaskins, the student author of the following selection, uses comparison and contrast to express a personal response to a roommate very different from herself.

I BELIEVE IN GRYPHONS

1   "Reality is just a figment of your imagination." That statement began the argument which would leave me unable to sleep and my roommate pounding her mattress in frustration.

2   I was trying to explain to Sue, my roommate, why I believe in gryphons; the problem was compounded by the fact that she had never heard of a gryphon before she came to college. Borrowing my basic argument from Robert Pirsig's Zen and the Art of Motorcycle Maintenance, I almost convinced her that anything a person really believed would be true—for that person. I did not say "anything one wanted to believe," but "anything one really believed, whether one wanted to believe it or not." That was the crux of the argument, for it did not matter then whether one's reality was truly "real" or

"imaginary" according to traditional definitions. She knew no
way to answer this reasoning, and it upset her. I hoped it
would make her take some time to examine her own beliefs; as
for myself, I spent the next few hours lying in bed following
the idea down several newly-discovered paths of thought.

3   We don't think alike, Sue and I, but it is actually fairly
rare that any two people picked at random do think alike.
Ideas like the one I brought into that night's discussion just
tend to emphasize the differences. For instance, we are both
science majors, and the scientific method is a useful and
respected tool for us both. For me, it has stayed a tool,
with faults and limitations like any carpenter's hammer. For
her, it seems to have grown into a way of life, a religion fed
by the daily ministrations of science teachers and society:
"Nothing exists which cannot be measured; so nothing which
cannot be measured exists." Perhaps that is why she got so
frustrated when I used logic to defend my belief in magic, in
gryphons and gods, in all those inhabitants of the imagination
which seem to have so very much more life than the most
rigorously proven scientific theories.

4   Our daily behavior often gives clues to our basic beliefs.
I lead a mentally active life, almost constantly reading,
writing, thinking or talking, and often doing several of these
at once. I stay up all night, when I get the chance, to
discuss ideals and philosophies of life with anyone who is
interested. If no one is interested in these, I'll discuss
just about any topic, and I rarely go to bed before one
o'clock even when no one will talk with me; my mind is
sharpest at night. Sue, on the other hand, seems to lead a
mentally passive life. She rarely reads, except for
classwork, and puts little creative effort into her
activities--she writes five letters (a normal activity for us)
in the time it takes me to do one. Sue often sits listening
to music and staring at nothing, but she will only rarely
discuss what is on her mind. And she is almost unfailingly
asleep before eleven o'clock.

5   One might expect from the above description that I take the
lead when we do things together, and sometimes this is true.
For instance, what Sue considers "crazy" escapades--such as
calling a stranger in the middle of the night and talking for
two hours, simply because he had the same name as a
philosopher I remembered from economics last year--are usually
my ideas. Just as often, however, she encourages me to go
with her to club callouts and meetings when I otherwise would
have stayed home to read a book. And generally it takes some
prodding and coaxing from each of us to "get up our nerve."
Yet, for the most part, we spend our evenings studying.

6   Beyond college, Sue has few plans. She is a biology major because she enjoyed the subject in high school, but she has given little serious thought to a career. In contrast, I came to college with one purpose in mind: to learn whatever it takes to qualify me for the space program. I became a physics major, figuring that would be the most straightforward approach. These facts seem to influence our outlook on life also, for Sue has a somewhat pessimistic view of the future, while I am an almost constant optimist. Yet there is plenty of good nature beneath Sue's pessimism, and it needs only a "crazy" influence like me to bring it out, just as it took the influence of several of my friends to develop and nurture my optimistic craziness.

7   Sue refers to my way of living, compared to her own, as a "natural high"--if she didn't know better, she says, she'd swear I was taking drugs. I refer to her way of living as "pre-digested"--if I didn't know better, I'd swear she had terminal apathy. But I'm trying to help her grow into an individual. I think we're succeeding. I know the experience is helping me to grow as a person who cares, not merely about the exterior, "real" world perceived by my senses, but also about the interior, "fantasy" world perceived by my mind. I call it "believing in gryphons."   --Denise Gaskins

EXPLORING CHOICES

Content and Organization

1. Which comparison and contrast plan does the writer use?
2. What is the function of paragraphs 1 and 2?
3. Point out the writer's thesis. What is the relation of her thesis to her title?
4. Note the writer's conclusion. How does it reaffirm and interpret her thesis?
5. What specific aspects or characteristics of her roommate and herself does the writer focus on? Has she stressed similarities, or differences?
6. Point out the transitional words and phrases the writer uses when she wishes to indicate a contrast between herself and her roommate.

Style

1. Note that in paragraph 3, the writer begins one sentence with "for me," and the next with "for her." Why do you think she uses these parallel sentence openers? What if she had replaced "for her" with phrasing such as "Sue, in contrast, thinks of the scientific method . . ."? Do you see a difference in effect? Explain.

2. Note the writer's use of quotation marks. Explain their different functions.

3. Point out the series of prepositional phrases in the final sentence of paragraph 3. Why do you think the last item of the series is longer than the others?

4. Note the writer's use of the dash in the final paragraph. What function does it serve? Could the writer have used parentheses instead? Explain.

Essay B

In the following essay, Bruce Catton, a professional historian, uses a comparison-and-contrast pattern to explain the differences between two military leaders.

GRANT AND LEE: A STUDY IN CONTRASTS

1   When Ulysses S. Grant and Robert E. Lee met in the parlor of a modest house at Appomattox Court House, Virginia, on April 9, 1865 to work out the terms for the surrender of Lee's Army of Northern Virginia, a great chapter in American life came to a close, and a great new chapter began.

2   These men were bringing the Civil War to its virtual finish. To be sure, other armies had yet to surrender, and for a few days the fugitive Confederate government would struggle desperately and vainly, trying to find some way to go on living now that its chief support was gone. But in effect it was all over when Grant and Lee signed the papers. And the little room where they wrote out the terms was the scene of one of the poignant, dramatic contrasts in American history.

3   They were two strong men, these oddly different generals, and they represented the strengths of two conflicting currents that, through them, had come into final collision.

4   Back of Robert E. Lee was the notion that the old aristocratic concept might somehow survive and be dominant in American life.

5   Lee was tidewater Virginia, and in his background were family, culture, and tradition . . . the age of chivalry transplanted to a New World which was making its own legends and its own myths. He embodied a way of life that had come down through the age of knighthood and the English country squire. America was a land that was beginning all over again, dedicated to nothing much more complicated than the rather hazy belief that all men had equal rights, and should have an equal chance in the world. In such a land Lee stood for the feeling that it was somehow of advantage to human society to have a pronounced inequality in the social structure. There should be a leisure class, backed by ownership of land; in turn, society itself should be keyed to the land as the chief source of wealth and influence. It would bring forth (according to this ideal) a class of men with a strong sense of obligation to the community; men who lived not to gain advantage for themselves, but to meet the solemn obligations which had been laid on them by the very fact that they were privileged. From them the country would get its leadership; to them it could look for the higher values—of thought, of conduct, of personal deportment—to give it strength and virtue.

6   Lee embodied the noblest elements of this aristocratic ideal. Through him, the landed nobility justified itself. For four years, the Southern states had fought a desperate war to uphold the ideals for which Lee stood. In the end, it almost seemed as if the Confederacy fought for Lee; as if he himself was the Confederacy . . . the best thing that the way of life for which the Confederacy stood could ever have to offer. He had passed into legend before Appomattox. Thousands of tired, underfed, poorly clothed Confederate soldiers, long-since past the simple enthusiasm of the early days of the struggle, somehow considered Lee the symbol of everything for which they had been willing to die. But they could not quite put this feeling into words. If the Lost Cause, sanctified by so much heroism and so many deaths, had a living justification, its justification was General Lee.

7   Grant, the son of a tanner on the Western frontier, was everything Lee was not. He had come up the hard way, and embodied nothing in particular except the eternal toughness and sinewy fiber of the men who grew up beyond the mountains. He was one of a body of men who owed reverence and obeisance to no one, who were self-reliant to a fault, who cared hardly anything for the past but who had a sharp eye for the future.

8   These frontier men were the precise opposites of the tidewater aristocrats. Back of them, in the great surge that had taken people over the Alleghenies and into the opening Western country, there was a deep, implicit dissatisfaction with a past that had settled into grooves. They stood for democracy, not from any reasoned conclusion about the proper ordering of human society, but simply because they had grown up in the middle of democracy and knew how it worked. Their society might have privileges, but they would be privileges each man had won for himself. Forms and patterns meant nothing. No man was born to anything, except perhaps to a chance to show how far he could rise. Life was competition.

9   Yet along with this feeling had come a deep sense of belonging to a national community. The Westerner who developed a farm, opened a shop or set up in business as a trader, could hope to prosper only as his own community prospered—and his community ran from the Atlantic to the Pacific and from Canada down to Mexico. If the land was settled, with towns and highways and accessible markets, he could better himself. He saw his fate in terms of the nation's own destiny. As its horizons expanded so did his. He had, in other words, an acute dollars-and-cents stake in the continued growth and development of his country.

10   And that, perhaps, is where the contrast between Grant and Lee becomes striking. The Virginia aristocrat, inevitably, saw himself in relation to his own region. He lived in a static society which could endure almost anything except change. Instinctively, his first loyalty would go to the locality in which that society existed. He would fight to the limit of endurance to defend it, because in defending it he was defending everything that gave his own life its deepest meaning.

11   The Westerner, on the other hand, would fight with an equal tenacity for the broader concept of society. He fought so because everything he lived by was tied to growth, expansion, and a constantly widening horizon. What he lived by would survive or fall with the nation itself. He could not possibly stand by unmoved in the face of an attempt to destroy the Union. He would combat it with

everything he had, because he could only see it as an effort to cut the ground out from under his feet.

12   So Grant and Lee were in complete contrast, representing two diametrically opposed elements in American life. Grant was the modern man emerging; beyond him, ready to come on the stage, was the great age of steel and machinery, of crowded cities and a restless, burgeoning vitality. Lee might have ridden down from the old age of chivalry, lance in hand, silken banner fluttering over his head. Each man was the perfect champion of his cause, drawing both his strengths and his weaknesses from the people he led.

13   Yet it was not all contrast, after all. Different as they were—in background, in personality, in underlying aspiration—these two great soldiers had much in common. Under everything else, they were marvelous fighters. Furthermore, their fighting qualities were really very much alike.

14   Each man had, to begin with, the great virtue of utter tenacity and fidelity. Grant fought his way down the Mississippi Valley in spite of acute personal discouragement and profound military handicaps. Lee hung on in the trenches at Petersburg after hope itself had died. In each man there was an indomitable quality . . . the born fighter's refusal to give up as long as he can still remain on his feet and lift his two fists.

15   Daring and resourcefulness they had, too; the ability to think faster and move faster than the enemy. These were the qualities which gave Lee the dazzling campaigns of Second Manasses and Chancellorsville and won Vicksburg for Grant.

16   Lastly, and perhaps greatest of all, there was the ability, at the end, to turn quickly from war to peace once the fighting was over. Out of the way these two men behaved at Appomattox came the possibility of a peace of reconciliation. It was a possibility not wholly realized, in the years to come, but which did, in the end, help the two sections to become one nation again . . . after a war whose bitterness might have seemed to make such a reunion wholly impossible. No part of either man's life became him more than the part he played in their brief meeting in the McLean house at Appomattox. Their behavior there put all succeeding generations of Americans in their debt. Two great Americans, Grant and Lee—very different, yet under everything very much alike. Their encounter at Appomattox was one of the great moments of American history.

—Bruce Catton

EXPLORING CHOICES

Content and Organization

1. The first part of this essay uses the block method of organization, the second part, the alternating method. How is this shift in strategy justified by Catton's material and purpose? Did you find it disorienting?
2. Ordinarily, contrasts are more telling than comparisons. Yet Catton begins with contrasts and then moves on to comparisons. Why is that suitable given his theme and viewpoint here?

3. How much do you actually learn about Grant and Lee as individuals? Why does Catton focus so heavily on the differing concepts of America that they represent?
4. Using brief notes, try to line up Catton's comparisons and contrasts in two sets of two columns each, one set headed "Grant/Lee," the other "frontier men/tidewater aristocrats." What does such an outline demonstrate about Catton's coverage of his subject?
5. Does Catton appear objective and impartial in his treatment of the two men and the two ways of life? If so, how does he maintain that sense of fairness?

Style

1. Comment on Catton's use of transitions, especially on those which signal the direction of the essay's major sections.
2. Catton's opening and closing paragraphs depend heavily upon the overused adjective "great." Is Catton's imagination flagging at these points, or is this an appropriately chosen repetition? Explain your response.

Essay C

In the following essay Jennifer Schmidt, a student author, uses a comparison-and-contrast pattern to persuade readers that one type of preschool training is superior to another.

THE ADVANTAGES OF MONTESSORI SCHOOLS

1 Since its introduction in the early part of this century, the Montessori method of child education has been one of the most controversial approaches to teaching the preschool child. A child educator who practiced in Italy, Dr. Maria Montessori believed that teachers should focus on the individual child rather than on a whole group of children simultaneously, the common practice in traditional classrooms. The most important and most effective form of education, she felt, was self-education; discipline, as a result, would arise from self-control rather than from the authoritarian command, "Do as I say!"

2 Because Montessori's approach to preschool education differs so greatly from traditional American methods of early childhood education, her philosophy is still fiercely debated in our society. Though some of her ideas have been adopted, many are still considered eccentric by the American parent and the American educator because American society still tends to view children almost as possessions or objects, always in need of adult control, while Montessori viewed children as

individuals with rights and needs of their own. However, an examination of the educational needs of children reveals that the Montessori school is more conducive to learning than is the traditional American nursery school because the Montessori method reflects a more accurate understanding of the nature of the child.

3   Just what is the nature of the child and what are his needs with respect to learning? To begin with, it appears that children learn more from self-teaching than from teaching by another. We see this most clearly when the young child cries "Let me do it!" as he struggles with a recalcitrant zipper or shoelace. What this illustrates is the child's need to learn by doing. He cannot learn by observing or by having things done for him; instead, he must learn in his own "real-life" context. Children best learn mathematics, for example, in the context of their own experience, not in the context of the classroom. The understanding of numbers grows from the child's need for them. Johnny may learn to count quite easily by selecting the correct number of plates to set the table for a family meal, but he may have difficulty learning to count using number symbols on paper—particularly if, to use Swiss psychologist Jean Piaget's developmental scheme, he is still in the preoperational stage of cognitive development.

4   In the Montessori school, children learn by experiencing real situations. They learn about hot, warm, cool, and cold, for instance, with their own senses: they feel the various temperatures in the form of metal cylinders filled with various temperatures of water. In contrast, many traditional nursery schools still teach temperature by using picture symbols such as the sun, or a steaming bowl of soup, or snow, and then talking about them. As a result, children in these schools learn concepts secondhand rather than through direct experience.

5   In addition to learning through direct experience, children schooled in the Montessori method also learn and develop at their own rate. We know from the work of Jean Piaget that, while children go through the same sequence of stages in their cognitive development, not all of them reach the various stages at the same time. Consequently, the learning rates of children differ. In the Montessori school, Piaget's ideas are respected. There, each child works on an individual task of his own choice for as long or as short a period of time as he needs in order to master a skill. For example, Johnny may work with the movable alphabet (a set of loose, cutout letters) all day, while Mary may work on several projects,

such as the Cuisinaire blocks (a set of differently sized and colored cubes and rectangles used to learn mathematical relationships), books, and the temperature cylinders. In contrast, children in traditional nursery schools are taught in groups. As a result, the child whose cognitive development is more advanced—the "gifted" child—as well as the child whose cognitive development lags behind—the "slow learner"— are both hurt. The gifted child is held back, reduced to the average learning level of the class, while the slow learner is pushed to keep up and is therefore not permitted time to master one concept fully before being confronted by a new one.

6   Another advantage of the Montessori school is its approach to discipline. The Montessorian believes that true discipline is self-control, which the child learns by understanding his importance as an individual. Seeing that he is respected by the adults around him, he is better able to respect others and to acknowledge that they have the same rights as he himself enjoys. In contrast, the child in the traditional nursery school sees discipline as something imposed, usually by an adult who utters commands. And because the child often learns by imitation, the model he hears becomes the model he uses. Receiving the "do as I say" message from the teacher in charge, he is likely to convey the same message when he interacts with other children.

7   What we know about the development of children tells us that Montessori schools are better able to accommodate the child's natural growth than are traditional nursery schools. If, as I have argued, children learn best by doing rather than by watching, and by learning at their own rate rather than from the will of an adult, then the Montessori method is best suited to their needs. This does not mean that all children should be enrolled in Montessori schools, but it does suggest that Montessori's methods should be more widely understood and applied in all schools that take early childhood education seriously.
                                                            —Jennifer Schmidt

EXPLORING CHOICES

Content and Organization

1. How does the title alert the reader to the purpose of the essay?
2. Which comparison and contrast pattern does the writer use? Do you think it serves her purpose best? Explain.

3. What is the function of paragraphs 1 and 2? What do these paragraphs suggest about the audience the writer is addressing?
4. Point out the writer's thesis. How does her thesis control the subsequent development of the essay?
5. Point to the writer's use of examples. Do you think she uses enough? Do the examples persuade you that the writer is knowledgeable about her subject?
6. Note the writer's use of authority. Does she identify her authority? Does her use of authority help to support her argument? Explain.
7. Point out the transitional words and phrases the writer uses when she shifts from one item of comparison to another.
8. Point out how the transitional sentence at the beginning of paragraph 5 repeats old information at the same time as it introduces a new idea.
9. Summarize the writer's argument. Is her argument adequately interpreted in her conclusion? Explain.

Style

1. Note the writer's use of parentheses in paragraph 5. What is their function? Could the writer have removed them and simply set off her material with commas? Explain.
2. The writer begins paragraph 3 with a question. Why do you think she does so?
3. Note the writer's use of the dash in paragraph 5. What function does it serve? Could the writer have used commas instead? Explain

WRITING SUGGESTIONS

1. You have been asked by the editor of your local newspaper to contribute a piece designed to inform others about good buys. The editor is especially interested in having you consider items like home computers, racing bicycles, motorcycles, cars, television sets, and stereos. Choose one of these items and compare and contrast two of its brands or types. You may wish to argue that one brand is better than another, or you may want to describe the features of each and then allow readers to make up their minds. In either case, remember that your reader depends on your expertise to make the best choice.
2. Explain to the members of your class the differences and similarities between two hobbies, two modes of exercising, two movies with a common theme, two major styles of playing tennis (or any sport), two current music styles, two political figures, two rock stars, or two roommates you have had. Before you begin writing, consider your readers' interests, expectations, and degree of knowledge about your subject.

CLASSIFICATION

Try to sort our your reading in the past year. Perhaps you've read a biography, a novel, or a travel account; perhaps you've been limited by time or inclination to magazines or the newspaper. However you characterize your preferences, you'll find yourself using generic terms or categories to identify the type of reading you've done—just as Brustein did with the horror films he'd seen. Thinking this way is called *classification:* you take a subject—in this case, reading—and arrange its parts into groups according to an element shared by each member of the group. You can classify almost any general subject that can be divided into parts or kinds. For example, before you go to the supermarket, you might classify the food you will buy into meat, dairy products, produce, pastry, and so on. If you're a tidy soul, and you've been collecting magazines, you can arrange them according to their specialties, such as news, sports, gardening, or cooking. For a camping trip you'd probably classify the different kinds of gear you'd need: cooking equipment, bedding, shelter, and so on.

In classification, the subject is usually plural—not a student, but students, not a particular automobile, but automobiles. Each plural subject is then divided according to a single principle of classification. If you wished to classify the students on your campus, you could group them by religious preference, by housing arrangements, by dating habits, by political loyalties, by leisure or professional interests, and so on. Depending on your aim, you would choose *one* of these ways to discuss in your essay. A paper for a political science class whose purpose might be primarily informative might concentrate on students' political preferences. Another designed to express a personal point of view to your peers might focus on the eating habits of students. In the first case, your categories would be already established: you could choose traditional party names to group the political preferences of students, or you might establish a political spectrum ranging from reactionary to radical. In the second case, however, you would probably have to come up with your own categories, especially if you wished to introduce a humorous note.

For example, to illustrate the degree of poverty among students, one writer chose to classify them according to what they ate for Sunday dinner when meals at the dorm were not served. She concluded that the poorest were the Carbonators, since they could afford only a coke for their Sunday dinner, the next poorest were the Carbohydrators, who could afford starchy food, and the least poor were the Proteiners, who could afford the most expensive cuts of meat. Note that she chose a single principle of classification (students classified according to what they ate for their Sunday dinner). If she had included how students studied on Sunday night (Carbonators, Carbohydrators, and Grinds), or what they wore on Sunday night (Carbonators, Carbohydrators, and The Suit and Dress Crowd), she would have misclassified students because she would have used more than one principle of classification.

The Structure of Classification

In addition to having a single principle of classification, an essay designed primarily to classify will often have a principle of arrangement that will govern the order in which the writer discusses each type. The most common is the most-to-least arrangement or vice versa. Such a pattern may use number (the largest number, the fewest or smallest or least number) or quality (the most serious or dangerous or beautiful, the least serious or dangerous or beautiful) or size (the largest, the smallest) or importance (the most important, the least important). At times, the principle of arrangement will be joined to an enumeration pattern which announces that the types will be listed sequentially, as, for example, "The first type, and the most serious. . . ." "Second in order of seriousness. . . ."

A classification essay begins with an introduction that announces the principle of classification. The introduction is followed by a discussion of type 1, 2, 3, and so on, in which the principle of arrangement is explored. The conclusion summarizes the implications of the principle of classification.

Essays for Analysis

Essay A

John Holt wrote extensively on educational problems. In this selection, he examines three kinds of discipline children encounter as they mature.

From FREEDOM AND BEYOND

1   A child, in growing up, may meet and learn from three different kinds of disciplines. The first and most important is what we might call the Discipline of Nature or of Reality. When he is trying to do something real, if he does the wrong thing or doesn't do the right one, he doesn't get the result he wants. If he doesn't pile one block right on top of another, or tries to build on a slanting surface, his tower falls down. If he hits the wrong key, he hears the wrong note. If he doesn't hit the nail squarely on the head, it bends, and he has to pull it out and start with another. If he doesn't measure properly what he is trying to build, it won't open, close, fit, stand up, fly, float, whistle, or do whatever he wants it to do. If he closes his eyes when he swings, he doesn't hit the ball. A child meets this kind of discipline every time he tries to *do* something, which is why it is so important in school to give children more chances to do things, instead of just reading or listening to someone talk (or pretending to). This discipline is a great teacher. The learner never has to wait long for his answer; it usually comes quickly, often instantly. Also it is clear, and very often points toward the needed correction; from what happened he can not only see that what he did was wrong, but also why, and what he needs to do instead. Finally, and most important, the giver of the answer, call it Nature, is impersonal, impartial, and indifferent. She does not give opinions, or make judgments; she cannot be wheedled, bullied, or fooled; she does not get angry or disappointed; she does

not praise or blame; she does not remember past failures or hold grudges; with her one always gets a fresh start, this time is the one that counts.

2   The next discipline we might call the Discipline of Culture, of Society, of What People Really Do. Man is a social, a cultural animal. Children sense around them this culture, this network of agreements, customs, habits, and rules binding the adults together. They want to understand it and be a part of it. They watch very carefully what people around them are doing and want to do the same. They want to do right, unless they become convinced they can't do right. Thus children rarely misbehave seriously in church, but sit as quietly as they can. The example of all those grownups is contagious. Some mysterious ritual is going on, and children, who like rituals, want to be part of it. In the same way, the little children that I see at concerts or operas, though they may fidget a little, or perhaps take a nap now and then, rarely make any disturbance. With all those grownups sitting there, neither moving nor talking, it is the most natural thing in the world to imitate them. Children who live among adults who are habitually courteous to each other, and to them, will soon learn to be courteous. Children who live surrounded by people who speak a certain way will speak that way, however much we may try to tell them that speaking that way is bad or wrong.

3   The third discipline is the one most people mean when they speak of discipline—the Discipline of Superior Force, of sergeant to private, of "You do what I tell you or I'll make you wish you had." There is bound to be some of this in a child's life. Living as we do surrounded by things that can hurt children, or that children can hurt, we cannot avoid it. We can't afford to let a small child find out from experience the danger of playing in a busy street, or of fooling with the pots on the top of a stove, or of eating up the pills in the medicine cabinet. So, along with other precautions, we say to him, "Don't play in the street, or touch things on the stove, or go into the medicine cabinet, or I'll punish you." Between him and the danger too great for him to imagine we put a lesser danger, but one he can imagine and maybe therefore wants to avoid. He can have no idea of what it would be like to be hit by a car, but he can imagine being shouted at, or spanked, or sent to his room. He avoids these substitutes for the greater danger until he can understand it and avoid it for its own sake. But we ought to use this discipline only when it is necessary to protect the life, health, safety, or well-being of people or other living creatures, or to prevent destruction of things that people care about. We ought not to assume too long, as we usually do, that a child cannot understand the real nature of the danger from which we want to protect him. The sooner he avoids the danger, not to escape our punishment, but as a matter of good sense, the better. He can learn that faster than we think. In Mexico, for example, where people drive their cars with a good deal of spirit, I saw many children no older than five or four walking unattached on the streets. They understood about cars, they knew what to do. A child whose life is full of the threat and fear of punishment is locked into babyhood. There is no way for him to grow up, to learn to take responsibility for his life and acts. Most important of all, we should not assume that having to yield to the threat of our superior force is good for the child's character. It is never good for *anyone's* character. To bow to superior force makes us feel impotent and cowardly for not having had the strength or courage to resist.

Worse, it makes us resentful and vengeful. We can hardly wait to make someone pay for our humiliation, yield to us as we were once made to yield. No, if we cannot always avoid using the Discipline of Superior Force, we should at least use it as seldom as we can.

4   There are places where all three disciplines overlap. Any very demanding human activity combines in it the disciplines of Superior Force, of Culture, and of Nature. The novice will be told, "Do it this way, never mind asking why, just do it that way, that is the way we always do it." But it probably *is* just the way they always do it, and usually for the very good reason that it is a way that has been found to work. Think, for example, of ballet training. The student in a class is told to do this exercise, or that; to stand so; to do this or that with his head, arms, shoulders, abdomen, hips, legs, feet. He is constantly corrected. There is no argument. But behind these seemingly autocratic demands by the teacher lie many decades of custom and tradition, and behind that, the necessities of dancing itself. You cannot make the moves of classical ballet unless over many years you have acquired, and renewed every day, the needed strength and suppleness in scores of muscles and joints. Nor can you do the difficult motions, making them look easy, unless you have learned hundreds of easier ones first. Dance teachers may not always agree on all the details of teaching these strengths and skills. But no novice could learn them all by himself. You could not go for a night or two to watch the ballet and then, without any other knowledge at all, teach yourself how to do it. In the same way, you would be unlikely to learn any complicated and difficult human activity without drawing heavily on the experience of those who know it better. But the point is that the authority of these experts or teachers stems from, grows out of their greater competence and experience, the fact that what they do *works,* not the fact that they happen to be the teacher and as such have the power to kick a student out of the class. And the further point is that children are always and everywhere attracted to that competence, and ready and eager to submit themselves to a discipline that grows out of it. We hear constantly that children will never do anything unless compelled to by bribes or threats. But in their private lives, or in extracurricular activities in school, in sports, music, drama, art, running a newspaper, and so on, they often submit themselves willingly and wholeheartedly to very intense disciplines, simply because they want to learn to do a given thing well. Our Little-Napoleon football coaches, of whom we have too many and hear far too much, blind us to the fact that millions of children work hard every year getting better at sports and games without coaches barking and yelling at them.

—John Holt

EXPLORING CHOICES

Content and Organization

1. What reasons can you deduce for Holt's decision to discuss the Discipline of Nature first, the Discipline of Culture second, and the Discipline of Superior Force third? Would another organizational pattern have been as effective? Why or why not?

2. How does Holt define each of these types of discipline? What method(s) of development does Holt employ in defining each?
3. What procedure do you suppose Holt used to arrive at his classification of discipline? Were his three categories preexisting ones, or were they devised by him?
4. Are the three categories, taken together, comprehensive, or would you add others? Explain.
5. According to Holt, when may discipline by force be legitimately used? What are its drawbacks?
6. What purpose does Holt's fourth paragraph serve in relationship to the rest of the selection?

Style

1. Holt begins many sentences in his first two paragraphs with the same word or words ("If" and "She does not" in paragraph 1, "Children" and "They" in paragraph 2). Is this repetition effective? Explain.
2. Comment on the transitional devices in paragraph 1. Comment on his use of the comma and the semicolon to hold his sentences together in paragraph 1. Are you bothered by the comma splice at the end of the paragraph? Why or why not?
3. Examine the gender of the pronouns Holt employs throughout the essay. Why, for example, might he have used the masculine pronoun for the student of ballet? Would you have handled the choice of masculine and feminine pronouns differently?

Essay B

In the following selection, the student author uses classification to develop an amusing essay about the food-begging habits of various types of dogs.

MENDICANCY

1   Mendicancy exists worldwide, from the sophisticated international variety (the Salvation Army), to the most innocent, homespun variety (Rover at the dinner table). It is to Rover that the following discourse is dedicated.

2   There are several categories of canine mendicants—the strong and silents, the huffers and puffers, the mumblers and grumblers, the whimperers and whiners, and the yippers and yappers. Each class, from the gargantuan strong and silents to the Lilliputian yippers and yappers, has successfully developed a begging style appropriate to its size, guaranteeing at least one handout per meal.

3   First, the strong and silents. These are the dogs ranging in size from twenty-seven inches to thirty-six inches measured at the shoulder—the Great Dane, St. Bernard, bloodhound,

German shepherd. Obviously, whatever they want, they get; therefore, they can afford to be strong and silent. Who is going to argue with two hundred pounds of Great Dane drooling over the top of the table, staring a diner steadfastly in the eye, indicating clearly that he is deeply in need of that hamburger? Few argue; most share.

4   Second, the huffers and puffers. These dogs measure twenty-three inches to twenty-five inches at the withers; therefore, their begging techniques are in keeping with their slightly smaller size. The Siberian husky, golden retriever, and Irish setter have a less passive approach than the strong and silents toward dinnertime panhandling. Because they are a few inches smaller and many pounds lighter than the strong and silents, the huffers and puffers, in order to insure their handout from the table, have to jazz up their begging style by adding some noise, an inoffensive muted sound resembling a cough caught up in an unexpected hiccup. Since this class stands just about even with an eater's elbow, a huff and puff combined with a friendly head-to-elbow nudge causes food to spill from fork to floor into the mouth of the waiting huffer and puffer.

5   Third, the mumblers and grumblers. The most characteristic representative of this class stands twenty to twenty-two inches--the boxer, Norwegian elkhound, Old English sheepdog. Smaller than the huffers and puffers by two or three inches, this class cannot afford to simply huff and puff; they have to develop a more vocal approach in order to meet their goal-- food, preferably the human variety. A winning technique for this group is the head-in-the-lap routine combined with the sub-glottal mumble and grumble, a vocal cross between a playful growl and a pathetic grunt. A little chin-ribbing and paw-slapping on the knee adds further dynamite to their modest vocal pleadings, causing even the most hardhearted diner to wilt and casually slip a scrap of fat into the eagerly awaiting jaws of this canine beggar.

6   Fourth, the whimperers and whiners. The most pathetic of this class are the cocker spaniel and the bassett hound. They stand fifteen inches, coming only to just below the average diner's knee cap. Since this class of dog is even further down the size scale than the huffers and puffers, mere begging has to be abandoned in favor of a more dramatic vocal repertoire. The chin-on-the-knee routine fails utterly here, because this class of beggars cannot reach up that far unless they stand on their hind legs, resting their front paws on the diner's lap, or, worse, on the table. This technique usually

causes irritation in the eater, who will brusquely push the mendicant aside. Vocal shenanigans prove to be best here. The typical whimperer and whiner most likely will begin with a shy, almost halfhearted, pitiful little whimper similar to that of an infant who begins to feel the early pangs of hunger. If this timid little begging overture fails to produce the desired result––a tidbit––the household pet will intensify his efforts to a penetrating, plaintive whine resembling the angry wail of an insistently hungry infant. In most instances, the whine will do it. A dainty morsel will be dropped to stifle the whimpers and whines.

7   Last, the yippers and yappers. These are the toy poodle, the Lhasa apso, and the dachshund, poor little mites who can barely be seen, measuring a scant ten inches. Since they are the least imposing of all the breeds, they must be the most violent in their attempts to receive their fair share of handouts from the dinner table. When they are on the move for food, they are in constant motion, leaping and jumping like salmon thrashing up a stream, twirling in ever-faster circles like a whirlpool in a river, turning back flips like acrobats in a circus, all the while uttering those piercing yips and yaps. Diners have discovered that the only two things to be done with a yipper and yapper dancing and prancing about are to kill it or feed it. Most choose to feed it.

8   We can see from this account that to mooch a tasty tidbit from the dinner table, each type of dog has developed a begging style compatible with its size, ranging from the seriously quiet approach of the strong and silents to the insanely hysterical approach of the yippers and yappers. If, as Darwin once said, the survival of a species depends on its ability to adapt, then these hounds show the adaptive instinct in play. How else would they have survived if they had not known in some mysterious way how to use their special traits to wheedle food out of even the most resistant diner?

—Lorraine Labate

EXPLORING CHOICES

Content and Organization

1. Point out the thesis of the essay. Where is the thesis repeated?
2. What principle of classification has the writer used? What if the writer had introduced matters such as the temperaments or the exercise habits of different types of dogs? Would these matters be appropriate, given the principle of classification she uses? Explain.

3. What principle of arrangement has the writer used? How does she apply this principle to the dogs she classifies?
4. Point out the writer's enumerative pattern and circle the transitional words she uses to carry it through.
5. Determine whether the writer's enumerative pattern is appropriate to her purpose. Can you think of other purposes where the enumerative pattern would be useful?
6. How many categories does the writer develop? Is each given equal treatment? What features does the writer discuss for each category?
7. In her conclusion, the writer alludes to the biologist Charles Darwin without identifying him. Why do you think she did so? Is the allusion relevant to the theme of the essay?
8. Note the title. What other titles might the writer have used? Which do you prefer?

Style

1. In paragraph 2 the writer calls the yippers *Lilliputian.* What does this word mean? What is its origin?
2. Point out the similes the writer uses in paragraph 7. Are these similes appropriate to the idea the writer is considering? Explain.
3. Note the final sentence of paragraph 3. Why do you think the writer chooses to make it so brief?
4. Note that the writer uses phrases and words such as *mooch, jazz up, chin-on-the-knee routine, head-in-the-lap routine.* What tone do these choices convey? Is this tone appropriate to the writer's purpose? Explain.
5. Point out the various synonyms the writer uses for *Mendicancy,* the title of her essay.
6. Point out the various ways the writer characterizes sound throughout the essay. Do you find her description of sound effective? Explain.
7. Paragraphs 3, 4, 5, 6, and 7 begin with incomplete sentences Do you feel the writer's choice is appropriate? Why or why not?

WRITING SUGGESTIONS

1. Consider several hobbies of which you have firsthand knowledge and classify them according to how easily a novice could acquire the skills they involve.
2. Using cars as your subject, take several representative models and classify them according to how economical they are.

DEFINITION

Definition is used in all types of writing. Whatever your writing purpose, you might need to define. Any time you use unfamiliar or ambiguous words, you will want to clarify or explain your meaning. Keep in mind, though, that the use of definition depends on the audience: knowing that audiences differ in degree of information, training, and general knowledge can help you determine when a definition is needed and when it is not. In the letters (Chap. 1) written to a foreign student who knew nothing about American currency, the writers continually defined the worth, appearance, and uses of the penny, aware that cultural differences made such definition imperative. An American reader who shared the cultural experiences of the writers would not have needed this kind of information. In the first case, too little definition would have been mystifying, in the second, too much would be patronizing.

One way to determine the need for definition is to ask yourself the following questions about your audience: Are my terms already known to my audience or will they be unfamiliar? Do my terms have more than one meaning so that my audience can take them to mean something I don't intend? Am I using my terms somewhat differently from common usage? If you are addressing a general audience, you may find it useful to define the following:

> scientific terms
> historical allusions
> mythological personages
> specialized terms associated with an academic discipline
> terms related to a specific operation, business, hobby, or profession
> terms so new they may be unfamiliar

If after probing your audience you find definition is in order, you will sometimes want to use a formal or logical definition. In this type of definition the word to be defined is related to its general class and is then distinguished from other members of that class by one or more differences. A student who set out to explain the role of the Federal Aviation Administration began his paper with the following formal definition:

Term   *Class*

The Federal Aviation Administration is a governmental agency whose

Differentiation

task is to investigate aviation accidents and set safety standards.

Another student whose purpose was to describe the properties of one type of chemical pollutant began his paper in this way:

Term   *Class*
Kanechlor 400 is a harmful polychlorinated biphenyl whose

     Differentiation
main component is tetrachlorobiphenyl.

More common is the brief definition in which equivalent words or phrases set off by commas are placed just after the term being defined, such as in these student examples:

Wort, a fluid consisting of enzymes and sugar, is boiled with hops during the beer-making process.

When he finally reaches the mesentery, a paper-thin covering of the internal organs, he tears a hole into it with a pair of forceps, exposing the intestines.

The one-sentence definition is convenient and useful. At times, however, you may want to define your term more fully. The following definitions, most by students and a few by professional writers, show you how you can:

Compare its current meaning to its former meaning

The term "Lager beer" used to mean a method of fermentation whereby the beer was poured into wooden kegs and was allowed to ferment slowly in the cool air. Today the term refers to all beers that are refrigerated (not frozen) while fermenting.

Examine the classes belonging to it

Asked to give a definition of a lie, most people will reply, "something other than the truth." Though all lies share this quality, they differ in their degree of seriousness. We can follow this difference if we consider three categories of lies, ranging from the least serious to the most serious: white lies, rumors, and perjury.

Clarify it through example

My friends and I have coined the word "bastidiousness" to describe a thoughtless or mean action. "Bastidiousness" means taking up the last two unrestricted parking spaces on campus with a Volkswagen that could easily fit into one half of a single space. It means smoking cigars, eating garlic, and not taking a bath for two weeks when you live in close quarters with a roommate.

Place it in the context of a process

If producing hybrid corn is your aim, the de-tasseling of corn means removing the tassels from six rows of corn and leaving the next two rows of another variety of corn with the tassels on. This process prevents the six rows of corn from pollinating themselves and allows the two rows of another type of corn to pollinate them instead. A hybrid corn which contains the best qualities of both is the result.

Explore its derivation or etymology

Chromatography, the partitioning of substances on the basis of their relative solubility between two solvents, has become a valuable aid in the separation and identification of organic compounds. Chromatography received its name from the Greek word *chrom,* meaning color, and *graph,* meaning drawn or written. It was invented to explain the very first experiments in which plant pigments were observed to separate into colored bands of material.

Explain what it is not

Southerners may fit the foxy-country-lawyer mold of the immortal Senator Sam J. Ervin Jr. of North Carolina. Ervin is to Koch as bourbon and branch water is to needled beer.

—Jerry Adler, "So What Are Street Smarts?" *Newsweek*

Separate it into its component parts

A molecule of the nucleic acid DNA is a long, thin double helix, each strand of which is a chain of nucleotides. Each nucleotide is characterized by a chemical group known as a base: adenine (A), guanine (G), thymine (T) or cytosine (C). Genetic information is encoded in the sequence of those bases.

—Pierre Chambon, "Split Genes," *Scientific American*

Locate its distinguishing characteristics

Great leaders are almost always great simplifiers, who cut through argument, debate and doubt to offer a solution everybody can understand and remember. Churchill warned the British to expect "blood, toil, tears and sweat"; FDR told Americans that "the only thing we have to fear is fear itself"; Lenin promised the war-weary Russians peace, land and bread. Straightforward but potent messages.

—Michael Korda, "How to Be a Leader," *Newsweek*

The Structure of Definition

When definition becomes the major purpose of a paper, the essay is considered an extended definition. The patterns of such papers vary. In fact, many will blend several of the patterns you've already encountered. A paper that sets out to define a liberal (or a conservative or a radical), for example, may use causal analysis to trace the origins of political liberalism, classification to distinguish types of liberals, comparison and contrast to set off the liberal from the conservative or radical, and narration to provide illustrative anecdotes of how a liberal thinks and acts. Any one of these patterns may become the major pattern of the entire paper. A writer whose purpose was to distinguish a principled liberal from a pragmatic liberal would probably rely for the most part on comparison and contrast. But if the major purpose were to illustrate the typical behavior of a liberal, narration might be a more useful pattern.

Essays for Analysis

Essay A

In the following selection, British writer Laurie Lee provides an extended definition of an abstract term.

APPETITE

1   One of the major pleasures in life is appetite, and one of our major duties should be to preserve it. Appetite is the keenness of living; it is one of the senses that tells you that you are still curious to exist, that you still have an edge on your longings and want to bite into the world and taste its multitudinous flavours and juices.

2   By appetite, of course, I don't mean just the lust for food, but any condition of unsatisfied desire, any burning in the blood that proves you want more than you've got, and that you haven't yet used up your life. Wilde said he felt sorry for those who never got their heart's desire, but sorrier still for those who did. I got mine once only, and it nearly killed me, and I've always preferred wanting to having since.

3   For appetite, to me, is this state of wanting, which keeps one's expectations alive. I remember learning this lesson long ago as a child, when treats and orgies were few, and when I discovered that the greatest pitch of happiness was not in actually eating a toffee but in gazing at it beforehand. True, the first bite was delicious, but once the toffee was gone one was left with nothing, neither toffee nor lust. Besides, the whole toffeeness of toffees was imperceptibly diminished by the gross act of having eaten it. No, the best was in wanting it, in sitting and looking at it, when one tasted an inexhaustible treasure-house of flavours.

4   So, for me, one of the keenest pleasures of appetite remains in the wanting, not the satisfaction. In wanting a peach, or a whisky, or a particular texture or sound, or to be with a particular friend. For in this condition, of course, I know

that the object of desire is always at its most flawlessly perfect. Which is why I would carry the preservation of appetite to the extent of deliberate fasting, simply because I think that appetite is too good to lose, too precious to be bludgeoned into insensibility by satiation and over-doing it.

5   For that matter, I don't really want three square meals a day—I want one huge, delicious, orgiastic, table-groaning blow-out, say every four days, and then not be too sure where the next one is coming from. A day of fasting is not for me just a puritanical device for denying oneself a pleasure, but rather a way of anticipating a rarer moment of supreme indulgence.

6   Fasting is an act of homage to the majesty of appetite. So I think we should arrange to give up our pleasures regularly—our food, our friends, our lovers—in order to preserve their intensity, and the moment of coming back to them. For this is the moment that renews and refreshes both oneself and the thing one loves. Sailors and travellers enjoyed this once, and so did hunters, I suppose. Part of the weariness of modern life may be that we live too much on top of each other, and are entertained and fed too regularly. Once we were separated by hunger both from our food and families, and then we learned to value both. The men went off hunting, and the dogs went with them; the women and children waved goodbye. The cave was empty of men for days on end; nobody ate, or knew what to do. The women crouched by the fire, the wet smoke in their eyes; the children wailed; everybody was hungry. Then one night there were shouts and the barking of dogs from the hills, and the men came back loaded with meat. This was the great reunion, and everybody gorged themselves silly, and appetite came into its own; the long-awaited meal became a feast to remember and an almost sacred celebration of life. Now we go off to the office and come home in the evenings to cheap chicken and frozen peas. Very nice, but too much of it, too easy and regular, served up without effort or wanting. We eat, we are lucky, our faces are shining with fat, but we don't know the pleasure of being hungry any more.

7   Too much of anything—too much music, entertainment, happy snacks, or time spent with one's friends—creates a kind of impotence of living by which one can no longer hear, or taste, or see, or love, or remember. Life is short and precious, and appetite is one of its guardians, and loss of appetite is a sort of death. So if we are to enjoy this short life we should respect the divinity of appetite, and keep it eager and not too much blunted.

8   It is a long time now since I knew that acute moment of bliss that comes from putting parched lips to a cup of cold water. The springs are still there to be enjoyed—all one needs is the original thirst.   —Laurie Lee

EXPLORING CHOICES

Content and Organization

1. The author suggests a number of very succinct definitions of the term *appetite*. What are a few of them?
2. Check a standard dictionary for its definition of *appetite*. What new concepts does Lee's add to it?

3. What is the writer's central thesis? Where in the essay is it most explicitly stated?
4. What, according to Lee, is the relationship between appetite and self-denial?
5. In what particulars does Lee's definition of appetite diverge from your own? What does that suggest about the validity of an extended definition?

Style

1. Comment on the metaphor at the end of paragraph 1. Why is it particularly apt to an introductory paragraph on appetite?
2. Lee uses a fragment for the second sentence in paragraph 4. What would have been the difference in effect if he had combined that sentence with the first so that it read: "So, for me, one of the keenest pleasures of appetite remains in the wanting of a peach, or a whisky, or a particular texture or sound, and not in the satisfaction"?
3. Comment on whether you find the piling up of adjectives in paragraph 5 effective. Why or why not?
4. Find several examples of rich, almost flowery language in Lee's essay. Are these appropriate or not to the subject?

Essay B

In the selection below, the novelist and poet May Sarton considers the meaning of solitude by focusing on its benefits.

THE REWARDS OF LIVING A SOLITARY LIFE

1   The other day an acquaintance of mine, a gregarious and charming man, told me he had found himself unexpectedly alone in New York for an hour or two between appointments. He went to the Whitney and spent the "empty" time looking at things in solitary bliss. For him it proved to be a shock nearly as great as falling in love to discover that he could enjoy himself so much alone.

2   What had he been afraid of, I asked myself? That, suddenly alone, he would discover that he bored himself, or that there was, quite simply, no self there to meet? But having taken the plunge, he is now on the brink of adventure; he is about to be launched into his own inner space, space as immense, unexplored and sometimes frightening as outer space to the astronaut. His every perception will come to him with a new freshness and, for a time, seem startlingly original. For anyone who can see things for himself with a naked eye becomes, for a moment or two, something of a genius. With another human being present vision becomes double vision, inevitably. We are busy wondering, what does my companion see or think of this, and what do I think of it? The original impact gets lost, or diffused.

3   "Music I heard with you was more than music." Exactly. And therefore music *itself* can only be heard alone. Solitude is the salt of personhood. It brings out the authentic flavor of every experience.

4   "Alone one is never lonely: the spirit adventures, walking/In a quiet garden, in a cool house, abiding single there."

5   Loneliness is most acutely felt with other people, for with others, even with a lover sometimes, we suffer from our differences of taste, temperament, mood. Human intercourse often demands that we soften the edge of perception, or withdraw at the very instant of personal truth for fear of hurting, or of being inappropriately present, which is to say naked, in a social situation. Alone we can afford to be wholly whatever we are, and to feel whatever we feel absolutely. That is a great luxury!

6   For me the most interesting thing about a solitary life, and mine has been that for the last twenty years, is that it becomes increasingly rewarding. When I can wake up and watch the sun rise over the ocean, as I do most days, and know that I have an entire day ahead, uninterrupted, in which to write a few pages, take a walk with my dog, lie down in the afternoon for a long think (why does one think better in a horizontal position?), read and listen to music, I am flooded with happiness.

7   I am lonely only when I am overtired, when I have worked too long without a break, when for the time being I feel empty and need filling up. And I am lonely sometimes when I come back home after a lecture trip, when I have seen a lot of people and talked a lot, and am full to the brim with experience that needs to be sorted out.

8   Then for a little while the house feels huge and empty, and I wonder where my self is hiding. It has to be recaptured slowly by watering the plants, perhaps, and looking again at each one as though it were a person, by feeding the two cats, by cooking a meal.

9   It takes a while, as I watch the surf blowing up in fountains at the end of the field, but the moment comes when the world falls away, and the self emerges again from the deep unconscious, bringing back all I have recently experienced to be explored and slowly understood, when I can converse again with my hidden powers, and so grow, and so be renewed, till death do us part.

—May Sarton

EXPLORING CHOICES

Content and Organization

1. May Sarton includes the quotation "Alone one is never lonely." Explain what this means in light of her essay's main point.

2. What is the greatest blessing of the "solitary life"? What phrases in the essay best express this?

3. The last line borrows its phraseology from the traditional marriage ceremony. Who is the "us" Sarton refers to? Why is the allusion to marriage appropriate?

4. As does Lee in his essay, Sarton defines partly by delineating the disadvantages of a term opposite to hers. What does she see as some of the possible drawbacks of too much "togetherness"?

Style

1. Why might Sarton have chosen to begin an essay on "aloneness" with an anecdote about a pleasant conversation with an old acquaintance?
2. Comment on the appropriateness of the metaphor in paragraph 3.
3. The concluding paragraph is one long sentence. What does its structure and rhythm contribute to the idea the author is conveying?

Essay C

In the following essay, a student provides his personal understanding of a common term's meaning.

WHAT IS FARMING?

1   When the word farming is mentioned, people immediately think of crops and animals. Webster's New World Dictionary defines it as "the business of operating a farm; agriculture." To me, however, the word farming means more than just producing crops or operating a farm. To me, farming means working in partnership with nature to produce an edible product from the earth that will provide the necessary nourishment to sustain human life.

2   In Gulliver's Travels, Jonathan Swift writes "that whoever could make two ears of corn or two blades of grass to grow upon a spot of ground where only one grew before, would deserve better of mankind, and do more essential service to his country than the whole race of politicians put together." Swift's view illustrates my own definition of farming. Like him, I believe that a farmer makes nature more productive and that he is essential to mankind. A farmer plants a seed in the ground and nurtures it to maturity, using his knowledge of soil chemistry to achieve the maximum yield possible. He applies nitrogen, potassium, phosphorous, and fertilizer to enrich the soil's productivity. He applies herbicides and cultivates in order to prevent the intrusion of weeds which will lower his yields. If the weeds persist, he, his family, or hired labor will walk through the fields and hoe or pull the weeds out by hand. Stubborn weeds will be killed with an aerial application of herbicide.

3   Even if the farmer manages to control all of the weeds, he may still face the problem of insect infestation. To eradicate the insects before they destroy his crops, he must first identify the pest and then purchase the appropriate insecticide. The method of application may be either ground spraying if the crops are relatively small, or aerial spraying if the crops have grown too large to permit equipment to move through the fields. If the farmer can accomplish this part of the farming operation in conjunction with the natural resources available to him, he will, as Swift says, "make two ears of corn or two blades of grass to grow upon a spot of ground where only one grew before."

4   Once the farmer's crops reach maturity, the grain will be harvested and processsed into food that can be consumed. Corn, for example, will be milled into flour. This flour, in turn, will be further processed and sold to a baker. The baker will combine the flour with other raw materials that also had their start in the farmer's field into bread. The bread will then be purchased by a retailer who will sell it to the consumer. In the end, the crop that the farmer struggled to produce will provide nourishment to the people who consume it, and the farmer will have fulfilled his role of producing an edible product from the earth that will sustain human life.

5   On the surface, the meaning of the word <u>farming</u> appears simple. But when the meaning is analyzed in detail, we can see that farming is a very complex process necessary to human life. If there were no farming, the human race would quickly perish. The Federal Land Bank explains the meaning of farming best when it says, "Farming is everybody's bread and butter."

—David Fraser

EXPLORING CHOICES

Content and Organization

1. Point out the writer's thesis. Explain how the writer uses negation (not X but Y) to establish his thesis.
2. In paragraph 2 the writer cites a passage from a literary work. How does this quotation serve his purpose?
3. Explain the process the writer traces to develop his definition. Does the process confirm his thesis? Explain.
4. Explain how the thesis controls the details the writer uses in paragraphs 2, 3, and 4.

5. The main point of paragraph 2 appears in the middle of the paragraph. Why do you think the writer placed it there instead of at the beginning of the paragraph?

Style

1. In paragraph 2 the writer begins two sentences with *He applies.* Do you find this repetition monotonous? Explain.
2. The last sentence of paragraph 2 shifts to the passive voice. If the writer had used the active voice ("He will kill stubborn weeds") what would be the difference in effect?
3. Point out other places where the writer uses the passive voice. Explain the connection between the passive voice and the pattern the writer is using.

WRITING SUGGESTIONS

You found in the preceding student example that extended definitions often express a point of view, sometimes to correct a too-narrow definition ("Farming is more than. . . ."). A point of view is also implied each time a writer attaches a quality to a term (a good movie, a great leader) or distinguishes between closely related terms (love and infatuation; avarice and frugality); or expresses a personal interpretation of a term ("Cramming is the best way to pass college courses with the least amount of effort and time.").

Following are some ways you can use an extended definition to express a point of view:

1. Explain sportsmanship to a group of high school athletes trying out for the varsity team.

2. Define the characteristics of a good teacher or coach for a committee empowered to recommend faculty appointments.

3. Advise your classmates on the difference between true, as opposed to fair-weather, friends or fans.

4. Advise your instructor about the characteristics of a good grading system.

If your purpose is to explain the meaning of a term without expressing an attitude, try defining a technical term (cybernetics, gerontology, in vitro fertilization) to the nonspecialist. Before writing, use the topics of invention on pp. 40–42 to explore your subject. Not only will they help you gather material for your paper, but they will suggest various patterns you can use to develop your definition.

MIXED PATTERNS OF DEVELOPMENT

As you saw in Brustein's essay at the beginning of this chapter, the patterns of development we have just outlined are often blended, depending on the writer's purpose. This is true as well in the following essay on epilepsy which enlightens the general reader about the disease before suggesting ways to treat the victim. To do this, the student author defines the disease, classifies its various types according to the degree of intensity of the seizure, and explains how attitudes toward the disease have changed.

Essay for Analysis

ONE OF US

1   Have you ever climbed a tree, ridden a bike or a skateboard? Have you ever played football? Many of us have; they are just common, everyday activities. But did you ever fall out of that tree? Did you ever lose your balance on that bike or skateboard? Did you ever suffer a jarring tackle in that football game? If so, you have experienced something akin to a disease that afflicts over eight hundred thousand Americans. What is it that can affect these people at any time, even when engaged in a seemingly harmless activity? The answer is, epilepsy.

2   Epilepsy has been with man for thousands of years. Socrates, Alexander the Great, William the Conqueror, Julius Caesar, Napoleon——all had the disease. At one time the disease was considered a mark of honor: in ancient Rome, historians tell us, epileptics were given high governmental positions, for it was thought that when they suffered a seizure, they were in direct communication with God. Centuries later, however, the badge of honor became a stigma, transformed into the perverse view that the epileptic spoke not to God but to the devil. Indeed, in the late Middle Ages, epileptics were institutionalized for insanity and demonic possession.

3   Even though this image of insanity has faded, people still feel uneasy about epilepsy, largely because the disease seems so mysterious. And, indeed, its exact cause is unknown,

though childhood diseases such as measles, mumps, and chicken pox can contribute to it, as can alcoholism, poor nutrition, a severe blow to the head, lead poisoning, and birth defects. Contrary to some popular thinking, epilepsy is not contagious, nor is it inherited, though a tendency to the disease seems to be congenitally transmitted.

4   The development of the electroencephalograph, an instrument which monitors the electric waves given off by the tissues of the brain, has taught us a good deal about epilepsy. What happens to an epileptic during a seizure is comparable to what happens to a fuse box when the circuits are overloaded. A buildup of electrical impulses occurs, causing an overload and short—circuit. Neither the fuse box nor the brain can handle the extra input: the first suffers a blackout, the other, a loss of consciousness.

5   Epileptic seizures are of three kinds. The most serious and prolonged is the "grand mal" seizure during which the victim suffers severe muscle spasms and a lack of consciousness ranging from two to five minutes. Less severe is the psychomotor seizure. During this seizure, the victim drops what he is doing and wanders aimlessly, unaware of where he is going or of where he has been. Though he suffers a blackout, he does not endure convulsions. The final type of seizure has been nicknamed the "daydreaming seizure." This usually occurs in young children, often reprimanded for daydreaming when, in fact, they are experiencing an epileptic seizure. During this five— to twenty—second interval, the child stares blankly into space.

6   Understanding the physiology of epilepsy can help erase its social stigma; even more, it helps us respond to a victim should a seizure occur in our presence. If we remember that there is no known way to control or cut short a seizure once it has begun, we can help the epileptic best by not moving or restraining him, taking care at the same time to remove any nearby sharp object. Unless it appears that one seizure is following another, it is not necessary to call a doctor, since the seizure must run its course. Above all, when the seizure is over, we can reassure the victim and allow him to sleep. In this way, we let him know that nothing extraordinary has happened, that he has suffered a momentary blackout from which he'll quickly recover. We tell him, in other words, that except for this minor affliction, he is fully capable of leading a life as rich and full as he wishes to make it. Such reassurance is the most precious gift we can give him.

—Nancy E. Hintz

Content and Organization

1. What patterns of development does the writer use in paragraphs 2 and 5? Why is each used?
2. Why do you think the writer begins her discussion of epilepsy by indirectly describing its effect?
3. Paragraphs 4 and 5 discuss the physiology of epilepsy. Try placing these paragraphs after paragraph 2. Is this placement as effective as the placement the writer chose? Explain.
4. In which paragraph does the writer state directly that her readers should adopt a different view of the epileptic? Is this placement effective? Could it have appeared earlier?
5. Explain the connection between the title and the purpose of the essay.

Style

1. The essay opens with a series of questions. Try changing these questions into statements (such as, "Many people have climbed a tree, ridden a bike, used a skateboard, and played football"). Which strategy is most effective? Which is most likely to influence the writer's audience? Why?
2. The second sentence of paragraph 2 begins with a list of names. In her first draft, Nancy phrased the sentence this way: "Some famous people who've had the disease were Socrates, Alexander the Great, Julius Caesar, William the Conqueror, and Napoleon." Which sentence do you prefer? Why?
3. In paragraph 4 the writer compares epilepsy to a fuse box. Explain the appropriateness of this comparison to the writer's subject, purpose, and audience.

WRITING SUGGESTIONS

Mixed patterns of development are commonly found in papers that argue a course of action or attempt to uphold the validity of an opinion. The following suggestions lend themselves to multiple patterns.

1. Argue for expanded facilities for less popular sports by defining these sports, classifying them according to the space and equipment they require, giving reasons why they have been ignored or downgraded, and comparing or contrasting them to more popular sports.

2. Support or oppose the drinking age law of your state by describing the law, comparing or contrasting it to the laws of other states, and analyzing the causes and effects of its enactment.

3. Criticize or support the local driver's license bureau by analyzing the causes and effects of its efficiency or inefficiency, using anecdotes to illustrate either, tracing the process of getting a new license or renewing a license, and examining changes (if any) in procedures for getting a license.

4. Question the construction of a new shopping mall by defining its characteristics, comparing it to existing malls of similar size, and analyzing its effects on the environment and community.

CHOOSING PARAGRAPHS

As readers and writers, most of us have an intuitive "paragraph sense." If you read a passage in which the author shifts to a new idea without beginning a new paragraph, or if, in this same passage, you find several unrelated ideas, you are likely to feel uneasy. If, on the other hand, you are the writer, you are likely to begin a new paragraph instinctively when you finish one idea and are ready to move on to the next. You may not always be conscious of the shape and structure of a paragraph when you first draft it; such conscious control usually does not come, at least for those whose vocation is not writing, until they begin to revise. Yet when you write you do have an intuitive sense of how to create paragraphs just as, when you read, you appreciate an author's control over paragraphs.

WHAT IS A PARAGRAPH?

To test the assumption that you have an intuitive sense of what constitutes a paragraph, examine the following passage from a student essay. Try to determine where a paragraph division would logically occur.

```
            LAETRILE: A CONTROVERSIAL DRUG

    (1) Second only to cardiovascular disease, cancer is the
most dreaded killer.  (2) Over one hundred clinical types of
cancer claim approximately 370,000 lives each year; even more
dramatically, cancer claims over 1,000 lives each day.  (3) An
overall cure for this catastrophic disease remains elusive,
though some cancers will respond to certain types of medical
treatment.  (4) These treatments, however, are often long and
painful, and they involve serious side effects that are often
as distressing as the disease itself.  (5) As a result, many
people search for an alternative that will be quick and
painless.  (6) One such alternative is Laetrile, a compound
derived from the kernels of apricots that supposedly kills
cancer cells.  (7) The usefulness of Laetrile has been
questioned in several studies designed to test the
effectiveness of the drug.  (8) According to the National
Cancer Institute, Laetrile showed no anti-cancer activity when
it was tested on animals.  (9) Equally, investigators reported
in 1981 that when Laetrile was used with 156 patients who had
advanced cancer and could no longer be treated by traditional
methods, it not only failed to cure the disease but it had
toxic side effects on many patients.  (10) Despite these
studies, however, public interest in the drug is increasing,
```

largely because people treated with Laetrile still credit it with saving their lives. (11) Today, approximately 50,000 Americans use Laetrile. (12) Although the Food and Drug Administration has banned Laetrile in interstate commerce, twenty-seven states have legalized the manufacture, sale, and consumption of Laetrile within their borders. (13) Moreover, many Americans travel to Mexico, where Laetrile is legal and readily available, to obtain the drug.

EXPLORING PARAGRAPH SENSE

1. Which sentence did you choose to mark the beginning of a new paragraph? Why? How does your decision compare to the decisions of others in your class?
2. On the basis of your paragraph division, try to define the characteristics of a paragraph.
3. Take the group of sentences that you designated as a new paragraph and try to determine how the sentences are related. From this, can you refine your definition of what a paragraph is?

SENTENCES THAT MARK NEW PARAGRAPHS

In your attempt to define paragraph divisions in the preceding passage, you may have decided that sentence 7 marked the beginning of a new paragraph. Let's attempt to define the characteristics of this sentence: "The usefulness of Laetrile in cancer treatment has been questioned in several studies designed to test the effectiveness of the drug."

The sentence immediately preceding sentence 7 simply describes and defines Laetrile as an alternative cancer treatment. Though the word *supposedly* in sentence 6 suggests that the writer will question the effectiveness of Laetrile, the sentence does not really address this idea. Only in sentence 7 does the writer raise the question of effectiveness directly, thereby shifting from Laetrile as an option in cancer treatment to the question of whether Laetrile is, indeed, a remedy. We might say, then, that sentences which mark a *content shift* often head new paragraphs.

A second marker for sentences that begin new paragraphs is *degree of generality*. Note that in sentence 7 the writer mentions several studies but does not name them. Only in sentences 8 and 9 does the writer describe and name the particular studies. Compared to sentences 8 and 9, then, sentence 7 is more general; the phrase *several studies* is an umbrella term which covers the specific items that follow.

A third way to characterize a sentence that begins a new paragraph is to note its *relation to the other sentences* in the paragraph. Sentence 7, for example, is not only more general than sentences 8 and 9, but it also determines their content; it announces that it is the "master" sentence to which the other sentences in the paragraph are subordinate. For this reason, the master sentence of a paragraph is often called a *topic sentence,* because it defines the major idea or topic of the paragraph. Other sentences in the paragraph may amplify, describe, explain, or modify the topic sentence, but they cannot introduce ideas unrelated to it. You might say, then, that the topic sentence controls the *unity* of the paragraph; it helps the writer determine what belongs in the paragraph, and it announces to the reader that the paragraph will explore a single idea.

PARAGRAPH UNITY AND THE TOPIC SENTENCE

The topic sentence guides the development of the paragraph. A good topic sentence structures the selection process, helping the writer discover what is pertinent and appropriate to the idea being presented and what is not. Like a strategically placed road sign, the topic sentence steers the writer in the proper direction, preventing, perhaps, a wrong turn or a turn that leads less directly to the goal.

You can see how a topic sentence unifies a paragraph in the following example:

Topic sentence

Animals caught in quicksand often do not get out by themselves. A dog generally succeeds, but it must be encouraged to work hard and not wait for its master's help. A horse will usually fight its way to safety, making frantic, rabbit-like jumps. The rider or driver must know where to guide it, however, for it can soon become exhausted and then rapidly sink in the sand. A loaded or harnessed mule will lie down on its belly with its feet tucked under as soon as the ground gives beneath it. In that position the animal will not sink. The mule's hooves are so small and narrow that it cannot struggle if it is at all weighted down. Once freed of any equipment, it can usually be urged to get itself out of the morass. It is a good idea to station a horse, preferably a mare, on the nearest firm land as a guide and further inducement.

—Gerard H. Matthes, "Quicksand," *Scientific American*

Note how the writer precisely establishes the point of his paragraph. The subject of the topic sentence is not animals in general, but animals caught in quicksand. All other animals are ignored; they have no part in the drama the writer wishes to record. The predicate also restricts the statement the writer is making about his subject. If he had said "Animals caught in quicksand have trouble," he would certainly have interpreted his subject, but he would have left us puzzled about the particular trouble the animals faced. Instead, he tells us immediately that they "do not get out by themselves," in effect banishing other troubles the animals might have encountered: swarms of stinging bees, a consuming thirst, panic, and so on.

The topic sentence determines which examples and supporting details appear in the body of the paragraph. The general word *animals* in the topic sentence of the "Quicksand" paragraph is later specified: within the paragraph we are introduced to a dog, a horse, and a mule. Moreover, these animals are discussed only in relation to their need for help when they are mired in quicksand. No other idea is allowed to intrude.

Composing Effective Topic Sentences

As we've discussed, a good topic sentence is a general statement that is sufficiently restricted to allow the writer to focus on one idea. If this restrictive quality is absent, a writer may not have an adequate guide for developing the rest of the paragraph. Note, for example, the difficulties a writer faces with a topic sentence such as "Television is an entertaining medium." At once, there is the problem of selecting material about the subject. After all, television is by no means a unified whole: not only is it divisible into corporate forms such as network television, cable television, or public television, but it is characterized by variety in programming. To uncover these distinctions and to gain a firmer notion of focus, the writer needs to define the subject more precisely.

The writer's interpretation of the subject also needs further definition. *Entertaining* is a general adjective that summarizes without explaining. Like *terrific, interesting, unusual,* and other evaluative adjectives, it is a blanket term that offers an easy escape from the need to be more exact. This is not to say that general adjectives should never be used in topic sentences, but only to suggest that when you use them, you must always explain their exact meaning.

FOLLOW-UP ACTIVITIES

1. Help the writer who wishes to write about television devise alternative topic sentences that would remedy the vagueness of the original version. Consider making a general statement either about a specific television program or about a type of program such as the situation comedy, the detective thriller, or the sporting event. For example:
    a. The plot of "General Hospital" has recently taken a bizarre turn.
    b. Daytime soap operas appeal to our human interest in gossip.

2. If a paragraph lacks a clear topic sentence, it can ramble, moving from one idea to another without establishing connections. You'll find this problem in the following student paragraph. As you read it, see if you can discover a unifying focus. Depending on the focus you uncover, you may find that some details need to be eliminated, either because they are unrelated—or only faintly related—to the general idea.

```
    Since 1967, only a few people have been executed in this
country.  The death penalty was first used in Egypt in 1500
B.C. because a criminal was practicing black magic.  Because
there is no federal statute that prevents capital punishment
at the present time, a number of states have adopted laws
allowing for it.  The use of the death penalty has aroused a
lot of controversy.  The crucial question is whether the death
penalty is a deterrent to crime, or whether it is not.  Though
studies investigating the problem are many, their conclusions
are ambiguous.  Statistically, it is very hard to prove or
disprove the fact that capital punishment is directly related
to the fluctuations of the crime rate.  By using alternative
equations and a variety of variables, both adversaries and
proponents of the deterrence theory can support the justice of
their position.
```

PARAGRAPH ORDER

So far, you have examined paragraphs that begin with a general statement and then move to specifics to explain, support, or amplify the opening idea. The movement is from general to specific, or from synthesis to analysis. Let's explore the type of logical thinking reflected in this process.

A general statement reflects a conclusion based on particulars. If, for example, you find that a carton of Grade A eggs costs ninety-eight cents at the beginning of the month and ninety-eight cents at the end of the month, you might reasonably conclude that the cost of these eggs has remained stable. Or, if you've noticed that John, a fellow student, pleads illness each time he's supposed to make a report to an important student committee, you might conclude that John is a malingerer. In each case, you've moved from the specific to the general, devising a conclusion broad enough to summarize and interpret the meaning of what you've observed.

Now let's say, in the case of John, that you want to write a memo documenting his poor performance, perhaps because you think he should be replaced on the committee. With this purpose in mind, you might begin with your conclusion, noting that John needs to be replaced because he has consistently shirked his duties. Since such an assertion is serious and requires evidence, you would then move from your general impression to instances confirming that John did, indeed, fail to meet his obligations. In doing so, however, you reverse the specific-to-general order of thought that led to your conclusion.

General-to-Specific; Specific-to-General

The position of the topic sentence can reflect either method of thinking we've just described. A paragraph that begins with a topic sentence follows a general-to-specific pattern; a paragraph that ends with a topic sentence follows a specific-to-general pattern. Many beginning writers feel most comfortable with the general-to-specific pattern, probably because it gives them greater control of paragraph unity. But as they mature and feel more confident of their writing skills, they will often try the specific-to-general pattern, especially when they want to achieve a special effect.

The student writer of the following paragraph chose a specific-to-general pattern because it contributes to the drama of the thesis. To emphasize that the violence of modern life is beyond the control of the victim, she begins by listing examples of criminal assaults. Only after she has recorded these chilling instances does she offer her interpretation of their meaning. By then, the reader is prepared to grant the justice of her view.

> Each day the newspaper catalogues a number of assorted
> crimes: an elderly man beaten senseless on the stoop of his
> apartment building, a storekeeper shot after handing over his
> day's receipts to a thief, a teenager raped in an elevator, a
> passing pedestrian knifed by a brawling drunk, train
> passengers held hostage by a group of political terrorists.
> The utter randomness in the choice of victim not only shocks
> the reader but alarms him. If such things occur, he thinks,
> and with this frequency, what is to prevent them from
> happening to him, or to those he loves? And the answer, quite
> realistically, is, of course, nothing. For as the newspaper
> reports it, the choice of victim is not dictated by anything
> under the victim's control—his personality or position, for
> example—but merely by his presence at the time and in the
> place the attacker is ready to act. The motivation comes
> entirely from the inner promptings of the criminal himself,
> not from anything originating in a particular victim.

Topic sentence and restatement

> Newspapers reveal to the reader just how completely he is at
> the mercy of the next man's whim. They provide endless
> documentation for the idea that life and its ends are entirely
> haphazard.

The position of the topic sentence need not be confined to the beginning or end of a paragraph. At times, writers will place the topic sentence elsewhere if the major idea they wish to present requires some prior explanation or preparation—a lead-in that sets the stage—or if they wish to gain a particular effect. Note that the student writer of the following paragraph provides a more dramatic account of the filth of modern Venice—the main idea of the paragraph—by first providing a contrasting image.

Topic sentence

> Venice, the ancient city of merchants, recalls Marco Polo, the craft of glass blowing, and exquisite handmade lace. But what thoughts the city of Venice brings to mind and what it is are totally different. Rather than being the incomparable showpiece of Europe, Venice is now its cesspool, its outskirts a tangled network of grass and weeds intertwined with heaps of debris: glass, paper, remnants of exploded tires, and parts of cars long junked. Entering the city, one experiences a true Venetian welcome: a flock of innumerable pigeons, which could replace the winged lion as the city's symbol, pelt the visitor with droppings and feathers that settle on the city's already considerable layer of dirt and filth. Of course, the Venetians themselves take little or no notice of this sad spectacle.

FOLLOW-UP ACTIVITY

Point out the topic sentence in each of the following student paragraphs and note its position. Try to determine the reason for its placement.

Paragraph A

> Both Paris and Madrid have royal palaces surrounded by sunny gardens whose sculpted shrubbery, patterned flower beds, statues, pools, and fountains are reminiscent of the splendor of the gardens of Versailles. But the Parisian gardens are more extensive than those in Madrid and more accessible to the public. The Jardin des Tuilleries outside the Louvre often attracts visitors to the museum eager for a refreshing stroll. Equally, the Luxembourg Gardens outside the Palais de Luxembourg are a favorite meeting place, especially on Sunday afternoons. In Madrid, in contrast, the Palacio—a neoclassic residence once occupied by Felipe II, the first of Spain's Bourbon monarchs—has gardens at its front and back, but in typical Spanish elitist tradition, the ones at the back are closed to the public, and the ones open to the public aren't really spacious enough to stroll in. Still, it's pleasant to sit and think awhile on a marble bench outside the Palacio, gazing at the flat and rounded tops of sculpted shrubbery, perhaps throwing a peseta into a pool of water for good luck.

Paragraph B   Wheels have always been another important element in Jim's life. As soon as he could afford it, he bought a cheap, secondhand Chevy convertible that he tinkered with and kept polished and soon traded for a late model Camaro with mag wheels and time payments. It wasn't long until he had a motorcycle, too, which he kept in the living room when he wasn't riding it. As he got used to the "bike," he began to seek out the bike trails and eventually the racing tracks. He bought a 1934 Ford pickup to carry the bike to the racetrack. For a season, we were enmeshed in track dust, cycle noise, worry, and excitement. Jim never won a race, but he was never injured, either. However, after a friend of his slid his cycle into a fence post and was nearly killed, Jim decided to sell his motorcycle.

Paragraph C   Although the major cost of cheese production is incurred during the ripening process, another significant cost is the marketing research. In order to encourage consumers to buy more cheese, producers must be aware of the consumer's food-buying and consumption habits. Often, they will hire food specialists to develop new recipes using cheese in meat dishes, breads, or desserts. Borden, for example, developed Cheez Kisses, which are bits of cheese food shaped and wrapped like candy, to encourage children to develop a preference for less sweet-tasting, nutritional snacks. Often, too, they use advertising to inform the public of the new ways to use cheese. These ads may be aimed at showing the nutritional value of cheese, the economy of using cheese as a meat substitute, the versatility of cheese as it is used to "dress up" plain food, or the variety of ways cheese can be quickly used to prepare an elegant dish.

Using Time Order

Though the topic sentence is a feature of many paragraphs, it is by no means universal. Leaf through a novel, a short story, a manual of instructions, and you'll probably find paragraphs without topic sentences. In writing that emphasizes a sequence of events or actions, time order becomes the principal method of arrangement.

To see how the time order of the whole essay influences the structure of individual paragraphs, examine the following student essay that explains a surgical procedure to the general reader. Because the writer aims to describe the stages or steps of a process, he organizes most of his paragraphs according to the order of time.

1   It is yet two hours before sunrise when the dull pain in your side awakens you. As you struggle to the medicine cabinet in the bathroom, you try to remember what you had eaten the night before that might have given you such indigestion. Having taken two tablespoons of Pepto Bismol, you are now convinced that the problem is corrected and return to bed, only to be kept sleepless by a steadily worsening pain.

2   With each passing hour of the day, the pain increases. You develop a fever and some nausea and soon decide to contact your family doctor. He sees you immediately, takes your temperature, palpates your abdomen, tells you that it is probably appendicitis, and insists that you be admitted to a hospital as quickly as possible.

3   Within two hours you find yourself in a spotless hospital room. A nurse draws blood from a vein in your arm in order to take a white blood cell count. A high number of white blood cells indicates an infection, and viewed with respect to the other symptoms, strongly suggests appendicitis. After a few other routine tests, such as an electrocardiogram to make sure that your heart is healthy enough to withstand anesthesia and surgery, the surgeon enters the room to give you the bad news. He explains that it is necessary for you to have surgery to remove an inflamed appendix, a diagnosis that is indicated primarily by your tender abdomen, high white cell count, and fever. He also tells you that there is nothing to worry about; he has done several hundred appendectomies during his career, and it is a rarity when something goes even slightly wrong. Before you have a chance to ask too many questions, a nurse injects you with a drug that quickly makes you drowsy.

4   An attendant wheels you into the operating room on a four-wheeled cart. While the surgeon and his assistants spend ten to fifteen minutes scrubbing and sterilizing their hands and arms, an attendant positions you correctly on the table, removes all traces of hair from your abdomen with a razor, applies antiseptic liberally to the skin, and places small, green sterilized towels around the area to be operated on, draping an opening where the surgeon will work. The anesthesiologist finally administers an anesthetic which will not only put you to sleep but will also relax your muscles as much as possible, enabling the surgeon to cut through and separate them with ease. The anesthesiologist will monitor your vital signs during the operation and will usually be the first to know if anything goes wrong.

5   Once the surgeon decides that everything is ready, he will begin the operation. He is in complete charge of the operation and gives the order to the surgical team consisting of a scrub nurse who hands the surgeon and his assistants the instruments they need quickly and efficiently, a circulating nurse who will run after any extra instruments that might be needed during the operation, one or two assistants, and the anesthesiologist.

6   The surgeon begins the operation by making a few inch–long incisions with a scalpel. He then cuts through a layer of fat, then a layer of muscle to gain entrance to the body cavity. When he finally reaches the mesentery, a paper–thin covering of the internal organs, he tears a hole into it with a pair of forceps, exposing the intestines. Reaching into the wound with two fingers, he finds the swollen appendix and draws it carefully into the opening. His greatest concern is that he not accidentally rupture the inflamed appendix, which would result in an internal infection known as peritonitis, a serious and potentially fatal complication. Deftly, he ties the appendix off from the colon to which it is attached. With a scalpel, he cuts the connecting tissue and lifts the severed appendix from the hole.

7   While the surgeon has accomplished this very quickly and efficiently, his assistant has been busy tying knots around the small arteries that leak blood into the wound. The surgeon now stitches a knot over the stump that remains in the colon and stitches the opening completely shut. He then stitches the mesentery, the muscles, and, finally, the skin. With that, he has finished the hard part of his job. All that remains for him is to make sure that you, the patient, make an uneventful recovery.

8   Two or three days later, you return home and after about two weeks you are as healthy as you were before, little realizing that the appendicitis surgery, so easy and routine for the surgeon, has prevented your premature death. A hundred years earlier, when such surgery was not available, you would have surely lost your life.   —Major Ryan Gross

EXPLORING CHOICES

Content and Organization

1. What writing strategies does the writer use to maintain time order at the beginning of and within each paragraph? Pay particular attention to the adverbs of time (*when, before, after, while, then,* and so on).

2. Note that the title of the essay suggests the writer's thesis. Point out how the writer reaffirms this thesis in his description of the surgeon and of the surgical procedure he performs.
3. Note that the writer makes the reader a participant in the action by using the second person *(you).* Why do you think he does so? What does this strategy suggest about the audience he is addressing?

Style

1. Point out the verb series in paragraph 2, sentence 3. Instead of combining these verbs in one sentence, the writer might have split them up into two or three sentences. Try doing so. What difference in effect do you find? Which do you prefer?
2. The words *mesentery* and *peritonitis* in paragraph 6 are each followed by a comma and a noun phrase. What is the function of this noun phrase? How does its use indicate that the writer is considering the needs of his audience?
3. Point out the adverbs in paragraphs 5, 6, and 7 that describe actions. Try placing these adverbs elsewhere in the sentence. What is the effect of your change? Which do you prefer? Why?
4. In what tense is the essay written? Consider changing the tense so that the first few sentences read, "It was yet two hours before sunrise when the dull pain in your side awakened you. As you struggled to the medicine cabinet in the bathroom, you tried to remember what you had eaten the night before. . . ." What difference in effect do you find? Which do you prefer? Why?

Using Topical Order

A paragraph organized by topic begins with a general idea or topic which the remainder of the paragraph explores in detail. Such paragraphs are often closely related to the thesis that announces the major idea of the essay.

The following essay is a character sketch that opens with a general statement or thesis summarizing the writer's impression of the subject. As you read it, notice that the subsequent paragraphs are organized topically: each begins with a general idea that restates one of the points raised in the thesis statement.

BARBIE DOLL

Thesis

1   Barbara and I occupied the same college apartment for six months, but I never felt I knew her. She was as pretty, well-molded, and inscrutable as a living Barbie doll. Her hair, undyed, was the glinting gold color of cornsilk, styled

in a shoulder—length pageboy that never drooped or frizzled, even after a steam shower. If she wore rollers or used a curling iron, they were never seen by anyone but her. When she emerged from her bedroom each morning, every strand was in perfect order. Her eyes were as bright—blue as the marble eyes of a doll, her nose straight, tip-tilted, and unfreckled. Her lashes and brows should have been pale with that blonde hair, but were carefully mascaraed and penciled each morning, including weekends and holidays. Her skin was porcelain—fair, her cheeks blushed pale pink. She never appeared garishly made—up or exaggerated, but always looked a bit too perfectly colored to be a real person.

Topic sentence   2   Barbara's clothing enhanced her doll—like appearance. Although only twenty years old, she detested pants, preferring kilts or A—line skirts or tailored dresses worn with nylons and patent leather, small—heeled shoes. The one time she wore a pair of slacks to go bicycle riding with her boyfriend, she looked (and said she felt) strange, sloppy, and ill at ease.

Topic sentence   3   If Barbara had personal feelings, emotions, doubts, and opinions, as she must have had, we who lived with her never knew them. Her china face held a perpetual impersonal smile, her voice was light and cheerful, but without warmth. Whenever one of her three roommates became ill, she would appear periodically in the bedroom with a cheery "Feeling better?" but would never think to bring a cup of tea or pick up the art history assignment or stay and chat. If she ever felt ill or depressed, we were unaware of it. She seemed impervious to human maladies and untouched by those of others.

Topic sentence   4   In a society where college students are known for their volubility and free expression of feelings, she seemed withdrawn. She led a textbook existence, doing enough work as an art history major to insure passing grades, relaxing on weekends with her boyfriend (about whom, of course, we learned nothing beyond his face, his "hello" at the door, and the fact that he was a student at a nearby college). Her one outstanding talent was an ability to sew smart, well—tailored clothes, but she never shared her skills or consulted us on possible patterns. We never talked of Picasso, of Renoir, of Breughel, though their prints hung in both our rooms and might have been a common interest. She never shared her classroom insights and rarely mentioned her schoolwork.

5   I have not painted a full picture of a human because Barbara never allowed those she lived with to see her as one. We were never able to penetrate the Barbie doll mask of perfect features and superficiality to find the person breathing inside.

—Carole Kagan

Choosing Paragraphs   **163**

Content and Organization

1. Note that the writer constructs a three-part thesis to announce her impression of her roommate. How does this thesis control her choice of topic sentences in paragraphs 2, 3, and 4?
2. How does the writer's thesis control the arrangement of each of her paragraphs? Could the paragraphs be arranged differently? Explain.
3. You have learned that much like a thesis statement, a topic sentence can be reduced to particulars. Point out how the writer uses her topic sentences to generate supporting details.
4. What words or phrases does the writer use throughout the essay to emphasize that her subject resembles a doll?

Style

1. Note the use of parentheses in paragraphs 2 and 4. Why do you think the writer has used them? Try removing them to see how the sentences read. Do you prefer the alternative forms? Why or why not?
2. In paragraph 1 the writer uses the compound word *porcelain-fair.* Is this word in the dictionary? If not, is the writer justified in using it?
3. Note the use of dialogue in paragraph 3. What if the sentence were changed to read, "When one of her roommates became ill, she would appear periodically in the bedroom to ask how she felt. . . ." Which do you prefer? Why?
4. Why do you think the writer chooses to use the phrase *textbook existence* in paragraph 4? What image does it evoke?

Using Spatial Order

At times, you may need to organize your paragraph according to how people and objects are related spatially. As you will see in the following examples, spatial arrangement has no single pattern. Sometimes the writer chooses to move from left to right or from right to left, from bottom to top or from top to bottom, from outside to inside or from inside to outside, from far to near or from near to far. Whatever pattern you choose, you need to be sure that it can be easily followed by the reader and that it is appropriate to the subject.

Following are several examples of student paragraphs that use spatial order. The first two, taken from the same essay, describe a gypsy. Note that the first, which describes the gypsy's clothes, moves from bottom to top, beginning with the gypsy's skirt and ending with the scarf around her neck. In the second paragraph, however, the writer chooses a reverse order, describing first the gypsy's earrings and moving downward to her rings and bracelets.

Paragraph A

(1) I had once heard from a friend that gypsies wore seven skirts, never washing them but simply rotating them, putting the bottom one on top to air out. (2) Mary's skirt, probably once a bright carmine velvet, was a murky burgundy–maroon. (3) Tucked into the waistband, a heavy blouse, deteriorated from crisp white to shadowy gray, still had most of the lace and embroidery around the collar, cuff, and yoke intact. (4) Over the blouse she wore a heavy, elaborately appliquéd black velvet vest. (5) Here and there a thread of the appliqué work was hanging, the ribbon drooping to reveal a spot of velvet blacker that the rest. (6) Around her neck was a green–blue silk scarf tied in front, its ends stuffed into the neckline of her blouse.

A STYLE ASIDE

1. Note that in sentences 2 and 3 the writer separates the subject from the verb with intervening modifiers set off by commas. Following are some alternative positions for these modifiers. Compare them to the writer's version and decide which you prefer.

   (2) Probably once a bright carmine velvet, Mary's skirt was a murky burgundy-maroon.

   (3) Deteriorated from crisp white to shadowy gray, a heavy blouse tucked into the waistband still had most of the lace and embroidery around the collar, cuff, and yoke intact.

2. Try moving the modifiers "Over the blouse" (sentence 4) and "Around her neck" (sentence 6) elsewhere in their respective sentences. Does the alternative work? Why or why not?

3. Note that the writer often modifies the colors she uses to describe Mary's garments (such as, "crisp white"). Try eliminating these modifiers or substituting others. What effect do you gain or lose by making these changes?

4. Point out the two compound words the writer uses to describe a color. Why do you think she does so?

Paragraph B

(1) As heavily as the air hung in the room, so hung the
ornate gold earrings from Mary's pierced lobes. (2) The holes
in Mary's ears had been pinpricked when she was a baby, but
had stretched to open slashes a half-inch in length. (3) Her
lobes, pulled down by years of progressively heavier earrings,
reached down below her jaw line, the earrings no longer
hanging free but resting on her shoulders. (4) On four of her
gnarled fingers she wore rings that would rival a sultan's
treasures. (5) A huge star sapphire, a diamond the size of an
aspirin, a piece of carved jade as big as a teaspoon bowl, a
garnet as wide as a nickel, vied for attention on those bony
hands. (6) Two or three gold bracelets of forge-chain
patterns circled each wrist, weighting the arms so that they
lay heavy in her lap. (7) Perhaps it was true that gypsies
wore their bank accounts as jewelry.

A STYLE ASIDE

1. Why do you think the writer chose to repeat the word "hung" in sentence 1? Would the word "dangled" have served her purpose as well? Why or why not?

2. Note the general word "rings" in sentence 4. How does the writer specify the word in sentence 5?

3. Note the number of similes in sentence 5. Why do you think the writer has used them? Can you think of others that might work as well? Try eliminating some of them. Are you satisfied with your alternative?

4. In sentence 5 the phrase "on those bony hands" ends the sentence. Try putting the phrase at the beginning of the sentence. Is there a difference in effect?

5. Note the phrase "vied for attention" in sentence 5. Try substituting "caught my eye" or "glittered" or another word or phrase you can think of. Are they as effective as the phrase the writer chose? Why or why not?

6. Explain the purpose of the final sentence, which does not directly describe Mary's jewelry as do the other sentences in the paragraph.

In the next example, the writer is describing a tavern, using outer to inner movement to coordinate his two paragraphs. Note, however, that within each paragraph, the spatial movement is different: the first uses a far-to-near-order, while the second uses an up-and-down order.

Paragraph C

```
    The tavern was just a large wooden box on the flat ground.
There was nothing else visible except the surrounding wall of
shadows off in the distance.  In the dirt driveway lay a
replica of an early wagon wheel, its once-fresh coat of
varnish faded and engraved with graffiti.  On the left and
right of the tavern entrance large upholstered booths that had
evidently outlived their usefulness sat anchored in mud.
    Inside, two large overhead fans pretended to keep the tavern
cool.  The large black bar spanning the thirty-foot width of
the tavern faced the swinging doors.  Behind it, a wall-to-
wall mirror covered with a layer of dust greeted the tavern's
guests with a cloudy self-portrait.  The mirror boasted two
signs: one read "Beer $.45," the other, "Boilermakers $1.05."
```

A STYLE ASIDE

The preceding paragraphs were written in several drafts. In the revision, the writer changed a number of verbs and in one instance combined sentences. Compare these changes in the sentences below. Which version is more effective? Why?

Original: A replica of an early wagon wheel was in the dirt driveway. Its once-fresh coat of varnish was faded and engraved with graffiti.

Revised: In the dirt driveway lay a replica of an early wagon wheel, its once-fresh coat of varnish faded and engraved with graffiti.

Original: Inside were two large overhead fans that tried to cool the tavern.

Revised: Inside, two large overhead fans pretended to keep the tavern cool.

Original: The mirror had two signs, one advertising beer, the other, Boilermakers.

Revised: The mirror boasted two signs: one read "Beer $.45," the other, "Boilermakers $1.05."

PARAGRAPH COMPLETENESS

Paragraphs that satisfy readers provide a thorough discussion of a subject. A skeletal paragraph that merely outlines a subject is likely to be dismissed; readers will find such a paragraph boring at best, at worst a kind of confession that the writer has not mastered the subject.

One way to develop your paragraphs is to retrace the thinking process involved in composing a topic sentence. Recall that, much like a thesis statement, a topic sentence is an interpretive summary drawn from lower-level material. It says that you have examined a group of particulars and have concluded that they have a common meaning. The meaning you arrive at is your generalization, your interpretive conclusion, but if you retrace your thought you will see that your interpretation is based on material you have examined earlier.

You can see how a thinking process that moves back and forth between the general and the specific is reflected in the following student paragraph. Note that the paragraph opens with a topic sentence that interprets the subject, in this case *toxic waste*. This general interpretation is then supported by specific information—the particulars from which the writer drew the conclusion stated in the topic sentence.

The effects of toxic waste are quite serious. In Woburn, Massachusetts, two city water wells were shut down when they were found to be contaminated with trichloroethylene, an industrial solvent known to cause cancer. Deaths from cancer rose 17 percent in five years among Woburn residents, and state officials are now in the process of finding out just how widespread the town's health problems really are. In Elizabeth, New Jersey, an abandoned chemical dump crammed with thirty-four thousand barrels of toxic waste caught fire and blew up. Dozens of firemen were overcome by the smoke, and hundreds of nearby residents reported symptoms of chemical poisoning. In Gray, Maine, a strange odor from the water led to the discovery that wells in the area had been contaminated by seepage from a local hazardous waste disposal site. The chemicals identified in the water were dimethyl sulfide, a toxic chemical used for industrial cleaning and paint stripping, and two industrial solvents, trichloroethane and trichloroethylene, the latter of which is known to depress the central nervous system, and to cause mental confusion, nausea, and gastrointestinal problems.

To use your topic sentence to advantage in developing your paragraph, ask yourself what ideas and information helped you formulate your interpretation. Try to be specific in answering your question. If your answer is as general as your topic sentence, you may still end up with an un-developed paragraph. Note, for example, that the following paragraph on toxic waste is far less effective than the preceding one because it relies on general assertions rather than on detailed information for support.

> The effects of toxic waste are quite serious. The pollution of drinking water, for example, can lead to serious health problems. Similarly, toxic fumes can lead to chemical poisoning, resulting in damage to the central nervous system.

Reviewing the topics of invention described in Chapter 2 can also help you develop your paragraphs. Patterns of thinking such as comparison and contrast, definition, and classification can be used not only to discover ideas but to develop them. The paragraph on toxic waste, for example, is developed through causal analysis: it establishes that toxic wastes have harmful effects. In the following paragraph you will see how a student uses comparison to develop the idea that East and West Berlin share a number of characteristics:

> East and West Berlin still have a few things in common. Both are considered the first cities of their respective countries. Both are inhabited by Germans sharing the same language, customs, and traditions, Germans proud of the cultural inheritance of Bach and Goethe, Germans dedicated to hard work. The hardworking Germans of West Berlin have rebuilt their city into the number-one city in Europe, center of culture, industry, and international commerce. The hardworking Germans of East Berlin have raised their standard of living above that of the Russians who won the war. Both sections of the city are tourist centers, attracting guests from all over the world. Germans of both sectors are anxious to forget the Hitler Holocaust and re-earn the respect of the other countries of the world. Both hesitate to sing the first verse of their national anthem, "Germany, Germany above all things in the world!" for fear of being misunderstood. Germans of both sections of the city hate and fear the Communists and hope to get rid of them, thereby reuniting Berlin.

Another technique that can help you develop full paragraphs is to examine your sentences to see if you can find general terms (normally a feature of topic sentences) that can be used to generate more specific details. We can see this process at work in the following student paragraph that describes a person. Note that it begins with the word *remarkable* and then specifies this generalizing adjective with a less general phrase that is then further specified. In all, the paragraph illustrates five levels of generality.

General adjective.	(1) The most <u>remarkable</u> woman I have ever known is my grandmother Rosina.
Explains remarkable *and introduces the idea of independence.*	(2) After my grandfather died, Rosina suddenly shed her submissive image and <u>became an independent woman.</u>
	(3) Her first act of independence was <u>to pull up stakes.</u>
Examples of pulling up stakes.	(4) She gave up her apartment in our two-family home and went off to Italy to live near a distant relative.
	(4) Two years later she traveled to Algeria, France, Denmark, and Germany, always alone and always making her own travel arrangements.
	(4) Now she's living in a tiny town in Canada, but she's always leaving it to visit remote logging camps in the Hudson Bay area, picturesque fishing villages in Newfoundland, or whatever other exotic place strikes her fancy.
Explains independence.	(3) She'll take <u>no advice from anyone</u> or allow any interference in her affairs.
Example of refusing to take advice.	(4) When my uncle tried to dissuade her from traveling to North Africa because of the discomforts she might encounter, she <u>promptly told him to mind his own business.</u>
Detailed response to uncle.	(5) "When you pay my bills, you can tell me what to do," she snapped, "but until then kindly look after your own affairs and not mine."
Example of refusing to take advice.	(4) The same waspish comment met my mother's plea that she return home to watch her grandchildren grow up.
	(5) "I've my own growing up to do," she wrote, "and I haven't as much time as they have."

PARAGRAPH COHERENCE

Imagine listening to a friend who is describing a boating accident and suddenly, in the midst of the narrative, begins to tell you about a chess game he'd played the night before. Chances are the abrupt and unexpected shift would puzzle you. What, you'd probably ask, is the connection between boating and chess? If your friend could explain, you'd probably attribute his lapse to one of those mental leaps we sometimes make when we think our audience is as familiar with our experience as we are. If he couldn't, though, you might question his grasp of reality because, like most of us, you consider coherence a mark of normal behavior.

If coherence is essential in even the most ordinary conversations, it is especially so in writing, where the opportunity to back up and explain something inadvertently omitted or to make clear the relationship between one sentence and another simply doesn't exist. You can, of course, correct the omission when you revise, but if you have completed your work, you cannot alter the sequence of words on the page. As a result, you need to take special care that your sentences and paragraphs are firmly linked to one another. You can do this by using the following *coherence devices*.

Repetition

To gain coherence you can repeat key words or phrases or, to avoid monotony, you can substitute synonyms and pronouns for key words you've already used. Here is how one student used repetition:

> Early in our relationship, Judy informed me that she did not really belong in the modern world, for at heart she was a "Victorian." I doubt if Judy ever read a true Victorian novel or knew much about Victorian history, but she created for herself a very clear idea of what it meant to be a Victorian. Being Victorian meant standing for hours in the dead of night, gazing out the window, as I often woke to find her, dressed in a long, flowing nightgown. Being Victorian meant using a typewriter which printed scripts and handing in beautiful, scrupulously neat homework assignments which took hours to prepare, but were usually done wrong. Unfortunately, being Victorian did not entail being meticulously clean. At first, when I noticed her clothes growing dingy, I would volunteer to do her laundry with mine, but as I grew more involved with college life, I just let her wardrobe get dingier. When Judy felt the way people do when they need a shower, she would skip the shower and double her dosage of perfume. At night, when she crawled quietly into her upper bunk while I slept in the lower, it was not her movement that awakened me but her rank odor.

Examining the paragraph, you can see that a key word in the passage is *I;* the reader is always aware that each descriptive detail is filtered through the writer's perception. The roommate's name is also a key word, announced in the opening sentence and repeated twice at strategic spots in the paragraph. Another key word is *Victorian,* repeated seven times because it provides the clue to the roommate's eccentric behavior. Note, too, that when the writer shifts to her roommate's lack of cleanliness, she repeats the word *dingy* (in the comparative form, *dingier*) and the word *shower* to remind us of Judy's slovenliness.

The pronouns and synonyms in the passage also provide continuity. *I* and *me, she* and *her,* appear throughout; we are never allowed to forget who is speaking and the person she is speaking of. Note also how the writer avoids repeating the word *clothes* by using the synonyms *laundry* and *wardrobe.*

Parallelism

Another way to ensure paragraph continuity is to repeat sentence openers. In the preceding student paragraph, for example, the writer begins two sentences with the phrase "Being Victorian" and a third with "Unfortunately, being Victorian." Words matched in this way are *parallel.*

The repetition of similar grammatical structures is another form of parallelism that can connect sentences. In the following student paragraph, the grammatical similarity of the italicized sentences effectively links one sentence to the other:

> The multilingual character of American culture goes back to the early settlers who were the first to transport the customs and traditions of a foreign land to the "new country." They did this in part by retaining and teaching the language of their origins. French missionaries and nuns taught French in Canada and Maine. The Germans taught German in Pennsylvania. The Spanish taught Spanish in Florida and the Southwest. Latin, Greek, and Hebrew——the three languages of scholarship in the colonial period——also contributed to our early polyglot culture. Indeed, they were so prized that in the early years of Harvard and Yale, commencement addresses were delivered in these so-called "pure" languages.

Parallelism is especially useful when the writer seeks emphasis as well as coherence. In the following paragraph, the repeated word *all,* combined with parallel structure, gives special weight to the central idea of the passage:

> National security is modern incantation. As in any incantation, the words have both power and mystery. In the name of national security, all things can be threatened. All risks can be taken. All sacrifices can be demanded. Break-ins, wiretaps, deception of Congress, assassination attempts

on foreign leaders—indeed, the Watergate cover-up and the
intervention in Vietnam—were all ordered in the name of
national security.   —Richard J. Barnet,
                                "Challenging the Myths of
                                National Security," New York
                                Times Magazine

Transitional Words and Phrases

A common means of achieving coherence is the transitional word or
phrase. If, for example, writers wish to illustrate the point they are making
(as we are doing in this sentence), they are likely to use words or phrases
such as *for example, for instance, for one thing.* Or they may introduce a
comparison with transitional signals such as *in comparison, likewise, similarly, in the same way.* Keep in mind that for each direction your thought
takes, you can choose among a number of signal words, some multisyllabic
and rather formal, others shorter, lighter, and less obtrusive. For example:

contrast: nevertheless, on the other hand, however, yet
time and sequence: now, earlier, first, last
addition: furthermore, in addition, also, moreover
emphasis: to be sure, without doubt, surely, certainly
summary or conclusion: in summary, in brief, to conclude, accordingly
space: above, below, opposite, behind
reason, result: thus, therefore, as a result, consequently

Transitional Sentences Within Paragraphs

Sometimes, continuity in a paragraph requires an internal transitional sentence, especially if the writer wishes to present an idea that is related to, but
slightly different from, the preceding ideas. You saw this important marker
in the student paragraph on Judy, where the writer shifted from Judy's "Victorian" posing to her slovenly habits.

Being Victorian meant using a typewriter which printed scripts
and handing in beautiful, scrupulously neat homework
assignments which took hours to prepare but were usually done
wrong. Unfortunately, being Victorian did not entail being
meticulously clean. At first, when I noticed her clothes
growing dingy, I would volunteer to do her laundry with mine,
but as I grew more involved with college life, I just let her
wardrobe get dingier.

If you tried reading this passage without the transitional sentence, you would no doubt find yourself puzzled. What, you might ask, is the connection between Judy's homework assignments and her dirty clothes? With it, however, you see that the writer has introduced the idea of contrast to prepare for the details that follow. Note, too, that the idea of contrast is both set off from, and connected to, the preceding sentences. To alert the reader to change, the transitional sentence begins with the adverb *Unfortunately.* And to show that this change is related to the preceding sentences chronicling Judy's "Victorian" illusions, the writer repeats the phrase *being Victorian,* as well as the word *being,* later on in the sentence. As you can see, a transitional sentence points in two directions: backward to old information and forward to new.

You can see the importance of the transitional sentence if you compare the following student paragraph in two drafts. After you have read both paragraphs, point out the transitional sentence the writer includes in his revision. How does this sentence alert the reader to the detail that follows? What words connect it to the sentences that precede it?

First Draft

```
    It is true that the younger the child the more sleep it
requires.  The average sleep time for infants is sixteen
hours.  A study by Dement showed that sixteen-year-olds tended
to sleep about ten hours and that young adults slept about
eight hours.
```

Revision

```
    It is true that the younger the child, the more sleep it
requires.  The average sleep time for infants is sixteen
hours.  As children mature, however, they require less sleep.
A study by Dement showed that sixteen-year-olds tended to
sleep about ten hours and that young adults slept about eight
hours.
```

Transitional Sentences Between Paragraphs

To clarify connections and relationships, transitional sentences are often required *between,* as well as *within,* paragraphs. Such transitions may take a variety of forms as you will see in the following student paragraphs. At times, a paragraph that introduces a new idea will repeat a word or phrase from the last sentence of the preceding paragraph:

Repeated phrase.

```
Children's programs, existing almost as long as television
itself, present many violent scenes that give impressionable
children false ideas of physical invulnerability.
    The suggestion of physical invulnerability is aided by
animation and special effects.
```

An analysis of some of the clothing styles discarded and embraced by the counterculture reveals that this revolution in fashion was in large part a result of <u>changes</u> in values.

Repeated word.   One of the most fundamental of these <u>changes</u> was the attack on the class structure of society.

Or the idea of the preceding sentence can be repeated in different words:

When watching <u>Open City</u>, the film-goer never has to take an active part in interpreting the film.

Idea of preceding   The <u>passive role of the audience</u> is also reinforced by the
sentence rephrased.   types of editing used throughout the film.

For this reason, if scholarships were awarded for academic achievement alone, too few blacks would be in the top 25 or 35 percent of the class (the percentage of each class which now receives scholarship aid) to maintain affirmative action quotas.

Idea of preceding   If <u>blacks are not awarded financial aid</u>, attending an Ivy
sentence rephrased.   League school will become an impossibility for them.

The transitional sentence can also repeat words or phrases that appear *before* the final sentence of the preceding paragraph:

Before the invention of modern technology and chemicals, the meat industry lacked the necessary tools to handle meat butchering and processing safely. In 1906, when Upton Sinclair's <u>The Jungle</u> was published, meat was stored carelessly and inadequately in old wooden barns with leaking roofs and improper temperature settings. Although the meat was well salted, <u>its poor storage conditions often led to rapid spoilage and the eventual invasion of rats. The inspection of meat before and after butchering was also very poor</u>. Many times sick and diseased animals were butchered and sold because inspectors did not detect their illnesses. As a result, bad meat would often be sold, which, in turn, led to the illness and, sometimes, to the death, of consumers. In addition to <u>improper storage and inspection</u>, the shipping methods of the early meat industry were also inferior.

If an essay depends on enumeration (*one type of, one reason for, one advantage of,* and so on), transitional sentences between paragraphs will often refer to the subject of the analysis. Following, for example, is the last sentence of an introductory paragraph concerned with the decline of a small town. Since the writer's purpose is to give reasons for this decline, each subsequent paragraph begins with a transitional sentence that repeats the idea of the introductory paragraph.

```
Eyeing these once-majestic buildings, a visitor might wonder
what has caused their plight: Why has Williamsport been
neglected and rejected by local residents?
    Perhaps the earliest contributor to the demise of
Williamsport was the automobile. . . .
    Modern Williamsport was also doomed because of its lack of
industry. . . . Still another reason why Williamsport died
was that its small businessmen and craftsmen became obsolete,
unable to compete with the influx of modern inventions. . . .
```

FOLLOW-UP ACTIVITIES

1. Underline the transitional markers in the following sentences and identify each type.
   a. Like the football player, the male ballet dancer must also train rigorously, although his training begins earlier, usually no later than the age of twelve. (Type: _____)
   b. The price of milk is therefore significant to the cheese producer because it takes approximately one hundred pounds of milk to make ten pounds of cheese. (Type: _____)
   c. Making beer requires a number of steps. First the barley grain is dumped into a large vat where steeping occurs. The grain is then transferred from the vat to a bin where the germination of the seed takes place. (Type: _____)
   d. The 1960s brought us shoes with leather spikes that provide better traction. As a result, all runners began to run times that were faster and faster. (Type: _____)
   e. Because they were poorly constructed, nearly half the planes in service during World War I fell out of the sky without being shot down. In fact, they were their own worst enemy. (Type: _____)

2. What methods are used to achieve coherence in the paragraphs below? Underline or circle transitional words and phrases, strategies of repetition, and parallelism.

Paragraph A

    In New York from dawn to dusk to dawn, day after day, you can hear the steady rumble of tires against the concrete span of George Washington Bridge. The bridge is never completely still. It trembles with traffic. It moves in the wind. Its great veins of steel swell when hot and contract when cold; its span often is ten feet closer to the Hudson River in summer than in winter. It is an almost restless structure of graceful beauty which, like an irresistible seductress, withholds secrets from the romantics who gaze upon it, the escapists who jump off it, the chubby girl who lumbers across its 3,500-foot span trying to reduce, the 100,000 motorists who each day cross it, smash into it, shortchange it, get jammed up on it.   —Gay Talese, "New York," *Esquire*

Paragraph B

The ancient belief in plant perception often led to tree worship. Communities of long ago worshiped trees as gods and felt that trees were vital to their existence. The Romans worshiped fig trees. Whenever a fig tree appeared to be withering, crowds would gather in a mass gesture of concern. An ancient Norse myth concerned a tree named Yggdrasil. The Norse believed that Yggdrasil was the tree of existence, of life, and of knowledge, sorrow, and fate--the source of all things including time and space. The Norse and the Romans shared the belief that pain suffered by the trees would result in misfortune for the community.

3. Circle the internal transitional sentence in both of the following student paragraphs. Explain how it represents a shift in thought from the idea with which the paragraph begins, as well as how it blends old and new information.

Paragraph A

Times have changed. The advent of Western civilization and education has changed the life of the Nigerian woman for the better. Nigerian fathers have recognized the need to educate their daughters as well as their sons, and there have been instances where daughters in the family have shown greater promise and achieved greater success in life than the sons. The Nigerian woman is no longer relegated to the background in the political life of the country. Right now two women are serving on two of the twelve state cabinets. Even when they do not hold political office, they sometimes exert political pressure. It's now a common practice for women to lead delegations to high government officials to demand things like improved sanitary conditions for the community.

Paragraph B

The change in the physical education department's curriculum in particular provided me with a striking contrast between the old "uptight" Lincoln and the new "progressive" Lincoln. I myself had spent four years in physical education classes running away from dodge balls, soccer balls, basketballs, and flung baseball bats, quaking in fear lest I be chosen to demonstrate a particular athletic skill in front of the rest of the class. If I were a student today, I would no longer need to fear exposure. All of the gym sports are now organized into elective classes; girls are no longer forced to play field hockey or climb ropes as part of a calisthenics program. Instead, they can sign up for tennis, figure control, or yoga.

4. Compose a transitional sentence that will link the second partial paragraph to the paragraph preceding it.

Paragraph A

```
    Tennis has obviously increased in popularity in the past few
years.  It does not take a tennis fanatic to realize that
there are many more tennis courts now than before, with many
more people using them.  Even the old court behind the grade
school, with cracks in its surface and holes in its nets, has
a line of people waiting to play whenever there is a sunny
day.
```

_____

```
No longer can players stay on a court for an unlimited amount
of time.
```

Paragraph B

```
    In the nineteenth century the traveling circus that
performed in a tent was a prosperous venture, delighting
millions of people.  Some favored the aerialist who courted
danger with high-wire acts or trapeze stunts.  Others loved
the side shows exhibiting the freaks of nature—the bearded
lady, the Siamese twins, "the tallest man on earth."  All this
has changed.  In this century the number of traveling circuses
has gradually declined until now only a few circuses remain.
For many reasons, traveling circuses have become a fading form
of entertainment.
```

_____

```
Too many days of rain could be disastrous.
```

Paragraph C

```
    Puerto Rican culture has suffered drastic changes since it
came in close contact with American culture.  Even though
Puerto Rico became an American colony in 1898 as a result of
the Spanish American War, it did not feel the impact of
American culture until it became a strategic point for the
defense of the hemisphere, just before the Second World War.
At that time large numbers of soldiers and technical personnel
arrived, bringing strange customs which changed the Puerto
Rican way of life, not always for the best.
```

_____

```
Traditionally the Puerto Rican father was the head of the
family, and it was he who made all important decisions.
```

INTRODUCTORY PARAGRAPHS

Writers often find the opening paragraph the most difficult to compose. A chief reason for their uneasiness is the need to enlist the reader's attention while providing a deft and succinct account of purpose. Both, of course, require close attention to audience and occasion: the introductory paragraph of a letter to the editor of a local newspaper obviously requires a different format from the introductory paragraph of an academic paper addressed to a professor and written to demonstrate competence in a specialized subject. Because audience and occasion may differ widely from one paper to another, it is often useful to question the context of a proposed work before beginning to write. The questions about audience at the end of Chapter 1 are a guide to making the appropriate choice. Review them carefully before drafting your introduction.

You may, of course, answer these questions satisfactorily and still find yourself wondering how to begin. If you find this happening, it may be best to delay the writing of the introductory paragraph until you've worked through the body of the paper. Postponement may be useful: some students claim that only in the process of putting their thoughts into writing do they find the exact ideas they want to express. Working on the body of the paper, they say, gives them a firmer grasp of their writing purpose and allows them to return to the beginning to write an introduction that precisely captures their intention. If you choose this reverse-order route, keep in mind that it has some hazards: without an opening paragraph that states, however imprecisely, the purpose of your paper, you may find yourself grasping at every idea or impression that comes to mind, with the result that your paper may become disorganized. To compromise, write a rough draft of an opening paragraph that provides some notion of what you plan to do and then revise this paragraph after you've written the body of your paper.

There is no ready-made formula for composing an introductory paragraph; writers must consider countless variables. Nevertheless, strategies do exist that may help you. Following are some that students have used. As you read them, try to define your expectations as a reader; ask yourself what these paragraphs foretell about the content and development of the rest of the essay. If you can't tell much about the essay from each paragraph (some writers need more than one paragraph to announce their purpose), try to predict several possibilities.

1. Narrate a dramatic moment

> Adrift on the sea, the passengers watched the Titanic, her lights still ablaze, slowly sink forward. As the forward tilt grew steeper, the front funnel toppled with a deafening sound. Then the roar began, beginning with the tinkle of breaking glass, increasing to a thunder as everything moveable broke loose. Two minutes passed before the noise stopped. The lights had all gone out and her bulk stood out largely against the starlit night. Slowly, the great ship reared perpendicular out of the water and began slipping faster, picking up speed. At 2:20 A.M., April 15, 1912, the magnificent Titanic plunged two miles to the bottom of the North Atlantic.

2. Offer some startling statistics

Since 1963, Scholastic Aptitude Test scores have been on the decline among the American college-bound population. Math scores have dropped thirty-two points from an average of 502 to 470, and verbal scores have dropped even more dramatically by 49 points, from 478 to 429. Educators and parents have become increasingly alarmed by this phenomenon which they attribute to an overall inadequate educational system. But the reasons underlying this decline in SAT scores are far more complex than the simplistic notion of faulty schooling. Unless policy makers understand the precise causes for this decline, they will not be able to devise a useful program aimed at raising SAT scores.

3. Provide historical background

A thousand years ago, Basque seamen went out to sea in search of the whale, the mightiest creature man had ever known. Experience had taught them that this strange, warm-blooded, air-breathing monster that occasionally washed up on shore yielded valuable stores of oil and meat. The seamen pursued the "right" whale, which at that time was numerous along the coast, learned to kill and butcher it, and founded an industry that would influence the course of history. It came to be known as the whaling industry, and while it lasts, great whales are dying by the millions, the victims of man's greed.

4. Question a point of view

When the United States was founded, the authors of the Constitution, striving to protect the rights of the individual, drafted a Bill of Rights which, among other provisions, guaranteed the right to bear arms. Two hundred years ago, the right to bear arms was a symbol of personal freedom, protecting the individual citizen from government suppression and abuse, a legitimate concern in the context of 1787 politics. But is that two-hundred-year-old provision in the Constitution a legitimate concern today? Does the right to bear arms still protect individual freedom? The fact is that the right to bear handguns threatens the peace and security of individual citizens; handguns threaten the lives of those people they are supposed to be protecting.

5. Begin with a quotation

New Hampshire, October 6, 1979

State troopers and National Guardsmen used sticks, tear gas, and high pressure water hoses to combat more than 14,000 raging protesters at the Seabrook nuclear power plant during a three-day ordeal which resulted in twenty-three arrests and many broken bones.——AP News Item

Creys-Malville, France

A bloody clash between 5,000 riot police and some 20,000 anti-nuclear demonstrators at the site of the world's first commercial fast breeder reactor left one person dead and a hundred wounded.——AP News Item

Without a doubt, in the United States and abroad, the cry against nuclear power has become louder and more vehement in the last few years than ever before. Even on college campuses, you can see "No Bike" signs on sidewalks repainted to "No Nukes"——evidence that what was once heralded as the cleanest, most economical source of energy is now widely feared. What has brought about the protests against the seventy nuclear power plants operating in the United States, which generate about one eighth of our country's electric power, and the approximately 150 others scattered around the world? The reasons which first come to mind are quite obvious.

6. Summarize opposing views

A central issue in automobile safety is whether air bags should be dropped in favor of efforts to make the wearing of seat belts mandatory. Auto makers maintain that the feasibility and dependability of air bags have not been proved and that the same safety goals can be achieved by getting people to wear belts that already exist in 95 percent of all cars on the road. Proponents of air bags counter that there is plenty of evidence air bags can reduce highway injury and death more than seat belts, which, they claim, will never be adequately used, laws or not. Either way, the issue raises fundamental questions about the proper role of government in regulating the lives of its citizens.

7. Describe a firsthand experience

   The young man strode purposefully down the street, his eyes
staring straight ahead. He was quite tall, a few inches over
six feet, and was clad only in an old T-shirt, old faded blue
jeans that were ragged at the cuffs, weather-beaten and holey
tennis shoes, and a dirty brown winter coat that was two sizes
too large, its collar upturned to protect his neck from the
cold. He wore no hat, and the bitter March wind often blew
his long, tangled brown hair into his face. I watched him as
he passed by the small variety store in which I worked, his
long strides carrying him quickly past the wide windows, the
front doors, around the corner, past the side doors, and out
of my view. Although his jaw was set as if he were about to
reach his destination, I knew that he was going nowhere in
particular. He had passed by the store five times that
blustery afternoon, and was constantly walking the same route
over again through downtown. While other people his age were
enjoying their last months of high school and were saving
money from jobs for college expenses, he was wandering up and
down the streets, perhaps playing an occasional game of pool
at the local bowling alley. He was only eighteen years old and
was a bum with nothing of importance to do. I believe that he
knew just as well as I did that his life could have turned out
much differently. It had been only four years before that
wintry March day when he had been the best known and most
prominent member of his Shelbyville Junior High School class.

CONCLUDING PARAGRAPHS

If introductions are the most difficult to write, conclusions run a close
second, possibly because writers find themselves groping for something to
say that they have not already said. If they don't succeed, they may succumb
to the lure of the "In conclusion" format which mechanically recapitulates
the main points in the essay. Or, in search of a more satisfying closure, they
may insert new ideas, thereby running the risk of introducing irrelevancies.
Often, these problems arise when writers misconstrue the word *conclusion,* considering it equivalent to a final paragraph in a series of paragraphs
rather than to a way of thinking. The difference is between arriving at a destination and arriving at a meaning: the first simply requires movement from
one place to another, while the second requires reflection that reveals
significance. While a conclusion must be hooked to everything that precedes it, it nevertheless differs from other parts of the essay in that it sug-

gests or explores the *implications* of what has gone before. Even if it reemphasizes the main points of the essay, it does so not by restating them but by interpreting their meaning.

The easiest way to illustrate this important principle about conclusions is to see how it works. Following are the opening and closing paragraphs of an essay about the psychological differences between males and females. As you read, note how the two paragraphs are similar and how they are different. The questions that follow will help you make these distinctions.

The essay opens with a quotation which the writer uses to establish the purpose of the essay.

> *Captain to Laura:* ". . . If it's true we are descended from the ape, it must have been from two different species. There's no likeness between us, is there?"
> —*The Father,* by August Strindberg

So it has begun to seem, and not only in the musings of a misogynist Swedish playwright. Research on the structure of the brain, on the effects of hormones, and in animal behavior, child psychology and anthropology is providing new scientific underpinnings for what August Strindberg and his ilk viscerally guessed: men and women *are* different. They show obvious dissimilarities, of course, in size, anatomy and sexual function. But scientists now believe that they are unlike in more fundamental ways. Men and women seem to *experience* the world differently, not merely because of the ways they were brought up in it, but because they feel it with a different sensitivity of touch, hear it with different aural responses, puzzle out its problems with different cells in their brains.

. . . .

Perhaps the most arresting implication of the research up to now is not that there are undeniable differences between males and females, but that their differences are so small, relative to the possibilities open to them. Human behavior exhibits a plasticity that has enabled men and women to cope with cultural and environmental extremes and has made them—by some measures—the most successful species in history. Unlike canaries, they can sing when the spirit, rather than testosterone, moves them. "Human beings," says Roger Gorski, "have learned to intervene with their hormones"—which is to say that their behavioral differences are what make them less, not more, like animals.

—"Just How the Sexes Differ," *Newsweek*

EXPLORING CHOICES

1. Point out the thesis of the introductory paragraph. Is this thesis reaffirmed in the concluding paragraph or is it modified? Offer evidence for your response.
2. The introductory paragraph suggests that the essay will describe the research in male/female differences. Does the final paragraph summarize this research, or does it interpret its implications?

3. What evidence is there in the concluding paragraph that the writer has not fully accepted the hypothesis announced in the introductory paragraph?
4. Point out the allusions to animals in both paragraphs. What organizational purpose does the animal allusion in the final paragraph serve? What thematic purpose does it serve? How is the allusion related to the writer's view of the *significance* of the research he has described?

EDITORIAL ACTIVITIES

YOU ARE THE EDITOR

The first draft of the following paragraph begins with a topic sentence that remains undeveloped. When the editor pointed out that the topic sentence summarized the writer's prior knowledge and/or experience and could therefore be reduced to particulars, the student rewrote the paragraph, adding detail. After you have examined both paragraphs, point out how the revision specifies the general idea of the topic sentence.

First Draft

    For alumni, homecoming is instant nostalgia that blocks out
any unhappy memories of their former college life. It gives
them the means to recall only the good times and to believe
that the past is preferable to the present. In general,
alumni forget their personal problems and immediately start to
reminisce about all the good times they enjoyed when they were
students. They conveniently forget that they had problems as
well.

Revision

    For alumni, homecoming is instant nostalgia that blocks out
any unhappy memories of their former college life.
Remembering how their frat drank two hundred gallons of beer
one weekend, how their float was the most extravagant on
campus, how they worked to get their girl chosen to be queen,
they bask in the warmth of pleasant memories. What they will
not remember, though, is the hangover of Monday morning, the
hours of planning and work that went into constructing their
float, and the money spent just to ensure the election of that
"special girl." They conveniently forget that the good times
were laced with plenty of headaches.

The Topic Sentence and Supporting Detail

The topic sentence of the following paragraph is not supported by specific detail. Help the writer see how he can develop the paragraph fully.

> Leaving home for the first time to attend college has taught me to be independent. Not having a parent constantly checking up on me encourages me to make decisions for myself. Despite some minor inconveniences, such as doing the laundry and not having a car, leaving home and staying away for a lengthy period is completely satisfactory. Added to this great overall freedom is the fact that I have been able to meet a lot of new people.

Sequence and Transitions Within Paragraphs

The first draft of the following paragraph lacks an orderly sequence as well as transitional signals. Acting on his editor's advice, the student rewrote the paragraph. The discussion questions will help you see the changes he made.

First Draft

> (1) Many people claim that man has tamed the southeast portion of the Everglades by draining the area and farming it. (2) This advancement is now haunting the Everglades. (3) To grow food products on this land, large quantities of fertilizer had to be used. (4) The problem is that the city of Miami and other cities along the coast of Florida obtain their fresh water from the Everglades. (5) The water is now too polluted for public use. (6) Miami and other cities are now spending large sums just to find new water sources. (7) Man gained a small amount in the agricultural area, but he lost far more in other respects.

Revision

> (1) Many people claim that man has tamed the southeast portion of the Everglades by draining and farming it. (2) But this supposed advancement is now haunting the population living near the Everglades. (3) The problem is that the Everglades has traditionally supplied the city of Miami and other cities along the coast of Florida with fresh water. (4) But because farming the area has required large quantities of fertilizer, the water is now too polluted for public use. (5) As a result, Miami and other cities are now spending large sums of money just to find new water sources. (6) The problem shows that though man may have gained something when he transformed a part of the Everglades into a farming area, he lost far more in other respects.

1. Point out the difference in wording in sentence 2 of the original and the revision. What has been added in the revision? Why?
2. Note that sentence 4 of the first draft has become sentence 3 in the revision. Why do you think the writer shifted its position?
3. Note that sentence 4 of the revision is a combination of sentences 3 and 5 of the first draft. What words has the writer added to effect this fusion? What relationship between his ideas has he created by adding these words?
4. Point out the transitional signal in sentence 5 of the revision. Why do you think the writer has added it?
5. Analyze the differences in the final sentence of both versions. Point out the coherence devices the writer has used in the revision.

YOU ARE THE EDITOR

The following paragraphs lack orderly sequence and appropriate transitions. Offer the writers editorial advice on how to correct these problems. You may want to suggest changes in wording as you go along.

Paragraph A

The electric car has many advantages over the gas-powered vehicle. One of these advantages is that it is much more economical to run. It costs 1.5 cents per mile to run an electric car, while a gas-powered car costs 3.6 cents per mile. The cost to run a gas-powered car is more than twice the cost of running an electric vehicle. If the gas-powered car idles when it stops at a traffic light, it uses much more energy. The more economical electric car has the advantage of not using energy when it stops at traffic lights. An electric car can get between fifty to one hundred miles per charge, and since 54 percent of all automobile trips are less than five miles, an electric vehicle is an economical choice for a family's second car. The electric car is an excellent town car.

Paragraph B

Another feature of diesel engines that needs exploring is turbocharging. The Volkswagen corporation has already manufactured a turbocharged diesel Rabbit. Turbochargers basically use the exhaust gas pressure to turn a turbine that creates pressure to turn another turbine which, in turn, forces air into the carburetor. A Rabbit with a turbocharger gets an incredible 65 mpg on the highway and approximately 42 mpg in the city. Examples like this Rabbit are making auto manufacturers more eager to develop a similar turbocharging system for their diesels. A diesel Rabbit, without the turbocharger, is very unresponsive to pressure on the gas pedal. With a turbocharger, however, the diesel Rabbit is almost as quick and fast as its gas counterpart. As of now, General Motors turbocharges only a few of its gasoline models. The GM cars that utilize turbochargers are very fast. These cars perform like the high performance cars of the early '70s.

Using the Transitional Sentence

The first draft of the following paragraph lacks several transitional sentences. Point out how the writer, following her editor's advice, includes the needed sentences in her revision. The discussion questions will help you see the changes she made.

First Draft

(1) Assuming that she has selected the finer clothes Belden's has to offer and that they are right for her, we can safely say that no one at the Art Institute Lecture Series will know if she paid two hundred dollars for them at a retail store like Field's or one hundred dollars at a discount store like Belden's. (2) Shopping for clothes is a delightful experience at Field's. (3) It is quiet, the salesladies are helpful, and it isn't necessary to sift through the junk. (4) On the other hand, if price is a consideration for the well—dressed lady, Belden's can't be beat.

Revision

(1) Assuming that she has selected the finer clothes Belden's has to offer and that they are right for her, we can safely say that no one at the Art Institute Lecture Series will know if she paid two hundred dollars for them at a retail store like Field's or one hundred dollars at a discount store like Belden's. (2) But she will be aware that the shopping experience was different. (3) Shopping for clothes can be a delightful experience at Field's. (4) It is quiet, the salesladies are helpful, and the merchandise is neatly and attractively displayed. (5) In contrast, shopping at Belden's is often nerve—wracking: it is noisy, the salesladies are few and indifferent, and the merchandise is scattered haphazardly. (6) However, if price is a consideration for the well—dressed lady, Belden's can't be beat.

EXPLORING CHOICES

1. Note that sentence 2 of the revision does not appear in the first draft. Why do you think the writer added this sentence?
2. Note that sentence 5 of the revision does not appear in the first draft. Why do you think the writer added this sentence?
3. Note the structure of sentence 5 of the revision. How is its structure similar to the structure of sentence 4? What transitional signal does the writer use?

4. Note that sentence 4 of the first draft and sentence 6 of the revision are alike except for the transitional phrase. Why do you think the writer changed the transition in the revision?

YOU ARE THE EDITOR

The following paragraph lacks an orderly sequence and a transitional sentence. Offer the writer advice on how to correct these problems. You may want to suggest changes in wording as you go along.

```
Once drunk, Don became violent and
destructive, breaking everything in sight:
chairs, lampshades, even, in one instance, the
plywood door to his room.  We lived in housing
units where twenty guys would live together in
one building.  There was a small lounge in each
building with several lounge chairs, a table, and
some lamps.  In one semester, Don broke three
doors, two lampshades, one chair, and a table.
He was six feet two inches tall and pretty
strong, too.  So when he was drunk, he didn't
seem to have a very hard time breaking things.
One time when he was drunk, he took a swing at
someone and hit the wall with his hand.  This
resulted in two broken fingers for Don.
```

Devising the General Key Phrase

The writer of the following first draft neglected to include a general key phrase in his topic sentence and to devise an internal transitional sentence. When his editor pointed this out, the writer not only found the general phrase and sentence, but he used them to organize his paragraph more effectively. The discussion questions will help you see the changes he made.

First Draft

(1) The basketball player's offensive ability in the early years of the game was limited. (2) For instance, the jump shot was unheard of. (3) If you couldn't set shoot, you didn't shoot. (4) There was little room for action, since the rules limited play. (5) One such rule was, if you scored a basket both teams would meet at mid-court and put the ball back in play with a jump ball. (6) This stopping of the game kept the players from finding their real offensive potential. (7) Shooting accuracy was low in the early days. (8) The reasons for this is the shots were taken from longer range and the shooters usually used two hands to shoot the ball.

Revision

(1) The basketball player's offensive ability in the early years of the game was limited, often by restrictive rules. (2) One rule prohibited the jump shot. (3) If you couldn't set shoot, you didn't shoot. (4) Another rule limiting action required that following each point scored, play was to begin again with a jump ball in midcourt. (5) This stopping of the game kept the players from finding their real offensive potential. (6) Awkward practices also limited offensive ability. (7) For example, players often took shots from longer range and used two hands to shoot the ball. (8) This practice often resulted in low shooting accuracy.

EXPLORING CHOICES

1. What phrase has the writer added to the first sentence of the revision? Why do you think he did so?
2. Note sentence 2 of the revision. What has been added? What has been deleted?
3. Sentence 4 of the first draft does not appear in the revision. How has the writer incorporated the idea of this sentence in other places in the revision?
4. What type of coherence device does the writer use at the beginning of sentence 4 of the revision?
5. Sentence 6 of the revision does not appear in the first draft. Why do you think the writer added it?
6. Note that the ideas contained in sentences 7 and 8 of the first draft are reversed in the revision. Why do you think the writer changed their position?

The following paragraph lacks a topic sentence and an internal transitional sentence. Offer the writer advice on how to devise each. Compare your suggestions to the suggestions of other students.

When an adolescent reaches eighteen, he is given the right to vote for people he thinks can best represent him in government. An adolescent must be mature to use this right wisely, and there are many who do use it wisely. Also, an eighteen–year–old has the right to marry a person of his choice without parental consent. For the young male, this often means supporting a family, a grave responsibility which many carry through. There are many responsibilities associated with drinking. Intoxication can cause injury to others, but if a young adult is judged to have enough maturity to have a say in government and to support a family, he may also be judged to have enough maturity to realize the side effects of drinking and to deal with it accordingly.

WRITING SUGGESTION

Often you will encounter a problem that cries for a solution. It may be purely personal: a younger sister or brother who insists on tying up the telephone; an apartment mate who needs bright lights and loud music for studying late when you want to sleep; an aged parent who must be cared for physically or financially. At other times the problem may affect the community as well as you: the lack of commuter parking space on campus; an alarming increase in the number of daytime assaults in your neighborhood;

crowd control at rock concerts. Write an essay about a problem of interest and concern to your readers and to you, describing it as fully as possible through illustrations and examples. Then offer possible solutions, explaining in detail how the preferred solution will work.

TIPS FOR SELF-EDITING

When you have completed the first draft of your paper, ask yourself the following questions about your paragraph structure.

1. If I've written a thesis/support paper, are my topic sentences related to my thesis?
2. Do my topic sentences precisely reflect the idea I want to develop?
3. Are my paragraphs fully developed? If not, can I use my topic sentences to generate additional detail?
4. Are my sentences firmly linked to each other by coherence devices?
5. Have I included transitional sentences where necessary, either within or between paragraphs?
6. Does my introductory paragraph whet reader interest and outline exactly what I intend to write about?
7. Does my concluding paragraph interpret the significance of what I have written?

CHOOSING SENTENCES

While explaining why she chose writing as a vocation, Joan Didion said this about the sentence:

> To shift the structure of a sentence alters the meaning of that sentence, as definitely and inflexibly as the position of a camera alters the meaning of the object photographed. Many people know about camera angles now, but not so many know about sentences. The arrangement of the words matters, and the arrangement you want can be found in the picture in your mind. The picture dictates the arrangement. —"Why I Write," *New York Times Book Review*

For Didion, as for most professional writers, a sentence is not merely a unit that begins with a capital letter and ends with a period; it is a unit of meaning that depends for its sense on the arrangement of its words. To native speakers of English this seems obvious, since the meaning of an English sentence relies heavily on word order. Consider, for example, the difficulty you might face if you came across a series of English words arranged like this:

```
The crossed Mary street morning the of November 9 a clutching
purse her hand in.
```

Obviously, this sentence is garbled because the words do not follow a conventional order. You can understand the meaning of individual words, but the sentence as a whole remains unintelligible. To make it meaningful, you would have to rearrange it.

```
The morning of November 9, Mary crossed the street clutching a
purse in her hand.
```

or

```
Clutching a purse in her hand, Mary crossed the street the
morning of November 9.
```

or

```
Mary crossed the street clutching a purse in her hand the
morning of November 9.
```

or

```
Mary crossed the street the morning of November 9 clutching a
purse in her hand.
```

Each sentence now makes perfect sense because each follows normal English word order: articles precede nouns, prepositions precede their objects, and the subject precedes the predicate. Note, however, that the sentences are not alike. Though all contain the same words, each is different from the other because in each a segment of the sentence appears in a position different from its position in the others. This tells you that the English sentence is highly flexible, often containing elements that can be moved. It is this mobile quality that interests Joan Didion. For her, and for you if you are a native speaker of English, the conventions of English word order come naturally; neither she nor you would be likely to write the garbled sentence in the example. What takes practice, however, is arranging sentence elements to reflect your exact meaning. How you choose to order your words, phrases, and clauses matters greatly, Didion says, because choice reflects purpose, "the picture in your mind."

FOLLOW-UP ACTIVITY

Examine the four sentences in the preceding example and determine which emphasize time and date and which emphasize the purse Mary was carrying. Which position in the sentence do you consider most emphatic? Which the least emphatic?

THE BASIC ENGLISH SENTENCE

A review of the basic English sentence illustrates how its elements can be expanded, combined, and adapted to reflect the writer's exact meaning. The core of most sentences consists of a subject and predicate. The predicate can be a single verb or, more often, a verb and its complement (a direct object, a predicate noun, a predicate adjective).

    S   V
Politicians squabbled.

   S   V   C
Tom washed the dishes.   (direct object as complement)

     S V C
The child is gifted.   (predicate adjective as complement)

     S   V   C
Mr. Brown is a grocer.   (predicate noun as complement)

EXPANDING THE BASIC ENGLISH SENTENCE

One way to expand the basic structure of a sentence is to add modification. Take, for example, the minimal sentence "Politicians squabbled." Such a sentence is grammatically complete: it sets forth a subject—what the sentence is about—and a predicate—what is being said about the subject. On occasion, the minimal sentence can be effective: it is focused and emphatic. Generally, however, it will be embedded in a more complicated structure in which modifying words, phrases, and clauses will limit the meaning of each core.

Adding Word, Phrase, and Clause Modifiers

Examine the following sentences. Note that the second expands the subject and predicate of the first by adding modifying words and phrases.

> Politicians squabbled.

> The local politicians squabbled over the proposed rule to limit debate in the City Council.

A modifier limits or qualifies a word or group of words; it adds precision by restricting meaning. The skeleton sentence "Politicians squabbled," for example, tells little of the politicians or of the nature of their disagreement. But when a word modifier is added to the subject and several phrase modifiers to the predicate, you learn a good deal more about who these politicians were and what they were arguing about. Moreover, this expanded sentence by no means exhausts the possibilities. You can, for example, add a modifying clause at the beginning of the sentence:

> *As soon as the election was over,* the local politicians squabbled over a proposed rule to limit debate in the City Council.

You can modify the subject further by adding a noun phrase:

> As soon as the election was over, the local politicians, *a group divided by sharp political differences,* squabbled over a proposed rule to limit debate in the City Council.

You can modify the predicate further by adding additional prepositional phrases:

> As soon as the election was over, the local politicians, a group divided by sharp political differences, squabbled *into the wee hours of the morning* over the proposed rule to limit debate in the City Council.

and by adding an adverb:

> As soon as the election was over, the local politicians, a group divided by sharp political differences, squabbled *vehemently* into the wee hours of the morning over the proposed rule to limit debate in the City Council.

Degree of sentence expansion depends, of course, on purpose and context. What this example shows is that modifying words, phrases, and clauses are useful: by providing additional information, they can make a statement more precise and less apt to be misunderstood.

FOLLOW-UP ACTIVITY

Expand the subject and predicate of each of the following sentences by using word, phrase, and clause modifiers.

1. The dogs barked.
2. The family fled.
3. War broke out.
4. The girl smiled.
5. Cars crashed.

Coordination

Another way to expand the basic English sentence is to add coordinate elements. These elements are called coordinate because they share the same grammatical value: a coordinate of a noun is a noun; a coordinate of an adjective is an adjective, and so on. Following are the basic patterns expanded to include an additional coordinate element:

> The politicians and townspeople squabbled.
> *(subject expanded with coordinate nouns)*
>
> Tom scraped and washed the dishes.
> *(predicate expanded with coordinate verbs)*
>
> *Tom washed the dishes and glassware.*
> *(direct object expanded with coordinate nouns)*
>
> The child is gifted and well-mannered.
> *(predicate adjective expanded with coordinate adjectives)*
>
> Mr. Brown is a grocer and part-time musician.
> *(predicate noun expanded with coordinate nouns)*

Note that in the preceding examples the coordinate elements are joined by the coordinating conjunction *and.* Other conjunctions that join coordinate elements are *but, for, nor, or, yet,* and *so.*

Coordination can be used to expand words, phrases, and clauses. It can also be used to join sentences.

Tempers flared. Fights broke out.
Tempers flared, *and* fights broke out.

The girls came. They stayed only a few minutes.
The girls came, *but* they stayed only a few minutes.

You can join the crowd and feel a part of things. You can stay away and feel isolated.
You can join the crowd and feel a part of things, *or* you can stay away and feel isolated.

She spoke fluent French. She failed to gain the support of the French community.
She spoke fluent French, *yet* she failed to gain the support of the French community.

He did not enjoy their endless chatter. He did not relish their childish games.
He did not enjoy their endless chatter, *nor* did he relish their childish games.

Employers organized. Workers did the same.
Employers organized, *so* workers did the same.

These examples illustrate that coordinating conjunctions join clauses of equal weight and emphasis. They announce equivalence: one idea is as important as the other. They also announce that each clause is grammatically complete and could stand alone if you removed the coordinating conjunction and substituted a period for the comma:

Tempers flared. Fights broke out.

The girls came. They stayed only a few minutes.

To do so, however, runs the risk of blurring connections between ideas. In the first example, removing the conjunction *and* eliminates an important causal connection between the two clauses. In the second, deleting *but* eliminates the idea of contrast.

Subordination

Subordination can also be used to expand a sentence. Note that the word *subordination* contains the prefix *sub,* meaning that the subordinate element is secondary to or dependent on a primary element. For the purposes of sentence expansion, subordination means that a primary sentence can be changed into a secondary clause or phrase and embedded in another sentence. Take, for example, these two basic sentences:

She broke the window. She is an impulsive person.

To make explicit the implied relationship between these two primary clauses, you would add the subordinating conjunction *because* to the second sentence and then attach the revised structure to the first sentence as a dependent element. The expanded sentence would then read:

She broke the window because she is an impulsive person.

Whenever a subordinating conjunction is used, it signals rank or hierarchy; one idea is subordinate to, or of lesser importance than, another. As a result, the clause in which it appears is grammatically dependent on the main clause.

If John does well in the semifinals, he is likely to win an athletic scholarship.

After John did well in the semifinals, he won an athletic scholarship.

Because John did well in the semifinals, he won an athletic scholarship.

Even though John did well in the semifinals, he failed to win an athletic scholarship.

Each of these sentences begins with a subordinate clause which is grammatically dependent. If you were to insert a period where the comma appears and so divide each sentence into two, you would find that the meaning of the initial clause would be unfinished. It provides important information, to be sure, but it is information that needs to be clarified by the main clause.

As you can see in the preceding examples, subordinating conjunctions announce logical relationships between dependent and independent clauses. These relationships are of different kinds. In the first sentence the subordinating conjunction *if* expresses the relationship of *condition:* it tells under what circumstances John will win the scholarship. In the second sentence, the subordinating conjunction *after* expresses a *time* relationship: it tells us that one event followed another. In the third sentence, the subordinating conjunction *because* establishes *cause* or *reason:* it tells *why* John won the scholarship. In the fourth sentence, the subordinating phrase *even though* expresses *contrast;* it demonstrates that one event or condition conflicts or contrasts with another.

FOLLOW-UP ACTIVITY

Often expanded sentences will include both subordinate and coordinate clauses, as well as word and phrase modifiers. Examine the following student sentences and point out the basic subject and predicate in the independent clause or clauses of each. Then identify the various means the writers have used to expand each element.

1. If the company were to dispose of hazardous wastes at only half of the new sites, it would have to insure itself for about $220 million, about 4.6 percent of its total equity, and such insurance would be very hard to get.

2. Because he had suffered intense privation during the war, his beard had turned silvery white prematurely, but its color was deceiving, for he was no decrepit old man by any means.

3. A few hours after preparing a large Christmas meal, she gave birth, and she decided soon after that the baby would be baptized on Easter Sunday.

4. When the Rangers score, the cheers cascade from the green seats to the ice, but when they let an opponent slip in behind the defense, Bronx raspberries vibrate from the rafters.

5. Meals were always prompt at my grandmother's house, and they followed the same pattern whether or not she had guests.

6. Whenever a fig tree appeared to be withering, people would gather in a mass gesture of concern, and they would kneel in reverence, praying for recovery.

PARALLEL STRUCTURE

To expand the basic sentence, you can also use parallel structure. In parallel structure, two or more coordinate elements are arranged in similar coordinate structures. Parallelism can be applied to elements of any grammatical value, as the following student sentences illustrate:

A series of nouns

Champagne,
hors d'oeuvres,
and canapes were served at the party.

A series of adjectives

John is flamboyant,
impulsive,
and rambunctious.

A series of infinitive phrases

The intricately designed chairs beckon you
to come in,
to sit in their perfect curves,
to run your hands over their smooth surface.

A series of subordinate clauses

According to today's patient, the friendly,
dependable family doctor who once visited the
home has been replaced by a cold, callous
physician, a person who requires office visits
in lieu of home visits,
who rarely takes the time to
explain an ailment,
who often will keep a patient
waiting for hours.

A series of verbs

He travels all over the region,
goes fishing and, occasionally, hunting,
does some farm work,
and even cuts and splits wood for the fireplace.

Parallel structure requires that nouns be paired with nouns, adjectives with adjectives, clauses with clauses, infinitives with infinitives, and so on. Forgetting this important rule results in a break in parallelism. Note, for example, how the italicized element in the following student sentences introduces a grammatical form different from the others in the series:

The modern ball, on the other hand, is smooth, light, and *bounces very* easily. *(The sentence pairs two coordinate adjectives with a verb plus modifier. Revised to correct the faulty parallelism, the sentence might read: "The modern ball, on the other hand, is smooth, light, and bouncy.")*

The outstanding features of this auto are its spaciousness, its economy, and it is virtually maintenance free. *(The sentence pairs a clause with two coordinate nouns. Revised to correct the faulty parallelism, the sentence might read: "The outstanding features of this automobile are its spaciousness, its economy, and its reliability.)*

Correlative constructions such as *both . . . and, either . . . or, neither . . . nor, not only . . . but also* equally require parallel grammatical forms, as in the following examples:

In spite of the extraordinary expense, the manager neither asked permission nor even informed the company of the course he had taken. *(The correlative construction "neither . . . nor" requires the parallel verbs "asked . . . informed.")*

He was both headstrong and vain, unable to control either his temper or his boundless lust for power.
(This sentence has two correlative constructions: "both . . . and" used with parallel adjectives; and "either . . . or" used with parallel nouns.)

In the following two student sentences, the writers have neglected to use parallel structure in their correlative constructions:

```
I feel I should have the option of turning to my classical
music stations, since I can't afford either a stereo or to go
to concerts every night.
```
(A noun, [stereo], is paired with an infinitive [to go] within the "either . . . or" construction. Revised to correct faulty parallelism, the sentence reads: "I feel I should have the option of turning to my classical music stations, since I can't afford either a stereo or tickets for nightly concerts."

```
These shows are both interesting and provide little-known
facts about their subject.
```
(In this sentence an adjective, [interesting,] is paired with a verb, [provide,] within the "both . . . and" construction. Revised to correct the faulty parallelism, the sentence might read: "These shows are both interesting and informative.")

THE USES OF PARALLELISM

Once you have mastered the grammatical requirements of parallel structure, you will find it an effective way to expand your sentences and to give them sophistication and polish. To do both, keep in mind that parallelism can be used for different purposes. One of its uses is *to connect similar ideas,* as in the following sentence where the writer constructs a series of prepositional phrases to outline the multiple functions of vehicles:

> Vehicles are able to transport men by unprecedented speed over and beneath the surface of the earth, on or below the ocean waves, through the air, and even to the moon and planets.
>
> —Jeffrey Marsh, "Engineers and Society,"
> *Commentary*

Parallelism can also be used to *specify a general word.* In the following sentence, note how the noun series following the colon helps to define the general word *aristocracy* introduced in the opening clause:

> It lacks all the essential characteristics of a true aristocracy: a clean tradition, culture, public spirit, honesty, honor, courage—above all, courage.
>
> —H. L. Mencken, "A Glance Ahead,"
> in *The Vintage Mencken*

Coordinate nouns can also provide *lower-level* descriptive detail, as in the following student example where the general word *goodies* in the main clause is amplified and expanded in the noun series:

We invariably came back from our walks with armloads of goodies: buckets of plums, muscadines, strawberries or blackberries, shocks of broomstraw, holly and evergreen for Christmas decorations, and pocketfuls of hazelnuts, chestnuts, or walnuts.

The following student sentences represent the same principle, but this time the writers have added considerable modification to expand each noun within the series:

Sentence A

```
Trays and trays of Italian delicacies crowd every counter: Rum
babas swimming in deep pools of rum; freshly deep-fat fried
San Guiseppe fritters flavored with lemon and richly sprinkled
with confectioner's sugar; zabaglione cream puffs filled to
overflowing with golden yellow custard or whipped cream
flavored with Marsala wine; cialde, a rolled waffle stuffed
with chocolate custard, lemon custard, or cheese custard;
tarts made from fresh ricotta cheese flavored with bits of
lemon rind and candied citron; zeppole, a fragrant farina
pastry with a hint of Marsala, shaped in a ball, deep-fat
fried to a golden brown and sprinkled with confectioner's
sugar; cannolli, a deep brown, crunchy rolled pastry shell
stuffed with a creamy ricotta cheese filling generously laced
with bits of chopped pistachio, diced chocolate, and candied
fruits.
```

Sentence B

```
Before me stood a vast array of antique cars:  Packards, long
and wide, sporting interior windshields between front and back
seats; ancient Cadillacs adorned with brass headlights and
radiators that had been polished to glow like golden jewels;
Auburns and Dusenburgs, their huge, ribbed chrome exhaust
pipes sticking out from long hoods covering polished U-12
engines; gigantic Henderson motorcycles, with four cylinder
in-line engines powerful enough to propel a small car; and
even an 1896 Hogenlocker, looking more like a sewing-machine-
powered baby buggy than an automobile.
```

Another way to use parallelism to specify a general word is to set off lower-level coordinate material with dashes.

Sentence A

The clutter behind him in the room—the Old-fashioned glass with its corrupt dregs, the choked ashtray balanced on the easy-chair arm, the rumpled rug, the floppy stacks of slippery newspapers, the kid's toys here and there broken and stuck and jammed, a leg off a doll and a piece of bent cardboard that went with some breakfast-box cutout, the rolls of fuzz under the radiators, the continual crisscrossing mess—clings to his back like a tightening net.

—John Updike, *Rabbit, Run*

Sentence B

```
Many creatures--frail, solitary sandpipers, nervous herons,
crayfish hiding until nightfall in their wet burrows, muskrats
feeding upon cattail roots and pickerelweed leaves--inhabited
the narrow black strip of shoreline which encircled the pond.
```
—Student sentence

To specify a general word, you can also use a series of parallel clauses. Note in the following student sentence how the word *cafe* becomes increasingly specific as the writer introduces detail in parallel clauses, each of which begins with a synonym for the cafe *(a building, a place, a place)*.

Sentence C

```
There was also Mar Yu's cafe, a neat brick building where no
food was served; a place teenagers rented, pooling quarters
and dimes to gather the needed five dollars to rent it for a
night of dancing; a place traveling evangelists hired for
revivals, exhorting us to forsake our sinful ways.
```

Parallelism can also *suggest continuous movement* when the predicate verb is compounded. The effect of such a strategy is to compress time, giving the sense of a single action. Observe these student sentences:

Sentence A

```
She reached to the low, cloth-covered table in front of her,
slowly picked up a heavy silver coffee pot, centered a tiny
china cup under its spout, and filled it with steaming coffee.
```

Sentence B

```
Upon entering the classroom, he would quickly flop into his
desk chair, carelessly toss his briefcase atop a mound of
books and papers covering his desk, and then frantically
search for his yellow legal pad--his memory, in reality--
shoved into his bottom desk drawer between yesterday's stale
ham sandwich and today's newspaper.
```

The effect of the following clause series is much the same:

Sentence C

```
Almost without warning, the tiller was out of my hand, the
sail was filling with water rather than air, the deck was
perpendicular to the sea, and I was in the water.
```

A series of parallel predicate verbs can also *connect a series of actions not restricted to a specific moment*. Note these student sentences:

Sentence A	The troop helped adults get out the vote, prepared lists of safety rules for the troop meeting place, displayed collections of drawings and paintings, made pillow covers, discussed why active games and sports were important to health, and prepared skits showing how to welcome a girl from another country into the community.
Sentence B	The manufacturer must maintain sanitation and health standards, create interest in his product, develop new markets, and expand his company in order to remain competitive in the industry.

Parallelism can also *organize the details that support a general statment*. Again, observe these student sentences:

Sentence A	The circus performers were a daring lot: Collin Murphy walked the highwire blindfolded and without a balancing pole; Elvin Baile ran on the outside of a giant wheel (fittingly called the wheel of death) eighty feet in the air; and Tito Giona threw doubles, triples, and even a quad (four complete revolutions) to his catcher on the flying trapeze.
Sentence B	All was right with the world it seemed to us, despite evidence to the contrary: dirty slush, scattered garbage, and broken glass littered the desolate street; winos and junkies huddled here and there in sheltered alleyways; distant sirens wailed forebodingly.

In the following example, the writer has not only constructed parallel clauses to support a generalization but has used the same word at the beginning of each clause. This strategy is called *anaphora*. Note how it emphasizes the details that support the generalization.

Sentence C	The neighborhood is antiseptic: no spreading maples or oaks rise above the houses; no birds perch on the roofs; no garbage cans line the curb; no sidewalks bear the chalky traces of past hopscotch games.

FOLLOW-UP ACTIVITIES

1. Point out the parallel coordinate elements in the following student sentences.

    a.   Bleachers are filled with all types of people: children playing tag under the wooden seats, teenagers chattering while eagerly watching the time clock countdown, adults scanning the field to find their son (the football player) warming up with the rest of the team.

b. Jeans accent the gentle curves of the hips, the fullness of the buttocks, the strength and gradual taper of the legs.

c. From nails hammered into the lumber hang household items ranging from mirrors to belts, from cowboy hats to show bridles, from baling twine to garden hose, from makeshift clotheslines to tennis shoes.

d. She arrives at church at least a half hour before the organ prelude, marches her mammoth frame to the front pew, struggles out of her black, voile coat, plops down on the end seat so that her back is against the arm rest, and folds her coat neatly on the space next to the pew back.

e. A water supply gets contaminated when waste materials on or in the ground are dissolved by rain and are either carried over the ground by runoff (to eventually reach streams) or are carried down to the groundwater system by percolation.

f. His blue eyes blazed with determination to suffocate any weed strangling his marigolds, to murder any grub worm invading his tomatoes, to scourge any blight sabotaging his corn.

g. Her wispy gray hair straying from its strict Grecian knot, her pure white brow, her patrician nose and thin, sensitive mouth often gave strangers a false impression of impracticality or unworldliness.

h. On the field, he kicks the hard rubber ball, dribbles it, steals it from between his playmates' legs, and tackles pitilessly, aiming at being the first to score.

i. In contrast, my mother's old neighborhood was always teeming with activity: children playing stick ball in the streets, senior citizens sitting in beach chairs along the curb, neighbors shouting from one balcony to another.

j. The pointed sloping figures of her account books were not only aesthetically pleasing but accurate as well.

2. Compose a sentence using parallel structure to support a general word or a generalization. Compose another sentence using parallel structure to summarize a series of actions or to establish a sense of continuous movement.

THE PERIODIC SENTENCE

The periodic sentence is also an effective method of sentence expansion. A periodic sentence is constructed so that the main clause appears at the end, preceded by subordinate or modifying elements. It is the reverse of the loose sentence, which starts with the main clause and ends with the subordinate elements.

Loose sentence:

>   (main clause)   (subordinate clause)
> **She looked at him disdainfully when he offered to light her cigarette.**

Periodic sentence:

>   (subordinate clause)   (main clause)
> **When he offered to light her cigarette, she looked at him disdainfully.**

If you said the periodic sentence aloud, you would probably stress the final clause because the order of such a sentence is climactic: it saves its main point for the end. This delay can be a powerful means to emphasize a point, especially if the writer builds suspense by compounding the introductory subordinate elements. At times, these introductory elements may rapidly set forth the particulars of an argument whose significance emerges only at the end of the sentence. The following periodic sentence, for example, compounds four parallel subordinate clauses (headed by the adverb *when*) to outline current deficiencies in the teaching profession, and then shifts to the emphatic main clause to explain their meaning:

> When a profession reinforces mediocrity through union-labor tactics and seniority rule; when school boards respond to city budget cuts by reducing classroom staff; when society continues to demand a cafeteria-style list of social, cultural and medical services from the schools, and when teachers shy away from healthy competition and academic evaluation, is it any wonder that none of my graduating honor students is seeking a career in education?
> —Stephanie H. Dahl, "Crisis in the Classroom," *Newsweek*

In the hands of skilled writers, the grammatical structure of the periodic sentence can directly reflect the theme or idea of the sentence, resulting in what Virginia Tufte calls a *syntactic symbol,* or a sentence organized so that "the very act of reading suggests some aspect of what the sentence names or describes." If you remember that the periodic sentence relies on delay of the main idea, you can see how Martin Luther King, Jr. uses this syntax in the following sentence to question the patience urged upon blacks in quest of their civil rights. The waiting that blacks are advised to practice becomes the waiting that readers must themselves do as they process a sentence that suspends its main thought until the end.

Perhaps it is easy for those who have never felt the stinging darts of segregation to say, "Wait." But when you have seen vicious mobs lynch your mothers and fathers at will and drown your sisters and brothers at whim; when you have seen hate-filled policemen curse, kick, and even kill your black brothers and sisters; when you see the vast majority of your twenty million Negro brothers smothering in an airtight cage of poverty in the midst of an affluent society; when you suddenly find your tongue twisted and your speech stammering as you seek to explain to your six-year-old daughter why she can't go to the public amusement park that has just been advertised on television, and see tears welling up in her eyes when she is told that Funtown is closed to colored children, and see ominous clouds of inferiority begin to form in her little mental sky, and see her beginning to distort her personality by developing an unconscious bitterness toward white people; when you have to concoct an answer for a five-year-old son who is asking: "Daddy, why do white people treat colored people so mean?"; when you take a cross-country drive and find it necessary to sleep night after night in the uncomfortable corners of your automobile because no motel will accept you; when you are humiliated day in and day out by nagging signs reading "white" and "colored"; when your first name becomes "nigger" and your middle name becomes "boy" (however old you are) and your last name becomes "John," and your wife and mother are never given the respected title "Mrs."; when you are harried by day and haunted by night by the fact that you are a Negro, living constantly at tiptoe stance, never quite knowing what to expect next, and are plagued with inner fears and outer resentments; when you are forever fighting a degenerating sense of "nobodiness"—then you will understand why we find it difficult to wait.

—"Letter from Birmingham Jail,"
in *Why We Can't Wait*

The periodic sentence can also be used in description to blend idea and form. In the following sentence, the verb *swells* used in the main clause to characterize a person is also true of the sentence, which swells as the writer piles prepositional phrase upon prepositional phrase to document the dominant quality of the person being described.

Over his lavendar collar, crushed upon a purple necktie, held by a diamond hoop: over his ammunition belt of tooled leather worked in silver, buckled cruelly around his gasping middle: over the tops of his glossy yellow shoes Braggioni swells with ominous ripeness, his mauve silk hose stretched taut, his ankles bound with the stout leather thongs of his shoes.

—Katherine Anne Porter, "Flowering Judas,"
in *Flowering Judas and Other Stories.*

FOLLOW-UP ACTIVITY

Though the periodic sentence is a somewhat formal structure that should be used infrequently, you will find that practice in its construction will increase your control of sentence syntax and rhythm. Following are some periodic sentences students have written. Compose similar ones, taking care to insert the required punctuation. When you have finished, share your sentences with others in the class.

Sentence A

> When you've been rudely roused from your sleep to stand shivering your turn at the latrine; when you've marched all day in the blistering sun with fifty pounds of gear on your back; when you've eaten a dinner of dehydrated mush mixed with water, then you will know what it means to serve in the U.S. Army.

Sentence B

> Once you have heard the agonizing squeal of a rabbit as a wolf snaps its neck or watched a young calf slowly gasp for the last time; once you have seen life ebb from a foal as it struggles desperately for the milk it cannot swallow, then you will know the bitterness of death.

Sentence C

> During the growing season, when the ripened vegetables gleam in the sunlight, and when the corn, wheat and pastures have turned a deep shade of green, the farm looks its best.

Sentence D

> To go out when you want and to stay out as late as you want, not having to answer to anyone; to speak out on any issue without fear of reprisal; to have friends of your own choosing, however questionable their reputations—this is to know freedom from a parent's shadow.

Sentence E

> To crouch in a cramped, leaky boat, fingers aching from hours of trolling; to fight surging whitecaps while the wind whips your face; to writhe each time your collar brushes your sunburned neck and then to watch helplessly as your prey fights clear of your bait—this is to know the agony of fishing.

ANTITHESIS

If you are working with contrasting ideas, you will find the antithetical sentence a good way to sharpen and clarify the relationship between opposing elements. In antithesis, contrasting ideas are juxtaposed or set side by side in balanced or parallel structures. Here is an example of an antithetical sentence written by a student:

> Blood flows more easily and quickly through veins that are _relaxed_ and _open_ than through those that are _tense_ and _constricted_.

In this sentence, one set of paired adjectives is contrasted with another. The structure is balanced: *relaxed* is balanced by *tense* and *open* is balanced by *constricted.*

In the following student example, the coordinate predicate adjectives in the first clause are balanced by their contrasting equivalents in the second clause:

```
The entire nature of the apple is forthright, firm, assertive;
the pear is subtle, yielding, timid.
```

Note that to maintain parallelism of idea as well as of grammar, the writer carefully arranges the second series of adjectives to match the order of the first series:

Clause 1		Clause 2
forthright	vs.	subtle
firm	vs.	yielding
assertive	vs.	timid

In the next student sentence, the second clause is balanced against the first to emphasize contrast. Note the parallelism of the antithetical elements: *cook* is paired with its opposite *non-cook;* and *complete with Cuisinart* is paired with its opposite *complete with Craig Claiborne's guide:*

```
Merri has since gone on to become a gourmet cook, complete
with Cuisinart; while I have become a non-cook, complete with
Craig Claiborne's guide to New York restaurants.
```

Antithetical clauses can gain emphasis when the introductory element of each clause is repeated. In the following student sentence, contrast is heightened by the repetition of the prepositional phrase *to the people* at the beginning of each clause:

To the people of China, acupuncture is a long-established tradition; to the people of the United States, it has only recently gained recognition.

In the following sentence, contradictory qualities of character are emphasized by parallel noun phrases, each of which balances one feature of personality against its opposite. Such a structure magnifies and underscores contrasting elements, giving them added weight and substance and intensifying the opposition between them:

Fulbright is, indeed, a complicated man, a man of many contradictions—a searing sarcasm and a courtly manner; long digressions on points that interest him; and yet impatience and even condescension toward those whom he considers dim; intense curiosity and a low boredom threshold; becoming modesty and a peacock's pride; a deep- and wide-ranging intellect and yet a peevish turn; . . .

fierce bursts of energy and periods of moodiness bordering on depression;
. . . . And, finally, both arrogance and self-doubt.

> —Daniel Yergin, "Fulbright's Last Frustration,"
> *New York Times Magazine.*

The antithetical clauses in the following sentence emphasize the difference between the past and the present. A pattern such as this is a succinct way to capture historical differences ("then and now"). Note how the parallelism of repeated elements ("they were once . . . they are now") magnifies distinctions and keeps the contrast firmly in the reader's mind:

> It is said they were once slaves, they are now free; they were once subject, they are now sovereigns; they were once outside ·of all American institutions, they are now inside of all and are a recognized part of the whole American people.
>
> > —Frederick Douglass, "Address to the People
> > of the United States," in *The Life and
> > Writings of Frederick Douglass*

Another way to construct an antithetical sentence is to use different forms of the same word, as in the following sentence where *natural* is contrasted to *unnatural, shame* to *shameful.* The formal name for the repetition of words derived from the same root is *polyptoton:*

> To live is to grow old. It is a natural process, not an unnatural disaster. To be handicapped in some way may be a shame—but it is not shameful.
>
> > —Editorial, *New York Times.*

FOLLOW-UP ACTIVITIES

1. Write a sentence about a person you know well who exhibits contradictory behavior. Put the idea of contradiction in your base clause and then document the contrast in parallel phrases or clauses.
2. Try a "then and now" sentence to illustrate changes in clothing styles, cars, dating patterns, or any other subject.
3. Compose sentences similar to the student-written sentences above that employ antithesis.

THE FREE MODIFIER

The free modifier is another option that will help you expand your sentences, especially when you want to add narrative or descriptive detail. This type of modifier is called *free* because it can usually be moved to different positions in the sentence.

It can appear at the beginning of the sentence:

Drifting and soaring with the air currents, pelicans fill the sky.

It can appear at the end of the sentence:

Pelicans fill the sky, *drifting and soaring with the air currents.*

It can be embedded between the subject and the predicate:

Pelicans, *drifting and soaring with the air currents,* fill the sky.

The preceding sentences can be divided into two parts: a base clause and a free modifier. For example:

(base clause)   (free modifier)
Pelicans fill the sky, drifting and soaring with the air currents.

Note that the base clause is grammatically complete: it contains a subject (*pelicans*) and a main verb plus object (*fill the sky*).

Within this structure, it is possible, of course, to add additional modifying detail. You can, for example, expand the base clause by adding adjectives:

Snowy Canadian pelicans fill the darkened sky.

Or you can add adjectives plus a prepositional phrase:

The snowy Canadian pelicans of the island fill the darkened sky.

Unlike the free modifier, however, these modifiers are *bound,* that is, their positions are fixed in the sentence. Try moving them about, and you will find the clause confusing. A sentence which read "Of the island the pelicans snowy Canadian fill the sky darkened" would leave you mystified.

Free and bound modifiers, then, differ in two important ways:

Free modifier:

1. Can often be placed before, after, or within the base clause.

2. Is usually set off from the base clause by punctuation (usually with a comma or, if it is embedded between the subject and predicate, with two commas).

Bound modifier:

1. Occupies a fixed position.

2. Is not set off by punctuation.

Learning to use free modifiers will not only give you added flexibility in constructing your sentences but will help you make an image vivid and precise. Note, for example, how the student whose sentence was adapted to illustrate the free modifier deftly uses it to suggest the swift and continuous motion of the pelicans:

> In search of unsuspecting fish, pelicans fill the sky,
> drifting and soaring with the air currents. Precisely
> calculating the exact second at which to dive, they fold back
> their strong wings and descend with blinding speed, breaking
> the surface of the water and zooming aloft with another catch
> even before the splash has settled.

FOLLOW-UP ACTIVITY

Identify the free and bound modifiers in the following student sentences. Point out the base clause in each. Try moving the free modifiers to other positions in the sentence. Do some positions seem better than others? Explain.

1. Her hands, twisted and knotted from age, hard work, and arthritis, slithered toward me.

2. Like a great aluminum buzzard, it dropped out of the sky, skimming over the last yards of grass before skipping to a halt near the end of the runway.

3. To my astonishment, Herr House once pranced around the room, flapping his flabby arms and giggling to himself as he sang an Italian opera.

4. Marie sits quietly, her charcoal pencil poised delicately in her hand, her sketch pad propped on her crossed legs.

5. Slowly, she trudged up the hill, her hands clasped behind her back.

THE CUMULATIVE SENTENCE

Understanding the structure of the cumulative sentence will add to your skill in constructing free modifiers. The cumulative sentence consists of a base clause followed by one or more free modifiers. It moves from whole to parts, or from general to specific: the base clause states a general or abstract idea which the free modifiers then specify. As a result, a sentence of this kind contains several levels of generality, the most general being the base clause, the least general, the free modifiers. We can see this movement in the following student sentence:

```
1    Geiser serves his regular customers with special care,
  2      scraping the tops of steaks for those who insist on it,
  2      handing free frankfurters to the little tikes,
  2      adding an extra quarter pound of sausage to the order.
```

In this sentence, the base clause contains the general phrase *with special care,* telling how the shopkeeper serves his customers. Were the sentence to end here, a good deal would be lost, since we would know nothing of what this special care entailed. With the free modifiers, however, the writer specifies meaning, so that we come to see what particular actions the shopkeeper takes to satisfy his regular customers. The general part of the sentence, then, is the level 1 base clause, which is made specific in the second-level free modifiers, each of which is numbered 2 because each is parallel to the other: each begins with an *-ing* word which specifies the meaning of *special care.*

Sometimes, the sequential order of events will require that a second-level free modifier precede the base clause, as in the following example:

```
  2      Careening out of the lot,
1    the car rumbled down the deserted alley,
  2      weaving from side to side.
```

Here *Careening out of the lot* appears before the base clause because it describes an action that comes before the event mentioned in the base clause: the car must leave the lot before it can enter the alley.

Free modifiers may also be arranged to achieve a particular effect. In the following sentence the student writer places all the free modifiers before the main clause in order to give the clause special emphasis:

```
  2      Their hair mussed,
  2      their clothes wrinkled,
  2      their eyes dull and half-shut,
1    they had the look of the recently sick.
```

The Verb Phrase

The verb phrase is a type of free modifier frequently used in narrative and descriptive writing. It consists either of a present participle (words ending in *-ing*) or a past participle (words ending in *-ed, -d, -en, -n*) and the accompanying complements or modifiers.

The present participle verb phrase

```
1    The elephant moved with little more than turtle-speed from one end of
     the enclosure to the other,
  2      *waving* a weak trunk,
  2      and *stirring* less dust than a prairie dog.
```

Here the free modifiers consist of two verb phrases, each headed by a present participle (*waving* and *stirring*) and each following the base clause.

The past participle verb phrase

> 2   Rusted and misshapen,
> 1   the mattress spring capping the pile of garbage swayed precariously with each gust of wind.

In this example, the verb phrase is headed by two coordinate past participles (*rusted* and *misshapen*) which precede the base clause.

FOLLOW-UP ACTIVITY

Add several verb phrases to the following sentences, taking care to insert the required punctuation. Try experimenting with both present and past participles. You may also want to place your verb phrases in different positions to see what effects you achieve. Example:

> Uncle Avery drummed his thick sausage fingers on the floor.
> (*Base clause*)

> *Spying Sam the cat curled up on the hearth,* Uncle Avery drummed his thick sausage fingers on the floor, *luring the cat from his safe position.*
> (*Base clause with two free verb phrases*)

1. Roberta handled the snake gingerly.
2. The old man gently lifted his great-granddaughter to his chest.
3. The storm waves thundered against the rocks.
4. Timidly, the nervous job seeker sidled into line.
5. The tired woman leaned against the railing.
6. Mrs. Brown ran her house with efficiency and economy.
7. My grandmother dined out rarely.
8. These soldiers will march away and go through the motions of combat.
9. I started to explore the barn.
10. He threw back his head and laughed shrilly.

The Free Absolute Phrase

Much like an independent clause, an absolute phrase consists of a subject and predicate. It differs, however, in that its predicate lacks a main verb. To change a complete sentence into an absolute, you can either delete a form of the verb *to be*, (*is, are, was, were*), or you can change the main verb into a present participle (an *-ing* word). You can see how absolutes are formed when the following sentences are combined:

She limped toward the door. Her hands were trembling.
She limped toward the door, her hands trembling.

Combining the two sentences changes the second sentence into an absolute because the verb *to be* (*were*) has been deleted. Though the absolute still has a subject (*hands*) and a predicate (*trembling*), it is no longer an independent clause.

Here is another example:

The single students hang wildly patterned curtains in the window. Their bold, orange stripes, black and red checkerboards, and big, yellow sunflowers dazzle the eyes of the passersby.

The single students hang wildly patterned curtains in the window, their bold, orange stripes, black and red checkerboards, and big, yellow sunflowers dazzling the eyes of the passersby.

When the two sentences are combined, the second sentence becomes an absolute because its original main verb *dazzles* has been changed into the present participle *dazzling*.

Note the difference between the free absolute phrase and the free verb phrase:

The woman tottered down the stairs, her body swaying from side to side.
(*Base clause plus free absolute phrase.*)

The woman tottered down the stairs, swaying from side to side.
(*Base clause plus free verb phrase.*)

Examining both sentences, you can see that the present participle *swaying* functions differently in each sentence. When it appears as part of the free absolute phrase, it functions as the predicate following the subject "body." When it appears as a verb phrase, it functions as the first word of the phrase.

FOLLOW-UP ACTIVITIES

1. The following example illustrates how a group of sentences can be combined into a single sentence composed of a base clause and free absolute phrases. What words and punctuation have been deleted in the revised sentence? What punctuation has been added? How many absolutes has the writer used? Point out the subject and predicate of each absolute.

The ruins of the Catholic cathedral still stood. Its walls were caved in and blackened by fire. Its iron girders were exposed to the sky.

The ruins of the Catholic cathedral still stood, its walls caved in and blackened by fire, its iron girders exposed to the sky.

2. Add at least one free absolute phrase to each of the following sentences.

    a. As the light turned green, he drove away.
    b. By late afternoon, he reached the top of the mountain.
    c. Hé paused outside the Guidance Office.
    d. He yanked at the jammed door.
    e. The girl sat at the edge of the sandbox.
    f. He caught the ball with his left hand.
    g. She moved steadily between the stove and the refrigerator.
    h. I ducked my head and walked bent over.
    i. He slid into third.
    j. Traffic inched along in just one lane.

The relationship of absolutes to the base clause. Absolutes are usually related to nouns in the base clause. A base clause, however, may have more than one noun, as in: "The waves beat furiously against the house." The writer who wishes to attach an absolute free modifier to a base clause of this kind has the choice of which noun to modify. If she chooses *waves,* her sentence might read, "The waves beat furiously against the house, their roar a warning that nature still had the upper hand." If, however, she selects *house,* the absolute would take a different turn: "The waves beat furiously against the house, its walls shuddering with each attack."

To show how absolutes can modify different nouns in the base clause, Martha Solomon has constructed the following set of sentences:

1. Randy gave Ruby an engagement ring, his eyes sparkling with pride.

2. Randy gave Ruby an engagement ring, her face revealing her surprise.

3. Randy gave Ruby an engagement ring, its tiny diamond shining brightly.

4. The committee elected Tom president, its members happy to have the decision over.

5. The committee elected Tom president, the office being the most prestigious it could bestow.

6. The girls painted the barn red, their hands and arms becoming splattered with paint.

7. The girls painted the barn red, its dried boards soaking up enormous quantities of paint.

Each of the following base clauses contains two nouns. Construct two sentences with free absolutes for each, one modifying the first noun, the other, the second. Be sure your absolutes contain a subject and a predicate.

1. The house was surrounded by a brick wall.
2. Flowers lined the walk.
3. The speaker congratulated each graduate.
4. Their friends were housed in a dormitory.
5. A stereo system sat atop a table.

The position of the free absolute phrase.   Like the free verb phrase, the absolute can appear in different positions in the sentence. Note these three sentences by Ernest Hemingway, all from his story "Big Two-Hearted River."

> *His mouth dry, his heart down,* Nick reeled in.
> (Absolutes placed *before* the base clause.)

> Nick climbed out onto the meadow and stood, *water running down his trousers and out of his shoes, his shoes squlchy.*
> (Absolutes placed *after* the base clause.)

> He took the sack off, over his head, *the trout flopping as it came out of water,* and hung it so the trout were deep in the water.
> (Absolute *embedded* between the first and second predicate verb.)

Using Verb Phrases and Absolutes

The verb phrase and the absolute have been discussed separately in order to clarify the structure of each. In actual practice, however, skilled writers will often give their sentences density and texture by using both the free verb phrase and the free absolute phrase in a single sentence. Following are two student examples:

> (verb phrase)
> *Sitting in front of his new TV,* he would wait patiently,

> (absolute phrase)
> *his feet propped up on worn-out, corduroy-covered pillows,*

> (absolute phrase)
> *his head leaning against the back of the sofa.*

> Each week for two full hours, this grotesque little creature shuffled

> (verb phrase)   (absolute phrase)
> around his classroom, *waving his hands furiously, his words showering us like pelting rain.*

Combine the following sentences. The first sentence of each of the following groups will be the base clause (and will remain unchanged), while the others can be changed into verb phrases or absolutes. Experiment with placing your verb phrases and absolutes in different positions. See also if you can use both verb phrases and absolutes in a single sentence.

Example:

He was a man in slow motion. He was quivering and pushing. He was straining every muscle to do as he was told. His stubby black oxfords, scuffed and dusty but in good condition, slid an inch at a time.

Quivering and pushing, he was a man in slow motion, straining every muscle to do as he was told, his stubby black oxfords, scuffed and dusty but in good condition, sliding an inch at a time.

1. Cracked mortar binds the gray and black stones of the horse-hitch. Its rusty iron hoop is firmly planted on the top. Its jutting stones on the knobby cylinder are smoothed by decades of exposure to the weather.

2. I stepped out of the front door and onto the sidewalk. There were tears in my eyes. I had two dollars in my jeans' pockets. I was sick of my parents' drinking.

3. Bill marched down the road. His St. Bernard heeled obediently to the left. His wife Sally was ten paces behind. His black cat Boris sedately brought up the rear.

4. I was forced back to reality when I walked past the ragamuffins sitting on the street corners. Their dirt-lined hands were outstretched. They were begging for pennies.

5. A man of about thirty-five slumps on the bottom step. He cradles his brown paper bag which ineffectively covers his wine and whiskey bottle nestled inside. His head bows occasionally.

6. The boys ran to the playground. They dashed between baby carriages and stopped cars. They shut out the annoyed cries of the passersby.

7. Uncle John pumps monotonously. He sits in a carved oak rocking chair. The wide planked floor is smoothed and worn into a saucer where his feet have touched for the past sixty years.

8. Finally, there is the sound of the players clashing on the field. Their cleats are creaking and their helmets are clacking. They are battling as though their lives depended upon the outcome of the game.

9. Her black skin is stretched across the hollow of her jaws. Her face is creased with lines. Her skin is slick with sweat as if oiled.

10. These relics now line the inside of the garage. They look like ominous mechanical monsters. They look like they are preparing for attack.

SENTENCE VARIETY

The advantage of having a variety of sentence patterns in your repertoire is that they multiply your options, whatever your writing purpose. Being able to choose among these options is especially important in achieving sentence variety, a significant feature of good writing. To rely exclusively on one or two sentence patterns is not only monotonous, but it neglects the many ways you can use language to express your exact meaning. By skillfully alternating your patterns, you can maintain reader interest, and you can mold the sentence to fit your thought.

Varying Sentence Patterns

The following student paragraph illustrates how some of the sentence patterns considered in this chapter can be used to enhance sentence variety.

```
    (1) I know from firsthand experience in the boxing ring what
it is like to be stunned.  (2) Hit with a very hard punch, my
head begins to vibrate and my knees become weak and rubbery.
(3) Dazed and groggy, I grope blindly for the ropes, hoping to
recover my equilibrium and balance.  (4) A dream world
swallows me: cats strumming guitars on rooftops, parrots
doing the dinner dishes, a horse working the computer.  (5)
How long it takes me to recover usually depends on how hard I
was hit.
```

Analyzing these sentences, we find that sentence 1 is a basic subject-verb-complement sentence with embedded modification. Sentence 2 begins with an introductory modifier followed by two coordinate clauses. Sentence 3 is a cumulative sentence which begins with adjective modifiers followed by a base clause and ends with a free verb phrase. In sentence 4 the basic subject-verb-complement structure of the main clause is followed by parallel phrases. Sentence 5 is a balanced sentence composed of the parallel elements "How long . . . how hard." In all, the student has used a variety of patterns to make the paragraph lively and interesting.

Varying Sentence Openers

Another way to gain variety in your sentences is to vary your sentence openers. You don't need to worry that each sentence begins differently but only that sentences following each other show some variation.

The way you choose to open your sentences will, of course, depend on their context. Your choice will also depend on knowing what elements of a sentence can be moved to different syntactical positions. Take, for example, one of the sentences discussed earlier in connection with subordination:

> Even though John did well in the semifinals, he failed to win an athletic scholarship.

Note that the subordinate clause with which the sentence begins could easily be placed after the main clause without disturbing the logical relationship between the clauses:

> John failed to win an athletic scholarship, even though he did well in the semifinals.

The ease with which this subordinate structure can be moved shows that its placement is a matter of stylistic choice. One important consideration in making this choice is sentence variation. Note what happens when the first sentence is given a context.

> Though John worked industriously to perfect his stroke, his hard work proved fruitless. Even though he did well in the semifinals, he failed to win an athletic scholarship.

Examining both sentences, you can see that each begins with an introductory subordinate clause. In this case, the alert writer, knowing that he could shift the position of his clauses to achieve variation, would reverse the order of the clauses in the second sentence. Revised, the sentence would read:

> Though John worked industriously to perfect his stroke, his hard work proved fruitless. He failed to win an athletic scholarship, even though he did well in the semifinals.

You can see how the plasticity of sentences can be used to promote sentence variety in the two drafts of the following student paragraph:

First Draft

```
    (1) I got off the bus and waved goodbye to my friends as the
big yellow machine lurched forward, leaving behind a black
cloud of smoke.  (2) I looked toward our house for a long
minute, then crossed the street, stopping to pick up a stick.
(3) I sat on the fence of our house for a while, waving my
hand around, pretending I was a fairy and the stick was my
wand.  (4) I thought that somehow, magically, the wand would
transform my mother and father into a loving couple again.
(5) I got down and walked to the house, stopping to tie my
tennis shoe strings which seemed loose.  (6) I unlocked the
door noiselessly and crept into the living room.
```

```
      (1) I got off the bus and waved goodbye to my friends as the
big yellow machine lurched forward, leaving behind a black
cloud of smoke.   (2) For a long minute, I looked toward our
house, then crossed the street, stopping to pick up a stick.
(3) I sat on the fence of our house for a while, waving my
hand around, pretending I was a fairy and the stick was my
wand.   (4) Somehow, I thought, the wand would magically
transform my mother and father into a loving couple again.
(5) I got down and walked to the house, stopping to tie my
tennis shoe strings which seemed loose.   (6) Unlocking the
door noiselessly, I crept into the living room.
```

EXPLORING CHOICES

1. Compare sentence 2 of both versions. What change do you find?
2. Compare sentence 4 of both versions. What change do you find?
3. Compare sentence 6 of both versions. What change do you find?
4. On the basis of your comparisons, describe the methods the writer used to develop sentence variety in the revision.

You have seen how an element within a sentence can be moved to an initial position to provide sentence variation. Another method, illustrated by sentence 6, is to change the structure of an initial element ("I unlocked the door noiselessly" changed to "Unlocking the door noiselessly"). A third method is to combine sentences. Note, for example, how joining the two sentences in the following example eliminates the repeated opener:

These costs often inspire taxpayer resistance. These costs include hiring special educators, purchasing special equipment, and removing architectural barriers.

The cost of hiring special educators, purchasing special equipment, and removing architectural barriers often inspires taxpayer resistance.

Yet another way to vary sentence openers is to invert the word order of a sentence. Normally, the English sentence follows a subject-verb-complement order. Occasionally, however, the verb or complement precedes the subject. Keep in mind, though, that the effect of placing a sentence element in an unusual position is usually emphatic. If you choose this method, you will need to be sure that you want such an effect.

Following are two versions of consecutive sentences. In the first version, the sentence opener is repeated. In the second the writer eliminates this repetition by shifting the complement to the initial position. Consider the difference in emphasis the shift produces:

I probed my impressions of Jean. I already knew that she was guilty.

I probed my impressions of Jean. That she was guilty, I already knew.

Varying Sentence Length

Varying the length of sentences is another way to achieve sentence variety. This method depends not on counting words but on understanding the function and effect of different sentence lengths. Of special importance are the uses of short sentences.

You can make a relatively brief sentence memorable by using it to summarize the idea of a longer sentence. Note how the brief second sentence in the following student example tersely interprets the preceding idea:

> This difference in audience orientation helps explain the slick professionalism sought by bluegrass groups: they are dealing with a relatively sophisticated audience rather than with an audience of farmhands out for a good time. An evening of bluegrass music is a cultural event, not a social get—together.

The sentence fragment can also be effective among longer and complete sentences. Note, for example, how the fragments in the following passage echo the gasps of the runner, who has just finished a race. Note, too, that the student writer begins four fragments with the same word to emphasize the resemblance of the series.

> As I cross Intramural Drive, the race ends. I double over, hands on knees, fighting for air. No congratulations. No medals. No glory. Just pain. I cough violently and spit away a portion of the flood trying to drown me. I shake as the perspiration—soaked turtleneck clings to my body. The four flights of stairs which I had raced down only an hour ago now become a major obstacle between me and my room. I conquer them slowly and carefully, ignoring the puzzled looks of those going down for breakfast. I open the door to my room. Rolling over on one elbow, my roommate looks at me and simply says, "You're crazy."
> No argument.

The short sentence can also be an effective way to contrast ideas, either within or between sentences:

(1) Human history has moved in a series of stages as we have tried to understand the world around us. (2) The first views we know about attributed to in-

visible spirits all the inexplicable things that happened to rocks and rivers, to plants and animals, and to people. (3) The spirits could not be dominated, they had to be placated. (4) Later, the idea of a multitude of animate spirits was transformed into a vision of gods and goddesses with more-or-less human forms and superhuman attributes. (5) They were not indifferent to people. (6) They could reward and punish. (7) Then came the idea of a single godhead, a unity of man and nature.

—Flora Lewis, "The Quantum Mechanics of
Politics," New York Times Magazine

In sentence 3, two short coordinate clauses expressing antithetical ideas are combined in a single sentence. Sentences 5 and 6 also express antithetical ideas, but this time the writer sets these ideas off in two short sentences, repeating the opener of each to emphasize their close relationship.

Short clauses joined by a semicolon can be used for special effect. Such structures are called *paratactic* because they dispense with the coordinating conjunction that usually joins coordinate clauses. In the following paragraph, the student writer, recalling a childhood incident, accents her anxiety by using a series of brief clauses in her first sentence, each of which echoes her mounting panic. The paragraph ends with a similar structure. Note how the writer uses *anaphora* (the repetition of the same word in successive clauses) to build rhythmic emphasis:

```
I was alone; I was afraid; I was in the dark; I wanted my
parents.  I screamed uncontrollably, wheeled around and around
the room until I couldn't see through my dizziness, beat on
the door until my fists ached, begged and yelled until I was
hoarse, and finally cried hysterically from the window for
anyone on the street to help me, free me.  No one heard; no
one listened.
```

The following paragraph taken from a book review uses the same strategy in several sentences, but this time the short, bare clauses are designed to imitate the style and personality of the writer being reviewed:

And there, almost always, he would stop. He was true to himself; but he had only half a life. He was very modest; he ruled his art accordingly; his best and most famous stories are of the shortest kind; he refused to stretch his inventive talents. He ended one of his best stories, "The Open Window," with this description of the heroine, a girl of 15 years: "Romance at short notice was her specialty." His, too.

—John Lukacs, "Review of The Complete
Works of Saki by H. H. Munro,"
New York Times Book Review

EDITORIAL ACTIVITIES

Editing to Correct Faulty Parallelism

Following are some student sentences that require editing. Help the writer correct the faulty parallelism in each.

1. Both are used by man for enjoyment and also as a money-making investment.
2. Many high school bandsmen are in band either because their parents make them stay in it, or some just stay in it for the easy ''A.''
3. When I was a lot younger, I stopped playing and running around long enough to eat, or when my mother decided it was past my bedtime.
4. A healthy person tends to be optimistic, cheerful, and lively, but one who eats poorly is irritable, cynical, and sleeps too late to accomplish anything.
5. In her spare time, she likes to paint, to go to museums, and a good game of tennis.
6. Many things accounted for his success, such as desire, the roles he played, and probably the biggest thing was style.
7. The actors were both snobbish and they thought a lot of themselves.
8. It also gave basic instructions on how to ski, making it all sound so easy and fun.
9. Not only is this unfair to the married students, but the conditions under which the single students live constitute a health hazard.
10. Changing this forward approach into a backward spin requires the tightening of the stomach muscles and to throw the arms backward.
11. We have a large amount of coal, but it is hard to handle, it pollutes, and the mining of it kills large numbers of people.

Using Free Modifiers

The first draft of the following paragraph would have a richer texture and a more sophisticated sentence structure if the writer had used the verb phrase and the absolute in key places. Acting on her editor's advice, the student rewrote the paragraph. The questions that follow will help you see the changes she made.

(1) At the start of her last lap, Eryn Forbes quickens her pace. (2) Her spikes bite into the all-weather track as she pushes for more speed. (3) She swings through the first turn and into the backstretch without looking behind her. (4) She pumps her arms as the good luck medal on the chain around her neck bounces vigorously against the red "Portland Track Club" insignia on her white shirt. (5) Eryn's stride is rapid and the redness in her cheeks is the only hint that pain lies deep behind her brown eyes. (6) Outwardly relaxed and inwardly fighting fatigue, Eryn sprints past the home stand and snaps the finish line, far ahead of her competition.

Revision

(1) At the start of her last lap, Eryn Forbes quickens her pace, her spikes biting into the all-weather track as she pushes for more speed. (2) Without looking behind her, she swings through the first turn and into the backstretch, pumping her arms, the good luck medal on the chain around her neck bouncing vigorously against the red "Portland Track Club" insignia on her white shirt. (3) Eryn's stride is rapid, the redness in her cheeks the only hint that pain lies deep behind her brown eyes. (4) Outwardly relaxed and inwardly fighting fatigue, she sprints past the home stand and snaps the finish line, far ahead of her competition.

EXPLORING CHOICES

1. What changes in sentence 2 of the first draft do you find in the revision?

2. How does the free modifier help the writer integrate material from sentence 4 of the first draft into sentence 2 of the revision?

3. Compare sentence 5 of the first draft and sentence 3 of the revision. What words have been deleted in the revision? What punctuation has been added?

4. Count the number of commas in both versions. Which has more? Why?

YOU ARE THE EDITOR

The following paragraph could be strengthened by the use of verb phrases and absolutes. Advise the writer where to place them. Note that there is no single pattern that is correct. If you compare your revision to the revisions of others in the class, you will probably find different versions. Discuss these versions to determine which you think is best.

The lights began to spin and my knees buckled beneath me. Weightlessly, I floated slowly to the cold cement as I focused momentarily on the maze of faces peering at me. I could hear them talking and see them gawking. There I was, prostrate on the mall floor with an invisible boundary around me. No one would dare cross the line. Each would fear contact with me. I lifted my mittened hand toward the crowd. My eyes pleaded for help, but I was rejected like a leper. The shoppers passed on after they had seen enough. The space they left vacant was quickly filled by other thrill seekers.

Editing for Sentence Variety

In the following paragraph, the writer begins many of her consecutive sentences with the subject "he" followed by a verb. When her editor pointed out that she could vary her sentence patterns by combining some of her sentences, she rewrote the paragraph. Compare the versions to see which sentences were combined in the revision.

First Draft

(1) Gramps is an exceptionally frugal man. (2) He hates to break in new clothes and bedding he has received as gifts. (3) He rationalizes, "My old things are good enough for me." (4) He has closets crammed with new clothes he refuses to wear. (5) He wears the same pair of pants and suit jacket almost every day, gray, straight-leg, cuffed pants and a plaid, square-shouldered jacket. (6) He also persists in using the same worn towel and sheets over and over again. (7) It's miraculous they come out of the wash in one piece.

Revision

(1) Gramps is an exceptionally frugal man. (2) Although his closets are crammed with new clothes and bedding he's received as gifts, he refuses to use them, rationalizing, "My old things are good enough for me." (3) Consequently, he's worn the same clothes for as long as I can remember, a pair of gray, straight-leg, cuffed pants and a plaid, square-shouldered jacket. (4) He also persists in using the same worn towel and sheets over and over again. (5) It's miraculous they come out of the wash in one piece.

YOU ARE THE EDITOR

Some of the consecutive sentences in the following paragraphs begin with the same pattern. Advise the writers on how to vary their sentence openers.

(1) William T. Schindler was the proprietor of the Middletown corner store where he worked from nine to five Monday through Saturday. (2) He took his job seriously and deviated very little from the day's routine. (3) Every time you entered the store, you'd be sure to see him stationed in front of an orderly shelf. (4) He would stand erect, his face gaunt, his cheeks hollow. (5) His eyes were likely to be fixed on the log book in front of him where he carefully marked the day's transactions. (6) He would write in the numbers neatly, using a perfectly pointed pencil with an unused eraser.

(1) Recovering from second-degree burns, I went back to work, replacing the destroyed parts on the machines so that the bowling alley could reopen on schedule in forty-eight hours. (2) Working twelve hours, three employees and I completed sixty-two of the seventy-two lanes that needed to be repaired. (3) When we had finished, another team headed by Duke went in to repair the remaining machines. (4) When I arrived two hours before the scheduled reopening, however, I found Duke in the bar, drunk and without a single lane done. (5) As a result, the company lost close to ten thousand dollars.

EDITING FOR SENTENCE ECONOMY

One of the editor's chief tasks is to encourage and promote sentence economy. Keep in mind that sentence economy is not the same as sentence length. A long sentence can be as economical as a short sentence. The key to determining economy is not to count words but to see if each word succinctly contributes to meaning.

Sometimes sentence economy is achieved by combining two or more consecutive sentences into a single sentence. At other times sentences can be made more compact by pruning elements *within* the sentence. The editorial activities that follow will help you see some of the strategies an editor uses to achieve sentence economy.

Combining Sentences

Deletion. One way to tell if sentences can be combined is to check the endings and beginnings of consecutive sentences. If you find a word or words repeated, or if a pronoun at the beginning of the second sentence refers to an antecedent near the end of the first sentence, the chances are that the two sentences can be combined by deleting the repeated element.

Compare the following sentences. What words have been deleted in the revision? Why? What punctuation has been added in the revision? Why?

Sentences A:
First Draft

The trees were cut into twelve-foot logs and loaded onto the log boat. The log boat was a long sled with smooth wooden runners in front.

Sentences A:
Revision

The trees were cut into twelve-foot logs and loaded onto a log boat, a long sled with smooth wooden runners in front.

Sentences B:
First Draft

The student side of the crowded street is filled with the newest and most expensive sports cars and psychedelic vans. They are parked so close together that it is impossible to walk between them.

Sentences B:
Revision

The student side of the crowded street is filled with the newest and most expensive sports cars and psychedelic vans, parked so close together that it is impossible to walk between them.

YOU ARE THE EDITOR

Using the strategy of deletion to combine sentences, apply your editorial skills to the following student sentences. Be sure to insert the comma in the appropriate place in your revision.

1. An example of such a technique is the use of embeds. Embeds are words that are embedded into an advertisement but that cannot be seen by the casual observer.

2. While training, the distance runner must concentrate on building a solid distance base. This distance base is obtained by pounding out many long miles during after-school excursions.

3. Many performers use some type of balancing device. This device is usually a balancing pole anywhere from twenty-three to forty feet long.

4. The horse stalls are bedded with shiny yellow straw. This straw is an assurance that each animal has a clean living area.

5. Meanwhile, two farm dogs, not seeming to mind the snow, dashed across the creek littered with ice floes. Perhaps they were in search of a rabbit whose round pellets betrayed his presence.

6. How could this team of great athletes become turned around so quickly? One year they are bidding for the Super Bowl, and the next year they are fighting to keep out of last place.

Deletion plus substitution. At times, deleting repeated words or phrases from the second sentence will require substituting another word or words before the sentences can be combined. Consider the following examples:

Sentences A:
First Draft

Every thirteen seconds, the mechanical arm reaches up and places four bottles on a conveyor belt. The belt moves four bottle widths at a time in synch with the swooping arm.

Sentences A:
Revision

Every thirteen seconds, the mechanical arm reaches up and places four bottles on a conveyor belt that moves four bottle widths at a time in synch with the swooping arm.

Sentences B:
First Draft

The music at a rock concert is loud and ear-shattering. The music excites the wild crowd even more.

Sentences B:
Revision

The music at a rock concert is loud and ear-shattering, exciting the wild crowd even more.

FOLLOW-UP ACTIVITIES

1. What words have been deleted in the revisions of sentences A and B?
2. What words have been substituted for the deleted words?
3. What changes were made in punctuation?

Using the strategy of deletion plus substitution to combine sentences, apply your editorial skills to the following student sentences. Be sure to insert any necessary punctuation in your revision.

1. At the end of the war, many of the rail systems of Europe had been completely destroyed. This destruction forced European countries to rebuild their systems from scratch.

2. Unclean needles that are inserted into the body cause infection. This infection usually results in swelling and irritation at the site of insertion.

3. Usually, in nine out of ten cases the injured are women. Women are generally weaker than men.

4. When the entire chair has been sanded, it is ready for the final step. This step entails staining the chair the desired tint.

5. After a single season of jumping, he became involved in exhibitions given by a local club. The members of this local club were paid to jump at shows and county fairs.

6. Contaminants that have been introduced into the groundwater can move horizontally or vertically. This movement depends on the comparative density and natural flow pattern of the water already contained in the aquifer.

7. The case involved Amy, a hearing-impaired student. Amy was given a government-supplied hearing aid that allowed her to understand approximately three out of every five words spoken by her teacher.

Deletion plus rearrangement.   Another way to combine sentences is to shift the position of the retained material. This strategy is especially effective when elements of the second sentence modify the subject of the first sentence. To make this relationship clear, the retained material should be embedded between the subject and predicate of the first sentence.

Consider the following example. What words have been deleted in the revision? Where has the retained material of the second sentence been placed in the revision?

First Draft

A cedar plaque hangs over the doorway of each cottage. Each plaque bears the name of a tree in the area.

Revision

A cedar plaque bearing the name of a tree in the area hangs in the doorway of each cottage.

YOU ARE THE EDITOR

Using the deletion plus rearrangement technique to combine sentences, apply your editorial skills to the following student sentences.

1. Although overeating is the main factor, other factors may contribute to obesity. An unbalanced diet, lack of exercise, and genetic inheritance may also contribute to obesity.

2. Our apartment is on the upper west side of the city. It is located right at the junction of the Harlem and Hudson rivers.

3. Great white lotus blossoms float on the pool's water. These lotus blossoms are the Asian version of the water lily.

4. A much-used cooking substance appeared to be linked to the disease. This cooking substance was rice-bran oil.

5. Mainstreaming is opposed by many classroom teachers. Mainstreaming is the integration of handicapped students into the regular classroom.

6. The ratchet is placed between the two ends of wire and cranked up and down. The ratchet is a twelve-inch metal mechanism with a brass crank on its end.

7. Two major theories describe the process of learning a prejudice. These theories are proposed by leading social psychologists Gordon Allport and Mary Ellen Goodman.

Addition. Combining sentences may require the addition of a subordinating conjunction that will clarify the logical relationship between the sentences that have been joined. Two types of subordinating conjunctions most often neglected in student writing are those showing cause or reason (*because, since*), and those showing contrast (*although, even though*).

Consider the sentences below. What word has been added in the revision? What relationship does it establish between the first and second clause?

First Draft

Recently, a Cessna 172 ran off the runway and dived directly into a group of trees. The snow covering the runway had made it difficult to bring the plane to a halt.

Revision

Recently, a Cessna 172 ran off the runway and dived directly into a group of trees because the snow covering the runway had made it difficult to bring the plane to a halt.

YOU ARE THE EDITOR

Using the strategy of addition to combine sentences, apply your editorial skills to the following student sentences. Explain how the word you have added clarifies the relationship between the clauses.

1. She required constant supervision and was destined to spend the rest of her life in an overstuffed, understaffed institution. Kathy was determined to do more than just exist.

2. We fifth graders would often tell our parents how terrible Sister was. They would shake their heads in disbelief.

3. If I went to a party with him, I was always sorry. Bob would drink excessively, as usual.

4. Traveling on side roads is much safer than traveling on a crowded freeway. However, accidents do occur.

5. We decided this area was relatively well off. Only a few poor children raced to scoop the manure onto boards.

Pruning Sentences

If editors find that the number of words in a sentence can be reduced without distorting meaning, they will use either deletion or deletion and substitution strategies to make the sentence more compact. In the first case, they will recommend that excess words be cut; in the second, they will recommend that words be removed and replaced by other words and phrases that will convey meaning more directly and succinctly.

Deleting redundant words and phrases.   Words in a sentence may sometimes repeat the sense of other words in the same sentence. When this happens, the sentence is redundant; it is padded with extra verbiage and needs to be pruned. Take, for example, the sentence, "Soon my feelings of disappointment turned into feelings of bitterness." The nouns *disappointment* and *bitterness* are words that stand for particular emotional states. To use the phrase *feelings of* with these nouns is to repeat what is already implied. Applying the strategy of deletion to this sentence eliminates unnecessary repetition and allows for a tauter structure, reducing a sentence of ten words to a sentence of six: "Soon my disappointment turned into bitterness."

Compare the following two sentences. Point out the words deleted in the revision and explain the reason for their deletion.

First Draft   Hopping with a rabbit-like gait, she disappeared from sight.

Revision   Hopping rabbit-like, she disappeared from sight.

Deleting the expletive.   The expletives *there is* (*are*) and *it is* can also lead to redundancy. Expletives are fillers which occupy the subject position but are not the actual subject of the sentence. Sometimes expletives are useful: they can give greater emphasis to the subject by postponing it. In the sentence "There are those who would uphold the death penalty, and there are those who would abolish it," the repeated expletive "there are" helps to emphasize "those," the subject of both clauses.

An expletive may also be a convenient way to announce or summarize a related group of ideas, as in the sentence "There are three reasons for abolishing the death penalty." Often, however, the expletive simply becomes a stretcher that lengthens the sentence without contributing to meaning. Compare, for example, "There were no other bands in the Midwest that could compare in size and quality" (a sentence with 15 words), to "No other bands in the Midwest could compare in size and quality" (the same sentence pared to 12 words). The *there were* construction of the first sentence postpones the subject for no reason. Removing it shortens the revised sentence and makes the relative pronoun (*which*) unnecessary.

Compare the following two sentences. Point out the words deleted in the revision and explain the reason for their deletion.

First Draft   There is no place I know of that could compare to the coldness and loneliness of my grandmother's nursing home.

Revision   No place I know compares to the coldness and loneliness of my grandmother's nursing home.

Deleting relative pronouns.   Deletion can also be used to eliminate relative pronouns such as *who, which,* and *that*. Often these pronouns are unnecessary because the relationship they signal is conveyed by the structure of the sentence. In the following revised sentence, the relative pronoun *that* is twice deleted, allowing for a sentence whose meaning remains intact with fewer words.

First Draft   Steel-cased air conditioners protrude from wood-framed windows that are too large for the modern contraptions that they are forced to accommodate.

Revision   Steel-cased air conditioners protrude from wood-framed windows too large for the modern contraptions they are forced to accommodate.

Deletion may also be in order when relative pronouns are followed by a verb phrase or by a verb plus adjective. "The boy who is leaning against the fence lives down the street" can be pared to "The boy leaning against the fence lives down the street." "A college which is close to home is best for students who are timid" can be shortened to "A college close to home is best for timid students."

Compare the following two sentences. Point out the words deleted in the revision and explain the reason for their deletion.

First Draft   These are only two of the instances where foreign children who were left on their own could have been harmed by lack of parental supervision.

Revision   These are only two of the instances where foreign children left on their own could have been harmed by lack of parental supervision.

YOU ARE THE EDITOR

Apply your editorial skills to the following student sentences by deleting excess words. Explain the reasons for your revisions. Try to stay as close to the writer's meaning as possible.

1. Though Patty is a girl with a very competitive drive, she is not disdainful of others' feelings.

2. Set on safety, I raced for my bike, my body leaping into the seat.

3. There are many people who lack the skills necessary to enter the electronics industry.

4. Her demeanor has always been one of coldness.

5. Mary told me that there was no one else who was planning to run for the nomination.

6. As long as people have disposable income, they will continue to purchase clothing on the basis of the style and color of the clothing rather than on the utility of the garment.

7. Silver Creek High School is the only school in the community that has fewer than two thousand students who attend school.

8. There are stipulations in some apartment leases that prevent renters from hanging pictures.

9. There is a kind of halcyon innocence that seems to descend on this little street.

10. Swimmers need strong psychological willpower to survive morning practice.

11. There were young boys who were dressed in brightly colored shirts and knee-length pants with long white socks.

12. My body fatigued from the climb, I decided to assemble my lean-to.

13. My mother told me he didn't usually come to town every day anymore.

14. The days that we spent in the North Woods would have been perfect had it not been for the mosquitoes that were enormous and hungry.

15. Those who were suspended were known for the pranks that they continually played.

Substituting adverbs for adjectives. Sentence wordiness can often be corrected by substituting adverbs for adjectives. Usually, this form of reduction eliminates superfluous prepositional phrases as well. In the following example, note how changing the adjective *haphazard* in the first draft to the adverb *haphazardly* in the revision eliminates the need for the prepositional phrase "in a . . . fashion."

First Draft

The entire town, in fact, is laid out in a somewhat haphazard fashion.

Revision

The entire town, in fact, is laid out somewhat haphazardly.

Compare the following two sentences and explain how the revision differs from the first draft.

First Draft

Each of the girls responded to the test in different ways.

Revision

Each of the girls responded to the test differently.

Substituting verbs for nouns. Another way to gain sentence economy by using the deletion and substitution strategy is to change nouns into verbs. Compare:

He had a preference for the music of Slim Whitman and Ernest Tubb.

He preferred the music of Slim Whitman and Ernest Tubb.

Sentence 1 has thirteen words, sentence 2 has ten. The difference can be traced to a simple substitution: the noun *preference* of the first sentence has been changed to the verb *preferred* in the second. To retain the noun is to load the sentence with deadwood—an inactive verb ("had") an article ("a") and a preposition ("for"). Changing it into a verb removes the extra words.

Compare the following two sentences and explain the deletion plus substitution strategy used in the revision.

First Draft

The club members had a thorough discussion of the matter.

Revision

The club members discussed the matter thoroughly.

Substituting the active voice for the passive voice. Misuse of the passive voice can also lead to wordiness. Compare:

Passive Voice:

The ticket was reluctantly paid for by me. (8 words)

Active Voice:

I reluctantly paid for the ticket. (6 words)

Active and passive voice refer to verb forms. When the doer of the action is the subject of the sentence, the verb is active and the sentence is in the active voice. When the subject of the sentence is acted upon, the verb is passive and the sentence is in the passive voice. Note that in the preceding examples the passive voice requires more words because its verb combines a form of *to be* ("was") with the past participle ("paid"); and it requires the prepositional phrase ("by me") to signal the subject acted upon. In this case, the passive construction leads to an unemphatic wordy sentence. Changing it into the active voice emphasizes the doer of the action (the subject "I") and removes unnecessary words.

The passive voice does, of course, have its uses. If the writer's purpose is to emphasize the receiver rather than the doer of an action, the passive voice is indispensable. Historical accounts which emphasize events often use the passive voice: "During the labor struggles of the 1890s, strikers were imprisoned, and strikebreakers were brought in to replace them." Similarly, accounts which describe the evolution of a process or that give instructions on how to complete a process will often use passive constructions, since in these cases the doer of the action is less important than the action itself. (The student essay "Not Kid's Play" in Chap. 3 show appropriate uses of the passive voice.)

The passive is appropriate too when the doer of the action is unknown: "The houses were vandalized for three weeks in a row," and "Fires had been set in a three block radius." The writer could have written "Vandals vandalized, etc." or "Arsonists set fires, etc." but these constructions would shift the emphasis to an anonymous doer when the event is of greater concern.

The choice between the passive and the active voice may be determined by rhetorical considerations. Consider, for example, the difference in emphasis between these two sentences:

Gun control legislation has been persistently opposed by the National Rifle Association.

The National Rifle Association has persistently opposed gun control legislation.

The first sentence suggests that the writer's major purpose is to discuss gun control legislation. The oppostion of the National Rifle Association is of secondary importance. In contrast, the second sentence reverses emphasis, suggesting that the NRA is the writer's major subject. The construction the writer chooses will depend on purpose and context.

Although a passive voice is useful, it is best to use it sparingly. The passive voice is a major source of wordiness, often encouraging a heap of static nouns and verbs. Note in the following sentences how the change in voice from passive to active removes considerable deadwood, making for a livelier and more emphatic sentence:

Passive Voice:

Smiles are passed to and fro between shoppers along the street as their extra change is dropped into the Salvation Army bucket.

Active Voice:

Shoppers along the street exchange smiles as they drop their extra change into the Salvation Army bucket.

Another reason to beware of the passive voice is that it often leads to dangling modifiers. A modifier dangles when it has no obvious word or words to modify. Consider this sentence:

Looking upward, the huge, silvery blimp can be seen lumbering around the stadium.

In this sentence, the participial modifier *Looking upward* requires a subject in the main clause who is doing the looking. The shift to the passive voice gives the blimp this function, a meaning the writer does not intend. Changing the main clause from passive to active corrects the problem: "Looking upward, I saw a huge, silvery blimp lumbering around the stadium."

Compare the following two sentences and explain how the revision differs from the first draft.

First Draft

Once satisfied with just an audible sound, perfection is now demanded, forcing electricians to eliminate various distortion-producing factors.

Revision

Once satisfied with just an audible sound, the public now demands perfection, forcing electricians to eliminate various distortion-producing factors.

YOU ARE THE EDITOR

Using one or more of the three deletion plus substitution strategies (substituting adverbs for adjectives; substituting verbs for nouns; substituting the active voice for the passive voice), apply your editorial skills to the following student sentences. In each case, explain the strategy you've used. Try to stay as close to the writer's meaning as possible.

1. Many of us found amusement in watching customers bend over to obtain the coin.

2. Ms. Lisa stood at the end of the line of owners and managers, presenting a slight grin.

3. In these committees, each bill is studied, considering every detail possible.

4. They threw looks of utter contempt at them.

5. Using the handy brush attached inside the cap, the cement may be applied easily and neatly, leaving the paper as smooth and wrinkle-free as it was before coating.

6. When the final pile of logs was laid on the fire and good-nights were said, I wished my tent weren't so far away from the fire and my friends.

7. In order to be a successful student, more than simply a good teacher is necessary.

8. When I was about four years old, my father found himself in the financial position to buy a house on Green Street.

9. The need and desire for a Girl Scout troop was made evident by the pleas of the junior girls in my church.

10. As time has passed, man has seemed to set a trend towards the more humane treatment of the criminal offender.

11. Her apron already on, she briskly moved about the kitchen, making efficient use of her time.

12. The earliest forms of punishment aimed at the elimination of undesirable behavior.

13. Yet, within a moment, upon her husband's entrance into the room, she turns into a twentieth-century housewife.

WRITING SUGGESTION

Think of an event which you witnessed but in which you were not a direct participant. Recall its atmosphere or the feeling it evoked, and then try to describe it vividly, using different sentence patterns for variety and special effect. You will see how one student managed both in the following essay. As you read it, consider especially the writer's skillful use of the cumulative sentence.

THE FINAL HEAT

It was the evening of the most crucial track meet of the indoor season. I was lounging with my team at the far end of the windowless armory, numb in the wake of the exhaustion and defeat which we, as a team, had suffered. The semifinals were over; we were awaiting the final heat of the 220 yard dash—an all-out sprint consisting of one lap around the boards. Eight teams had qualified, but everyone in that stadium knew that the contest was between two schools: Jackson and Boys' High.

All day the atmosphere had been tense. The armory, a fire hazard by any standard, was packed beyond legal capacity. Since my arrival that morning, I had witnessed at least four sporadic fights. The tension in the air seemed the result of far more than mere school rivalry; it verged on a kind of bottled-up hysteria.

When the gun went off for that final 220, the entire crowd jumped to its feet like one enormous animal. The runner from Jackson took the lead off the blocks, pumping his knees up to his chest, his thin torso slicing the air, fetid now with the accumulated smoke of several thousand cigarettes. The Boys' High sprinter followed him down the straightaway, shedding himself of the pack like a fullback who had found his hole, his chest thrust forward at an impossible angle. They leaned into the turn, their bodies moving in perfect synchronization, looking like two riders on the same high-speed, tandem bike.

As they shot out onto the final straightaway, the Boys' High runner made his move. Forsaking the rail, he crept up on the outside, his face contorted, knowing that his performance

during the next five seconds would either win or lose a race
which was the culmination of a season's effort. Head down, he
started moving, gaining a few inches with each step, his
swollen chest eclipsing and then passing that of the Jackson
sprinter. His involvement was total; I'm sure he never saw
the bottle coming. . . .

Flashing out of the second tier of onlooking faces, a green
Coke bottle caught the glare of the overhead lights for just a
second, before streaking past the lowered face of the leading
runner, missing him by inches, and shattering into a thousand
fragments on the hardwood floor. The noise had reached such a
crescendo that I never actually heard the bottle shatter.

Neither runner broke stride. Boys' High won. The
maintenance crew was called out, and an intermission of
fifteen minutes was announced by a metallic voice over the
loudspeaker.
                                        --Bill Christophersen

---

TIPS FOR SELF-EDITING

While revising your essay, examine your sentences carefully, using the following guide to determine their effectiveness:

1. Are my sentences varied? Have I alternated sentence openers? Have I varied my sentence length to achieve a specific purpose or effect?

2. Are my sentence patterns effective? Do they reflect my exact meaning?

3. Are my sentences concise? Can I combine sentences to achieve further sentence economy? Can I pare my sentences to achieve further economy?

4. Do my sentences show the logical relationships I intend? Have I used coordination where appropriate? Have I used subordination where appropriate?

5. Have I used modification appropriately? Do some sentence elements require further modification, less modification?

CHOOSING WORDS

*I*n the early stages of writing, words may come easily, probably because you want to get your thoughts down on paper rapidly for fear of losing them. Later, while revising, you may stop to consider whether the words you have chosen are accurate, effective, or appropriate. The answer may be complex, not only because there is no simple equation between an idea and a word, but because word choice depends on context: to choose words well you need to keep in mind your subject, occasion, and audience. In this chapter we will consider some characteristics of words that will help you make the appropriate choice.

DENOTATION AND CONNOTATION

Many words have both denotative and connotative meanings. The denotative meaning of a word is its literal or dictionary sense; connotative meaning arises from the associations and suggestions a word brings to mind. Take, for example, the word *rose,* which the *American Heritage Dictionary* defines as "Any of numerous shrubs or vines of the genus *Rosa,* usually having prickly stems, compound leaves, and variously colored, often fragrant flowers." Such a definition avoids feeling or emotion. It defines the botanical object, not its web of associations. Yet, while the rose is a literal object in nature that may be defined by its formal characteristics, it is also something which evokes human feelings and is associated with love, delicacy, fragrance, vigor, and many other qualities. Poets are quick to exploit this verbal resonance, often through metaphor. When Shakespeare writes of a character that "He wears the rose/Of youth upon him," he is using the word *rose* connotatively, transferring its suggestion of natural vitality to the human form.

Because many words have meanings beyond the merely literal, choosing the appropriate word requires sensitivity to its range of associations. To be sure, some words are neutral and have no connotations unless a personal experience triggers a particular response. A painful episode in a dentist's office might color the word *dentist* for the patient, but generally the word *dentist* simply denotes a doctor who treats teeth. Many words, however, have connotations that are pleasant or unpleasant, positive or negative. Consider the connotative differences in the following descriptions of the same person:

> Much like his frugal parents, he husbanded his money, remaining thrifty to the end of his life.

> Much like his miserly parents, he hoarded his money, remaining stingy to the end of his life.

Obviously, each sentence creates a different impression. The first approves its subject: words like *frugal, husbanded,* and *thrifty* suggest wise economy, a virtue. In contrast, the second is distinctly unflattering; we may applaud conserving money, but for most of us, the penny-pinching implied in words like *miserly, hoarded,* and *stingy* is a major fault. In each instance, then, word choice represents a judgment. Many words do not simply point to things and ideas but imply the writer's favorable or unfavorable attitude toward them.

The value of being sensitive to connotation is twofold: it can help you choose words responsibly and accurately; and it can alert you to how people may use words to manipulate and influence you. Each day you are asked to buy certain products, to vote for certain people, to support certain proposals. To evaluate these appeals, you need to be aware of the part played by connotation. You may be skeptical if you find the writer relying primarily on slanted or loaded words to gain your consent.

FOLLOW-UP ACTIVITIES

1. The denotations of the following word groups are roughly similar, but their connotations differ. Explain the connotative differences in each group.

   overweight, fat, plump, well-nourished
   slender, skinny, thin, lean
   aggressive, contentious, pushy, belligerent
   purloin, pirate, steal, pilfer
   peppery, lively, spirited, testy
   shy, diffident, reserved, withdrawn
   indigent, poor, destitute, impecunious
   debate, quarrel, argue, contend

2. The brand names of products are often chosen for their connotative value. Group the following names according to the feelings, beliefs, and attitudes to which they appeal. Discuss the connotations of each group.

Right Guard	Ultraban	Ultima
Minute Rice	Corn King	Safeguard
Princess Gardner	UniRoyal	Wind Song
Rolaids	Nestlé's Quik	White Cloud
Lady Borden	Easy-Off	Mountain Dew
Royal Crown Cola	Handiwrap	Toastmaster
Sea Breeze	Minutemaid	Moon Drops
Imperial Margarine	Waldorf	A Touch of Class

GENERAL AND SPECIFIC WORDS

When we learn to speak, we usually learn to name general categories before we learn to name the specific objects belonging to those categories. To a two-year-old child, collies, German shepherds, and cocker spaniels are simply dogs; oaks, elms, or sycamores are lumped together as trees; hyacinths, roses, and pansies are all flowers. Later, as our control of language becomes more sophisticated, we learn to distinguish between general words that name a class and specific words that refer to a member of that class. We also learn that the terms *general* and *specific* are relative: *dog,* for example, is more specific than *animal* but is more general than *collie.* You can see how the same word may be both general and specific by ranking the words in the following lists by their degree of specificity:

food, nourishment, cake, dessert, baked Alaska

pneumonia, unwholesome condition, disease, infirmity, virus infection

music, sound, composition, Beethoven's Fifth Symphony, symphony

ABSTRACT AND CONCRETE WORDS

The terms *abstract* and *concrete* are used to distinguish between words that refer to qualities, characteristics, and concepts that we know only intellectually, and to objects and things that we perceive through our senses. If you say a person is *dimpled* or *sunburned* or *tall,* you are using concrete words to describe features you can see. If, however, you say that the same person is *vain* or *intemperate* or *impetuous,* you are using abstract words that refer to mental concepts. Though the person's behavior may persuade you that she is vain, the word *vain* of itself has no sensory referent: it cannot be seen, touched, heard, felt, or tasted.

Abstract and general terms are indispensable to human communication. They summarize actions and objects that would otherwise be too tedious to list. They also allow you to find meaning and pattern in human life. Consider the difficulty you would have if you lacked the word *vain* to characterize someone's behavior. You might say that such a person preened before the mirror, or could talk about no one other than himself, or boasted of his exploits—but without the word *vain* you could not identify what these separate actions had in common. You could list facts, but you could draw no conclusions about their meaning.

Actually, words labeled *abstract* and *general* reflect a mental process known as *abstracting.* Whenever you classify, you are abstracting. If you say, for example, that chairs, beds, sofas, and tables are all furniture, or that

France, Belgium, New Zealand, and Algeria are all nations, you are selecting or abstracting from the members of each group a feature they have in common. Similarly, when you speak of a quality such as loyalty, you are classifying a series of actions, saying that one action resembles another and that both characterize a form of behavior called *loyalty.*

The process of abstracting is central to writing: you abstract each time you formulate a thesis that summarizes the main idea of an essay. When you express your thesis as a generalization, you are saying that selected features of your experience have something in common. You find similarities which you join under a heading general enough to cover each separate instance or feature.

The process of abstracting can take place on many levels. If you speak of *virtues,* you are using a more abstract term than *loyalty,* since loyalty is only one of the many kinds of behavior generally characterized as virtuous. Similarly, *entertainment* is more abstract than *TV comedy,* and *vehicle* is more abstract than *Corvette.* The abstraction ladder (p. 248) devised by S. I. Hayakawa illustrates how a specific cow named Bessie can be classified in terms that become increasingly abstract.

Understanding the abstraction ladder can help correct an overreliance on abstract and general language, a tendency in some writing. You do, of course, need such language, not only to interpret experience but also to formulate and discuss complex ideas. A student who writes "The use of alternative equations and variables allows both proponents and adversaries of the deterrence theory to support the justice of their position" justifiably uses an abstract vocabulary to discuss the death penalty, a complicated issue. In this case, the writer's word choice responds to the demand of the subject. But consider the following student sentence: "On a campus where conservatism, tradition, and the omniscient reality of life prevail, one feels a sense of stability as well as security." Here the writer attempts to express a personal response to college life, but the series of lifeless abstract nouns actually prevents the expression of individual perception. In this case, reliance on abstract language smothers the writer's voice and leads to impersonal prose that could be written by anyone.

Balance is the key to using language that is neither too abstract nor too concrete. To rely exclusively on the abstract is to seal off thought from the particularities of experience, but to select only concrete terms is to record facts without interpreting them. You can avoid both hazards if you remember that abstract and general words are usually reducible to lower-level statements. A class word may be reduced to specific members of that class; and an abstract word is an inference that often derives from sensory experience. If you have assembled a series of details that have no clearly formulated relationship, you probably need to move up the abstraction ladder to find general terms that would clarify their connection. Conversely, if you've written a series of abstract statements, you need to move down the abstraction ladder to find lower-level examples and details.

ABSTRACTION LADDER
Start reading from the bottom up

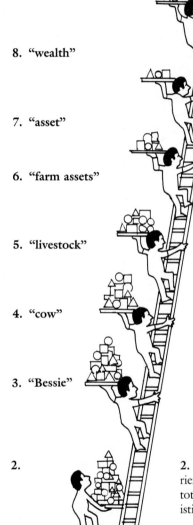

8. "wealth"

7. "asset"

6. "farm assets"

5. "livestock"

4. "cow"

3. "Bessie"

2.

8. The word "wealth" is at an extremely high level of abstraction, omitting *almost* all reference to the characteristics of Bessie.

7. When Bessie is referred to as an "asset," still more of her characteristics are left out.

6. When Bessie is included among "farm assets," reference is made only to what she has in common with all other salable items on the farm.

5. When Bessie is referred to as "livestock," only those characteristics she has in common with pigs, chickens, goats, etc., are referred to.

4. The word "cow" stands for the characteristics we have abstracted as common to cow_1, cow_2, cow_3 . . . cow_n. Characteristics peculiar to specific cows are left out.

3. The word "Bessie" (cow_1) is the *name* we give to the object of perception of level 2. The name *is not* the object; it merely *stands for* the object and omits reference to many of the characteristics of the object.

2. The cow we perceive is not the word, but the object of experience, that which our nervous system abstracts (selects) from the totality that constitutes the process-cow. Many of the characteristics of the process-cow are left out.

1. The cow known to science ultimately consists of atoms, electrons, etc., according to present-day scientific inference. Characteristics (represented by circles) are infinite at this level and ever-changing. This is the *process level*.

FOLLOW-UP ACTIVITY

Point out the blend of abstract-general language and concrete-specific language in the following passages:

Passage A

```
    My high school, built in 1942, is being constantly
modernized.  Sophisticated PET computers were purchased for a
new computer science course.  The old military green lockers
were torn out and replaced with royal blue, orange, yellow,
and scarlet ones, color-coordinated to the freshly painted
walls.  A $250,000 all-weather asphalt track, calibrated in
metric distances, a new basketball floor, and $60,000 in
racing style starting blocks and record boards for the pool
have all been added in the past three years to keep the
athletic teams up-to-date.
                                        --Student paragraph
```

Passage B

It's not unthinkable to assume that as language evolves, so, too, will its excesses be pruned to fit the streamlined image of future man. Yet the opposite appears to be true. In language, we Americans are becoming intolerably pompous and boring. A life preserver today has evolved into "a personal flotation device." A tape recorder we listen to in a car is "a contemporary communication device incorporated into the automotive experience." There are Americans who no longer clarify anything. They prefer to disambiguate it, because that is two syllables longer. At Fort Devens, Massachusetts, the guardhouse—imagine this, the guardhouse—has become "a correctional custody facility." The Navy's no better. An admiral, recommending that suggestive books and movies be kept off ships, says that to have them on board "is to underline deprivation in an already deprivational situation," thereby disambiguating fuzzy notions about the reason why war is hell: It's a deprivational situation.

—Edwin Newman, "Torrents of Babel," *Omni*

Passage C

A Gesternblatt evening is, above all, an *event*. In no particular is this as apparent as in the food. It's exotic; it's inventive; it's expensive beyond imagining; it's a fantasy. Roe of oyster; truffles spread around like Fritos; partridges *en brioche;* salmis of hare, pheasant, antelope; a cheese board that would daunt General de Gaulle; whatnots of sugar spun to a fineness that a Murano glassblower would envy. Great vintages of claret and Rhenich cascade down aristocratic throats with the foamy fury of the Reichenbach Falls. It's extravagant. It's wondrous strange to behold.

—Michael M. Thomas, "Mrs. Fish's Ape,"
Vanity Fair

LANGUAGE AND STYLE

Style is a slippery word that defies precise definition because it's used in so many different ways. In one sense style suggests distinctiveness, as when we speak of a style of clothing or furniture. Another sense implies elegance or opulence, as when we say that someone lives "in style." In yet another sense, style may mean a habitual or characteristic way of doing something or of behaving, as when we refer to someone's "lifestyle."

Style in writing also has a range of meanings, depending on whether it refers to the writer, to the audience, or to the occasion. To speak of Ernest Hemingway's style is to suggest that Hemingway used certain forms of language that marked his prose off from the prose of other writers. It is also to suggest that Hemingway's style reflects his personality and beliefs. The concrete words and spare sentences that Hemingway preferred not only reveal his character but express his belief that only the concrete items of the physical world are real.

Style in writing also refers to the strategies writers use to achieve a certain effect. Throughout this text, you have seen how words, sentence structure, tense and voice, punctuation, and the arrangement of sentences and paragraphs can produce emphasis, specificity, and vividness, often to suggest a feeling or emotion. You have also seen how certain constructions can reduce clarity and effectiveness. In either case, style is closely related to the response the writer hopes to evoke in the reader.

Style also refers to levels of language, ranging from *casual* to *informal* to *formal.* Used in this sense, it directs attention to occasion and to audience. Because different occasions require different language choices, most of us command a range of styles. A letter to a friend describing a car accident will differ considerably from a report of the same accident filed with an insurance company. A report on nutrition for a health class will differ in style from a description of one's personal eating habits. The key element is appropriateness: just as most of us choose one set of clothes for a wedding and another for a tennis match, so, too, do we match language to the writing occasion.

Comparing Casual and Formal Style

To recognize how casual style differs from formal style, compare the following paragraphs. Note especially how they differ in vocabulary and sentence structure. Consider the occasion that would be appropriate to each.

Paragraph A

```
    My friends had it all figured out:  Les and I would "duke it
out."  We were the two youngest ones in the crowd, and Kevin
and the older guys were kind of curious to see who would lose.
I didn't give a damn about the whole thing.  Les was a decent
guy and pretty smart as well.  I figured from the glance he
```

gave me that he knew as well as I did that we were going to
have to act as entertainment for the others, but what the
hell, why not . . . ? Rickey was going to be my coach and
Carey his coach. That was all right by me: they were both
blowhards, but Rickey was a little less cocky, and I liked him
better. He had given me my first football a few years back.

—Student paragraph

Paragraph B

Specifically, the Polish drama lies in an unprecedented descent from national grandeur to national annihilation. At its height in the sixteenth century, Poland came near to establishing itself permanently as one of the great powers of Europe, and perhaps the freest among them, only to lose everything in the partitions of the eighteenth century and to plunge into an abyss which threatened the nation with irrevocable servitude, indeed extinction. Ever since, the aspiration of the Poles has been to refute the apparently final verdict of history and restore their national greatness. This quest, moreover, produced a cultural tradition that is a somewhat bizarre and uniquely Polish amalgam of libertarian democracy, Baroque Catholicism, and Romantic patriotism.

—Martin Malia, "Poland's Eternal Return,"
New York Review of Books

No doubt you've pegged paragraph A as an instance of the casual style. The slang terms "duke it out," "blowhard," as well as expressions like "what the hell," "didn't give a damn," suggest an oral quality—the language that might be used in conversation with a friend. The vocabulary as a whole is concrete and the sentences are either a single brief clause or several brief clauses joined by coordination. The writer speaks in the first person *I* and reports his own sensations and feelings. His purpose is to recreate an adolescent experience, and so he chooses language that an adolescent would be likely to use.

Paragraph B illustrates the formal style. As you have probably noted, the passage contains no slang or popular expressions. There is an abundance of abstract words and phrases ("unprecedented descent," "irrevocable servitude," "national annihilation") and specialized terms ("libertarian democracy," "Baroque Catholicism") that suggest an audience of educated readers. The sentences are relatively long, with considerable modification, and they are carefully connected with transitions. Because the passage occurs in a review of a series of books dealing with the history of Poland, it is impersonal: the writer does not speak in his own voice nor does he attempt to convey his impressions directly.

The Informal Style

The informal style is appropriate to a wide range of writing occasions and purposes. It is the one you will use in most of your writing. The following student paragraphs illustrate a few of its possibilities:

The Phillies certainly were physically tired when the World Series began. They had won the Eastern Division with only two days left in the regular season and then entered the National League Championship "Series that would not end" against the Houston Astros, a five-game war in which all three of the Phillies' victories were come-from-behind. The Royals, on the other hand, clinched their division early in the season and took the American League pennant with a three-game sweep of the Yankees, which allowed the Royals to rest while the Phillies struggled with the Astros. But what the Phillies lost in strength they gained in character; the last-week win of the division and the extra-inning play-off games taught the Phillies to "never say die." This attitude was quite obvious. The Phillies came from behind in three of their four World Series wins, the most impressive being the game five winning hit by Manny Trillo, with two strikes and two outs in the ninth inning. The Phillies were tired from the demands of rallying to beat Houston, but with the same determination they showed in the Astrodome, they overcame their fatigue to win the Series.

Often when I am in my room at home, the glint of light reflecting off the metal edge of my Hart skis catches my eye, making me stop and think back as to why I took up downhill skiing as a hobby. Looking at the well-waxed, limber skis with their shiny Marker bindings mounted on them, a pair of aluminum ski poles, and the sleek black leather ski boots all sitting in that ski rack specially designed for my car, reminds me of all the money I have wrapped up in this particular interest of mine. I know I didn't take it up because it was cheap. So just why did I take up downhill skiing?

As these passages show, informal style stands midway between casual style and formal style. The vocabulary is in the middle range, neither slangy nor learned. Occasionally, popular expressions are used ("never say die," "come-from-behind"). Sentence patterns are varied, ranging from the simple and short ("This attitude was quite obvious") to more sophisticated structures characterized by balance and parallelism ("But what the Phillies lost in strength they gained in character"; "Looking at the well-waxed, limber skis, . . . a pair of aluminum ski poles," etc.). The voice may be personal or impersonal, depending on the degree to which the writer wishes to emphasize personality.

TONE AND DISTANCE

Closely related to the level of style you choose is the tone of your writing, your attitude toward your subject and audience. One element of tone is the degree of distance you maintain between yourself and your reader. If, for example, you use a casual style that draws on expressions more common in speech than in writing, your tone would be conversational, as if you were speaking to a small group of friends. As a result, there would be little distance between you and your readers. Informal style also permits this sense of intimacy. In the following paragraph the student writer urges his classmates to become proficient in a foreign language. To do so, he uses the second person ("you") throughout, conveying the impression that he is appealing to his readers directly.

> Chances are, if all things are equal, foreign language ability will be the one asset that raises you above all the other job applicants. Make no mistake: a foreign language is a good "selling point" and a clear advantage in a job-scarce economy. Businessmen who want to clinch those overseas deals, stewardesses on international flights, police and firemen working among foreign-born populations, advertisers who must promote products abroad, radio announcers who must pronounce names correctly, and scientists who must rely on science journals—over 30 percent of which are in a foreign language—to keep abreast of current developments in their field, are just a few of the people who perform their jobs more effectively with a foreign language. Furthermore, it is possible that your company or firm may wish to transfer you to one of its foreign branches. In this age of expanded international trade, it is to your advantage to have even a working knowledge of a foreign language.

Sometimes, the distance between writer and reader is wider, as in the following student paragraph where the writer wishes to explain various elements of her subject. As a result, the passage is toneless, colored neither by an authorial voice nor by any attempt to appeal to the reader:

> Trypanosomiasis, better known as sleeping sickness, is a painful and many times fatal disease that infects a wide area across Central Africa. Carried by the tsetse fly, the disease at one time was known only in a few isolated areas. But as

felled tropical forests gave way to moisture-laden savanna woodlands--excellent breeding grounds for the moisture-hungry tsetse--the disease gradually spread. Above all, the advent of colonialism in the nineteenth century spurred its growth, for the colonialist built modern transportation systems that helped introduce trypanosomiasis to many previously uninfected regions. Today, the disease attacks more than ten thousand people each year, seven thousand of whom die from its ravages. As a result, many of the nations affected have embarked on elaborate programs of control, diagnosis, and treatment.

Your writing occasion and purpose will largely determine the level of style you choose and the degree of distance you maintain between yourself and your reader. Once you make these choices, your chief concern will be consistency. You will not, for example, want to inject a conversational tone in a context that requires distance. Consider the following passage where the student writer forgets this important consideration:

Once ex-cons are released from prison, most of them try to get their act together again. They try to find a job, any job that would bring them some measure of stability and give them a sense of importance. But they don't find one. All their prospective employers treat them like lepers. After all, they might cut out with stolen loot. This is what it boils down to. It doesn't matter whether an ex-con is the best electrician or salesman around. What does matter is the word ex-con. It turns off all employers. This is discrimination, but what can ex-cons do about it? Nothing! Nothing except return to doing something they already know how to do, which is committing crime. What happens after they are arrested, you should already know. At least, you should know since you or society are the ones who indirectly drive the ex-cons back to their former life. They were rehabilitated. Do you really think they wanted to go back to a life of crime just so they could be put right back where they were only a few months ago? No! Of course they didn't. Because of you, me, and society, they were driven, indirectly forced, to commit a crime and to be sent back to prison.

The passage is taken from an essay addressed to a general audience and designed to analyze public attitudes that hinder the integration of ex-convicts into society. The level of style appropriate to the writer's subject, occasion, and audience is therefore informal, best illustrated in the sentence "They try to find a job, any job that would bring them some measure of stability and give them a sense of importance." The subject, moreover, requires distance between the writer and reader. The problem the writer is discussing is widespread in society and not the particular attitude of any one person. Note, though, that the writer loses sight of this almost from the start by introducing slang and stock expressions ("ex-con," "get their act together," "cut out," "boils down to," "turns off") often used in informal conversation but inappropriate in this writing context.

Reliance on a conversational tone in this passage eventually leads the writer to abandon any pretense of distance and to address the reader directly, implying the reader's personal responsibility for the problem being analyzed. The tone becomes shrill, almost as if the writer were wagging a finger at the reader. General readers who expect reasonable arguments would find this tone distasteful. In this case, the writer's purpose and material require a more detached attitude.

FOLLOW-UP ACTIVITY

Test the assumption that the personality of writers may be glimpsed in their style by examining the diction and other language strategies of these personal ads, taken from Raymond Shapiro's *Lonely in Baltimore*. If you find that each projects a particular personality, try writing your own ad that is similarly individual.

1. **JUST LISTED:** 28-year-old real estate professional, tall, thin, brown hair, blue eyes, with these amenities: Eastern values, clean living, ambition, family orientation. Mind/body in great location. Interesting; no payments, nothing assumable. Offered in exchange for smiling, blue-eyed blond, American type, 18–25. Flexible terms.

2. **AVERAGE . . . FEMALE,** 28, average looks, standard height, common traits, usual interests, typical ambitions, moderate income, and ordinary lifestyle seeks a normal, everyday kind of guy.

3. **WHY A VOID? WHERE IS SHE?** Male, mid-thirties, everything going, looks, brains, creativity, boom-boom style, arts, etc. seeks female counterpart. Trim, feminine, aware—Before we all disintegrate in pollution and war—Saw a gray hair yesterday! Oh wow, help!

4. **EXIGUOUS HEIRESS,** 25, anomalous, well-read. Last scion of decaying stock. Seeking corrigible male, cerebral, cynical, compassionate, etc. for desultory correlation. Prefer genius.

5. **YOUNG, FIFTYISH FEMALE** fancies synergistic companionship with witty, wiry, famished fellow who appreciates protean life, flowers, food, freckles. No fickle fakes, fat cats, or fubsy fuddy duddies. Slightly bent or balding OK, but mentally awake.

6. **WIDOWER, 51, NO CHILDREN,** worth $100,000. Seeks lady same age bracket—no children, same financial position.

FIGURATIVE LANGUAGE

A figure of speech is an intentional deviation from ordinary language. A figure can create a picture that helps readers understand the essence of an idea or grasp the essential quality of a thing or person. It can make the strange familiar or the familiar strange. Used with care, the figure will add freshness and vitality to your writing.

Figures of speech often involve comparisons. Three commonly used figures are *simile, metaphor,* and *personification.*

Simile

The simile explicitly affirms the resemblance (introduced by *like* or *as*) between two dissimilar things. It is a useful way to reinterpret the abstract in terms of the concrete, the general in terms of the specific. In the following sentence, the student writer uses the general term *rootless* to characterize actors. Though the term is itself a figure of speech since it ascribes to people a quality usually associated with plants, the writer gives it added figurative power by animating it, drawing on an image from physics to suggest incessant motion:

> Actors are rootless beings, circulating from "gig" to "gig" like electrons in a highly charged magnetic field searching for a nucleus, briefly combining, and then ionizing apart again.

A simile can add vividness and specificity to an already concrete image, as in the following student sentences:

> When she was angry, her shriveled lips would come together like a leather pouch gathered tightly shut by drawstrings.

> One squirrel scampers up mammoth tree trunks while another, stopping to camouflage itself, sits up on its hind legs like a stuffed souvenir from a past hunt.

> The sea is like a vast blue-green carpet needing no upkeep, sweeping or cleaning, for it has survived longer than the toughest wool or burlap.

> On the far side of the pond stands a slender weeping willow as graceful as a water nymph, her tapered fingers probing the water's surface as if seeking something lost.

Metaphor

Like the simile, the metaphor compares dissimilar things, but unlike the simile, it does so implicitly, dispensing with *like* or *as.* To understand how metaphor works, take the student sentence, "When angered, Beth would simmer, then boil, and finally erupt." The verbs in this sentence are used metaphorically. Volcanoes *simmer, boil* and *erupt;* people do not. When two unlike things are compared so that the qualities of one are said to be the qualities of the other, we have the metaphoric equation. In the case of the preceding student sentence, you accept this departure from literal meaning for good reason: it is a more dramatic and faithful account of one kind of human behavior. And more succinct, too. To render the thought literally, you could say, "When angered, Beth would keep her feeling to herself until it grew so intense that she was forced to express it," but such a paraphrase is not only pallid in comparison, it actually fails to capture the full sense of anger pent up and released.

At times, a metaphor is carried beyond the single sentence. When this happens, we have the *extended metaphor.* Though the extended metaphor requires considerable skill and control, student writers often use it effectively. As you read the following example, consider the writer's implied comparison and point out how he maintains it throughout the passage.

```
     Outside, the familiar cadence of heavy-breathing headers
     rumbled in the distance, and I knew some punk was about to
     drag.  His hopped-up car growled.  A crack of the accelerator
     and the beast snarled, a second crack and he roared, his paws
     of rubber gripping the cool asphalt.  Raging with pent-up
     fury, he stormed the highway, ready for the kill.
```

Personification

Personification is a type of metaphor that attributes human qualities to objects or ideas. It is common in everyday speech. To speak of the *eye* of a needle, the *head* of the table, the *arm* of a chair, the *foot* of a bed, is to personify the inanimate object by giving it human characteristics. Such expressions are so common, however, that they have lost the power to surprise. They are dead metaphors that have become permanent fixtures of the language.

Used freshly, personification can add color and vigor to your writing. Here are three possibilities, each demonstrated by a student passage:

Personification can define a response to a personal experience

```
     Carmone Street is a cobblestoned crone who would feel at
     home in Little Italy.
```

While tying my tennis shoes, I glanced over at my polished
boots. They looked so proud, standing spotless and perfectly
straight, as if at attention.

Personification can support a point of view.   In the following passage, the writer uses personification to argue the folly of the Concorde, the
supersonic passenger plane.

The birth of the Concorde took a long time, twenty years in
fact, and it was a costly experience for her parents, who paid
almost three billion dollars in physicians' fees for her
health and well-being. In fact, she was so costly that one
parent (England) tried to abort her but thought better of it
after the other (France) threatened to sue for breach of
contract. Thus, the Concorde was a problem even in her foetal
stage.

Personification can explain characteristics and attributes.   In the
following essay, the student writer skillfully outlines the characteristics of
two types of trees by giving them the power of speech. In this case,
personification becomes the major strategy of the entire essay.

TREES ON A HILL

1   The story I am about to tell you is a bit bizarre, and I
would not blame you if you were to think me crazy. The story,
however, is a true one.

2   I was lying on a hill in the park one day when I heard some
voices behind me. Turning quickly, I glanced up the hill. To
my surprise, I saw only two trees that appeared to be talking
to each other. The tree on my right was a maple tree and the
one on my left an oak. I crept closer to try to hear what
they were saying. When I got close enough to hear them, I
realized they were having an argument.

3   The oak tree stated, "I am a German Oak and have been on
this hill for twenty-five years. I have seen many romances.
I have had hearts carved into my hard wood to prove these
romances existed. My short, broad leaves have provided shade
for many couples in love lounging in the hot summer sun. My
seed, the acorn, feeds many squirrels throughout the winter.
I am, therefore, the most important tree on this hill."

4   The oak tree was just getting his last word out when the
maple tree replied with vehemence, "I beg to differ with you.
I am a Sugar Maple, sir, and have seven rings around my
middle. I, too, have seen many romances, although no one has
carved hearts into my soft wood. I acknowledge that you have
been here a much longer time than I, but I am able to provide
the same amount of shade with my huge three-pointed leaves.

My seeds are also very important. They are not required for the existence of any animal, but they do amuse many people. They throw them in the air and watch them flutter to the ground like helicopters. I have seen many kids split the ends of my seeds and stick them on their noses and pretend they are Pinocchio. This provides psychological relief for humans. I feel by providing this relief I am the most important tree on this hill."

5   "Hogwash!" exclaimed the oak. "I may not provide psychological relief, but my beauty entertains many. In the fall my leaves turn a brilliant red. My leaves are so beautiful that people make time in their busy schedules just to come to the park to admire me. My wood is helpful to people, also. Oak is known as the hardest wood and is used in any sturdy furniture. It is definitely not like your flimsy wood."

6   "My wood is not flimsy," interrupted the maple tree. "It just is not as hard as yours. It does not need to be as sturdy because my main function is to release gallons of sap so that people can make it into maple sugar and maple syrup. If my wood were hard, these people could not tap me to get my sticky treasure. And about those leaves. The people do not come to see your leaves, but they do come to see mine. My leaves take on a deep golden color the splendor of which could not be matched by any shade of red. You, my friend, are just a side show."

7   I decided to leave quickly before they started throwing branches at each other. Halfway down the hill, I met a ranger. Without mentioning the talking trees, I asked him about the merits of the arguments I had heard. Was the German oak more important than the sugar maple, or vice versa? The ranger smiled at my naiveté. "Nature," he explained, "gives us abundance without rank. The key is difference, not importance." I thanked him politely and went on my way, wondering why those silly trees had failed to understand this simple truth.

—Charles Files

FOLLOW-UP ACTIVIITES

1. Try using the verbs below metaphorically. Remember that metaphors compare unlike things. The verb *battled,* for example, keeps its customary or literal meaning in the sentence "The soldiers battled for control of the hill." When, however, it appears in the sentence "He battled the traffic," it is used metaphorically.

launched	flooded	stung
boiled	pawed	slaughtered
clawed	oozed	drowned

2. The following passage lists the metaphors a researcher in artificial intelligence uses to make graphic his conception of the human mind. When you have read the passage, try composing a similar set of metaphors for such things as a dormitory, a popular meeting-place, a sports event.

> Hofstadter has no shortage of metaphors for the mind. An ant colony. A labyrinth of rooms, with endless rows of doors flinging open and slamming shut. A network of intricate domino chains, branching apart and rejoining, with little timed springs to stand the dominoes back up. Velcro-covered marbles bashing around inside a "careenium." A wind chime, with myriad glass tinklers fluttering in the cross-breezes of its slowly twisting strands.
>
> —James Gleick, "Exploring the Labyrinth of the Mind," *New York Times Magazine*

SOME HAZARDS OF WORD CHOICE

Choosing words wisely implies having a variety of options. It also implies elimination, since to select is also to discard. Reasons for making one choice rather than another may vary, but one that often guides skilled writers is the degree to which a word or phrase may be stale, pretentious, or evasive. The hazards of word choice they commonly try to avoid are the *stock figure,* the *cliché, jargon,* and *euphemism.*

The Stock Figure

Overheard conversation:
Student 1:

> I worked like a dog half the night to get my paper done for Professor X. He's a nice guy, but he's hard as nails when it comes to meeting deadlines.

Student 2:

> Well, at least you got it done. The one I have due next week has been sitting on the back burner for days. I'll be in hot water if I put it off much longer.

This simple exchange illustrates our habit of using language figuratively, even in casual conversation. The speakers freely used expressions such as "working like a dog," "hard as nails," putting something on a "back burner," being in "hot water," knowing they would not be taken literally.

English is full of these figurative expressions. Consider how often we compare people to animals: a person may be shy as a kitten, proud as a peacock, blind as a bat, strong as a horse, fleet as a hare. Such comparisons are woven into the fabric of language; they are the homespun of everyday speech. Just as we inherit the vocabulary and syntax of English when we learn to speak, so, too, do we inherit its stock figures.

Because stock figures are prepackaged expressions that can be easily transferred from one context to another, using them in writing often entails the loss of a personal voice. The predictable figure suggests anonymity; it announces that one voice is like any other and that all sing the same refrain. In your personal life, you probably resist this facelessness, finding ways to express your individuality. You need to do the same in your writing. To write well, you should examine the world through your own eyes and sort out your way of seeing and thinking from what others have thought and said.

Clichés

Like worn-out metaphors, clichés have been used so often that they have become stale. Ceremonial occasions are apt to inspire this kind of formulaic language. Consider the commencement speaker who advises graduates to *leave the innocence of youth behind and travel the rough and tumble road of life with courage and fortitude.* Or the speech of the aspiring presidential candidate who promises that he will *stem the tide of America's decline and usher in a new era of peace and prosperity for rich and poor alike.* Frank Sullivan's cliché expert testifies to how the idea of love can be, and often is, expressed in the all-too-familiar catch phrase.

THE CLICHÉ EXPERT TESTIFIES ON LOVE

Q: Mr. Arbuthnot, as an expert in the use of the cliché, are you prepared to testify here today regarding its application in topics of sex, love, matrimony, and so on?

A: I am.

Q: Very good. Now, Mr. Arbuthnot, what's love?

A: Love is blind.

Q: Good. What does love do?

A: Love makes the world go round.

Q: Whom does a young man fall in love with?

A: With the Only Girl in the World.

Q: Whom does a young woman fall in love with?

A: With the Only Boy in the World.

Q: When do they fall in love?

A: At first sight.

Q: How?

A: Madly.

Q: They are then said to be?

A: Victims of Cupid's darts.

Q: And he?

A: Whispers sweet nothings in her ear.

. . . .

Q: What happens after that?

A: They get married.

Q: What is marriage?

A: Marriage is a lottery.

Q: Where are marriages made?

A: Marriages are made in heaven.

Q: What does the bride do at the wedding?

A: She blushes.

Q: What does the groom do?

A: Forgets the ring.

Q: After the marriage, what?

A: The honeymoon.

Q: Then what?

A: She has a little secret.

Q: What is it?

A: She is knitting a tiny garment.

Q: What happens after that?

A: Oh, they settle down and raise a family and live happily ever afterward, unless—

Q: Unless what?

A: Unless he is a fool for a pretty face.

Q: And if he is?

A: Then they come to the parting of the ways.

. . . .

Q: Mr. Arbuthnot, your explanation of the correct application of the cliché in these matters has been most instructive, and I know that all of us cliché-users here will know exactly how to respond hereafter when, during a conversation, sex—when sex—when—ah—

A: I think what you want to say is "When sex rears its ugly head," isn't it?

Q: Thank you, Mr. Arbuthnot. Thank you very much.

A: Thank you, Mr. Untermyer.

—Frank Sullivan, *A Pearl in Every Oyster*

The word *cliché* is French for stereotype plate, a metal plate cast from a page of type that permits multiple reproductions. Its basic meaning corresponds to the familiar English word *stereotype*. In ordinary conversation, the cliché can be a quick and convenient way to express an idea. In writing, however, clichés are best avoided; indeed, discriminating readers and listeners may dismiss cliché-ridden discourse at once because the use of trite or hackneyed terms usually reveals a mind too lazy or too tired to formulate a fresh way of saying something. This is why careful writers· are wary of clichés, which they may use unwittingly simply because they come to mind so easily. Usually, clichés appear in first drafts when you want to get your thoughts down on paper rapidly. While revising, though, you need to examine your words carefully with an eye to editing out commonplace language.

1. The following student essay is an adaptation of a fable, an animal tale that expresses a moral. Its major strategy is personification—in this case, giving human qualities to animals. To give the tale added humor, the writer also deliberately cultivates the cliché. As you read the essay, point out the clichés.

THE ARROGANT SPARROW

1   Once upon a time, there lived a sparrow named Claude. He came from an upper-middle-class nest and was the son of a very happy Mr. and Mrs. Finch. Before Claude was born, the Finches were a contented and peaceful couple. Mr. Finch worked his tail feathers off at a nearby pillow factory, but he enjoyed his work and soon earned enough seed to buy a fine straw nest for himself and his loving wife. Mrs. Finch worked hard to keep the nest clean, and on special days she would cook up one fine mess of seed stroganoff.

2   All of this was shattered when Claude was born. He never obeyed his parents and rarely listened to a peep from them. He walked by his elders with a turned-up beak. Even more, he fouled his own nest by skipping flying school and earthworm anatomy, considering himself too important for these ordinary tasks. As time went on, Claude grew lazier, fatter, and increasingly arrogant.

3   Soon autumn came, and Mr. and Mrs. Finch prepared to move to their summer home in Florida. Claude, however, insisted that since he was superior to the other birds, he would not go. His parents squawked and fluttered, but to no avail. So, while the other birds of a feather were flocking south together, Claude lay in bed popping seeds and drinking a six-pack of Birdweiser Beer.

4   With all the other birds gone, Claude was in fine feather; food was plentiful, and he ate to his heart's content. However, one night it got very cold, and Claude awoke to find a layer of snow on the ground and on himself. The once-plentiful food was now buried, and the already frigid air was getting colder by the minute. Realizing that he should, perhaps, have gone south with the others, Claude exclaimed, "This cold white stuff is for the squirrels!" and began his flight to Florida.

5   The bitterly cold air made flying difficult for such a fat and lazy bird. To make matters worse, a huge storm of freezing rain soon broke, caking his wings with ice. Prepared to meet his maker, the fat, arrogant sparrow plummeted to the ground, crashing into an abandoned corn field. He shivered, wondering how something so terrible could have happened to such a wonderful bird as himself. But luck was with him, for he found to his surprise that he had landed in a pile of cow dung. It was foul-smelling but warm, and soon his icy wings and cold feet began to thaw. He knew that he would survive because of his new-found "home."

6   Feeling renewed, Claude began to sing, attracting the attention of a nearby farm cat. Because the farm cat knew that the birds had already gone south for the winter, he found the sight of a live bird lying in a pile of cow dung curious indeed. Walking over to this oddity, the sly cat asked Claude what exactly he was doing. Claude replied, as arrogant as ever, that it was only through his own considerable bravery that he had survived the cold and snow. At once sensing the arrogance and stupidity of the bird, the cat remarked, "Oh, great one! But you are so dirty! Let me lick you clean so that you can look as great as you really are!"

7   Claude agreed readily, feeling flattered. He strutted over to his new-found valet, proud of this added feather in his cap. Quickly, the farm cat pounced and gobbled him up.

8   The morals of this story are:

1. Not everyone who gets you out of dung is your friend.
2. If you're up to your ears in dung and like it, keep your mouth shut.
3. The next time you feel arrogant think of this story and don't be an arrogant son of a finch.

--Mark Laubenstein

2. Following are some clichés collected by Eric Partridge under the headings *Doublets, Alliteration,* and *Battered Similes.* Read the lists and try to add to each category.

Doublets	*Alliteration*	*Battered Similes*
far and wide	bag and baggage	as fit as a fiddle
heart and soul	might and main	as cool as a cucumber
null and void	rack and ruin	as large as life
to pick and choose	slow but sure	as old as the hills
tooth and nail	safe and sound	as steady as a rock
sackcloth and ashes		as thick as thieves
six of one and half a dozen of another		

3. Clichés are so familiar that usually we can anticipate the entire expression once we've heard the first word. To test your level of cliché recognition, fill in the blanks below.

Mary was sick and _____ of being maligned by people she once thought her tried and _____ friends. Putting her desk in _____ order, she stormed in to the office manager and laid her cards _____. "I've been with this company through thick and _____," she protested, "and it hasn't been a bed of _____. I've put my shoulder to _____ and worked my fingers _____, trying to keep this place from going _____. And all I get for my pains is a stab in _____ from people who would let this company go to the _____ without lifting a _____ to save it. It makes my blood _____ to see a bunch of fools rotten _____ calling the _____ in this office."

The office manager listened to this tirade without blinking an _____. Trying to soothe the troubled _____, he purred, "Mary, I know you've succeeded by the sweat _____. If you hadn't burned the candle _____ when the company was on its last _____, it probably would have gone off _____. You're the salt _____, second to _____ in your loyalty to the firm. No one could step into _____ and do as good a job. Be assured that I will take the bull _____ and speak to the office staff."

Mary heaved a _____ of relief and thanked the office manager from the bottom _____.

Jargon

Jargon refers to two types of language. It may refer to the special vocabulary of a trade or profession; or it may mean long-winded and pretentious language that aims to sound authoritative and weighty, often at the expense of sense. The distinction is between technical language and *gobbledygook,* a word coined by a congressman to express his distaste for the bloated prose of government officials. The first is essential to specialists speaking to other specialists in their field; technical language captures with exactness and economy precise meanings that would otherwise take many more words to convey. Gobbledygook, in contrast, is an attempt to *sound* technical or scientific without a corresponding weightiness in substance. Its ponderousness often hides a relatively simple idea that can be translated into straightforward language.

Technical language easily degenerates into gobbledygook when non- or pseudo-specialists use its special terminology as buzzwords designed to

DOONESBURY

by GARRY TRUDEAU

dazzle a popular audience. Used for this purpose, the specialized term loses its appropriateness and becomes a strategy for hiding meager ideas in high-sounding words. "Doonesbury" provides a good example of the use of buzzwords.

The chief features of gobbledygook are wordiness, excessive use of the passive voice, and a reliance on polysyllabic words. Following are some examples with their translations.

The fact of rapid deterioration of musical skill when not in use soon converts the employed into the unemployable.	Musicians out of practice can't hold jobs.
Nearly all operations in the industry lend themselves to performance by machine, and all grades of men's clothing sold in significant quantity involve a very substantial amount of machine work.	Much men's clothing is machine made.

Within the cleaning plant proper the business of the industry involves several well-defined processes, which, from the economic point of view, may be characterized simply by saying that most of them require separate handling of each individual garment or piece of material to be cleaned.

Each article sent to the cleaner is handled separately.

—Samuel T. Williamson, "How to Write Like a Social Scientist," *Saturday Review*

Though most students avoid the overblown style, it is easy to succumb to the mistaken notion that a big word is better than a short one, or that a phrase is more impressive than a single word. Big words are not of course inherently bad. The student who writes "PCBs are extremely stable compounds; under environmental conditions they do not react chemically to oxidation, reduction, nitration, isomerization, and nucleophilic reactions" is using a number of polysyllabic technical words, but their use is justified because they precisely capture her concept. When, however, big words are used for their supposed glitter and have no connection to the idea expressed, they are best eliminated or recast. Consider the following student sentences:

```
The industrial army has blitzed the suburban kaleidoscope and
the once sensuous places of special quietude are now wasting
away into the flux of contemporary technology.

Restricted expressions in collegiate life are disclosed by the
imposition of limitations on research and report options by
college instructors.
```

In the first example, reliance on fine-sounding big words leads to obscurity. A guess at the writer's intention suggests the rather trite idea that "Technology has destroyed the peace of the countryside," but it would be only a guess likely to tax the reader's patience. Standing in the way of clarity are sonorous but empty phrases like "suburban kaleidoscope," "sensuous places," and "special quietude," as well as vague and garbled metaphors. In the second sentence, meaning is obscured by the writer's addiction to static, polysyllabic nouns that encourage cumbersome prepositional phrases (five in a relatively brief sentence), the passive voice ("is disclosed"), and nouns modifying nouns ("research and report options"). Recast, the sentence seems to mean "College instructors limit the free expression of ideas by restricting students to a certain type of research or report." Note that the revision substitutes the active for the passive voice ("College instructors" become the agent of the action), uses the single word "students" in place of the vague phrase "collegiate life" and introduces the verb "limit," thereby eliminating the phrases "by the imposition of limitations."

1. The following parody is a jargonized version of " 'Twas the Night Before Christmas." As you read it, recall the words of the original and point out how the writer has transformed them into gobbledygook.

'TWAS THE NIGHT BEFORE CHRISTMAS
(IN A MANNER OF SPEAKING)

'Twas the nocturnal segment of the diurnal period preceding the annual Yuletide celebration,
And throughout our place of residence,
Kinetic activity was not in evidence among the possessors of this potential, including that species of domestic rodent known as *Mus musculus.*
Hosiery was meticulously suspended from the forward edge of the woodburning caloric apparatus,
Pursuant to our anticipatory pleasure regarding an imminent visitation from an eccentric philanthropist among whose folkloric appellations is the honorific title of St. Nicholas.

The prepubescent siblings, comfortably ensconced in their respective accommodations of repose,
Were experiencing subconscious visual hallucinations of variegated fruit confections moving rhythmically through their cerebrums.

Hastening to the casement, I forthwith opened the barriers sealing this fenestration,
Noting thereupon that the lunar brilliance without, reflected as it was on the surface of a recent crystalline precipitation,
Might be said to rival that of the solar meridian itself,
Thus permitting my incredulous optical sensory organs to behold
A miniature airborne runnered conveyance drawn by eight diminutive specimens of the genus Rangifer.

Piloted by a miniscule, aged chauffeur so ebullient and nimble
That it became instantly apparent to me that he was indeed our anticipated caller.
With his ungulate motive power traveling at what may have been more vertiginous velocity than patriotic alar predators,
He vociferated loudly, expelled breath musically through contracted labia, and addressed each of the octet by his or her respective cognomen:

"Now Dasher! Now Dancer! . . . " et al.,
Guiding them to the uppermost exterior level of our abode,
Through which structure I could readily distinguish the concatenations of each of the 32 cloven pedal extremities.
As I retracted my cranium from its erstwhile location and was performing a 180 degree pivot,

Our distinguished visitant achieved with utmost celerity a downward leap-entry
by way of the smoke passage.

Clenched firmly between his incisors was a smokingpiece
Whose gray fumes, forming a tenuous ellipse about his occiput, were suggestive
of a decorative seasonal circlet of holly.
His visage was wider than it was high,
And when he waxed audibly mirthful, his corpulent abdominal region undu-
lated in the manner of impectinated fruit syrup in a hemispherical con-
tainer.

Without utterance and with dispatch,
He commenced filling the aforementioned hosiery with various of the aforementioned articles of merchandise extracted from his aforementioned previously dorsally transported cloth receptacle.

He then propelled himself in a short vector onto his conveyance, directed a
musical expulsion of air through his contracted oral sphincter to the
antlered quadrapeds of burden,
And proceeded to soar aloft in a movement hitherto observable chiefly among
the seed-be ring portions of a common weed.
But I overheard his parting exclamation, audible immediately prior to his vehi-
culasion beyond the limits of visibility:
"Ecstatic Yuletide to the planetary constituency; and to that selfsame assemblage
my sincerest wishes for a salubriously beneficial and gratifyingly pleasurable period between sunset and dawn."

—Roger Devlin, *Tulsa Tribune*

2. Translate the following examples of gobbledygook into plain English.

Example A

It is obvious from the difference in elevation with relation to the short depth
of the property that the contour is such as to preclude any reasonable developmental potential for active recreation.

Example B

Verbal contact with Mr. Blank regarding the attached notification of promotion has elicited the attached representation intimating that he prefers to decline the assignment.

Example C

Voucherable expenditures necessary to provide adequate dental treatment
required as adjunct to medical treatment being rendered a pay patient in inpa-
tient status may be incurred as required at the expense of the Public Health
Service.

Example D

"We are wondering if sufficient time has passed so that you are in a position to
indicate whether favorable action may now be taken on our recommendation
for the reclassification of Mrs. Blank, junior clerk-stenographer, CAF 2, to assistant clerk-stenographer, CAF 3?"   —Stuart Chase, *Power of Words*

Euphemism

A euphemism is an attractive or pleasant expression substituted for one generally thought offensive. References to bodily functions which seem too coarse to be expressed directly are excellent candidates for euphemisms, as typified by terms such as *kings and queens, lavatory,* and *john.* Drunkenness may be made more palatable in less offensive terms such as *inebriation* or *intoxication* or, more breezily, *under the weather.* Since the fact of death is too distasteful for most people to face directly, it is often shrouded in a host of expressions, often metaphors, designed to soften its impact *(deceased, passed away, called to heavenly rest, kicked the bucket, threw in the sponge, played his last card).* Indeed, Jessica Mitford writes that the funeral industry, aware of the human inclination to avoid the straightforward mention of death, has obligingly manufactured many euphemisms to gloss over this unpleasant truth:

> . . . a whole new terminology . . . has been invented by the funeral industry to replace the direct and serviceable vocabulary of former times. Undertaker has been supplanted by "funeral director" or "mortician." (Even the classified section of the telephone directory gives recognition to this; in its pages you will find "Undertakers—see Funeral Directors.") Coffins are "caskets"; hearses are "coaches," or "professional cars"; flowers are "floral tributes"; corpses generally are "loved ones," but mortuary etiquette dictates that a specific corpse be referred to by name only—as, "Mr. Jones"; cremated ashes are "cremains." Euphemisms such as "slumber room," "reposing room," and "calcination—the *kindlier* heat" abound in the funeral business.
> —Jessica Mitford, *The American Way of Death*

The connotations of words play a major role in the development of euphemism. Consider, for example, the difference between Internal Revenue Bureau, the original name of the U.S. tax collecting agency, and Internal Revenue Service, a name later adopted. Obviously *Bureau* and *Service* have vastly different connotations, the first bringing to mind an anonymous bureaucracy, indifferent, perhaps, to individual need, while the second takes on an aura of benevolence, as if the IRS were offering assistance to the taxpayer. Or take the fleet of police cars in one community boldly lettered *Public Safety* instead of the more common *Police,* no doubt in an effort to substitute the idea of devotion to public well-being for the negative feelings sometimes aroused by the usual term. Or, in another example, consider the plight of a poor young woman, evidently seeking financial aid from a government agency, who writes,

> I used to think I was poor. . . . Then they told me I wasn't poor; I was needy. They they said it was self-defeating to think of myself as needy, that I was cultur-

ally deprived. Then they told me deprived was a bad image, that I was under-privileged. Then they told me that underprivileged was overused, that I was disadvantaged. I still don't have a dime—but I have a great vocabulary!

> —Quoted in William and Mary Morris, *Harper Dictionary of Contemporary Usage*

Public agencies are not alone in discovering the power of words to influence our thinking and response. The workplace offers many other instances where words designating a profession or job have been deliberately upgraded to enhance social status. H. L. Mencken, an astute student of the American language, has collected a wide assortment of these occupational euphemisms:

> The old-time newsboy is now a *newspaper boy,* which seems to be regarded as somehow more dignified; a dog catcher is a *canine control officer* in Peoria, Illinois; and a *humane officer* in Tulsa, Oklahoma; . . . . A janitor is a *superintendent, custodian, engineer-custodian* or custodial engineer. . . . In 1940 the International Brotherhood of *Red Caps* changed its name to the United *Transport Service Employees of America*. In 1939, when the surviving customers' men in the offices of the New York stockbrokers formed an Association of *Customers' Men* there was a diffidence about their title, which had suffered grievously from the town wits; they soon adopted *customers' broker*. Three years before this the hod carriers of Milwaukee had resolved to be *mason laborers,* and only a few months later the Long Island Federation of Women's Clubs decreed that housewives should become *homemakers*. In 1942 some reformer in Kansas City launched a crusade to make it *household executive*. In 1943 the more solvent spiritualists of the country, fretting under the discreditable connotations of their name, resolved to be *psychists* thenceforth.
>
> —H. L. Mencken, *The American Language*

When euphemism arises from snobbery or from linguistic politeness, it is probably harmless and may even do some good. A janitor who prefers to be known as a *custodian* may do a better job if pride in name carries over to pride in work. To tell a lazy student that he is an *underachiever* may obscure the truth somewhat, but it may also encourage greater effort by suggesting an untapped potential. Other forms of euphemism, however, are not so innocuous. When euphemism is used to hide or evade or distort the truth, it can have powerful social consequences. The language of politics and government, for example, illustrates how words can be used to sanitize or cover up questionable behavior and actions. A public official repeatedly caught lying claims he has a *credibility gap* or that the statements in question are *inoperative;* a recent IRS plan to monitor the spending habits of the American public is called *gathering lifestyle information;* documents an administration wishes to keep secret (a suspect word in the lexicon of democracy) are dubbed *classified;* spying is *covert activity;* a nuclear attack on military targets a *strategic nuclear exchange.* During the Vietnam War, the Pentagon renamed bombing a *protective reaction,* transformed concentration camps into *pacification centers,* and promoted an illegal invasion as an *incursion.*

The following satirical sketch by the popular columnist Art Buchwald offers a classic account of the art of naming to obscure or deceive.

WEAPON-NAMING KEEPS PENTAGON PLANNERS BUSY

You may have noted that the new name for the MX missile is "The Peace-keeper." As much thought went into what to call the missile as to where to put it. You can say what you want about our military planners, but when it comes to naming mega-death weapons they know their business.

An entire military establishment is involved in thinking up new names for weapons. It is one of the most important divisions in the Pentagon, because when Defense is acquiring new hardware it doesn't want to tip off the taxpayer that it is buying a weapon that can obliterate millions of people.

Digby Trident, who is in charge of market research at Defense, told me: "We spend a lot of time and money thinking up names for our new weapons. The more innocent the name, the better chance we have of the public accepting it."

"How do you work?"

"Let's take the 'Cruise Missile.' The name was selected over others after a great deal of market research in on-the-street interviews. The pollsters asked people first how they felt about a new, improved 'Hiroshima Plus Missile' and received an overwhelmingly negative reaction. Then they were questioned how they'd like one called 'Sudden Death.' The male respondents said the name appealed to them because it reminded them of professional football. But most females said the first thing that came to their minds was a lot of families being wasted."

"Women always tend to be more squeamish when it comes to war," I agreed.

"Finally we asked what came to mind when they saw the words 'Cruise Missile.' The majority of those questioned said it made them think of a nice boat on a smooth sea. Eighty percent said they would buy a ticket on a cruise missile, even if they didn't know where it was going."

"How did you come up with the name 'Trident' for the new nuclear submarine?"

"We had originally named it 'Killer Shark.' But it turned out that several dovish senators on the Armed Services Committee had seen the film 'Jaws' and decided to withhold appropriations for it. Since we didn't have another name ready for it and were fighting a deadline, the Admirals said, 'We don't care what you call it, Trident. We've got to have it.'

"The Admiral who was scheduled to testify on the submarine in front of the committee is hard of hearing, and thought we had named it 'Trident.' So that's what he called it when he made his case before the senators, and they loved it. There are a lot of people around here who thought I fixed it so I could have a class of submarine named after me, but I'm completely innocent."

"Where did you find the name 'Peacekeeper' for an MX missile?"

"A couple of months ago we got a call from the White House saying the President planned to make a decision on the MX basing system, and go public with it on television. He was leaning toward the Air Force theory that if you packed 100 missiles in a 20-mile strip, and the Soviets attacked them, the explosion of the first Soviet missile would destroy the other incoming Russian missiles. Then we could fire our MX missiles at the U.S.S.R. with impunity.

"We first thought of calling [it] the 'Fratricide Missile,' but when we test marketed that name we found people thought it meant killing your brother. Then the White House called back and said the President wanted to use the MX missiles as a chip in disarmament talks in Geneva, and he would like a name that would not only alleviate the fears of American Catholic Bishops, but also give a message to the Soviets that we were serious about wanting to cut down on the arms race. So we came up with 'Peacekeeper' which is probably the greatest brand name for a nuclear weapon that we ever thought of."

"It makes you want to buy one for a baby," I said.

"It tells the whole story, as far as we're concerned. It's got the carrot AND the stick."

"What's the carrot?"

"The name 'Peacekeeper.' "

"And what's the stick?"

"The missile itself. With 10 nuclear warheads on each, we've got the greatest sabre-rattler in the business."

It is generally best to avoid using euphemisms unless your writing purpose requires a degree of tact. If, for example, you are writing a paper explaining the services available to people who have lost the use of an arm or a leg, you could refer to these people as disabled or handicapped or crippled. Though for your purposes the last word is the most precise since it excludes other kinds of permanent infirmities, it may nevertheless be an unwise choice in view of its negative connotations. In most cases, however, you will find that choosing the straightforward term will not only save you from wordiness but will give your writing the honesty and clarity that good readers normally expect.

EDITORIAL ACTIVITIES

Editing Jargon and Overwriting

Simplify the following student sentences by substituting direct language for jargon and pretentious diction. Try to stay as close to the writer's meaning as possible.

1. After careful consideration of all the input received from a variety of sources, I concluded that a candidacy by me for the office of president of student government would indeed be viable.

2. I can remember our peals of laughter and then the momentary suspension of this merriment as the segmented sound of cracking glass made its way from the auditory channels to the brain.

3. It is not possible to realize what amount of seclusion is attainable in an urban situation without having stayed in this little abode.

4. It was this physical nausea that forced me to take an introspective look at the reasons behind my extreme aversion to housework.

5. From the time she walked through the door to that infinitesimal moment when my mind could perceive and respond to the stimuli created by her presence, she had become my heart's love.

6. I am assailed by visual sensations that cause a surging tingle of excitement.

7. Before they finally leave their domicile, the sun will have climbed to its heavenly peak.

Editing Clichés and Slang

The following student sentences contain clichés or slang. Use your editorial skills to suggest substitutions. At times, you may find a single word will be appropriate, at other times, you may have to recast the sentence. Try to stay as close to the writer's meaning as possible.

1. If people could, like him, be conscientious and benevolent, he wouldn't stick out like a sore thumb.

2. He not only does not help his friends, he often puts them down.

3. The class was so unruly that the directions of the swimming instructor went in one ear and out the other.

4. Pressure from his parents convinced Brad that he should make a clean breast of what he had done.

5. Those who call the shots should be willing to take responsibility for their decisions.

6. When we missed the train, we were left high and dry.

7. Dressed in the latest of fads, Susie always attracts attention by her way out costume.

8. Tom gives 100 percent of himself in every athletic event.

9. He goes off the deep end every time someone asks him about his brother's suicide.

10. Individuality seems to have fallen by the wayside, and most people buy clothes, whether suitable or not, just to be in fashion.

Editing General-Abstract Words

In the following passages, you'll see how students revised their first draft by moving down the abstraction ladder. Point out how the revision provides a better blend of abstract-general words and concrete-specific words.

Passage A: First Draft

    By the time we straggled to the top, the darkness had lifted. On all sides the mountainous landscape was taking form suddenly but irregularly out of the grey. We were overcome with visual imagery.

Passage A: Revision

    By the time we straggled to the top, the darkness had lifted. On all sides the landscape was taking form suddenly but irregularly out of the grey. In the distance loomed a mountain, mostly green but also white with snow from the top to a quarter of the way down its sides. You could see where the trees, challenged by the snow, had stopped growing. They were mostly pine or evergreen trees, green with thick branches, as sweet smelling as soap, and soft to look at in the distance.

Passage B:
First Draft

Unlike the other buildings in the neighborhood, Mrs. Babcock's is not modern. Large and ostentatious, it seems more appropriate for haunting than for restoring. In good weather Mrs. Babcock can be seen on the front porch, drinking a cup of tea and petting her ancient dogs.

Passage B:
Revision

Unlike the other buildings in the neighborhood, Mrs. Babcock's is a Victorian monstrosity. A twenty—three room mansion with as many garrets, turrets, and minarets as any Disneyland nightmare, it seems more appropriate for haunting than for restoring. If the day is not too blustery, Mrs. Babcock might be seen on the crumbling front porch swing, drinking a cup of Formosa oolong ("the only tea I'll drink") and petting her ancient twin beagles, Calvin and Chester.

YOU ARE THE EDITOR

Point out how the following student sentences could be strengthened by the inclusion of specific-concrete words. You may suggest that the writer keep the general-abstract word and *add* specific-concrete words, or you may suggest that the writer *substitute* specific-concrete words for the abstract-general ones used. Here is how one student writer, acting on his editor's advice, substituted a noun series for the general word *sounds* in the sentence "The sounds were sharp and distinct":

The gurgle of the water behind the transom, the smacking of the bow upon the waves, the creaking of cleats and blocks, and the rush of air through the rigging were sharp and distinct.

1. Brad played several different musical instruments during his senior year in high school.

2. Rare is the fire escape that is not laden with potted greenery of all sorts.

3. I awoke the next morning to the sound of life all around me.

4. An old man clad in a bizarre outfit munches a yellow mound of popcorn.

5. Everyone who leaves the University in the future will be a more rounded and educated person.

6. Elaborately decorated doormen direct you to lobbies bedecked with objects of art.

7. The architecture of the campus buildings is appealing to the eye, and such things as the sports complex and the fountain on the mall would improve the looks of any campus.

8. Her gracious manner impressed the assembled guests.

WRITING SUGGESTION

Write an essay describing a place that has made a deep impression on you. Try to suggest its character or dominant quality (this will be your thesis). The following student essay will suggest some possibilities. As you read it, note how the writer uses figures of speech to evoke the atmosphere of the place he is describing.

AERODROME

An airport is a personable place. Brightly lit, she beckons, intruding upon the solitude of the night sky. Planes are strangers gliding to meet her. As they come near, they appear to be her sole concern. They are taken in and cared for.

Runways appear as welcoming arms preparing to receive a guest, the glow of their lights an invitation. The yellow ribbon of the centerline becomes a rope to be towed by. Aircraft follow the rope trustingly, knowing they won't be misdirected.

Planes wait on the ramp, poised, gently pushing against the chocks, ready for flight. The ramp is dark, with faint shafts of light spilling upon it from other areas. Linemen move as dim figures, barely visible in the light. They are phantoms, unobtrusive, silent, unknown, betrayed only by the dull thump of the fuel hoses they maneuver to feed their charges.

Hangars rise in the distance, dominant and majestic, dwarfing their surrounding structures. Bathed in a soft light, their sand-colored walls shelter and protect the slumbering aircraft, like a mother watching over her children. They are the airport's sentinels, her guardians, her way of showing that an airport is a hospitable place, warm, generous, and helpful.

—William Johnson

TIPS FOR SELF-EDITING

While revising your first draft, examine your word choices for appropriateness, accuracy, freshness, degree of specificity, and honesty. The following questions will help guide your analysis:

1. Is my word choice appropriate to my audience and occasion? Have I observed the appropriate level of style?

2. Have I used words responsibly? Are my words free from slanting, from euphemism?

3. Have I avoided jargon and stock expressions?

4. Are my words concise and direct?

5. Does my word choice reflect a balance between abstract-general words and concrete-specific words?

6. Have I used figurative language where appropriate?

3

MAKING CHOICES

A Peer Editor Workshop

A PEER EDITOR WORKSHOP

*T*he preceding chapters have illustrated the many choices writers make, from the moment they begin to think about a subject to the time they complete their writing. To make these decisions well takes skill and practice, and even with years of writing experience, many writers seldom succeed the first time. They are habitual revisers who regard change as fundamental to the composing process.

Many writers rely heavily on the response of a respected reader to help them determine how well they've succeeded. Often, they revise on the basis of this response. In this section, you'll have a chance to be the reader who will guide the writer's revision. First you'll see how drafts of four student essays have been annotated by an experienced editor. This will help you understand how editors help writers improve their work. You will then see how the writers revised their essays on the basis of the editor's comments. Following each revision is an unedited essay for you to read and annotate.

THE EDITOR AT WORK

The tone of an editor's comment, as you'll see, is especially important. Editors assume that writers want to express something important. They believe that writers are serious and deserve serious attention. Consequently, good editors are never flippant or dismissive, nor are they indifferent to what a writer has done well. When they note flaws, their remarks are supportive, aimed at helping the writer produce a better piece of writing. When they note the strengths of an essay, they do so not only because they find good writing pleasurable, but because they know that praise builds confidence and encourages the writer to try again.

In addition to maintaining a respectful tone, editors are careful to make their comments specific. Comments that are vague or that simply express a feeling or reaction don't give the writer much guidance. Moreover, editors often phrase their comments as questions rather than commands. In the essay that follows, for example, the editor is concerned that the writer has introduced ideas that don't seem relevant to his major point or thesis. The editor's comment begins with a question ("Are this paragraph and the next one related to your thesis?") and then explains the reason for the question. Note the difference if the editor had simply used a deletion symbol or had written, "Delete these paragraphs because they do not contribute to the point of your paper." The questioning technique introduces a tentative note that encourages the writer to review and rethink, perhaps to adopt the editor's suggestion, perhaps not. The command, in contrast, promotes passivity and unthinking obedience. Though the questioning technique is not always feasible, editors use it as often as possible because it encourages dialogue and independent thought.

Editors comment on the content, purpose, organization, and style of an essay—for the most part in the margin, occasionally within the text. They also write observations at the end of the essay that acknowledge what is especially effective and what needs further work. Some marginal comments simply describe what the editor has noticed without suggesting change: an editor may write, "These three sentences begin in the same way," or "You've used the passive voice three times in this paragraph." Such comments are neutral: they simply draw attention to matters the author may have overlooked. Others, though, express a judgment, pinpointing what the author has done well or what may be problematic. Comments that note weaknesses will often suggest specific ways to revise.

The Editing Process

When you begin your peer editing, keep in mind that you are already able to recognize good writing. Knowing this will help you respond honestly to an essay's strengths. Our experience tells us that however inexperienced student writers may be, they always manage to do something well, and you, as an editor will want to confirm the skills they already have. With this in mind, read the essay through first without marking anything, just to get the full sense of what the writer is trying to say. Then go back and point out specific features that you consider especially effective. Did you notice a strong metaphor or verb, a good example, plenty of detail to support an idea? Did the introduction hold your attention? Did it give you a clear idea of what the essay would be about? If you're working on a copy of the essay, you might want to circle or underline those strong features and then, in the margin, tell the author as fully as you can why they work.

After you've provided some positive comments, review the essay again, but this time pay attention to any elements that puzzle you. Perhaps you don't find a main idea or perhaps the main idea is poorly stated; perhaps some logical connections are missing; maybe a certain word throws you off; maybe there are not enough clues and information for the audience the writer seems to have in mind. Whatever the source of confusion, express your uncertainty. You might want to begin by saying, "This is unclear to me" or "I'm not sure what you are trying to say," and then go on to tell the writer why. If you can think of an alternative that you think is better, write it down. Your suggestion may not be adopted, but it's sure to make the writer rethink her original choice.

Once you've pointed out the strengths and whatever you find confusing, consider the *order and development* of the writer's ideas. Examine the paragraphs to see if they're related to the main idea and, if so, whether they're in the most effective order. See how well each paragraph is developed. Has the writer used enough facts, details, or examples to support his ideas? Look closely at the conclusion. Does it fully but succinctly reinterpret the point of the essay? In each case you'll be considering how well—or if—something works, not whether it's right or wrong.

You'll also want to examine the effectiveness and accuracy of *word choice, sentence structure, grammar,* and *mechanics.* Are there any words or phrases that seem tired or stale? Are there extra words that could be omitted? Are the sentence patterns varied? Are there sentences that could be combined? Are there errors in grammar or mechanics? If so, you may want to indicate needed changes with the correction symbols and proofreaders' marks that appear on the inside back cover.

After you have made your comments in the margin, write a brief paragraph that summarizes your response to the essay. What did you find especially effective? What needs further work? Try to give the writer as much help as possible by making your comments specific.

THE EDITING PROCESS: POINTS TO REMEMBER

1. Read the essay through without making notations.

2. Point out the essay's strengths.

3. Identify anything you find confusing.

4. Comment on the effectiveness of organization and development.

5. Comment on the effectiveness and accuracy of word choice, sentence structure, grammar, and mechanics.

6. Summarize your response in a final comment.

Peer Editing and Self-Editing

Practicing your peer editing skills on the essays that follow will prepare you to read the work of your classmates with a critical eye. Your peers will profit from your help, as you will from theirs. And there's an added bonus. You'll find as you go along that learning to become a skilled editor will improve your own writing. You may not always be aware of the interchange, but as the comments of the following students show, there are many ways in which peer editing and self-editing reinforce one another.

```
     I've learned a lot about introductions from my peer
editing--what works and what doesn't work.  I now write about
four revisions of the first paragraph of each essay (I used to
toss them off) because I feel that it sets up the ideas for
the rest of my paper.  Why do I revise?  Well, I want to
express exactly what I mean.  After all, if I think that what
I have to say is important enough for someone to read, then
it's important to make it clear.            --Rosemary Rozman
```

Awkward sentences and repetition--that's what I think peer editing has taught me to look for in my own writing. Now I reread every paragraph (start to end) before I start a new one. This helps me make sure I'm making sense. I also read my paper out loud every four or five paragraphs (drives my roommate nuts).

                                                        --Matt Booty

   I act like a peer editor when I read my own writing because I'm always thinking of what someone else might say. Here's how I do it. First I write a rough draft without making a single change. Then, to give myself an upper, I go back to see what I like ("Lori, you're a genius," I tell myself in the margin). Then starts the real work--getting it right so my reader won't have trouble following what I'm trying to say. I'll experiment with different sentence structures and word order. I'll rearrange what I've written and then, if I'm on another page and a thought hits me which belongs on the first page, I'll go back and add to or change that part. I guess what I've learned most from peer editing is that you can't take anything for granted. It has to be all there. --Lori Bubb

   Well, to be completely honest, writing an essay is like pulling teeth. I guess you could say writing is not my favorite sport. But I think peer editing has helped me get over a couple of blocks. One of them is having enough to say. When I see how other people fill out their ideas, I get ideas for my own writing. I also discovered that I'm pretty good at tinkering with someone else's sentences, and that has given me the confidence to rework my own sentences.   --Karen Lichtle

AN EDITOR'S CHECKLIST

   Here are reminders of the questions editors ask when they examine an essay. Remember that you'll want to consider these questions in the context of the editing process outlined above.

CONTENT AND PURPOSE

1. Does the essay have a main idea? Is the main idea effectively stated?

2. Is the main idea of the essay adequately supported by facts, details, examples, or related information?

3. Is the title effective? Does it alert the reader to the major theme of the essay?

ORGANIZATION AND DEVELOPMENT

1. Is each paragraph related to the main idea?

2. Does each paragraph have a clear focus?

3. Are the paragraphs logically arranged? Is there a better pattern of arrangement?

4. Is each paragraph fully developed?

5. Are the paragraphs coherent? Is there continuity within the paragraph as well as between paragraphs?

6. Is the introduction effective? The conclusion?

STYLE

1. Are the tone and level of style appropriate to the occasion and audience?

2. Is the language direct, clear, and fresh?

3. Is the language too abstract or concrete to suit the writer's purpose and audience?

4. Are words that may be unfamiliar to the intended reader defined?

5. Are the sentences effective? Should they be revised for emphasis, clarity, or variety?

6. Are the sentences concise? Should words be deleted, substituted, rearranged, or added?

7. Does the essay observe standard grammar and mechanics, unless the writer is seeking a special effect?

WORKSHOP ESSAYS

The first drafts of the student essays in this section have been annotated by an editor. They will help you see how editors help writers improve their work. You will then see how the writers revised their essays on the basis of the editor's comments. Compare the revision to the first draft to determine the changes the writer made.

Following each revision is an unedited essay for you to read and annotate. When you have finished editing, compare your comments to those of others in the class. If there is disagreement, determine which comment is better. Keep in mind that sometimes different recommendations can be equally effective.

Writing purpose.   Mark LaPack, the author of the following essay, is responding to an assignment that asks him to express a point of view about a current practice or fad. Himself a dedicated cyclist, Mark decided to argue that cycling was a far better way to promote physical fitness than jogging. He had two kinds of readers in mind when he wrote the essay: those who are looking for some form of exercise and those who are already joggers.

First Draft

RIDE! DON'T RUN

1   Running. Biking. Both activities provide a

very popular and healthy form of exercise. [Or do

they?] Both are good exercises for developing and

Doesn't this sentence somehow question the value of both exercises? Is this your intention?

toning the leg muscles. Both are great aids for

losing weight. Both are important developers of

the cardiovascular system. And both increase

Good use of parallelism to emphasize similarity

mental alertness and sharpen the senses. [But why

is riding a bicycle a much healthier form of

exercise?]

Don't you have to prove this before you state it as a fact?

2   Cycling is healthier and more efficient than

running for many reasons, but to be fair,

bicycling can be an expensive form of exercise.

The serious bicycle enthusiast may spend as much

as $600 and up for top quality, chrome-molybdenum

or aluminum alloy ten-speed racing bikes such as

those made by Nishiki, Fugi, and Raleigh.

However, the serious runner may wear out two or

three pairs of $35 to $40 Nike or Puma brand

running shoes in a year. He may also spend over

$100 on an Olympic style running suit. But just

as in running, most people ride bicycles for

Are this paragraph and the next one related to your thesis? Both seem to support the idea that there are disadvantages to bicycling — not benefits as your first paragraph suggests.

reasons other than competitive ones. For these people, ten-speed bicycles may be bought at prices starting at about $60.

Since it is illegal to ride on sidewalks, another obstacle for bicyclists is the danger of automobiles. To solve this problem, most public parks have bike trails, and a lonely, virtually traffic-free, country road is no further than twenty minutes away from all but the largest cities.

Many athletes are turning to bicycling to replace running in both their on- and off-season training. They have found that bicycling is more efficient and less strenuous on the leg joints than is running. Tony Starks, a senior finalist in the 1980 NCAA wrestling tournament and Indiana Central University's first All-American, switched from running to bicycling to train in the off-season before his senior year. [He found that by cycling, his ankle and knee joints strengthened considerably.] Eric Heiden's training included 100 miles per week of bike riding, aiding him in securing five Olympic gold medals and in shattering the world record in the 10,000 meter speed skating event by a phenomenal 6.20 seconds.

Unlike joggers,
∧Cyclists do not develop[the everyday problems that face joggers such as] blisters, bone bruises,

Does this Paragraph deal with the thesis you've announced in your opening paragraph? **3**

Should this paragraph follow the next one? Isn't it better to show the disadvantages of running before showing that athletes have substituted bicycling for running to keep in shape? **4**

Doesn't this sound as if the ankle and knee joints are bicycling? I would omit "by" and put "strengthened" after "cycling."

5

shin splints, sprained ankles, and stress

fractures. [These are] problems that result from

the friction between the ground and the feet and

legs of the runner. [Only smooth, rhythmic

motions work the muscles of the legs of the

cyclist. The cartilage in the joints is not

damaged by the constant pounding on stark

pavement.] The internal organs themselves [are not

deteriorated] by each reverberating jolt of each

descending footfall, as are those of many long-

distance joggers and runners. Many runners,

including Frank Shorter, a gold and silver

medalist in the 1972 and 1976 Olympics

respectively, begin to urinate blood. [This

condition is] caused by the destruction of small

amounts of muscle, integumentary tissue, and

organs. Bloody urine may occur after a long,

vigorous run, or it may occur after several years

of jolting and jostling the internal organs while

striking the ground with each stride.

6   Bicycling is a more fluid, rhythmic exercise,

and punishing jolts [are eliminated.] The basic

idea of exercising or keeping in shape for

competitive and noncompetitive reasons [is

preserved,] without many of the injuries and the

damages to the joints and internal organs that

result from?
are attributed to running.

If you omit the bracketed material and put a comma after "fractures," you can combine these two sentences.

Can you show the logical relationship between these two sentences by making the first sentence a subordinate clause and attaching it to the second?

If you stay with "cyclists" as your subject, you can substitute the active for the passive voice.

If you substitute "a condition" for the bracketed material and put a comma after "blood," you can combine this sentence with the one above it.

If you use a "that eliminates, etc." clause, you can avoid the passive.

Can you use the active voice?

Mark:

Your point that bicycling is a better way than jogging to build physical fitness is nicely argued. Your examples are good, and you are very specific about the hazards of jogging. I think, though, that you can make your case stronger if you organize your material more effectively. Paragraphs 2 and 3 seem to wander from your main point -- and even to chip away at your thesis. Do you really need them? If so, can you find another place to put them? I think, too, that your argument would have a greater impact on the reader if you first showed the hazards of jogging (par. 4) before you gave examples of athletes who had switched from jogging to bicycling.

Try in your revision to tighten your sentence structure. In some cases, you can combine your sentences, in others, you can eliminate wordiness by switching from the passive to the active voice.

Revision

RIDE! DON'T RUN

1   Running. Biking. On the surface, both activities provide popular and healthy forms of exercise. Both develop and tone the leg muscles. Both are great aids for losing weight. Both are important developers of the cardiovascular system. And both increase mental alertness and sharpen the senses. Despite these surface similarities, however, they do not equally promote health. For many reasons, bicycling is a healthier exercise than running.

2   Unlike joggers, cyclists do not develop blisters, bone bruises, shin splints, sprained ankles, and stress fractures, problems that arise from the friction between the ground and the feet and legs of the runner. Because they rely on smooth, rhythmic motions to work the muscles of their legs, cyclists also avoid damage to the cartilage of leg joints that often results from constant pounding on stark pavement. Moreover, cyclists do not suffer damage to internal organs that often afflicts long-distance runners and joggers. Many runners,

including Frank Shorter, a gold and silver medalist in the 1972 and 1976 Olympics respectively, begin to urinate blood, a condition caused by the destruction of small amounts of muscle, integumentary tissue, and organs. Bloody urine may occur after a long, vigorous run, or it may occur after several years of jolting and jostling the internal organs while striking the ground with each stride.

3   Many athletes are turning to bicycling to replace running in both their on- and off-season training because they have found that bicycling builds powerful legs with less stress on the leg joints. Tony Starks, a senior finalist in the 1980 NCAA wrestling tournament and Indiana Central University's first All-American, switched from running to bicycling to train in the off-season before his senior year because he found that bicycling strengthened his ankle and knee joints considerably. Eric Heiden's training included 100 miles per week of bike riding, aiding him in securing five Olympic gold medals and in shattering the world record in the 10,000 meter speed skating event by a phenomenal 6.20 seconds.

Bicycling is a fluid, rhythmic exercise that eliminates
4   punishing jolts. Moreover, bicycling preserves the basic idea of exercising or keeping in shape for competitive and noncompetitive reasons without the risk of injury to joints and internal organs that often results from running. If you can afford a decent bicycle which costs anywhere from $60 to $300, you will probably enjoy a far healthier form of exercise than jogging can offer. Take my advice: "Ride! Don't run."

                                                      --Mark LaPack

YOU ARE THE EDITOR

Writing purpose. Like Mark LaPack, the author of the following essay is expressing a point of view about a current practice, in this case, the practice of some college instructors to give early finals. The essay is addressed to concerned students as well as faculty.

THE INJUSTICE OF EARLY FINALS

As each semester comes to a close, one must

prepare for final exams. These spine-tingling

affairs usually take place during a specified

week when, and only when, these important tests

are supposed to be scheduled. However, some professors find it an advantage to present final exams before the final exam week begins. When this is done, it puts the student at a disadvantage in many ways.

Of course finals scheduled before finals week make for one less test to study for and one more out of the way. That may seem like an advantage to some, but to most people, there is a different perspective in which to look at this issue. Prior to finals week there are many assignments and classes to finish up and to attend. Thus, one's time is in great demand. Hours for studying, uninterrupted by classes to attend, and everything else to finish, are rather hard to come by. Anyone will testify to the fact that when the end of the semester comes, there is much to accomplish, and not much time in which to accomplish it all. When an early final is added to this already full schedule, the result is hectic.

Professors which take part in this early final practice reason that some students will be glad to get one out of the way. The professors themselves I'm sure don't mind getting done earlier. It's possible that the professors do not realize the position they are putting the students in. Maybe they don't realize how tight a student's schedule can be before finals week begins, and that in fact the professors believe they are doing the students a favor by getting an exam out of the way. However, by scheduling early final exams, the professors are helping no one but themselves.

Finals week is designed as a week when no classes are to meet. Therefore an extra 15-20 hours are saved by each student and they can be used to study. Since final exams require a lot of extra study apart from that spent normally on each class, these extra hours during final exam week are more than welcomed by students. They are a necessity. Because of this it is unfair to permit these tests to be held while classes are still in progress.

Another reason that may seem trivial but nonetheless is an influencial factor in the discussion of finals, is the overall atmosphere that exists during finals week. Extra quiet hours are enforced and the normally crazy atmosphere of a college campus changes drastically. Students which have to prepare for final exams do not have this atmospheric advantage. They may have just the opposite of an atmosphere to contend with. Everyone seems to take it easy and have a good time just before they must begin the drudgery of studying for

finals. Therefore a less than studious
atmosphere is presented to those having early
finals.

Early final exams put a student at a
disadvantage in many ways. It may make for one
less on their mind during finals week, however,
it is by no means an advantage. The student who
is forced to take an early final most likely
could have done better had the final been taken
during the regular finals week. The atmosphere
during finals week does not exist for the benefit
of those who must take early finals. Students
with early finals must try to prepare themselves
while continuing with their classes and
assignments. For these reasons, it is unjust
that finals are permitted to be given before the
finals week officially begins. In the end this
benefits only the professor.

Writing purpose.   The author of the following essay is interested in
medicine generally and in sports medicine in particular. Writing for
nonspecialists who are curious about new developments in medical
research, she attempts to explain a new procedure in the treatment of
cancer.

First Draft

A POTENTIAL CURE FOR CANCER
Do you need this?

1   One [of the most] recent discoveries in
Do you need this?
cancer research has been in [the field of]
immunology. Doctors have developed a specialized
immune cell called a <u>hybridoma</u> which will fight
against cancer cells in the same manner that

other immune cells destroy viruses or bacteria that cause other diseases. Doctors are very hopeful about the use of hybridomas because they promise to be more effective and there are fewer *Don't these need to be parallel?* dangerous side effects than the current treatments with chemotherapy or radiation.

2   When a person "catches" a virus, the body's white cells will attack the foreign cells because *Can you think of an opening sentence that would state the point of this paragraph?* they recognize that they do not belong in the body. When a person has cancer, however, the white cells do not recognize the tumor or cancer cells as being foreign, because they began as normal cells within the body. Another reason the immune system does not fight against cancer is that in some way cancer suppresses the system so that it does not function efficiently.

3   The process of developing hybridomas begins with locating the cancer cells in the patient. Some of these cells are extracted and then injected into a healthy mouse. Since the cancer cells are foreign to the mouse, its immune system begins to respond and develops cells to attack the cancer.

4   Once the mouse develops immune cells which will fight the cancer, researchers must isolate and extract them and then produce them [in a large *Don't you mean a quantity large enough to destroy the cancer?* quantity in order to use them against the cancer in the original patient.]

5   Even under ideal conditions, however, the
immune cells would reproduce very slowly on their
own. [So researchers fuse the original immune

Can you combine these sentences to clarify the reason for the procedure?

cells with cancer cells. Cancer cells multiply
very quickly.] When the two are combined
researchers are able to produce the needed
amounts of the new cells. They are called
hybridomas because hybrid is a new form created

Good definition!

from two different parents and oma means cancer.

6   After the hybridomas have been grown in
sufficient quantities, they are injected into the
original cancer patient. Since these [contain

I think you mean they are partly composed of the patient's cancer cells.

parts of the patient's own cancer cells,] they are
not rejected and are allowed to work as part of
the immune system. They travel through the body
until they find the cancer cells they are
designed to destroy. The effectiveness of this
treatment depends on how far the cancer has
progressed. So far, it has been successful
against cancer in early stages but has not worked

If you substituted "possibly" for the bracketed material, you could combine the last two sentences in this paragraph.

well against more developed cancer. [This is
possible] because in later stages, when cancer has
spread to other areas of the body, the hybridomas
may not recognize the cancer in its new site.

7   Doctors are continuing experiments with
this new treatment in an attempt to refine and
improve it. One method they may use to improve
it is to combine hybridomas with chemotherapy. A

major side effect of chemotherapy is that the
chemicals damage other body cells that are
similar to cancer cells, especially fast-growing
cells like hair and the linings of the stomach
and intestines. Since hybridomas cluster only
around cancer cells, [if the chemicals could be
bonded to the hybridomas, they would be confined
to the cancer site.]

So what, then, would be the effect of confining them to the cancer site?

Can you begin the sentence with the bracketed material?

8

The treatment of cancer with hybridomas is
still experimental and the combination of
chemotherapy and hybridomas is just beginning to
be researched. Since the early results of these
experiments have been |so successful,| doctors are
confident that they are very close to finding a
cure for cancer.

Can you hedge a bit? Hybridomas are not always successful, as you note.

Jane:

   You've explained a complicated process rather well.
The background you provide in paragraphs 1 and 2
is especially useful to readers who are not
medical specialists. You need, though, to clarify
your ideas in a couple of places. Paragraph 2 would
benefit from a topic sentence that would signal
its focus. Some of the ideas in paragraphs 4, 5,
and 6 need to be rephrased to sharpen your
meaning. You might also consider hedging your
conclusion. If, as you say, the new procedure
is not always successful, you need to acknowledge
this in your summary.

1   One recent discovery in cancer research has been in
immunology. Doctors have developed a specialized immune cell
called a hybridoma which will fight against cancer cells in
the same manner that other immune cells destroy viruses or
bacteria causing other diseases. Doctors are very hopeful
about the use of hybridomas because they promise to be more
effective and to have fewer dangerous side effects than
chemotherapy or radiation.

2   Until the discovery of hybridomas, the body's immune system
would not destroy cancer cells. When a person "catches" a
virus, the body's white cells will attack the foreign cells
because they recognize that the foreign cells do not belong in
the body. When a person has cancer, however, the white cells
do not recognize the tumor or cancer cells as being foreign
because they began as normal cells within the body. Another
reason the immune system does not fight cancer is that in some
way cancer suppresses the system so that it does not function
efficiently.

3   The process of developing hybridomas begins with locating
the cancer cells in the patient. Some of these cells are then
extracted and injected into a healthy mouse. Since the cancer
cells are foreign to the mouse, its immune system begins to
respond and develops cells to attack the cancer.

4   Once the mouse develops immune cells which will fight the
cancer, researchers must isolate and extract them and then
produce them in a quantity large enough to destroy the cancer
in the original patient. Even under ideal conditions,
however, the immune cells reproduce very slowly on their own.
To speed up the process, researchers fuse the original immune
cells with cancer cells because cancer cells multiply very
quickly. When the two are combined, researchers are then able
to produce the needed amounts of the new cells. These new
cells are called hybridomas because hybrid is a new form
created from two different parents and oma means cancer.

5   After the hybridomas have been grown in sufficient
quantities, they are injected into the original cancer
patient. Because they contain, in part, the patient's own
cancer cells, they are not rejected and are allowed to work as
part of the immune system. They travel through the body until
they find the cancer cells they are designed to destroy. The
degree of their effectiveness depends, however, on how far the
cancer has progressed. So far, they have been successful
against cancer in early stages but have not worked well
against more developed cancer, possibly because in later

stages, when cancer has spread to other areas of the body, the hybridomas made from cancer cells extracted from one site may not recognize the cancer in its new site.

6   Doctors are continuing experiments with this new treatment in an attempt to refine and improve it. One method they may use to improve it is to combine hybridomas with chemotherapy. A major side effect of chemotherapy is that the chemicals damage other body cells that are similar to cancer cells, especially fast-growing cells like hair and the linings of the stomach and intestines. If the chemicals could be bonded to the hybridomas, they could be confined to the cancer site, since hybridomas cluster only around cancer cells. As a result, healthy cells would not be destroyed.

7   The treatment of cancer with hybridomas is still experimental and the combination of chemotherapy and hybridomas is just beginning to be researched. Since the early results of these experiments have been encouraging, doctors feel hybridomas may be a potential cure for cancer.

—Jane Rubesch

YOU ARE THE EDITOR

Writing purpose.   The essay below explains how a drill team is trained. The author is writing for college students who have watched drill teams but who are unaware of the painstaking work involved in their training.

ALL THIS FOR FOUR MINUTES?

The use of the drill team to complement the

marching band in field and track shows has more

than doubled over the past ten years in college

and high school bands. In these shows the drill

teams work around the band as a secondary or

special effect unit. Just recently, however,

drill teams have developed an image of their own,

presenting spectacular floor shows without the

band. These drill teams consist of flag, rifle,

and majorette corps. The shows they present

demand practice, training and precision from each member and usually take anywhere from fifty to two hundred hours to perfect.

The first step in producing a drill team show is choreographing a routine that effectively uses the music and conglomerates the three units within the team. This routine is choreographed by team captains. It usually centers around several intricate maneuvers. Such a maneuver could be a difficult head chop. In this stunt, rifles are tossed, flags are passed between the rifler and the twirler, and finally rifles are caught. The extreme difficulty of such a move produces a crowd-arousing effect if it is carried out with no major flaws. A simple flash move done perfectly and with snap can also have a spectacular effect. So can creative patterns and floor coverage.

Once the captains have choreographed the show, they must then spend several days simply teaching the marching part of the show. In these sessions drill team members use no equipment and concentrate entirely on marching maneuvers, floor patterns, and the general flow of moving from one formation to the next.

Only after the marching drill has been learned are equipment and routines, usually falling in sequences of eight or sixteen counts, taught. It takes several hours of going through each sequence again and again before the team is able to go through the entire show without stopping. These practices are primarily concerned with continuity, the overall flow of one routine to the next. After the routine is learned, music, marching, and routine are then synthesized.

The next step is to perfect the show. This step is probably the most difficult and time-consuming element of the entire production. The objectives of this stage are uniformity and precision. Instead of being thirty-six individuals or three separate units, the group becomes one single team, working together for one purpose. Hand positions, body carriage, and even facial expressions must all be identical. Simple head moves must be practiced over and over for precision. Rifles must be tossed the same height, and flags positioned at the same angle. Precision, the key word in a good drill team show, is reflected in the snap and uniformity of the entire group.

Before the performance boots are polished, sashes straightened, and make-up applied. A formal inspection usually lasting twenty minutes is conducted by captains while the drill team stands at attention.

Once the show begins concentration and pride are of utmost importance. The crowd does not exist to the performer who must direct all her attention to each part of the show. Pride usually comes naturally, the thrill and glamour of being in the limelight reflected in the performance. Perhaps it is this feeling of pride and glamour that makes the intense hours of grueling practice for the four-minute show worth the trouble.

Writing purpose.   Larry Crawford, the author of the essay below, is a car buff. Asked to write an essay that would clarify and explain the differences between two things, he decided to write about two synthetic automotive fuels. Larry decided to address his essay to readers who were looking for a way to end American dependency on foreign fuel resources but were unaware that recent developments in fuel technology offered one such way.

First Draft

SYNTHETIC [SYNDROME] *Is this the word you want?*

1   Because the world has become increasingly dependent on the vast oil reserves in the Middle East, [Ahab the Arab] has been able to charge *Can you think of a less derogatory way to refer to people in the Middle East?* exorbitant prices for his "black gold." Concerned citizens and industries of the United States who cannot trust [Ahab's dependency] have *Doesn't this sound as if Ahab is dependent?* decided to search for alternative fuel sources to decrease this country's need for foreign crude. One such application of [this newly discovered] *Have you mentioned what has been discovered?* technology is in the field of automotive transportation, [providing synthetic fuels for

What does this phrase modify?

sources of travel.⎤ Examples of two different synthetic fuels are hydrogen and electricity. Although many years of experimenting and testing are needed before mass production of either begins, both appear to be practical substitutes for gasoline. They differ, however, in several important ways.

Good transition.

2 One distinct difference between hydrogen and electric vehicles is the power plant needed for the two fuels. In a hydrogen car, an electric motor turns on an engine which provides heat to two tanks filled with liquid hydrogen. The hydrogen is pumped in between two tanks, liberating the hydride ion which is sent to the carburetor, mixed with oxygen, and burned like regular gasoline in the piston chamber, causing the drive shaft and wheels to turn. In an electric automobile, a large electric motor is turned by the power provided by a bulky battery, causing a similar shaft to turn and giving the wheels motion.

3 The fuels also differ in the amount of mileage they get. A hydrogen-powered Cadillac Seville made by the Billings Energy Corporation is able to cruise sixty miles per tank of hydrogen. A fully charged auto equipped with two tanks of hydrogen liberating the ion hydride can travel one hundred miles. Once this supply runs

chemically to completion, a new supply can be

generated and introduced into the car in thirty

Can you think of a transition that would move the reader from hydrogen-powered vehicles to electric vehicles?

minutes.∧ Electric vehicles are capable of

running for an entire day on a full charge but

must sit overnight to rejuvenate the battery. On

a cold day, the electric car must use part of its

battery supply to provide heat to the vehicle,

which reduces the overall mileage attainable.

Can you interpret this information for the reader? Which gets better mileage?

4 The cost of these alternate fuel sources

also differs. Hydrogen fuel can be used in an

existing gasoline engine system. A Dodge Omni

can be purchased for fifteen thousand dollars to

These consecutive sentences open in the same way.

run on either by the flip of a switch. An

electrolyzer unit, which converts water to

hydrogen, must also be purchased for an

additional fifteen thousand dollars because the

hydrogen required is not produced in large

Is this the best position for the modifier?

quantities [as of today] The twin tanks which

hold the hydrogen are capable of lasting the

car's life. Batteries that run the electric

vehicle must be changed every two years and are

Can you provide more information about the cost of these batteries?

costly to replace. [The battery required is so

bulky that only one passenger can ride with a

driver. This can prove inconvenient on a long

Are these details related to cost, the main point of your paragraph?

This sounds as if the alternate fuels are already being widely used. Is this the point you've made in your paper?

vacation]

5 [The search for alternate fuels continues to

relieve the dependency on Ahab's crude oil.] The

fuels may be underdeveloped for mass use but if

given time to be researched, could prove highly
effective. [Both synthetic fuels are clean; they *Have you discussed these ideas earlier?*
do not pollute the atmosphere as do fuels derived
from oil. Their use could thus prove purifying.
By choosing such fuels we benefit the
environment.]

Larry:
You've provided some good information for readers who know little or nothing about recent developments in fuel technology. You need, though, to interpret some of your facts. What do they add up to? How do they support your idea that the fuels you describe may, indeed, be feasible alternatives? You also need to modify your tone, especially in the first paragraph when you refer to people in the Middle East. Look closely at your conclusion. Does it introduce ideas you haven't really discussed?

The Essay Revised

SYNTHETIC SUBSTITUTES

1   Because the world has become increasingly dependent on the
vast oil reserves in the Middle East, countries producing this
oil have been able to charge exorbitant prices for their
"black gold." Fearful of this dependency, industries in the
United States have decided to search for alternative fuel
sources to decrease this country's need for foreign crude.
One result of this search has been the development of
synthetic fuels to power automobiles. Examples of two
different synthetic fuels are hydrogen and electricity.
Although many years of experimenting and testing are needed
before mass production of either begins, both appear to be
practical substitutes for gasoline. They differ, however, in
several important ways.

2   One distinct difference between hydrogen and electric
vehicles is the power-plant needed for the two fuels. In a

hydrogen car, an electric motor turns on an engine which provides heat to two tanks filled with liquid hydrogen. The hydrogen is pumped in between two tanks, liberating the hydride ion which is sent to the carburetor, mixed with oxygen, and burned like regular gasoline in a piston chamber, causing the drive shaft and wheel to turn. In an electric automobile, a large electric motor is turned by the power provided by a bulky battery, causing a similar shaft to turn and giving the wheels motion.

3   The fuels also differ in the amount of mileage they get. A hydrogen-powered Cadillac Seville made by the Billings Energy Corporation is able to cruise sixty miles per tank of hydrogen. A fully charged auto equipped with two tanks of hydrogen liberating the ion hydride can travel one hundred miles. Once this supply runs chemically to completion, a new supply can be generated and introduced into the car in thirty minutes. The electric car is not as efficient. Although it can get between fifty to one hundred miles per charge, it can run only one day on a full charge and must be recharged overnight. Moreover, on a cold day, the electric car must use part of its battery supply to provide heat to the vehicle, thereby reducing the overall mileage it can get.

4   The cost of these alternate fuel sources also differs. Hydrogen fuel can be used in an existing gasoline engine system. For fifteen thousand dollars, a Dodge Omni can be purchased that will run on either gasoline or hydrogen simply by flipping a switch. An electrolyzer unit which converts water to hydrogen must also be purchased for an additional fifteen thousand dollars because, as of today, the hydrogen required is not produced in large quantities. The twin tanks which hold the hydrogen are capable of lasting the car's life. At this point, the cost of running an electric car appears to be higher. Most electric cars built today are kit-made cars bought from the manufacturer and assembled by the buyer. The Bradley Automotive Company, for example, offers an electric car for around eight to nine thousand dollars. This relatively reasonable cost, however, is increased by the need to purchase new batteries frequently. The battery presently in use is the lead-acid battery which has a short life span and can be recharged only a few times. However, General Motors is now working on a zinc-nickel battery capable of over three hundred charges and discharges and twice as powerful as the present lead-acid battery. If they are successful in making this battery problem-free, the cost of running the electric car would probably be lower than the cost of running the hydrogen-powered car.

5   Though synthetic fuels such as hydrogen and electricity are
not yet ready for mass use, current research indicates that
they could prove highly effective, especially if their cost is
reduced. If they fulfill their promise, America will no
longer be dependent on Middle East crude oil. Maybe then we
won't have to worry any more about gas lines and high gasoline
prices.
                                            --Larry Crawford

YOU ARE THE EDITOR

Writing purpose.   The following essay is written from the perspective of
the hunter who wishes to explain differences in the firearms hunters use.
The essay is written for the non-hunter who might consider taking up the
sport, or for the reader who is simply curious about the author's subject.

SHOTGUNS AND RIFLES

     Shotguns and rifles in America today are

becoming increasingly more popular. To the

average person, the outward appearances of these

two guns look extremely similar. To the hunter,

however, there is a great deal of difference.

     The outside of a shotgun and rifle are very

similar. They both have a forearm, stock,

trigger, and barrel; and both come in pump,

automatic, and bolt actions. Yet there are many

differences, starting with the barrel.

     The barrel of a shotgun is usually twenty-

eight inches long and comes in either plain or

ventilated rib. The rifle barrel, on the other

hand, is usually twenty-two inches long and is

always plain barrel. The sights on a shotgun

barrel consist of a series of beads, while the

sights on a rifle barrel consist of a small bead on the end of the barrel and a rear sight which is the shape of a capital "V." Even the insides of the barrels are different. The inside of a shotgun barrel is smooth, while the inside of a rifle barrel contains little grooves called "rifling" to give the bullet a rotating motion as it leaves the barrel.

Both shotguns and rifles fire different sizes and types of shells. The shotgun shell consists of a brass rim approximately one inch high on top of which there is a three—inch—high plastic casing. All shotgun shells are center fire, while the smaller rifle shells are rim fire. The projectiles a shotgun fires is called a "shot." This shot consists of various amounts of lead pellets, ranging in size from 00 buck to number 9 shot. (The size of a shot is determined by the diameter of the pellet.) The rifle projectile, on the other hand, is called a bullet. The bullet consists of tightly packed grains of lead, the size of which is determined by the number of grains the bullet contains (usually between 100 to 300).

Both the shotgun and the rifle are used for hunting and target shooting, yet there is a difference. In hunting, one uses the shotgun when one needs a quick, short shot which is not

very accurate. The main types of hunting done
with a shotgun are rabbit, quail, pheasant, and
squirrel. Due to the quick, erratic moves of
these animals one needs a quick generalized shot,
exactly what the shotgun was designed for. In
hunting, the rifle, however, is used where a
long, accurate shot is needed. The main types of
hunting done with a rifle are deer, varmint, and
big game hunting. Because of the distances
involved and the accuracy needed for this type of
hunting, the rifle works perfectly.

Another difference contrasting the rifle to
the shotgun is the cost. The price of a shotgun
can range from $38.95 up to and in excess of
$5,000. The average shotgun costs about $200.
The price of a rifle may range from $19.85 to
over $1,000 with the average rifle costing around
$125. The price of ammunition makes a difference
too. The price of a box of shotgun shells
consisting of twenty-five, costs in excess of
$5.75 while the cost of a box of .22 caliber
rifle shells costs around $3.06 for a box of one
hundred.

Purely looking at guns, one can't possibly
see all the differences, but to the serious
hunter there is a different gun suited just for
the job he needs.

Writing purpose.　The purpose of the following essay is to give instructions. An experienced soccer player, the author seeks to give advice to the novice soccer player on how to kick the soccer ball properly.

First Draft

HOW TO PLAY SOCCER CORRECTLY *Is this the title you want? Your essay seems to be about kicking the soccer ball correctly.*

1　　I have been told by many people that soccer is easy to play. They think that all the beginning player needs to do is to get out on the field and start playing. As an experienced soccer player, I [cannot be persuaded to believe] *Can you condense this?* that this is true. Someone who wants to play soccer well needs some basic knowledge about the *Agr/Pn* game before they begin to play.

2　　One of the basics [which I will deal with a *Do you need this?* little] is properly kicking the ball. There are fundamentally two styles of kicking, these are *cs you might try a colon and list the kicks.* instep and shoelace kicks. The instep kick is used to direct the ball for accuracy, while the shoelace kick is used for power shots. The instep kick uses the instep of the shoe which has the most area of contact with the ball. Since most of the area of the shoe is touching the ball, better ball control [can be obtained and *Would the active voice be better here?* better accuracy achieved.] However, more accuracy means less power. ∧The shoelace kick uses the

Can you help the reader move from one kick to the other? You might use the idea of power as a transition.

shoelaces of the shoe and therefore the full swing of the leg is employed and the power. However, accuracy is diminished because the

shoelaces do not provide as much of a contact
surface as the instep does.

3   If you keep these two basic kicks in mind,
you will be ready to start your training. First,
put the ball in front of you and place your left
foot very close to the left side of the ball.
Then turn your right foot perpendicular to your
left foot and turn the instep to the ball.
Without much follow-through, kick the ball with a
quick stroke. [Keeping in mind] *Do you need this?* to direct the ball
forward, kick it dead center; to the left, kick
it right of dead center; and to the right, kick
it left of dead center. [This is the instep kick.] *Shouldn't this sentence appear at the beginning of the paragraph?*
To keep the ball low to the ground position your
body over the ball as much as possible without
hindering your kicking motion. To give the ball
flight, lean backward a little and kick it below
dead center.

4   For the power shots which employ the
shoelaces, put the ball in front of you. Place
the left foot approximately two to two and one-
half feet from the left side of the ball or as
far left as possible, with the right leg
extending to the ball. Lean to the left, putting
the entire weight on the left leg, and, taking
the right leg stiffened straight, swing it to the
ball with the shoelaces facing the ball. [Keeping

Not a full sentence. Try beginning the sentence with "Keep."

in mind at all times that your eyes should be peeled on the ball.] Then, with all the strength possible, kick the ball with a short burst of power and without a long follow-through. The ideal placement of the ball is about waist high, with the ball traveling as fast as possible. [In attempting] this ideal, you need to kick the ball slightly below dead center and as hard as possible, but this takes practice.

Don't you mean "to achieve"?

Can you make these tips more emphatic by using a colon to introduce them?

5   The tips that will aid you in bettering your performance are keep your eyes on the ball at all times, know where you want it to go before you kick it, and do not kick it with the toe. [The toe kick is never taught in sooooer, therefore no one should ever come across the occasion to use it.] The follow-through [is not emphasized] because the kick is mostly in the moment the shoe is in contact with the ball. The rest of the kick is a waste of motion, what little follow-through there is, is natural.

cs

Do you need this sentence?

You use the second person ("you") as your subject in the opening sentence. If you continue using it as your subject, you can eliminate the passive voice.

cs

6   Practice should begin slowly and then gradually [work up] as the leg becomes accustomed to the strain. It is a good idea to do calisthenics before and after the practice because calisthenics [are muscle flexing actions that relieve muscle tension.] If you follow all these procedures, you may not become a star

Do you mean increase?

Can you tighten this sentence by deleting "are"? What do calisthenics do?

soccer player, but you will find a place for

yourself on the soccer team.

Robert:

You obviously know a good deal about soccer, and your directions are generally clear. At times, though, you neglect to highlight a central point in your discussion. In paragraph 3, for example, you discuss the instep kick, but the reader doesn't know the point of your discussion until midway in the paragraph. Try also to make your discussion more emphatic by paring unnecessary words. Consider punctuation as well: you tend to join two independent clauses with a comma.

The Essay Revised

HOW TO KICK A SOCCER BALL CORRECTLY

1   I have been told by many people that soccer is easy to play. They think that all the beginning player needs to do is to get out on the field and start playing. As an experienced soccer player, I don't believe this is true. Someone who wants to play soccer well needs some basic knowledge about the game before he begins to play.

2   One basic thing a beginner needs to know is how to kick the ball properly. There are two basic types of kicks: the instep kick and the shoelace kick. The instep kick is used for accuracy, while the shoelace kick is used for power shots. The instep kick is done with the instep of the shoe, an area which has the most contact with the ball. Since most of the shoe is touching the ball, the player gets better ball control and therefore achieves greater accuracy. However, more accuracy means less power. A more powerful kick is the

shoelace kick made with the shoelaces of the shoe. This kick is more powerful because it allows the full swing of the leg. However, accuracy is diminished because the shoelaces do not provide as much contact area as the instep does.

3   If you keep these two basic kicks in mind, you will be ready to start your training. To do the instep kick, put the ball in front of you and place your left foot very close to the left side of the ball. Then turn your right foot perpendicular to your left foot and turn the instep to the ball. Without much follow-through, kick the ball with a quick stroke. To move the ball forward, kick it dead center; to move it to the left, kick it right of dead center; to move it to the right, kick it left of dead center. To keep the ball low to the ground, position your body over the ball as much as possible, without hindering your kicking motion. To give the ball flight, lean backward a little and kick it below dead center.

4   For the power shots which employ the shoelaces, put the ball in front of you. Place the left foot approximately two to two and one-half feet from the left side of the ball or as far left as possible. Lean to the left, putting the entire weight on the left leg, and, taking the right leg stiffened straight, swing it toward the ball, with the shoelaces facing the ball. Keep in mind that your eyes should be peeled on the ball at all times. Then, with all the strength possible, kick the ball with a short burst of power and without a long follow-through. Ideally, you should try to place the ball waist high and have it travel as fast as possible. To achieve this ideal, you need to kick the ball slightly below dead center and as hard as possible, but this takes practice.

5   To improve your performance, try following these tips: keep your eyes on the ball at all times, know where you want it to go before you kick it, and do not kick it with the toe. You don't need to worry about the follow-through because the power of the kick depends on the moment the shoe is in contact with the ball. The rest of the kick is a waste of motion; what little follow-through there is, is natural.

6   Practice should begin slowly and should gradually increase as the leg becomes accustomed to the strain. It is a good idea to do calisthenics before and after the practice because calisthenics flex muscles, thereby relieving muscle tension. If you follow these procedures, you may not become a star soccer player, but you will play a good enough game to guarantee yourself a place on a soccer team.

—Robert Watson

Writing purpose.   Like the preceding essay, this one offers advice, this time to the inexperienced buyer of home stereo equipment.

```
            HOW TO BUY A STEREO
     As a stereo buff, who has been through the
hassle of buying a stereo, a little advice for
anyone just entering the market; be prepared to
answer a few basic questions about your wants and
needs.  In the next few paragraphs, I would like
to discuss the basics of stereo buying by
describing and answering the basic questions.
     First, one must understand what stereo
really is.  Stereo is the reproduction of a
source (tape, record) with two distinct signals,
which gives a three-dimensional sound.  While
most natural sounds are mono (one signal only),
stereo is a product of man's technological
advancement.  Its quality of sound ranges from
poor, as found in many consoles and plastic
compact units; to exceptional, as found in
today's component systems.
     Since only components are capable of high
fidelity sound, I will focus my discussion about
this type only.  A basic component system
consists of an amplifier, which amplifies the
signals from the source; a pair of speakers,
```

which emit the amplified signals; a turntable,
which rotates a record at a constant speed; a
cartridge, which is mounted on the tonearm of the
turntable and picks up the signals from the
record; and a tape deck which is capable of
reproducing signals from a magnetic tape.

Now that you know what stereo is, you can
begin to answer the basic questions. The first
and most important question is; how much do you
want to spend? Component systems range in price
from $400 to well over $1000. The amount you
spend depends on what you can afford; however,
the most important thing to remember on cost is
to make sure you spend your money proportionally.
In other words if you spend a total of $700 don't
spend $600 on the amplifier alone and scrimp on
the rest of the system. On the average the cost
should be broken down in somewhat of the
following percentages: amplifier 35%, turntable
and cartridge 15%, speakers 25%, tape deck 25%.

The second question to ask yourself is;
What amount of use will the system receive? The
amount of use will affect how much you spend on
the system. You would not spend $1000 on a
system that will be used only once or twice a
year. Also the type of use will affect what type
of components you will need. For example, if you

prefer hours of uninterupted music, then you
might consider buying a receiver (an amplifier
and radio in one unit) instead of an amplifier,
whose sources must be constantly changed.

A third question to ask yourself is; what
kind and type of space do you have? If you have
a small room an amplifier with perhaps twenty
watts would be sufficient in supplying room—
filling sound. However, if you have a large
room, with sound—absorbing rugs and drapes,
perhaps sixty watts would be needed. Also if
space is limited big speakers would not be
needed. Today's smaller speakers are more
efficient than the big ones of a few years ago.

Another important question is: where to
buy your system? As a general rule buy your
system through a stereo dealer; rather than at a
department store or discount store. The reason
for this is that, unfortunately, stereo's, like
other electronic items, need service once in
awhile. Most department and discount stores
can't service what they sell; so they send them
to the factory for service. This takes up a lot
more time than a stereo store with in shop
service.

Now that you have answered all the basic
questions, you are ready to buy your first

component system. If you analyze carefully the
basic questions of cost, use, space and where to
buy; you will probably purchase a system capable
of reproducing high fidelity sounds for years to
come.

4

MAKING CHOICES

Special Assignments

PERSUASION

Almost all writing is persuasive, if its intent is to make readers share your perceptions of reality and experience it as you have. Even most narrative and descriptive writing tries to evoke from readers a response parallel to the writer's. Consider, for example, this sentence from William Gass's *In the Heart of the Heart of the Country* in which he pictures an everyday event in a small town with such detail that the reader comes to share his attitude:

> Their hair in curlers and their heads wrapped in loud scarves, young mothers, fattish in trousers, lounge about in the speedwash, smoking cigarettes, eating candy, drinking pop, thumbing magazines, and screaming at their children above the whir and rumble of the machines.

The description compels the reader to experience the aridity of these women's diminished and numbing lives. Such writing may be called persuasive, though in a different way from an essay which argues that no woman's life can be complete and self-fulfilling unless she pursues a career outside her home. The descriptive account seeks to influence subtly, while the other seeks to influence directly, or even to encourage the reader to take action.

Much persuasive writing does not hold categorically that one thing is right and true while the other is wrong and false. Instead, it insists that one position is better than or preferable to another. Argumentative writing may simply evaluate or judge an issue: "*General Hospital* is the best program on daytime television" or "Some media newscasters are more competent than others." Some persuasive writing, however, includes a plea for change: "TV violence must be curbed because it aggravates aggressive tendencies in children" or "TV anchors should present the news in a less biased fashion." In either case arguing such propositions poses a problem, for the reader may agree or disagree with the opinion expressed.

PERSUASION AND AUDIENCE

Keeping your intended readers in mind will help you choose suitable appeals or bases upon which to ground your argument and will help you arrange them skillfully. Before you begin to write, try to target your audience: do you want to address your fellow students, the readers of a local newspaper, the readers of a specialized journal or magazine? Once you've pinpointed your readers, consider their degree of knowledge about, and interest in, the issue you are exploring; try to determine what views they already hold and how firmly they hold them; ponder the degree to which these views correspond to your own; think of the kinds of appeals to which your readers would be likely to respond. Above all, remember that you need to *earn* your readers' agreement, which requires gathering abundant evidence to support your point of view.

A rule of thumb in framing a suitable appeal is to put yourself in the readers' shoes: look at the issue you're evaluating from their point of view. Identifying with your readers has a number of advantages. For instance, it can help you question your own views. If you begin with the assumption that your readers may not share your point of view and may in fact be able to marshal counterarguments to refute it, you'll be more sensitive to flaws and loopholes—and to discovering ways to strengthen your position. Identifying with your readers can also help you find a common ground on which to meet them. Your purpose in persuasion is not to alienate readers but to have them agree with your proposal. The best way to do this is through conciliation, which means acknowledging, if only partially, the value of opposing arguments and seeking a compromise.

Being sensitive to your readers will also help you control the tone of your argument. Tone reveals the writer's attitude toward the audience; that attitude is crucial in establishing the bond that will help you gain your readers' assent. If you patronize your readers by assuming a condescending tone, or if you imply that they are part of the problem you are exploring, you risk alienating them. No one likes to be talked down to or chided. If, on the other hand, you consider your readers intelligent and judicious, fully able to assess the merits of your arguments, you will encourage a full, possibly sympathetic, hearing of your views.

ETHICAL AND EMOTIONAL APPEALS

To persuade your reader, you can use three types of appeal: *ethical, emotional,* and *logical.* Often you will want to use all three in the same essay. The ethical appeal is designed to foster readers' confidence in your truthfulness and integrity as a writer. Readers are more likely to be swayed by an argument if they perceive you as someone who uses evidence accurately and fairly, who is evenhanded and willing to consider opposing views, and who is forceful without being dogmatic. Ultimately, the ethical appeal rests on the *image* that you project in your effort to gain the reader's consent. Just as a defense attorney might rely on a character witness to strengthen a case, so, too, in persuasive writing the image of yourself you convey gives witness to your character. It can have a forceful impact on your audience.

The emotional appeal seeks to stir the reader's feelings. It relies not so much on reasoned arguments as on evoking sympathy or distaste, two basic emotions that can move readers to approve your arguments or to disapprove of your opponent's arguments. Emotional appeals can, of course, be abused. To resort to name-calling in order to conjure up an unflattering image of an opponent is one kind of abuse. If, on the other hand, you are arguing for harsher, mandatory punishments for drunk drivers and you write about children left homeless and orphaned when their parents were killed by a drunk driver, you would seek to arouse justifiable indignation. Emotional appeals per se are not bad. It is only when they are used unscrupulously, or when they replace cogent reasoning, that we should question their use.

The following article questions the power of federal bureaucrats. As you read it, point out its emotional appeal and determine whether or not the appeal is justified.

THE DESK

1   When editorial writers and politicians discuss bureaucracy, they talk about it with a capital B—the massive, faceless, red-tape-clogged Bureaucracy of chamber of commerce after-dinner speeches. But when I think of bureaucracy, I think of Martha.

2   Martha is a retired woman who lives in Augusta, Ga. She survives, but barely, on a small social security retirement check. A friend once told her that because her income was so low, Martha was also eligible for Supplemental Security Income (SSI). Reluctantly—she is a proud woman—Martha applied.

3   There is a desk in the Augusta Social Security Administration office; Martha sat down on the "client's" side of it. She was, she timidly told the caseworker who sat opposite her, at her wit's end. She just couldn't make ends meet, not with today's prices. She had never asked anyone for charity before—he had to understand that—but she needed help and had heard that she was entitled to some.

4   The caseworker understood. Gently, he asked Martha the questions he needed to fill out her application. Everything was in order—except why did she have this $2,000 savings account? For her burial, she told him. She had always dreaded dying as a ward of the state, so for almost 50 years she had saved—a dollar a week when she had it—to finance her own funeral.

5   But, the caseworker said, we aren't allowed to give SSI to people with more than $1,500 in the bank; that's the law. Don't be silly; the law couldn't apply to burial money, said Martha, scared and defensive in her embarrassment. The caseworker saw her point, but there was nothing he could do; the law did not—and realistically could not—distinguish between money for funerals and money for high living. Anxious to help, he advised her to go out and blow $500 on a color television—on anything—just to bring her savings down to $1,500. Then, he said, she would be eligible for SSI. Appalled by this perverse advice, Martha left.

6   Martha is one of several dozen people I have talked to over the past three years, ordinary people from a variety of regions, classes and backgrounds. I talked with them because, as a political scientist and a political journalist, I was interested in finding out what the world of government and politics looks like from the citizen's-eye view. To my surprise, that world contained little of the issues and personalities that pollsters ask about and pundits fulminate about. Instead, it was a world dominated by bureaucracy—not Bureaucracy, mind you, but rather the specific government agencies that these citizens had to deal with in their personal lives—too often, they felt, and with too little satisfaction.

7   Most ironic was the image of government that was born of these experiences. As any scholarly treatise on the subject will tell you, the great advantage bureaucracy is supposed to offer a complex, modern society like ours is efficient, rational, uniform and courteous treatment for the citizens it deals with. Yet not only did these qualities not come through to the people I talked with, it was their very opposites that seemed more characteristic. People of all classes—the rich man dealing with the Internal Revenue Service as well as the poor woman struggling with the welfare department—felt that the treatment they had received had been bungled, not efficient; unpredictable, not rational; discriminatory or idiosyncratic, not uniform, and, all too often, insensitive, rather than courteous. It was as if they had bought a big new car that not only did not run when they wanted it to, but periodically revved itself up and drove all around their yards.

8   Are they right? Would that things were that simple. But we taxpayers can't even make up our minds what the problem is with bureaucrats: are they lazy do-nothings, snoozing afternoons away behind the sports section, or wild-eyed do-everythings who can't *ever* sleep unless they have forced some poor soul to rearrange his life to conform with one of their crazy social theories?

9   As for the bureaucrats, they seem no less blinded by anger than we. Frequently, they dismiss the unhappy citizens they deal with as sufferers of what one political scientist calls "bureausis"—a childish inability to cope with even the simplest, most reasonable rules and regulations. Like children, they add, we demand a lot but expect somebody else to pay.

10   Yet there are no callous bureaucrats or "bureautics" in Martha's story, nor were there in most of the stories I heard. What there is, though, is a desk. On one side of it sits the citizen—a whole person who wants to be treated as a whole person. Special consideration? Of course. Bend the rules a little? Certainly, I'm unique. And she is unique, as is every other person who approaches government from her side of the desk.

11   Across from her sits the bureaucrat. His perspective is entirely different. He is there not as a friend or neighbor, but purely as the representative of his agency, an agency whose only business is to execute the law. His job is to fit this person across the desk into a category: legally eligible for the agency's services or not; if so, for what and on what terms? He cannot, *must* not, look at the whole person, but only at those features that enable him to transform her into a "case," a "file," a "client" for his agency. That way she can count on getting exactly what any other citizen in her category would get from the government—nothing more, nothing less. And do we really want it any different? Would we rather that low-level bureaucrats had the power to give or refuse public services purely as they saw fit?

12   The desk, whether physical or metaphorical, is there in every encounter between Americans and their government. It turns unique and deserving citizens into snarling clients, and good-hearted civil servants into sullen automatons. More than anything else, I suspect, it explains why we and our government are at each other's throats—why taxpayers pass Proposition 13s and public employees strike like dock workers. *It* is the bureaucracy problem, and if what I heard from the people I talked with is representative, the bureaucracy problem is the crisis of our age.

13   I only wish I had the solution.   —Michael Nelson, *Newsweek*

THE LOGICAL APPEAL

The logical appeal uses a chain of reasoning to establish the validity of the view proposed. Reasoning is thinking that relies on two mental processes: *induction* and *deduction*. When we think inductively, we examine particulars and then arrive at a conclusion or generalization that interprets their meaning. Conversely, when we think deductively, we reason from the general to the specific. Actually, both forms of thought are intimately related, as Thomas Henry Huxley advises:

1   Suppose you go into a fruiterer's shop, wanting an apple,—you take up one and, on biting it, you find it is sour; you look at it, and see that it is hard and green. You take up another one, and that too is hard, green, and sour. The shopman offers you a third; but, before biting it, you examine it, and find that it is hard and green, you immediately say that you will not have it, as it must be sour, like those that you have already tried.

2   Nothing can be more simple than that, you think; but if you will take the trouble to analyze and trace out into its logical elements what has been done by the mind, you will be greatly surprised. In the first place, you have performed the operation of induction. You found that, in two experiences, hardness and greenness in apples went together with sourness. It was so in the first case, and it was confirmed by the second. True, it is a very small basis, but still it is enough to make an induction from; you generalize the facts, and you expect to find sourness in apples where you get hardness and greenness. You found upon that a general law that all hard and green apples are sour; and that, so far as it goes, is a perfect induction. Well, having got your natural law in this way, when you are offered another apple which you find is hard and green, you say, "All hard and green apples are sour; this apple is hard and green, therefore this apple is sour." That train of reasoning is what logicians call a syllogism, and has all its various parts and terms,—its major premise, its minor premise, and its conclusion. And, by the help of further reasoning, which, if drawn out, would have to be exhibited in two or three other syllogisms, you arrive at your final determination, "I will not have that apple." So that, you see, you have, in the first place, established a law by induction, and upon that you have founded a deduction, and reasoned out the special conclusion of the particular case.

—"The Phenomena of Organic Nature,"
Darwiniana

Inductive Reasoning

The implications of Huxley's last sentence are important, since he stresses that even in deductive essays you think inductively *before* you start to write: in the process of developing and formulating a generalization, your thinking and reflection must follow an inductive pattern—unless you actually have no position until you discover it through writing (an unlikely way to begin an argumentative essay). Say, for instance, that the dangers posed by drunk drivers are much on your mind. You've read in the newspaper and heard on TV statistics claiming that up to 75 percent of all fatal traffic accidents involve drinking, and that arrests of drunk drivers are up 30 percent over last year. In the past six months, there's been a high incidence of fatal accidents caused by drunk drivers. This especially troubles you, since you've seen so many friends driving away from parties after having had too much to drink. And then there are the innocent victims, perhaps even someone you knew. From all these bits of evidence, both statistical and personal, you conclude that "Drunk drivers should be kept off the streets"—a proposition which could serve as the basis for a persuasive essay.

Let's work further with that provisional thesis in an attempt to arrive at something more substantive than the argument—which hardly anyone would question—that drunk drivers are a menace to safety. One approach would be to ask *how* drunk drivers could be kept from behind the wheel of a car: Mandatory suspension of their license if arrested for driving while intoxicated? Longer suspension for repeat violations? Lifetime suspension for drunk driving that results in injury to others? Mandatory prison sentence for reckless homicide? Maybe even making bar owners and bartenders culpable for allowing intoxicated patrons to drive away from their premises? In a persuasive paper whose purpose is to examine these alternatives and demand a reform in state laws dealing with drunk drivers, your initial generalization ("Drunk drivers must be kept off the streets") and the feeling and thinking which led to that conclusion might all be included in your introductory paragraph. The initial generalization, arrived at inductively, might be refined to read: "Drunk drivers should be kept off the streets by mandatory punishment for first offenders and increasingly harsher penalties for repeat offenders." The remainder of the paper could then examine the pros and cons of various punishments and their appropriateness for specific offenses.

As this instance makes clear, when you sit down to write a persuasive essay, you do not begin in the dark. A process of inductive thinking that moves from an awareness of specifics (facts, examples, impressions, and so on) to a generalization drawn from them inevitably *precedes* the actual writing. This inductive process may have been germinating over a prolonged period, so that the generalization had already been formed long before you set pen to paper. Whether you finally choose to organize your paper deductively (moving from general to particular) or inductively (moving from particular to general), the specific ideas and feelings that led you to your generalization can now be used as supporting evidence for that proposition. If, however, by withholding a formal statement of your position until nearly the end of the paper, you can create the impression that you are arguing inductively, you will be able to carry readers along with you step-by-step, gradually earning their agreement. Such a method is particularly useful if the issue under debate is complex or if your position is an especially thorny one and likely to be unpopular.

Deductive Reasoning

The deductive thought process can be represented schematically by means of a *syllogism*. A syllogism, as Huxley noted, has three parts: a *major* premise, or generalization that is either universally self-evident or arrived at through experiential data; a *minor premise,* or more particular instance of the major premise; and a *conclusion,* which results from applying the major premise to the minor premise. A syllogism, then, expresses the logical movement of thought occurring when you reason from two premises, or propositions—the second more specific and less inclusive that the first—to a valid conclusion. Putting your own arguments into syllogisms *before* you begin writing can help in structuring your papers, since the major premise,

> Huxley's "All hard and green apples are sour,"

the minor premise,

> "This apple is hard and green,"

and the conclusion,

> "Therefore, this apple is sour,"

can be equivalent to the main topic headings in an outline, each of which could then be expanded through appropriate details. More important, reducing your argument to a few skeletal sentences will help make any inconsistencies or illogicalities obvious, and so serve as a check or gauge of your reasoning process. The following student letter to the editor of a campus newspaper illustrates the way an argumentative paper uses details to fill out the bare bones of a deductive argument.

```
To the Editor:
  Recently, the Board of Trustees, charged with establishing
the regulations governing university residence halls, has been
petitioned to change current rules limiting hours of
visitation.  Those who've asked for the change want open
visitation.  In effect, this means no restrictions at all.
  Those who clamor for an open visitation policy believe that
because they are adults who have paid for their rooms, they
should be allowed to have guests at any time.  What they don't
acknowledge is that such a system would interfere with the
rights of their roommates.  Consider the plight of the
roommate who wishes to study in his/her dormitory room, only
to find that a visitor (usually of the opposite sex) wishes to
socialize.  Or, worse yet, consider that roommate's problem
when he/she is asked to sleep elsewhere.  To be sure, the
roommate can always say "no," but refusing inevitably leads to
arguments and bad feelings, hardly a good atmosphere for
```

```
people who must live together.  Even if the rights of
roommates could somehow be respected, the most serious problem
with an open visitation policy would still remain:  namely,
security.  Open visitation could endanger every female
dormitory resident if male visitors were allowed to roam the
halls at all hours.  At best, it might mean encountering a
male in the bathroom at three in the morning.  At worst, it
could open the door to physical assault.
   The risk is not worth taking.  The Board of Trustees should
continue its limited visitation policy.
```

Margaret Alberson

The student's deductive reasoning might be stated in this way:

> The Board of Trustees must not allow anything that infringes upon the rights and security of all dormitory residents.
> Open visitation infringes upon dorm residents' rights and security.
> Therefore, the Board of Trustees must not allow open visitation.

As you notice, the student never actually states her generalization, reached through a process of induction, that the university administration is obliged to protect the rights and security of all students, but it is implied. In other words, she uses a general principle arrived at through a prior inductive process as the basis for her deductive argument. The body of her letter—paragraph two—develops the special instance by citing examples of violations of the right to privacy or security, and then the letter ends with the conclusion she draws. If you accept the truth of this student's initial generalization, then you must admit the *validity* of her logical argument. That does not mean, however, that you must agree with her position or find it convincing; you might maintain that, even with open visitation, steps could be taken to protect the rights and safeguard the security of dormitory residents. So even though the argument is logically valid, the conclusion is still open to dissent; there remain legitimate areas of disagreement that the writer should foresee and might be expected to answer for those who believe differently.

FALLACIES IN ARGUMENTATION

As you write persuasive prose, you must guard against *fallacies of reasoning* if your argument is to be intellectually sound and convincing. You will need to avoid, for instance, such fallacies as:

1. *Hasty generalization* or overgeneralization on the basis of irrelevant examples, insufficient evidence, or misinterpretation of statistical data: "All test tube babies are certain to be girls since the half dozen already born are."

2. *Overdependence on emotional appeals* or stereotyping at the expense of reasoned argumentation: "Any God-fearing man or woman knows that alcohol is a tool of the devil."

3. *Circular reasoning* or repeating in different words what you are attempting to prove: "Capital punishment is cruel and unusual punishment because it takes another's life."

4. *Begging the question* by assuming what must be proven: "Mark Twain's *Huckleberry Finn* should be banned from the schools because it is racist."

5. *Ad hominem attacks* on the personal integrity and character of your opponents rather than on the issues they represent: "Candidate X not only is divorced but also has been arrested for driving while intoxicated and so cannot serve us well as mayor."

6. *Implying that no other alternatives exist* by stating your thesis as an either/or proposition: "Either the United States must spend more money on space exploration, or the Soviets will dominate the universe."

7. *Inferring a causal relation* where probably none exists: "Weather patterns on Earth have become more extreme ever since man started traveling in outer space"; or suggesting that one event caused another simply because it coincided with it or preceded it in time (*post hoc ergo propter hoc*): "The feminist movement has led directly to an increase in the divorce rate."

Read carefully the following newspaper column with an eye to possible fallacies:

ANTI-SMOKING PUSH A FEMINIST PLOT?

1   Recently, preparing to fly home on a plane, I was asked at the ticket counter whether I wanted to sit in a smoking or non-smoking section. When I answered that it didn't matter to me one way or another, the young lady became distinctly miffed.

2   A poster in the lobby outside my office had proclaimed Tuesday, Nov. 16, as smokeless, "The Great American Smoke Out."

3   At one of my favorite restaurants, Monday is supposed to be smokeless: no pipes or cigarettes, and, barbarously, no cigar after lunch.

4   The Catholic Church used to decree a meatless Friday, but that's gone by the boards. But some sort of new religious impulse seems to be insisting on a smoke fast day.

5   One national columnist given to faddish things has gone completely around the bend on the smoke issue, announcing with righteous indignation that after a cigar-smoking guest had left the columnist's home, he and his wife had taken

down all the curtains and sent them to the cleaners. Mere half-measures, I say. He should have burned them, á la Savonarola.

6   In the recent voting, a tough anti-smoking measure appeared on the California Ballot; though, in a sudden spasm of common sense, it lost heavily.

7   What's going on?

8   I think we can forget about the health aspect.

9   Sure, there's a correlation between smoking and some kinds of cancer, but there's a correlation between driving and sudden death, and between drinking and various complaints, and we don't see any anti-driving or anti-drinking campaign being mounted—at least nothing comparable to the anti-smoking business.

10   We did have Prohibition once, a complete failure. No one pays any attention to the 55 mph speed limit, not even the cops, its absurdity being generally recognized.

11   It's true, of course, that smoke at close quarters can be a nuisance, especially in a restaurant; but people have been smoking ever since explorers brought the leaf to Europe, and have been smoking in public ever since about 1920. The anti-smoking outcry, on the other hand, is relatively recent.

12   For a long time, indeed, think of Humphrey Bogart, Greta Garbo, or Marlene Dietrich, a cigarette was positively fashionable.

13   I have a couple of suggestions. Surely the anti-smoking crusade is the current focus of puritan feeling. The Maoist puritans, when they were in the saddle, abolished smoking and even tried to abolish sex, and the anti-smoking crusade here has comparable puritan roots. There always seems to exist a faction which hates the small pleasures of other people.

14   But I think there's another angle to the smoking business. Though many women smoke, smoking is much more a masculine activity, cigarettes, yes, but especially pipes and cigars.

15   The anti-smoking campaign may thus be an aspect of feminist self-assertion, and have distinct anti-male content.

16   The "smoke filled room" is not female. And feminist self-assertion has been typically moralistic and puritanical. Smoking can be a macho symbol, so it has to go. Better watch out, boys. Taking away the cigarettes, pipes and cigars is very likely only the first step.
             —Jeffrey Hart, *The Indianapolis Star*

EXPLORING FALLACIES

1. How has Hart organized his argument? Point out the transitional devices and comment on the logical coherence of his article. Where there are no apparent transitions, on what basis are the ideas linked together?

2. What fallacies can you point to in his argument?

3. Hart argues his point by using four analogies or extended comparisons. Identify them. Are they qualitatively equivalent and thus defensible analogies for Hart's position?

4. How would you refute Hart's article? What is the main charge you would level against this column as an example of persuasive writing?

5. Describe the tone of this article. Is there any evidence Hart is being satiric? If so, could the problems you detected with his argument be excused on the basis that he is not being totally serious with his readers, but rather tongue-in-cheek?

6. One method for checking the validity of your arguments or those of others is to restate them in *syllogistic form,* composed of a major premise, a minor premise, and a conclusion. This helps to reveal any glaring problems in a chain of reasoning. The final three paragraphs of Hart's essay put into syllogistic form would look something like this—and would point up immediately the circularity of his argument:

Feminists are out to destroy all macho symbols.
They have successfully waged war against smoking (which is a macho symbol).
Therefore, feminists will destroy all other macho symbols as well.

In your own writing, you usually will not state your ideas this bluntly, with the directness of syllogistic form, since it lays your argument open to immediate scrutiny. More often, you are likely to formulate *enthymemes,* or modified syllogisms that submerge the major premise by employing *because* clauses. If, for example, you were to write, "Because of the dry, cool days and even colder nights most of the summer, the harvest will be later and less abundant than usual," your readers would supply mentally the unstated premise that warm, wet weather promotes an early, plentiful crop. If Hart had used the enthymeme, he might have said: "Because feminists successfully outlawed smoking, which is a macho symbol, they will eventually destroy all other evidence of masculinity as well"—leaving the reader to supply the unwarranted generalization that feminists are against all evidences of masculinity. Now go back over Hart's essay and restate some of his arguments in either syllogistic form or enthymemes. Does this help reveal any problems in logical argumentation that you did not detect before?

SUPPORTING YOUR POSITION

The introduction of a persuasive paper does what any good introduction must: secures the reader's attention; perhaps provides some background on the nature of the controversy; overtly states the thesis or the writer's position or solution to the problem; and maybe indicates the method and arrangement of the argument to follow. The conclusion, though it need not necessarily summarize the writer's position, typically demands intellectual agreement and perhaps even moves the reader to make some change or take some action, while hinting at the larger ramifications of the issue. But the center of any persuasive essay, whether inductive or deductive in its organization, must be the presentation of support for your position (detailed evidence drawn from experience, statistics, testimony of experts in the field, and so on) and the refutation of the opposing position.

Structuring Argumentation

Once you have gathered a reasonable amount of supporting detail you can decide how to arrange the evidence most effectively. Ordinarily, it is best to save your strongest arguments for the end. If you are able to produce only one or two reasons in favor of your thesis, then perhaps you should stop and question whether you really have sufficient evidence to persuade an audience. Almost always, however, you move in a climactic order that plays your trump card or strongest, most compelling point last. The organizational pattern of the support section of your paper would look like this:

> Thesis
> Least compelling evidence
> Stronger evidence
> Still stronger evidence
> Strongest supporting evidence

FOLLOW-UP ACTIVITY

In order to sharpen your skills at amassing evidence to support a proposition, complete each of the following theses with several clauses beginning with *because* that could serve as lead-ins to paragraphs supporting the generalization. Then arrange each series of *because* clauses in an appropriate order, from weakest to strongest.

1. The presidency should be limited to a single six-year term because . . .
2. College athletes should be paid a salary just as professional athletes are because . . .
3. Mothers of school-age children should not work outside the home because . . .
4. Fraternities and sororities promote democratic living because . . .
5. Colleges have an obligation to offer remediation to those students inadequately prepared by the public schools because . . .

REFUTING THE OPPOSITION

Writers can often neglect an important fact: the way that you forestall and refute the likely arguments of your opponents can be almost as vital to a successful persuasive essay as the presentation of the supporting material for your own position. In short, there can be no solid argumentation without refutation, simply because there are at least two sides to every issue that's worth the time and effort of a persuasive paper. If you were on a high-school debate team, you may remember when the coach made you prepare to debate both sides of an issue: both for and against federal aid to farmers; both for and against election of the President by popular vote rather than by the electoral college; both for and against foreign aid to totalitarian or dictatorial regimes. You may find it necessary to use the same process when you develop the refutation section of a persuasive essay. Of course, sometimes coming up with arguments in favor of the side you didn't think you held may change your mind on a position, and you must then redraft the paper supporting a thesis you once thought you opposed!

FOLLOW-UP ACTIVITY

In order to sharpen your refutation skills, list the major arguments you can think of *on both sides* of each of the following issues.

1. College scholarships should be awarded solely on merit.
   College scholarships should be given only to the financially needy.
2. There should be a flat-rate income tax for all citizens.
   The graduated income tax should be retained.
3. Motorcyclists should be legally required to wear helmets.
   Motorcyclists should not be legally required to wear helmets.
4. The U.S. should impose quotas on the importation of Japanese cars.
   The U.S. should not impose quotas on the importation of Japanese cars.
5. Final exams adequately measure a semester's work.
   Final exams are an insufficient measure of a semester's work.

Strategies of Refutation

The two papers which follow—the first by an expert, the second by a student—both concern the one-time debate over the 65 mph as opposed to a mandatory 55 mph speed limit. Since they adopt opposite sides on the issue—the first pro, the second con—they might be read as refutations of each other. Keep this in mind as you read them.

FIFTY-FIVE IS FAST ENOUGH

1   In 1972, the winning car in the Indianapolis 500 was clocked at an average speed of 162.962 m.p.h., a record that stands today. The car, which I own, was driven by my friend Mark Donohue. Three years later, Donohue crashed and was fatally injured while practicing for the Grand Prix in Austria. He was not yet 39.

2   Professional race drivers deliberately accept the risks of high speed and the ever-present possibility of sudden death behind the wheel. But for thousands of ordinary motorists every year, death on the highway is all too often unnecessary.

3   I am a lifelong racing enthusiast, first as a driver and today as a car builder and team owner. I am also a firm believer that speeding motor vehicles belong *only* on racetracks, not on public highways. Yet one of our most effective safeguards against needless highway slaughter—the national 55-m.p.h. speed limit—is today under severe attack from increasingly vocal skeptics around the country.

4   Some leaders of the anti-55 movement ought to know better. These are the racing enthusiasts who have been conducting a national publicity campaign to discredit and repeal the 55 limit. Their campaign, aimed at dedicated racing fans, has been very influential. And why not? Auto racing is currently the country's fourth most-popular spectator sport. Already this year, bills to raise the speed limit have been introduced in six states.

5   Active in the anti-55 campaign are two of the largest-circulation magazines for motor-racing fans, *Car and Driver* and *Road & Track.* Last September, John Tomerlin, *Road & Track's* highway-affairs analyst, told a national meeting of state traffic-safety officials that the federal government's claim that 55 saves lives and fuel cannot be documented. Also figuring in the campaign against the law were delegates to the Republican National Convention, who adopted a platform plank attacking the national speed limit as an invasion of states' rights.

6   In addition, critics contend that enforcement costs too much and diverts police from more important work, that it is creating a nation of scofflaws since no one obeys it, and that it amounts to "Big Brotherism." Let's examine these charges:

7   *Charge:* The 55-m.p.h. limit is just another example of Washington-imposed Big Brotherism.

8   *Fact:* Shortly after the Arabs shut off the oil in October 1973, the Emergency Highway Energy Conservation Act became law, requiring all states to impose a highway speed limit of 55, or risk losing federal highway funds. But 28 states had already jumped ahead of Big Brother by imposing 55 (and in some cases, 50) on their own. The National Governors Association and the heads of all state law-enforcement agencies continue to support the 55 limit. And public-opinion polls consistently show that about 75 percent of drivers also support it.

9   *Charge:* The 55 law doesn't save lives.

10   *Fact:* Though the speed limit was imposed to save fuel, not lives, its safety benefits became apparent shortly after it was enacted. In 1974, the first year of 55, auto fatalities dropped by more than 9000. Critics say that the reduction was because Americans drove less in 1974 than in 1973. But the decrease in miles traveled was only 2.5 percent, compared with a 16-percent fatality drop.

11   Traffic engineers attributed the reduction in highway accidents to something called "traffic pace." When all drivers travel at about the same speed, which tends to happen under the 55 law, there is no need to weave from lane to lane to pass. But when speed limits go up, the faster cars are continually zooming around the slower ones, creating prime conditions for accidents.

12   And consider this: If you do have a crash at 70 m.p.h. or faster, your chances of survival are 50-50. Cut your speed to between 50 and 60 m.p.h., and the odds climb to about 31-to-1 in your favor.

13   According to the U.S. Department of Transportation, strong enforcement of 55 could forestall as many as 415,000 injury-producing accidents over the next ten years, and save up to 32,000 lives.

14   *Charge:* Drivers ignore the 55 limit.

15   *Fact:* A certain percentage of drivers *always* exceed the speed limit. Yet the latest speed-monitoring reports from states around the country indicate that the average speed on roads posted for 55 is less than half-a-mile-an-hour over the limit.

16   *Charge:* Police are taken off more important work to enforce 55, and the law costs too much to enforce.

17   *Fact:* The U.S. National Highway Traffic Safety Administration reports that "no significant redistribution of resources results from the 55-m.p.h. speed limit." Police are *not* being pulled off more important duties to enforce 55. And critics who argue that enforcement of the speed limit wastes tax dollars aren't aware that states spend only a small percentage of their law-enforcement budgets for 55. In any case, states will always have to enforce *some* kind of speed limit, whether it is 40, 55, or 70. The cost doesn't vary significantly for different speeds.

18   *Charge:* The 55 limit saves an insignificant amount of fuel.

19   *Fact:* The exact amount of savings varies with the vehicle, but cuts in fuel use when speed is reduced from 70 to 55 m.p.h. commonly range from 15 percent to 30 percent.

20   In 1978, the Department of Transportation estimated that Americans were saving 1.5 billion gallons of motor fuel a year as a result of 55. Recent analyses, which take into account today's more fuel-efficient engines, show that savings of motor fuel attributable to 55 now amount to 3.4 billion gallons a year—about 3 percent of our total comsumption.

21   Critics claim time and money would be saved if trucks and buses were exempt from 55. Again, wrong. According to fleet companies, slower speeds improve fuel mileage for trucks and buses, and cut maintenance costs. For example, Consolidated Freightways, the nation's second-largest regulated motor carrier, changed gear ratios to limit top speed on its rigs to 57 m.p.h., and thus realized 8 percent better fuel economy. United Parcel Service conducted fuel-consumption tests with identical tractor-trailers, one driven at 55 m.p.h. and the other at 65 m.p.h. The 55-m.p.h. truck got 32-percent better fuel economy. And so it goes around the country: truck fleets *are* saving because of the 55 law.

22   Americans have had seven years to evaluate the 55-m.p.h. speed limit. *All* the evidence is favorable. The law saves gas. *And* lives.

—Roger Penske, *Reader's Digest*

AM I GOING TO MAKE IT HOME TONIGHT?

1   In the waning months of 1975, the 55—mph speed limit went into effect nationwide. Those who argued in its favor cited energy conservation and increased safety: the lower speeds, they argued, would lead to reduced use of gasoline and to fewer traffic accidents and deaths. What they didn't consider was the loss of valuable time and the economic hardships the law would impose. Nor did they foresee that the law would be unpopular and virtually impossible to enforce.

2   Even the argument that the 55—mph speed limit reduces highway accidents and deaths is questionable. The United States has the best superhighway system in the world. Entrances and exits are gradual. There is no cross traffic going in opposite directions. Guard rails are built along cliffs and mountains. The lanes are extra wide and there are always two lanes with wide paved shoulders running in the same direction. These superhighways are safe at speeds in excess of 75 mph. What a waste not to use these highways to their full potential.

3   Equally, the improved features of auto design ensure increased safety. All new cars have shoulder and seat belts as well as safety glass. Steel—belted radial tires, as well as collapsible steering columns and padded dashboards, are also standard equipment on most cars. The fact is that these modern cars are safe in a collision even at speeds higher than 55 mph.

4   Yet even if the 55—mph speed limit saves lives, it isn't worth the loss of time it entails. In places like Nevada, Arizona, Utah, Colorado, New Mexico, Texas, and Wyoming, towns 60 miles apart are not uncommon. Getting from one town to another is therefore time—consuming even without a 55—mph speed limit. Moreover, these areas are sparsely populated: one can drive for hundreds of miles and not pass a single car. Finally, the roads are flat and visibility is usually five to ten miles. It does not make sense to drive 55 mph in an area that has few people, fewer cars, and where distances between population centers are relatively great.

5   The economic hardship produced by the 55—mph speed limit also makes the law questionable. Take the case of an owner—operator truck driver who must make his truck payments and pay his bills by the month. Since he gets paid by the mile, the more miles he drives a month, the more money he makes. To see what the 55—mph speed limit means for this driver, let us compare two truckers on a run from New York to Los Angeles.

Assume the work week to be 120 hours long. No matter how fast
the truck is going, the drivers will spend the same amount of
time eating and sleeping. Both truckers are paid $.50 per
mile. Trucker A will average 55 mph (getting four miles to
the gallon), and trucker B, 75 mph (getting three miles to the
gallon). The distance between New York and Los Angeles is
3,000 miles.

6   It takes Trucker A 60 hours to get to Los Angeles. Using
950 gallons of diesel at $1 a gallon, he gets $1,500 for the
trip and spends $40 for food. As a result, his net pay for
the trip is $510. Because the work week is 120 hours long,
Trucker A has enough time to flip back to New York and make
another $510. When the week is over, his total net pay for
the week's work is $1,020.

7   Let us now consider the case of Trucker B, who drives 75
miles per hour. He leaves New York and arrives in Los Angeles
in 40 hours. Getting three miles per gallon, he uses 1,000
gallons of diesel fuel. He also spends $40 for food and, like
Trucker A, gets paid $1,500 for the trip. Subtracting his
expenses, he finds he has made $470, which is $40 less than
Trucker A. But because he has more hours to spend on the
road, he can flip back to New York and make another $470, and
then flip back to Los Angeles for yet another $470, bringing
his net to $1,410 for the week. For the same amount of
driving time, Trucker B makes $390 more a week than Trucker A.
This translates into $19,500 more a year.

8   If the economics of lifting the 55-mph speed limit were not
persuasive enough, there is the matter of enforceability. The
fact is that the 55-mph speed limit is impossible to enforce
because radar is used in 95 percent of all speeding
convictions, and radar is inaccurate. Radar sends out a beam
that bounces off an object, comes back to a receiver, and
reads out in miles per hour. There are many things wrong with
this system. Not only is the readout affected by CB radios,
heaters and air conditioners, and faulty ignition systems, but
it is influenced by distance, by the size of the object, and
by the material from which the object is made.

9   Assuming that the readout comes back and is correct, the
question still remains: whose speed is being read? Radar is
most sensitive to size; therefore, the bigger object will get
the readout, not the fastest or closest. Radar will pick up a
tractor trailer at 7,650 feet, but it won't pick up a Firebird
Trans Am until it gets within 1,820 feet, and it can't track a
Corvette until it gets within 520 feet. The reason for this
is the shape and the material of the car: the lower and more
pointed the car is, the harder it is for radar to pick it up.

10   As a result of these problems, it is possible to be arrested for someone else's speed. If the police see a Corvette at 600 feet and point the radar gun at it, they will not get a reading. If, however, there is a truck, not yet visible, approaching 7,600 feet away and going 75 miles per hour, the police will get the truck's reading because the radar has gone through the Vette and bounced off the not yet visible truck. As a result, the driver of the Vette gets pulled over for doing 75 when, in fact, he might have been obeying the law.

11   Perhaps the most important factor determining whether a law is good or not is the attitude of the people towards it. In this case, the facts speak for themselves. Since the 55-mph speed limit went into effect, sales of radar detectors and CBs have skyrocketed. Moreover, people have begun to hate the police: once known as "Bears," a rather neutral tag, they are now called "Porky Pigs," a title that certainly expresses distaste. The same aversion is evident in movies like <u>Smokey and the Bandit</u>, popular because they are about breaking the 55-mph speed limit and putting one over on the police. Clearly, the American people do not like the 55-mph speed limit. It is a headache and deserves to be abolished.

—Charles Sanders

EXPLORING REFUTATION

1. Both the professional and student essay begin by stating briefly the likely arguments of their opposition. Why?

2. Characterize the nature and source of the evidence each writer uses to support his position.

3. What pattern do you detect in the arrangement of the persuasive material in each of the essays? Why does each writer *end* with the point he does—Penske with the argument of fuel economy and Sanders with the argument of the public's poor attitude toward the police because of the 55-mph speed limit? Are these points the most compelling arguments of each? If not, where do their most persuasive arguments occur?

4. Locate some issues on which Penske and Sanders present diametrically opposite points of view. In these instances, whose position are you more likely to accept? Why?

5. These two papers were not written in response to one another. But if they had been, how successfully does Sanders refute Penske's arguments? How successfully does Penske answer Sander's position?

6. Do you find these two arguments equally convincing? If not, what considerations other than content and style enter into your judgment about the success of each argument? Does the fact that Penske was a race-car

driver and was once chairman of the Automotive Safety Foundation have any bearing on your attitude toward his argument?

7. Examine the title of each essay. Comment on its appropriateness as a lead-in to what follows.

Structuring Refutation

When you organize the refutation part of your essays, you face the same decisions about arrangement of points as in organizing proofs. Generally, it is wise to begin the refutation by conceding any unassailable, irrefutable points on the side of your opponents. After that, you would move from the arguments most difficult to refute because they have some validity, to those easiest to refute because they are weaker. In outline format, the refutation section of your paper would look like this:

> Concede opponent's unassailable arguments
> Refute opponent's strongest argument
> Refute next strongest argument
> Refute next strongest
> Refute opponent's weakest argument
> Reiterate your position

Often, instead of first supporting your position and then refuting that of your opponents, you will find it more logical and effective to refute the opposing arguments at the same time as you support your own, especially if this prevents needless repetition of material. When you swing back and forth between pro and con, you will use transitional words and phrases such as *indeed, but, however, moreover, nevertheless, besides, on the other hand,* and *therefore* to introduce the arguments in favor of your position. And you will use transitions such as *to be sure, of course, some may hold, one must admit,* or *still* either to concede points or to introduce arguments against your proposition.

FOLLOW-UP ACTIVITIES

Choose a few of the five topics in the exercise on page 333 and organize, in outline form, the proofs for your position and refutations of the opposing position in a logical and effective manner, sometimes employing the alternating method.

To understand how refutation can be used as the principle of organization in a persuasive essay, examine the following student paper.

A HANDGUN FOR PROTECTION?

1   When the United States was founded, the authors of the Constitution, striving to protect the rights of the individual, drafted the Bill of Rights, which, among other provisions, guaranteed the right to bear arms. Two hundred years ago, the right to bear arms was a symbol of personal freedom, protecting the individual citizen from government suppression and abuse, a legitimate concern in the context of 1787 politics. But is that two-hundred-year-old provision in the Constitution a legitimate concern today? Does the right to bear arms still protect individual freedom? The fact is that the right to bear handguns threatens the peace and security of individual citizens; handguns threaten the lives of those people they are supposed to be protecting.

2   According to the latest statistics, 27,000 Americans die from guns yearly: approximately 11,000 Americans are murdered with guns each year, and another 13,000 commit suicide using guns. Moreover, handguns are the biggest culprit, used in 92 percent of all murders involving a gun. Yet the sale of handguns continues to rise. Americans own over 30 million pistols and handguns, and 2 million new handguns are sold annually at a rate of one every 16 seconds. These facts help explain another grim statistic—every 19 minutes an American is killed with a handgun. In fact, 67 percent of all murders are committed with handguns.

3   Recent Harris and Gallup polls indicate that 67 percent of all Americans favor stricter gun controls, while 41 percent favor an outright ban on handguns. Yet countless gun control bills before Congress fail to gain substantial support. Why? If the voice of the people is not being heard, then whose voice is heard? The fact is that many special interest groups, spearheaded by the National Rifle Association, lobby vigorously to prevent the passage of gun control legislation. The crux of their argument is based on the Constitutional right to bear arms, a right, they claim, that protects individual freedom. Granted, if gun control were legislated, the right to own handguns would be taken away; however, the right to live would be granted to many of the 27,000 Americans now senselessly killed with guns each year.

4   Opponents to gun control legislation argue that citizens need handguns to protect their property from intruders and prowlers. But are they really protected by handguns? A report presented to the American Public Health Association in 1973 refutes this claim: "A gun kept by a civilian for protection is six times more likely to kill a family member or

friend than an intruder or attacker." A recent study by two professors at Case Western Reserve University found that at least 70 percent of the people killed by handguns are shot by people they know, most often a relative or an acquaintance.

5 Opponents of stricter gun controls argue that the statistics about deaths are meaningless, because if an individual plans to commit a murder, he will do it even if a handgun is not available. This is probably true. But the fact is that most murders with handguns arise in the context of a quarrel with little or no planning. If handguns were banned, the deaths caused by heated arguments could be reduced. If, for example, the most accessible instrument were a knife instead of a gun, the rate of death would be significantly reduced. A wound from a gun is more deadly than a knife wound; in fact, a gun is five times more lethal than a knife.

6 Perhaps the strongest argument given by opponents to handgun control is that it would be nearly impossible to enforce such a law; only the law-abiding citizens would sacrifice their handguns, not the professional criminals. This argument seems valid. The problem of policing gun control seems mindboggling, considering that over 30 million handguns are already owned by Americans. Strict handgun controls would probably not prevent premeditated murder. The professional criminal and assassin would find a gun. However, outlawing handguns would greatly reduce crimes of passion, which account for 70 percent of all homicides in the United States. In addition, it would be difficult for a disturbed personality like Sara Jane Moore or Arthur Bremer to buy a pistol.

7 Finally, the argument that banning handguns will inhibit hunters is false because handguns are not good weapons for hunting. In fact, many small handguns like the "Saturday-night special" are designed for one purpose—to kill people. "Saturday-night specials" are short-barreled, cheaply made weapons that sell for about twenty-five dollars and usually fire small-caliber bullets. If the sale, manufacture and possession of the ammunition necessary to fire these weapons were outlawed, if all handguns and handgun ammunition were outlawed, then the most basic of all human rights would be protected—the right to live.

8 Robert J. di Grazia, the Boston Police Commissioner, recently stated that the handgun is "no longer merely the instrument of crime; it is now a cause of violent crime." Easily accessible handguns do not protect the rights of individuals. Handguns are designed to kill people. Statistics prove that handguns usually injure or kill the people they are supposed to protect. Stricter gun control

legislation banning the sale and possession of handguns will
not eliminate violent crimes. However, banning handguns will
greatly reduce the casualties resulting from a weapon designed
for one ominous purpose--to kill people.

--Eric Witherspoon

EXPLORING CHOICES

Content and Organization

1. Where does the thesis or proposition of the essay appear? What discussion precedes it? What is the function of this preliminary discussion?

2. What is the function of paragraph 2? Could paragraph 2 be placed elsewhere in the essay? What appears to be the writer's purpose in placing it just after he asserts his thesis?

3. The statistical evidence used in paragraphs 2 and 3 serves different purposes. What is the nature of this difference? Could the writer have altered the order of his presentation of this evidence? Explain.

4. The writer does not document the statistical evidence he cites. Do you consider this a failing? Explain. Do you think there are other places where the writer should have documented his sources?

5. Explain how refutation serves as an organizing principle of the essay.

6. What principle, if any, appears to control the order in which the writer refutes his opponents' positions while supporting his own?

7. At times, the writer affirms the accuracy of an opposing argument. Where does this strategy appear? How does it affect the tone of the essay? Does this strategy increase or decrease your confidence in the course the writer is urging?

8. Point out the writer's use of authority. Are you inclined to accept the credentials of the authorities he cites? Why or why not?

9. The essay follows a problem/solution format: the writer first attempts to establish the need for gun control legislation before defining the specific kind of legislation required to meet this need. What arguments does he use to establish need? What specific legislation does he propose?

10. Though the writer agrues for gun control legislation, he is primarily interested in controlling a particular kind of gun. Do you think he would have made his case stronger if he had defined the limits of the gun control legislation he is advocating early in the essay? Explain.

11. Paragraph 7 defines the particular gun the writer wishes to control. Should this definition appear elsewhere? Explain.

12. In paragraph 4, the writer refutes the argument that handguns protect citizens from prowlers by citing a study which claims that handguns are far more likely to kill friends and family than intruders. Is his refutation valid and logical? Explain.

13. In paragraph 6, the writer points out that though handgun control would be difficult to enforce, it would nevertheless "greatly reduce crimes of passion." Is his conclusion warranted? Explain.

Style

1. Point out the writer's use of questions. What rhetorical purpose does this strategy serve?
2. In paragraph 6, the writer alludes to two people without identifying them. Can the writer assume that these people will be known to other college freshmen, the audience for his essay?
3. Note the writer's use of phrases such as *ominous purpose, senselessly killed, grim statistics.* What is the effect of such phrases?
4. Point out the writer's use of the dash. Account for its purpose and effect in each instance.

The following problem/solution essay relies on causal analysis as the basis for its argument: in it, the author first details the causes of the problem, and then outlines the probable effects of the solution he proposes. As a review of the concepts discussed in this chapter, read and respond to the article:

HOW TO SAVE SOCIAL SECURITY

1   The social-security system is in trouble. Expenditures and receipts are in uneasy balance and the situation is likely to grow worse in the decades ahead. Young workers are understandably concerned because social-security taxes take a big bite out of their paychecks with no guarantee that the economy will be able to provide them with equivalent benefits when they retire. Retired persons fear that a sudden crisis in funding may force a rollback in their main source of support. The fears are justified, but I believe there is a way out.

2   The basic problem is that the system is not, and was never intended to be, a "save for retirement" insurance plan. It is a "pay as you go" system. The taxes paid by current employees (and their employers) are not invested in a fund to finance their retirement. Instead, current taxes are used to pay benefits to the workers of earlier generations who have already retired. When the number of retired persons is small relative to the number of workers, no problems arise. But when the number of retired persons grows much more rapidly than the number of workers, large increases in taxes and/or decreases in benefits are needed to keep the system in balance.

3   What is going wrong? In large part the system is the victim of demographic changes that it did not cause, but that it must respond to. Longer life expectancy and declining birthrates are the main factors undermining the financial foundations of the system. Since it was designed in the 1930s, there has been a significant increase in the proportion of the population that reaches retirement age. More recently, death rates at post-retirement ages have also decreased appreciably. Between 1968 and 1977 life expectancy at 65 jumped from 12.8 to 13.9 years for men and from 16.3 to 18.3 years for women. Congressional action in 1956 and 1961 that created an early-retirement option at 62 has also increased the retiree-worker ratio. Currently, fewer than half of all workers wait until 65 to begin collecting benefits.

4   Until now the increasing number of retirees has been offset in part by the rapid growth of female-labor-force participation and by the massive influx of the baby-boom cohorts into the work force. These sources of additional labor will begin to dry up in the years ahead. Although the female-labor-force participation rate is likely to remain high, it is virtually impossible that it will *increase* as rapidly as it has in the past. Even more important, because of the decline in the birthrate, which began many years ago, the number of young people who reach working age during the 1990s will be approximately 7 million less than it was in the 1970s.

5   What can we do? Politicians are understandably reluctant to reduce benefits or to raise taxes, but unless some action is taken a crisis is likely to develop—one that would set generation against generation and would prove extremely disruptive to the society. Some experts would like to see a change to a fully funded "save for retirement" insurance system. While such a system has some advantages, it is not feasible to make such a radical change. In order to create a funded system while maintaining benefits to those who have already retired, the current generation of workers would have to bear an enormous increase in taxes. From both a political and an economic point of view, that is neither a viable nor necessarily a desirable option.

6   Fortunately, there is a simple and effective way to put the system back on a sound financial footing without raising taxes or reducing benefits to retired persons. Beginning soon we should gradually and steadily raise the age at which workers become eligible for retirement benefits. For instance, legislation passed next year could state that in 1983 the eligibility age for so-called early retirement would be 62 years and two months, eligibility for standard retirement would be 65 years and two months and that these ages would increase by two months every year for the following seventeen years. Thus, by the year 2000 the key eligibility ages would be 65 and 68. This simple, gradual change would provide a large financial boost to the social-security system without causing significant disruption to workers, families or firms. In the long run the effect would be comparable to a major increase in social-security taxes because the ratio of workers to retired persons would be much larger than if we allow the eligibility ages to remain as they are now.

7   Would raising the age of eligibility change retirement patterns? There can be no doubt that it would. Opinions differ regarding exactly how retirement decisions are influenced by ill health, inflation, unemployment and other factors, but the *timing* of retirement clearly depends upon social-security eligibility. Withdrawal from work is much greater at 62 and 65 than in the years just before and just after those ages. Moreover, once Congress changes the social-security ages, most private-pension plans would probably adapt, thus reinforcing the effect. Mandatory retirement, it should be noted, has already been changed by Congress from 65 to 70.

8   There is nothing sacred or magical about reaching 62 or 65—Congress picked those ages, and Congress can change them. The use of 65 as a standard retirement age goes back to the nineteenth century when Bismarck chose it for the new German social-security system. This was at a time when most people began work before the age of 15 and most died before ever reaching 65. At present in the United States very few youngsters begin full-time work until finishing high school, and a substantial fraction do not begin until they are well into their 20s. Furthermore, given present trends in life expectancy at older ages, persons retiring at 68 in the year 2000 can probably expect to enjoy as many years in retirement as did the worker who retired at 65 in 1960.

9   The problem is clear. So is the solution. All that is required is the political courage to act *before* a crisis is actually upon us.

—Victor R. Fuchs, *Newsweek*

EXPLORING THE PERSUASIVE ESSAY

1. What purposes does Fuchs accomplish in paragraph 1? What image does Fuchs convey of himself in this paragraph—especially through the tone of the last sentence—and throughout the entire essay? What difference would it have made if Fuchs had titled his article, "Can Social Security Be Saved?" Would the more ambiguous title have been preferable? Explain.

2. In paragraph 2, Fuchs outlines the problem with the current social-security system. State the problem as he sees it in your own words. How appropriate is his terminology, "pay as you go," as a description of the current system?

3. What are the causes, as Fuchs sees them, of the present problem? What is the main source for his evidence in paragraphs 3 and 4?

4. Paragraphs 5 and 6 move from the problem to possible solutions. The first of these two paragraphs suggests alternative solutions that Fuchs would reject. Has he refuted them adequately? How convincing do you find Fuchs' own solution and why?

5. What objections, if any, could you raise toward his solution that he has failed to refute in his essay?

6. Paragraph 7 lists the effects if Fuchs' solution were adopted. What are they?

7. What function does paragraph 8 serve? As background to the problem, we might have expected it to occur earlier. Why do you suppose he placed it at this point in the essay rather than near the beginning?

8. How would you characterize the substance and intent of the concluding paragraph? Why do you suppose that Fuchs decided not to summarize his argument? Is this an effective strategy?

EDITORIAL ACTIVITIES

Following are the first draft and revision of a persuasive paper on the validity of intelligence tests. The questions will help you understand and assess the changes that the student made.

I.Q. TESTS

(1) There has been recent controversy over the validity of I.Q. tests. (2) Many authorities feel the use of such intelligence tests is unfair to the individual. (3) The validity questions raised are important because the future education of many human beings is involved.

(4) Those who wish to continue using I.Q. tests feel the only way to measure potential is by measuring current abilities. (5) Yet, these same people define intelligence as "the entire repertoire of acquired skills, knowledge, learning sets, and generalization tendencies considered intellectual in nature that are available at any one period in time." (6) I.Q. tests measure only our abilities on a verbal scale. (7) Also, this verbal scale does not measure innate capacity, mainly because no such measure exists. (8) Thus, many abilities of the individual human being are not being correctly evaluated by such tests.

(9) In addition, the proponents of testing believe tests measure abilities which develop in a culture. (10) While this may be true, one must also look at the fact that America is multi-cultural. (11) So, do these tests recognize such facts and measure intelligence according to individual cultures? (12) Not really. (13) Even though attempts have been made by various test designers to take into account these cultural influences, there still exists a mutual agreement between both sides of the test issue that a test cannot be totally free of cultural bias.

(14) Finally, perhaps the strongest argument given by the supporters of I.Q. tests is that these tests can help discover those children who may benefit from special help. (15) As long as these children have had the kind of assumed background that may require this special help, I.Q. tests can be useful. (16) Even so, we must be very cautious since I.Q. tests are also known to misclassify too many minority children. (17) Thus, such tests may be useful only if all conditions are considered.

(18) To sum up, the controversy over I.Q. tests does raise
some valid questions about their measuring abilities. (19)
While it is true these tests can aid the detection of mental
impairment, they do not measure creativity or innate
abilities, nor do they exclude environmental factors which
result in cultural biases. (20) Therefore, in my opinion,
intelligence tests are only useful for those children who are
truly impaired.

Revision

I.Q. TESTING?

(1) Recently, controversy has arisen among educational
psychologists over the fairness and validity of I.Q. tests as
a measurement on which to base decisions about educating and
employing individuals. (2) Many authorities in the field
legitimately hold that these intelligence tests can measure
only existing capabilities, are culturally biased, and
unfairly label people as impaired. (3) These objections
appear to be valid, and thus call into question the continued
dependence on these exams as determiners of people's futures.
(4) Those who argue for continuing to use I.Q. tests feel
that future potential can be projected only from measuring
current abilities. (5) Yet, these same people define
intelligence as "the entire repertoire of acquired skills,
knowledge, learning sets, and generalization tendencies
considered intellectual in nature that are available at any
one period in time." (6) To accommodate both of these two
beliefs, however, I.Q. tests would need to measure not only
verbal aptitude and math skills, but also creative abilities
or acquired skills, such as artistic performance, musical
talent, and originality of thought. (7) But this is clearly
not the case, since I.Q. tests can measure neither creative
abilities nor innate capacities. (8) Thus, many potential
abilities of the individual are not being correctly evaluated
by such tests.
(9) In addition, the proponents of I.Q. testing believe that
these tests adequately measure abilities which develop across
and within an entire culture. (10) While this may be so, we
must remember that America is multi-cultural. (11) These
tests, then, are not really designed to consider that
multiplicity. (12) Even though various experts in test design
have attempted to take into account these cultural influences,
everyone agrees that no test can be totally free of cultural
bias.
(13) Finally, perhaps the strongest argument proponents of
continued I.Q. testing can put forth is that these tests can

discover which children benefit from special help. (14) If these children do, indeed, suffer only from physical or emotional problems, then I.Q. tests can be useful in assessing this. (15) However, we must be very cautious, since these tests have been known to misclassify too many minority children as physically or mentally impaired who simply have lacked the proper environmental stimuli for educational growth. (16) Therefore, such tests are useful only if all conditions possibly affecting individual performance are considered.

(17) The controversy over I.Q. tests has, indeed, raised valid questions about their measuring ability. (18) While these tests can aid in the detection of mental impairment, they cannot measure creativity or innate abilities; neither can they be free from cultural bias since they fail to take into account environmental factors. (19) In my opinion, therefore, if one really wants to assign a number to a person's intelligence, the best way is to teach and observe the person for a time to see if and what he learns. (20) This approach would benefit both teacher and student alike, since it would foster a one-to-one relationship of trust and caring.

—Carole Hruskocy

EXPLORING CHOICES

1. What has the student accomplished by her additions to sentence 1?
2. How does the new material in sentence 2 help indicate to the reader what the writer's purpose and approach will be?
3. What new words in sentences 2 and 3 are explicit indicators of the writer's point of view?
4. What seems to be the purpose of the additional material in sentence 6 in the revision?
5. Point out the minor revisions in paragraph 3. In what ways is each of these an improvement over the original?
6. What points has the student clarified by her revisions in paragraph 4?
7. The last two sentences of the revision add material not in the original. What is the function of this addition? Is this new conclusion stronger than the earlier one? Is it appropriate to what has come before?
8. What other additions to the content or modifications in the organization or style would you suggest the student make if she revised her paper again?

YOU ARE THE EDITOR

The following student essay overgeneralizes, lacks specificity in the writing and use of examples, and inadequately refutes the opposing viewpoint. As the editor, give the student detailed advice for making the paper a more compelling piece of persuasive writing.

PRIORITIES

1   America as a country has been greatly blessed with an abundance of natural beauty. Our country can boast an outstanding variety of rugged mountains, dense forestland, countless lakes and rivers, and a tremendous variety of trees, plants, flowers, and wild animals. Nature itself is one of our most important natural resources, and the utmost should be done to protect it from the senseless destruction often inflicted upon it by our modern society. However, there comes a time when the needs of the American people must be put before the preservation of our environment. This is not to say that I condone strip mining or acid rain or offshore oil drilling, only that I believe that sometimes those who most wish to preserve our natural environment often overlook the prevailing needs or desires of everyone else.

2   An example of this occurred several years ago when a huge dam project in Tennessee was halted because it was found that construction of the dam would endanger the life of the snail darter, a

small fish few people had ever heard of and even fewer cared about. However, due to the efforts of a small group of environmentalists, the construction of the dam was blocked. Of course all animals, however insignificant or small, are important and should be protected. But was it really more important to save the snail darter than provide millions of people with cheaper electricity and thus at least a somewhat improved standard of living? Do all those people paying higher electrical bills in Tennessee pay them with a sense of pride and satisfaction because they know the snail darter is safe?

3   There are many times when the push for progress comes in conflict with our natural environment, as our many polluted rivers, barren woodlands, and stripped mountains bear witness to. In most cases the damage is senseless, unnecessary and avoidable, and man is to be faulted for his lack of concern about his environment. But in those cases when the betterment of the American people is the primary motive for the damage done to our environment and a totally justifiable need for damaging the environment for the sake of society can be proven, then perhaps it is time for the environmentalists to step aside just once and allow the wishes of the majority to be exercised.

4   Controversy is bound to arise whenever the

question is raised as to whether damaging our
environment is justifiable and totally necessary,
and in most cases it usually isn't. We probably
really don't need any more forests and fields
torn up for new shopping malls or fast food
restaurants or parking lots, and most of our
current problems such as acid rain could probably
have been avoided in the first place if more
concern or farsightedness had been exercised.
This doesn't mean, though, that progress is
always bad and must be checked. As long as
progress can be made in a reasonable fashion and
with utmost concern for the environment in mind,
it should be allowed to do so. Cooperation and
trust, not loathing and mistrust, must exist
between industrial leaders and environmental
leaders to overcome existing problems and to
avoid future ones. Above all, it must be
realized and accepted that once in a while the
needs of the people must come before the
preservation of the environment, however unfair
or distasteful that may seem to some. People
are, after all, our most important natural
resource, and perhaps if as much concern were
shown to them as is given to saving the whales or
baby seals or snail darters, our country would be
in better shape than it is today.

WRITING SUGGESTIONS

1. You are an amateur photographer on the scene of a natural disaster or accident which claims several lives. The photos you take of the victims and grieving survivors are potential prizewinners, and a press service offers to pay you highly for them. But the survivors beg you to respect their privacy. Write a letter either to the survivors justifying your decision to sell the pictures despite their pleas, or to the representative of the press expressing your reasons for refusing to put the pictures in the public domain.

2. You are working for an ad agency and have been assigned to write advertising copy for a new product or service (candy bar, cologne, restaurant, resort hotel). Prepare two versions of the copy, one arranged inductively, the other deductively. Include with the copy a brief essay in which you argue for the superiority of one version of your copy over the other, and explain how your ad is appropriate for the targeted audience.

3. You are working for the board of a group of local realtors in an area where houses are not selling well. They ask you to prepare a small brochure, addressed to young singles or married couples, persuading them to invest in their first home or condominium rather than continue renting an apartment. Convince your audience that even the disadvantages of owning their own home outweigh the advantages of renting.

THE ESSAY EXAMINATION

*T*hroughout this book we have discussed the choices available to you as a writer at every stage of the composing process. When you write an essay examination, however, your choices will be limited: the essay questions and the unusual writing conditions will ordinarily predetermine the general content and even the organization of your response. Furthermore, the constraints of time usually prevent extensive revision, so that you need to make do with careful proofreading before the bell rings. Everything from prewriting to proofreading is severely condensed; what under other circumstances would be a first draft, now becomes a final draft. Consequently, taking an essay examination is perhaps most like writing an in-class theme for which you are given only a hint of the topic beforehand. All these limitations on time, topic, and approach prove restrictive; fewer choices are open during an essay examination or when writing an in-class paper than during almost any other type of writing.

Since there is so little time for prewriting and invention during the exam period, the studying done beforehand must substitute for the thinking and planning stages—but without the false starts characteristic of this stage of the process. Studying is a time to bring the course material into focus, to synthesize the main ideas or currents. Because the actual exam time is short, most essay examinations ask you to bring together a considerable amount of material by seeing relationships that were left implicit or only hinted at during the semester. For example, a course in adolescent psychology might contain units on peer pressure; individuation through the rejection of authority; sexual adaptation; discovering role models; and motivating teenagers to learn. The final exam might ask you to choose the theorist whose approach to adolescence seems most comprehensive and useful, and then to justify your choice. Your preparation for the exam involves foreseeing possible topics or subjects that an instructor might use to measure how well you have integrated the material that you have been studying.

PREWRITING TIPS

Even if reviewing for an essay exam includes dreaming up—and maybe even writing responses to—possible questions, the anxiety of the exam situation can never be totally alleviated. No matter how long or hard you prepare, or how well you think you know the material, there's still that inevitable moment of distress when you first encounter the question sheet.

Some of this distress can be eased by following a few common sense suggestions.

1. Before writing any answer, look over the *entire* exam carefully. Most essay examinations offer a choice of topics, allowing you to eliminate any that you can't answer or feel uncertain about handling. Seeing the whole exam before you write, and knowing all the topics you will be covering, may give you ideas you can jot down and reserve for later. It may also help you apportion your time according to the difficulty and importance of the questions.

2. Choose those questions you can answer best and—if possible—write on them first. If nothing else, this helps increase your confidence.

3. If you still feel uneasy about some topics you've chosen—or if you've been given no choice at all—begin by writing on those that are most familiar; the process of answering these may help dredge up material for the others.

TYPES OF QUESTIONS

Most questions on an essay examination require that you synthesize a large volume of material within a short period of time and in a conventional format. As a result, certain kinds of questions tend to recur on essay examinations no matter what the academic discipline. Broadly speaking, essay questions are *informational, relational,* or *critical.* The categories will often overlap, especially as your answers become more sophisticated.

Informational questions might ask you to narrate a sequence of events, to trace a pattern, to define a movement, to describe a process, to review the literature in a certain field. At their least challenging, such questions might do little more than measure retentiveness by requiring you to give back in an orderly fashion what you have read in outside assignments or heard in class. On a more challenging level, they will ask you to demonstrate that you have reflected upon the material in an insightful way. Here are some examples of informational questions:

Trace the major events and figures in the Women's Suffrage movement.

Choosing a particular form of cancer, describe what the predictable process of metastasis would be.

Define the baroque style in art, drawing on examples from painting, sculpture, and music.

Outline the ethical problems that might arise in connection with in vitro fertilization.

Relational questions require that you show the connections between things by comparing, by contrasting, by explaining causal sequence, or by applying an abstract concept to a specific case. For example, you might be asked one of the following:

> What similarities can be seen between American involvement in Southeast Asia in the 1960s and American involvement in Central America in the 1980s?

> Distinguish between the evolutionary theories of Darwin and Lamarck.

> What is the relationship between inflation and full employment?

> How would Karl Marx respond to the British type of socialism attempted in the post-World War II period?

Critical questions imply judgment or interpretation; they require you to assess, evaluate, or prove something. Falling into this category would be such questions as:

> Some researchers trace autism in children to a lack of parental warmth and affection during infancy. Assess the validity of these findings.
> Support, refute, or modify the assumption that "We cannot have decontrol of natural gas without higher prices for consumers."

You can see, however, that even informational or relational questions may involve judgment. If, for instance, your answer includes an evaluation of a scholar's contribution to a field of study, or if you assert that one theory is more important than another, your essay becomes not just informational or relational but also critical. Deliberately interjecting a point of view may, in fact, become the spine that supports the entire essay.

Discussion questions—a favorite among instructors—call for an informational or relational or critical response, or any combination of the three. This question's only explicit direction is the word *discuss*. This kind of essay question puts you at a slight disadvantage: you must spend extra time analyzing what precisely is being asked for. In other words, you must understand the implications of the question and look for clues about an appropriate method of attack. Taking a few moments for analysis and reflection will usually pay off, since the more you see about the possibilities for answering a *discuss* question, the fuller your response is likely to be. Let's examine a few very simple examples. If a question reads, "Discuss black holes," most students will immediately see that the minimum requirement for responding to such a question is an informational definition in the form of a detailed description. An insightful student would also see possibilities for a relational response that would discuss this mysterious phenomenon in terms of a similar one that is better understood, or for a more critical answer, would evaluate contending theories about the nature of black holes, their formation, and so on. If another question reads, "Discuss depression," most students will again easily see that the response must describe depression, its causes, its symptoms, and its treatment, which might best be handled in a structure combining causal and process analysis. Yet this question, too, allows for and even invites a critical assessment of varying opinions about the causes of depression (mental? physical?) and its treatment (counseling? drugs? diet?).

But what of *discuss* questions whose clues about an appropriate approach are not so obvious, and which seem to allow a greater range of choices? In a course on the detective film, for instance, students found this question on their final examination:

> One critic has written: "In the detective story the heroes . . . have perceived that the dilemmas they see outwardly are essentially internal dilemmas and they have to be perceived from within." Discuss.

If you analyze this question, which asks students to interpret a body of data, you will see several possible approaches. One answer could be descriptive: providing three or four examples to support the critic's hypothesis of detectives who experience largely internal dilemmas. A second approach, which would measurably improve upon the first, could be relational: not only comparing but contrasting a range of detectives (perhaps Sam Spade in John Huston's *The Maltese Falcon,* Philip Marlowe in Howard Hawks' *The Big Sleep,* and Harry Moseby in Arthur Penn's *Night Moves*) for whom internal dilemmas seem more or less central, thereby suggesting a need for a balanced view of the critic's thesis. A third approach, which would build upon and be richer and more satisfying than either of the others, would venture into an evaluation of how this critic's insight has altered the traditional analysis of the detective hero, thus adding to our understanding of a whole body of films.

FOLLOW-UP ACTIVITIES

1. Review some of the essay exams you have taken recently, and try to categorize or characterize the types of questions asked.
2. Write some examination questions appropriate for the courses you are taking. Categorize these as well.

A METHODOLOGY FOR THE ESSAY EXAM

The cardinal rule for taking an essay exam is always to understand, as precisely as possible, what the question asks. Then respond to that—and not to some mythical question you would prefer to answer. Many students, when faced with an exam topic, tend to start writing immediately, putting down everything even remotely related to the subject, hoping that they will eventually hit on what the examiner wants. But this blitzkrieg method is never the best strategy. Remember, most exam questions only delimit a topic or a subject for investigation; invariably it is necessary for you to develop a tentative thesis about the subject *before* beginning to write. After that, jot down, in a sparse outline, the key terms that will keep you from forgetting the main points and the most relevant supporting details. The question itself will usually help determine not only the nature of the information needed but also the pattern of your answer. Almost any structural pattern demanded by an essay question will be a variation of one of those discussed in detail in Chapters 3 and 7.

When reading essay responses, most instructors look for clear and unambiguous statements of facts and ideas, as well as a logical and appropriate overall shape. Most topics can be handled, depending on the complexity of the material, within a four- or five-paragraph format of introduction, body, and conclusion. The overall movement of most essay exam answers will usually be from general to particular, or from abstract to concrete. It is probably easiest for the writer, and especially for the reader who might look for highlights at the beginning of each paragraph, if individual paragraphs also follow the general to particular movement.

The introductory paragraph need not be crafted especially to attract the attention and interest of your reader; such attention can be assumed. It must, however, still indicate the general idea and signal the direction the essay will take. The topic sentence will reveal the choices you have made—always within the limitations imposed by the question—about what you will discuss and the methodology you will employ. By developing a focused opening, you can, to some extent, bring the question under *your* control. If, for example, you are asked to discuss the conditions that led to the Civil War and begin by stating, "Economic factors overshadowed the political and even racial causes of the Civil War," you have limited your consideration to the three broad categories of economic causes, political causes, and racial causes—each of which would be discussed in a separate paragraph. More than that, you have led your reader to expect that you will treat these causes in an ascending order of importance: political, racial, and economic.

The supporting details included in the central paragraphs of your answer need to be chosen more selectively than in ordinary out-of-class writing. Although you might be able to think of four or five points that could logically come under each of your three categories of political, racial, and economic causes, you may have time to mention and explain only the two or three most important under each heading. And when you reach your conclusion, it will be necessary not just to reiterate your thesis that economic factors overshadowed political and racial ones, but to emphasize *why* this was the case.

Sometimes, while writing an answer, you may even develop a new perspective or insight; if that happens, then a strong concluding paragraph will be your only opportunity—since you lack the luxury of starting over—to state or explain your thesis more fully. In short, as with all good expository writing, your task in the essay exam is to set down your best ideas concisely and succinctly, to organize them cogently, and to support them with the most significant and relevant detail.

THREE ESSAY EXAMS

Let's examine some student papers written in response to several types of examination questions.

Exam A

Discuss the theme of initiation in two short stories by Hawthorne and two by Melville.

You will notice immediately that the topic allows some latitude: there is a required subject (initiation as a thematic motif), although the particular type of initiation is left open. The question also specifies that the writer examine two works by each author, although, once again, the choice of which stories to discuss is left to the writer. Although the question would seem to demand no more than a purely informational response, it lends itself as well to comparison and contrast, a relational response.

As you read the following essay, notice the writer's strategy in his opening paragraph: he repeats the topic, and then suggests the general thrust of his thesis, though he goes into little detail at this point, except to say that differences will emerge. After devoting a paragraph to each of the stories he names in his introduction, he uses the conclusion to make the elements of his thesis more concrete—as if he refined and discovered the specifics of his thesis while writing the answer. The sense that the *writer's* understanding of the subject grew as he answered the question strengthens the answer's impact on the reader.

Effective *transitions* are especially important in writing exam essays because they indicate the writer's ability to synthesize material and to recognize relationships among the ideas. For example, in the following essay the first sentence in paragraph 3 connects the central character of the second story with the protagonist of the first, while the third sentence hints at a contrast between the two. Referring to ideas introduced earlier is, you will notice, one of the strengths of this answer:

1   The theme of initiation is an important one throughout the works of both Hawthorne and Melville as evidenced by the stories "My Kinsman, Major Molineux," "Young Goodman Brown," "Billy Budd," and "Bartleby the Scrivener." As we shall see, though, the types of initiation and their effects on the different characters vary dramatically.

2   In Hawthorne's "Major Molineux," Robin arrives in the city as a naive country hick, in search of his esteemed kinsman. He fancies himself a "shrewd youth" when, in fact, he is quite immature. Throughout the tale, he is laughed at by the townspeople, yet he cannot understand the reason for their laughter. Not until he sees his kinsman tarred and feathered does he begin to laugh with the rest of the town. Laughter represents, of course, knowledge of the human condition. Robin, when he laughs with the rest, is accepting the fact that there is both good and evil in everyone. He is being initiated into adulthood.

3   Hawthorne's Young Goodman Brown, like Robin, is naive and innocent. However, as he journeys through the forest, he meets the Devil and is initiated into the dark side of human nature. Brown, though, cannot accept this; he loses all of his faith in mankind. " 'My Faith is gone!' cried he. . . . 'There is no good on earth. . . . ' " Brown refuses to accept the duality of human nature and is cast out of the chain of humanity.

4   Melville's Billy Budd is also very young and innocent. He is indeed a bud—a flower that has not yet bloomed. Aboard the Rights-of-Man he is sheltered from evil; however, aboard Indomitable he is exposed to the real world and evil, personified by Claggart. Yet even though he is being initiated into an evil world, he doesn't fully realize that this evil exists. He is intrinsically good and cannot even recognize evil. Even as he is about to be executed, he remains eternally cheerful by saying, "God bless Captain Vere!"

5   Melville's "Bartleby" might also be viewed as a story about initiation, for in it the lawyer is initiated from a world of logic, reason and "the head" into one of illogic, unreason and "the heart." While our other initiates were transplanted physically from a sheltered world to the cruelties of the real world, the lawyer's journey is a mental one. The beginning of the story finds him a man of great intellect, a student of Cicero. As the story progresses, though, he becomes more and more compassionate as he begins to realize the plight of Bartleby. His transformation is evidenced by his use of

Bartleby's vocabulary, especially "prefer." He begins to
really know his own heart.

6   Thus we have seen Robin initiated into a world of adulthood
and responsibility, Brown and Billy Budd initiated into a
world of evil (and good), and the lawyer initiated into a
world of compassion.   —John Schmidt

EXPLORING CHOICES

1. Locate the transitional sentences in paragraphs 4 and 5. Discuss the function of each of these within the paragraphs and within the essay as a whole.
2. The one-sentence concluding paragraph could have served as the last sentence of the introductory paragraph. If it had been placed in that position, would the essay have been strengthened or not? Why?
3. The concluding paragraph suggests that three different patterns of initiation are apparent in these stories. Do the writer's categories adequately summarize the material he has presented?
4. Can you detect any reason behind the order the writer has chosen to discuss the four stories? Might another order have been as good or better?
5. This essay falls into the comparison/contrast pattern, and the writer has used the block pattern of development. Would an alternating structure have been preferable?

Exam B

Following are two reviews of a film by Woody Allen. If you were editing an Arts and Leisure page for your local newspaper, which one would you run and why?

1   Some critics have soured on Woody Allen's recent movies, accusing him of foisting his identity problems on the public. So Woody seems to have decided: "You want identity problems? I'll give you identity problems." His new film, *Zelig,* deals with the biggest identity crisis in the history of identity. It's also an amazing technical tour de force, a movie unlike anything Woody or anyone else has ever made. It's a documentary film, but a documentary about a fictitious character named Leonard Zelig, a once celebrated but now forgotten hero of the '20s. Like Orson Welles in "Citizen Kane," Woody understands the strange power in old movie images. In "Zelig" he combines wonderful old clips with his own imitations of old movies and newsreels, plus all sorts of optical trickery. The result is a brilliant cinematic collage that is pure magic, and that allows

Woody to satirize all sorts of things, from nostalgia, psychoanalysis and the American dream to critics, himself and much more.

2   Woody is Zelig, the most bizarre nut case of the '20s. Known as the Incredible Changing Man, or the Human Chameleon, Zelig has no personality of his own but takes on the characteristics, physical as well as mental, of whomever he comes in contact with. The son of a Yiddish actor known for his role of Puck in "the orthodox version of 'A Midsummer Night's Dream,' " Zelig becomes a black trumpet player in a jazz band, takes on Caruso's most famous role, Canio in "I Pagliacci," invades Yankee Stadium to take his cuts with Babe Ruth and Lou Gehrig. Zelig becomes the darling of psychiatrists worldwide, who marvel at his protean malady. Placed next to an obese man, the frail Zelig balloons up to 250 pounds; encountering an Indian, he sprouts feathers and a Mohawk profile. It's hard for psychiatrists to deal with his syndrome because in their presence he *becomes* a psychiatrist, describing his studies with Freud. "We broke over the concept of penis envy," explains Zelig. "Freud felt it should be restricted to women."

3   The superschizo becomes a superstar. There are Zelig dolls with many guises. A dance craze, The Chameleon, sweeps the country. A billboard shows Zelig saying, "We smoke Camels." Then a young woman psychiatrist, Dr. Eudora Fletcher (Mia Farrow), cures him through the twin powers of psychiatry and love. Happiness is a single personality. Then disaster strikes. Three wives appear from Zelig's fragmented past. Moral opinion is outraged. Disgraced, Zelig disappears only to emerge again, hilariously, from the very crossroads of history itself.

4   One of Woody's satiric targets seems to be his buddy Warren Beatty who in "Reds" interviewed "witnesses" to interpret the life of John Reed. Woody interviews heavies like critics Susan Sontag and Irving Howe, novelist Saul Bellow and psychoanalyst Bruno Bettelheim. They all explain Zelig in terms of their own concerns: Bettelheim, speaking in tones of profound compassion, sees the ever-changing Zelig as "the ultimate conformist."

5   Woody is clearly having fun with the critics who see his movies as Rorschach tests by which to decipher the Allen psyche. Still, it appears that in some way he does see himself as a modern Zelig, fated to deal with the great questions of life with the Silly Putty of a comic sensibility. That sensibility is in fine fettle in "Zelig," aided by Woody's colleagues like cinematographer Gordon Willis and composer Dick Hyman.

6   The picture teems with scores of perfectly chosen actors, led by Mia Farrow's sweetly abashed psychiatrist and Patrick Horgan's perfect voice-over narration. The trick effects are as good as anything in "Star Wars"; the masterly blend of real and fake in "Zelig" creates a time-warp universe as effective as anything in the work of writers like Borges or Calvino. And Woody is funnier, our most intelligent comic and most comic intelligence. His Zelig is a romantic who desperately wants the supreme cocktail of reality mixed with glory—the Great Gatsby as schlemiel.

—Jack Kroll, "Happiness Is a Single Self," *Newsweek*

1   "Cole Porter was fascinated by him," recalls a witness. "He wrote a song: *You're the Top, You're Leonard Zelig.* But he couldn't find anything to rhyme with Zelig."

2   Cole Porter was not alone. In his time, the '20s and '30s, the whole world was bewitched by the strange case of a human chameleon so eager to be liked that he developed the capacity literally to change accent, shape and even color in order to ingratiate himself with whomever he happened to be with. One day Scott Fitzgerald noticed him at a Gatsby-like Long Island party; the next, he was sitting in with a black jazz band at a Chicago speakeasy. Soon enough, Presidents and prize fighters, pundits and publishers were seeking him out. And where they led, the newspapers, the admen, Hollywood and all the other hustlers followed.

3   To tell the story of a first-generation American, who like many of his ilk would undergo any contortion in order to join the national mainstream, Woody Allen (who plays Zelig) has chosen a form that is utterly original in conception and exhilarating in execution. It is a parody of a television documentary, one of those compilations of old newsreels, scratchy recordings and animated stills held together by a voice-over narration. This material is supported by modern interviews, shot in jarring color, in which aged witnesses (among them Mia Farrow, who plays his psychiatric savior) testify about Zelig's life. They are abetted by modern "experts," among them Saul Bellow, Susan Sontag, Irving Howe and Bruno Bettelheim, in effect playing themselves playing themselves. Like Allen, they have perfect pitch. But Allen skewers not only the modern TV form but the loopy manner of the show's antique sources. Dick Hyman contributes songs like *You May Be Six People, But I Love You* that catch the flavor of hasty topicality, and cinematographer Gordon Willis recaptures the conventions of oldtime photography. The match between his footage and genuine historical shots is perfect.

4   *Zelig* is the culmination of a long quest by Allen. He is virtually the only celebrity who has continually investigated the values and liabilities of his own status. Three years ago, in *Stardust Memories,* he attempted to order these thoughts on film and was roundly criticized for so doing. In that story of a comedian oppressed by his own fame, he was unable to achieve the distance and objectivity he needed. *Zelig's* form provides both. Acutely satirizing mediaspeak, the film hilariously exposes the vulgarizations and misleading distortions of that language. At the same time, it touchingly demonstrates that celebrity is a kind of victimization, capable of claiming the souls of those who have some skill or talent, no matter how strange or silly, that is marketable.

5   Like all of Allen's best work, *Zelig* is, finally, a comedy of manners—public manners in this case, not private ones as in *Annie Hall* or *Manhattan.* In Yiddish it means blessed, and *Zelig* is, surely, in the midst of a typical American summer at the movies when almost everything is a loud assault on the senses, a benison. It is both a welcome wooing of sensibility and intellect and a film that will be recalled long after Labor Day has come and gone.

—Richard Schickel, "Meditations on Celebrity," *Time*

Here is how one student responded:

1   Both Jack Kroll, in "Happiness Is a Single Self" from <u>Newsweek</u>, and Richard Schickel, in "Meditations on Celebrity" from <u>Time</u>, have only praise for the newest Woody Allen film, <u>Zelig</u>. However, whereas Kroll only teases the reader with bits from the movie, Schickel provides an insight into the movie in order to demonstrate its excellence.

2   In order to establish why Schickel's review is superior to Kroll's, some criteria must first be established. A review, in general, is a brief commentary that touches on the major aspects of the film. This could include sketching in the plot and discussing the quality of the actors' performances, the script, the direction and editing, and the technical aspects such as special effects. A good reviewer will go beyond this, though. He will try to give the prospective viewer an idea of what the film is about without ruining all the surprise. He might do this by delineating major themes or by hinting at the message implicit in the film or by providing a wider context in which to review the single film. Such a preview of more than just the film's highlights would give the reader a good basis on which to decide whether to see the film, as well as alert him about some issues he might keep in mind to make seeing the movie a richer experience.

3   Both these reviewers indicate the major points that make the film stand out, including the originality of both story and style. Their descriptions are punctuated by a great number of superlatives; "perfect" is a prominent example. Kroll does not rise above this kind of compliment, though. He is content to mention the fictional Zelig's background, specific examples of the cinematographic trickery, and major plots twists. His analysis of what Allen is trying to do with the movie is limited to a sentence: ". . . [Allen] does see himself as a modern Zelig, fated to deal with the great questions of life with the Silly Putty of comic sensibility."

4   Schickel also gives us the basic points, though in a more concise fashion. He doesn't waste space talking about the fact that Allen is able to convey his points in a most hilarious manner; he assumes that Allen's particular brand of satire is well known. Instead, he concerns himself with giving the reader an idea of what <u>Zelig</u> is all about. Describing the film as "the culmination of a long quest by Allen," he argues that Allen has been trying for years to explore both the good and bad sides of being a celebrity. But up until now, according to Schickel, Allen has been unable to accomplish

this successfully. By providing this perspective on Allen, Schickel is better able to inform the reader and potential moviegoer of exactly what sort of film experience Zelig is. This gives a clearer sense of the film's content, a much harder task than indicating the film's quite apparent cinematic quality.

--Robert Duke

EXPLORING CHOICES

1. Point out the student's thesis statement. What does it indicate about how the rest of the essay will be organized?
2. Where in the essay does the writer support his thesis? How convincingly has he used details from the two reviews to back up his judgment about their relative merit? At what specific points could further details have been usefully added?
3. What is the function of paragraph 2? Is it more or less general than the rest of the answer? What would have been the difference in effect if the writer had put that paragraph first? Would that have improved the essay or not?
4. The last two sentences of paragraph 4 can be seen as the essay's conclusion. Should they have been given a separate paragraph? If so, might the conclusion have been expanded, and in what way?

Exam C

The period from about 1763 to about 1776 might be viewed as a period of constitutional crisis within the British empire. During this period the colonists altered their ideological perspective, developed new aspirations and expectations, and were eventually faced with revolution as the only way left to chart their own course. Discuss this thesis with an emphasis upon the ideological or constitutional beliefs, convictions, and assumptions held by the "radicals" and in relation to the views of the British administration. Were there changes in the colonists' views? Can one identify certain important moments at which the changes occurred?

Following is one student's answer:

1   The years from 1763 to 1776 can be characterized as a period of continual confrontation between the colonists and the British administration whereby the colonists were forced to recognize, articulate, and adamantly defend their beliefs and convictions. The colonists groped their way through a maze of unexpressed political views and perceptions brought to the

fore by actions taken by the British Parliament. The maturation and sophistication of their views ultimately charted the course that left the colonists with one alternative: revolution. By analyzing the ideological and constitutional beliefs, convictions, and assumptions the "radicals" had and examining what gave birth to them, one can contrast the radicals' views to those held by the British.

2   As a result of direct steps taken by the British Parliament, the colonists were forced to alter their ideological perspective and thus begin the formation and articulation of an "American" ideology. It is important to recognize that the historical experience of the British was far different from that of the colonists: the British had already gone through an evolution during which Parliament asserted its supremacy; in contrast, the colonists' experience closely resembled that of the early Anglo–Saxons. They were autonomous, self–governing, experienced in civic responsibilities––via legislative assemblies and jury duties––and had developed political and social elites and a flexible political system for solving their own internal conflicts and incorporating many citizens into the participatory system. Thus, when Parliament passed the Sugar Act of 1764 and the Stamp Act of 1765, the colonists were predisposed to perceive them as a threat to self–government.

3   The "radicals" like Samuel Adams saw the Sugar Act as challenging the doctrine of "no taxation without representation" and viewed it as a tax rather than a regulation of trade. Many viewed the Sugar Act as an ill–advised economic policy that would hurt the economy and called for its repeal. While we see this distinction between economic expediency versus constitutional principle with the passage of the Sugar Act, it is not until the Stamp Act that the constitutional question became more controversial. The radicals felt that Parliament did not have the right to tax the colonists who were not represented "actually" in Parliament. One can also see the colonists willing to allow the British the right to regulate their trade (external taxation––duty), but determinedly steadfast in their resolve not to allow Parliament to tax them internally; they see it as their constitutional right to be represented by the legislature that taxes them. The radicals seem to change their ideological perspective in a subtle way: they view the Ancient Constitution as an embodiment of the natural rights of man and as a way of protecting them, for a constitution limits the legislature and the executive.

4   In response to the actions Parliament took between 1765 and
     1776, the colonists engaged in various forms of protest to
     alert the Parliament and George III of their discontent. But
     gradually they began to realize that they were having little
     impact on the British government and would have to go even
     further. The radicals held a Stamp Act Congress in 1765 to
     provide a forum from which ideas and views could be shared and
     compared. In this time of formulating just how the American
     Colonies should react to acts that could serve as precedents
     for greater erosion of the autonomy of the colonial
     governments in the future, the proliferation of pamphlets was
     an additional source of furthering unity among the colonists,
     who were not single-minded in their support for revolution.
     The boycott the colonial radicals engaged in after the Stamp
     Act Crisis educated them that the Mother Country was
     vulnerable economically as well as psychologically to
     challenges to her authority. The Stamp Act Crisis also
     precipitated the passage of the Virginia Resolves which
     triggered the passage of similar resolves by other assemblies.
     All the resolves claimed that Parliamentary taxation was
     unconstitutional and would thus be resisted; and they claimed
     that anyone who affirmed Parliament's power to tax was an
     enemy of the people.

5   In addition to these movements to resist the Stamp Act, the
     colonists used riots to undermine the authority of Parliament.
     The Sons of Liberty organized or institutionalized the mob
     riots to keep them orderly and more effective as political
     weapons. The efforts to resist the Act and force its repeal
     (the merchants in Britain who were hurting financially due to
     the boycott demanded its repeal also) were successful;
     however, with Parliament's persistence in avoiding the
     "constitutional question" and advocating its supremacy over
     the colonial governments, especially the assemblies which were
     independent of the vast British patronage system, the
     relationship between the Mother Country and her colonies
     deteriorated further. The 1767 Townshend Duties on imported
     goods resulted in the colonial Non-Importation Agreements
     which, in short, united the colonists in their efforts to
     boycott England. After the Boston Massacre, the Boston Tea
     Party, and the Boston Port Act, the colonists seemed to accept
     the fact that Parliament and George III were not going to
     recognize their rights as Englishmen. In effect, by
     protesting and violating the various acts of Parliament and
     asserting their own rights to govern, the colonists were
     questioning Parliament's power and sovereignty in America.

6   In the decade before the Revolutionary War, the colonists
        were ready to break with the Mother Country and devise their
        own governmental structure: a republic. It had become an
        "either-or" dilemma: either the colonists would remain slaves
        of Parliament and be content with the liberties she might wish
        to grant them, or the colonists could declare total
        independence and chart their own course to "freedom and
        liberty for all," choosing revolution to institutionalize
        their convictions and beliefs.   --Diana Berkshire

EXPLORING CHOICES

1. Examine and categorize the question. Is it informational? Relational? Critical? What patterns of development would it demand or permit?
2. Examine the opening paragraph of the student's answer. How does it indicate the method she has chosen to respond to the question? What does it reveal about how she has understood and interpreted the question?
3. What is the student's basic pattern of development throughout the essay? Look especially at paragraphs 4 and 5.
4. Examine the last sentence of paragraph 3. Is its purpose transitional? If not, how does it function—within the paragraph and in the essay as a whole?
5. At what points in the answer has the student stated her thesis? Look at the details she used to support that thesis; are they sufficient in both quantity and quality?
6. Reexamine the question. Are things asked that the student has chosen not to address in her answer? If so, does this weaken the response? Could she have chosen a significantly different pattern of development and approach to the question? If so, what would it be?

Holistic Evaluation of Essay Exams

Although the three exams you have just read and analyzed were written for courses in diverse fields, it is possible to evaluate them qualitatively, in comparison to one another. Do so, using as your criteria:

the adequacy of the response as an answer to the question
the student's command of the material

the appropriateness of the method of organizing that material
the use of details to support generalizations
clarity and correctness of the writing

Is one of the essays markedly superior (or inferior) to the others on the basis of these criteria?

WRITING SUGGESTIONS

To gain practice in writing an essay exam, choose one of the following questions and respond to it, using the principles discussed in this chapter.

1. Analyze the two advertisements for bedding (pp. 372–373), one from Martex and the other from Wamsutta. Pay particular attention to the audience being appealed to in each. What differences do you see in the devices employed by the two ad agencies? Which is the more effective ad?

2. The following passages appear in essays collected under the title, *Men in Difficult Times,* edited by Robert A. Lewis. Read them carefully, and then respond to the question at the end.

   Despite the emphasis on toughness and skill, girls are able to fit into Little League baseball with little difficulty. Boys see baseball as a goal-oriented activity, and any help toward that goal will be viewed with favor. The only difficulty in terms of complete acceptance of girls into the Little League structure comes from parents . . .
   —Gary Alan Fine, "Little League Baseball and Growing Up Male"

   From a historical viewpoint, one sees that conventional wisdom advises that the crucial figure in the child's early years is the child's mother. Partly because of this, the traditional nursery school or child-care setting has been operated and staffed by women. This view holds that women through their "innate" nurturing abilities were destined to be with young children. As a result, men have been socialized away from the field of early childhood education.
   —Katherine Lowe, "Male Teachers and Young Children"

   Discuss the sociological factors underlying the exclusion of girls from participation in Little League baseball and of male teachers from the preschool classroom.

The Good Night Sheet

A sheet is something you sleep with. Martex never forgets. That's why we've created a whole new collection of peaceful patterns to help lull you to sleep.

And every Good Night Sheet feels as blissfully, smooth and restful as it looks.

Because they're made exclusively of dreamy, no-iron Dacron® and combed cotton.

Get Good Night Sheets at fine stores everywhere. Like the one you see here, Sheep.

Of course, we can't guarantee our Sheep will put you to sleep, but we can promise you won't spend the whole night counting them.

West Point Pepperell

MARTEX
You can tell the difference with your eyes closed.

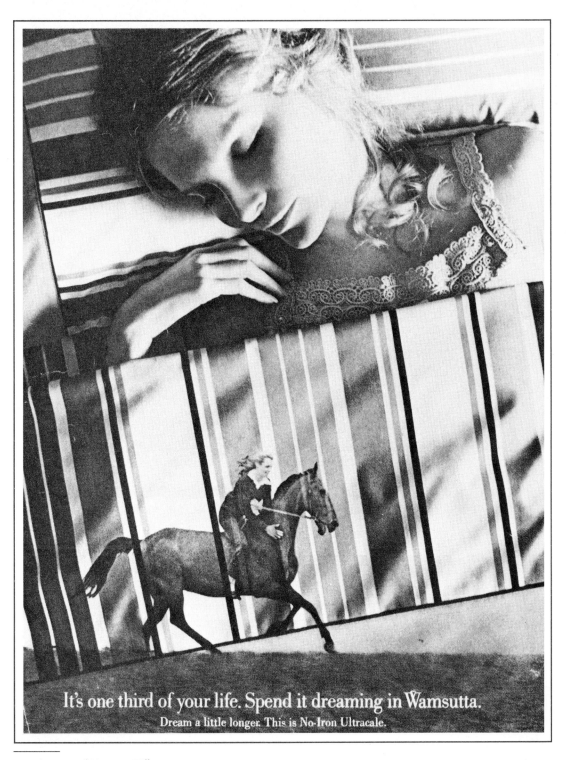

It's one third of your life. Spend it dreaming in Wamsutta.
Dream a little longer. This is No-Iron Ultracale.

Courtesy of Wamsutta Mills.

TIPS ON TAKING THE ESSAY EXAMINATION

Before you write:

1. Choose the questions you know most about and apportion your time.

2. Analyze and understand exactly what each question asks.

3. Jot down your thesis statement for each answer.

4. Make notes on the main supporting details you will use.

5. Decide on the best pattern of organization for your essay, and arrange the details accordingly.

As you write:

1. Be open to new ideas generated in the writing process and incorporate them at appropriate points.

2. Take into account opposite points of view; at least acknowledge their existence even if you cannot entirely refute them.

After you write:

1. Proofread for minor errors in grammar and mechanics.

2. Check for transitions, adding ones if necessary to increase the orderly flow of your essay.

3. If your essay lacks a conclusion, add one either to reemphasize your main point or to accommodate related ideas that came to you in the process of writing.

9

WRITING THE BOOK REVIEW

*O*f all the essays you might be asked to write in the course of your college career, the one most familiar to you is probably the book review. No doubt you have read reviews written for a popular audience in your favorite magazine or in the daily newspaper; perhaps later, when you have completed your training in your chosen field, you will read reviews written for specialists in your area of expertise. In either case, you read reviews to learn what books have been recently published, what a particular book is about, and, above all, whether or not a book is worth reading.

Your threefold purpose in reading a review can serve as a preliminary guide to the writing of your own reviews. Especially important is the matter of analysis and evaluation. A review does not merely summarize the contents of a book, though summary certainly has its place. Rather, at its best, a review becomes a dialogue between you and the book you are reviewing; it suggests your interpretation of the book, as well as your critical evaluation of its merits. Sometimes, these features are combined with summary: reviewers will interpret and evaluate the work in the course of narrating the book's events (if it is fiction) or recapitulating the book's arguments and ideas (if it is nonfiction). At other times, reviewers will summarize first and comment later. Which method you will choose will depend on the type of book you are reviewing as well as on your personal inclination.

THE ELEMENTS OF A REVIEW

Though reviews do not follow a single pattern, most include the following features:

A **bibliographic headnote** that generally provides the following information:

> Title
> Author
> Place of publication: Publisher. Number of pages. Price.
>
> (Published reviews usually do not include date of publication. If you are reviewing a book that is not current, you should include this information after you identify the publisher.)

Here is an example of a bibliographic headnote:

> *Dresden 1945: The Devil's Tinderbox*
> By Alexander McKee.
> New York: E. P. Dutton. 322 pp. $18.95.

The **reviewer's name** that may appear after the bibliographic headnote or at the end of the review.

Background information that identifies the genre (novel, biography, memoir, etc.), the author's other books and the place of the book under review among them, the author's credentials or special expertise, related books by other writers, the author's purpose and theme, and perhaps the potential audience for the book. The type of book being reviewed as well as the length of the review will determine how much background the reviewer will choose to include.

A **summary** that tells how the book is organized and succinctly condenses its key ideas and arguments, or, in the case of fiction, its plot. Fiction reviewers generally avoid revealing how the plot is resolved. This portion of the review is often rich in example and may include brief quotations.

An **interpretation** that comments on the meaning of the material: what the events, ideas, or arguments add up to; how the people in the book are to be perceived.

An **analysis** that considers questions of *how* the book means, rather than simply *what* it means. Analytical comments deal with the arrangement of the material, the structure of the plot or argument, and the author's style and tone.

An **evaluation** that considers how well the book fulfills its purpose and whether or not it has met the reviewer's expectations. This section of the review will most clearly express the reviewer's personal response.

SAMPLE REVIEWS (FICTION)

The following review of Ann Tyler's novel *The Accidental Tourist* illustrates the general features of a review. As you read it, note especially how the reviewer interweaves summary and commentary.

Review A

The Accidental Tourist
By Anne Tyler.
New York: Knopf. 355 pp. $16.95.

The markings on Anne Tyler's recent novels are as distinctive as those on a Japanese print, or on the back of a silver spoon. The first stands for "Baltimore." The next reads "delicate balance of comedy and pathos." The third: "tensions of domesticity." The last: "temptations of order and chaos." In "Morgan's Passing" and "Dinner at the Homesick Restaurant," eccentric or extravagant characters dream of a more orderly life. In "The Accidental Tourist," Tyler reverses her perspective: the orderly life, taken to an extreme, becomes a deadening cocoon; the dream of redemption involves life of "color and confusion."

As the novel opens, Sarah Leary tells Macon, her husband of 20 years, that she wants a divorce. The previous year, their son had been murdered and Sarah is depressed by the world's evil. She thinks Macon doesn't care. Much later, she expands on her theme: "It's like you're trying to slip through life unchanged . . . You're like something in a capsule." She's right: there's something muffled about Macon's approach to living; he's a finicky, dithering man, fond of his little methods, reflexively correcting other people's grammar.

Most authors would be hard put to rouse sympathy for such a protagonist, but Tyler knows how: she makes Macon the author of a series of anti-guidebooks, books for the businessman who'd rather not leave Baltimore just to go to Rome, London or Paris. Macon's logo is an overstuffed armchair with wings. "Armchair travelers dream of going places," his publisher says. "Traveling armchairs dream of staying put." Macon's "Accidental Tourist" books tell a traveler how to see as little of a city as possible (they presume he'll never venture into the countryside). They tell him where to find American fast-food joints, how to avoid anything foreign. The only safe thing to eat in France, says Macon, is Salade Niçoise. On planes, eat little and "always bring a book, as protection against strangers. Magazines don't last. Newspapers from home will make you homesick, and newspapers from elsewhere will remind you you don't belong."

When Sarah leaves, Macon reverts contentedly to childhood, living with his sister and brothers, who avoid life just as busily as he. Any plot at this point needs a spoon to stir it; Tyler produces a familiar one. Muriel Pritchett, who trains Macon's dog for him, is one of Tyler's eccentrics. A ragged young woman with a damaged child, she's as appalling as she is appealing. Muriel embodies what Shaw called the Life Force. There's something heroic about the way she exposes her mangled past as if it were a book from which she must read aloud at once, something heroic, too, about the nakedness of her designs upon Macon. Macon moves in with her and her son, always keeping shy of commitment. But holding back won't work—not in life, certainly not in a novel.

It would be rash to say that "The Accidental Tourist" is the best of Tyler's 10 novels, but it's certainly as good as any she has done. Her comedies are of the very best sort, which is to say that they are always serious, that they combine the humor of a situation with a narrative voice that allows itself moments of wit. (Of a very young woman confronted by a children's game, she writes: "all the guests [joined] in except Brad's wife, who was still too close to childhood to risk getting stuck there on a visit back." Again: "Her face was a type no longer seen . . . How did women mold their basic forms to suit the times? Were there no more of those round chins, round foreheads, and bruised, baroque little mouths so popular in the forties?") Tyler cares for the frailty of her characters and exults in their resources. She knows that living is a messy business that will not long accommodate an antiseptic tourist like Macon. Macon must stop falling into his life; he must take charge of it. Tyler presents him with a fateful, clear-cut choice. Neither alternative is free from pain, nor from the pain he must cause another. The point is, he must choose and take the consequences, and he does. Like most novelists—think of Henry James, sending Isabel Archer back to her husband—Tyler spares us the sight of what happens next.

—Peter S. Prescott, *Newsweek*

Note that the review of Tyler's book includes the following elements:

> a bibliographic headnote;
>
> a reference to the title, author, and genre;
>
> information about the author (the characteristics and concerns of her earlier books; the place of *The Accidental Tourist* among them);
>
> an announcement of the book's theme ("the orderly life, taken to an extreme, becomes a deadening cocoon");
>
> information about the book's content (summary of plot, brief sketches of the major characters);
>
> an interpretation of the events and characters (Muriel Pritchett is both "eccentric" and "heroic"; she is "as appalling as she is appealing");
>
> commentary on the author's style and tone (comic with serious overtones; witty; compassionate);
>
> an evaluation of the book's merits (despite the familiarity of some of the plot devices, "certainly as good as any [book] she has done");
>
> the reviewer's name.

FOLLOW-UP ACTIVITY

Following is another review of *The Accidental Tourist* by Anne Tyler. Keeping in mind the general features of a book review, point out the passages that illustrate each feature. Consider, too, how the various features are interwoven.

Review B

The Accidental Tourist
By Anne Tyler.
New York: Knopf. 355 pp. $16.95.

Watching Anne Tyler grow as a novelist is a riveting experience—like a slow-motion movie of a flower opening, familiar yet awesome. She published her first novel in 1964, and during the 21 years and 10 novels since then, her work has steadily progressed toward excellence. *The Accidental Tourist* is, quite simply, her best novel yet. Her place in American fiction is now secure. This is clear. Less easy to pinpoint, however, are the subtle changes from novel to novel—so subtle, in fact, that one almost fears to crush the flower in attempting to find out what makes it so exquisite.

Like many of her novels, this one is set in her hometown of Baltimore. Macon Leary has just separated from his wife, Sarah. (Macon's job, which gives the novel its title, is writing guidebooks entitled *The Accidental Tourist in . . .* for businessmen.) The murder of their son Ethan precipitated their separation but is a catalyst rather than an exploitive central trauma. The plot turns on Macon, his life alone, his pets—including a charismatic but aggressive corgi named Edward—and his gradual involvement with a brassy dog-trainer named Muriel. The Leary family, Macon's brothers and sisters, are entwined in the story as are his estranged wife and his colorful publisher, Julian Edge.

How bleak are outlines! Tyler's prose is spare, unmannered, but simply evocative: "He didn't take the elevator: he felt he couldn't bear the willy-nilliness of it. He went down the stairs instead." Macon Leary is a man who likes to be in control of his environment, as does his sister Rose with her kitchen so alphabetized that "you'd find the allspice next to the ant poison." Macon is so compulsive—washing his clothes as he showers so as not to waste water—that he verges on the grotesque, but, infinitesimally, Tyler pulls Macon back: "At moments—while he was skidding on the mangled clothes in the bathtub or struggling into his body bag on the naked, rust-stained mattress—he realized that he might be carrying things too far."

Disorganized, warm, vulgar Muriel comes to redeem Macon from the small private hell he is assiduously building for himself. We are allowed a glimpse of compromise, even of possible happiness for Macon.

Anne Tyler's characters have strange private obsessions and work them out in odd ways, but at the same time the elements of Everyman are firmly in place. They eat at Burger King and get frozen pipes in their basements. Their powerful presence comes from the arrangement of the recognizable pieces, the creation of complex characters built of familiar sorrows, frustrations, and satisfactions. The image of the novelist piecing together a jigsaw puzzle is too crude, too lacking in delicacy for Anne Tyler. Hers is the work of a mosaic artist, where every tiny fragment is crucial to the glowing whole.

—Brigitte Weeks, *Ms.*

EXPLORING CHOICES: COMPARING REVIEWS

1. Compare the lead paragraphs of the two reviews of *The Accidental Tourist.* How do they differ?
2. Point out the background information in each review. Which is fuller?
3. Which of the two reviews provides the clearest sense of the novel's major characters?
4. Which reviewer most fully interprets the novel's theme(s)? Are the reviewers' interpretations alike? different? Explain.

REVIEWING NONFICTION

Though the major features of a review appear in both fiction and nonfiction reviewing, there are two elements of a nonfiction review that deserve special mention. One concerns the authority of the book's author, of considerable importance since many works of nonfiction deal with subjects that require special knowledge and expertise. The alert reader will therefore want to know the authors' qualifications. Are they experts in the field? Do they have professional affiliations that testify to their authority? A reviewer of nonfiction will address these questions briefly, usually by citing the author's professional background.

Another matter of concern is faithfulness to the author's ideas, especially if the ideas are controversial. Reviewers therefore take special care to distinguish between their own comments and the actual agruments of the author. To make sure that the author is properly credited and to avoid any possible ambiguity, careful reviewers will usually repeat the author's name in attributive phrases such as "Brown writes," "Brown argues," or "Brown points out."

SAMPLE REVIEWS (NONFICTION)

Below are reviews of an autobiography, a history, and a study of a current problem. Each clearly identifies the author's background. But as you will see, the discussion of the author's ideas varies because the books under review differ in form and purpose.

Review A

Just Barbara: My Story
By Barbara Woodhouse.
New York: Summit Books. 189 pp. $16.95.
Reviewed by Monica Dickens

Walkies! Come along now, all you dog owners and PBS watchers! Heads up, choke chain collar on, off we go, nose by the left heel, ears up, eyes bright. Don't mess about there, the man with the Yorkshire terrier, keep him alert!

For Barbara Woodhouse fans, this brisk, chatty autobiography will be a meeting with an old friend. For others, it will mean discovering an astonishing British woman whose rapport with animals seems to descend from St. Francis. "Just Barbara: My Story" is a condensation of previously published work about her life with animals: a sort of potted Barbara, extremely entertaining and likable.

As a child, she preferred animals to dolls and cared for sick birds and mice in her nursery. Making up stories for younger children, she discovered that an exciting tone of voice got them hooked. This was the genesis of her "*What* a good dog!" training method of lively praise and gaiety.

The only female student, she passed unscathed through agricultural college, armored with her mother's old-fashioned philosophy: "If any man did kiss me on my doorstep with more passion than should be shown except in the privacy of one's marriage bedroom, he was out there and then." Did the men on the huge Argentine cattle ranch where she worked for a year get the same treatment? They broke their wild horses with rough cruelty, so Mrs. Woodhouse showed how it could be done with kindness and love, using the magical trick taught her by an old Indian—blowing down her nose into the animal's nose, the way horses talk to one another.

In Argentina, she trained her first Great Dane to work with sheep. Back in England, after she was settled with her doctor husband and three children on the farm where she still lives, she trained her famous Danes Juno and Junia. Through obedience contests and charity demonstrations, she and the dogs got into show business, with dozens of dog food commercials, and films and chat shows and finally the 1980 BBC series "Training Dogs the Woodhouse Way." It became such a cult in the States that people planned their social life around it, as with "Upstairs, Downstairs," and gleefully added "Walkies!" to their vocabulary, and "Sit!"

Lovely she is, an energetic, warm woman with a spiritual gift that brings her very close to all living things, including humans. A writer she isn't. She rollicks along, dealing briskly with great dramas like diabetes: "To make a long story short, I knew I was dying." High fever? The cows must be milked, so wrap up and take the germs out into the cold. "They soon find a more comfortable body to invade!"

Cosy anecdotal exclamation marks erupt through the book like short, sharp yelps: "It's a small world!" "Goodness knows why!" All right, her style is naïve and simple, but her brilliantly successful style with dogs is simple too, very direct and honest, so the dog knows exactly what to do and gets praise when he does it. Her style with people is equally direct, her training classes orchestrated to her classic motto: "No bad dogs, only bad owners."

Cheerily, she ends this engaging story of her life and four-legged loves by telling us that for the most part "I think I have completed everything I have wanted to do."

Good girl, Barbara—*what* a good girl!

EXPLORING CHOICES

1. Examine the lead paragraph. What strategy is the author using to get the reader's attention? Evaluate its effectiveness.
2. Point out the background information. Where does it appear?
3. Explain how the reviewer interweaves summary and evaluation.
4. Where does the reviewer quote directly? What is each quotation meant to illustrate?
5. How would you describe the reviewer's tone? Do you find it appropriate for the book she is reviewing?
6. Evaluate the one-sentence paragraph that concludes the review. Do you find it effective? Why or why not?

Review B

The Bill James Historical Baseball Abstract
By Bill James
New York: Villard Books. 619 pp. $24.95.

Most serious baseball fans are closet CPAs. Throw out any name—Hack Wilson, who starred for the Cubs in the 1930s, or Shoeless Joe Jackson, who played for the Sox between 1910 and 1920—and the true fan will toss back a welter of statistics (batting averages, stolen-base totals, game-winning RBIs, etcetera) with a facility that an IRS agent would admire. That Wilson played 50 years ago and Jackson 70 years ago is of no consequence; numbers are how we stay connected to the game.

But ask a fan to describe Jackson's uniform, the fielder's glove he wore, or the ballparks he played in, and you will most likely draw a blank. Most of us cannot even recall a National League without the hated New York Mets. What a welcome resource, then, is *The Bill James Historical Baseball Abstract*. It is a chatty, colloquial history of the game, told decade by decade, from 1870 to the present.

James is best known for his annual statistical analyses of current ballplayers and their teams, and in the *Abstract* numbers again play a major role. Half the book is devoted to determining, once and for all, the greatest ballplayers of all time. It is thrilling to learn, for instance, that no one—not Willie Mays, not Mickey Mantle—hit more home runs or collected more RBIs in the 1950s than the great Duke Snider.

But it is the remaining half of the book that is so intriguing. It is a collection of short, breezy pieces based on the assumption that major-league baseball is equally the story of its anonymous support players—the Carmen Fanzones and Bill Tuttles who round out the teams of every era.

From James's copious research of newspapers and periodicals of the day, we learn what each generation of fans saw when they visited the nation's ballparks. We discover, for example, that turn-of-the-century ballplayers dressed in sack-like, high-collared uniforms that were belted at the side, and that they wore handmade spikes that looked somewhat like hiking boots. We learn, too, that in 1880, nine balls constituted a walk and the pitching rubber was only 50 feet from home plate.

James's enthusiasm for his subject is infectious. He recounts with gusto the best World Series of each decade, the off-field baseball issues of the day, and anecdotes that shed light on each era, including the kind of person most likely to play the game. He describes the players from 1910 to 1920, for example, as shysters, con men, carpet baggers, drunks and outright thieves. I'm sure they were only a tiny portion of the whole baseball populace, but they are the ones who gave the decade its character, and they are the ones who are remembered.

This book is written with great humor, much wisdom, and a folksy scholarship that is especially welcome at a time when baseball seems more a boardroom endeavor than our national sport. The *Abstract* is an encyclopedia, in the best sense of the word.

—Ron Berler, *Chicago Magazine*

EXPLORING CHOICES

1. Who would be the likely reader of the book? How do you know? How do the first two paragraphs establish the book's possible audience?
2. What background information does the reviewer provide? Where does it appear?
3. According to the reviewer, the book presents information that is new. What is this information?

4. Point out the reviewer's evaluation of the book. How does he combine summary and evaluation?
5. Identify the examples used to illustrate the book's content. Do you consider them effective? Explain.

Review C

The Third Sex: The New Professional Woman
By Patricia A. McBroom.
New York: Morrow. 282 pp. $16.95.

Whoever persuaded anthropologist Patricia A. McBroom to call her book *The Third Sex* did her dirt. The title evokes those 1960s tomes that described working women as dropouts from their sex—members of some unhappy new subdivision of humanity—and advised them to go back home if they valued their mental health. It's not that kind of book. For that matter, it's no longer that period of history. Today most people would agree with McBroom that business and professional women are no stranger than the men who left farms and factories generations ago for white-collar jobs. They, too, suffered identity crises.

But the women face tougher, subtler problems, which *The Third Sex* probes with great insight. At work, the women agonize over using the "masculine" power they need to function. At home, they recoil from the prospect of motherhood because—aside from its career conflicts—they dread a return to "feminine" weakness. To a modern woman conditioned by old notions of a selfless role, motherhood is a state so high that she isn't good enough for it and so low that she doesn't want it.

Because all successful societies must reproduce, McBrown talks a lot about motherhood. If motherhood is used as a measure, women who achieve business or professional success are failures. Half a century ago, the reproductive rate of such achievers barely topped zero. By 1982 a Korn/Ferry International study of 300 executive women recorded a rise, but only to 39%. McBroom says these nonreproducing careerists not only fail to pass on their abilities and values but also could threaten society at large as more recruits join their ranks.

The careerist's attitude toward being a mother also turns out to be something of a litmus test. McBroom based her book on extensive interviews with 44 women bankers, brokers, and other financial managers in New York City and San Francisco. Of this sample, the 15 who had children were the happiest with their lot and the most successful. Perhaps children produced the kind of balance that enabled the women to succeed, or perhaps the same qualities accounted for both children and success. But some kind of link is clearly there.

So is another link. Unlike most of the childless women, who recalled mothers dominated by their fathers, the 15 with children had strong mothers. They made key decisions or shared power with their husbands. Several of the 15 even had strong grandmothers. The memory apparently helped them play a nurturing role without feeling weak and a forceful role without feeling male, and to enjoy both. How to achieve this outlook is the problem that still stymies most business and professional women.

Usefully, the author reminds us where our sex roles come from. In primitive warrior societies, the biologically expendable men do the fighting, boss the women, and remain distant from the children. The women perform much of the work, applaud the men, and rear the children. Men learn to be tough—to others as well as to themselves—and women learn deference to equip them for their roles. Western society, which grew out of a warrior culture, widened this split in the 19th century when industrialization took work out of the home and prosperity permitted upper- and middle-class women to concentrate on the domestic virtues. The model woman was servant and guardian angel.

That was still the ideal when Betty Friedan's 1963 book, *The Feminine Mystique,* started the movement to promote women from support systems to individuals. In terms of career, the movement succeeded for women such as McBroom's exemplars. But a corporate lifestyle that makes no allowance for families skews their personal lives. And the old division between the male role (strong, self-centered, and distant) and the female (weak, altruistic, and warm) hobbles them psychologically. It hobbles men, too, but that's another book.

McBroom's diagnosis is so good that one looks forward to her prescription. But her "modest proposal" abruptly leaves the real world. Corporations, she writes, must "move in fundamental ways to balance their requirements with family life, or watch reproduction dwindle among the daughters of the middle class." They must give parents more family time, more flexible hours, and more stable work locations. Women must surrender their primary rights over children, including the legal preference for custody in divorce. Men must become true partners in child-rearing, to recover the qualities they lost as distant males and because shared family rights and duties will destroy the warrior ethos, with "far-reaching effects on the social order."

Well, I just don't see corporations changing their hard-driving ways for the sake of the birthrate. And the legal preference for mother's custody is eroding fast, so women may not mind giving it up. But will men choose to take on child-care tasks that could limit their careers in unchanged corporations? McBroom argues that they will, to guard their right to child custody now that more women are also able to provide support. That's pretty thin. Few people act on the basis of what might happen in case of a future divorce.

Society doesn't change in that programmed fashion, however desirable the change. It changes in bits and pieces—as it is beginning to do now. A number of companies offer parental leaves and lighter schedules for mothers of young children. Others will offer them if the labor market gets tight.

In a different political climate, laws may require some corporate concessions to family life. Emotionally, many men are closer to their children than their fathers were to them and less involved with their work. That alters the definition of sex roles for themselves and everyone they know. As more women do "a man's job" in "a man's way," the numbers affect how they—and others—feel about what they're doing. It's not neat or inevitable, but it seems to be happening. Slowly.

—Irene Pavl, *Business Week*

1. In the lead paragraph, the reviewer quarrels with the author's title. Why? How does this opening strategy provide important background information?

2. In summarizing the content of the book, the reviewer focuses on the problems it explores. What are these problems? Where are they announced?

3. Where does the reviewer explain the author's research? Should this information appear earlier? Explain.

4. Point out the medical metaphor in paragraph 8. How does it help to organize the reviewer's discussion of the book's strengths and shortcomings?

5. Where does the reviewer quote the author's words? What connection do you see between the quotation and the purpose of the paragraph in which it appears?

6. Why does the reviewer end the review with the single word *Slowly?* How does this unusual usage emphasize the reviewer's criticism of the book?

ORGANIZING A REVIEW

Many reviews follow a general format for the lead paragraph, the body of the review, and the conclusion. Here are some suggestions for the items you might wish to include in each section as you shape your own review. Remember that except for the bibliographical headnote, these items can be differently arranged, depending on the type of book you are reviewing.

Bibliographic Headnote

Begin with a bibliographic headnote that states the book's title, author, place of publication, publisher, number of pages, and price.

Lead Paragraph

Mention the author, title and genre.

If you are reviewing a work of nonfiction, state the author's professional affiliation or his/her special credentials.

Indicate the book's main argument, idea, or theme.

Try to get the reader's attention in the opening sentences. Here are some possibilities that student reviewers have used:

Begin with a dramatic event chronicled in the book

Few Americans are familiar with the Allied destruction of Dresden, Germany, on February 13 and 14, 1945. And it was destruction. As Alexander McKee describes it in Dresden 1945: The Devil's Tinderbox, ten million cubic meters in the heart of the city were totally leveled. An occasional chimney stood among the rubble, but that was all. Why this ruthless action was undertaken is the question McKee tries to answer. He concludes that the raids were meant to destroy the morale of the German people.

Begin with a quotation taken from the book

"Now we have a problem in making power credible, and Vietnam is the answer." With these words, reported in Stanley Karnow's Vietnam: A History, President Kennedy tried to define the purpose of American policy in Vietnam. A reporter for Life magazine in Southeast Asia before and during the Vietnam War, Karnow tells us not only what that policy was but how and why it developed. He tells an unhappy tale of mistaken policy decisions at home and of mismanaged military decisions on the battlefield.

Begin by characterizing the book

Sometimes candid, sometimes humorous, and always arrogant, Mayor, by Edward Koch, is a memoir written by one of the world's most powerful and authoritative city leaders. Early in his career as mayor of New York City, Koch began taking notes on matters he thought "important and interesting." Now, as the end of his second term approaches, he has published an account of his reign that is bound to offend his enemies and delight his supporters.

Begin with a comparison

The phrase "space, the final frontier" is apt to conjure up images of Captain James T. Kirk on the bridge of the Enterprise; the Columbia rising into a clear Florida sunrise; Neil Armstrong taking the first step on the moon. Can earthbound humanity, we think, do anything as spectacular? Those who think not should read Tracy Kidder's work of literary journalism, The Soul of a New Machine. A tale of microchips and microcodes, of sassy, high-powered "adding machines" and bug-ridden kludges, it describes a world of computers every bit as exciting as the world of space.

Body of the Review

Include some background information: the author's previous books, related books by other authors, the occasion or event that led to the writing of the book.

Examine the organization of the book and summarize its main points, interpreting these as you go along. Use brief quotations to give readers the flavor of the book or to highlight an especially important feature. If you are reviewing a work of nonfiction that argues for a particular point of view, be sure to distinguish your ideas from the ideas of the author.

Conclusion

Comment on the style and tone of the book.

Single out a feature you found noteworthy or, conversely, shallow or weak.

Indicate your response to the book: what you learned, what questions it forced you to ask, what feelings it evoked. If your response is largely negative, express your disappointment and tell the reader why. If you find some features commendable and others questionable, express your ambivalence. In closing, you can advise the reader directly whether or not to read the book, or you can let your response imply your recommendation.

Identify yourself as the reviewer.

A SAMPLE REVIEW

In the following review, Ann Ryder, a student interested in horticulture, examines a reference book for gardeners. As you read her review, note especially how she shapes her material to meet the needs of her audience.

```
Right Plant, Right Place
By Nicola Ferguson.
New York: Summit Books. 292 pp. $14.95.

   Right Plant, Right Place, by Nicola Ferguson, is a reference
book for gardeners.  But its seemingly ordinary subject is
made unusual by its approach and organization.  Ms. Ferguson,
herself a gardener with a charming though small garden in
Edinburgh, Scotland, found that she needed help when she set
out to select plants for a location that was damp, had chalky
soil, and faced north.  But when she went to the literature
```

for guidance, she discovered that the books were organized by plant names followed by a description of growing conditions. This meant she had to leaf through entire volumes to get a list of plants suitable for her garden in Edinburgh. So she decided that a book with a different organization was needed, and she set out to supply it. Right Plant, Right Place is the result. Open it at random and you'll see chapter headings like "Plants Suitable for Heavy Clay Soils," "Plants Suitable for Crevices in Paving," "Winter Flowering Plants," etc. Such an organization allows gardeners to retrieve information readily.

In addition to its useful organization, Right Plant, Right Place is a complete landscape plant selection guide that profiles over fifteen thousand trees, shrubs, and herbaceous ornamental landscape plants. Each plant featured is illustrated by a color photograph. Latin names are always given while common names are noted in parentheses. Following the common names are shorthand notations for height, sun, life cycles, flowering times, and colors. A short paragraph examines the qualities of the plant.

The book contains three main indexes and several listings, another feature that makes it invaluable. The index of botanical names lists in alphabetical order the Latin names of all plants found in the book. Another, though shorter, index lists the common names. The third index lists subject headings under which plants that are "featured elsewhere in the book" are listed. A list of sixty-three suppliers' addresses, a master list of species grown in the United States and Great Britain, a metric conversion table, and a key to abbreviations and symbols complete the book's highly organized structure.

Though the book as a whole is excellent, it has several shortcomings. Since the photos are often close-ups of flowers, the inexperienced reader has no way of visualizing overall form. Another difficulty is that the key to abbreviations and symbols is buried in the back of the book instead of placed on the inside cover, where the reader can find it easily. For a book organized by environmental conditions, there is surprisingly little discussion of the causes of these conditions. The author assumes that readers can accurately diagnose the physiological and environmental properties of their gardens.

The drawbacks are minor. For the professional horticulturist, as well as for the avid amateur, Right Plant, Right Place is a splendid guide. It's likely to become a standard work that will be consulted by everyone interested in gardening.

—Ann Ryder

EXPLORING CHOICES

1. To whom is this book likely to appeal? How do you know?
2. The lead paragraph describes the circumstances that led to the writing of the book. Do these circumstances establish the author's expertise as well? Why or why not?
3. Why does the reviewer focus on the organization of the book? What connection does she establish between the book's organization and its purpose?
4. Examine the summary of the book's content in paragraphs 2 and 3. How is the information organized?
5. Where does the reviewer express disappointment in the book? Are her reservations persuasive?
6. What is the reviewer's recommendation? Is it expressed directly or indirectly?

TIPS FOR SELF-EDITING

1. Have I included background information such as the type of book I am reviewing, the author's credentials, the author's other books, related works by other authors, the author's intended audience?

2. Have I defined the author's purpose?

3. Have I accurately summarized the content of the book?

4. Have I suggested how the book is organized?

5. Have I commented on the author's style and tone? Have I conveyed the flavor of the book by quoting from it briefly and judiciously?

6. Have I illustrated the book's ideas and themes with appropriate examples?

7. Have I indicated the strengths and/or shortcomings of the book?

8. Have I organized my material logically and coherently? Have I written clearly, correctly, and in an appropriate tone?

WRITING THE CONTROLLED RESEARCH PAPER

*T*hough the controlled research paper might simply convey information, it more often expresses a point of view or position; in this, it resembles the persuasive essay. Unlike the simple persuasive essay, however, the controlled research paper carefully blends what others have said on the subject with the ideas of the writer. The two basic meanings of research reflect this interaction. In one of its senses, the prefix *re-* means to repeat or to do something over again, as in the word *reread.* Seen from this angle, research means a review of the existing literature, a survey of what has been learned or thought about the subject. But the prefix *re-* also means *anew,* as in the word *rebuild.* In this second sense, research is not merely a compilation of what has been thought and said but a reinterpretation of the subject, a rethinking or reevaluation in which you add your informed point of view to the judgment of others.

THE NATURE OF CONTROLLED RESEARCH

When you begin a research paper, the first step—after choosing and narrowing your topic—is usually a trip to the library to check the bibliographies and card catalogue. In undertaking a controlled research assignment, however, the trek to the library is unnecessary, since the required materials are already at hand or easily collected. Because the number of sources for a controlled research paper is deliberately limited, you are less apt to spend time reading peripheral material or chasing up blind alleys. Your sources might be primary, secondary, or both. *Primary materials* may include speeches, eyewitness accounts or autobiographies, statistical or computer data, case studies, works of literature, or artwork (paintings, sculpture, music, films). *Secondary sources,* so called because they comment on primary materials, include news reports and analyses, biographies, journal articles, reviews, and critical books.

In the controlled research paper, your review of the literature will be limited to relatively few documents. Collecting materials for such a paper might be as simple as following, over a period of days or weeks, a series of feature articles, editorials, and letters to the editor in a newspaper or magazine, and then developing your own perspective on the subject. Or it might mean reading a collection of essays on a subject in a college reader, and then taking a stand on an issue in light of what you have read. Or it might involve using a *casebook,* a collection of articles assembled on a single subject, so that the gathering of materials can be bypassed.

For a controlled research assignment, you will therefore concentrate much of your early effort on reading and understanding a limited amount of material: a few secondary sources and perhaps, depending on the nature of the assignment, some primary material. The procedure during the prewriting and invention stages of your paper will involve analyzing, evaluating, summarizing, and synthesizing what others have written and then incorporating it with your own ideas.

Analyzing the primary and secondary material involves not only understanding clearly what an author has said but also formulating your own ideas and perspective about the material.

Evaluating the secondary sources means reading them critically with an eye to how adequately and how fairly they treat the topic.

Summarizing the secondary sources involves expressing the central ideas in your own words and then observing the extent to which you agree or disagree with them.

Synthesizing means pulling together the primary and secondary sources, discovering common threads, and seeing what light they throw upon one another, as well as how they mesh—or fail to mesh—with your own perceptions.

Incorporating involves deciding how you can most cogently use the secondary material: as a jumping-off point; as support for your own position; as something to criticize or argue against.

Although you have come to terms with and assimilated the ideas in the source material, what *you* think must still take center stage in the essay, only now it is framed by the larger perspective of what others have thought and written.

A CASEBOOK: PRIMARY SOURCES

In this chapter, in order to sharpen your analytical skills, you will work with two poems, Robert Frost's " 'Out, Out—' " and Karl Shapiro's "Auto Wreck," as well as with a small collection of secondary material in the form of brief essays and excerpts from critical works.

Robert Frost based his fine narrative poem " 'Out, Out—' " on a newspaper account he had read entitled "Sad Tragedy at Bethlehem." Asked to write an appreciative response after reading the two versions of the event, one student chose to assess the difference in emotional impact between reading the poem and reading the news report. He conveyed his main point through an analogy in the opening sentence of his essay: "Reading 'Sad Tragedy at Bethlehem' is like looking at a poster outside a movie house; reading " 'Out, Out—' " is like going inside and seeing the film." Following are both the news article and the poem for you to consider.

SAD TRAGEDY AT BETHLEHEM/RAYMOND FITZGERALD A VICTIM OF FATAL ACCIDENT

Raymond Tracy Fitzgerald, one of the twin sons of Michael G. and Margaret Fitzgerald of Bethlehem, died at his home Thursday afternoon, March 24, as a result of an accident by which one of his hands was badly hurt in a sawing machine. The young man was assisting in sawing up some wood in his own dooryard with a sawing machine and accidentally hit the loose pulley, causing the saw to descend upon his hand, cutting and lacerating it badly. Raymond was taken into the house and a physician was immediately summoned, but he died very suddenly from the effects of the shock, which produced heart failure. . . .

—*The Littleton Courier,* 31 March 1901

'OUT, OUT—'

The buzz saw snarled and rattled in the yard
And made dust and dropped stove-length sticks of wood,
Sweet-scented stuff when the breeze drew across it.
And from there those that lifted eyes could count
Five mountain ranges one behind the other
Under the sunset far into Vermont.
And the saw snarled and rattled, snarled and rattled,
As it ran light, or had to bear a load.
And nothing happened: day was all but done.
Call it a day, I wish they might have said
To please the boy by giving him the half hour
That a boy counts so much when saved from work.
His sister stood beside them in her apron
To tell them 'Supper.' At the word, the saw,
As if to prove saws knew what supper meant,
Leaped out at the boy's hand, or seemed to leap—
He must have given the hand. However it was,
Neither refused the meeting. But the hand!
The boy's first outcry was a rueful laugh,
As he swung toward them holding up the hand
Half in appeal, but half as if to keep
The life from spilling. Then the boy saw all—
Since he was old enough to know, big boy
Doing a man's work, though a child at heart—
He saw all spoiled. 'Don't let them cut my hand off—
The doctor, when he comes. Don't let him, sister!'
So. But the hand was gone already.
The doctor put him in the dark of ether.
He lay and puffed his lips out with his breath,

30   And then—the watcher at his pulse took fright.
No one believed. They listened at his heart.
Little—less—nothing!—and that ended it.
No more to build on there. And they, since they
Were not the one dead, turned to their affairs.

—Robert Frost

FOLLOW-UP ACTIVITY

Using as your topic the student's idea about the news account being a poster and the poem being the film, what details would you use from both the article and the poem, and under what categories would you arrange them? Consider the tone and emotional impact of both article and poem.

Karl Shapiro's poem "Auto Wreck" is similar enough in subject matter to " 'Out, Out—' " that it can profitably be compared to Frost's poem from any number of perspectives. You could, for example, compare and contrast the persona or the narrator in each poem; or the poets' attitudes toward death. Think about other possible points of comparison with Frost as you read Shapiro's poem.

AUTO WRECK

Its quick soft silver bell beating, beating,
And down the dark one ruby flare
Pulsing out red light like an artery,
The ambulance at top speed floating down.

Past beacons and illuminated clocks
Wings in a heavy curve, dips down,
And brakes speed, entering the crowd.
The doors leap open, emptying light;
Stretchers are laid out, the mangled lifted
10   And stowed into the little hospital.
Then the bell, breaking the hush, tolls once,
And the ambulance with its terrible cargo
Rocking, slightly rocking, moves away,
As the doors, an afterthought, are closed.
We are deranged, walking among the cops
Who sweep glass and are large and composed.
One is still making notes under the light.
One with a bucket douches ponds of blood
Into the street and gutter.
20   One hangs lanterns on the wrecks that cling,
Empty husks of locusts, to iron poles.
Our throats were tight as tourniquets.
Our feet were bound with splints, but now
Like convalescents intimate and gauche,

Writing the Controlled Research Paper **395**

We speak through sickly smiles and warn
With the stubborn saw of common sense,
The grim joke and the banal resolution.
The traffic moves around with care,
But we remain, touching a wound
30   That opens to our richest horror.

Already old, the question Who shall die?
Becomes unspoken Who is innocent?
For death in war is done by hands;
Suicide has cause and stillbirth, logic.
And cancer, simple as a flower, blooms.
But this invites the occult mind,
Cancels our physics with a sneer,
And spatters all we knew of denouement
Across the expedient and wicked stones.
—Karl Shapiro

FOLLOW-UP ACTIVITY

Choose either of the topics previously suggested, or one of your own involving both poems, and develop a thesis that could be supported in a brief paper. What specifics from each poem would you use in discussing your topic?

WRITING SUGGESTION

On the basis of Shapiro's poem, write a news account of the accident; you will, of course, need to invent names and so on. How does your story differ from the poem in the material it includes or omits? In its tone? In its emotional impact on the reader?

A CASEBOOK: SECONDARY MATERIAL

Whenever you work with secondary sources, you must understand, interpret, and evaluate what others have said about the subject. If you have read attentively and critically, then you should be able to express concisely, in your own words, the central points made by the earlier writer. When you convey in a condensed, concentrated form the essential ideas of an article or of a self-contained excerpt from a longer work, then you have written what is called an *abstract* or a *précis*. Let's look, for example, at a brief discussion of Frost's " 'Out, Out—' " by Gemino Abad:

A Formal Approach to Lyric Poetry/Gemino H. Abad

> Frost's . . . poem takes significantly its title from Macbeth's response to the news of Lady Macbeth's death, i.e., his reflection on life's brevity and meaninglessness. But it is not a meditation on that theme; (234) it depicts quite clearly an incident to which we respond emotionally, i.e., not only with pity toward the boy who dies so young but also with a kind of horror that life could end so suddenly. "And then is heard no more." The pity is underscored most especially by the boy's recognition, "though a child at heart," that now "all [is] spoiled," and by his appeal to his sister, though "the hand was gone already." The horror does not lie merely in the gruesome details of the accident ("But the hand!") nor in the unexpectedness of the disaster (note, for instance, the busy yard and the peaceful and beautiful scenery at the poem's outset, or the fact that since "day was all but done," the boy might have been given a half hour of free time). It is evoked most especially toward the poem's close as the boy's life ebbs away until there is "No more to build on there" and everyone turns to his affairs "since they were not the one dead." The narrator's tone—wryly humorous ("As if to prove saws knew what supper meant" or "Neither refused the meeting"), laconic ("No more to build on there"), sardonic ("since they/Were not the one dead, turned to their affairs")—informs the representation with an emotional restraint which intensifies the pathos and the horror of the event.

Since the passage is brief, you should be able to abstract it in a single sentence. You may at first formulate something like the following: "Frost's poem generates an emotional response of pity for the victim and horror over the gruesomeness and suddenness of the event." If you go back and look at the passage in light of this initial formulation of your abstract, however, you discover that, while it accurately represents what Abad says about the effect of " 'Out, Out—,' " it fails to mention the techniques of the poet to which Abad attributes this effect. So your initial précis, though correct as far as it goes, is incomplete. Try again: "The wryly understated and sardonic tone of Frost's poem actually intensifies our emotional response of pity for the victim and horror over the gruesomeness and suddenness of the event." This sentence of fewer than thirty words now conveys the essence of Abad's paragraph. Notice that in abstracting you have done the opposite of what you do in writing when you support a generalization: here, you have *subtracted* the supporting details to arrive at the kernel or core of meaning, which is then stated in your own words.

Descriptive and Critical Abstracts

Most of the abstracts you read, as well as most of those you write, might be called *descriptive* in nature; that is, they express as succinctly and comprehensively, and as objectively, as possible the essential idea(s) and the major supporting details of the original—whether paragraph, article or essay, book chapter, or even full-length work. Other abstracts are, however, what might be called *critical,* because along with providing a concise summary they respond subjectively to the original work, commenting very briefly on such matters as the author's development of ideas or even on the style of writing. But whether you are writing a descriptive, objective abstract or a critical, subjective one, your first step must be to read the original work analytically, unravelling precisely what the author says so that you can then restate it briefly in your own words.

To adequately write any abstract usually requires reading the original more than once; perhaps the first time through, you might want to read fairly rapidly to get a sense of the entire passage, and then, on the second reading, either underline selectively, or preferably jot down brief notes. As a rule of thumb, the original author's thesis will become the topic sentence of a one-paragraph abstract, while the topic sentence of each paragraph in the original work will become the supporting details for your topic sentence:

Original		Abstract
Thesis statement	becomes	Topic sentence
Topic sentences	become	Supporting details

Both the descriptive and the critical abstract are concise summations of the thoughts of another, interpreting *what* the author means. Added to that interpretation in the critical abstract will be analysis and evaluation of *how* the author conveys the meaning. In other words, the critical abstract is a product of reading that approaches the work with some skepticism, holding the author accountable at every step along the way. The critical reader examines the author's assumptions, the beliefs or principles underlying a piece of writing, to see if they are valid. The critical reader is concerned also with the writer's biases. Furthermore, the critical reader demands that all generalizations be supported by facts; that such evidence be sufficient in quantity and quality; that no important facts are omitted; that statistics are used fairly and assessed accurately; and that any opposition arguments are noticed and adequately refuted. Finally, the critical reader might question the authority and qualifications of an author, as well as notice strengths and weaknesses in an author's style.

Since the critical abstract, like the descriptive one, must remain brief, any subjective judgments need to be presented in as few words as possible—usually appearing as modifiers. Here are some evaluative words and phrases that you might find useful when writing a critical abstract:

For commenting upon an author's qualifications: *noted authority; well-informed; ill-equipped; unreliable*

For assessing a writer's objectivity: *fair; open; prejudiced; slanted*

For judging an author's assumptions: *warranted; justified; unwarranted; questionable*

For evaluating a writer's argument: *compelling; convincing; unconvincing; one-sided*

For remarking on an author's use of evidence: *abundant; telling; un-substantiated; manipulated*

For noticing a writer's style: *clear; energetic; muddy; confusing*

As you know, a writer's thesis statement may appear at one of several points in an essay—the beginning, middle, or end. It might be stated at the beginning and then repeated or reiterated in different words at the end. Or it might not be stated explicitly at all, so that the readers must arrive at it in their own minds. When writing an abstract, it is not necessary that you retain the original author's pattern of development; especially if the original moves inductively (from specific to general), you may want to position your restatement of the author's central idea nearer to the beginning of your abstract rather than keep it at the end. Nor is it essential that your abstract retain the proportions of the original by supplying, for instance, one sentence for each paragraph. A large part of writing any abstract involves deciding what to retain and what to omit: in general, you include central points while omitting the author's examples and restatements of ideas.

Sometimes, an instructor might want you to survey the existing literature written over a period of years on a given subject, and then present your findings in a series of abstracts drawn together into an *annotated bibliography*. To do this, you first read the relevant articles, book chapters, and so on; then you write a separate précis for each item; and, finally, you compile your abstracts, arranging them either alphabetically by the last names of the authors, or chronologically by the date they first appeared in print.

TIPS FOR WRITING THE ABSTRACT

1. Read the selection you are abstracting analytically, perhaps making brief study notes in the process.

2. Formulate the author's thesis in your own words.

3. Decide which of the writer's supporting details you will include and which you will omit.

4. Decide on the best arrangement of ideas so that your abstract will have a coherence of its own.

5. Make certain that you express the ideas as succinctly as possible; if it is absolutely essential to include phrases from the original, be sure to enclose them within quotation marks.

Rule of Thumb: Original author's thesis = your topic sentence; author's topic sentences = your supporting details.

Below is a paragraph from David F. Noble's "A Neo-Luddite Plea" (*Harper's,* November 1984), followed by five one-sentence abstracts that students wrote of it. Evaluate each of these abstracts for conciseness and inclusiveness.

Among our inherited blinders is the identification of technological advance with social progress, an idea espoused by liberals and socialists alike. Late-twentieth-century Americans need not be reminded that this belief is suspect and invites a fundamental re-evaluation. Given the social costs—military, ecological, and socioeconomic—it would be wise to call a halt to rapid, undirected technological advance, if only until we regain our bearings. But there is another inherited blinder, the conviction that technological advance cannot be stopped because "You can't stop progress." In reality, this is a bizarre and relatively recent Western notion invented to disarm critics of capitalism, which can be readily refuted by reference to centuries of socially interrupted technological development.

1. The fallacy that identifies technological advance with social progress suggests that "We can't stop progress," when it might be wise to curb undirected technological advance.

2. Our technological advances must be evaluated and we must foresee where we want them to take us.

3. Unlimited technological advance is not necessarily the same thing as social progress, and, despite a belief to the contrary, it can be halted.

4. The blind advance of technology without any thought of how it will affect the advancement of the society should and can be halted.

5. We have failed to restrict technology because of two commonly-held beliefs: the belief that technological advance causes social progress, and the belief that you can't stop technology from progressing.

Following are three additional commentaries—two on Frost's poem and one on Shapiro's. Read them carefully and thoughtfully, and write a succinct yet comprehensive abstract for each.

Robert Frost's New Testament/Marie Borroff

The tragic story told in " 'Out, Out—,' " a poem which Frost never would read aloud because it was "too cruel," is predicated on the denial of this process whereby labor becomes one with love. The narrow viewpoint of the adults, the "they" for whom the boy is working, is implied from the beginning in the speaker's description of the scene:

> And from there those that lifted eyes
>   could count
> Five mountain ranges one behind the
>   other
> Under the sunset far into Vermont.

Here the phrase "lifted eyes" ("raised their eyes" would have been equally satisfactory metrically, and perhaps more idiomatic) is reminiscent of Psalm 121:1, "I will lift up mine eyes unto the hills." The point is that "they" do not lift their eyes; the sunset is ignored. The boy is not allowed that extra "half-hour" at the end of the day that would have meant so much, and it is during this enforced continuation of work that the accident occurs which maims him and then ends his life. "They" are thus responsible; (48) it is significant that the boy appeals not to "them," but to his sister, to save his hand when the doctor comes. The loss of the hand is obviously ironic in that it renders the boy useless for work: "No more to build on there." He now sees "all spoiled," but all is spoiled at the outset in a world dominated by so rigid a work ethic; life in such a world is indeed, in the Shakespearean phrase alluded to by the title, "a tale . . . signifying nothing." At the end of the poem, the speaker, far from indicating approval of "their" stoical acceptance of bereavement, dismisses them with contempt as they turn to their "affairs."

Frost's 'Out-Out'/Weldon Thornton

Robert Frost's " 'Out, Out—' " has been included in several poetry textbooks with comments or questions which imply what seems to me a mistaken interpretation of the poem. Most of the editorial comments suggest that the themes of the poem are the uncertainty and unpredictability of life and regret at the apparently meaningless death of the young boy. . . .

But scrutiny of the poem reveals several details not explained by this interpretation, and suggests a psychological complexity which it misses. As we look into the poem, we realize that the young boy is deftly characterized and that his accident is not entirely accidental. The poem reveals a psychological drama played out between the boy and his family. The climax of this drama is the boy's moving his hand into the saw, in an inarticulate and self-destructive protest against the insensitivity of the family which wishes to hurry him into the responsibilities of adulthood. . . .

All day the boy has been at work, and all day the feeling has been growing within him that he is held captive by the work and by the parents who keep him at it. He feels that he is being kept from things he wants to do, that life is being stolen from him. His sister's call to supper provides just the break in the continuity of the day's work which permits the boy's subconscious impulse to act on the dissatisfaction it has been harboring: he moves his hand toward the saw. That this is what the boy does should be clear from the way Frost describes it, when he says the saw

As if to prove saws knew what supper meant,
Leaped out at the boy's hand, or seemed to leap—
He must have given the hand. However it was,
Neither refused the meeting.

In this undeniably realistic poem, the personification of the saw most reasonably implies what the other lines say, that the boy gave the hand. Not that the boy intended to kill himself; what he rather wanted was not death but harm, some basis for saying "Look what you have done to me, have made me do to myself." And this view is supported by the boy's next action: "The boy's first outcry was a rueful laugh, / As he swung toward them holding up the hand / Half in appeal, but half as if to keep / The life from spilling." Only half of the boy's thought is on saving his life; with the other half he holds toward them "in appeal" the emblem of the life they have deprived him of.

When the boy cries to have the already severed hand saved, his cry is not to the parents but to his sister, since he feels that she, also called into labor and responsibility too soon, will understand him better than they. But of course it is too late, and the boy dies. The point of his death, however, is not the inscrutability of fate and the tenuousness of human existence. Rather it is the waste of life brought on by the well-meaning but insensitive parents' rushing the boy out of childhood into adulthood.

Doors Leap Open/Alice Coleman

In answer to the question, "To what is the ambulance compared in the first sentence or first seven lines?" [of Shapiro's "Auto Wreck"], some students thought of an airplane by association with beacons, flashing lights, heavy curve, and words like *dips down* and *floating*. Others identified a large, death-like bird, some thought Death himself was personified, and others insisted it was just an ambulance. All agreed that the images were vivid: sound pictures—"silver bell beating"; color pictures— "ruby flare pulsing out red light like an artery" and "illuminated clocks"; motion or kinesthetic words— "floating," "dips," "brakes speed," and "enters crowd." The total effect suggested urgency, danger, and shortness of time.

In the second sentence (lines 8–10), we discussed the reason for the passive voice, since no particular persons are mentioned when the "doors leap open," "stretchers are laid out," and the "mangled lifted and stowed into the little hospital." This impersonality adds to the feeling of fear, dread, and haste. The third and last sentence in the stanza (lines 11–14) increases the ominous tone, for the bells, which had been softly beating, are now tolling, the bodies now are referred to as "terrible cargo" while the doors closed, "as an afterthought," as though care no longer mattered. Whereas the tone may be impersonal, the mood is tragic.

The point of view in the second stanza shifts abruptly to those who are spectators. After discussing the meaning of "We are deranged," the class noticed the poet's juxtaposition of this statement with the contrasting comment that the attending "cops" (632) (a surprising word to some students) are "large and composed" as they go about their business. Their routine duties are self-evident except for the reference in the last line (21) to "empty husks of locusts," used in relation to the wrecked cars. Biology students pointed out that the locusts leave their frail, shell-like husks conspicuously empty; we concluded that the unlovely insects who once inhabited the husks could be compared to the frivolous, predatory, short-lived individuals who have been carried away as "terrible cargo." Subtly, the poet is influencing our thinking. . . .

In the last stanza we find several ambiguous phrases: The question "Who shall die?" is already old, since this immediate accident is already beyond recall. But other people have asked many times before why death occurred at a particular moment and on a particular spot. . . . Lines 33 to 35 were relatively easy to grasp, but we spent considerable time on the last four lines:

> But this invites the occult mind,
> Cancels our physics with a sneer,
> And spatters all we know of denouement
> Across the expedient and wicked stones.

"This" refers to the accident which makes us probe the mysteries of the "occult" mind, suggesting that all the reliable, mathematically proven laws of physics are no longer applicable. "Denouement" is translated to mean resolution, catastrophe or the final ending of us all, but why are the stones both "expedient" and "wicked"? Why stones instead of other building materials? Although stones make a suitable highway, still the use of "wicked" connotes a moral judgment, implying that the poet may question the people who have laid the stones, the pathway to death. When we recalled similar accidents in newspapers, we recognized that the journalist does not have time, nor would it be appropriate, to employ the imagery which makes the scene come alive in the poem. Only a poet would dare to use the symbolic and dominant image of red with ruby flares, lights pulsing like arteries, blood being spattered in the gutter, wounds being probed, and closely related, the illuminated clocks and the closing of the lighted door. Each image compounded our awareness of violence, bodily injury, and of life cut short. The poet's use of the bell first beating, then tolling, his use of the hospital metaphor, and his references to death in forms of war, suicide, and cancer are all unpleasant, but they made the scene unforgettable. Only a skilled poet could condense so much emotion into so few lines.

REFERENCES WITHIN THE CONTROLLED RESEARCH PAPER

Since you work with relatively few sources in writing a controlled research essay, and especially since your instructor or reader is likely to be as familiar with these materials as you are, you'll want to choose the simplest, most straightforward method for acknowledging the origin of ideas not your own. This usually entails putting the relevant information about the author, title of work, and citation of specific page within the text itself, foregoing any notes or list of references at the end of the paper. Say, for instance, that you want to include the gist of your abstract of Abad's commentary on " 'Out, Out—.' " To do that, you might write: "Gemino Abad believes that the understated tone of Frost's poem intensifies our emotional response of pity for the victim and horror at the suddenness of the event" (*A Formal Approach to Lyric Poetry,* p. 234). If you introduced your précis of Abad's observation by saying, "In his critical study, *A Formal Approach to Lyric Poetry,* Gemino Abad argues that . . . ," the content within parentheses could be reduced to simply citing the page: (p. 234). Some instructors may want more information within the text, requiring details of publication (place and date), along with a citation of the page number within the parentheses; others may want both internal citations plus a list of references at the end.

A SAMPLE CONTROLLED RESEARCH PAPER

The following controlled research paper focuses on several differences between the Frost and Shapiro poems: in their attitude toward death; in the way they engage or distance the reader's emotions; and in the way they editorialize or let the action speak for itself. The questions at the end will direct you to consider how the student writer has balanced her own ideas with those of the critics you have just read.

TWO FACES OF ACCIDENTAL DEATH

1   Both Robert Frost in " 'Out, Out—' " and Karl Shapiro in "Auto Wreck" confront the fact of accidental death, each poet painting a vivid scene and concluding with an editorial comment. Frost's and Shapiro's commentaries, however, fall at opposite ends of the spectrum: Frost attacks our preestablished notion of an accident as a cruel, yet blameless, fate, while Shapiro probes our sense of the "occult" (to use his word) and our helplessness in the face of a seemingly irrational and inexplicable accident.

2   In order to support his editorial comment, Frost begins his poem at the scene of the accident, well before it occurs, and he can thus influence our attitude toward the characters and events. Frost's speaker intends to place blame for the accident on the adults who deny the child his boyhood. In her commentary on " 'Out, Out—,' " Marie Borroff rightly suggests that "the narrow viewpoint of the adults, the 'they' for whom the boy is working, is implied from the beginning in the speaker's description of the scene" in lines 4–6; she continues, saying, "The point is that 'they' do not lift their eyes; the sunset is ignored" ("Robert Frost's New Testament: Language and the Poems," Modern Philology, 47). Sunset is a traditional symbol of approaching death, and so this disregard on the adults' part both foreshadows the dark event to come and hints that the unaware adults may be at fault. This foreshadowing is repeated in lines 10–12, where the adults again disregard the day's end as well as the boy's feelings in regard to that end. The speaker strongly implies that had the adults been more sensitive to the boy's needs and desires, then the accident would not have occurred. By noting their insensitivity twice before the accident, the speaker has prepared the reader to believe that this event was not merely an ill turn of fate—especially since the boy is hurt by the very tool with which he is working for the adults.

3   "Auto Wreck," on the other hand, builds no case of guilt. The impersonal, non–allusive title, like a headline, establishes that the wreck has already happened, and the reader must follow the ambulance to reach the scene of the accident that could have happened to anyone. This lack of identification is quite different from the personal identification the reader makes with the boy in the Frost poem. Whereas the speaker in " 'Out, Out—' " biases our view in order to support his case of blame, the speaker in "Auto Wreck" impersonalizes the accident so that the final stanza of the poem will be more meditative and possess a wider philosophical application.

4   Given his intention, Frost's opening is more effective than Shapiro's. In her essay " 'Doors Leap Open' " from the English Journal, Alice Coleman says that the first seven lines of Shapiro's poem suggest "urgency, danger, and shortness of time" (631). "Quick soft silver bell," however, creates a delicate, almost Christmasy image; "floating down" and "Wings in a heavy curve, dips down" again suggest delicacy and style, perhaps implying the delicacy with which an ambulance driver must maneuver. Furthermore, the bird–like or angel–like images diminish a feeling of urgency and danger. On the other hand, "dark," "ruby flare," and "red light" are all signs of danger; "pulsing," too, is a particularly appropriate verb— referring both to the motion of the light and to the bleeding victims. In her comments on lines 8–14, Coleman perceptively asserts that Shapiro's use of passive verbs creates an "impersonality [that] adds to the feeling of fear, dread, and haste" (631). The paramedics are at work, and there is not time for names. The ambulance is personified as the "doors leap open," and the bell tolls once, signaling death, so that there is now no need for speed. The speaker extends the impersonality to the point of never referring to the accident victims as people—they are "the mangled" and the ambulance's "terrible cargo" in line 12. It is not until the ambulance doors are closed that "Auto Wreck" emerges from the impersonal passive voice to the emotionally vulnerable active voice.

5   Frost seems to avoid the passive as intentionally as Shapiro
uses it—a surprising difference when one considers that there
is markedly less action taking place in " 'Out, Out—' " than
in "Auto Wreck," and that Frost is recounting the past whereas
Shapiro drags us through the present. Just as Shapiro's
speaker personifies the ambulance, so Frost's speaker
personifies the saw:

> the saw
> As if to prove saws knew what supper meant,
> Leaped out at the boy's hand (lines 14-16).

The personification, however, is immediately retracted:

> or seemed to leap—
> He must have given the hand (lines 16-17).

This retraction is imperative in establishing Frost's ultimate
downplaying of the role of fate in the boy's accident. Some
critics, like Weldon Thornton in The Explicator, probe the
boy's dissatisfaction over parental restraint as motivation
for feeding his hand to the saw (May 1967, Item 71). Along
with Borroff, I prefer to think that Frost is even more
emphatic in laying the blame for the boy's action directly on
the adults who caused his dissatisfaction. This reading is
supported by the lines which immediately follow the accident.
The adults have been insensitive right from the beginning, and
the speaker draws out this insensitivity to its cruelest
point, ending the account with mention of their indifference
as they turn back to their work. This final look at the
adults confirms our bias against them, which has been
heightened throughout the poem as the speaker persuaded us to
give our emotional support to the boy and boyhood in general.

6   Shapiro supports his final comment in a less intricate way.
Whereas Frost's speaker, by his understanding sympathy, pulls
us close to the boy, Shapiro's speaker turns away from the
victims once the ambulance doors are closed. In the third and
longest stanza of "Auto Wreck," there is a drastic shift in
viewpoint, signalled by the word "We," which forces us away
from the victims and into ourselves. Shapiro's speaker does
not subtly suggest emotions. Instead, he tells us
straightforwardly that the witnesses, and by extension the
readers, are "deranged." I find Frost's subtlety more
effective rhetorically than Shapiro's straightforward
statement. Shapiro would have better written more lines like
18 and 19, which are full of imagery. I can see, smell, and
feel the blood—and the impersonality of it—running in the
street. The image of spilt blood being douched into the

gutters imposes far more horror than does the speaker's demand that we feel horrified. In short, Frost's summing up is more effective because his generalization springs from the specific details rather than being imposed upon them.

7   The final stanza of "Auto Wreck" is the most impersonal of all. "Who shall die?" the voice asks, implying that any one of us may be next. To the speaker, death is not intolerable if there is an explanation. Even cancer, though beyond our control, works in a way that we can recognize and study. But accidental death? This comes as a shock,

>   And spatters all we know of denouement
>   Across the expedient and wicked stones (lines 38–39).

Upon reading the conclusion of "Auto Wreck," it becomes obvious why Shapiro begins the poem after the incident. The real climax of "Auto Wreck" comes in the last two lines. Yet "Auto Wreck"'s clincher is similar in format to " 'Out, Out—' "'s. Both express the poets' ultimate insight. Their outlooks, however, are at opposite ends of the same spectrum: in Frost's poem, the accident has a human cause and we can assign blame, whereas in Shapiro's, the accident calls into question whether there is any reason for suffering, which is more unsettling. Yet, from the viewpoint of emotional impact, Frost's poem makes a deeper impression on my memory.

—Carolyn Sigall

EXPLORING CHOICES

1. Write a brief abstract of this student paper; it should include a formulation, in your own words, of the writer's thesis.
2. Does the writer explicitly state her thesis at any point in the paper? If so, where?
3. Is the writer's central idea sufficiently different from those of her sources to make the paper original? Does the writer supplement the ideas of others with her own?
4. Has the writer used her sources carefully? Has she distorted or misrepresented their points?
5. How has the writer used her sources? To take issue with and argue against? To support her own ideas? Do the quotations from the sources add to the paper, or are they used only for effect? Might the writer profitably have used others?
6. Are the sources smoothly integrated with the writer's own words? In paragraph 5, where the writer summarizes, has she summarized accurately? How adequately does she evaluate her sources?

7. Has the writer satisfactorily prepared you for the concluding sentence of her paper? If not, what else might she have done to gain your agreement?

WRITING SUGGESTION

Following is a casebook of four editorials written in response to a proposal passed by the National Collegiate Athletic Association that would set stiffer academic requirements for college athletes. The proposal, requiring a C average in a high-school core curriculum and a minimum SAT score of 700, met with a controversial reception, especially from black educators who felt that it was inspired by an attempt to reduce the current dominance of blacks in college football and basketball. The following editorials—two in favor of the NCAA proposal and two against—address other related issues as well: the exploitation of athletes by colleges and universities; the fairness of standardized tests in measuring the ability of minority students; and the adequacy of high schools in preparing students for college. After reading them carefully, write a brief controlled research essay developing and supporting your point of view on some issues raised by the NCAA decision and these editorials. Try to incorporate material from at least three secondary sources.

A Casebook: The NCAA Statement of Academic Requirements

The Virginian-Pilot, Thursday, January 20, 1983

Last week the major universities and colleges within the National Collegiate Athletic Association decided to toughen admission standards for athletes. To win a scholarship and compete as a freshman, a high school senior now must have a C average, have completed a core curriculum including math, English and social and physical sciences, and scored a minimum of 700 on the Scholastic Aptitude Test or 15 on the American College Testing exam.

These are not especially demanding standards; indeed, they could be criticized for being too low. No one has said that, however. The charge against the new requirements rather is that they are too high.

This is the charge levied by a number of black university presidents. Their focus is on the standardized tests, and their complaint is the now familiar one that the tests are slanted with regional, racial and class biases and fail to take into account creativity, motivation and potential. Right now, blacks average 652 on the SAT. The black university presidents believe that the 700 standard will force many black athletes to attend minor schools or perhaps to forgo college altogether.

It is arguable, however, whether the tests are biased against blacks; strenuous efforts have been made to make sure they are not. Objections to the tests often sound merely like excuses for poor performance. There is every reason to believe, as Jesse Jackson says, that higher expectations lead to higher achievements. Black athletes, contrary to what some black educators seem to imply, are capable of doing better academically.

Furthermore, the NCAA has taken a responsible approach to improving the admissions standards. For one thing, it will be three years before the new requirements take effect; that should be long enough for aspiring college athletes of any race to ready themselves, and for high schools to take more seriously their academic obligations to athletes. Also, requiring completion of a strengthened basic curriculum should help all athletes score higher on the SAT or the ACT. Indeed, it is probable that this requirement will have a spillover effect, helping non-athletes as well.

Finally, the NCAA approved a measure that will allow athletes who don't meet the new requirements to receive athletic scholarships under certain conditions. These athletes can't play or practice their sport during their freshman year, and they will qualify for eligibility during their three remaining years only if they meet what's academically required for all freshman athletes. All of this amounts to a second chance for academically deficient senior high school athletes.

The NCAA has taken a step in the right direction. Too many athletes have contributed athletically to universities, but gained little or nothing from their academic experience, because they were unprepared for it. Horror stories abound about athletes who have been to college but know nothing more than how to dribble or run a pass pattern. The new standards should give some meaning to that terribly devalued term, "student-athlete."

Reno Gazette-Journal, Tuesday, January 18, 1983   Bruce Bledsoe

Dealing fairly with university student athletes is not easy, especially when these athletes are minorities.

On the one hand, athletic scholarships offer financial assistance to deserving students whose grades do not merit traditional scholarships, but who are nonetheless college material.

On the other hand, athletic programs clearly have abused students in many universities. Unqualified for college on any terms, these students have been eased through the system until their athletic eligibility is used up, then allowed to drift away or flunk out. The university gets a winning team and considerable income from filling the stands for its sporting events, but the student gets four wasted years and little hope for future job success.

This abuse of the athlete and the twisting of ethical and educational standards for glory and money have become a national scandal. It is little wonder college presidents at the recent National Collegiate Athletic Association convention decided to try to shore up the educational standards of their schools.

And yet, in taking a tough stand, the presidents and those who supported them have tilted too far in the other direction. Instead of simply protecting the student athlete and the educational system, they have acted in a manner prejudicial to minorities.

Blacks are furious, and with good reason. They object strongly to the rigidity of the new admission requirements for Division I schools, especially the requirement that freshmen must score 700 on the SAT test or 15 on the ACT college entrance exam to be eligible for athletics. Blacks claim this is unfair to minorities—and, indeed, it does seem unfair.

Minorities, because of cultural conditioning, often do not do as well on standard tests as white students, even though their potential might be as good. It seems strange the NCAA should be placing more emphasis on these tests at a time when many other parts of society are giving them less emphasis or restructuring them to give bright minority members a better chance of succeeding.

Minority spokesmen believe racial prejudice is involved, and point out that the American Council on Education Committee which put forth the proposal was solidly white. Prejudice is difficult to prove, but it does seem odd that no minorities were included in the discussion. Whether the creation of an all-white committee was due to specific intent or social blindness, it was wrong.

This does not mean that all committee recommendations were inadequate, nor that Proposal 48, as adopted by the NCAA delegates, was without merit. There is certainly nothing wrong with requiring a student athlete to have had a 2.0 (C) average in high school, or to have had 11 core curriculum classes, such as English, math, science and history.

But certainly these achievements over a high school career should weigh more heavily than scores on a one-time-only test. SAT and ACT test results should be considered, but specific scores on these tests should not be mandatory.

In trying to help minorities—and other students—the truly important thing is to give them a chance. This is often done with nonathletes by permitting students with questionable high school academic achievements to take a crack at college on a probationary basis. If they cannot succeed, then they are dismissed. But at least they are given the opportunity to try. Student athletes should have the same opportunity.

The NCAA has tried to get around this by adopting a loophole, whereby an athlete who does not meet Proposal 48 requirements can receive a scholarship anyway, but lose his first year of athletic eligibility. If he succeeds academically as a freshman, he can play the next three years.

But this loophole is not very satisfactory. It takes away one year of athletic practice from the student, making the average athlete valuable to a team only in his last year or two. This makes Division I schools less likely to accept minority athletes. But beyond this, the loophole calls into serious question the standards of Proposal 48. It is an admission in afterthought that No. 48 is not very good.

At its next convention, the NCAA definitely should revise No. 48 and eliminate the test score requirements. This would keep educational requirements strong but eliminate a requirement that is blatantly prejudicial to minorities.

The Boston Globe, Saturday, January 29, 1983

The National Collegiate Athletic Assn. has taken the initiative to tighten academic standards for prospective college freshmen in answer to the increasing concern among educators that athletes are being exploited. Effective in 1986, the new rule will require high school seniors to achieve a combined score of 700 on the Scholastic Aptitude Test before they are eligible for intercollegiate athletics.

While the NCAA's intent is honorable, its move to play the benevolent overseer may prove to be harmful to the student-athlete. Imposing minimum standards not only increases the barriers for minorities and educationally disadvantaged students, it shifts the focus from the root of the problem: the failure of universities and colleges themselves to take responsibility for the education of their athletes.

No doubt immediate action is called for. Only two percent of college athletes sign professional contracts in football, basketball or baseball. The remaining 98 percent too often are abandoned by the institutions that coddled them scholastically through four years of athletic performance. With a brief adieu the door slams. A worthless piece of parchment is too often the only tool for survival.

The NCAA proposes either the 700 combined minimum on the SATs or 15 out of 36 on the American College Test and requires that athletes maintain a minimum 2.0 (out of 4.0) while taking a core curriculum in college.

The use of standardized tests to screen athletes is a negative and ill-conceived approach. Black educators who vehemently oppose the law may be justified in their belief that the tests are culturally biased. A 1981 study by the New York College Board reveals that approximately 56 percent of blacks scored below 700 while only 14 percent of whites scored below the cutoff. Controversy over the validity of these tests as indicators of potential and ability still rages.

Gregory Anrig, president of the Educational Testing Service, which develops the SATs, praises the NCAA for having the courage to deal with the problem but feels there are "better and fairer ways" to accomplish those ends.

"The idea of a cutoff is wrong. The SAT is not designed for a cutoff score. It's designed to be taken into consideration as one measure and not by itself," he said.

If measures taken by the NCAA are not fair, what is the solution? Ideally, colleges and universities should impose normal admission standards on their athletes, then accept the responsibility of their scholastic progress.

To ensure that institutions are not exploiting their athletes, NCAA accrediting bodies should keep pressure on schools and take action when needed. Academic accrediting bodies should also monitor the way schools they review handle athletes; the central problem here is, after all, academic and not athletic.

The NCAA approach blames the victim, penalizing athletes whose talents are already exploited by colleges and universities.

Appropriate sanctions should be applied to the exploiters, through prohibitions against participation in NCAA supervised athletics. The choice is whether to penalize those who abuse the system, or as the NCAA has proposed, to penalize those who suffer its abuse.

Rapid City Journal, Thursday, January 20, 1983

It's regrettable that a new National Collegiate Athletic Association rule which toughens academic standards for athletes has been tagged with a "racist" label.

The new rule requires that athletes must have completed a high school "core curriculum" of math, English, social and physical sciences. They must also score 700 points of a possible 1,600 points on the Scholastic Aptitude Test (SAT) or 15 of a possible 36 on the American College Test (ACT). Last year the national average was 992 on SAT and 18.4 on ACT.

The NCAA also adopted what amounts to a loophole by specifying that athletes who do not meet the new requirements will be permitted an athletic scholarship but cannot compete their first year.

Supporters of the rule view it as an effort to put pressure on secondary schools to prepare student athletes for a college life without basket-weaving courses.

Opponents contend, however, that the average scores for black students on SAT and ACT tests trail those of other students and therefore the tests contain a cultural bias.

Coaches of some of the nation's top college athletic powers are divided on the issue.

Coach Tom Osborne of the Nebraska Cornhuskers, who opposed the rule, considers the test discriminatory against students whose schools or family life did not encourage academic attainments or the majority culture's speech patterns.

Osborne says if the new requirements had been in force, one-third of the athletes currently in the Big Eight conference would not have been allowed to compete as freshmen.

Joe Paterno, coach of the national gridiron champion Penn State, is on the other side of the argument. He charges that for 15 years black athletes have been "raped" by a system which exploits their talents without developing their minds. More and more black athletes are frustrated later in life because they didn't get what they should have gotten out of college. He predicted athletes will take up the challenge of meeting the new requirements.

Other perennial football powers such as Notre Dame and Alabama also voted for the new requirements.

We agree with those who contend the new rule will be a step toward reestablishing the integrity of institutions of higher learning many of which have been wracked with athletic recruiting scandals. In all too many instances, "student" no longer applies in the term "student-athletes."

It's time that something was done to correct the system which places a 17-year-old in an environment he is ill-prepared for. The NCAA is to be congratulated for reducing the chances that young men and women will be exploited for their athletic ability and then go unprepared to meet the challenges which will confront them when their playing days are over.

WRITING THE LIBRARY
RESEARCH PAPER

Some writing purposes depend on what you have experienced, observed, or imagined as the source of material. Even if your purpose is to explain or persuade, you may still draw mainly on firsthand experience. For much of your writing, then, you are your own authority. But for projects that involve complex or unfamiliar material, you will need to depend on outside authorities for facts and ideas before you can make any reasonable judgment of your own. For such writing activities, you will first need to research the topic, reading widely to discover what specialists in a field have thought and said. Only after this thoughtful examination of a problem or question will you be able to reach your own conclusions.

PREWRITING THE RESEARCH PAPER

Most of you remember writing something called the *term paper* in high school. If those term papers were simply a compilation of undigested information—ten typewritten pages of paraphrase, summary, and quotation from two or three sources—they share little with the library research paper. Research, as we are using the term here, involves surveying what is known about a subject as well as rethinking and reinterpreting the subject. Researchers first *recover* information and ideas in order to become knowledgeable about the contributions of others to the subject they are studying. Then they *add* to the literature, indicating that they have made an informed judgment about their subject and are contributing their own perspective and assessment.

An example from the legislative process illustrates both steps. When legislative bodies amend a law or propose a new one, they first gather authoritative testimony, statistical data, past judicial decisions, government reports, case studies, and other relevant material. The accumulated evidence—the product of research—allows for an informed decision and reduces the possibility of error. The report they compile is therefore both a summary of past assessments of an issue and a recommendation for a future course of action.

Though your own research purpose may not involve urging a course of action, you will find it useful to follow both steps: to demonstrate that you are informed about your subject, you should review the relevant literature; in addition, you will want to take a position on a question open to conflicting interpretation, even if you cannot solve the issue conclusively. In this way, rather than simply repeating or synthesizing the ideas of others, you will have something valuable of your own to contribute.

Choosing a Topic

The first choice in an extended research paper is the selection of a topic. You will write best if you settle on a topic that interests you; indeed, the success of your project may hinge on this choice. Research requires considerable effort and time, and your willingness to make this investment depends on the appeal your topic holds for you. An absorbing topic is a powerful motivator: it will spur you to read widely and to ponder the issues; it will give you the imaginative boost that distinguishes good research from the merely perfunctory; it will make the difference between an assignment fulfilled merely to satisfy an obligation and an assignment fulfilled because you find your project intrinsically fascinating and important.

Before you commit yourself to a topic, take time to explore half-formed ideas, hints, and intuitions that point to a subject you might want to research. Spend time in the library examining a variety of materials—periodicals, journals, books, government documents, and so on. Browsing in the library may suggest a new topic, or it may sharpen and shape a topic you've already considered. In any case, you will want to make sure you can find sufficient information on the topic. If, for example, you considered exploring the effectiveness of gun control legislation recently enacted in some communities, you would probably find little data to guide your investigation, though you would find many impassioned arguments on one side or the other. In this case, the topic is too recent to have produced the evidence you need to make a reasonable judgment.

Framing a Research Question

General topics are broad entities not sharply focused enough to be the subject of research: they mark off boundaries or denote an area of inquiry. Following are some topics that have recently been popular with students. Note that they are in an outline form that includes a number of subtopics under each heading.

Ecology
animal trapping
crop rotation
endangered species
wilderness areas

Energy
gasohol
nuclear energy
solar energy
wind energy

Education
bilingual education
competency testing
public and private education
sex education
teacher salaries

Health and Physical Fitness
alcoholism
anorexia and bulimia
crash diets
jogging
smoking

Pollution
acid rain
PCBs
toxic waste

Sports
college athletics
little league
superstar salaries

These topics and subtopics are a convenient way to categorize human experience. For you as a researcher they represent potential areas of investigation. You may be drawn to some of the categories because they fit your professional or personal interests. Note, however, that none of these categories, whatever the degree of specificity, represents an *actual* topic of research. If you were to settle on one of them, you would know little more than the broad area you wanted to study. To transform a general topic into a research topic, you need to formulate a research question that will pose the exact problem you propose to investigate. Following are some research questions students have chosen, based on two of the preceding general topics:

Energy

1. What are the advantages of gasohol as a fuel?
2. Is nuclear energy worth the risk?
3. Is solar energy a useful alternative to conventional means of home heating?

Health and Physical Fitness

1. What evidence is there that crash diets may injure health?
2. What are the causes of anorexia and bulimia?
3. What evidence exists that alcoholism can be cured?
4. What evidence is there that lowered cholesterol levels reduce the risk of heart disease?

FOLLOW-UP ACTIVITY

Following is a list of topics, some more specific than others, that have recently provided subjects for students' research papers. Consider each with a view to narrowing it to a usable focus by asking a specific question about some facet of the topic. For example, if you were intrigued by "Today's Best Sellers," you might discover a specific area for your research by asking: "Why has the public embraced novel X even though the reviewers generally dismissed it as worthless?"

Student Drinking
The Occult
Men and Feelings
Children and Divorce
Fraternity Hazings
UFOs

Television Violence
Sex in Advertising
Merit Pay
Pay for College Athletes
Plea-Bargaining
Gun Laws

Euthanasia   Over-the-Counter Drugs
The Volunteer Army   Marijuana and Cancer Treatment

TIPS FOR DEVELOPING A RESEARCHABLE QUESTION

1. Aim for the lowest possible level of generality. "Do toxic wastes threaten the environment?" is better than "Is pollution a serious problem?"

2. Treat your research question, especially if it involves a yes/no answer, as an initial hypothesis that may or may not be confirmed in the course of your investigation. Doing so will help you review the evidence responsibly. If you have made up your mind before you begin, you may be tempted to ignore evidence that does not fit your preconception.

3. Recognize that your research question may have an underlying assumption that you will need to address in planning your paper. A question such as "What steps need to be taken to control acid rain?" implies that acid rain needs to be controlled. Establishing the validity of this assumption would be an important feature of the paper.

On page 442 you will find a research paper entitled "Energy: Is the Answer in the Wind?" Steven Primack, the writer, knew from the start that his general topic would be energy. He was especially interested in alternative energy sources because he felt that shortages of conventional energy were certain to arise in the near future. Browsing in the library, he found a short article in a weekly news magazine about harnessing energy from the wind, and this idea attracted him: he recalled being fascinated by the old, out-of-use windmill on his grandparents' farm when he was a child. He decided to formulate the following research question: "Is wind energy a feasible way to supplement more conventional energy sources?"

To help you understand the sequence of activities involved in planning and writing a research paper, the following will describe Steve's step-by-step research procedure.

Developing a Bibliography

After formulating his research question, Steve did some preliminary digging in the library to develop a *bibliography,* a list of books and articles to consult in the process of arriving at a thesis about his topic. When you set out, you may have little knowledge about a topic, few ideas about what you will say, and only a vague notion of what your attitude toward the problem will be. Reading what others have said helps clarify and refine your thinking by generating new ideas; by forcing you to sharpen ideas you had only partially formulated; and by scrutinizing ideas you had not critically examined. The process of reading and notetaking is a large part of the discovery process that precedes the writing of the library research paper.

On his first trip to the library, Steve decided to gain an overview of his subject by acquainting himself with what one of the major encyclopedias, such as *Americana* or *Britannica,* had to say. He knew that encyclopedia entries usually conclude with suggestions for further reading that can help develop a bibliography. Steve now felt ready to make a preliminary list of reading materials. He had two possible strategies for developing his reading list: he could consult one of the standard reference guides for his field of research—which would provide titles of specialized articles on wind energy—or he could go to the card catalog, which would give him the names of books on the subject in his college library. Since he knew little about the technical aspects of his topic, he first wanted general sources that would serve as an introduction, so he began by checking the *Library of Congress Subject Headings,* which would direct him where to look in the card catalog.

Using the Library of Congress subject headings.   The two-volume *Library of Congress Subject Headings* is usually available near the card catalog. Skimming down the three columns under the headings that included the word "Energy," Steve did not see any mention of "wind." He did, however, notice that the words "Power resources" appeared frequently, and so he checked under that in the *Subject Headings,* finally discovering a reference to "Wind power." Turning to "Wind power," he saw that it is, indeed, listed as a heading he would be able to find in the subject catalog. The entry from the *Library of Congress Subject Headings* suggested that he might see also (*"sa"*) the cards under the subject headings "Air-turbines" and "Windmills," and indicated that a half-dozen broader subject headings (such as "Natural resources" and "Renewable energy sources"), designated *"xx,"* might provide some background information.

> **Wind power**
> *sa* **Air-turbines**
>   **Windmills**
> *xx* **Air-turbines**
>   **Natural resources**
>   **Power (Mechanics)**
>   **Power resources**
>   **Windmills**

Sometimes browsing through the *Library of Congress Subject Headings* can be a useful means of limiting—or even of finding—a topic. If you have in mind a general subject such as "Energy" for a research assignment, the subheadings designated by "see also" will suggest narrower and more specific topics with subject card entries of their own.

Using the card catalog. Having found the appropriate subject heading, "Wind Power," Steve went to the card catalog. The card catalog is arranged in three ways: by *subject,* by *author,* and by *title.* Shuffling through the subject catalog cards under "Wind Power," he found cards for numerous titles, including three that were book-length *bibliographies,* listing printed material in the field.

If you are unfamiliar with the information contained on the three types of catalog entries, the following sample cards for the same book will help:

Subject Card

```
                      WIND POWER

     621.45    Naar, Jon.
     N11n         The new wind power / by Jon Naar ; foreword
               by Robert Rodale. -- Harmondsworth, Middlesex,
               England ; New York, N. Y. : Penguin Books,
               1982.
                  251 p. : ill. ; 23 cm.
                  Bibliography: p. 239-242.
                  Includes index.
```

Author Card

```
     621.45    Naar, Jon.
     N11n         The new wind power / by Jon Naar ; foreword
               by Robert Rodale. -- Harmondsworth, Middlesex,
               England ; New York, N. Y. : Penguin Books,
               1982.
                  251 p. : ill. ; 23 cm.
                  Bibliography: p. 239-242.
                  Includes index.
```

Title Card

```
                The new wind power.

621.45      Naar, Jon.
N11n            The new wind power / by John Naar ; foreword
            by Robert Rodale. -- Harmondsworth, Middlesex,
            England ; New York, N. Y. : Penguin Books,
            c1982.
                251 p. : ill. ; 23 cm.
                Bibliography: p. 239-242.
                Includes index.
```

Many of the volumes for which Steve found subject cards were housed in the campus engineering library, and others sounded far too technical. But he made notations about four or five that appeared to be basic introductions, carefully copying on a notecard the relevant information for each—author, title, publisher, location, date—along with the call number indicating where the book was shelved. One of his cards looked like this:

> 621.45
> C783w
>
> Coonley, Douglas R. *Wind:*
> *Making It Work for You.*
> Philadelphia, The Franklin
> Institute Press, 1979.

Consulting reference guides and indexes.   To retrieve a reference to the article he had browsed through earlier from the news magazine, as well as to find other articles on his subject that appeared in journals, Steve consulted the standard index, the *Readers' Guide to Periodical Literature.* In the volume covering the years 1981/82, he found the following entry under "WIND power":

WIND power
See also
Windfarms, Ltd
Windmills

8,000-foot wind-power tower. E. F. Blase and J. H. Kaimon. il Pop Sci 219:68-9 D '81
Harnessing the wind. il Nat Geog [sp energy issue] p38 F 81
PURPA: a new law helps make small-scale power production profitable [Public Utilities Regulatory Policies Act] P. Gipe. il Sierra 66:52-5 N/D '81

Renaissance for wind power. C. Flavin. il Environment 23:31-41 O '81
"Wind farm" east of Portland. Others will be coming to the West. il Sunset 167:44-5 S '81
Wind farm's first sprout [turbine] V. E. Smay. il Pop Sci 219:111 N '81
Wind power book [excerpt] J. Park. il Mother Earth News 71:174-7 S/O '81

Once again, he noted the relevant information for each item he thought might be of interest, so that he could find the magazines by using the serials listing. One of his bibliography cards looked like this:

"Harnessing the Wind," National
Geographic (Energy Issue),
February 1981, p. 38.

Along with the bibliographies devoted to particular subjects—and for which you will find entries in the card catalogue—specialized indexes devoted to periodical literature in particular fields are also available. You may want to consult one or more of the following reference works:

Applied Science and Technology Index, 1913–
Art Index, 1929–
Biography Index, 1947–
Biological and Agricultural Index, 1916–

Book Review Digest, 1905–
Business Periodicals Index, 1958–
Dramatic Index, 1909–1949
Education Index, 1929–
Essay and General Literature Index, 1900–
General Science Index, 1978–
International Index, 1907–1065
   (Became *Social Sciences and Humanities Index,* 1965–1974; split into
   Humanities Index, 1974–   and *Social Sciences Index,* 1974–   )
Monthly Catalogue of United States Government Periodicals, 1895–
Music Index, 1949–
*MLA International Bibliography of Books and Articles in the Modern
   Languages and Literature,* 1921–
Poole's Index to Periodical Literature, 1802–1906
Retrospective Index to Film Periodicals, 1930–1971

There are also indexes to newspapers such as the *London Times Official Index, The National Newspaper Index,* and the *New York Times Index.* For a thorough list of major reference works in your field, consult one of the "bibliographies of bibliographies," such as E. P. Sheehy's *Guide to Reference Books,* 9th ed. (Chicago: American Library Association, 1976).

Searching the computer databases.   Manual searches through specialized bibliographies lining a library shelf or at the back of other volumes, together with going through the card catalogs, are generally adequate for the undergraduate researcher. But they also have certain disadvantages: they are time-consuming; they are subject to inaccurate citations if information is not transcribed with great care; and they can hardly ever be exhaustive. If Steve had felt that his search of the relevant bibliographies and the catalog had not turned up enough items, or if he sensed that he was missing something important, he might have used his library's computerized information retrieval system. A library contracts with a publicly available vendor to access their *databases,* which are collections or files of bibliographical citations for the published literature in many specific areas or fields.

    To initiate a computer search, Steve would first complete a request form, providing a librarian trained as a computer search specialist with the pertinent information: the subject or a brief description of his project; key words or descriptors that would be fed into the computer; and any limitations on the citations he wanted, for example, only those written in English, or only those published within a certain time period. After formulating a strategy on how to proceed, the searcher would type the key words into the terminal, properly equipped with a modem or receptacle for a telephone receiver. This allows the terminal direct, or on-line, access to the computer database via the telecommunication network.

    The specialist performing a computer search for Steve chose to search the ERIC database (a database that stores education materials). She used as her descriptors "wind energy and/or wind power." From that one database she uncovered three citations, called "postings" or "hits." After she logged off, the vendor, or owner of the computer contracted with by the library, mailed a printout of these citations, none of which Steve had unearthed by the usual methods:

```
Print 3/7/1
DIALOG File1: ERIC - 66-83/Dec (Item  1 of   1) User 2360   9feb84


EJ273302  SE532513
A Two-Way Spinoff.
Aviation/Space, v9 n5-6 p58-65 Fall-Win      1982
Available from: Reprint: UMI
Language: English
Document Type: JOURNAL ARTICLE (080); GENERAL REPORT (140)
A  unusual  technology  transfer,  involving  sailboats and
commercial  wind  energy  systems,  highlights  space-related
spinoffs  for  home,  consumer,  and recreational use.  These
include  clothing  for   cooling   athletes,   high-intensity
lighting,   an  advanced  welding  tool,  and a water filter.
(Author/JN)


ED221406  SE039381
Toward  a  Regional Geography of Renewable Electrical Energy
Resources.
Pryde, Philip R.
Jun 1982   41p.
EDRS Price - MF01/PC02 Plus Postage.
Language: English
Document Type: CONFERENCE PAPER (150); RESEARCH REPORT (143)
Geographic Source: U.S.; California
Journal Announcement: RIEFEB83
It  is  postulated  that  many  types  of  renewable  energy
resources,   like  fossil  fuels,   are  amenable to regional
availability analysis. Among these are hydropower, geothermal,
ocean temperature gradient, wind,  and direct solar energy.  A
review  of  the  spatial  attributes  of  each of these types
reveals areas of the United States  that  contain  comparative
advantages  for  the  conversion  of  one  or  more  of these
alternative  forms  into  electrical  energy.   Combining  the
results of five separate studies produces a generalized map of
alternative  energy  supply  regions within the United States.
(Author/JN)


ED219244  SE038587
Energy Bingo.
Canipe, Stephen
[1982   19p.
EDRS Price - MF01/PC01 Plus Postage.
Language: English
Document Type: TEACHING GUIDE (052)
Geographic Source: U.S.; North Carolina
Journal Announcement: RIEDEC82
Rules  are  provided  for  this bingo game focusing on terms
related to solar,  coal,  nuclear,  hydro,  and  wind  energy.
Playing cards and calling cards (to be cut out by the teacher)
are also provided. (JN)
```

If Steve had requested additional citations, the search specialist could have tried other databases, such as ENERGYLINE or POWER. But each of these searches, which can be done in a matter of minutes, would have cost Steve more money. Depending on the length of time a search takes, and the amount of information finally printed off-line and then mailed to you, a computer search will cost anywhere from a minimum of $5 or $10 up to $75, so it is always wise to get an estimate before beginning the search. Despite the savings in time and the greater efficiency and accuracy, you might decide that a computer-based search is simply not warranted for your project.

The following list of databases will give you some idea of the extent of the bibliographical resources available via computer:

AMERICA: HISTORY AND LIFE (U.S. and Canadian history and current affairs)

CANCERLIT (all aspects of cancer)

COMPENDEX (worldwide engineering—all disciplines—and technical literature)

ECONOMIC LITERATURE INDEX (worldwide information, in English)

ENVIROLINE (all aspects of the environment)

FEDERAL INDEX (all federal government and congressional activities)

HISTORICAL ABSTRACTS (history and related social sciences from 1450 to the present)

LIFE SCIENCES COLLECTIONS (biology, biochemistry, ecology, microbiology)

MAGAZINE INDEX ARTICLES (news reports, editorials, biographical pieces, reviews)

MATHFILE (pure and applied mathematics, computer science)

MEDLINE (biomedical literature)

MICROCOMPUTER INDEX (use of microcomputers in business, education, home)

PHILOSOPHER'S INDEX (aesthetics, epistemology, ethics, logic, metaphysics)

PSYCHINFO (psychology and behavioral sciences)

SCISEARCH (science and technology)

SOCIAL SCISEARCH (social sciences)

SPORT (recreation, sports medicine, physical education)

Also available via computer are the *Book Review Index* and the *Newspaper Index*.

Taking Notes

The ideal procedure in writing a library research paper is to use the ideas of others not as a substitute for original ideas, but to supplement and complement your own. This goal should govern both the quantity and quality of notetaking. Today, with the ready availability of photocopy machines, it may seem easier to reproduce entire articles or chapters from books instead of taking notes. But this simply delays the process of assimilating the material, of mastering the subject and making it your own. The better method is to start taking notes on your reading immediately, but *selectively*. Initially, you will take down too much information, but as you see your thesis more clearly, you will become more judicious and begin to sense what will be of use in writing the paper. As you read, some things will seem so sharp and well said that you will copy them down word for word, so that you can quote them later, either as support for your own position, or as something to criticize. Faced with other passages, you may want to record just the most striking phrases, or summarize them in your own words. You will also want to note your own ideas as they emerge and develop during your reading.

The cardinal rule for making notes of quotations is absolute letter-for-letter accuracy. Researching his paper on wind energy, Steve came upon the following sentence in Coonley's book that he felt he would want to quote in his paper (as it turned out, he never used it). Since he already had a full reference—title, publisher, year—to Coonley's book on a separate bibliography card, he made a notecard, indicating only the author's last name along with the specific page number:

Problems with Development

Coonley:
"Three critical considerations for the future of energy are wind rights, energy storage systems, and wind system manufacturers."
(p. 71)

Organizing Notecards

You will notice that, at the top of the notecard, Steve added a *subject heading*. This not only indicates, in brief, the focus of the material on the card—"Problems with Development"—but also provides a category around which he can group cards containing similar information. Once he completes his research, Steve will probably already have developed even more topic headings than will finally appear in his outline. Grouping his notecards in this fashion *during* the process of reading rather than after it, and periodically rereading them, will help him determine when he has enough material on a given facet of his topic. Likewise, it will help him synthesize and draw tentative conclusions, as well as reveal what aspects of his subject he needs to explore further. If, while taking notes, he sees the categories into which the material naturally falls and the relationships among these categories, then the process of organizing the material and achieving transitions from one point to the next will be easier. If he's lucky, he may even discover that the outline—when he reaches that stage—falls easily into place because he has made the extra effort to keep his materials organized as he goes along.

What follows is a second notecard with an appropriate subject heading, containing material that Steve thought he would allude to in his finished paper:

Naar :
Wind Energy in America
(19th Century)

"Right after the Civil War there was a great surge in windmill technology and use: to pump water for the new railroads and to irrigate the new territories of the West." (p. 43)

Paraphrase, Summary, and Quotation

Reading and notetaking help you comprehend and analyze the reasoning process of others and paraphrase or summarize the ideas you have encountered. Often you will want to put what you read into your own words rather than quote directly. When you *paraphrase* a passage from someone else's writing, you render it almost word for word, idea by idea, but in your own language, whereas when you *summarize* you also express the main idea of the passage in your own words though in considerably briefer form. In an article on wind energy, Steve read the following:

> It is deplorable also that labor unions do not see the potential for employment in this new, low-technology labor-intensive industry. Instead, they use their political influence in a shortsighted way to support nuclear energy, where the ratio of jobs to invested capital is low, but where some jobs are immediately available. —David R. Inglis, "The Answer Is Blowing in the Wind," *The Progressive,* 46.

If he had included a paraphrase of this passage in his paper, it would have read something like this:

> We should view with regret the shortsightedness of labor unions for not recognizing the possibilities for workers in this relatively non-technical, labor-oriented enterprise. Rather, they mistakenly expend their political clout in support of nuclear industries where--even though the proportion of jobs is small in relation to the total money being poured into that field--some positions are already open (Inglis 46).

You notice immediately that the paraphrase is longer and less sharp than the original, partly because the writer must avoid repeating the author's original words. In general, therefore, a passage important enough to paraphrase is important enough to quote directly. To avoid excessive reliance on lengthy quotations you can use summary, which is more succinct than paraphrase. What follows are two summaries of the original paragraph, the first more complete than the second in its inclusion of details:

> Unfortunately, labor unions, with their focus on immediate job opportunities, have been more interested in supporting the nuclear industry--despite the relatively small number of jobs in proportion to the total money involved--than the less technical yet more labor-oriented windpower industry (Inglis 46).

> Sadly, labor unions have promoted the nuclear industry, with its immediate job openings, at the expense of the windpower industry, which would be more feasible for their workers (Inglis 46).

Whether you paraphrase, summarize, or quote directly from the work of another, you must represent the ideas honestly and without distortion. You must also provide accurate documentation of the original source. Therefore, all of the preceding three passages of paraphrase or summary, and the following two passages which use selective quotation, are followed by an internal citation.

> One proponent of the wind energy industry chides the labor unions for supporting nuclear energy rather than recognizing "the potential for employment in this new, low-technology labor-intensive industry" (Inglis 46).

In this last passage, the quoted material is integrated smoothly and effortlessly into a summary that provides a context for the reader. This passage can serve as a model for the artful blending of summary and quotation in your research writing. You may decide not to quote a passage in full; if so, you can delete unwanted words or phrases, or even whole sentences, by using ellipsis marks (. . .) to indicate where you have omitted parts of your source. For example, you might write the following:

```
From the perspective of David Inglis, "It is deplorable . . .
that labor unions do not see the potential for employment in
this new, low-technology labor-intensive industry.  Instead,
they use their political influence . . . to support nuclear
energy, . . . where some jobs are immediately available" (46).
```

This partial quotation, of course, must be followed by a citation, just as a paraphrase, summary, or full quotation would be.

In typing the final copy of your paper, lengthy quotations—those passages running to five lines of text or more—should be indented ten spaces from the left margin and typed double-spaced, as Steve does on pages 3 and 10 of the following research paper. Such long quotations from your sources should be used sparingly so that you do not appear to be "padding" your paper. Whenever possible, it is good to shorten quoted passages by using ellipsis marks, eliminating all but the words essential in conveying the point.

DOCUMENTING RESEARCH

As a writer, you have a responsibility to give credit for facts, theories, and opinions that are as much the property of others as their houses or cars. If you fail to do so, you are guilty of *plagiarism,* that is, of presenting other people's ideas as if they were your own. You document not only so that your reader and other researchers can see the relationship between your ideas and those of others, but also so that later researchers can find your sources and use them in their own work. No one, of course, expects you to indicate a precise source for facts that everyone knows; the statement, "George Washington was the first president of the United States," requires no documentation. But when you employ the results of someone else's experiments or investigations, or the fruits of their thinking and reflection on a problem, you must adopt a proper form for attributing those conclusions or ideas to their original source. When you quote someone's words directly, you can easily see the necessity for proper attribution; if, however, you summarize or paraphrase the findings of others, you are under the same obligation. In that case, you must make it absolutely clear to the reader where the material of others ends and where the original material begins. A general reference at the end of a paragraph may be inadequate if it camouflages this distinction.

Proper documentation of your research need not be as formidable a task as you might suppose; ordinarily it means mastering just a few simple forms. In most disciplines, the older method of footnoting has been replaced by a simpler, less cumbersome method that incorporates the essential details—the name of the author, the specific page reference, and the date—directly within the text. In writing his paper on wind energy, Steve was advised by his instructor to use the documentation method described in the *MLA* (Modern Language Association) *Handbook,* the system most frequently employed when writing in the humanities. (The second student research paper included in this chapter makes use of the APA [American Psychological Association] method of documentation, which has slight differences in emphasis.) An important rule of thumb: once you adopt a system of documentation, use it consistently throughout the paper.

MLA Parenthetical Citations

Under the MLA system for citation of sources, you include the author's last name and the page reference for your source, within parentheses, in the text of the paper. Notice that the name and page number are *not* separated by a punctuation mark:

```
One proponent of the wind energy industry chides the labor
unions for supporting nuclear energy rather than recognizing
"the potential for employment in this new, low-technology
labor-intensive industry" (Inglis 46).
```

When the writer's name already appears in your sentence, you cite only the page number within parentheses:

```
From the perspective of David Inglis, "It is deplorable . . .
that labor unions do not see the potential for employment in
this new, low-technology labor-intensive industry" (46).
```

If the source you are citing is anonymous, you use a key word from the title, along with the page reference, as in ("Harnessing" 38). And if two or more works have the same author, you distinguish between them by placing a key word from the title between the author's name and the page: (Inglis, "Answer" 43) and (Inglis, "Power" 17).

Explanatory or Content Notes

Even in papers which use parenthetical documentation, a writer may append *explanatory* or *content notes,* which usually take one of two forms: either they direct the reader to other sources of additional material on the subject; or they provide more detailed information than the writer wishes to include within the body of the paper. In the paper on wind power, for example, the writer briefly surveys the history of wind energy in the United

States. For readers who desire greater detail, he could have added a footnote number in the body of the paper and appended the following content note at the end:

> ²For a more complete history of wind power from the
> Persians to the present day, see Flavin (8-11).

The other type of explanatory footnote might have been included in the second research paper on the relation between physical exercise and mental conditioning. In this paper, the student summarizes a scientific study which concluded that men become "more imaginative, more self-sufficient, and more emotionally stable" through programmed exercise. The data on which this conclusion was based appears in the form of statistical tables in the article she consulted; for interested readers, she might have added an informational note containing some of this data, as in the following:

> ³Ismail and Trachtman's study (1973) showed that by the
> end of the exercise program, the emotional stability factor of
> low-fitness participants had risen from 4.6 to 5.4; the
> imaginative factor from 5.3 to 6.1; and the self-sufficiency
> factor from 6.4 to 8.0 (81).

MLA Bibliographical References

The bibliography page at the end of a library research paper, which lists all of the works referred to within the essay, and only those works, is usually headed simply "Works Cited." Mastering the basic form for citing books and articles from periodicals will enable you to write correct bibliographical references for the majority of works. Since a "Works Cited" page is arranged in alphabetical order, for each *book* you provide:

the author's name, last name first, followed by a period;

the title of the book, underlined, followed by a period;

and the publication information: including the city, followed by a colon; the publishing house, followed by a comma; and then the date of publication followed by a period.

In all bibliographical references, every line after the initial one is indented five spaces. Here is an example:

> Rhode, Eric. A History of the Cinema from Its Origins to
> 1970. New York: Hill and Wang, 1976.

The bibliographical citation for an *article* from a journal provides:

the author's name, last name first, followed by a period;

the title of the article in quotation marks, with a period within the end quotes;

the title of the journal, underlined;

the publishing information, consisting of volume number and—in cases where issues have been continuous—the issue number separated by a period; and then the date of publication within parentheses, followed by a colon;

and finally the inclusive pages of the article, followed by a period.

```
Burkman, Katherine H. "Hirst as Godot: Pinter in Beckett's
     Land." Arizona Quarterly 39.1 (1983): 5-14.
```

If you include more than one work by the same author in your "Works Cited," a line substitutes for later mentions of the author's name (see p. 456, for example), with the works arranged in alphabetical order by title.

Although the two basic bibliographic forms will largely meet your requirements, you may occasionally need to use one or more of the following forms:

For a book by two authors:

```
Cavett, Dick, and Christopher Porterfield.  Cavett.  New York:
     Harcourt Brace Jovanovich, 1974.
```

For a book by three or more authors:

```
Spiller, Robert E. et al.  Literary History of the United
     States.  4th ed.  New York:  Macmillan, 1974.
```

For an essay or a chapter in a book:

```
Staples, Robert.  "Research on the Black Male:  A Resource for
     Change."  Men in Difficult Times.  Ed. Robert A. Lewis.
     Englewood Cliffs, N.J.:  Prentice-Hall, Inc., 1981, 275-
     278.
```

For a monograph or pamphlet:

```
Bigsby, C. W. E.  Tom Stoppard.  Writers & Their Work 250.
     London:  Longman Group Ltd., 1976.  [Bigsby's monograph
     is number 250 in the Writers & Their Work series; since
     that information is not part of the pamphlet's title, it
     is not underlined.]
```

For an encyclopedia entry:

Pierce, John R. "Satellite Communication." Encyclopaedia
    Britannica. 1982 ed.

For an article in a monthly magazine:

Awiakta, Marilou. "What Is the Atom, Mother? Will It Hurt
    Us?" Ms. July 1983: 44–48.

For an anonymous article in a weekly magazine:

"The Manufacture of Marilyn." Time 24 Jan. 1983: 77.

For a newspaper article:

Eckhouse, John. "Latest computer buzzword? Ergonomics." San
    Francisco Examiner 19 June 1983, Sec. D: 1, 9.

For a newspaper editorial:

"The Fear of AIDS." Editorial. New York Times 25 June 1983:
    22.

For a book review:

Clemons, Walter. Rev. of Clare Booth Luce, by Wilfrid Sheed.
    Newsweek: 22 Feb. 1982: 74.

For a film or theatre review:

Kael, Pauline. "Wrapping It Up." Rev. of Fanny and Alexander
    dir. by Ingmar Bergman. The New Yorker 13 June 1983:
    117–121.

For an interview:

Cranston, Alan. Personal Interview. 9 June 1982.

For an item in the Congressional Record:

Cong. Rec. 30 June 1982, S7739.

THE PROSPECTUS AND THE PAPER

Preparing the Prospectus

After Steve had developed his bibliography and done some of the reading, he prepared a *prospectus*. A prospectus is a preliminary version of a research paper that condenses the main points the writer will include in the completed version. Doing a prospectus can be useful for several reasons. First, it can reveal whether the writer has a manageable topic, an appropriate research question, and a well-formulated thesis. Second, it anticipates the possible shape and pattern of organization of the finished paper. Third, it permits an informed editor to suggest strategies for completing the task: perhaps pointing out weak links in the argumentation; or suggesting areas that need further exploration; or making observations about improvements in style. Steve's prospectus begins on p. 435.

EXPLORING THE PROSPECTUS

While not originally written as a prospectus, these introductory paragraphs from Elaine Dutka's, "X-Rays: The Inside Picture" (*Cosmopolitan,* May 1981, p. 104) share the same relation to her article as a whole that a prospectus does to a research paper. As you read, ask yourself what details might be added, what points expanded, and what material would require documentation in a full essay on the subject.

> X-rays are taken of over half the population each year. They're used by dentists to check for impacted teeth, jaw fractures, and tooth alignment and by doctors to diagnose everything from tumors to tuberculosis to heart disease. No one disputes that, since their discovery in 1895, x-rays have saved millions of lives . . . nor that all radiation involves an element of risk. Which side of the x-ray debate you come down on depends on just how much risk you perceive.
>
> Defenders of present x-ray practices claim dangers are minimal compared to the benefits derived. They cite improvements in x-ray equipment, the elimination of controversial mass screenings, and the growing consciousness among doctors of the potential long-range effects of radiation. What's more, regulatory agencies such as the Bureau of Radiological Health and the Environmental Protection Agency (EPA) protect the public from radiation abuse.
>
> The critics sound a different note, insisting that the American public is still exposed to a lot more radiation than is necessary, and that x-ray equipment, though better than it used to be, still varies in quality from machine to machine. Many doctors and dentists are still ignorant of radiation danger charges this more cautious group, and even those who are aware of it often overprescribe x-rays in reaction to patient demand.

X-rays should be used only when the potential for good far exceeds any potential hazard. Often this is something the patient herself must determine—she should find out why an x-ray exam has been ordered, and if adequate precautions have been taken to get a maximum of information with a minimum of radiation.

The format of a prospectus—as you will see from the sample which follows—calls for a definition of the problem or question, a brief discussion of its background, a summary of some of the experts' views, both pro and con, and an initial formulation of the writer's own point of view. Preparing the prospectus enabled Steve to see the link between persuasive writing he had done earlier and the long research paper he was currently preparing; helped provide clearer definition and purpose to the rest of his reading about the subject; and eventually fed into the process of outlining the research paper.

Energy: Is the Answer in the Wind?

PROBLEM: A problem in the past and most notably
                           of recent years has been deciding what
                           conventional and alternative energy sources
                           to use and in what proportion. With fuel
                           prices subject to sudden fluctuations
                           because of the whims of suppliers, other
                           energy sources are being considered. One
                           of these potential sources, wind power, has
                           been studied in great detail recently with
                           many positive results. Proponents point to
                           the tremendous long-range benefits of
                           obtaining energy from the wind. Opponents,
                           however, argue that development of this
                           source of energy will take too long. As of
                           today, the government does not regard wind
                           energy as having enough potential to fund
                           it sufficiently for large-scale
                           development.

BACKGROUND: Wind energy on a large scale in the
                           United States got its start in 1939 when a
                           turbine firm, the S. Morgan Smith Co. of
                           Pennsylvania, began the construction of a
                           megawatt-scale wind-powered electric

generator. By 1945, the firm had compiled ample preliminary data. However, in that year, when a part in the generator failed that could not be replaced, the construction was concluded short of its completion. It was decided at the time that it would be uneconomical to build similar machines because of the lower cost of hydroelectric power (Inglis 44–45). Also, nuclear power was getting its start at this time, and the U.S. government decided to promote its development instead.

Most projects with wind turbines in the 1950s and 1960s were eventually abandoned because of their poor economic return. This was a time when fossil fuel was very inexpensive, and wind power could not compete. More recently, however, research on wind power has been very productive. The most promising design thus far has been a tornado-type wind turbine developed by Dr. James Yen. Yen's design does not involve any oversized propellers, but rather a large tower that will collect the wind currents and create a tornado effect when it is heated from below

(Kocivar 78–80). However, this innovative design has not yet been tested on a large scale because of insufficient funding.

ALTERNATIVE VIEWS: Opponents of large-scale use of wind power usually say that it is impractical. The initial cost of construction is high, and wind power loses out in the competitive market to the more conventional generating methods of today. However, if fuel prices increase once again, the utilization of alternative energy sources will look more inviting. Other arguments against wind power are that wind is not always available, and that a storage device would be necessary.

Proponents feel that wind power, if sufficiently funded, could meet a small but significant part of our energy needs before the end of the century. Once installed, a wind-powered electric generator is extremely cheap to operate, assuming that proper storage of the power is provided for. Yen's tornado turbine has been proven on a small scale to provide measurable electricity, and once it is scaled up he feels that its capital cost will be comparable to that of a big fossil-fuel plant.

WRITER'S
VIEW:

Wind is only one alternative to the energy problem, but its plentiful supply makes it very inviting. According to federal government estimates, the potential energy harnessable from the wind is thirty times that of current electrical power generation in the U.S. alone (Carrol 44). With this much energy available, it seems that some of it must be utilized. Wind-powered generators have proven effective in Europe on a much smaller scale than the U.S. would need to employ, but they still have proven economically feasible. What stands in the way now is lack of government funding. If wind power were aided to the same extent that nuclear power currently is, it would most definitely be contributing to the energy needs of the nation.

WORKS CITED

Carrol, Frank. "The Muzzled Wind." USA Today January
    1980: 43–45.

Inglis, David R. "The Answer Is Blowing in the Wind." The
    Progressive 41.1 (1977): 43–46.

Kocivar, Ben. "Tornado Turbine Reaps Power from a
    Whirlwind." Popular Science January 1977: 78–80.

1. Has the writer set forth clearly what the purpose of his paper will be? Has he defined key terms clearly?
2. Does the prospectus provide sufficient background about the problem so that it can be easily understood?
3. Does the prospectus adequately indicate and explain viewpoints on both sides of the question? Viewpoints contrary to the writer's?
4. Are there additional places in the paper where the writer should have cited a source to indicate an idea that was not his own?
5. On the basis of this prospectus, what is the likelihood that the student will compose a satisfying paper? What advice could you give the student about the direction he should go from here? What remains to be done? What other avenues of inquiry might he pursue?
6. Does the student's point of view about the problem differ enough from that of the "experts" he cites to provide a somewhat original perspective for the reader? To help the reader think about the problem in a new way?
7. As you read the student's outline and the final copy of his paper, try to determine the relationship between these final steps and the prospectus. When he wrote the prospectus, does it seem that he had already completed most of his work? How closely does the outline follow the organization of the prospectus? At what points in the final paper has he added to or significantly modified the material in the prospectus?
8. On the basis of your discoveries in answering question 7, would you say that the writing of the prospectus has been a valuable step for this student? Why or why not?

Writing the Research Paper

After Steve had finished the reading, notetaking, organizing, and outlining of his paper, he was ready to begin the actual writing. Through tempted to take a break from his work, Steve began writing a first draft immediately after finishing his prewriting; he knew that the fresher the ideas were in his mind, the more effective the paper would be. Steve's finished paper, which follows on p. 442, will help you see how he used his prospectus to organize his material. You will also see how he incorporated his research sources into the body of the paper.

TIPS FOR PREWRITING
THE LIBRARY RESEARCH PAPER

Before doing outside reading:

1. Refine the question or problem that is the focus of your research.

2. Record your initial ideas about the subject.

During your reading:

1. Restrict your notetaking to those ideas directly pertinent to your question.

2. Write a brief abstract of each source, evaluating its potential contribution to your understanding of the problem.

After completing your reading:

1. Categorize the sources according to their perspective on the question; note areas of agreement and disagreement, and synthesize the current thinking on the subject.

2. Add to your initial ideas any new ones that have developed during your reading.

3. Alter or revise your original ideas, if necessary, on the basis of your outside reading.

4. Write a prospectus of your paper; after receiving suggestions by your instructor and peers, do additional research if necessary.

Before writing your first draft:

1. Formulate and refine a precise statement of your thesis.

2. Determine what to include and what to omit from the material you have gathered.

3. Devise an appropriate pattern of organization to accommodate your material.

4. Decide how you can make best use of your secondary sources: As background on the problem? As a jumping-off point to introduce your own perspective? As support for your position on the question? As something to take issue with?

5. Consider what your conclusions will be, emphasizing especially original ideas that do not appear anywhere in the secondary material you consulted.

Energy: Is the Answer in the Wind?

by

Steven L. Primack

Freshman Composition II

Ms. Fitch

April 25, 1986

Outline

Thesis: Because of wind power's potential as an alternative energy source, the federal government should provide substantially increased funding for research and development, especially of Yen's tornado turbine design.

I. Introduction

    A. Overview of the problem

    B. Brief history of wind power in the U.S.

    C. Current expenditures on wind energy research

II. Wind turbine designs

    A. Yen's tornado turbine

        1. Description of process

        2. Advantages of design

    B. More traditional windmills

III. Arguments against dependence on wind power

    A. Low output

    B. Need for storage device for ''windless'' periods

    C. Interference with TV reception

    D. Noise disturbance

IV. Factors impeding progress in developing wind power potential

    A. Lack of research

    B. Utility companies' lack of cooperation

    C. Insufficient funding

V. Conclusion

Energy: Is the Answer in the Wind?

After the horse, ox, and himself, man's primary
mechanical energy source before the industrial
revolution was wind. It has a role to play again
("Harnessing the Wind" 38).

In recent years, a serious concern has arisen over
which alternative energy sources to use and in what
proportion. One of these possible sources, wind power, has
been studied in great detail and with many positive
results. Proponents of wind power point to the tremendous
long-range benefits of harnessing energy from the wind.
Opponents, on the other hand, argue that development of
this source of energy will take too long. As of today, the
government does not look upon wind energy as promising
enough to justify a level of funding sufficient for
ensuring large-scale research and development.

Wind energy as a potential source of power in the
United States got its first big boost in 1939 when a
turbine firm, the S. Morgan Smith Co. of Pennsylvania,
began constructing a megawatt-scale wind-powered electric
generator. By 1945 the firm had compiled ample data.
However, in the same year, when a part in the generator
failed that could not be easily replaced, the project was
aborted short of completion. It was decided that, compared
to the cost of hydroelectric power, wind-powered machines

were not economical (Inglis, "Answer" 44–45). Also, nuclear power as a major energy source for the future was getting its start, and the U.S. government decided to promote its development instead, with the result that wind power has been forced to take a backseat ever since. At present, the federal government spends "billions of dollars on nuclear energy . . . contrasted to the tens of millions spent on wind . . . energy" (Carrol 45). Furthermore, the majority of funds expended on wind energy today are not even spent on the best designs; most of the money has gone to develop the large propeller machines, but only because that model has been built most often in the past. So although research into wind power has been very productive of late, the soundest designs have been given only minimal funding.

The most promising model thus far is a tornado-type wind turbine tower designed by Dr. James Yen. Yen's design does not involve any oversized propellers; instead, a large tower collects the wind currents and creates a tornado effect by being heated from below. Energy is derived from the "tornados," and then electricity is produced from that energy (Kocivar 78–80).[1] This innovative design, however, has not yet been tested on a large scale because of insufficient funding. At full size, the turbine tower might be as large as 1800 feet high and 600 feet wide. The biggest model tested as of today is tiny by comparison—only 20-foot—yet it has operated very successfully.

According to Kocivar, Yen sees many practical and
economic advantages to his turbine over and above the
increased power supply:

> --Since the tower is stationary and
> omnidirectional, it can be made in large sizes of
> lightweight materials but still withstand strong
> winds. When the winds get too high, all the
> vanes can be opened to relieve structural
> loading.
>
> --Large towers mean large unit capacity. This
> reduces the cost of feeding power into utility
> grids.
>
> --The tower can be mass-produced in modules on
> assembly line and erected on location, perhaps by
> helicopters, reducing costs.
>
> --For energy storage, the vertical shaft could be
> coupled to a system of flywheels that would keep
> providing power when the wind slows or
> stops. . . .
>
> --Since the turbine would be close to the ground
> and in a protective shell, it would not create a
> safety hazard. The turbine's proximity to the
> ground would also make it easier to service (80).

Yet by far the biggest advantage of the tornado turbine is
the cost. To put Yen's turbine into operation would, by

Kocivar's calculation, involve a capital expenditure of "$65 to $500 per kilowatt" as opposed to around "$300 per kilowatt for big fossil-fuel plants" (80). Once in operation, though, the tornado turbine would obviously be less expensive as an energy source than a fossil-fuel operation.

Yen's tornado turbine has, it is true, many advantages over the more traditional windmill; yet updated old-fashioned windmills, if located in an ideal geography, can still be very effective. For example, in Boone, a small town in North Carolina, an electricity-generating windmill with two 100-foot blades can, under optimal conditions, generate 2000 kilowatts of power, which is a sufficient amount to serve about five hundred residential customers (Sheils and Buckley 66). Especially in regions where electrical power is extremely costly, wind power can be a most advantageous alternative. In these areas, small wind-power devices can easily be used economically by individual residents. An eight-kilowatt generator designed by Windworks, Inc., under a Department of Energy contract, is probably the finest small wind energy device. The estimated cost is anywhere from $10,000 to $15,000, but, as Lindsley writes, "in some areas of high-cost electrical power . . . and where suitable winds prevail, the wind generator might be cost effective after three to four years of operation" (84).[2] It would seem, then, that most designs for home use could be economical once the initial expenditure is covered.

Since, however, there are inherent limits to the maximum size of the blades on a windmill, Yen's design holds more promise than any of the other windmills designed so far. When windmill blades get too long, they tend to shake themselves to pieces. But without great length, the output of power from a windmill will obviously be limited. In contrast to traditional windmills, a tornado turbine should be able to compete nicely with the power plants that depend on fossil fuels.

The best location to look for wind power is obviously where the strongest winds blow, and so offshore wind power is an attractive possibility. Since "A floating unit would automatically face into the wind by riding on its mooring the way an anchored ship does" (Inglis, "Power" 20), having the windmill floating on the water solves one of the difficulties associated with land-based windmills. To study the feasibility of offshore wind power, a contract was awarded to one firm, Westinghouse--a company which, unfortunately, has a heavy investment in nuclear energy. Predictably, therefore, the report was largely negative. Yet because of this single study, offshore power has not been investigated or developed very seriously. As Inglis comments, if "two or more parallel studies" to the

Westinghouse one had been undertaken, perhaps the bias in favor of nuclear development could have been avoided and efforts in generating offshore wind power would be much further along than they are at the present time ("Power" 18).

Even with the many obvious advantages of the various wind-power machines, opponents of wind power point to some equally apparent drawbacks. One argument against the large-scale use of wind power questions its practicality. Most windmill-type wind turbines (not, however, Yen's tornado turbine design) are, granted, quite impractical insofar as output is concerned. As Inglis notes in a second article, it would require in excess of five hundred two-megawatt wind turbines, each having 200-foot blade spans, in order to generate the amount of energy produced by one of the monster fossil-fuel plants now in use ("Answer" 45).

Another argument against widespread use of wind power reminds us that wind is not consistently available, and storage devices would thus be essential in regions where winds are not strong. One solution to this problem would simply be to provide some type of backup system to produce energy when the wind is not sufficient. A possibly productive example of this can be found in Yen's tornado turbine; " 'by coating the walls of the tower [to] get energy through heat convection to the vortex,' " Yen would produce solar radiation as a substitute for extended periods of reduced wind (qtd. in Kocivar 80).

One difficulty that has already arisen with existing windmills is that television reception has been adversely affected in nearby areas. Because the frequency at which the wind turbines operate approximates that of television, interference is likely within a mile radius of the operating windmill. Since, however, having cable TV service can compensate for this, the problem of interference with television reception should be minimal (Torrey 13). In addition, complaints have been received about the disturbing noise from wind turbines already in operation. Although scientists have not yet found a way around this problem with the more traditional windmills, Yen believes that the towers of the tornado turbine-type structures could themselves be " 'soundproofed sufficiently to make them habitable' " (qtd. in Kocivar 80).

Along with these reasons put forth by opponents to wind power, Flavin suggests that a number of other facts and fears are impeding progress toward greater dependence on wind power as an alternative energy source. These include: (1) a lack of initiative in gathering the information necessary before long-range plans about wind utilization can be formulated; (2) a hesitancy on the part of utility companies to want the excess electricity produced by the wind fed into their power lines; (3) a severe lack of funding for research; and (4) a concern among environmentalists that wind turbines would use cropland and mar the scenic wilderness (36-40).

What most stands in the way of wind power research and development, however, is money. Most projects with wind turbines in the 1950s and 1960s were eventually abandoned because of their poor economic value. That was a time, of course, when fossil fuel was very inexpensive, and wind power simply could not compete. Throughout the 1970s, the lack of interest in wind power could be attributed to the initial cost of constructing a wind turbine, which was too high to compete with the more common generating methods. However, as fuel prices increased, the utilization of alternative rather than conventional energy sources began to look more inviting.

Government expenditures for wind power research have been increasing recently. In 1979, $60 million in Department of Energy funds went towards designing large wind generators; by 1981, the figure jumped to $80 million ("Written" 59). And the Wind Energy Systems Act passed in 1980 allocates $900 million over an eight-year period for developing windpower systems ("Harnessing" 38). This money must be spent wisely to ensure the greatest return on the taxpayers' dollars. As was pointed out earlier, however, most of the federal government's money for wind energy has

been spent on windmills——this despite the fact that most
experts working with wind power agree that the tornado
turbine system is potentially far superior to more
traditional windmill designs (Carrol 45).

Given sufficient funding——and assuming that these
funds are spent on the most promising designs——the most
optimistic proponents of wind power feel that it could
satisfy a substantial part of our energy requirements
"before the end of the century" (Inglis, "Answer" 45). The
summary paragraph of a mathematically based article in
Science states well the future value of wind power: "Wind
energy is seen to offer a potential far larger than many
other self-renewing energy sources" (Gustavson 13).

Wind is only one alternative answer to the energy
problem, but it is in plentiful supply, which makes it very
inviting. "According to Federal government wind power
publications," writes Carrol, "the wind energy harnessable
in the U.S. alone, at low altitudes, is 30 times greater
than present electrical power generation" (44). With this
much energy potentially available, some of it certainly
should be utilized. Wind-powered generators have proven
effective in Europe on a smaller scale than what the U.S.
would need to employ, but they still have proven
economically feasible.

Wind power may not single-handedly be able to solve
our present and future energy problems, but any additional

source such as wind needs to be tapped. As we have seen, wind power has disadvantages, but as other energy sources become either more expensive or more open to opposition on environmental and/or safety grounds, the advantages of energy from the wind may well outweigh the possible drawbacks. What now stands in the way is the lack of adequate government funding. If wind power were funded like other energy sources, such as nuclear power, it would most definitely contribute substantially to the energy needs of the nation. Flavin states the challenge as well as anyone has:

> In fact, wind energy has so much potential that a small amount of government support over the next several years might yield a vibrant and self-sufficient industry that could continue the effort on its own. Failing to continue government support right now would be like stopping work on a major bridge when it is only a few meters short of completion. Governments that limit their research funds to the most undeveloped and problematic technologies will miss the opportunity to provide a final push to wind power and to other renewable energy sources that could make a substantial contribution in the next two decades (46).

Considering the potential of wind power for the future, it seems inevitable that governments will rise to this challenge. In ongoing research and development, Yen's design, since it is the most workable of the wind turbines, should be given the most attention. In general, everyone needs to remember, as Carrol has remarked, that "The fuel bill for wind power is zero and wind never gets used up—there is always more. . . . It needs only to be actively promoted to provide the means to overcome our dependence on oil and OPEC" (45).

NOTES

[1]For diagrams of Yen's tornado turbine system, see Kocivar (78, 80).

[2]Not all estimates are this optimistic. According to an article in Time, "in windy regions where electricity costs are high, a standard $5,000 home windmill . . . ought to be able to pay for itself in perhaps ten years" ("Written" 59).

WORKS CITED

Carrol, Frank. "The Muzzled Wind." USA Today January
    1980: 43–45.

Flavin, Christopher. Wind Power: A Turning Point.
    Worldwatch Paper 45. Washington, D.C.: Worldwatch
    Institute, July 1981.

Gustavson, M. R. "Limits to Wind Power Utilization."
    Science 204.4388 (1979): 13–15.

"Harnessing the Wind." National Geographic (Special Energy
    Issue) February 1981: 38.

Inglis, David R. "The Answer Is Blowing in the Wind." The
    Progressive 41.1 (1977): 43–46.

_____. "Power from the Ocean Winds." Environment
    20.8 (1978): 17–20.

Kocivar, Ben. "Tornado Turbine Reaps Power from a
    Whirlwind." Popular Science January 1977: 78–80.

Lindsley, E. F. "Advanced Design Puts New Twists in
    Windmill Generator." Popular Science October 1979:
    84.

Sheils, Merrill and Jerry Buckley. "Welcome to 'The
    Monster.'" Newsweek 23 July 1979: 66.

Torrey, Volta. "Blowing Up More Kilowatts from Wind."
    Technology Review 82.4 (1980): 12–13.

"Written on the Wind." Time 21 July 1980: 59.

1. The title the student chose for his paper is a good one, not least because it alludes to a folk song popularized in the 1960s. But you may have noticed that it is a rephrasing of the title of Inglis's 1977 article. Should it have been footnoted? Why or why not?
2. Consider the epigraph the student has chosen for his paper; does it give away too much of the student's position too soon? Why or why not?
3. Is the student's description of Yen's design on pages 2 and 3 and the process by which the tornado turbine generates energy clear to you as a nonspecialist? Should it have been described at greater length? Should a drawing have been included rather than just the source for a drawing, as mentioned in note 1?
4. On page 3, the student quotes a long passage from Kocivar's article about the advantages of Yen's design. Would it have been better to summarize this material, or to omit some of it by using more ellipsis marks as the student did with the quotation on page 2?
5. How successfully does the student answer the arguments of those against large-scale development of windpower on pages 6 and 7?
6. On page 7, the student summarizes several things that Flavin says are impeding windpower research. Should he have added his own response to Flavin's position? What is implied by the student's not commenting?
7. What arguments does the student put forth to support his position that the federal government should greatly increase its funding of research into wind energy? Are they sufficient to convince you?
8. Comment on the student's strategy of including the long quotation from Flavin as part of his conclusion. Would it have been preferable for him to conclude with his own words rather than someone else's? Why or why not?
9. In general, has the student achieved a proper balance between summary and quotation of the opinions of others and his own ideas? Has he always made it perfectly clear, through adequate and correct documentation, which ideas are his own and which are not?
10. Why do you think the student chose to include the information within explanatory footnote 2 rather than place it in the text of the paper? Is this a defensible strategy?

ALTERNATIVE METHODS OF DOCUMENTATION

Some academic disciplines, as well as some instructors, may require you to use a documentation system different from the one that Steve employed in his paper on wind energy. Together with the MLA system, the following two alternative methods—the APA and the standard footnote/endnote forms—should equip you to handle most of your research assignments.

APA Parenthetical Citations

Several fields, particularly those in the social sciences such as psychology, sociology, and political science, employ the documentation method set forth in the *Publication Manual of the American Psychological Association* (APA). As with the MLA parenthetical method, with the APA system the reader need not look at the bottom of the page or the back of the paper to find the source for the writer's information or ideas. Instead, "shorthand" references to the essential information—author's last name, date of publication, and page number—appear directly in the text. Because those involved in scientific research must depend on the most up-to-date data in their investigations, in APA citations—as well as in bibliographical references—the date is given a position of preeminence. Notice also that the page number is preceded by either "p." or "pp." for "page" or "pages," respectively:

> Inglis (1977) chides the labor unions for supporting nuclear
> energy rather than recognizing "the potential for employment
> in this new, low-technology labor-intensive industry" (p. 46).

With the name/date/page citation format, the writer can choose to incorporate either or both of the first two items within the body of the sentence itself, so that only the page reference need be placed in parentheses at the end. Where more than one work by the same author is cited, a short version of the specific title is included within the parenthetical reference. At the end of each paper, the reader finds a list headed "References," including *only* the sources actually cited, that gives full bibliographical information for each item.

APA Bibliographical Citations

Although the general order of the list of "References" remains alphabetical, as it does on the MLA "Works Cited" page, if there are two or more works by the same author, these are arranged in chronological order. So that you will readily see the difference between bibliographical citations using the APA system and those employing the MLA method, we are giving correct APA citations for the same works we used earlier in this chapter. You will notice some major differences, particularly in the handling of the author's name and the system of capitalization.

To write a bibliographical reference to a *book* using the APA form, provide:

the author's name, last name first, with initial(s), the period serving as the stop;

the date within parentheses, followed by a period;

the title of the book as it appears on the title page, underlined with only the first word and proper nouns capitalized, followed by a period;

the publishing information: city, followed by a colon, and then the publisher, using shortened form, followed by a period.

Note that each line after the first is indented two spaces. Here is a sample:

```
Rhode, E.  (1976).  A history of the cinema from its origins
    to 1970.  New York:  Hill & Wang.
```

If there is a volume number or edition number, that information is placed within parentheses immediately after the title and before the period.

A reference to an *article* published in a scholarly journal takes this form under the APA system:

the author's name, last first, followed by initial;

the date within parentheses, followed by a period;

the title of the article, *without* quotation marks and with only the initial word and proper nouns capitalized, followed by a period;

the name of the journal, underlined, followed by a comma;

the volume number, underlined, followed by a comma, and the inclusive pages, with a period after. Here is an example:

```
Burkman, K. H.  (1983).  Hirst as Godot:  Pinter in Beckett's
    land.  Arizona Quarterly, 1983, 39, 5–14.
```

The following list provides samples of the most often used bibliographical references, in the proper APA form; again, compare these with the corresponding MLA form.

For an essay or a chapter in a book:

```
Staples, R.  (1981).  Research in the black male:  a resource
    for change.  In R. A. Lewis (Ed.), Men in difficult times.
    Englewood-Cliffs, N.J.:  Prentice-Hall.
```

For a monograph or pamphlet:

Bigsby, C. W. E. (1976). Tom Stoppard (Writers & Their Work 250). London: Longman.

For an encyclopedia entry:

Pierce, J. E. (1982). Satellite communication. Encyclopaedia Britannica.

For an article in a monthly magazine:

Awiakta, M. (1983, July). What is the atom, Mother? Will it hurt us? Ms., pp. 44–48.

For an article (anonymous) in a weekly magazine:

The manufacture of Marilyn. (1983, January 24). Time, p. 77.

For a newspaper article:

Eckhouse, J. (1983, June 19). Latest computer buzzword? Ergonomics. San Francisco Examiner, Sec. D., p. 1, cols. 2–5 & p. 9, cols. 1–4.

For a newspaper editorial:

The fear of AIDS (editorial). (1983, June 25). New York Times, p. 22, cols. 1–2.

For a book review:

Clemons, W. (1982, February 22). Rev. of Clare Boothe Luce by Wilfrid Sheed. Newsweek, p. 74.

For a film review:

Kael, P. (1983, June 13). Rev. of Fanny and Alexander directed by Ingmar Bergman. New Yorker, pp. 117–121.

For an interview:

Cranston, A. (1984, June 9). Personal interview.

The following student paper demonstrates the APA documentation form in use.

Exercise: The New—Old Answer to Mental Wellness

by

Becky Burton

Freshman Composition II

Mrs. Altschaeffl

January 23, 1985

Exercise: The New-Old Answer to Mental Wellness

Walking to and from classes, I pass an average of twenty-five joggers per day. The running tracks on campus are always crowded. Early last month, I looked into an aerobic dance class and found an entire gymnasium so packed with people jumping up and down to the beat of Neil Diamond that I could not even see the instructor. However, when I took physical education back in high school (long before this fitness craze began), we figured out how to reduce our laps to one half the assigned number without the teacher noticing. Why is there now this widespread interest in physical fitness? The answer: Because exercise, along with helping us stay comfortable in our "Calvin's" jeans, has beneficial effects on our mental well-being. Psychiatrists are even beginning to use exercise programs in the treatment of mental depression (Wallis, Galvin & Thompson, 1983).

In researching the benefits of physical fitness, I discovered that nearly every advocate of regular exercise refers to physical health and, in the same breath, comments on what it accomplishes mentally. Kathryn Lance (1977), author of Running for Health and Beauty, started running regularly when she was twenty-nine years old. By the time she had been running a year, she had lost ten pounds without dieting, had stopped smoking, and was in excellent physical shape. She also states, "My disposition was far better. I no longer flew off the handle at little things (well, hardly ever). I was much less nervous. After a hard day of working at my desk, I would go to the Y, start running, and feel the tension melt away from my neck and shoulders" (p. 5). James Fixx (1977), a marathon runner and well-known editor and author, after traveling the countryside and talking with different runners, generalized: "Everyone, it seemed, was secretly interested in—in a surprising number of cases obsessed by—what goes on in runners' minds and how the sport changes people" (pp. 13-14). He then talks about the psychology of running and how different people have described their changed mental states to him. Why does exercise affect one mentally, and why is this phenomenon suddenly becoming noticed?

For many athletes, the connection between physical fitness and mental well-being is not a new idea; they have known for centuries that exercise is an important part of a well-rounded life. The Greeks, for example, put great emphasis on maintaining the body's condition. Even the word "recreation" suggests these benefits: re-creation. Until recently, many of us, however, have been caught up in a world without personal exercise, and recreation has consisted largely in watching others participate in sports. When stress rears its persistent head, we can take tranquilizers, turn to smoking or alcohol, or even ignore

it—for a while. But these methods have never been
adequate solutions, because of their harmful side effects.
We are becoming a generation interested in helping
ourselves. The bookstores are filled with books telling us
how to become better organized, how to be better parents,
and so on. And in our quest to overcome tension, stress,
and mental depression, we are rediscovering the age-old
answer: physical fitness. Even some large corporations
are seeing the positive effects of exercise for their
tension-riddled executives and are installing fitness
centers in their corporate offices (Wallis, Galvin &
Thompson, p. 54).

But why does exercise benefit us mentally as well as
physically? It is easy to understand why our thighs become
thinner, our heart stronger, and our endurance greater,
since the muscles controlling those areas are exercised.
Would it not seem logical, then, that the thing most
beneficial to our mental condition would be intellectual
exercise?

On the contrary, the brain is also an organ which
depends on certain physiological processes. As Tom
Griffin, M.D. (1982), reminds us concerning the brain,
" 'While it's only 2% of the body's mass, it requires 20%
of the body's oxygen . . . the nerve cells in the brain are
actually using 100 times more oxygen than the average cell
in the rest of the body' " (cited in Mazer, p. 62). The

brain does not receive this oxygen when we are continually sedentary, but only when our heart is pumping blood to the brain and supplying it with the necessary amount of oxygen.

In addition to the oxygen that the brain requires in order to function properly, other changes occur in the brain during physical exercise that are directly related to our mental state. Professors Ismail and Trachtman (1973) at Purdue University conducted extensive research on the effects of exercise upon personality. The mental changes that occurred among the subjects of the experiments during a rigorously controlled and monitored program of exercise were attributed to two factors—one of which I will discuss here and the other later in this paper. The first, or physiological factor, was the increase in the level of "glucose essential to the brain's nutrition" (p. 82). In addition, as Fellman (1981) reports, a number of chemicals called neurotransmitters, such as adrenaline, norepinephrine, serotonin and the endorphins, are essential in bridging the gaps between the nerve cells in the brain; anxiety can disturb these substances and create depression. In particular, it was found that levels of MHPG, a breakdown product of the neurotransmitter, are low in people suffering from depression, and that exercise can cause these levels to rise (p. 70). Furthermore, exercise raises serotonin levels, which are normally low in depressed persons, and it provides a natural release for adrenaline, whereas inactivity prohibits release of the secretion. Fellman cites the conclusion of Jerome Mammorstein, M.D., that " 'Exercise is a balance factor. It promotes conservation of energy and an overall reduction in chronic anxiety. You feel better mentally and experience a sense of emotional wellbeing' " (p. 73).

The last of the above-mentioned chemicals are the endorphins. No one seems to be making hard and fast rules regarding them, as their properties, particularly as natural pain blockers, are still being studied. In research carried out at the New Mexico Health Enhancement and Marathon Clinics Research Center in Albuquerque, N.M., fifteen runners of a 28.5 mile race were tested for betaendorphin levels before and after their running. A 100% increase in the level of the natural painkiller occurred, and the higher level remained in effect for three or more hours. Since novice runners experienced a greater change than veterans, it would seem that endurance training over an extended period stabilizes this substance—which may be responsible for the legendary " 'runner's high' "— within the body (Appenzeller, 1981, p. 13).

Another hormone whose level was significantly lower in depressed persons, catecholamine, was studied by this same group, and it was noted that levels increased 300% above baseline after seven miles into the race and 600% above by the end. The level did not remain elevated for more than one hour, however, and further studies regarding this change are still underway (p. 13).

The physiological effects of exercise upon the brain are, therefore, very real and important. Equally important is the psychological effect. Kathryn Lance's tension really melted away--through the release of adrenaline secretions--but what about the psychological effect she noticed after her physical activity?

The personality study on participants in the fitness program at Purdue concluded that men became more imaginative, more self-sufficient, and more emotionally stable by the end of the program. Ismail and Trachtman attribute some of the change to a second group of factors, this one psychological rather than physiological in nature: "a man confronts a psychologically difficult challenge and overcomes it." They conclude: "In confirming what exercise enthusiasts have claimed for thousands of years-- that physical activity can change the state of one's mind-- we have established a fact that is more important than the value of exercise. . . . The adult personality may be much more plastic than we thought" (p. 82).

Physical exercise not only produces immediate effects on the mind; it also provides us with long-term benefits. Studies at San Diego State University by David E. Sherwood and Dennis E. Selder (1979) concluded during tests on 32 runners and 32 non-runners between the ages of 24 and 59 that physical activity "might well help ward off decreased mental sharpness that tends to come with aging" (Health advantages of physical fitness, p. 214).

In addition to the obvious physical advantages that occur when we foresake a sedentary lifestyle, we increase our brain's ability to function, become psychologically healthier, are better able to handle stress, and keep our mind sharper later in life. Therefore, the next time you see individuals pounding the pavement in the pouring rain, don't assume that the vanity of a lithe body is their driving force. Most of their motivation, whether they know it or not, may be in their head.

References

Appenzeller, O. (1981, April). Does running affect mood? *Runner's World*, p. 13.

Fellman, B. (1981, May). Exercise your way to happiness. *Prevention*, pp. 68–73.

Fixx, J. F. (1977). *The complete book of running*. New York: Random House.

Health advantages of physical fitness. (1979, September 8). *Science News*, p. 214.

Ismail, A. H. and Trachtman, L. E. (1973, March). Jogging the imagination. *Psychology Today*, pp. 78–82.

Lance, K. (1977). *Running for health and beauty*. New York: Bobbs-Merrill.

Mazer, E. (1982, June). Feeling better all over. *Prevention*, pp. 59–64.

Wallis, C., Galvin, R. M. and Thompson, D. (1983, June 6). Stress: Can we cope? *Time*, pp. 48–54.

1. Should the writer have cited a source for her information about the Greeks and physical exercise on page 2? Why or why not?

2. Comment on the unity and coherence of the paragraph which begins at the bottom of page 2. Why does the writer introduce at this point her comment about self-help books and their popularity?

3. Point out the transitional devices—especially transitional paragraphs—that the writer employs throughout her paper, and assess their effectiveness.

4. On pages 4 and 5, the writer includes a good deal of scientific terminology and data. How well has she handled this material for nonspecialist readers? (Examine, for example, the methods she has used for defining her terms.)

5. Parts of this paper are written in an informal, anecdotal style, while other sections display a more objective, scientific tone. How well has the writer meshed her two styles into a pleasing whole?

Standard Footnote or Endnote Forms

Some disciplines in the humanities, such as history, philosophy, theology, and the fine arts, do not use either the MLA or APA systems of parenthetical citation. Instead of those simplified procedures for including name, page, and date references internally, they employ a system of *footnotes* or *endnotes* that you may be familiar with from high school. With this method, the notes for each page either appear at the bottom of the page (footnotes) or are grouped together at the end of the paper (endnotes), and are numbered consecutively. Because footnotes or endnotes contain complete information about each source, there is no need to append a Selected Bibliography to your paper—unless the instructor specifies otherwise. If you master the two basic forms for a citation to a book and to an article, then you should have no trouble writing correct notes for any reference.

The information in a footnote or endnote provides the name of the author, the title of the book or article, details about publication, and, most often, a reference to the specific pages cited. For a *book* you:

indent five spaces;

raise the note number a half-space;

give the author's name in normal order, followed by a comma;

give the title of the book, underlined;

follow this by a parenthesis which includes the city of publication, a colon; the name of the publishing company, a comma; and the date of publication;

end with a comma after the parentheses, followed by the page number and a period.

Any line after the first is not indented. Here is an example:

> [1]Eric Rhode, A History of the Cinema from Its Origins to 1970 (New York: Hill and Wang, 1976), p. 387.

The basic reference form for an *article* appearing in a periodical provides, after indenting and raising the note number:

the author's name in normal order, followed by a comma;

the title of the article in quotation marks, followed by a comma;

the name of the journal, underlined, followed by a comma;

the volume number, followed by the date within parentheses;

a comma after the parentheses, and then the page number without the "p." followed by a period.

Here is a sample:

> [2]Katherine H. Burkman, "Hirst as Godot: Pinter in Beckett's Land," Arizona Quarterly, 39 (Spring, 1983), 13–14.

Modifications of basic note forms.   These two basic forms are subject to modification in a number of minor ways as the situation demands:

If there is no author, begin with the title.

If there are two or three authors, give the full names of each; if there are four or more authors, give the full name of only the first, followed by "et al." as in the following examples:

> [3]Dick Cavett and Christopher Porterfield, Cavett (New York: Harcourt Brace Jovanovich, 1974), p. 115.
> [4]Robert E. Spiller et al., Literary History of the United States, 4th ed. rev. (New York: Macmillan, 1974), p. 1326.

If the book has been either translated or edited, provide the name of the translator, preceded by the abbreviation "trans.," or the name of the editor, preceded by "ed.," after the title, as in the following:

> [5]Wolfgang Hildesheimer, Mozart, trans. Marion Faber (New York: Farrar Straus Giroux, 1982), p. 227.

If the book is part of a multi-volume set or an edition after the first, provide that information (e.g. Vol. II or 2nd ed.) after the title, as in the following:

```
⁶Edward Nehls, ed., D. H. Lawrence:  A Composite
Biography, Vol. 1 (Madison:  Univ. of Wisconsin Press, 1957),
p. 11.
```

After the first citation of a book or article, it is unnecessary to repeat the full bibliographical information; the most common form for second and succeeding references is simply the last name of the author, followed by the page number, as in the following:

```
⁷Rhode, p. 526.
⁸Burkman, 5.
```

Furthermore, in instances where you will be referring repeatedly throughout your paper to one or two primary sources—as you will when writing a critical analysis of a primary work—you need give the full reference only in the first citation to the work; at subsequent points, place just the specific page reference in parentheses after the quotation. Your first citation of the work would take the following form:

```
⁹John Stuart Mill, The Subjection of Women, in Essays on
Sex Equality by John Stuart Mill and Harriet Taylor Mill, ed.
Alice Rossi (Chicago:  Univ. of Chicago Press, 1970), p. 239.
Further references to this edition appear within parentheses
in the text.
```

Frequently used standard note forms.   In addition to the preceding examples, the following notations provide examples of the standard footnote or endnote forms that occur most often. So that you can see the difference between the format of a note and a bibliographical reference, these examples correspond to the ones provided for frequently used MLA bibliography forms.

For an essay or a chapter in a book:

```
¹Robert Staples, "Research on the Black Male:  A Resource
for Change," in Men in Difficult Times, ed. Robert A. Lewis
(Englewood Cliffs, N.J.:  Prentice-Hall, Inc., 1981), p. 276.
```

For a monograph or pamphlet:

```
²C. W. E. Bigsby, Tom Stoppard, Writers & Their Work 250
(London:  Longman Group Ltd., 1976), p. 27.
```

For an encyclopedia entry:

    [3]John R. Pierce, "Satellite Comunication," Encyclopaedia Britannica, 1982 ed.

For an article in a monthly magazine:

    [4]Marilou Awiakta, "What is the Atom, Mother? Will it Hurt Us?" Ms., July 1983, p. 47.

For an anonymous article in a weekly magazine:

    [5]"The Manufacture of Marilyn," Time, 24 Jan. 1983, p. 77.

For a newspaper article:

    [6]John Eckhouse, "Latest Computer Buzzword? Ergonomics," San Francisco Examiner, 19 June 1983, Sec. D, p. 9.

For a newspaper editorial:

    [7]"The Fear of AIDS," Editorial, New York Times, 25 June 1983, p. 22.

For a book review:

    [8]Walter Clemons, rev. of Clare Boothe Luce by Wilfrid Sheed, Newsweek, 22 Feb. 1982, p. 74.

For a film or theater review:

    [9]Pauline Kael, "Wrapping it Up," rev. of Fanny and Alexander dir. by Ingmar Bergman, The New Yorker, 13 June 1983, p. 119.

For an interview:

    [10]Personal interview with Senator Alan Cranston, Washington, D.C., 9 June 1982.

For an item in the *Congressional Record*:

    [11]Cong. Rec., 30 June 1982, S7739.

TIPS FOR EDITING THE RESEARCH PAPER

Content:

1. Is the most important idea of the paper my own? Have I used the ideas of others to supplement, rather than substitute for, my own?

2. Have I organized my material logically and coherently? Have I provided adequate transitions between and within paragraphs so that the ideas progress smoothly from one to the other?

3. Is there a reasonable balance between my own words and the quotations from or summary of the works of others? Have I quoted purposefully, or only for effect?

4. Are quotations from others smoothly integrated with my own ideas? Have I introduced the secondary material so that its relevance is explained or interpreted?

Documentation:

1. Have I documented my paper correctly? Have I always given credit when I have used the ideas of others?

2. Would it have helped to summarize more rather than quote directly from my sources? In what instances? Have I summarized skillfully?

Style:

1. Have I used standard English throughout?

2. Have I varied my sentence patterns? My word choice?

3. Have I given the paper an interesting and appropriate title?

5

MAKING CHOICES

A Handbook for Revising and Editing

A HANDBOOK FOR REVISING AND EDITING

Mary Berthold

INTRODUCTION

Whether you are editing your own work or the work of your peers, you are constantly making choices. At times the choice seems to be simply a matter of wrong or right—not really a choice at all. To correct a faulty construction, you add a semicolon or delete a comma, change a pronoun form or reposition a modifier. But these corrections may leave you dissatisfied: the semicolon inserted to avoid a comma splice creates too abrupt a pause in the sentence; deleting the comma weakens the phrase that follows it; the *whom* required by the rules of grammar sounds stilted. Of course, the solution is not to let the error stand. The rules of grammar, punctuation, and mechanics reflect the conventions of standard written English—the type of English most widely used by writers and most widely understood and accepted by readers. By disregarding these conventions, you not only distract your reader (who focuses on the error rather than on the content), but you create the impression that you are careless or uninformed. If you want your writing to receive serious attention, you must meet your reader's expectations by conforming to conventions.

Fortunately, the conventions of standard written English do allow some choices. Should you find yourself dissatisfied with the result of correcting an error, you need to switch from mere correction to editing in a broader sense—from simply fixing the obvious error to finding ways to make the sentence not only error-free but effective.

Several considerations might influence your choice. First of all, sometimes the rule is flexible. Some fragments and comma splices are allowable; some ordinarily extraneous commas may be inserted for good reason. Next, the audience and content might make a difference: *who* may be preferable to *whom* in an informal context even though it violates the pronoun-case rule; abbreviations and figures not allowed in general writing may be preferred in technical writing; slang may be appropriate in an informal paper, jargon in a technical one. Finally, and most important, there are always choices of the method you use to correct an error: you may always restructure a sentence or group of sentences rather than simply add or delete punctuation or change a form.

The following sections on **Grammar and Sentence Structure** and **Punctuation and Mechanics** give you the rules, but they also show that the rules permit a variety of options. And since English is such a flexible language, you will certainly discover even more options within convention than the ones offered here. The final section on **Sentence Effectiveness** condenses some of the material on effective stylistic choices that *The Writer's Choices* explores in detail. It reminds you that even an error-free sentence may need editing to be effective, and it presents the stylistic considerations you should bear in mind as you edit for grammar, punctuation, and mechanics.

GRAMMAR AND SENTENCE STRUCTURE

MAJOR SENTENCE ERRORS

When you punctuate two sentences as if they were one (creating a comma splice or fused sentence) or when you set off a dependent part of a sentence as a complete sentence (creating a sentence fragment), you not only confuse the reader but create the impression that you do not understand what a sentence is. Even in the poorest student essays, however, only a small number of sentences are spliced, fused, or fragmented. These problems usually occur with particular kinds of constructions.

If you frequently make major sentence errors, study the types of errors you make. Maybe your comma splices occur only with words like *however* and *therefore,* which you mistakenly use as connectives. Or you may write fragments only with present participles (*-ing* forms), which you confuse with verbs. If you are unsure about identifying major sentence parts, review Chapter 5, which explains the various modifying elements you must be able to distinguish from the main clause. Reading out loud will also help you determine where one sentence ends and another begins. Once you have cleared up any misunderstandings about dependent and independent sentence elements, study the following examples and exercises to see what choices you have for revision, making it your goal to construct sentences that are not only grammatically complete but effective as well.

Comma Splice

You create a comma splice when you join two independent clauses with a comma:

> These dogs measure twenty-three inches to twenty-five inches at the withers, therefore, their begging techniques are in keeping with their slightly smaller size.

> Hearing Spanish and Italian spoken on a New York City street is commonplace, in my neighborhood you can also hear Greek, Japanese, and Chinese.

> Some of Montessori's ideas have been adopted, many are still considered eccentric by the American parent and the American educator.

> If you find these films silly or foolish or predictable, you are probably right, great themes are not often treated in an animated cartoon.

Replacing the comma with a period will always correct the grammatical error but may not be the most effective revision. Usually you have spliced the sentences in the first place because you sensed that they were too closely connected to be separated by a period. To revise, examine the relationship between the clauses to determine whether one of the following revisions is more appropriate:

1. Replace the comma with a semicolon:

These dogs measure twenty-three inches to twenty-five inches at the withers; therefore, their begging techniques are in keeping with their slightly smaller size.

(This revision is the standard one when the second clause is introduced by a conjunctive adverb; see Semicolon, p. 520.)

2. Add the appropriate coordinating conjuction (*and, but, or, for, yet, so*) after the comma:

Hearing Spanish and Italian spoken on a New York City street is commonplace, *but* in my neighborhood you can also hear Greek, Japanese and Chinese.

3. Subordinate one of the clauses:

Though some of Montessori's ideas have been adopted, many are still considered eccentric by the American parent and the American educator.

4. Replace the comma with a colon:

If you find these films silly or foolish or predictable, you are probably right: great themes are not often treated in an animated cartoon.

(This revision is appropriate when the second clause elaborates upon or completes the first; see Colon, p. 522.)

Comma splices are acceptable when the clauses are short (especially if they are parallel) and contain no internal commas:

Some memories fade quickly, some remain vivid for years.

I've won, I'm the hero of the day.

YOU ARE THE EDITOR

Edit the following student sentences: substituting a semicolon, colon, or period for the comma; inserting a coordinating conjunction after the comma; or subordinating one of the independent clauses. Then choose the most effective revision. Place a check beside any sentence that needs no revision (either because it is not a comma splice or because it is an acceptable one).

1. Citizens throughout the town signed petitions, schoolchildren picketed the Board members' homes.

2. He lives out of town, otherwise he would have come.

3. Some people disagree with the law, they believe marijuana is safer than cigarettes, which are legal.

4. Rain delays of baseball games are common, there has never been a snow delay until today.

5. Newspapers not only convey information, they also influence public opinion.

6. Because they have heard horror stories about nursing homes, some couples are determined to keep their aging parents at home, however difficult it becomes to care for them.

7. Inside is the baby animal ward, here children can see eggs hatch and watch the baby monkeys feed.

8. For high-school players, football is recreation, for professionals, it's a job.

9. All automobiles are basically the same, they have four wheels and move people from one place to another.

10. He went to Europe a reactionary, he returned a dedicated Communist.

Fused Sentence

A fused sentence is a comma splice without the comma—two sentences run together with no punctuation between them:

Some of Montessori's ideas have been adopted many are still considered eccentric.

If you frequently run sentences together, you can usually detect the break between them by reading your essay aloud. The choices for revision are the same as those for the comma splice. Unlike the comma splice, however, a fused sentence is never justifiable except in creative stream-of-consciousness writing.

Choose the most effective method to correct each of the following fused sentences: insert a semicolon, colon, or period between the independent clauses; join the clauses with a coordinating conjunction; or subordinate one of the clauses.

1. The citizens of Athens could own property and engage in politics they numbered about 160,000.

2. Henry is wounded and sent to a hospital in Milan Catherine is a nurse there.

3. Science helps scholars in many fields art historians, for instance, can detect a forged painting through radiocarbon dating.

4. The role of women has changed therefore family life has changed.

5. Melville's first voyage was on a merchant ship bound for Liverpool next he shipped on a whaler to the archipelagoes of the South Seas.

6. Santiago is not defeated although the marlin is eaten by sharks the old man demonstrates his own skill and endurance.

7. The book was not a success readers were looking for a simple adventure story they got a moral allegory.

8. It was clear that thieves had entered the tomb for some reason they had taken none of the treasures buried there.

9. Almost all the products have to be shipped to the Islands consequently the cost of living is very high.

10. Mount St. Helens erupted on May 18 residents of Yakima were still shoveling ash from their sidewalks a week later.

Sentence Fragment

Punctuating a word, phrase, or dependent clause as a complete sentence creates a sentence fragment:

Eliot's play, though set in the Middle Ages, will still have meaning for audiences in the twenty-first century. *While many of today's television dramas, though set in more recent times, will not.* (Dependent clause introduced by subordinating conjunction *while*)

When questioned, Jackson lied repeatedly. *Saying, for instance, that he had never met Schooley.* (Verbal phrase)

Although the stories have many similarities, they also have marked differences. *Some of which have already been mentioned.* (Relative clause)

Wind power can be a most advantageous alternative. *Especially in regions where electrical power is costly.* (Prepositional phrase)

The counselors had to be able to deal quickly with emergencies. *Anything from a camper's broken ankle to a skunk in the latrine.* (Appositive)

As the examples show, unintentional fragments most often occur when a modifying element is detached from the end of a sentence. Although punctuating the modifier as a complete sentence seems to show a lack of "sentence sense" (understanding of what a sentence is), it may in fact demonstrate an excellent sense of where a sentence needs to *end*: the detached modifier could often make the sentence too long or awkward; or it could dilute the strength of an emphatic closing word or phrase, or blunt the sharpness of a brief, incisive sentence. When the modifier does belong at the end of the sentence, it may have been detached because it was awkwardly worded and did not seem to fit there. Thus, although most fragments (and all the preceding examples) would be complete, grammatically correct sentences if the periods were simply replaced by commas, other revisions may be more effective:

1. Make the fragment a complete sentence:

    Eliot's play, though set in the Middle Ages, will still have meaning for audiences in the twenty-first century. However, many of today's television dramas, though set in more recent times, will not.

    When questioned, Jackson lied repeatedly. He said, for instance, that he had never met Schooley.

2. Reword the fragment and make it a phrase or clause within the sentence:

    Although the stories have many similarities, they also have, as we have seen, marked differences.

3. Reverse the position of the elements when you reattach the fragment to the sentence, placing the most important element at the end:

    Especially in regions where electrical power is costly, wind power can be a most advantageous alternative.

4. If the modifier seems to belong at the end of the sentence, try rewording it
    so that it fits smoothly into the sentence:

    The counselors had to be able to deal quickly with emergencies ranging from a
    camper's broken ankle to a skunk in the latrine.

Sometimes fragments are used intentionally for stylistic effect:

Exclamations

Just what I needed!

Questions and Answers

The problem this time? A sex-change operation.

Certain Transitions

So much for the causes. Now to the effects.

To return to the reasons for this policy.

First, the strong and silents.

Descriptive Details, Thoughts, or Feelings Set Down Impressionistically

Goldfinches arrived. A mad twittering like a zoo full of canaries. Invisible.
—Josephine Johnson, "April"

I used to ride Coke High only about five miles every morning when we were
rounding up horses. Hard miles of twisting and turning. About six hundred
miles a year.
—Barry Lopez, "My Horse"

Words and Phrases Set Off for Special Emphasis

The law saves gas. *And* lives.
—Robert Penske, "Fifty-five Is Fast Enough," *Reader's Digest*

Attica. San Quentin. All major penitentiaries. All potential threats to the
communities that surround them.

Suddenly, I felt myself sinking and then I knew. Quicksand.

YOU ARE THE EDITOR

The following excerpt from a student essay has been repunctuated so that it contains many sentence fragments. Edit the essay to eliminate the ineffective fragments. Be prepared to justify any fragments you retain.

Practicality was never our strong point. When it came to buying our first house, Bob and I were a realtor's dream. Easily led past a broken furnace to a leaded window. Or distracted from a leaking roof by a tree in bloom. Our eyes were blind to dry rot. But could focus miraculously on the pristine oak beneath ten layers of paint.

Our first house, of course, was full of charm. And possibilities. And age. It introduced itself to us in a never-ending series of revelations, always surprising and seldom pleasant. In the way of old houses. The furnace was the Rolls Royce of furnaces. As the realtor had assured us. The 1920 model, however. The sewer backed up twice in the first week. After that, twice a month. The downstairs toilet acquired an ever-renewable ring of sludge around the bottom. A bulge appeared in the ceiling. Alarmingly shaped like the bathtub directly above it. The kitchen linoleum began to come up in large hunks, leaving gooey black holes. After drinking gallons of wax without the hint of a shine. The refrigerator vibrated eerily in the

```
night.  Liquifying the ice cream and freezing the

eggs.  The woodwork was solid paint.  So far as

we could discover.  We got through the white,

beige, pink, and yellow layers; then we gave up.

When we hit green.  Somewhere below, there may

lurk genuine oak, but we won't be the ones to

find it.

    We decided to move.

    This time, we told ourselves, we'd be

ruthlessly practical.  No more houses with

"possibilities."  No more trade-offs of

essentials for charm.  The new house would have a

modern kitchen.  Also faultless plumbing.  Walls,

floors, paint and trim would be in perfect,

easily maintained condition.  No more handyman's

specials for us.  We'd been through that.  We

knew what we wanted.  A streamlined, practical

house.
```

AGREEMENT OF SUBJECT AND VERB

Singular subjects take singular verbs; plural subjects take plural verbs. This seemingly simple rule becomes complicated when you are not sure whether certain kinds of subjects are plural or singular. The following cases will help you determine the correct verb for a particular subject.

1. Compound subjects joined by *and*

   Verbs of singular or plural subjects joined by *and, both . . . and,* and *not only . . . but* are plural:

   > Unemployment and high inflation *have* changed consumers' spending habits.

   > Not only the wife but also the husband *take* care of the children.

Exception. If the compound subject is considered a single unit, use a singular verb:

Spaghetti and meatballs *was* his favorite meal.

Note. Phrases like *as well as, in addition to, along with,* and *together with* modify the subject; they do not compound it:

The *choice* of colors and patterns together with the weaver's skill *makes* this blanket a work of art.

As this example shows, you must be careful that other modifiers containing plural nouns (like *colors* and *patterns*) do not lead you to give a singular subject a plural verb.

2. Compound subjects joined by *or*

Verbs of subjects joined by *or, either . . . or,* and *neither . . . nor* agree with the subject closest to the verb:

His brothers or *he has* captured the title in the last six tournaments.

When the first subject is plural and the second singular, or when the two subjects are different persons requiring different forms *(I am, you are)*, you can rewrite to reduce the awkwardness:

He or his *brothers have* captured the title . . .

In the last six tournaments, either his *brothers have* captured the title, or *he has.*

3. *There is/are* structures and other inverted structures

The subject, which in this case comes after the verb, determines the form of the verb:

First came Lucy and Ethel; later there *were* Mary and Rhoda.

Inside *live* an old woman and fifty pet Pomeranians.

4. Noun clause as subject

The verb is singular:

What startled the children *was* the dogs.

5. Collective noun as subject

When the subject is a noun singular in form that refers to a group of people *(family, committee, board, jury)*, the verb is singular if the group is considered as a unit, plural if the group is considered as individuals:

The class *has* raised four thousand dollars for *its* class gift.

The class *were* ready to receive *their* diplomas. (In the latter case, adding the word *members* reduces awkwardness.)

6. Relative pronoun as subject

    Who, which, and *that* agree with their antecedents:

    He is the *man who releases* the balloons when the Brewers score a home run.

    He is one of the *men who release* the balloons . . .

    Exception.   When *only* comes before *one,* the verb following the relative pronoun is singular:

    He is the *only one* of the players *who* consistently *scores* over fifteen points a game. (Consider simplifying such structures: He is the *only player* who . . .)

7. Indefinite pronoun as subject

    Each, either, neither, and those pronouns ending in *-body, -one,* and *-thing (anybody, someone, everything)* are singular:

    Each of these wound-types *is* dangerous.

    All, any, some, and *none* are singular or plural depending on the number of the nouns they refer to:

    All of the *tickets are* gone.

    Some of the *sugar is* gone.

    Exception.   *None* is occasionally singular with a plural noun. In such cases, the context indicates what choice to make:

    None of the students *was* willing to be *the first* to burn *his* draft card.

    Note.   Eliminating "of" after the indefinite pronoun not only helps you avoid confusion over singular and plural but also gives you a more concise statement:

    Each wound-type is dangerous.

    All the tickets are gone.

    Some sugar is gone.

    No student was willing . . .

    Nouns referring to amounts *(percentage, number, majority)* are singular or plural on the same principle as *all, any,* and *some:*

A certain *number* of *drivers* always *exceed* the speed limit.

A high *percentage* of the American *diet consists* of empty calories.

YOU ARE THE EDITOR

Edit the following student sentences to correct disagreement between subjects and verbs. Place a check in front of any sentence that is correct. After you have corrected the verb form, rephrase the sentence if necessary to eliminate awkwardness or wordiness.

1. Green Bay is one of the cities that was considered for the award.

2. At the foot of the garden are a small pool and a gazebo.

3. A combination of logical arguments and emotional appeals are used to attract the prospective buyer.

4. The mother's life in addition to the child's were in danger.

5. He thought that neither the test grades nor the final exam were fair.

6. What bothered him most was the noisy parties held next door.

7. If you think that either of these statements reflect my opinion, you are wrong.

8. Jeff is the only one of the players who have been injured this season.

9. A majority of students fail the exam each year.

10. The committee are dining at home before meeting at the Village Hall.

PRONOUNS

Pronoun Agreement

Make sure your pronouns agree in person and number with the nouns to which they refer. In general, noun and pronoun antecedents that require a singular verb also require a singular pronoun form. The rules for number of compound subjects, collective nouns, and indefinite pronouns (Agreement of Subject and Verb, p. 486) will answer most of your questions about pronoun agreement. In speech and informal writing, plural pronouns (but not plural verbs) are often used with *everybody, everyone, anybody,* and *anyone.*

The following versions of the same sentence illustrate the kinds of problems you might encounter with pronoun agreement:

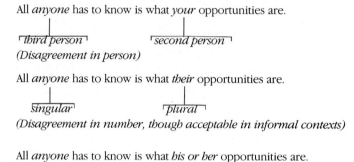

All *anyone* has to know is what *your* opportunities are.

┌third person┐   ┌second person┐
(Disagreement in person)

All *anyone* has to know is what *their* opportunities are.

┌singular┐   ┌plural┐
(Disagreement in number, though acceptable in informal contexts)

All *anyone* has to know is what *his or her* opportunities are.
(Grammatically correct, but awkward)

All *anyone* has to know is what *his* opportunities are.
(Grammatically correct, but unacceptable to some readers)

Although masculine pronouns have traditionally been used generically—to refer to any human being, male or female—today many readers consider it inappropriate to refer to both men and women with a masculine form. The awkward alternatives—*he or she, his or her*—can frequently be avoided if the antecedent is changed to a plural form:

All that *people* have to know is what *their* opportunities are.

In informal writing, the *you* form solves the problem:

All *you* have to know is what *your* opportunities are.

YOU ARE THE EDITOR

Edit the following student sentences so that each pronoun agrees in person and number with its antecedent noun. When you come across a masculine pronoun that is used generically, try to eliminate the reference to gender. Where relevant, indicate both the informal and formal forms. Place a check in front of any sentence that needs no revision.

1. The teacher asked everyone to pick up their books and leave the room.

2. Each of the hospitals must meet the needs of the community it serves.

3. Only some of the group had started their projects.

4. Anybody who has been through registration at a large school remembers all the hassles you went through.

5. What's wrong with a parent's sending their child to a school that teaches them religion?

6. Serve the party at table nine its salads.

7. The class looked forward to receiving its diplomas.

8. Every restaurant seemed to have their own seafood specialty.

9. A doctor who spends time with his patients is hard to find.

10. Management submitted its proposal to the union.

Pronoun Case

Most personal and relative pronouns take one form when they are used as subjects (*I, he, she, we, they, who*), another when they are used as objects (*me, him, her, us, them, whom*), still another when they are used as possessive modifiers (*my, your, his,* etc.). You will probably have trouble with the case of pronouns in only a few situations:

1. Compound subjects and objects

Check to see if you have the right form by omitting one item from the pair:

> One time, [Brent and] *I* trapped a bumblebee in a foil-lined Kool-Aid package; then we argued over whether it belonged to [him or] *me.*

2. Pronouns acting as, or modified by, appositives (nouns or pronouns that identify other nouns or pronouns)

Check the form by omitting the other noun or pronoun:

> *We* [students] need a representative. No one speaks for *us* [students].
>
> We don't think alike, Sue and *I. (Sue and* I *don't think alike.)*

You may discover that the sentence is more economical and effective if the appositive or the word it modifies is eliminated.

3. Pronouns used as complements of the verb *to be*

In formal writing, the subjective case is called for:

> Who was calling? It was *she. (formal)* It was *her. (informal)*

But "She was," a more natural and economical choice, would be appropriate in either kind of writing. In many cases you can check to see whether you have the correct form by reversing the sentence:

> The culprits were *he* and *I. He* and *I* were the culprits.

Unless you have a good reason for preserving the first version of such sentences, use the second, more natural one *(She was).*

4. *Who, whom, whoever, whomever*

In formal writing, the case depends on the relative pronoun's function *in its own clause:*

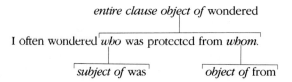

The entire *who* clause is the object of *wondered. Who* in is the subjective case because it is the subject of *was,* not the object of *wondered.* Notice how the rule applies in these examples:

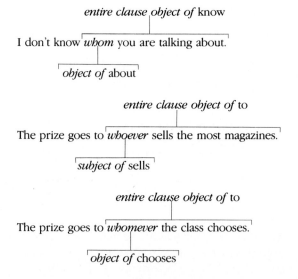

Whom and *whomever* are often replaced by *who* and *whoever* in informal writing. Frequently, even in formal writing, you can avoid the stilted *whom* or *whomever* by changing the structure of your sentence:

> The seller of the most magazines receives the prize.

> The class chooses the winner of the prize.

5. Pronouns that modify gerunds (verbal forms acting as nouns)

    Use the possessive case:

    > She was surprised by *my* calling the police.
    > *(She was surprised by my act of calling, not by me.)*

    > No one objects to *his* running for Mayor.
    > *(No one objects to the fact that he is running. The sentence does not say whether anyone objects to* him.*)*

    Don't confuse the gerund (*-ing* form acting as a noun) with the present participle (*-ing* form modifying a noun):

    > We caught a glimpse of *him* running through the woods.
    >   *object* *participle*

    > *(We caught a glimpse of* him, *not of the abstraction called "running." He happened to be running when we saw him.)*

6. Comparisons

    Choose the form that expresses the function of the pronoun in the elliptical comparative clause:

    > John likes her better than *I* [like her].

    > John likes her better than [he likes] *me*.

YOU ARE THE EDITOR

The following passage may be more elementary than one you would write for your college classes, but it illustrates some of the problems writers have with pronoun case forms. Some of the pronoun forms are correct; others are not. Edit the passage twice—once making it appropriate for formal usage, once for informal.

For Louisa Stokes's tenth birthday, her mother allowed her to invite whoever she liked to the Ice Capades. Louisa chose Amy and I. We children took the bus downtown to the stadium, where Mr. and Mrs. Stokes met us. At first Louisa sat between Amy and me, and her parents sat across the aisle from we children. But Amy objected that a tall couple sitting in front of Louisa and she interfered with them seeing the ice, so Amy and Louisa switched seats with Louisa's parents. That rearrangement resulted in me sitting next to Mr. Stokes, who I liked but who made me feel shy. Soon, however, I forgot whom was sitting next to me, as the lights dimmed and the skaters glided onto the ice. Only they and me existed. One skater was Dorothy Hamill, who I had seen on television and whom many experts thought was the best in the world. I don't know, though, who I liked best—the clowns or her. Mr. Stokes said later he thought the clowns were more skillful skaters than she.

Pronoun Reference

A pronoun should have a clear, unambiguous antecedent. Check your pronouns to be sure you have avoided the following pitfalls:

1. No antecedent:

    > We skated at the rink where *they* held the National Figure Skating Championships.

    The use of *they* to denote "whoever is responsible" is common in conversation and occasionally appropriate in writing that adopts a conversational tone. As a general rule, revise such sentences to eliminate the pronoun:

    > We skated at the rink where the National Figure Skating Championships were held.

2. Implied but unstated antecedent:

Childbearing should be postponed until the couple is economically stable and mature enough to raise *them.*

Them apparently refers to *children,* which should replace the pronoun.

3. Use of *this, that, which,* or *it* to refer vaguely to a whole clause:

A child demands extra time and money, and *this* can jeopardize a woman's job, social life, and financial security.

Revise to make clear *what* can jeopardize the job, etc.:

. . . and these extra demands can jeopardize . . .
A child's demands for extra time and money can . . .

If the reference is absolutely clear, and the alternative would be a lengthy clause or phrase, the general reference of *this, that, which,* or *it* is acceptable:

Those who favor nuclear energy often boast that not one individual has been killed because of a nuclear accident. Unfortunately, *this* is not the case.

4. Use of a possessive modifier as antecedent:

Skiing strengthens the skiers' legs and gives *them* a trim waistline.

Revised Skiing strengthens the legs and trims the waistline.

5. Use of an ambiguous antecedent:

When *he* was thirty years old, his only son died of pneumonia. *(Was the father or son thirty?)*

Revised His only son died of pneumonia at thirty.
or At thirty, he lost his only son to pneumonia.

Notice that at the same time you clarify the pronoun reference, you can often also make the sentence more concise.

YOU ARE THE EDITOR

Edit the following student sentences so that the pronouns have clear antecedents.

1. In Dickinson's poem, she describes the snow as a garment the countryside is wearing.

2. If Stewart wins the election, it will show that voters are against the nuclear waste plant.

3. In high school, they stressed creative writing, not grammar.

4. Many faces stare at you as you walk through the door, which makes you feel self-conscious.

5. At the city's present growth rate, it will soon be overpopulated.

6. Sara told her mother the news as soon as she got home from work.

7. When the gas fumes reached the furnace, it caused an explosion.

8. Last summer, I coached tennis at a large resort hotel, which was an excellent job for many reasons.

9. Matthew and Doug agreed that he should leave for home as soon as possible.

10. My mother is a perfectionist, and this has influenced me, which I think is fortunate.

SHIFTS

Unnecessary shifts, either within a sentence or from sentence to sentence, make your writing seem disconnected and confuse your reader.

Shifts in Pronouns

The section on pronoun agreement (p. 489) deals with agreement of pronouns and antecedents within a sentence. You should also make pronouns that refer to the same persons or things consistent from sentence to sentence. Avoid passages like this one:

A new *student* has a tough time on the first day of school. First of all, *they* don't know where any of the rooms are. Secondly, *you* don't know who to ask. If *he* doesn't have a schedule yet . . .

Shifts in Tense

When you refer to different time periods, you naturally shift tenses, even within a sentence:

Blackwell, who *is* now president of the Clinic, *was* formerly Chief of Staff at Mercy Hospital.

You also shift tenses to distinguish the timelessness of a general truth from the time when it was expressed or discovered:

Freud *concluded* that unconscious motives *underlie* much of our behavior.

Shifts in tense are also justified when you want to give a past incident the immediacy of the present, as in the following passage, where the tense shifts to the present as a motorcycle race begins:

He was in the left lane, I in the right, as my friend came between us and raised his arms. Everything is automatic now. My tach needle sweeps toward its 9500 rpm red line as my friend yells "Three!" over the deafening roar and lowers his arms. We hurl down the lane like rockets with near neck-breaking acceleration.

What you want to avoid are shifts made simply because of carelessness:

Melville's childhood was closely connected with the sea. He *plays* among the wharves and warehouses on the New York waterfront and *listened* to tales of whaling and seafaring life from his uncles and cousins. So it *seems* natural for him to become a sailor himself.

Another unintentional shift can occur when you describe incidents in a play, novel, or poem. The *present* tense is appropriate for such passages, and the *present perfect* (not the past) is then used to describe incidents preceding those described in the present:

In this pivotal scene, Huck and Jim *are* on a raft on the Mississippi. Both *have run* away . . . (*not* Both *ran* away)

Shifts in Mood

Mood (mode or manner) refers to differences in verb forms that indicate the way the speaker regards the action expressed by the verb.

The *indicative* mood states a fact (or what the speaker believes to be a fact) or asks a question. Although both statements and questions are considered indicative, you should avoid shifting from one form to the other within a sentence:

His purpose was to discover who was the Dark Lady of Shakespeare's sonnets.

To be consistent, the clause should be an indirect question:

His purpose was to discover who the Dark Lady of Shakespeare's sonnets was.

A concise revision avoids the clause altogether:

His purpose was to identify the Dark Lady of Shakespeare's sonnets.

The *imperative* mood expresses a request or order. It is easy to shift from the indicative to the imperative in describing a process:

The care label *should be examined.* Also *check* the seams to be sure they are ample and securely stitched.

The mood you use in such a case depends on whether your purpose is to instruct the reader (then the imperative is usually appropriate) or simply to describe how something is done by others.

Revised for Consistency

Examine the care label. Also *check* the seams to be sure they are ample and securely stitched.

The *subjunctive* mood expresses an action or condition that is uncertain or contrary to fact. Writers sometimes incorrectly shift the mood of such sentences to the indicative because the subjunctive forms differ from the indicative in only a few cases:

1. In *if, as if,* and *as though* clauses expressing a condition contrary to fact and in clauses after *wish,* the form of *to be* is *were* in the singular as well as the plural:

   If John *were* taller, he could win a basketball scholarship. (*not* If John *was* taller . . .)

   I wish I *were* less sensitive to criticism. (*not* I wish I *was* . . .)

2. In *that* clauses after verbs expressing a request, preference, suggestion, recommendation, or command, *be* is used for all forms of the verb *to be,* and the plural form of other verbs is used even when the subject is singular:

   He requested that the students *be* suspended.

   He insists that the paper *be* typed.

   I suggested that she *study* the directions more carefully.

   (*not* would *be,* should *be,* should *study*)

Shifts in Point of View

Unnecessarily shifting the grammatical subject of your clauses within a sentence or between sentences also shifts your reader's focus and results in confusion. Usually (but not always) such shifts involve a shift from the active to the passive voice:

> His *father* died, and *Melville* was forced to give up his schooling. His *mother and seven brothers and sisters* had to be supported. Several *jobs* were obtained, but *he* was not satisfied with being a bank clerk, shop assistant, or farm worker. The *sea* was what he then turned to. His greatest *work* was to derive from this subject.

Of course, no extended piece of writing can or should have a single grammatical subject for all its sentences. But if your sentences are *about* Melville, their grammatical subject should be Melville until there is a reason to shift focus. Varying your sentence openings with introductory clauses and phrases, and combining sentences can help you to avoid a succession of sentences beginning with *he:*

> When his father died, Melville was forced to give up his schooling in order to support his mother and seven brothers and sisters. Although he took several jobs (as bank clerk, shop assistant, and farm worker), he was not satisfied with them. He turned to the sea, which was to become the source of his greatest work. (*or* This was to become . . . , indicating a shift to *sea* as focus.)

YOU ARE THE EDITOR

Edit the following student passage to eliminate unnecessary shifts.

```
    Melville first shipped on a merchant vessel
bound for Liverpool.  Next comes a voyage on a
whaler to the South Seas, where several months
are spent living among cannibals.  These voyages
provide the raw material for nearly all of
Melville's subsequent works.  Typee and its
sequel Omoo, adventure stories based on the South
Seas experience, were published first.  Next he
published Mardi, the story of his first voyage.
Two more tales of travel based on his life at sea
follow.  Finally, put together all of your
```

knowledge and experience of the sea, and <u>Moby</u>

<u>Dick</u>, the epic novel of seafaring, is produced.

Melville achieved popular success with Typee

and <u>Omoo</u>. The reader enjoyed such exotic

stories; they look forward to a third work by the

promising author. But <u>Mardi</u> is a failure. The

average reader was looking for a tale of

adventure. They require that a book should be

entertaining and prefer that it does not contain

hidden meanings. Read this book, however, and

you find a moral allegory.

FAULTY PARALLELISM

Coordinate sentence elements (items in pairs and series) should have the same grammatical form:

> The obvious machinery—*combines* costing over thirty thousand dollars, *tractors* topping twenty thousand dollars, pickup *trucks* priced at ten thousand dollars, *plows, planters,* rotary *hoes*—must be replaced frequently to produce high quality crops.

> *He must buy* gasoline and diesel fuel *to operate* his tractors and combines and *he must face* the escalating cost of fertilizers *to continue* planting his corn and soybeans.

> But it is always preferable to take *a small issue and treat it imaginatively and thoroughly,* rather than *a burning issue and treat it vaguely and superficially.*

(Parallelism is treated fully in Chapter 5, pp. 200–206.)

Faulty parallelism occurs:

1. When coordinate elements are not expressed in the same grammatical form:

> Make no mistake; a foreign language is a good *"selling point"* and clearly *advantageous* in a job-scarce economy. *(noun, adjective)*

When we forsake a sedentary lifestyle, we *increase* our brain's ability to function, *become* psychologically healthier, *better able* to handle stress, and *keep* our mind sharper. *(verb, verb, adjective, verb)*

French missionaries and nuns taught French in Canada and Maine; in Pennsylvania German was taught by German immigrants; Spanish was learned from the Spanish in Florida and the Southwest. *(clauses of different patterns)*

To revise, use the same grammatical structure for each item in the pair or series:

Make no mistake; a foreign language is a good *"selling point"* and a clear *advantage* in a job-scarce economy. *(nouns)*

When we forsake a sedentary lifestyle, we *increase* our brain's ability to function, *become* psychologically healthier, *handle* stress more easily, and *keep* our mind sharper. *(verbs)*

French missionaries and nuns taught French in Canada and Maine; the Germans taught German in Pennsylvania; the Spanish taught Spanish in Florida and the Southwest. *(clauses of the same pattern: subject-active verb-object-prepositional phrase)*

2. When prepositions or infinitive markers *(to)* are omitted:

Others believe vitamins can provide neither a *cure* nor *relief of* colds.

To revise, you may add the necessary preposition to make the prepositional phrase complete and idiomatic:

Others believe vitamins can provide neither a *cure for* nor *relief of* colds.

But frequently, you can construct a more concise sentence by using verb rather than noun forms:

Others believe vitamins can neither *cure* nor *relieve* colds.

3. When elements of coordinating structures *(both/and, either/or, neither/nor, not only/but also)* are misplaced:

Physical exercise produces *not only immediate effects* on the mind; it *also provides* long-term benefits.

Revise so that each coordinating word is followed by the same grammatical form or structure:

Physical exercise *not only produces* immediate effects on the mind; it *also provides* long-term benefits.

or Physical exercise provides *not only immediate effects* on the mind *but long-term benefits.*

4. When elements that are not logically coordinate are expressed in coordinate form:

> According to my mother, my hair was *stringy, lifeless, impossible,* and *needed to be cut.*

> My Aunt Mary is a *woman* of strange habits and *who* visits us each month.

To revise, separate the non-coordinate element from the pair or series:

> According to my mother, my hair was stringy and lifeless—in a word, impossible. It needed to be cut.

Sometimes you will find that you have two levels of coordinate items:

> The chemicals *depress* the central nervous system and *cause* mental *confusion, nausea,* and *gastrointestinal problems.*

Sometimes you should subordinate rather than coordinate one element, leaving the element you want to stress in the main clause:

> My Aunt Mary, a woman of strange habits, visits us each month.

> *or* My Aunt Mary, who visits us each month, is a woman of strange habits.

Placing non-coordinate elements in coordinate form is common in speech and may be justified in informal, conversational writing:

> Les was a decent guy and pretty smart as well.

YOU ARE THE EDITOR

Edit the following student sentences to correct faulty parallelism.

1. Both cities are inhabited by Germans sharing the same language, customs, traditions, and who are proud of the cultural inheritance of Bach and Goethe.

2. The swim club gave me a chance to compete, make new friends, and kept me in good physical condition.

3. The winners of sweepstakes usually have a choice either of a sum of money or go on an exotic trip.

4. Old age is symbolized in the first stanza by autumn, twilight in the second, and finally the third, which deals with a dying fire.

5. A study based on not only written sources but also supplemented by oral history would add to our knowledge.

6. Mboya, a trade union leader and acceptable to the government, became Minister of Labor.

7. The winning runner receives a twenty-five dollar savings bond, second, ten dollars, third, five dollars, and twenty-five honorable mentions at one dollar each.

8. Michael failed to get into the premed program because of both his poor math grades and because he had not taken enough science courses.

9. Before the house was ready to live in, the roof had to be repaired, the chimney rebuilt, paint for the upstairs rooms, and a new heating system had to be installed.

10. Those at greatest risk are men who smoke, drink heavily, and whose relatives have had heart attacks.

INCOMPLETE CONSTRUCTIONS

Writers often omit words necessary for grammatical completeness or clarity in the following kinds of constructions:

1. Comparisons

Don't omit *than* or *as* in a double comparison:

Exercise is as important [as], if not more important, than diet.

or (less awkward):
Exercise is as important as diet, if not more so.

or Exercise is at least as important as diet.

Don't omit *other* when comparing members of the same class:

Bonzo won more points than any [other] dog in the show. *(Assuming that Bonzo was a dog in the show, he could not have won more points than he himself won.)*

Don't omit words necessary to make comparisons unambiguous:

Teachers are often more sympathetic to children than [to] parents.

or Teachers are often more sympathetic to children than parents [are].

(*As the two versions show, without* to *or* are, *the sentence could be understood in two different ways.*)

Don't omit words necessary to make the comparison logical:

Sara's coat was more expensive than [that of] her mother [*or* her mother's]. (*A coat cannot logically be compared to a person.*)

Don't omit one term of the comparison:

Davidson has more appeal to young professionals [than his opponent *or* than to labor].

(*The second term of the comparison may be omitted if a preceding sentence makes it clear:* Haynes gains most of his support from labor. Davidson has more appeal to young professionals.)

2. Pairs of idioms

Don't omit necessary prepositions in idiomatic compounds:

If deinstitutionalization is to succeed, we must change our attitudes [toward] and treatment of the mentally ill.

3. *That* clauses

Don't omit *that* when the omission may lead to misreading:

Patrick never believed [that] his father had willingly abandoned him. (*Without* that, *the reader may initially interpret* his father *as the object of* believed, *not the subject of* abandoned: Patrick never believed his father.)

Its four stories harmonize with other campus buildings at the same time [that] its own distinctive identity is maintained. (*Without* that, *the sentence appears to be two fused sentences that should be divided after* buildings.)

The witness said [that] on Friday he had not seen the defendant. (*Without* that, *it is unclear whether the witness made the statement on Friday or failed to see the defendant on Friday. See Misplaced Modifiers, p. 509.*)

YOU ARE THE EDITOR

Edit the following student sentences, inserting words necessary for grammatical completeness and clarity.

1. Some people believe that the unborn child's rights take precedence over the mother.

2. I've always found pleasure in just listening and watching the natural scene from the top of our hill.

3. More paper is produced in the Fox Valley region than any area in the world of its size.

4. Police did not suspect the woman had been murdered until they found bloodstains in the garage.

5. Like Mary, Jane's childhood is spent in an isolated setting.

6. The weather is as cold if not colder than yesterday.

7. More women are paricipants rather than simply spectators of sports events.

8. First baseman Morton was as fast if not faster than any player on the team.

9. The potential energy that can be harnessed from the wind is thirty times greater than current electrical power plants.

10. His concepts are compared with other scholars on the subject.

MIXED CONSTRUCTIONS

Sometimes a writer begins a sentence with one grammatical construction and ends with another:

By overfeeding fish can kill them.

Survival for most communes that stay alive have financial support from religious groups.

The writer needs to choose one structure and to stick to it:

Overfeeding fish can kill them.

By overfeeding fish, you can kill them.

Survival for most communes depends on financial support from religious groups.

Most communes that survive have financial support from religious groups.

Another type of mixed construction, called faulty predication, occurs when the predicate of a sentence (usually the verb *to be* and a complement) does not fit the subject in meaning and/or grammar:

> Another *example of violence* in sports *is where* a fight breaks out in a hockey game.

Since such sentences have often been written carelessly in the first place, an effective revision may involve recasting the entire sentence, as the following stages of revision show:

> Another example . . . is a fight breaking out . . .

> Another example . . . is fights during hockey games.

> Fights during hockey games provide another example of violence in sports. *(Final version)*

Faulty predication appears commonly in definitions:

> *Leukemia is when* the white blood cells multiply uncontrollably.

It also occurs in the redundant "reason is because" construction:

> The *reason* for leukemia *is because* the white blood cells multiply uncontrollably.

Although faulty predication may occur with other verbs, the verb *to be* is most frequently involved. Since this verb acts as a kind of "equal sign," you must be particularly careful that the subject and complement it joins fit together grammatically and semantically. Often another verb is a more effective choice, as some possible revisions of the preceding examples indicate:

> Leukemia is a condition in which the white blood cells multiply uncontrollably.

> Leukemia develops when the white blood cells multiply uncontrollably.

> Leukemia involves uncontrollable multiplication of the white blood cells.

YOU ARE THE EDITOR

Repair the mixed constructions in the following student sentences. If necessary, recast your corrected version to make it as effective as possible.

```
1.  Going to McDonald's conserves energy by not having so
    many stoves turned on for dinner.
```

2. Doctors report terrible incidents where children are abused.

3. About 150 new students resulted from the college's media campaign.

4. Through these noneducation courses will give education students competencies in subjects that will be useful to them as teachers.

5. A pretty sight is when you ski at night and see the lights of the surrounding towns.

6. If a researcher wishing to explore fully the leadership positions of women in tribal cultures must do field study.

7. A major problem caused by divorce is if a child has to grow up with only one parent.

8. The Northeast lost much of its attraction for business was due to the high cost of living and uncertain energy supply.

9. Studies on birth defects have proven to be caused, in many cases, by poor maternal nutrition.

10. Eating animal fats and smoking cigarettes are substances that may cause cancer.

MODIFIERS

Dangling Modifiers

Technically, a dangling modifier is any modifier that has no word in the sentence to modify; it therefore "dangles":

Black, poor, and uneducated, it is difficult to get a job. *(dangling adjectives)*

The air cleared quickly *after opening the door. (dangling present participle)*

Commonly, dangling modifiers are introductory verbal phrases (infinitives or participles) or elliptical clauses that do not modify the subject of the sentence:

To get to Julia's, a two-hour bus ride must be endured. *(dangling infinitive)*
Recently laid off, Michael's plans are uncertain. *(dangling past participle)*

After being refrigerated for four hours, it is necessary to beat the mixture thoroughly. *(dangling present participle)*

When only twelve, his mother died. *(dangling elliptical clause)*

When you revise the sentence to correct the dangling modifier, choose the method that expresses your thought most precisely, emphatically, and economically within its context:

1. Change the modifying phrase to a clause:

   When you are black, poor, and uneducated, it is difficult to get a job.

   The air cleared quickly *after I opened the door.*

   Since Michael was recently laid off, his plans are uncertain.

   When he was only twelve, his mother died.

2. Revise the main clause so that its subject is properly modified by the introductory phrase:

   To get to Julia's, *you* must endure a two-hour bus ride.

   Recently laid off, *Michael* has no definite plans.

   After being refrigerated for four hours, the *mixture* must be beaten thoroughly.

3. Recast the entire sentence:

   Anyone who is black, poor, and uneducated has difficulty getting a job.

   Opening the door cleared the air quickly.

   Getting to Julia's involves a two-hour bus ride.

   Note: Absolute phrases that modify the entire sentence need no revision:

   To sum up, the residents object to the day-care center.

   All things considered, we were lucky.

   Even allowing for inflation, the raise is quite adequate.

YOU ARE THE EDITOR

Edit each student sentence in the three ways suggested to eliminate dangling modifiers. Place a check beside the most effective revision.

    1. After waiting for four hours in the rain, no tickets were
        left.

2. Although hardly ever done, Greek slaves could become citizens.

3. A town is finally reached after driving many miles in this deserted landscape.

4. Having been alive for some eighteen years now, my experience of human nature is broad.

5. Instead of being carpeted, dingy gray linoleum covered the floors.

6. To get fresh vegetables and meat from the mainland, a weekly crossing on the ferry was made.

7. Listening to professional engineers, my understanding of what to expect in an engineering career increased.

8. Turning to your left, Lake Michigan comes into view.

9. Coming into the museum for the first time, the modernistic steel sculpture immediately caught my eye.

10. Discouraged by his poor grades, it seemed to John that his ambition to become a doctor was foolish.

Misplaced Modifiers

English is a flexible language: often the writer can place modifying words, phrases, and clauses in different positions to achieve a variety of effects (see Chapter 5 and Improving Emphasis, p. 564). But since English also depends to some extent on word order for meaning, careless placement of modifiers can distort or confuse the sense of a statement. A modifier is misplaced

1. When it appears to modify the wrong element:

I had to pass a house where a brutal murder had taken place *every morning. (A murder took place every morning.)*

Several children were located by social workers *who had been severely abused. (The social workers had been severely abused.)*

2. When it could modify either one of two elements *(squinting modifier):*

The witness said *on Friday* he had not seen the defendant. *(Did the witness make the statement on Friday or fail to see the defendant on Friday?)*

In general, place the modifier as close as possible to the element it modifies but not between two possible elements it might modify. Notice that you can make the relationship of the modifier clear and still rearrange other parts of the sentence to achieve the desired emphasis:

Every morning I had to pass a house where a brutal murder had taken place. A brutal murder had taken place in a house I had to pass *every morning.*

Several children *who had been severely abused* were located by social workers. Social workers located several children *who had been severely abused.*

Reposition the squinting modifier so that the meaning of the sentence is clear. Again, you usually have more than one choice:

On Friday the witness said he had not seen the defendant.

He had not seen the defendant, the witness said *on Friday.*

Or, if the other meaning is intended:

The witness said he had not seen the defendant *on Friday.*

He had not seen the defendant *on Friday,* the witness said.

Adding *that,* rather than repositioning the modifier, is also a solution when the modifier comes between a verb and a noun clause (see Incomplete Constructions, p. 503):

The witness said *on Friday that* he had not seen the defendant.

or The witness said *that on Friday* he had not seen the defendant.

Single-word adverbs such as *only, even, scarcely, almost, just, hardly,* and *merely* are frequently misplaced in conversation:

I *only* studied for half an hour. *(Logically, I only studied; I did nothing else.)*

In formal writing, such adverbs should be placed precisely:

I studied for *only* half an hour. *(I studied no longer than half an hour.)*

YOU ARE THE EDITOR

Edit the following student sentences in as many ways as you can to correct the misplacement of modifying words, phrases, and clauses. If a sentence contains a squinting modifier, edit to show both possible meanings.

1. I decided the next semester I would transfer to the School of Engineering.

2. In one of the longest continuous swims on record, Clarence Giles almost swam thirty miles.

3. The Chamber of Commerce donated money as well as many citizens.

4. Books and paintings have been found in attics worth thousands of dollars.

5. Eating small meals often will make the ulcer patient feel better.

6. Archaeologists located several unique vessels that the ancient tribe had used in religious ceremonies in 1978.

7. You should at least know a little of the country's native language that you are visiting.

8. Women can now have careers, whether married or single.

9. An antique plate was broken by a child that could have sold for over five hundred dollars.

10. Members of the Davis family only became severely ill after Nurse Toppan had treated them.

YOU ARE THE EDITOR (Review of Grammar and Sentence Structure)

Each of the following student sentences contains several errors in grammar and sentence structure. Edit each sentence in as many ways as you can to make it error-free. Then choose the most effective version.

1. Though only seen for a few seconds and a distance of sixty feet, the witness positively identified the defendant as its driver.

2. Each of the characters refuse to face reality. Jack Boyle not seeing the tragedy caused by his dream of wealth. Mary Boyle refused to believe Bentham had left her.

3. Moore, a California lawyer, defends the radicals and loses. According to some, the reason being because he was not accustomed and knowledgeable about the traditions of the Massachusetts courts.

4. It was hard to tell who was more frightened—them or us—we all just stop, wait, and then we heard a siren.

5. More compelling than any scene in the book is where the two girls witness a murder each has their own view of who was the aggressor, whom was being attacked, and why, the way he describes it, you can't be certain who is right.

6. Before someone over forty begins to run, have a physical examination to be sure you are healthy enough to do it.

7. An agreement must be signed before moving into the complex that enumerates both the tenants' and the management's responsibilities then you only deposit one hundred dollars and the apartment is yours.

8. The diction of both poets are similar, since they were written in the same period, however, each have their own distinct form.

9. By looking at the fast-food restaurants they go to can tell as much if not more about America's culture than a sophisticated poll.

10. There I was, climbing through the window. When in steps the housemother, whom I knew immediately would report me to the dean.

11. Any employee today is likely to experience the effects of recession. Such as getting laid off, fired, their hours reduced, or their company going out of business.

12. Deriving a large income from the paper industry and in the center of a prosperous agricultural region, economic slowdowns are not felt as much in Centerville as other parts of the country.

13. John felt as if he was in a nightmare he knew when he got on the stage he would forget his lines.

14. What distinguished the great Blondin were his many variations on the tightrope-walking stunt. Fortified with champagne, his trips across the Niagara River gorge were made blindfolded, pushing a wheelbarrow, with his hands and feet manacled, and once he cooked an omelette halfway across.

15. The crowning achievement was him walking a tightrope across the river with a man on his back, the Prince of Wales witnessed the event but refused Blondin's request that he would be the next passenger.

PUNCTUATION AND MECHANICS

PUNCTUATION WITHIN THE SENTENCE

Comma

Commas mark the pauses that you would make while reading sentences out loud. A sentence that lacks needed commas confuses the reader, who must slow down and perhaps reread in order to mentally supply the clarifying pauses:

> The young man was quite tall a few inches over six feet and was clad only in an old T-shirt old faded blue jeans that were ragged at the cuffs weather-beaten and holey tennis shoes and a dirty brown winter coat that was two sizes too large its collar upturned to protect his neck from the cold.

Notice how much more easily you can read the passage with the necessary commas put in:

> The young man was quite tall, a few inches over six feet, and was clad only in an old T-shirt, old faded blue jeans that were ragged at the cuffs, weather-beaten and holey tennis shoes, and a dirty brown winter coat that was two sizes too large, its collar upturned to protect his neck from the wind.

Even in a brief sentence, lack of a comma can cause misreading:

> Behind a wall-to-wall mirror greeted the tavern's guests. (*Without a comma after* behind, *the reader at first reads* mirror *as the object of* behind.)

By creating pauses, commas not only facilitate reading but also affect the pace and rhythm of your sentences, and the emphasis of certain words in them. A sentence without commas moves rapidly; one with several commas moves slowly, and the pauses marked by the commas give emphasis to the words they set off, as silence emphasizes a sound. Lewis Thomas illustrates this idea when he suggests putting in commas "as you go along":

> If you try to come back after doing a paragraph and stick them in the various spots that tempt you you will discover that they tend to swarm like minnows into all sorts of crevices whose existence you hadn't realized and before you know it the whole long sentence becomes immobilized and lashed up squirming in commas. Better to use them sparingly, and with affection, precisely when the need for each one arises, nicely, by itself.
>
> —"Notes on Punctuation," *New England Journal of Medicine*

Thomas had a stylistic reason for leaving out conventional commas in the first sentence and putting in unconventional ones in the second: he wanted to illustrate the effects of omitting or adding commas. You may also bend the rules at times, but first you must *know* the rules, and then you must have a good reason for bypassing them. The basic comma rules are listed here, and options are discussed under each one. When in doubt, you will not go wrong if you follow the basic rule. But try to exercise your ear and your judgment in deciding when to leave out conventional commas or insert unconventional ones.

1. Use a comma before the coordinating conjunction *(and, but, or, for, not, yet, so)* that joins independent clauses:

> Many people know about camera angles now, *but* not so many know about sentences. The arrangement of the words matters, *and* the arrangement you want can be found in the picture in your mind.
>
> —Joan Didion, "Why I Write"

(For additional examples, see pp. 519–20. For clauses containing internal punctuation, see Semicolon, p. 520.)

Writers frequently omit (or editors delete) the comma between short clauses:

> Suddenly, I felt myself sinking   and then I knew. Quicksand.
> [ ]

Sometimes the comma may be omitted even when the clauses are fairly long:

> Take a stroll in any large city   and you are likely to bump into people chatter-
> [ ]
> ing in a language unknown to you.

But don't omit the comma before considering the effect of the omission. No pause is necessary in the first example, and the absence of a pause in the second example emphasizes the immediacy of the narrator's realization. When the conjunction is *but* or *yet,* however, the pause marked by the comma is nearly always called for to emphasize the contrast between the clauses:

> The fears are justified, but there is a way out.

When the conjunction is *for,* the absence of the comma may lead the reader to expect a prepositional phrase instead of a clause:

> We waited hours   for the train had derailed.
> [ ]

When in doubt, retain the comma between short clauses.

The usual corollary to the rule about placing commas between compounded independent clauses is to omit the comma between a pair of compounded elements that are *not* independent clauses. A comma before the conjunctions in the following sentences would be inappropriate:

If she ever felt ill   or depressed, we were unaware of it.
                     [ ]

Guard rails are built along cliffs   and mountains.
                                  [ ]

Neither the fuse box   nor the brain can handle the extra input.
                    [ ]

She never shared her classroom insights   and rarely mentioned her
schoolwork.   [ ]

Again, however, when *but* is the conjunction, the comma is frequently effective to emphasize a contrast:

I remained undefeated, but for how long?

She never appeared garishly made-up or exaggerated, but always looked a bit too perfectly colored to be a real person.

And even when the conjunction is *and* or *or,* you should always use a comma when the second compounded element comments on or qualifies the first:

The credit, or perhaps the blame, for this "fitness craze" belongs to the media.

The career-seeker is the first type, and the least common.

Likewise, the comma may be inserted for special effect:

What is to prevent such things from happening to him, or to those he loves?

The pause created by the comma gives stress to both *him* and *those he loves.*

2.   Use commas to separate words, phrases, and clauses in a series:

Rouge, powder, and *lipstick* go on last.

They're *honest, humble, friendly,* and *grateful* for what they have.

No people in the world are *scrutinized, measured, counted,* and *interrogated* by as many *poll-takers, social science researchers,* and *government officials* as are Americans.

You *awake, flip* on the television set, and *flop* onto the sofa to watch a cartoon.

It is quiet, the salesladies are helpful, and *the merchandise is neatly and attractively displayed.*

(See Semicolon, p. 520, for series in which items already contain commas.)

Though the comma before the last item in the series is frequently omitted, it is best retained because it lets the reader know that the final item in the series, rather than a part of the preceding item, follows. *(It is quiet, the salesladies are helpful and knowledgeable, and . . .).*

With a series of adjectives before a noun, use commas between *coordinate adjectives* only—that is, between those that separately and equally modify the noun:

dry, flat countryside

lush, vigorous plants

slow, arduous process

calloused, work-roughened hands

placid, pink-faced Madonna

big, old, unkempt-looking house

You can reverse coordinate adjectives or place *and* between them (flat, dry countryside; dry and flat countryside); you cannot reverse noncoordinate ones or place *and* between them:

computerized data systems

padded office chair

cold steel frame

four sporadic fights

3. Use a comma after introductory elements:

Since my arrival that morning, I had witnessed at least four sporadic fights.

In the Montessori School, Piaget's ideas are respected.

Meanwhile, the animation director is constructing the "model sheets."

You may omit the comma after a single word or short phrase:

Within two hours you find yourself in a spotless hospital room.

Today the sun shone for the first time in two weeks.

Frequently, however, retaining the comma after brief introductory elements strengthens transitions:

> *A century ago,* farmers constituted approximately ninety percent of the total labor force in America.

> *Then,* the son of a farmer was expected to follow in his father's footsteps.

> *Today,* less than four percent of the people employed are farmers.

Regardless of the transitional effect, you may need the comma to prevent misreading:

> *Ever since I remember,* the Amish have been the butt of jokes.

> *Inside,* two large overhead fans pretend to keep the tavern cool.

> *Frequently,* drunk or drugged teenagers are picked up on Main Street.

When in doubt, retain the comma.

4. Use a comma before closing elements that add a qualification, contrast, or afterthought to the main idea of the sentence:

> Most solar energy designs for home use could be economical, *at least once the initial expenditure is covered.*

> An overall cure for this catastrophic disease remains elusive, *though some cancers will respond to certain types of medical treatment.*

> Wind power can be an advantageous alternative, *especially in regions where electrical power is extremely costly.*

The kinds of words, phrases, and clauses that are set off at the beginning of the sentence are less often set off at the end. If the sentences under rule 3, for instance, were reversed, none of the elements would require commas. In general, you must use your ear and your judgment to decide whether to use commas before closing elements.

5. Use commas to set off free modifiers (pp. 211–213), wherever they occur in the sentence:

> *Forsaking the rail,* he crept up on the outside, *his face contorted, knowing that his performance during the next five seconds would either win or lose the race.*

6. Use commas to set off nonrestrictive modifiers. Restrictive modifiers require no commas.

Nonrestrictive   The once-proud opera house, *dated 1894,* sags miserably.

Restrictive   The painting *dated 1894* is a forgery; the one *dated 1892* is genuine.

A nonrestrictive modifier adds nonessential information (the date of the opera house); it could be omitted from the sentence without affecting its basic meaning or clarity ("The once-proud opera house sags miserably"). A restrictive modifier identifies, or limits the reference of, the noun it modifies (in the second example, the specific painting referred to); it can't be detached from the sentence without making its meaning unclear ("The painting [which one?] is a forgery; the one [which one?] is genuine"). You can see the distinction and the differing punctuation in the following pairs of sentences:

> William Carlos Williams, *the poet,* was also a farmer.
> The poet *William Carlos Williams* was also a farmer.

> John, *who has been drinking,* should not drive.
> People *who have been drinking* should not drive.

> Many Americans travel to Mexico, *where Laetrile is legal and readily available.*
> Many Americans travel to countries *where Laetrile is legal and readily available.*

> In spring, *when the water is high,* the lake surges over the rocks.
> At times *when the water is high* the lake surges over the rocks.

> The waiters, *dressed in their white jackets,* are already arranging the chairs on the sidewalk.
> The waiters *dressed in white jackets* serve in the main dining room; those *in red* serve in the coffee shop.

7. Use a *pair* of commas to set off any parenthetical element within a sentence.

If the sentence would be clear and grammatically complete without a word, phrase, or clause within it, set that element off by a pair of commas—one at each end. Don't leave one of the commas out. Such parenthetical elements include transitional expressions (such as *however, therefore, then, first*), names in direct address, and interrupters like *I believe* and *he says,* as well as the free and nonrestrictive modifiers discussed in items 5 and 6.

> It would seem, *then,* that busing is not the solution.

> My house, *for example,* was encircled by a wall made of concrete with sets of iron bars bolted into the cement.

> The story, *however,* is a true one.

> You can see, *Dad,* that I've improved.

> This issue, *I believe,* has been obscured by the rhetoric of both parties.

> Trypanosomiasis, *better known as sleeping sickness,* is a painful and many times fatal disease.

> The armory, *a fire hazard by any standard,* was packed beyond legal capacity.

8. Use commas conventionally to set off quotations and parts of place names and dates:

"The problem," he said, "is all in your mind."

The conference took place in Columbus, Ohio, on Friday, October 27, 1979.

9. Insert commas where necessary to prevent misreading:

When she got back, there was an antiaircraft gun in her flower garden.

Besides, children who are in school seven hours a day need a break from lessons.

Those who can, work outside the home.

A Final Note on Commas: Do *not* use a comma to separate a subject from its verb, a verb from its object or complement, a preposition from its object, an adjective from the noun it modifies, or a conjunction from the clause or compounded element that follows it:

Over one hundred clinical types of cancer claim approximately 370,000 lives each year.   [ ]

You'll probably wonder if you've slipped through a crack in time.
                    [ ]
Our yard was about twenty square feet.
              [ ]
. . . a vast blue-green carpet.
                    [ ]
Aunt Mary refuses to part with her car even though it's about to fall apart.
                                            [ ]
Smoking can be a macho symbol, so it has to go.
                          [ ]

YOU ARE THE EDITOR

Edit the following student sentences to insert needed commas and delete unnecessary ones. If there is an option to use a comma or not, write the sentence both ways; then choose the version that seems most clearer and more emphatic.

```
1.  Armed with a college degree she returned to Portland her
    hometown, to teach, she hoped at the local high school.
```

2. On April 4 1983 John Firelli an eighty—six—year—old
   Portuguese immigrant, successfully fought off a teenage
   mugger only to suffer a fatal heart attack the next day.

3. Many of those far removed from the bomb's epicenter will
   perish, too far more slowly but just as inevitably
   succumbing to radiation sickness, starvation or exposure
   or dying of illnesses or injuries, that might have been
   cured, had ambulances doctors and drugs been available.

4. The front, or obverse of a coin, usually shows a profile
   portrait though sometimes, it may picture a building,
   animal or plant, that represents the place of issue.

5. Though dreaded from biblical times to the present leprosy
   in fact, is neither highly infectious, nor inevitably
   disfiguring.

6. Older people, who have poor eyesight and cannot enjoy TV,
   make up a small, but important, segment of the radio
   audience.

7. Lazy and overweight, as a teenager he rarely worked for
   his parents gave him everything he wanted.

8. The colorful, Italian Renaissance prince, Sigismondo
   Malatesta, was both a cousin of Parasina Malatesta who
   was beheaded by Niccolo d'Este, and a husband of
   Parasina's daughter Ginevra whom according to rumor he
   poisoned.

9. Believing in the goodness of natural man the Russian
   novelist Tolstoy held the view, that people should follow
   their natural instincts, and reject society's dictates.

10. Pieces of broken pottery or shards are labeled according
    to location, and set aside for the pot—mender who sorts
    them on the basis of clay—type color and design, and
    assembles those that he can, into complete vessels.

Semicolon

Use the semicolon to separate coordinate elements that require a stronger
mark of punctuation than a comma.

1. Use a semicolon between independent clauses not joined by coordinating
   conjunctions:

To the people of China, acupuncture is a long-established tradition; to the people of the United States, it is a new medical procedure.

If a violinist plays it, it's a violin; if a fiddler plays it, it's a fiddle.

No spreading maples or oaks rise above the houses; no birds perch on the roofs; no garbage cans line the curb; no sidewalks bear the chalky traces of past hopscotch games.

Understanding the physiology of epilepsy can help erase its social stigma; even more, it helps us respond to a victim should a seizure occur in our presence.

Notice that the clauses so joined are truly coordinate—equal in importance (though they do not have to be absolutely balanced grammatically). When the second clause amplifies the first without using a phrase like *for instance,* use a colon between the clauses (see p. 522). When neither is the case, consider subordinating one clause (see revisions for Comma Splice, p. 479). The semicolon is the standard punctuation when the second clause is introduced by a conjunctive abverb *(besides, consequently, furthermore, hence, however, instead, moreover, otherwise, still, then, therefore, thus, etc.):*

Obviously, whatever they want, they get; therefore, they can afford to be strong and silent.

Replacing the semicolon with a comma in any of these cases would result in a comma splice; dropping it altogether would cause fused sentences (see p. 481).

2. Even when two or more independent clauses are joined by coordinating conjunctions, use a semicolon between them if one clause or both clauses contain internal punctuation that makes the structure of the sentence difficult to discern:

The thriving commerce of such European capitals as Copenhagen and Amsterdam, where cars are banned from certain districts, suggests that economic consequences can be minimized; and an upgrading of public transportation should make private auto use less attractive by comparison.

3. On the same principle of using the stronger pause to mark off the larger elements in the sentence, use a semicolon between items in a series when the items contain internal punctuation:

Before me stood a vast array of antique cars: Packards, long and wide, sporting interior windshields between front and back seats; ancient Cadillacs adorned with brass headlights and radiators that had been polished to glow like golden jewels; Auburns and Dusenburgs, their huge, ribbed chrome exhaust pipes sticking out from long hoods covering polished U-12 engines . . .

4. Use a semicolon between items in a series even when the items contain no punctuation if you desire greater separation of the elements and thus greater emphasis on each:

> What might be called relational questions require the student to show a mastery of seeing the connections between things: by comparing; by contrasting; by explaining causal sequence; by applying an abstract concept to a specific item.

Except for the situations covered in rules 2–4, don't use the semicolon as a substitute for the comma, and never use it to replace the colon and dash, which have quite different functions (see the following two sections).

Colon

The colon is an economical means of signaling to the reader that an amplification of the preceding statement follows. The amplification may take a number of forms:

1. A statement that explains:

> At one time, epilepsy was considered a mark of honor: in ancient Rome, historians tell us, epileptics were given high government positions, for it was thought that when they suffered a seizure, they were in direct communication with God.

> A microphone is to a tape deck what a lens is to a camera: Microphones allow you to determine a point of view when taping.

> *(As these sentences illustrate, usage is divided on whether an independent clause following a colon is capitalized.)*

2. A statement that illustrates:

> There may be a few cosmetic differences: the fiddle may have catgut instead of wire-wound strings, embedded deposits of rosin under the fingerboard, and a honed-down bridge.

3. A single word or series that specifies a general word or phrase:

> The strangest thing about Aunt Mary is her *car:* a battered, old Ford.

> Soon the Saturday carnival will end and the streets of the North End will resume *their weekday guise:* rundown, slightly seedy, and quiet.

> We invariably came back from our walks with armloads of *goodies:* buckets of plums, muscadines, strawberries or blackberries, chocks of broomstraw, holly and evergreen for Christmas decorations, and pocketfuls of hazelnuts, chestnuts, or walnuts.

4.   A quotation:

> The summary paragraph of a mathematically based article in *Science* states the future value of wind power well: "Wind energy is seen to offer a potential far larger than many other self-renewing energy sources."

> *(If the quotation is brief and not introduced by an independent statement, a comma is used:* As the general said, "War is hell.")

Most students probably don't use the colon enough, reserving it to introduce numbered lists and formal quotations. As you can see in the preceding sentences, however, the colon is valuable especially as an economical transition: it can indicate the relationship between two statements in less than a word, and it lets you introduce a series of words or phrases without starting a new clause ("These are . . . ," "which include . . . ").

The colon does have limitations:

You can't use a pair of colons—as you use a pair of dashes—to enclose material within a sentence.

Except when the colon is used in a heading for an example or list (as, for example, in the preceding list of colon rules), an independent clause must come before the colon. A colon never goes between a verb and its object or complement:

> My most difficult subjects are physics, math, and chemistry.
> *not* My most difficult subjects are: physics, math, and chemistry.

You can't use a colon if the first element of a sentence is a series of words or phrases. Use a dash instead:

> Physics, math, and chemistry—those are my most difficult subjects.
> *not* Physics, math, and chemistry: those are my most difficult subjects.

The following sentence illustrates the distinction:

Independent clause precedes colon	In ordinary conversation, we can express our meaning in all sorts of extra-linguistic ways:
Series introduced by clause and colon	the lift of an eyebrow, the gesture or grimace, the stress, pitch, and intonation of the voice—
Summary comment on series introduced by dash	all can help to convey our meaning.

Dash

You can use the dash in a number of ways:

1. Especially in informal writing, use the dash as what Sheridan Baker calls a "conversational colon," for all the purposes of a colon (see the preceding section).

> She refers to my way of living, compared to her own, as a "natural high"—if she didn't know better, she says, she'd swear I was taking drugs. *(Dash introduces an explanatory statement.)*

> Many small handguns like the "Saturday-night special" are designed for one purpose—to kill people. *(Dash introduces a specifying appositive.)*

> There are several categories of canine mendicants—the strong and silents, the huffers and puffers, the mumblers and grumblers, the whimperers and whiners, and the yippers and yappers. *(Dash introduces specific examples of a general phrase.)*

> From all outward appearances, my older sister is about as ordinary as a dime-store guppy in a school of angel fish—not flashy, not causing any commotion, just swimming along in the background. *(Dash introduces an explanatory series.)*

2. When your sentence takes the opposite pattern—a series followed by a summarizing statement—use a dash instead of a colon in both formal and informal writing:

> Socrates, Alexander the Great, William the Conqueror, Julius Caesar, Napoleon—all were subject to epilepsy.

3. Use the dash to signal an abrupt turn of thought:

> We liked our cat Charlie—until he began to swell at the abdomen.

4. Use a *pair* of dashes to set off parenthetical expressions more emphatically or clearly than a pair of commas can:

> Electronically controlled harvesters—fast and efficient—have replaced hand-held scythes.

Dashes clearly mark off a parenthetical series (or other parenthetical element that contains internal commas) within a sentence:

> The basic machinery—combines costing over thirty thousand dollars, tractors topping twenty thousand dollars, pickup trucks priced at ten thousand dollars, plows, planters, rotary hoes—must be replaced frequently to produce high-quality crops.

Unlike commas, dashes can enclose a full sentence (statement, question, or exclamation) within the sentence:

> When she began, she knew that the subject interested her—she had been raised on a farm and knew the farming way of life intimately—but she was uncertain of how she wanted to treat her subject.

5. Use a dash to give extra emphasis to words or phrases by setting them off from the rest of the sentence:

> Such compassion was new to me—and strange, stranger than a life lived without the benefit of the machine.

> Our name, dear Miss Moore, is—Edsel.

The dash has many uses, but if you scatter dashes throughout your writing, you defeat their basic function—to emphasize certain elements by setting them off from their context. Consider your choices carefully before using a dash where a colon, comma, or parenthesis might go; and never use a dash to replace a period. Two other caveats:

Don't use a comma and a dash side by side:

> But as felled tropical forests gave way to moisture-laden savanna woodlands —excellent breeding grounds for the moisture-hungry tsetse— the
> [ ]   [ ]
> disease gradually spread. *(Notice that the dash absorbs the comma that would ordinarily appear after the introductory clause.)*

In typing, distinguish between the hyphen and the dash, which is typed as two hyphens, with no space before, between, or after them:

> The leaves—silver-white—have a pebbled texture . . .

Parentheses

Use parentheses to enclose explanatory details, examples, qualifications, and incidental remarks that do not require the emphasis of the dash but are too interruptive or incidental to be enclosed in commas:

> The masculine wardrobe is rounded out by a black summer hat (the thing looks like a cereal bowl upside down on a dinner plate) and—again black—a stocking hat for winter. *(descriptive detail)*

> Moore suggested a "Hurricane" series of cars named for birds—the Hurricane hirundo (swallow), the Hurricane aquila (eagle), the Hurricane accipiter (hawk), and so on. *(definition)*

Mendicancy exists worldwide, from the sophisticated international variety (the Salvation Army), to the most innocent, homespun variety (Rover at the dinner table). *(example)*

The narrator's tone—wryly humorous ("As if to prove saws knew what supper meant" or "Neither refused the meeting"), laconic ("No more to build on there"), sardonic ("since they/Were not the one dead, turned to their affairs")—informs the representation with an emotional restraint which intensifies the pathos and the horror of the event. *(quoted examples in literary analysis)*

—Gemino H. Abad, A Formal Approach to Lyric Poetry

About four months after the murder (or manslaughter, as it was later judged), my father decided to rent a house that was directly across from an Amish farm. *(qualification)*

Father glanced into the crowded room, blanched, and quickly went upstairs (he always found it hard to cope with more than one teenager at a time). *(incidental remark)*

Notice in the last example that a single period for the entire sentence comes *after* the closing parenthesis, even when the closing parenthetical remark is a complete sentence in itself. If a parenthetical remark is not appended to a sentence but comes between sentences, the period comes before the closing parenthesis:

In the end, I chose a rifle because it was cheaper. (A shotgun would have cost about seventy-five dollars more.)

Also notice in the other examples that no internal punctuation comes before the opening parenthesis; punctuation that would normally be required after the phrase or clause to which the parenthetical remark is appended comes after the closing parenthesis.

YOU ARE THE EDITOR

Edit the following sentences so that internal marks of punctuation (comma, colon, dash, parentheses, and semicolon) are used appropriately. Where you have a choice, write the sentence in several different ways, and indicate the respective choices you would make for different contexts (formal or informal, circumstances that may require special emphasis, etc.).

```
1.  The defendant is believed innocent (until proven guilty)
    thus, the burden of proof rests on the prosecution.
```

2. A conscientious well-disciplined runner's daily practice and it should be daily, has: three parts—warm-up exercises, the run itself and wind-down exercises.

3. On the one hand he loved his work—he also needed the money it provided—on the other hand he loved his children, and feared, he was neglecting them.

4. He had learned to handle a weapon, fly a plane and survive in a hostile jungle: yet in the ordinary tasks, involved in being a father husband and civilian employee he was utterly helpless.

5. Nowadays women, are urged to "fulfill" themselves, by working outside the home—however few jobs, that a former housewife can get, are very fulfilling.

6. After our miserable performance in class discussion it was clear, what we could expect and what we deserved, the next day, a pop quiz.

7. Scare tactics don't seem to work, in fact more people are smoking now, than ever before.

8. I wasn't prepared for the courses here; even though, I had gone to a demanding, highly reputable, boarding school.

9. The first part of the novel, introduces the reader to the Ramsey family, Mr. Ramsey, his wife based on Virginia Woolf's own mother, and their eight, very different children.

10. Petitions were signed; legal appeals filed; and the governor's mansion picketed: all to no avail, Sacco and Vanzetti who may well have been innocent, were executed in August 1927 seven years after their conviction.

11. Even if the detectives had investigated the case thoroughly; and it appears that they did not; it is unlikely, that they could have solved this carefully planned, professionally executed, crime.

12. Given sufficient information people are capable of making intelligent decisions, and solving their own problems—this assumption is basic in a democracy.

13. Most smokers: listen to their doctor's advice; read the warnings on the pack; hear the public-service announcements on TV; and light up another cigarette.

14. John never called again; nor did I see him, he seemed—to have vanished.

15. We seem to have saved an incredible collection of useless items over the years—children's toys, long since broken and discarded, school papers and report cards, outworn, outdated, snowsuits, sneakers, and prom dresses, concert programs (of performers now long dead), greeting cards snapshots clippings: all the detritus of three decades of family life.

END PUNCTUATION (Period, Question Mark, Exclamation Point)

Once you have learned to identify complete sentences (see Major Sentence Errors, p. 479), you can avoid the other potential trouble spots involved with end punctuation by following a few basic rules:

1. Use a period after all declarative and imperative sentences (the vast majority of all sentences) and after polite questions intended as statements or directions:

> Handguns are designed to kill people.
>
> Be prepared to spend as much as an hour a day practicing.
>
> Would you please fill out the questionnaire and return it in the enclosed envelope.

2. Use question marks after *direct* questions only:

> Whose speed is being read?

Don't put a question mark after an *indirect* question:

> Radar cannot always determine whose speed is being read. (*not* . . . determine whose speed is being read?)

If the first clause of a sentence is a statement and the last a direct question, use a question mark:

> I know the answer, but what is the question?

3. Use exclamation points sparingly, for genuine exclamations (forceful interjections; phrases, clauses, and sentences that express an unusual degree of strong emotion). Usually these occur in dialogue:

"Dumpkopf!" yelled the thoroughly soaked buggy driver.

Don't use exclamation points simply for emphasis:

I started sinking and then I knew. Quicksand. (*not* Quicksand!)

Every nineteen minutes an American is killed with a handgun. (*not* . . . killed with a handgun!)

In the first example, the fragment provides the needed emphasis; in the second the grim statistic itself is emphatic. As Lewis Thomas says (and illustrates) in "Notes on Punctuation":

If a sentence really has something of importance to say . . . it doesn't need a mark to point it out. And if it is really, after all, a banal sentence needing more zing, the exclamation point simply emphasizes its banality!

YOU ARE THE EDITOR

Insert the proper end punctuation in the following student sentences.

1. Would you please let me know what kind of clothes are appropriate for a trip to Honolulu in December____

2. If this is the attitude of a doctor, what can we expect of a poorly educated citizen____

3. The legislators spent the better part of a day debating whether the state should have a state bird; how much time have they devoted to the dumping of nuclear wastes in our state____

4. "You idiot____" he shouted____ "Don't you know that's an electric fireplace____"

5. We would like to know how many students are planning to register next semester____

APOSTROPHE

Since apostrophes are used to form possessives, contractions, and occasionally plurals, omitting or misplacing an apostrophe can affect meaning. Learning the rules can help you make the right choices.

1. Add *'s* to show possession in all singular nouns (even those ending in *s**), all singular indefinite pronouns (such as *everybody, someone else*), and all plural nouns that don't end in *s:*

    the *dog's* breakfast *(singular noun)*

    James's paper route* *(singular noun ending in* s*)*

    my *mother-in-law's* car *(singular compound noun)*

    everybody's worst subject *(singular indefinite pronoun)*

    someone else's locker *(singular indefinite pronoun compound)*

    women's clothing (*plural noun not ending in* s*)*

2. Add the apostrophe alone to show possession in plural nouns ending in *s:*

    the *Smiths'* yard

    the *horses'* hooves

3. Add *'s* to all nouns in a pair or series to show individual possession:

    John's and *David's* cars *(John and David each own a car.)*

    Add *'s* to only the last noun of a pair or series to show joint possession:

    John and David's car *(John and David jointly own one car.)*

4. Place an apostrophe where letters are omitted in contractions:

    it's (it is or *it has)*

    weren't (were not)

    who's (who is or *who has)*

5. Don't use an apostrophe in possessive pronouns:

    The decision is *theirs,* not *yours.*

    The cat kept scratching *its* ear.

    Whose purse is this?

---

*An alternative way of forming the possessive of singular nouns ending in *s* is simply to add an apostrophe: James' paper route. This alternative gives you an extra rule to remember, however; and the possessive so formed usually is not consistent with pronunciation.

6. Don't use an apostrophe to form plurals, except the plurals of letters, numerals, and words used as words:

> She got three *A's* on her report card.
>
> No *if's* or *but's* about it.

7. Use the *of* form of the possessive with most inanimate nouns and in other cases where the apostrophe form is awkward:

> the cellar *of the house* (*not* the house's cellar)
>
> the annual migration *of the geese* (*not* the geese's migration)
>
> the home *of mice* (*not* the mice's home)
>
> the positions *of the editors-in-chief* (*not* the editors-in-chief's positions)

YOU ARE THE EDITOR

Edit the following student sentences, inserting and deleting apostrophes where necessary and making other changes needed to form possessives and contractions correctly.

1. Many men in the consciousness-raising group resented their mothers-in-law's interference in their marriages.

2. The proposed highway would cut through the mooses' feeding grounds.

3. Since my mother and father's parents died before I was born, Ive never had any grandparents.

4. The wives criticisms centered on their husbands unwillingness to help with household tasks.

5. The teacher returned everybody elses' papers with As and Bs on them; he did'nt return her's at all.

6. I dont care who's dog it is; its not staying here.

7. Under joint custody, many children of divorced parents spend equal time in their mothers and fathers residences.

8. The waitress attitude was rude and her service slow.

9. The orders are sent from the various merchants computer's to the central distributors computer.

10. The Frederick's rarely quarrel, but sometimes Mrs. Fredericks' constant criticism's make Mr. Frederick snap back at her.

HYPHEN

For the most part, you use hyphens to satisfy convention; in such cases you may need to check the dictionary to see whether a compound word is hyphenated, written as one word, or written as two words. In other cases, you use hyphens to help readers grasp your meaning quickly. In these cases, if you use hyphens correctly to form compounds and to split words across lines, readers won't have to figure out whether "three year old children" means "children in general who are three years old" or "three children who are one year old." They won't confuse the *re-creation* of a nineteenth-century village with its *recreation*. They won't read *contra-* at the end of one line as a prefix and be brought up short by *ct* at the beginning of the next.

Use a hyphen with the following words and phrases:

1. Two or more words which together serve as a modifier in front of a noun:

slow-moving, traffic-snarled vehicles

black-and-tan coonhounds

four-wheel-drive tractors

twenty- to thirty-year-old males

(Notice in the last example that you insert a hyphen after parts of compounds that are completed later in the sentence.)

Don't hyphenate compound modifiers consisting of an *-ly* adverb and an adjective:

electronically controlled harvesters

2. Fractions and the numbers twenty-one through ninety-nine:

three-fourths

one hundred fourteen men and twenty-three women

3. Compounds formed with the prefixes *all-, ex-,* and *self-:*

> all-channel TV
>
> ex-husband
>
> self-explanatory

4. Compounds formed of prefixes and capitalized words:

> pre-Civil War
>
> anti-American

5. Most compounds formed of prefixes and words that begin with the last letter of the prefix:

> re-examine
>
> semi-invalid
>
> over-react

6. Words that will be misread without the hyphen:

> re-cover (the sofa), distinguished from
>
> recover (from an illness)

You also use a hyphen to divide a word at the end of a line. Several rules apply:

1. Divide only between syllables (and thus never divide a one-syllable word). Generally, you can divide a word after a prefix, *(pro-tect),* before a suffix *(organiza-tion),* and between double consonants *(rag-ged).* Check a dictionary to be sure of the syllabification.

2. Divide so that more than two letters stand at the end of one line and the beginning of the next. Thus, you cannot divide words like *ex-tract* and *en-er-gy.*

3. Divide compound words, whether they are hyphenated or not, only between the words that form them:

> self-satisfied, *not* self-satis-fied
>
> under-achievement, *not* underachieve-ment

YOU ARE THE EDITOR

A. Insert hyphens where needed in the following words and phrases. Place a check mark before the number of any item which requires no hyphens.

1. long or short term credit
2. carefully monitored experiment
3. fifty seven and one half
4. selflimiting
5. reestablish
6. resort the mail
7. hundred dollar bill
8. antiindustrial
9. double parked car
10. first, second, and third place winners
11. resort to violence
12. exPresident Carter
13. semifinal
14. antitrust
15. proCommunist
16. deescalate

B. Use your dictionary, if necessary, to determine the syllable division of the following words. Then insert hyphens wherever the words can be broken at the end of a line. (There may be more than one place.) Put a check mark before any word that cannot be divided at the end of a line.

1. worker
2. running
3. containment
4. pollution
5. alarming
6. onerous
7. location
8. self-cleaning
9. integument
10. grouped
11. buoyancy
12. mezzanine
13. encased
14. gullible
15. unadvised
16. pizza
17. proportion
18. irritatingly
19. necessity
20. mastermind

ABBREVIATIONS, CAPITALS, NUMBERS

Abbreviations

Use the following abbreviations, which are conventional in writing:

1. Abbreviations of titles with proper names:

    > Dr. Richard Selzer, Mr. Smith, St. Francis (*but* the doctor, the saint)

    You may use abbreviations such as *Prof., Sen., Rep., Gen.,* and *Capt.* before full names or before initials and last names, but not before last names only:

    > Prof. John Yu (*but* Professor Yu)

2. Abbreviations for academic degrees:

    > Richard Selzer, M.D.

    > She received her Ph.D. at Purdue after earning her M.A. at Ohio State.

3. Familiar acronyms and initials for organizations, people, objects:

    > UNICEF, FBI, IBM, SPCA, FDR, TV, CB

4. *B.C.* and *A.D.* with specific dates:

    > 100 B.C., A.D. 39

    A.M. or *a.m., P.M.* or *p.m.* with specific times expressed in figures:

    > 2:30 a.m. (*not* ten a.m. *nor* early in the a.m.)

    No. or *no.* and the dollar sign ($) with numerals only:

    > no. 4 (*but not* no. one *nor* the first no.)

    > $10.95 (*but not* $ten *nor* ten $)

In general, avoid other abbreviations:

1. Avoid Latin abbreviations such as *etc.* and *et al.*

    Except in footnotes, bibliographies, and parenthetical comments, use the English equivalents or other words or phrases that fit smoothly into your sentence:

that is (i.e.); compare (cf); for example (e.g.); and others (et al.); and so forth (etc.); versus (vs.)

2. Avoid using an ampersand (&) for *and* and such abbreviations as *Bros.* or *Inc.* except when referring to official names of business firms:

   Dombey & Son, Inc.

3. Avoid abbreviations for units of measurement

   Except in technical or scientific writing, which frequently uses abbreviations or symbols for units of measurement with figures, spell out *inch, foot, pound,* and the like. In informal writing, you may abbreviate long phrases if their abbreviations are commonly understood:

   miles per hour (m.p.h. or mph), cycles per second (c.p.s. or cps), revolutions per minute (r.p.m. or rpm)

4. Avoid abbreviations for place names; days, months, and holidays; names of people; names of divisions of texts (except in parenthetical references):

   MA for Massachusetts, St. for Street, Mt. for Mount

   Tues., Jan., Xmas

   Chas., Wm.

   pp., Ch., Vol.

   Exception. You should use *D.C.* after *Washington; U.S.A.; U.S.S.R.*

Capitals

You know that capitals are used at the beginnings of sentences and in proper names. The following list is a guide to capitalization of words and phrases you may be uncertain about.

1. Capitalize the first and last words of a title and all other words except articles (*a, an,* and *the*), and short (less than five letters) prepositions and conjunctions:

   All's Well That Ends Well; The Merchant of Venice; Much Ado About Nothing.

   Opinion is divided on capitalization of *the* before titles of newspapers and magazines: the *New Yorker* or *The New Yorker;* the *Christian Science Monitor* or *The Christian Science Monitor.*

2. Capitalize *all* the words except articles and short prepositions and conjunctions in place names and names of specific historical events and periods:

> South America (*but* northern Italy)
> Wyalusing State Park (*but* the state park at Wyalusing)
> the Allegheny River (*but* the river Allegheny)
> Park Avenue; the Ritz-Carlton Hotel
> the Church of the Holy Redeemer
> the Battle of Waterloo
> the Sixties; the Middle Ages (*but* the nineteenth century)

Do not capitalize such phrases as *the village hall, the municipal library, the county courthouse* unless they are used as titles without *the:*

> City Hall

3. Capitalize names of races, nationalities, and languages:

> Native American (*but* blacks, whites); Spanish; Swahili

4. Capitalize words that refer to a specific section of a work:

> the Table of Contents; the Preface; Chapter 1 (*but* the first chapter); Volume 4 (*but* the fourth volume); Act III (*but* the third act)

5. Capitalize *north, south, east,* and *west* and their derivatives only when they are part of a proper noun or when they refer to specific regions:

> North Dakota; the South; the Midwest; the Northeast (*but* head south; midwestern accent; northeasterly winds)

6. Capitalize days of the week, months, and holidays; but do not capitalize the seasons:

> Tuesday, January, Halloween (*but* spring, summer, fall, winter)

7. Capitalize titles that precede a proper name:

> President Ford, Uncle Joe, Captain Queeg, Professor Yu

As a general rule, don't capitalize such terms in other contexts:

> the presidential speech; my uncle; Queeg, the captain; John Yu, the professor.

Opinion is divided in the capitalization of high titles like President or King when not followed by a name: *"Mary Tudor was the Queen [or queen]."* Take your choice, but be consistent.

8. Capitalize names of *specific* institutions, political parties, religious denominations, committees, businesses, and movements:

> the University of Wisconsin ("He attended the University" if you are referring to a specific one, *but* "He had a university education"); a Communist (*but* communist philosophy); Christians; Christian beliefs; the Judiciary Committee (*but* "the citizens' committee studying the curriculum"); Ford Motor Company (*but* "an automobile company"); the Art Deco Movement

Numbers

Usage texts generally tell you to spell out numbers you can express in one or two words and to use figures for others: twenty-eight; fifty-three thousand; 146; 23,582. This is a safe rule for most of the writing you do in college. If you look at the practice of published writers, however, you will often find figures used for all numbers greater than ten, especially in informal writing; or figures used for all numbers greater than one hundred, even when they might be expressed in two words. In technical and scientific writing, figures are frequently used exclusively. Base your choice on your material and audience, but generally follow this guide:

Formal:	*Informal:*
three percent	3% or 3 percent
3-1/2 percent	3-1/2 percent
one-eighth	one-eighth
one through one hundred	one through ten
eleven	11
101	101
thirteen hundred	1300 (or 1,300)
1265 (or 1,265)	1265 (or 1,265)
thirty-four thousand	34,000
35,467	35,467
one million	1,000,000
thirty million	30 million

Whatever style you choose:

1. Don't mix figures and written-out numbers within a passage:

> There were 18 students in my class and twenty in yours.

Revised eighteen, twenty (formal)
18, 20 (informal)

> **Exception.** When two numbers (not in a series) immediately follow each other: four 2″ × 4″ posts; 148 three-year-olds.

2. Don't *begin* a sentence with a figure other than a date:

> 29 students signed up for the course last semester.

Revised　Twenty-nine students signed up . . .

> Last semester, 29 students signed up . . .

> A total of 29 students signed up . . .

3. Don't mix abbreviations or symbols with written-out numbers, even though you may use figures with unabbreviated words for units of measurement:

> $15.00 or 15 dollars or fifteen dollars

> $4,500,000 or $4.5 million or 4.5 million dollars

> 3% or 3 percent or three percent (*always write out* percent *for fractional percentages:* 3.8 percent, 2-1/2 percent)

> 3 × 5 cards or three-by-five cards

> 46°F. or 46 degrees F. or forty-six degrees Fahrenheit

> 6′2″ tall or six feet, two inches tall

Even in formal writing some types of numbers are conventionally expressed in figures:

Pairs or series of numbers that are compared:

> Student enrollment increased from 900 to 2,379. (*not* Student enrollment increased from nine hundred to 2,379.)

Exact dates:

> June 6, 1971 (*Without the year, you may write* June sixth.)

> 36 B.C.; A.D. 79

Time of day:

> 3:30; 9 p.m.; *but* nine o'clock, *not* 9 o'clock (*Don't add* o'clock *or redundant phrases like* in the morning *to* a.m. *or* p.m.)

Addresses:

> 525 First Avenue
> Madison, WI 53703

> 123 E. 125th Street
> New York, N.Y. 10025

Scores and statistics:

> odds of 3 to 1; a ratio of 5 to 3; They won 78 to 76 (*but* They won by two
> points.)

Dollars and cents:

> $1.25; $24.32

Pages and other numbered divisions of texts:

> *Othello*, Act II, Scene 1, lines 23–26; Chapter 4, pages 10–16; Volume 10 (*In
> parenthetical references:* II, 1, 23–26; Ch. 4, pp. 10–16; Vol. 10)

YOU ARE THE EDITOR

Edit each of the following sentences twice, following the conventions regarding abbreviations, capitals, and numbers for (1) *formal* writing and
(2) *informal* writing.

1. The locale of faulkner's novels is the south,
    specifically Yoknapatawpha county, an area of twenty–four
    hundred sq. m. bounded by the Rivers Talahatchie and
    Yoknapatawpha.

2. 15,611 people populate the major city of this imaginary
    area, which resembles Oxford, Miss.

3. Only two and a half % of the total population has a
    University education, and this group is largely
    concentrated in the extreme Western part of the Country.

4. You may be able to reach Wm. through his sister, who
    lives at Sixty–five N. Twenty–fifth St., Castille
    springs.

5. The temperature has been below fifteen ° Fahrenheit for 20
    days, and with heating oil at a dollar twenty–five a
    gal., I don't know how we'll last the Winter.

6. In nineteen seventy–two, king Sobhuza II of swaziland had
    one hundred and twelve wives.

7. It is said that Koo–an, the Japanese emperor, reigned for
    almost one hundred years, from three hundred and ninety–
    two to two hundred and ninety b.c.

8. 73 political parties registered for the italian elections of May nineteenth, 1968.

9. 5 blades 30″ long were once swallowed simultaneously to 2/3 of their length by Sandra dee Reed (lady Sandra) of florida, according to the nineteen-seventy-seven ed. of the Guinness Book of World Records, p. 45.

10. My favorite meal at the Neopolitan cafe is the italian Spaghetti, which is a bargain at two-fifty a plate.

11. The classes are held every Tues. evening at 7:30 p.m. and last for 2 hrs., according to the Daily Cardinal.

12. The first postcards were issued on Oct. first, 1869, but pinup girls did not appear on postcards until nineteen hundred.

13. During the 2nd W. W., about fifty-four million, 800 thousand people died, including twenty-two % of poland's population.

14. The earliest dated Cave Paintings were made in about twenty-five thousand b.c. in the périgord region of France.

15. I read Shakespeare without Tears by Margaret Webster, and now I understand some of Shakespeare's plays--e.g., the Comedy Of Errors, Measure For Measure, and Much Ado About Nothing, etc.--more clearly.

MECHANICS OF QUOTING

Uses of Quotation Marks

Use quotation marks to set off dialogue, brief quotations, minor titles, and words used in a special sense. Don't forget to put in the closing quotation marks.

1. Dialogue:

> My dad was kind of curious about Joe and Edna's own family. "How many kids by now, Joe?" he asked.
> "Just the two little ones—Marion and Leroy."
> "Oh, come on," came back Dad, "only two?" The Amish are better known for big families than Catholics.

Notice the punctuation and the lack of capitalization when the quoted sentence is interrupted. Notice, too, that when the speaker changes, you begin a new paragraph.

2. A word, phrase, sentence, or brief passage quoted from another writer or speaker:

> David E. Sherwood and Dennis E. Selder concluded that physical activity "might well help ward off decreased mental sharpness that tends to come with aging."

(Keep the opening capital letter if the quotation is a full sentence.)

For treatment of long quoted passages (block quotes), check your individual style manual or check with your instructor.

3. Poetry of one to four lines:

> Frost suggests the boy's dissatisfaction as early as line 5 when he says, "And from there those that lifted eyes could count / Five mountain ranges one behind the other / Under the sunset far into Vermont."

Notice the slash (/, with a space on either side) used to mark line division.

In the example, the three lines of poetry form a single sentence and fit naturally into the context. Unless this is the case, you should indent and single-space two or more lines of poetry:

> Frost implies this, when he says that the saw,
>
> > As if to prove saws knew what supper meant,
> > Leaped out at the boy's hand, or seemed to leap—
> > He must have given the hand. However it was,
> > Neither refused the meeting.

4. Titles of short works (generally those published within a larger work) and unpublished works. These include short poems; essays; short stories; chapters; magazine and journal articles; episodes of radio and television programs; songs; and unpublished dissertations, theses, and speeches. Underline other titles (see p. 546) except those of your own papers, which are not set off by either italics or quotation marks.

5. Words and phrases used in a special sense (usually to indicate that someone else's term rather than the author's is being used):

> The "radicals" like Sam Adams saw the Sugar Act as challenging the doctrine. *("Radicals" is the designation given to Adams and others like him at the time.)*

Les and I would "duke it out." *(The quoted phrase was Les and the writer's term for fighting at the time.)*

Don't use quotation marks apologetically around a word or phrase that is not appropriate (slang or a cliché, for instance). Reword instead. You may use quotation marks in definitions and to mark off words used as words, though underlining is more common (see p. 546). Whichever system you use, be consistent.

Punctuation Within Quotations

1. Place periods and commas *inside* quotation marks:

   The theme of initiation is an important one throughout the works of both Hawthorne and Melville as evidenced by the stories "My Kinsman, Major Molineux," "Young Goodman Brown," "Billy Budd," and "Bartleby the Scrivener."

2. Place colons and semicolons *outside* quotation marks:

   He fancies himself a "shrewd youth"; in fact, he is quite immature.

   Let us look at the reasons of those who argue that capital punishment is "cruel": . . .

3. Place exclamation points and question marks *outside* the quotation marks *when the entire sentence is an exclamation or question:*

   Did the murderer stop to consider that his treatment of the victim was "cruel"?

   How I resented being called "a gifted child"!

4. Place exclamation points and question marks *inside* quotation marks *when the quotation itself is an exclamation or question:*

   Discipline, as a result, would arise from self-control rather than from the authoritarian command, "Do as I say!"

   "This may be fine," you may say, "but will a foreign language help me in my chosen job?"

Notice that in such cases the punctuation of the quotation is also the end punctuation for the sentence as a whole, even though the sentence may be a statement rather than an exclamation or question. Occasionally, double punctuation will occur with quotations within a sentence, in which case the punctuation for the quotation goes within the closing quotation mark and the other punctuation goes outside of it:

This procedure was followed by the student who wrote the paper entitled "Energy: Is the Answer in the Wind?" which appears in Chapter 11.

5. Place *single* quotation marks around a quotation within a passage you are quoting.

> Buckley argues that the death penalty "cannot . . . be regarded as objectively 'cruel.'" *(Notice that the period comes inside both marks.)*

Use double quotation marks for quotations within a block quote.

Additions, Alterations, and Omissions in Quotations

When you put quotation marks around a passage, you are telling your reader that the quoted writer or speaker said *exactly* what is within the quotation marks. If you need to alter the quotation, you let the reader know that you have changed it by using square brackets ([ ]) or ellipsis marks (. . .).

1. Use square brackets to distinguish between your parenthetical comments and those of the writer you are quoting:

To add an explanatory word or comment:

> "When a little girl," Dickinson writes, "I had a friend [Benjamin Newton] who taught me Immortality; but venturing too near, himself, he never returned."

To add a word or to indicate you have changed the form of a word to make the quotation fit grammatically into your sentence:

> The pity is underscored most especially by the boy's recognition that, "though a child at heart," now "all [is] spoiled."

> Newton, according to Dickinson, "taught [her] Immortality."

Rather than adding *sic (thus)* in brackets to indicate a minor error in a quotation, most writers today silently correct the error unless it is important to call attention to it.

2. Use an ellipsis mark (three *spaced* periods, with a space before and a space after) to indicate an omission in quoted material:

> Perelman found "the effort of writing . . . more arduous all the time."

If the omission comes between two quoted sentences, omit the space before the first period, and add a fourth period:

"The fuel bill for wind power is zero, and wind never gets used up—there is always more. . . . it needs only to be actively promoted to provide the means to overcome our dependence on oil and OPEC."

(Generally, ellipsis marks are not used when the omission comes at the beginning or end of a quoted passage.)

Use a full line of spaced periods when you omit a whole paragraph or more of prose or a whole line or more of poetry.

YOU ARE THE EDITOR

Edit the following student sentences so that quotation marks, square brackets, and ellipsis marks are used properly and so that punctuation is placed correctly in relation to quotation marks. (For exercises involving titles, see p. 546 following Underlining.)

1. It was in the movie versions of the Holmes stories, not the originals, that Sherlock Holmes said, 'Elementary, my dear Watson.'

2. We should not ask, "how many credits does a student need to graduate"? but "what skills should a high-school graduate command"?

3. "Funny!" exclaimed Mr. Pickwick, involuntarily. "Yes, funny, are they not?", replied the little old man, with a diabolical leer.

4. "No longer," he wrote, "Can I stand by and watch you distroy [sic] yourself.

5. The following famous writers were included in what Gertrude Stein called the "lost generation:" Ernest Hemingway, Sherwood Anderson, and F. Scott Fitzgerald.

6. What does the senator mean when he speaks of "adequate defenses?"

7. Algernon Swinburne was called, among other things, ". . . the libidinous laureate of a pack of satyrs; Swinburne himself, however, was not above "bad-mouthing", labeling Emerson, for instance, a "foulmouthed gaptoothed old dog".

8. The final question was, "what cartoon character is famous for the line, "What's up, Doc?"."

9. Thus Dickens describes the technique of "catching a hat":
    "A vast deal of coolness, and a peculiar degree of
    judgment, are requisite . . . A man must not be
    precipitate, or he runs over it; he must not rush into
    the opposite extreme, or he loses it altogether. The
    best way is, to . . . get gradually before it, then make a
    rapid dive, seize it by the crown, and stick it firmly on
    your head."

10. Hamlet shows the same desire to be firm yet just when he
    says that he " . . . will speak daggers to her (Gertrude),
    but use none."

UNDERLINING (Italics)

Underlining in a hand- or typewritten manuscript is the equivalent of italics
in a printed work. Underline to distinguish the following kinds of words
and phrases:

1. Titles:

Books

The Turn of the Screw

Magazines, Journals, Newspapers

the *New Yorker;* the *New England Journal of Medicine;* the *New York Times* or
the New York *Times* (Opinion is divided on treatment of *the* as part of the title
of newspapers and periodicals and of the name of a city as part of a
newspaper's title.)

Plays

King Lear; The Cherry Orchard

Long Poems

Hiawatha; The Faerie Queene

*(Don't underline the Bible or names of legal or historical documents: the
Declaration of Independence; the Constitution.)*

Movies, Radio Programs, Television Programs

Terms of Endearment; Prairie Home Companion; Moonlighting

Works of Art and Long Musical Compositions

the *Mona Lisa,* Mozart's *Symphony No. 39 in E flat major*

Ships, Aircraft, Spacecraft, Trains

the *Nina, Pinta,* and *Santa Maria;* the *Hindenburg; Apollo XII;* the *Broadway Limited*

Use quotation marks around titles of short and unpublished works (see p. 542).

2. Words used as words:

But one spring I began to have trouble choosing *him* or *her* in a sentence.

In defining, you have a choice of using underlining or quotation marks for both the word and the definition, or underlining for the word and quotation marks for the definition:

Napiform means *shaped like a turnip.*

"Napiform" means "shaped like a turnip."

Napiform means "shaped like a turnip."
(*This choice is the most common.*)

Use quotation marks rather than underlining when you refer to words from a text you are analyzing:

In the fourth sentence, the adjective "splintery" appeals to the sense of touch, as does the phrase "sandpaper rough to the touch" of the final sentence.

3. Foreign words or phrases that have not become part of the English language:

deus ex machina, malgré lui, caveat emptor, idée fixe, but not bourgeois, status quo, cliché, karate, naive. (Check a recent dictionary to be sure.)

Do not underline foreign names of people or places.

4. Words and phrases you wish to emphasize:

We see this most clearly when the young child cries "Let *me* do it!"

All the evidence is favorable. The law saves gas. *And* lives.

Like any other means of emphasis, underlining loses its force if overused. Use this device sparingly, for words and phrases that deserve the added stress.

Add quotation marks and underlining as needed in the following student sentences.

1. On Fame the other night, the students presented a musical version of Shakespeare's Othello, which included a song called Desdemona.

2. The word sarcophagus comes from two Greek words, sarx and phagein; together, they mean flesh-eater.

3. Two bronze sculptures by Picasso, The Madman and Head of a Girl, are owned by the Musée des Beaux Arts in Paris.

4. Edwin Newman's Strictly Speaking contains a chapter on business language called The Capacity to Generate Language Viability Destruction.

5. The collision of the Andrea Doria and the Stockholm took place in heavy fog near the Atlantic coast.

6. The Armory Show became a succès de scandale, pitting the avant-garde against the bourgeoisie.

7. Truman Capote's story A Tree of Night was first published in Harper's Bazaar in 1945.

8. The record set includes Beethoven's Symphony No. 1 in C by the Berliner Philharmoniker conducted by Herbert von Karajan.

9. Tonic and milkshake have quite different meanings in New England and the Midwest.

10. A Sunday Afternoon on the Island of La Grande Jatte, a huge painting by Georges Seurat, hangs in the Art Institute of Chicago.

YOU ARE THE EDITOR (Review of Punctuation and Mechanics)

Edit the following sentences to correct errors in mechanics and punctuation. Where there is more than one correct choice, write the sentence in several ways, and decide which version you would use in different contexts (formal, informal, circumstances requiring special emphasis, etc.).

1. Shortly after three p.m. on April fifteenth 1920, paymaster, Frank Parmenter, and Alexander Berardelli his guard, walked down the quiet, main street of provincial south Braintree MA, carrying the 15,776.51-dollar payroll of the Slater and Morrill shoe company from its main office to its factory, a block away.

2. Conceit; arrogance; imagined heroism; rationalization: all these traits of adolescence are present in Henry Fleming the hero of Stephen Cranes novel, "The Red Badge of Courage".

3. Julie Harris starred in a 1 woman play about Emily Dickinson the poet, called The Belle Of Amherst.

4. No one, who has not experienced battle firsthand; and senator Day has not can adequately address the problems of the Soldier, on the front lines.

5. Mrs. Malaprop, a character in Sheridans play, "The Rivals", calls her niece: "as headstrong as an allegory on the banks of the nile;" this confusion of allegory and alligator is called a malapropism.

6. Edvard Munch worked at his painting The Sick Child from eighteen eighty-five to eighty-six but critics called it 'an unfinished attempt'.

7. On her brothers-in-law's advice she sued her exhusband for non support of her three, school age children.

8. After deliberating on the evidence for 5 hrs. the jury brought in it's verdict (guilty of murder in the first degree).

9. Ole Rolvaag, 1876–1931, who was himself a Norwegian immigrant, writes of: what it meant to be a pioneer, and what it meant to be a european in the new world—two, repeated themes in Norwegian American Literature.

10. The Dreyfus Trial in which capt. Alfred Dreyfus was convicted of treason in camera, became a cause célèbre at the end of the 19th century.

11. Another of David Hockney's paintings Picture Emphasizing Stillness, shows two men with their backs to a leopard, that is leaping toward them—between the men and the animal is written "They are perfectly safe. This is a still."

12. In the Years With Ross a biography of Harold Ross the editor of the New Yorker from 1925 to 1951, author, James thurber, records Ross' puzzled reaction to the stir caused by Shirley Jacksons story the Lottery, "Ill never print another story I don't understand"

13. A Night to Remember tells the story of the Titanic, a british liner, that sank in the north Atlantic South of Newfoundland on April Fourteenth, 1912 with a loss of over 15 hundred lives!

14. The Police took the 2 suspects to the scene of the crime, and had them enact the robbery before witnesses, who stood in the same positions, that they had held during the actual crime, thus the witnesses saw the men in the role of robbers, not merely as suspects: a circumstance that tended to elicit positive statements of identity.

15. The 2 person staff of the Nursery School is responsible for 12 3 year olds and 15 four year olds, from 7. A.M. in the morning until 4 o'clock in the afternoon.

16. Over the past three years he has lived in: Taos, N.M., Windsor Ont., Glenview Ill, Lubbock Texas and Bermuda.

17. At 12:00 o'clock midnight Aug. 22, 1927 in the death-house of Charlestown prison the State of Massachusetts perpetrated, what many believe to have been, the legal murder of Nicola Sacco and Bartolomeo Vanzetti.

18. One small room a few pieces of rented furniture and a monthly Social Security Check: could these be all the 86 yr. old woman had after a lifetime of hard work.

19. Where Have All the Flowers Gone? was a popular anti-war song during the 60s—it asks the question "when will they ever learn"?

20. If you read some womens' magazines, "The Ladies home Journal" and "Family circle" for instance over a period of time you get the impression that a woman is not fulfilling her role unless she: cooks gourmet—but cheap—meals daily; is completely available to her husband—and children (at all times); has a full time job and in her spare time of course turns out museum quality patchwork quilts and knitted sweaters.

21. The poor reception accorded the first performance of Madame Butterfly has several, possible explanations—Italian audiences were not accustomed to the oriental harmonies, in fact, outright dissonances that Puccini introduced, they were shocked by the love affair between a japanese girl, and an american sailor, they grew bored by an unusually long, 2nd Act.

22. As the book opens James expresses a wish to go to the lighthouse the next day; but his father says the weather will be too poor for a boat trip—this reaction crushes James, and represents mr. Ramseys typical attitude, toward anything, which interests his son.

23. Residents and campers in the area were warned of the coming eruption of mt. Saint Helens, nevertheless more than 50 people died and almost two hundred survivors had to be brought out by rescuers.

24. The opera, Lucia di Lammermoor based on sir Walter Scotts' novel The Bride of Lammermoor, had it's American *première* at the *Théâtre d'Orléans* New Orleans in the mid Nineteenth Century.

25. Many students today know that Caesar's statement "Veni, vidi, vici" means: "I came; I saw; I conquered;" how many however can relate the latin words to modern English terms, such as convenient, video or victorious.

SENTENCE EFFECTIVENESS

CHOOSING VERBS

1. Whenever possible, express the action (activity, movement, feeling, condition) in your sentences with verbs rather than nouns or adjectives:

Weak	The top eight firms in oil *are in control of* about 57% of the business.
Stronger	The top eight firms in oil *control* about 57% of the business.
Weak	Staking *causes an improvement in* air circulation and thereby *leads to a reduction in* the likelihood of disease infestation.
Stronger	Staking *improves* circulation and thereby *reduces* the likelihood of disease infestation.
Weak	A farmer's livelihood *is dependent on* investment.
Stronger	A farmer's livelihood *depends on* investment.
Weak	Some cancers *are responsive to* medical treatment.
Stronger	Some cancers *respond to* medical treatment.

Each of the weak sentences, of course, contains a verb; but the verb, rather than expressing the primary action of the sentence, serves as a weak link to a noun or adjective that does. Shifting the action from the verb to a noun or adjective weakens a sentence in two ways. First, since nouns and adjectives are static (simply naming or describing something that exists) and frequently the verb is static as well (*is* or *have,* describing a state of being), the sentence lacks force and movement. Second, since the sentence requires a verb to take the place of the one shifted to a noun or adjective, as well as a preposition and/or article, the sentence is wordy.

Sometimes, of course, a verb plus a noun phrase is more precise than a single verb. If you wish to describe a gradual decision, you may prefer to say "reached a decision" instead of "decided"; if you want to emphasize a cause-effect process, you may choose to say "causes a decrease" instead of "decreases." In such cases, you *are* following the rule by expressing the important action of the sentence ("reach" or "cause") in the verb.

2. In general, use the active voice rather than the passive.

Passive	Mathematics *is best learned* by children in the context of their own experience.
Active	Children *best learn* mathematics in the context of their own experience.

As you can see, the active voice is more direct and economical. However, the passive voice may sometimes be appropriate. Here is a quick review of the occasions when the passive voice is justified:

When you want to emphasize the receiver and the action received rather than the doer:

Indeed, in the last Middle Ages, *epileptics were institutionalized* for insanity and demonic possession.

When you want to emphasize the action itself, as in the description of a process:

As the tomato plants increase in size, they *should be staked.*

When you don't know the doer, or the doer is unimportant, as in technical writing:

These films are now ready *to be pumped* into your home.

When you need the passive to maintain appropriate emphasis or point of view:

Violins which *are not handled* with these correct techniques balk when commanded to produce classical music. When this happens, they *are* often sadly *swathed* in silk, *locked* into a velvet case, and *laid to rest* in the attic. *(focus on violins)*

The active voice would be appropriate only in a different context:

When I finally realized I wasn't going to be the next Isaac Stern, or even the first violinist in my high-school orchestra, I sadly *swathed* my violin in silk, *locked* it into its velvet case, and *laid* it to rest in the attic. *(focus on I)*

(See Chapter 5 for detailed treatment of the passive voice.)

A final hint on verbs: When you edit your paper, underline every verb of being *(be, been, am, is, are, was, were)* as well as forms of *have* and *make.* Ask yourself in each instance whether the verb is the best choice or whether it indicates an unjustified passive or a careless shift of action to a noun or adjective. You will probably be surprised at how many verbs you underline and how many you can revise.

YOU ARE THE EDITOR

Edit the following student sentences to strengthen verb forms. If you decide to retain the passive voice in some cases, be prepared to explain why you did so.

1. An announcement was made by the chairman that the special meeting would be closed to the public.

2. In hydroponic gardening, seeds are placed in a liquid growing medium, and the growing of crops takes place in small greenhouses, where they are not affected by the weather.

3. It has been discovered by researchers that many handicapping conditions are caused by a missing or extra gene.

4. In the injection process, liquid metal or plastic is injected into a mold.

5. The content of my report was not questioned, but the professor wanted the organization and style to be improved.

6. Most scholars express the belief that the medal was created by Antonio Pisano.

7. Unless the plastic rod is repeatedly buffed by machine, it will not be able to be moved smoothly in the cylinder.

8. The questioning of the witness was pursued relentlessly by the prosecutor.

9. To achieve eradication of insects before they cause destruction of crops, an identification of the pest must be made by the farmer before choice of the appropriate insecticide can be made.

10. The expectation of most parents is that both academic and extracurricular activities will be engaged in successfully by their children.

ELIMINATING AWKWARD SENTENCES

You can usually detect an awkward sentence by reading it out loud; such a sentence sounds wrong. It is often more difficult to find just what to revise to make it sound right. The awkwardness frequently results from inadvertently using some of the same devices (repetition and separation) that you use intentionally for emphasis. If your instructor diagnoses a sentence as *Awk,* look for one of the following symptoms:

1. Overcoordination

A sentence strung together with clauses connected by *and, but,* and *so* may sound awkward and confusing because no single element receives emphasis:

These centers employ a trained medical staff and aides, *and* their duty is to look after the patients, *but* some centers are understaffed, *so* not all patients get their full share of attention.

To revise, subordinate some of the elements in dependent clauses or modifying phrases:

> These centers employ a trained medical staff and aides *to look after the patients,* but *since* some centers are understaffed, not all patients get their full share of attention.

You might also split the sentences into two independent clauses:

> These centers employ a trained medical staff and aides to look after the patients; *since some centers are understaffed, however,* not all patients get their full share of attention.

If the clauses have the same subject or verb, use a parallel series:

> To register, you pay your fees, [and] then [you] pick up your registration materials, and finally [you] sign up for your courses.

Coordination can be an effective device for emphasizing a profusion of objects or activities or conveying a sense of tedium or sameness, as H. H. Munro ("Saki") does in a short story:

> It was a hot afternoon, and the railway station was correspondingly sultry, and the next stop was at Templecombe, nearly an hour ahead.
>
> —"The Story-Teller"

Awkward coordination, by contrast, results from inattention rather than conscious intent.

2. Tandem or overlapping subordination

Hanging a number of dependent clauses on each other also results in an awkward sentence:

> My other neighbor was Dave, *who* was always looking for work, *which* was scarce in a town *that* had no industry.

To revise, you can turn some of the clauses into modifying phrases or independent clauses:

> My other neighbor Dave was always looking for work, [which was] scarce in a town with no industry.

> Dave, my other neighbor, was always looking for work, but work was scarce in a town with no industry.

3. Successive prepositional phrases

    When your sentence has several prepositional phrases, one after another, it is usually wordy as well as awkward:

    > A survey was conducted of students by the committee on what they thought of the food and service in the cafeteria.

    Revise such sentences by changing passive verbs to active ones and replacing phrases with one-word nouns, verbs, and modifiers:

    > The committee surveyed students' opinions of the cafeteria food and service.

4. Separation of sentence elements

    An adverb phrase or clause between the subject and verb or between the verb and its object or complement interrupts the flow of the sentence, making it sound awkward:

    > The competition for a starting position, *because of the many superior players in the school,* is tough.

    Reposition the interrupting element to eliminate the separation:

    > Because of the many superior players in the school, the competition for a starting position is tough.

    A phrase or clause that separates the parts of a verb phrase or an infinitive also causes awkwardness:

    > Often, the gardener *can,* by growing resistant varieties, *anticipate* the problem of pests.
    >
    > There was no time to *bring* the issue of school bus transportation for handicapped children *up.*
    >
    > It is possible *to* more economically *obtain* garden soil by mixing your own.

    Revised
    > Often the gardener *can anticipate* the problem of pests by growing resistant varieties.
    >
    > There was not time to *bring up* the issue of school bus transportation for handicapped children.
    >
    > It is possible *to obtain* garden soil more economically by mixing your own.

    A single word or brief phrase that "splits" the infinitive is permissible, and even advisable, if its placement elsewhere would be awkward:

The school hopes to *more than* double the minority enrollment by 1986.

"More than to double" would be more awkward, and confusing as well; an alternative would be less economical: "The school hopes to increase the minority enrollment by over 100 percent by 1986."

Sometimes, of course, you may intentionally separate sentence elements for emphasis (see p. 567).

5. Noun clauses as complements

A noun clause after the verb *to be* makes a sentence sound awkward and is usually wordy as well:

My experience during my brother's illness is *what made me decide to become a nurse.*

My experience during my brother's illness is *why I decided to become a nurse.*

Usually you can eliminate the verb *to be* and make the verb of the noun clause your main verb:

My experience during my brother's illness made me decide to become a nurse.

or I decided to become a nurse because of my experience during my brother's illness.

6. Careless repetition of words or sounds

Repetition is a type of wordiness (see p. 566), but using the same word in two different senses or using two different words that sound alike can make even an economical sentence sound peculiar:

Only elders have the *right* to participate in the *rites.*

Revised Only elders may participate in the rites.

Participation in the rites is limited to elders.

When you *write,* be sure to use the *right* tense.

Revised When you write, be sure to use the correct tense.

The same problem results from repetition of sounds, when alliteration or rhyme is not intended:

Particularly packed with paper mills is my hometown, Appleton.

Like overcoordination and separation, repetition may be used for emphasis (see p. 566), and even the repetition of a word in two senses can be effective, when it is intended:

Here he was perched on a fawn leather stool, *neat* little foot on the rail, *neat* little fat hand holding what looked like a *neat* scotch.

—Anthony Burgess, *Earthly Powers*

7. Awkward negatives

Using *not* plus a phrase instead of a word that already has a negative form or that has a positive synonym is awkward:

Such behavior causes the child *not* to obey the parent.

Such use of *not* is even more awkward when it splits an infinitive or is used with a gerund and possessive:

The *child's not respecting* the parent causes him *to not obey* the parent.

Revise by using the existing negative forms or synonyms:

Such behavior causes the child to *disobey* the parent.

The child's *lack of respect* results in *disobedience.*

8. Awkward possessives

Two possessives together or a possessive *'s* attached to a modifier sounds awkward. Use the *of* form of the possessive or, if possible, drop the possessive altogether:

I headed for *John's brother's farm.*

Revised I headed for *the farm of John's brother.*

The *man upstairs' snoring* kept me awake all night.

Revised The snoring of the man upstairs kept me awake all night.

9. Overburdened sentence

Occasionally your sentence is awkward simply because it is trying to say too much:

Since the super-patriotism and anti-alien feeling in America due to World War I at the time of Sacco and Vanzetti's trial combined to cause the radical beliefs and foreign background of the two defendants to become a dominant issue which colored nearly all reports of the crime and subsequent proceedings, perhaps we can evaluate the case more objectively now apart from the high emotion that accompanied it in the 1920s.

The solution is to pull the sentence apart, writing one sentence for each main idea:

At the time of Sacco and Vanzetti's trial, near the close of World War I, super-patriotism and anti-alien feeling ran high in America. For this reason, the radical beliefs and foreign backgrounds of the defendants became an issue which colored nearly all reports of the crime and subsequent proceedings. Now, perhaps, distanced from the hysteria of the 1920s, we can evaluate the case more objectively.

Awkwardness also results from unnecessary use of the passive voice (p. 238), lack of transitions (p. 173), and wordiness (p. 234).

YOU ARE THE EDITOR

Edit the following student sentences below to eliminate awkwardness.

1. Who has the right to force a person who will not adapt normally to society on society?

2. The paper industry has made Appleton prosperous, but it has also polluted its air and water, yet industry officials are now installing pollution controls.

3. The content of the course on urban development in addition to architecture and landscape architecture extended to civil engineering and law.

4. Another poem which shares the structural characteristics of the other poems that we have been discussing but which is somewhat different, not in its form but in the emotion that it expresses, is Sonnet 2.

5. The defendants were radicals who were well known who had preached a revolutionary message that alarmed the conservative businessmen and provincial farmers who made up the jury.

6. The reason for Donne's poem's not being as simple as Shakespeare's sonnet is that the comparisons Donne makes are unusual.

7. The rest of the tourists preferred to rest, but I went with the tour guide on a guided tour, and we saw the colosseum and I was able to view the lions' victims' "waiting rooms" below the grandstand.

8. The investigator hopes when he arrives to arrive at an explanation for the midair collision.

9. He founded a school of Buddhist thought which came to be known as the Ching-chung School, which Tsung-mi described as a school of thought that taught that "one should be mindful of the three phases which correspond to morality, concentration, and wisdom."

10. The reason for the coach's not playing them in the final game was that they had missed the day before's practice.

EDITING FOR ECONOMY

An economical sentence is not the briefest possible expression of an idea, but its most *efficient* expression: it is a sentence in which every word serves a purpose. In the following examples you can see the difference between stripping down a passage to its bare essentials and eliminating unnecessary words:

Original passage:

> Of course, the doomsday machine didn't spring into existence all at once. The superpowers held no unveiling ceremony to announce to mankind that the preparations for the elimination of the human species were now complete. Yet when people turned their attention to the nuclear peril they tended to see it all at once, with astonishment and horror, as though they had suddenly turned around and found themselves looking at a ferocious beast in the room with them *(77 words)*
>
> —Jonathan Schell, "The Abolition," *New Yorker,* January 2, 1984

We could state the basic idea in far fewer words, but only by eliminating the details and devices of emphasis that make the passage vivid and memorable:

> The doomsday machine developed gradually. The superpowers did not just suddenly announce that it was complete. Yet when people noticed it, they tended to see it all at once, with astonishment and horror. *(33 words)*

If, on the other hand, we add words and phrases that are truly superfluous, we dilute the force of the original:

> Of course, [it is a fact that] the doomsday machine's existence did not come into being all at one time. The
>
> didn't spring into existence   once

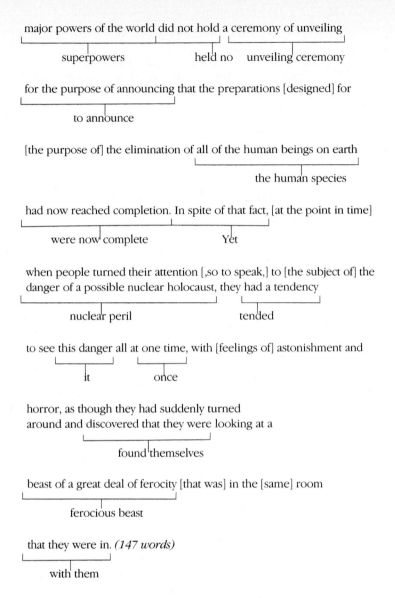

major powers of the world did not hold a ceremony of unveiling
    superpowers   held no   unveiling ceremony

for the purpose of announcing that the preparations [designed] for
    to announce

[the purpose of] the elimination of all of the human beings on earth
    the human species

had now reached completion. In spite of that fact, [at the point in time]
    were now complete   Yet

when people turned their attention [,so to speak,] to [the subject of] the
danger of a possible nuclear holocaust, they had a tendency
    nuclear peril   tended

to see this danger all at one time, with [feelings of] astonishment and
    it   once

horror, as though they had suddenly turned
around and discovered that they were looking at a
    found themselves

beast of a great deal of ferocity [that was] in the [same] room
    ferocious beast

that they were in. *(147 words)*
    with them

When you revise for economy, eliminate unnecessary words and phrases like the ones in the preceding passage, but not vivid details and emphatic constructions that contribute to effect. Chapter 5 details methods of expanding "bare" sentences and reducing wordy sentences. Here is a quick review of the kinds of words and phrases that may make your sentences wordy:

1. Repetitive words and phrases

Repetition of the same word:

Before [scuba-] diving, scuba-divers should carefully check their [scuba-diving] equipment [carefully].

Redundant words and phrases:

Though we tend to underestimate it, pneumonia can be a fatal disease [that causes death].

2. Expletives (There is/are; It is)

[There are] few students [who] can pass all their courses without studying at all.

3. Unnecessary relative pronouns

The most serious and prolonged is the *grand mal* seizure, [which is] characterized by severe muscle spasms and a lack of consciousness.

Holding steady as a rock in this tide of change is Mr. Morris Aronson, [who is] a sixty-five-year-old, bull-headed monument to a past era.

Many students now wear the chic, thin ties [that] they used to laugh at.

4. Phrases that can be expressed in single words

Use single-word adverbs and adjectives instead of prepositional phrases:

During this type of seizure, the victim drops what he is doing and wanders *in an aimless way* [*aimlessly*]

The plan is *of great importance* [*important*].

Use single-word conjunctions and prepositions instead of prepositional phrases:

by means of: by

due to the fact that: because

for the purpose of: for

for the reason that: because

in order to: to

in regard to: concerning; about

in terms of: in

in the event that: if

in the nature of: like

in virtue of the fact that: because

on account of: because

Use strong verbs instead of weak verb-and-noun phrases:

Wordy   We *made an investigation of* students' complaints.

Concise   We *investigated* students' complaints.

Wordy   School districts are *finding it a struggle to provide the funding* for needed programs.

Concise   School districts are *struggling to fund* needed programs.

(See Choosing Verbs, p. 550.)

Use single nouns and adjectives instead of noun phrases and relative clauses:

Wordy   The most common apostrophe errors are *the leaving out of* apostrophes *which are needed* and *the putting in of* apostrophes *which are not called for.*

Concise   The most common apostrophe errors are *omission of needed* apostrophes and *addition of unnecessary* ones.

5. Pretentious circumlocutions

Wordy   I envision my chief purposes for seeking advanced training at the college level to be threefold.

Concise   I want to go to college for three reasons.

6. Unnecessary passive forms

Wordy   Since the brushfire was *quickly put out* by me and my father, the fire department *did not have to be called.*

Concise   Since my father and I *quickly put out* the brushfire, we *didn't have to call* the fire department.

(See Choosing Verbs, p. 550.)

7. Deadwood or "Empty Words"

Some words are so broad as to have almost no meaning until attached (unnecessarily) to other words:

   appearance, area, aspect, character, facet, factor, feature, manner, state, type

When you find that such words are attached to more specific ones, you can usually delete them:

Wordy   His behavior aroused comments *of a critical nature.*

Concise	His behavior aroused *critical comment.*
Wordy	This wine has a unique *type of character.*
Concise	This wine is unique.
Wordy	I am majoring *in the field of* psychology, with a specialty in *the area of* learning disabilities.
Concise	I am majoring in *psychology,* with a specialty in *learning* disabilities.

Phrases such as "I believe" and "in my opinion" are another kind of dead-wood. Since you are the writer, the reader assumes that the paper expresses your view. If you wish to avoid sounding dogmatic on matters of opinion, qualify your statements by such words as *seems, appears, may, is likely.*

Most writers use wordy constructions in their first drafts. Bear in mind, as you revise, that "Ideas will best slide into a reader's mind when the word noise is least" (Jacques Barzun, *Simple and Direct*).

YOU ARE THE EDITOR

Edit the following student sentences to make them as economical as possible.

1. The school board was against the pool for reasons dealing with money.

2. Even when women were in their high-school years, they were prevented from being able to take whatever classes they wanted.

3. All the school board members unanimously gave their approval to fourteen resolutions which were proposed by the National Association of School Boards.

4. There may be psychological stress suffered by the victims if they are not given counseling.

5. The purpose of the program was to aid in the education of nurses and others in the field of public health and to work for the improvement of the health of the community.

6. When it becomes necessary for new products to be repaired or serviced, it may now be necessary for a worker to have additional training in order to perform the task.

7. The final conclusion of the committee was that students were failing to learn the most important essentials for success in college.

8. As far as I can see, the policies of the agency are reflections of the attitudes of government leaders.

9. The expectation of parents for their children to succeed in life is one of the reasons that they encourage their sons and daughters to go to college.

10. It has a similarity to the ancient medals in terms of its combination of Greek and Latin inscriptions.

IMPROVING EMPHASIS

Every sentence you write has some kind of emphasis. Much of what you read in this chapter tells you how to avoid emphasizing the wrong thing. An obvious grammatical error calls attention to itself and deflects attention from the idea you are expressing. A poor choice of punctuation can make your reader hurry past an important word or phrase or pause at one that needs no stress. An awkward sentence is usually awkward because it emphasizes some element that doesn't deserve emphasis: It may draw the reader's attention to a succession of prepositional phrases or of *ands* or *whiches,* or it may make the reader focus on a repeated word or phrase that deserves no stress. By avoiding these unintentional emphases, you improve the effectiveness of your sentences. You can strengthen your sentences even more if you know how to achieve the emphasis you want. Here are some ways to emphasize the important parts of your sentences:

Emphasis by Position

1. Put important words and phrases at the beginning and end of a sentence:

> *Cancer,* second only to cardiovascular disease, is the most dreaded *killer.*

Generally, the end of a sentence is the most emphatic position, the beginning the next most emphatic, the middle the least emphatic. Thus, observing the following rules will improve the emphasis of your sentences:

Avoid putting an unimportant idea at the end of the sentence:

> Venice is now Europe's cesspool, *rather then being its incomparable showpiece.*

Revised   Rather than being the incomparable showpiece of Europe, *Venice is now its cesspool.*

At night, when she crawled quietly into her upper bunk while I slept in the lower, it was her rank odor and not her movement *that wakened me.*

Revised   At night, when she crawled quietly into her upper bunk while I slept in the lower, it was not her movement that wakened me but *her rank odor.*

Avoid deemphasizing an important idea at the end of a sentence by putting it into a participial phrase, which makes a sentence trail off weakly:

After my grandfather died, Rosina suddenly shed her submissive image, *becoming an independent woman.*

Revised   After my grandfather died, Rosina suddenly shed her submissive image and *became an independent woman.*

Avoid a weak *There is/There are/It is* at the beginning of a sentence:

It is *traumatic* to see your own blood shed in an accidental wound.

Revised   Seeing your own blood shed in an accidental wound is *traumatic.*

There are *severe penalties* for racing in the streets.

Revised   The *penalties* for racing in the streets are *severe.*

Avoid beginning a sentence with a conjunctive adverb, unless you want to emphasize the adverb.

However, the Mediterranean people enjoyed the tomato's flavor and used it widely in their cooking.

Revised   The Mediterranean people, *however,* enjoyed the tomato's flavor and used it widely in their cooking.

2. Arrange items in a series from least important to most important (climactic order):

It lacks all the essential characteristics of a true aristocracy: a clean tradition, culture, public spirit, honesty, honor, courage—above all, courage.
—H. L. Mencken, "A Glance Ahead"

Braddock advanced too quickly, he advanced without adequate intelligence, he ordered his troops in the march in a long, thin line (flanks were left unguarded, a mistake in the wilderness), and, worst of all, he failed to secure high ground before entering into battle.

Sometimes, of course, the items in a series serve to describe, to present a sequence of actions, or to stress a proliferation of items of equal weight; then you would arrange the items by space, time, classification, etc.

Emphasis by Subordination

Put the main idea in the independent clause, which receives more emphasis in a sentence than dependent clauses or modifying phrases.

1. Avoid inverted subordination—putting the main idea in a subordinate clause and a lesser one in the main clause:

   Many mail-order garden suppliers sell egg cases of predatory wasps, *which can control tomato hornworms. (The purpose of the paragraph is to tell how to control various garden pests.)*

   Revised   *Tomato hornworms can be controlled by predatory wasps,* whose egg cases are sold by many mail-order garden suppliers.

   Such surgery was not available a hundred years earlier, *when you would have surely lost your life.*

   Revised   A hundred years earlier, when such surgery was not available, *you would have surely lost your life.*

2. Avoid putting the main idea in a modifying phrase:

   Women's magazines, *now concentrating on fitness,* show practically naked, sickeningly skinny models in leotards exercising their way to perfection.

   Revised   *Women's magazines now concentrate on fitness,* showing practically naked, sickeningly skinny models in leotards exercising their way to perfection.

3. Avoid coordinating ideas that are unequal in importance:

   Montessori's approach to preschool education differs greatly from traditional American methods of early childhood education, *and* her philosophy is still fiercely debated in our society.

   Revised   *Because* Montessori's approach to preschool education differs so greatly from traditional American methods of early childhood education, her philosophy is still fiercely debated in our society.

Emphasis by Repetition

Although careless repetition results in wordiness and awkwardness, intentional repetition can emphasize.

1. Repetition of a word, phrase, or clause

   Unemphatic   The buildings match, each four stories high, made of red brick, topped by black slate roofs with gables, and boasting white curtains in every window.

Emphatic	The buildings match, *each* four stories high, *each* made of red brick, *each* topped by black slate roofs with gables, *each* boasting white curtains in every window.
Unemphatic	Diners have discovered that the only two things to be done with a yipper and yapper dancing and prancing about are to kill it or *feed it.* Most choose *the latter course.*
Emphatic	Diners have discovered that the only two things to be done with a yipper and yapper dancing and prancing about are to kill it or *feed it.* Most choose to *feed it.*
Unemphatic	All that I could think of as I walked down the street was that *my hair was short.* It was snowing, and *that was all there was on my mind.*
Emphatic	All that I could think of as I walked down the street was that *my hair was short.* It was snowing, and *my hair was short.*

2. Repetition of structure

Parallelism:

Unemphatic	No one can deny that the perpetual crush of heavy traffic is *injurious to health; it is also bad for emotional well-being and offends aesthetic sensibilities.*
Emphatic	No one can deny that the perpetual crush of heavy traffic is injurious *to health, to emotional well-being,* and *to aesthetic sensibilities.*
Unemphatic	It's a violin when a violinist plays it, but when a fiddler plays it, then it's a fiddle.
Emphatic	If a violinist plays it, it's a violin; if a fiddler plays it, then it's a fiddle.
Unemphatic	The utter randomness in the choice of victim *shocks and alarms the reader.*
Emphatic	The utter randomness in the choice of victim *not only shocks the reader but also alarms him.*

Emphasis by Separation

Setting off an idea, phrase, or word gives it emphasis.

1. Give an important idea its own sentence:

Emphatic	In the name of national security, *all things can be threatened, all risks taken, all sacrifices demanded.*
More Emphatic	In the name of national security, *all things can be threatened. All risks can be taken. All sacrifices can be demanded.*

—Richard J. Barnet, "Challenging the Myths of National Security"

For the sake of emphasis, even a part of a sentence may be detached and punctuated as a complete sentence:

> It now boasted a Jardine header, K.C. alloy sprocket, King and Queen seats, sissy bar, and drawn-back handlebars lowered in the rear and extended in the front. *A chopper.*

But don't set off an unimportant idea in a sentence by itself:

Unemphatic   I never wanted to go to sleep. *I was like a lot of kids that way.*

Emphatic   *Like a lot of kids,* I never wanted to go to sleep.

2. Use a colon or dash to set off an element at the end of a sentence:

Unemphatic   Research is providing new scientific underpinnings for August Strindberg's visceral guess *that men and women are different.*

Emphatic   Research is providing new scientific underpinnings for what August Strindberg viscerally guessed: *men and women are different.*

Unemphatic   But then *the inspiration I needed* came to me.

Emphatic   But then it came to me—*the inspiration I needed.*

3. Use a pair of dashes to set off an element within a sentence:

Unemphatic   Break-ins, wiretaps, deception of Congress, assassination attempts on foreign leaders, *and, indeed, the Watergate cover-up and the intervention in Vietnam* were all ordered in the name of national security.

Emphatic   Break-ins, wiretaps, deception of Congress, assassination attempts on foreign leaders—*indeed, the Watergate cover-up and the intervention in Vietnam*—were all ordered in the name of national security.

—Richard J. Barnet, "Challenging the Myths of National Security"

4. Use unconventional commas, and separate commonly joined sentence elements by inserted words:

> If such things occur, he thinks, and with this frequency, what is to prevent them from happening to him, or to those he loves? And the answer, quite realistically, is, of course, nothing.

The comma before *or* would normally be omitted but is used here to stress the final phrase. In the second sentence, the unconventional (and in other cases awkward) insertion of adverbs between subject and verb and verb and complement, puts extra stress on *nothing.*

Emphasis by Varying Sentence Type and Pattern

Since most sentences are statements, sentences in other forms, such as a question, command, or direct quotation, are emphatic by contrast:

Unemphatic	I also took Latin.
Emphatic	Dare I mention that I also took Latin?
Unemphatic	She wanted to know how I could have done that to her.
Emphatic	"How could you do this to me?" she wanted to know.

Varying the normal subject-verb-object order of a sentence can also emphasize the word that is shifted:

Unemphatic	I *never* wanted to go through such an experience again.
Emphatic	*Never* do I want to go through such an experience again.
Unemphatic	I still carry *the scars* with me.
Emphatic	*The scars* I still carry with me.

Limit your use of such inversion, or your style will sound eccentric rather than emphatic.

Emphasis by Mechanical Devices

Occasionally, underlining a word or phrase gives it a needed stress you can't achieve by other means.

> But scientists now believe that men and women are now alike in more fundamental ways. Men and women seem to experience the world differently. (*Without the underlining, the word* experience *would lack stress because it is in the middle of the sentence.*)

In general, however, avoid using devices like capitals, underlining, quotation marks, and exclamation points for emphasis.

Of course, sentences are always more emphatic when they are concise rather than wordy, when their verbs are active rather than passive, when their words are concrete and precise rather than abstract and vague. (See Editing for Economy, p. 559, Choosing Verbs, p. 550, and Choosing Words, Ch. 6.)

YOU ARE THE EDITOR

Edit each of the following student sentences to make it more emphatic.

1. Sometimes there are special appearances made by the Green Bay Packers.

2. The United States was the first nation to land a human being on the moon, pioneered space communication technology, and has one of the most advanced space stations.

3. Over half the city's working population, people who without the mills would be out looking for work, are employed by the mills.

4. The person who founded the new school of Buddhist thought was a prince from Korea and was referred to as the ''monk Chin.''

5. Abortions should be allowed if prenatal examination reveals that the unborn child would be severely handicapped. I can't stress enough that the unborn baby has to be handicapped in some severe way before abortion should be allowed.

6. Wisconsin is the number-one dairy-producing state, although the paper industry is just as important as the dairy industry to Wisconsin's economy.

7. The opportunity to compete is the most challenging aspect of being a member of the club whether a person is a beginner or a more advanced swimmer.

8. In less than three minutes, two of the town's citizens had died violently, the little factory town had become the scene of a brutal crime, and its quiet main street had been transformed into an excitely noisy thoroughfare.

9. A factual piece of evidence on which the jury could hang a verdict of ''Guilty'' now was presented by the prosecution, which had so far established no concrete proof of guilt.

10. Unfortunately, more and more mothers with young children are going to work, leaving their children at worst alone at home or else at impersonal day care centers.

YOU ARE THE EDITOR (Review of Sentence Effectiveness)

Edit the passage below to strengthen verb forms, eliminate awkward sentences, and improve economy and emphasis.

I came from tiny Shelby High to the state university, and I had a feeling as though I had all of a sudden undergone a change from an angelfish in an aquarium to a minnow in the Atlantic when I arrived at the university. At first, it took an effort of all my power of will to not reverse the course of my future existence and return back in ignominious shame to my secure niche in Shelby. There were two things that made the biggest impression on me and caused me to feel intimidated about this university. One thing is that it is so large in size, and the other thing has to do with the subject of its variety. There is a total population of 1800 people in Shelby, compared to 40,000 people who are going to classes here on this campus. And while there are buses that take these people to and from all of their classes for the reason that the distances between classes can be too far to walk since the campus is so large, there isn't anywhere in Shelby that couldn't, by a walk of about fifteen minutes' time, be gotten to. There are concerts in Shelby that are publicized and advertised for months, and an audience of fifty is one that is considered to be large. There are classes which are held in large lecture halls here which have as many as five hundred individual students in them every day. There are over two hundred departments which you can take such diverse subjects as Swahili, Chinese calligraphy, and Pueblo pottery-making in. Some departments are so large that they have more students and they offer more courses and they employ more instructors than were present in the whole of my high school. The Agriculture Department alone, for instance, has many farms and labs and different buildings for classes as well, and it has about thirty different special areas of agriculture, such as the fields of agricultural economics, dairy science, and animal nutrition, that may be chosen by students to major in.

Apart from size, the variety of the university is impressive. I saw, on the first day I was here, in addition to a man who had once been a secretary of state and someone else who was the winner of a Nobel Prize, Indians wearing saris and turbans, Africans who had ritual scars on their cheeks, and followers of the Hare Krishna sect of religion who were wearing long robes of

saffron color and who had shaved their heads. I
even saw all different kinds of American students
who had a range from preppies all the way to punk
rockers. I took my first walk on campus and
passed a nuclear reactor, the nation's first
radio station, a tennis stadium that is famous
all over the world, a wildlife refuge, and a
lake. I would judge that all of this took place
inside of about the first fifteen minutes of time
of my walk. Not exactly the same as walking down
Main Street back home in Shelby.

ACKNOWLEDGMENTS

Abad—Gemino H. Abad, *A Formal Approach to Lyric Poetry.* University of the Philippines Press, 1978, pp. 233–34.

American Heritage—From definition for "rose," reprinted by permission from *The American Heritage Dictionary of the English Language,* Second College Edition. Copyright © 1982 by Houghton Mifflin Company.

AP News—"A Bloody clash between . . ." AP news item, dateline Creys Malville, France.

AP News—"State Troopers and National Guardsmen." AP news item, dateline October 6, 1979.

Barnet—Richard J. Barnet, "Challenging the Myths of National Security." *New York Times Magazine,* April 1, 1979, p. 25.

Berler—"The Bill James Historical Baseball Abstract" by Ron Berler. Reprinted by permission of the author.

Bledsoe—Editorial on NCAA Proposal 48 by Bruce Bledsoe from *Reno Gazette-Journal,* January 18, 1983. Reprinted by permission.

Boatright—Reprinted with permission of Macmillan Publishing Company and Texas Folklore Society from *Folk Laughter on the American Frontier* by Mody C. Boatright, pp. 38–39, 43, 87, 118, 132–134, 143–144. Copyright 1942, 1943, 1945, 1949, by Mody C. Boatright, and renewed 1970 by Mody C. Boatright. Copyrights renewed 1971, 1973, 1977 by Elizabeth K. Boatright, Mody K. Boatright and Frances B. Speck.

Boatright—*Sketches and Eccentricities of Col. David Crockett of West Tennessee,* 1833, p. 164.

Borroff—From "Robert Frost's New Testament: Language and the Poems" by Marie Borroff in *Modern Philology,* Volume 69, Number 1, pp. 47–48. Copyright © 1971 by the University of Chicago. All rights reserved. Reprinted by permission of the University of Chicago Press.

Boston Globe—Editorial on NCAA Proposal 48 from *The Boston Globe,* January 29, 1983. Reprinted courtesy of The Boston Globe.

Bronowski—J. Bronowski, *Science and Human Values.* Harper and Row, 1956.

Brustein—"Reflections on Horror Movies" in *The Third Theatre* by Robert Brustein. Copyright © 1958, 1960, 1961, 1965, 1966, 1967, 1968, 1969 by Robert Brustein. Reprinted by permission of Alfred A. Knopf, Inc.

Buchwald—"Weapon-naming keeps Pentagon planners busy" by Art Buchwald. Copyright © 1982 by the Los Angeles Times Syndicate. Reprinted by permission of the author.

Catton—"Grant and Lee: A Study in Contrasts" by Bruce Catton in *The American Story: The Age of Exploration to the Age of the Atom* edited by Earl Schenck Miers. Reprinted by permission of the U. S. Capitol Historical Society. All Rights Reserved.

Chambon—Pierre Chambon, "Split Genes." *Scientific American,* May 1981.

Chase—Hall, Milton, *Getting Your Ideas Across Through Writing,* Washington, Federal Security Agency, Training Manual No. 7, 1950. Cited in *Power of Words* by Stuart Chase. New York: Harcourt, Brace & World, 1953, p. 255.

Chronicle of Higher Education—From "Marginalia" in *The Chronicle of Higher Education,* July 28, 1982. Copyright © 1982 by The Chronicle of Higher Education. Reprinted with permission.

Coleman—From "Doors Leap Open" by Alice Coleman in *English Journal,* November 1964, pp. 631–633. Reprinted with the permission of the National Council of Teachers of English.

Coupe—Courtesy of Porsche Audi.

Dahl—From "Crisis in the Classroom" letter by Stephanie H. Dahl to *Newsweek,* May 23, 1983. Reprinted by permission of the author.

Devlin—" 'Twas the Night before Christmas (in a manner of speaking)" by Roger Devlin. Reprinted by permission.

Dickens—From a book review "A Woman's Best Friend," by Monica Dickens, *The New York Times,* November 9, 1986. Copyright © 1986 by The New York Times Company. Reprinted by permission.

Didion—Joan Didion, "Why I Write." *New York Times Book Review,* December 5, 1976.

Douglass—Frederick Douglass, "Address to the People of the United States."

Dutka—From "X-Rays: The Inside Picture" by Elaine Dutka as appeared in *Cosmopolitan,* May 1981. Reprinted by permission of the author.

Eric Database—Wind Energy search from *Eric* Database, ERIC-66-83/Dec. Reprinted by permission of *Dialog* Information Services, Inc.

Farbstein—W. E. Farbstein, *New York Times,* March 29, 1953, as cited in *Power of Words* by Stuart Chase. New York: Harcourt, Brace & World, 1953, p. 250.

Fine—Gary Alan Fine, "Little League Baseball and Growing Up Male." *Men in Difficult Times: Masculinity Today and Tomorrow,* Prentice-Hall, Inc., 1981, p. 73.

Frost—" 'Out, Out—' " from *The Poetry of Robert Frost* edited by Edward Connery Lathem. Copyright 1916, © 1969 by Holt, Rinehart and Winston. Copyright 1944 by Robert Frost. Reprinted by permission of Holt, Rinehart and Winston, Publishers.

Fuchs—"How to Save Social Security" by Victor R. Fuchs. Reprinted by permission.

Gass—William H. Gass, "In the Heart of the Heart of the Country." *In the Heart of the Heart of the Country.* Harper and Row, 1968, p. 176.

Gelman—From "Just How the Sexes Differ" by David Gelman from *Newsweek,* May 18, 1981. Copyright © 1981 by Newsweek, Inc. All rights reserved. Reprinted by permission.

Gleick—James Gleick, "Exploring the Labyrinth of the Mind." *New York Times Magazine,* August 21, 1983.

Hart—"Anti-Smoking Push a Feminist Plot?" by Jeffrey Hart. Reprinted by permission of King Features Syndicate.

Hayakawa—From *Language in Thought and Action,* Fourth Edition, by S. I. Hayakawa, copyright © 1978 by Harcourt Brace Jovanovich, Inc. Reprinted by permission of the publisher.

Hemingway—Ernest Hemingway, "Big Two-Hearted River." *The Nick Adams Stories,* Charles Scribner's Sons, 1972.

Holahan—"Why Did I Ever Play Football?" by David Holahan. Reprinted by permission of the author.

Hughes—Langston Hughes, "Salvation," *The Big Sea: An Autobiography.* Alfred E. Knopf, 1940.

Huxley—Thomas E. Huxley, "On Our Knowledge of the Causes of the Phenomena of Organic Nature." *Darwiniana,* Greenwood Press, 1968, p. 365–66.

Inglis—David R. Inglis, "The Answer Is Blowing in the Wind." *The Progressive,* 1977, p. 46.

King—From "Letter from Birmingham Jail—April 16, 1963" in *Why We Can't Wait* by Martin Luther King, Jr., pp. 83–84. Copyright © 1963 by Martin Luther King, Jr. Reprinted by permission of Harper & Row, Publishers, Inc.

Kroll—From "Happiness Is a Single Self" by Jack Kroll in *Newsweek,* July 18, 1983. Copyright © 1983 by Newsweek, Inc. All rights reserved. Reprinted by permission.

Lee—Laurie Lee, "Appetite," *I Can't Stay Long.* Atheneum, 1976.

Lewis—Flora Lewis, "The Quantum Mechanics of Politics." *New York Times Magazine,* November 6, 1983.

Los Angeles Times—"Figuring It Out by Degrees," *Los Angeles Times,* July 27, 1986. Copyright © 1986 Los Angeles Times. Reprinted by permission.

Lowe—Katherine Lowe, "Male Teachers and Young Children." *Men in Difficult Times: Masculinity Today and Tomorrow.* Prentice-Hall, Inc., 1981, p. 188.

Lukacs—John Lukacs, from a review of "The Complete Works of Saki." *New York Times Book Review,* March 28, 1976.

Malia—Martin Malia, "Poland's Eternal Return." *New York Review of Books,* September 29, 1983.

Matthes—From "Quicksand" by Gerard H. Matthes in *Scientific American,* June 1953, p. 101. Reprinted by permission.

Mencken—H. L. Mencken, "A Glance Ahead." *Notes on Democracy,* Alfred A. Knopf, 1926, p. 203.

Mencken—H. L. Mencken, "Euphemism." *The American Language,* Alfred A. Knopf, 1945.

Mitford—Jessica Mitford, *The American Way of Death.* Simon and Schuster, 1963.

Moore—"The Ford Correspondence" from *A Marianne Moore Reader* by Marianne Moore. Copyright © 1957 by The New Yorker Magazine, Inc. Reprinted by permission of Viking Penguin Inc. and The Estate of Marianne C. Moore.

Morris—William and Mary Morris, *Harper Dictionary of Contemporary Usage.* Harper & Row, 1975.

Nelson—"The Desk" by Michael Nelson. Reprinted by permission of the author.

Newman—From "Torrents of Babel" by Edwin Newman in *Omni,* October 1980. Copyright © 1980 by Edwin Newman, and reprinted with permission of Omni Publications International, Ltd.

New York Times—From Editorial "We Hear You, Mr. President" from *The New York Times,* September 11, 1983. Copyright © 1983 by The New York Times Company. Reprinted by permission.

Partridge—From Introduction to *A Dictionary of Clichés* by Eric Partridge. Copyright © 1978 by Eric Partridge. Reprinted by permission of Routledge & Kegan Paul Ltd.

Pave—"Corporate Women Have It All—But A Family LIfe" by Irene Pave. Reprinted from June 2, 1986 issue of *Business Week* by special permission, © 1986 by McGraw-Hill, Inc.

Penske—"Fifty-Five Is Fast Enough" by Roger Penske from *The Reader's Digest,* April 1981. Reprinted by permission of the author.

Pirsig—Robert M. Pirsig, *Zen and the Art of Motorcycle Maintenance.* Bantam Books, April 1974.

Porter—Katherine Anne Porter, "Flowering Judas." *Flowering Judas and Other Stories,* Random House, 1930.

Prescott—"Watching Life Go By" by Peter S. Prescott, *Newsweek,* September 9, 1985. Copyright © 1985 by Newsweek, Inc. All rights reserved. Reprinted by permission.

Rapid City Journal—Editorial on NCAA Proposal 48 from *Rapid City Journal,* January 20, 1983. Reprinted by permission.

Rowan—"Unforgettable Miss Bessie" by Carl T. Rowan. Reprinted with permission from the March 1985 Reader's Digest. Copyright © 1985 by The Reader's Digest Assn., Inc.

Ryder—Review of *Right Plant, Right Place* by Ann Ryder. Reprinted by permission of Ann Ryder.

Sarton—"The Rewards of Living a Solitary Life" by May Sarton, *The New York Times,* April 6, 1974. Copyright © 1974 by The New York Times Company. Reprinted by permission.

Schickel—"Meditations on Celebrity" by Richard Schickel from *Time,* July 11, 1983. Copyright 1983 Time Inc. All rights reserved. Reprinted by permission from *Time*.

Schneider—Alan Schneider, "Baltimore Boy 1930–1939," *Entrances: An American Director's Journey.* Viking, 1986.

Shapiro—"Auto Wreck" reprinted from *Collected Poems 1940–1978,* by Karl Shapiro, by permission of Random House, Inc. Copyright 1942 and renewed 1970 by Karl Shapiro.

Shapiro—From *Lonely in Baltimore: Personal Columns* collected by Raymond Shapiro. Copyright © 1983 by The Madison Press Limited and Raymond Shapiro. Used by permission.

Solomon—From "Teaching the Nominative Absolute" by Martha Solomon in *College Composition and Communication,* December 1975. Copyright © 1975 by the National Council of Teachers of English. Reprinted by permission.

Stafford—William Stafford, from "A Way of Writing" in *Field,* Spring 1970. Reprinted by permission.

Steinbeck—John Steinbeck, "The Creative Cross." *Sweet Thursday,* The Viking Press, 1954.

Strindberg—From "The Father" by August Strindberg in *Six Plays of Strindberg,* translated by Elizabeth Sprigge. Copyright © 1955 by Elizabeth Sprigge. Reprinted by permission.

Sullivan—From "The Cliché Expert Testifies on Love" from *A Pearl in Every Oyster* by Frank Sullivan, 1938. Reprinted by permission of the Historical Society of Saratoga Springs.

Talese—Gay Talese, "New York." *Esquire,* July 1960.

Thomas—Lewis Thomas, "Death in the Open," *The Lives of a Cell: Notes of a Biology Watcher.* Bantam Books, 1974.

Thomas—Michael M. Thomas, "Mrs. Fish's Ape." *Vanity Fair,* September 1983.

Thornton—From "Frost's 'Out, Out—' " by Weldon Thornton in *The Explicator,* Volume XXV, Number 9, May 1967, a publication of the Helen Dwight Reid Educational Foundation. Copyright © 1967 by *The Explicator.* Reprinted by permission of Heldref Publications.

Updike—John Updike, *Rabbit, Run.* Alfred F. Knopf, 1960.

Virginian Pilot—Editorial on NCAA Proposal 48 from *The Virginian-Pilot,* January 20, 1983. Reprinted by permission.

Review by Brigette Weeks of *The Accidental Tourist* by Anne Tyler. Reprinted by permission of Brigette Weeks.

White—E. B. White, "A Study of the Clinical 'We'," *Quo Vadimus? or The Case for the Bicycle.* Harper and Brothers, 1939.

Williamson—Samuel Williamson, "How to Write Like a Social Scientist." *Saturday Review,* October 4, 1947.

Yergin—Daniel Yergin, "Fulbright's Last Frustration." *New York Times Magazine,* November 24, 1974.

Index

Fine, Gary Alan, from "Little League Baseball and Growing Up Male," 373

Fitzgerald, F. Scott, 6

Footnotes, *see* Endnotes

Formal style, 250–52, 492–93

Fragment
    editing of, 485–86
    as sentence error, 482–84
    uses of, 223, 484

Fraser, David, "What Is Farming?" (student essay), 144–46

Free modifiers, 211–13, 225–26, 517

Freewriting, 28

Frost, Robert, " 'Out, Out—,' " 393–95

Fuchs, Victor R., "How to Save Social Security," 344–46

Fused sentences
    editing of, 482
    as sentence error, 481

G

Gaskins, Denise, "I Believe in Gryphons" (student essay), 119–22

Gass, William, from *In the Heart of the Heart of the Country,* 322

General and specific words, 246

Generality, levels of, 214–15

Generalizations, 329

Gibbs, Wolcott, 4

Gleick, James, from "Exploring the Labyrinth of the Mind," 260

Gross, Major Ryan, "Easy Surgery" (student essay), 160–62

H

Hanley, Sheila, "Letter to Mr. X" (student essay), 9–10

Hart, Jeffrey, "Anti-Smoking Push a Feminist Plot?" 330–32

Hasty generalization, 329

Hayakawa, S. I., from *Language in Thought and Action,* 247–48

Hemingway, Ernest, 6, 218

Hintz, Nancy E., "One of Us" (student essay), 147–49

Holahan, David, "Why Did I Ever Play Football?" 113–15

Holt, John, from *Freedom and Beyond,* 130–33

Holistic evaluation
    of "Letter to Mr. X," 7–10
    of essay exams, 370–73

"How to Buy a Stereo" (student essay for editing), 315–18

Hruskocy, Carole, "I. Q. Testing?" (student essay), 347–49

Hughes, Langston, "Salvation," 81–83

Huxley, Thomas Henry, from *Darwiniana,* 326

Hyphenation, 532–33

I

Illustration
    in essays: "A Study of the Clinical 'We,' " 95–97; "Death in the Open," 97–100
    as pattern of development, 94–100
    structure of, 95
    as topic of invention, 41

Indexes, 420–24

Induction, 326–28

Informal style, 251–52, 492–93

Inglis, David R., from "The Answer Is Blowing in the Wind," 426

"Injustice of Early Finals, The" (student essay for editing), 292–94

Interpretation, in book review, 377

Introductory paragraphs, 178–83

Italics, *see* Underlining

J

Jargon and gobbledygook
    explained, 265–67
    editing of, 268–70, 274

Johnson, Josephine, from "April," 484

Johnson, William, "Aerodrome" (student essay), 277

Journal keeping, 32–36

K

Kagan, Carole, "Barbie Doll" (student essay), 162–64

King, Martin Luther, Jr., from *Why We Can't Wait,* 207–08

Korda, Michael, from "How to Be a Leader," 139

Kroll, Jack, "Happiness Is a Single Self," 363–64, 366–67

L

Labate, Lorraine, "Mendicancy" (student essay), 133–36

La Pack, Mark, "Ride! Don't Run" (student essay), 288–91

Laubenstein, Mark, "The Arrogant Sparrow" (student essay), 263–64

Leacock, Stephen, 26

Lee, Laurie, "Appetite," 140–42

Lewis, Flora, from "The Quantum Mechanics of Politics," 224

Library
    as aid to invention, 32
    uses of in research, 417–25

Library of Congress Subject Headings, 418

Limiting a subject, 44–45

Littleton Courier, The, 394

Logical appeal, 326–29

Lopez, Barry, from "My Horse," 484

Los Angeles Times, 100–102

Losey, Mary, "Letter to Mr. X" (student essay), 8

Lowe, Katherine, from "Male Teachers and Young Children," 373

Luesch, Roger, "Letter to Mr. X" (student essay), 9

Lukacs, John, from "Review of *The Complete Works of Saki,*" 224

M

Malia, Martin, from "Poland's Eternal Return," 251

Marsh, Jeffrey, from "Engineers and Society," 202

Martex ad, 372

Matthes, Gerard, from "Quicksand," 154–55

Memory, in invention, 27

Mencken, H. L., from "A Glance Ahead," 202

Mencken, H. L., from *The American Language,* 271

Metaphor, 257

Miller, Philip D., "The Fort" (student essay), 88–89

Misplaced modifiers, 509–11

Mitford, Jessica, from *The American Way of Death,* 270

Mixed patterns of development, 147–50
    in essays: "Reflections on Horror Movies," 70–77; "One of Us" (student), 147–49

MLA parenthetical documentation
    for article, 430–31
    for book, 430
    explained, 429
    most common forms of, 431–32
    sample Works Cited page, 454–56

Modification, in sentence expansion, 196–97

Modifiers
    bound, 212
    clause, 196
    dangling, 239, 507–09
    free, 211–13, 517
    misplaced, 509–11
    nonrestrictive, 517–518
    phrase, 196
    restrictive, 517
    word, 196

Moore, Marianne, from *A Marianne Moore Reader,* 23–24

Morris, William and Mary, from *Harper Dictionary of Contemporary Usage,* 270–71

Munro, H. H., from "The Story-Teller," 554

N

Narration
    in essays: "Cherry-Red Stockings" (student), 33–36; "The Penalties of Pride (student)," 78–81; "Salvation," 81–83; from *Entrances,* 83–85; "The Final Heat" (student), 241–42
    as pattern of development, 77–85
    structure of, 77–78

NCAA Proposal 48, editorials about, 408–12

Nelson, Michael, "The Desk," 324–25

Newcomer, Meg, "Cherry-Red Stockings" (student essay), 36

New England Journal of Medicine, 513

Newman, Edwin, from "Torrents of Babel," 249

Newsweek, "Just How the Sexes Differ," 183–84

New York Times, 211

Noble, David, from "A Neo-Luddite Plea," 400

Note taking, for research
    organizing note cards, 426
    paraphrasing, 426–28
    quoting, 425
    sample note cards, 425
    summarizing, 426–28

Numbers, 538–40

O

On-line search, 422

On-the-spot observing, 30

Order
    climactic, 333
    general-to-specific, 157–58
    spatial, 164–68

Process analysis
    in essays: "Figuring It Out by Degrees,"
        100–102; "Not Kid's Play" (student), 102–05;
        "Easy Surgery" (student), 160–62
    as pattern of development, 100–106
    structure of, 100
    as topic of invention, 42
Proofreaders' marks, inside back cover
Pronouns
    agreement with antecedents, 489–90
    case of, 491–92
    editing of, 491, 494, 495–96, 499–500
    reference of, 494–95
    shifts in, 496
    use of, for coherence, 172
Prospectus
    defined, 433
    format of, 434
    purpose of, 433
    sample of, 435–40
Punctuation
    apostrophe, 529–31
    brackets, 544
    colon, 480, 522–23, 543
    comma, 479–80, 513–20, 543
    dash, 524–25
    ellipses, 544–45
    exclamation point, 528–29, 543
    hyphen, 532–33
    parentheses, 525–26
    period, 528, 543
    question mark, 528, 543
    quotation marks, 541
    semicolon, 480, 520–22, 543
Purpose
    and thesis, 44–45
    choosing a, 12

Q

Question marks, 528
Quotation marks, 541–45
Quotations
    ellipses in, 428, 544–45
    introducing, 427
    length of, 428
    in note taking, 425
    plagiarizing, 428
    punctuation of, 519, 523, 541–45
    in research papers, 426–29

R

Rapid City Journal, The, 411
Reader's Guide to Periodical Literature, 421
Reasoning
    deductive, 328–30
    inductive, 326–28
Reference works
    bibliographies, 419
    encyclopedias, 418
    indexes, 420–22
    Library of Congress Subject Headings, 418
Refutation
    arrangement of, 340
    importance of, 334
Reno Gazette-Journal, The, 409–10
Repetition
    for coherence, 171–72
    for emphasis, 171–72, 566–67
Research papers
    controlled research
        casebooks for, 393–96, 396–97, 401–03,
            408–14
        meaning of, 392
        nature of, 392–93
        note taking in, 398
        references in, 403–04
        student model of: "Two Faces of Accidental
            Death," 404–08
    library research
        choosing a topic for, 415
        developing a bibliography for, 417–24
        editing of, 474
        formulating a research question for, 415–17
        possible topics for, 415–17
        preparing a prospectus for, 433–40
        and prewriting, 414
        and reading, 418–23
        sample outline of, 443
        searching computer databases for, 422–24
        student models of: "Energy: Is the Answer in
            the Wind?", 442–57; "Exercise: The
            New-Old Answer to Mental Wellness,"
            461–69
Revising checklist, 59–61
Rowan, Carl T., "Unforgettable Miss Bessie," 90–93
Rubesch, Jane, "A Potential Cure for Cancer"
    (student essay), 294–99
Run-on sentences, *see* Fused sentences
Russell, Bertrand, 4
Ryder, Ann, Review of *Right Plant, Right Place*
    (student review), 388–90

S

Sanders, Charles, "Am I Going to Make It Home Tonight?" (student essay), 337–40

Sarton, May, "The Rewards of Living a Solitary Life," 142–44

Schell, Jonathan, from "The Abolition," 559

Schickel, Richard, "Meditations on Celebrity," 365, 366–67

Schmidt, Jennifer, "The Advantages of Montessori Schools" (student essay), 125–28

Schmidt, John, "Essay Exam Response" (student essay), 362–63

Schneider, Alan, from *Entrances* 83–85

Secondary sources
 casebooks of, 396–403

Semicolon, 480, 520–22, 543

Sentence editing
 to add free modifiers, 225–27
 of awkwardness, 553–59
 for economy, 228–41, 559–64
 for emphasis, 550–52
 of faulty parallelism, 225, 570
 of fragments, 485–86
 of fused sentences, 481–82
 for grammar and sentence structure (review), 511–12
 of shifts in person and number, tense, mood, point of view, 499–500
 for variety, 221–22, 227, 228

Sentence errors
 comma splice, 479–81
 dangling modifiers, 507–09
 faulty parallelism, 500–03
 fragment, 482–86
 fused sentences, 481–82
 incomplete constructions, 503–05
 misplaced modifiers, 509–11
 mixed constructions, 505–07
 shifts in person and number, tense, mood, point of view, 496–500

Sentence expansion
 through coordination, 197–98
 through modification, 196–97
 through subordination, 198–99
 see also Cumulative sentence; Free modifier; Parallelism; Periodic sentence

Sentences
 balanced, 209–11
 basic, 195–200
 combining of, 228–34
 cumulative, 213–14

 emphasis in, 207–08, 214, 564–70
 parallelism in, 200–207, 567
 parenthetical elements in, 518
 periodic, 207–09
 topic, 154–59, 168–69
 variety in, 220–24, 227--28

Shapiro, Karl, "Auto Wreck," 395–96

Shapiro, Raymond, from *Lonely in Baltimore,* 255

Shifts
 editing of, 499–500
 in mood, 497–98
 in point of view, 498–99
 in pronouns, 496
 in tense, 497

"Shotguns and Rifles" (student essay for editing), 307–10

Sigall, Carolyn, "Two Faces of Accidental Death" (student essay), 404–08

Simile, 256

Solomon, Martha, from "Teaching the Nominative Absolute," 217

Sources
 primary
  defined, 392
  casebook of, 393–96
  first reference to, 472
 secondary
  analyzing, 393, 398, 426
  casebook of, 396–403
  defined, 392, 396
  documenting, 428–32, 458–60
  evaluating, 393, 398, 426
  incorporating, 393, 427–28
  summarizing, 393, 427
  using, 393

Specificity, 170

Spivey, Tom, "A World of the Unexpected" (student essay), 61–63

Stafford, William, 1, 5

Steinbeck, John, from *Sweet Thursday,* 4–5

Stevens, Wallace, 4

Stock figures, 260–61

Structure, in writing, 13–15

Style
 defined, 250
 casual, informal, and formal, 250–52, 478, 490
 see also A Style Aside

Style Aside, A, 14, 17, 165, 166, 167

Subject card, 419

Subjects for writing, 26–36

Sullivan, Frank, from *A Pearl in Every Oyster,* 261–62

EDITORIAL ACTIVITIES

PROOFREADERS' MARKS

insert new material   ∧

insert comma   ⅄

insert semicolon   ⅄

insert colon   ∧
                                        ∨

insert period   ⊙

insert hyphen   ⹀